THE
CHILDREN

THE
CHILDREN

DAVID
HALBERSTAM

RANDOM HOUSE
NEW YORK

ALL RIGHTS RESERVED UNDER INTERNATIONAL AND PAN-AMERICAN COPYRIGHT
CONVENTIONS. PUBLISHED IN THE UNITED STATES BY RANDOM HOUSE, INC.,
NEW YORK, AND SIMULTANEOUSLY IN CANADA BY RANDOM HOUSE
OF CANADA LIMITED, TORONTO.

LIBRARY OF CONGRESS CATALOGING-IN-PUBLICATION DATA
HALBERSTAM, DAVID.
THE CHILDREN / DAVID HALBERSTAM.
P.   CM.
INCLUDES INDEX.
ISBN 0-679-41561-0
1. AFRO-AMERICANS—CIVIL RIGHTS—HISTORY—20TH CENTURY.   2. CIVIL
RIGHTS MOVEMENTS—UNITED STATES—HISTORY—20TH CENTURY.   3. CIVIL
RIGHTS WORKERS—UNITED STATES—BIOGRAPHY.   4. UNITED STATES—RACE
RELATIONS.   I. TITLE.
E185.61.H195   1998   323.1′196073—DC21   97-19974

RANDOM HOUSE WEBSITE ADDRESS: WWW.RANDOMHOUSE.COM

PRINTED IN THE UNITED STATES OF AMERICA ON ACID-FREE PAPER

2 4 6 8 9 7 5 3

FIRST EDITION

BOOK DESIGN BY LILLY LANGOTSKY

This book is dedicated
to the memory of three uncommon men
who played influential roles in my life
when I lived and worked in Nashville:

COLEMAN HARWELL 1905–1987

JENNINGS PERRY 1900–1987

KELLY MILLER SMITH 1920–1984

BOOK
1

THE CHILDREN

PROLOGUE

YEARS LATER THOUGH SHE COULD RECALL ALMOST EVERY PHYSICAL detail of what it had been like to sit there in that course on English literature, Diane Nash could remember nothing of what Professor Robert Hayden had said. What she remembered instead was her fear. A large clock on the wall had clicked slowly and loudly; each minute which was subtracted put her nearer to harm's way. What she remembered about the class in the end was her inability to concentrate, and the fact that both her hands were soaked with sweat by the end of the class and left the clear handprint of her fear on the wooden desk. It was always the last class that she attended on the days that she and her colleagues assembled before they went downtown and challenged the age-old segregation laws at the lunch counters in Nashville's downtown shopping center. No matter how much she steeled herself, no matter how much she believed in what they were doing, the anticipatory fear never left her.

It had been at its height the night before the first sit-in, on February 13, 1960. On that evening, she had sat alone in her room at Fisk University. Suddenly she was hit with an overpowering attack of nerves. What had she gotten herself into? she wondered. She was supposed to march that next day into downtown Nashville and challenge the existing white power structure. She, Diane Nash, a coward of the first order in her own mind, a person absolutely afraid not just of violence but of going to jail, was going to join a small group of black children and ministers and take on the most important and resourceful people in a big, very white, very Southern city. She and her friends, who had nothing and were nothing, were going to go up against white businessmen, who were rich and powerful and connected to the white politicians, who were their pals and who agreed with them on everything.

What had all of them been thinking in Jim Lawson's workshops on nonviolence? These men would have nothing but scorn for a bunch of black children venturing into their territory.

These were white men in their forties and fifties and sixties. They owned the police force of the city and they owned the judges who sat in the city's courts. And she, Diane Nash of Chicago, could not make a phone call to a single powerful person in all of America if her life depended on it, which indeed it might. She was now all of twenty-one and she was in way over her head. Somehow she had been caught in the camaraderie, and had begun to surface as someone outspoken and confident. The others, she knew, had already started to look up to her as a leader, but they had no idea how scared she was. It was a joke, she thought, it will never happen. We are a bunch of children. We're nice children, bright and idealistic, but we are children and we are weak. We have no police force, no judges, no cops, no money. Jim Lawson is a fine man and a good leader, she thought, but this is nothing but a dream. She could almost see those powerful white men, like the white men she had seen in movies, who sat around and knew how to make decisions, hearing the news that a small group of black students were insisting on being served at the lunch counters at downtown stores, and laughing at them. She felt pure terror in her heart at that moment, and if there had been any way she could disappear from the movement without causing great shame to herself and letting down these others, she would have done it. If there was anything besides the cause itself which kept her from bailing out, it was the growing loyalty she now felt to the others in this small and, she hoped, hardy group of young students who had become not merely her colleagues, but now, her friends. They had started out quite tentative with one another; they came from different parts of the country, went to different schools, and there were obviously significant differences in class among some of them. What they shared, however, was a powerful common purpose, one which was becoming a more dominant part of their lives every day: The more committed they were, the more their past differences seemed less important, and their new political kinship became the critical part of their daily lives. It was as if the longer they stayed in, the more they left their old world with their old friendships behind, and the more this new political incarnation became the single dominating part of lives which had suddenly been completely redrawn. Besides, she liked them: Rodney Powell was a medical student, serious and cerebral and well spoken. John Lewis was rural and shy, but he was already known by the others for the steadfast quality of his character—there wasn't anything he would not do for the cause. Curtis Murphy was full of laughter and charm. Gloria Johnson was obviously bright, but shy and a little stiff. Jim Bevel was provocative, a little older than the others, difficult, brilliant, but unpredictable, a young man whom the others both admired but found prickly. The more she knew them, the more she was impressed by them. Now, above all, she did not want them to think badly about her.

Besides, she shared their passion for the cause. She knew exactly why, despite her fear, she had joined up with them. Soon after arriving at Fisk the previous fall she had been taken to the Tennessee State Fair by one of the many young men vying for her attention. Since there did not seem a lot to do in Nashville socially, at least not compared with Chicago, or Washington, where for a time she had been a student, she gladly went along. There for the first time in her life she encountered signs for segregated rest rooms. WHITE ONLY, the sign had said, the first of those most odious signs she had ever beheld. And then COLORED. The humiliation she had felt was immediate—it was as if someone had slapped her face. What shocked her even more was that her date, who was from the South, did not seem surprised or offended; he quite willingly seemed to accept it. But for her the experience was so transcending, her anger so immediate and so complete that she was effectively politicized from that moment on. It was her first encounter with overt legal discrimination—she had known covert discrimination in Chicago, but she had always managed to look away. Worse, that terrible day at the fair had been followed up very quickly by other comparable humiliations. As a girl growing up in Chicago she had been accustomed to going downtown and shopping with her friends. There had been a certain aimlessness to those shopping trips. They would wander through the great department stores of the city, enjoying the role of shopper and viewer, and then they would have lunch at a restaurant in one of the stores. But when she tried to do this in Nashville she found that the store owners welcomed her money on most floors of the store but that she and her friends were not welcome in their lunchrooms. That had angered her every bit as much as the moment of humiliation at the state fair. After that she had begun to take notice of what was around her in downtown Nashville: In the center of the downtown there were black people eating their lunches while sitting on the sidewalk. That was yet another shock to her. She had come to the South almost casually, choosing Fisk because she was restless with her life at home. She had not thought very hard about the racial consequences of what she was doing—a black woman raised in the North moving to a region where the laws of segregation were just coming under legal and social challenge.

That was why when a fellow student had quite casually mentioned that a black minister was holding workshops designed to challenge the local segregation laws in downtown lunch counters, she had been an eager recruit. It was, she had thought at first, out of character to do this. It soon became obvious, however, that she was one of the most forceful members of this small band of students. By mid-February 1960 the others—the men—had come to her and asked her to be one of the two leaders of the group. The men were impressed by her in no small part because she was so brave and she exuded confidence. There she was, the others thought, the slightest of them, a girl at that, and she was fearless. Nothing stopped her. When they had been pummeled, she never considered turning back. Not for an instant. If anything, the harsher the attacks on them, the more determined she had seemed at their next meeting to go right back to the exact same place and show that they could not be intimidated by hate and violence. That violence would not deter them. The men in the group felt if she could stand up to the fear, then they could keep going back too. The truth was that she was always scared. Always. Her memories of sitting in Professor Hayden's class were among the clearest of her undergraduate days. She remembered watching the clock, and she remembered in great detail the mark her soaked palms left on the desk. She had had to will herself to leave the class, to become once again the fearless leader that they had turned her into and that they believed she was. If the others thought she was Diane the fearless, she knew better; she knew she was Diane the coward. As the clock had ticked in Professor Hayden's class she became more aware of the rising quality of anxiety she felt, and as she had left that class to venture forth once again as a leader of the movement, she could look down on her desk and see the wet handprint of fearless Diane Nash of Chicago.

It was not a lark for her. She had joined for serious reasons, and it—the commitment to a radical, nonviolent way to change America—became in different ways with different manifestations a lifetime devotion. From the start she had found a spiritual home in the Lawson group. If there was one source of strength she and the other young people in this embryonic movement had, it was, more than anything else, a belief in each other. A few, particularly those who attended the little black Baptist seminary nearby, had a special, immutable faith in their God to sustain them. Others did not. But all had gradually come to have faith in each other, even though in most cases their friendships were still quite tenuous. Some of the friendships born of those days would last a lifetime, and more than one marriage would come from this small group.

Most of them came from different towns and cities and states in the South. A handful of them were from the North. Most of them were black but a few were white exchange students attending black colleges. Because there were four black schools in the Nashville area, the students' links were to each other rather than to their schools, and years later they would not identify themselves as graduates of Fisk or A&I, or Meharry or American Baptist, but first and foremost as sit-in kids. Scorned and mocked and teased by many of their classmates in those early days for being do-gooders as they undertook this challenge, they formed what was in effect their own university.

They did not think of themselves in those days as being gifted or talented or marked for success, or for that matter particularly heroic, and yet from that little group would come a senior U.S. congressman; the mayor of a major city; the first black woman psychiatrist to be tenured at Harvard medical school; one of the most distinguished public health doctors in America; and a young man who would eventually come back to be the head of the very college in Nashville he now attended. Another of their group would become one of Martin Luther King's principal and most favored assistants, a young man who was so hypnotic a speaker that King often used him at major rallies as his warm-up speaker. Others would go on to lives which were relatively more mundane, and their days in this cause would remain the most exciting and stirring of their lives. A few became, if not casualties of those days, then men and women whose most exciting and most valuable moments had come when they were very young and whose lives never quite measured up to what some had believed was their early promise; they were not unlike brilliant combat leaders in America's wars who never handled in peacetime an existence which was routine as well as they had handled one fraught with danger.

The journey they were beginning had started with a limited enough objective: an assault on the segregated lunch counters in Nashville, a seemingly pleasant city in a border state. But there was an inevitable progression to their cause, and gradually it became something of a children's crusade as they and hundreds and thousands of black students like them throughout the country, knowing that the right moment had finally arrived, became part of a growing challenge to segregation in the South. As that assault grew it created among these young people its own new equation: They could not begin and end this quest with nothing grander than the right to eat lunch counter hamburgers. Each victory they gained demanded a further step; the totality of segregation as it existed in the American South in February 1960, when they began, meant that most of them would not be able to turn back, not at least for several years, and they would be caught in an escalating spiral in which they kept pursuing ever more dangerous challenges to the forces of segregation in ever more dangerous venues—in small towns and cities in the Deep South. They had begun by believing that by coming aboard and joining the sit-in struggle, they would be risking their bodies in some marginal and not very terrifying way in this semiprotected environment; within two years some of them would be risking their lives every day as the shock troops in the final challenge upon legal and political segregation in Alabama and Mississippi.

No one reflected that remarkable transformation from scared young black student to black student samurai more obviously than this shy, often timid young woman, Diane Nash. In Nashville in the beginning days of February 1960 she was frightened each day, scared that her fear would give her away to their enemies, to her friends, and to herself. Yet somehow she was able to overcome it and impress her peers. And this was just the beginning of what was to become her dramatic interior conversion: In a little more than two years, in the spring of 1962, she would have so overcome her normal psychic barriers of fear that she would stand in a Jackson, Mississippi, courtroom. There, already six months pregnant, surrounded by sworn enemies, accused on a trumped-up charge of contributing to the delinquency of a minor, because she and her friends had tried to integrate local facilities using high school students, she would stand her ground. In that Jackson courtroom she would boldly tell the white judge (a man duly stunned to find that the young integrationist he intended to slap into jail was in fact very pregnant) that it did not matter whether she went to jail or not, because her child was going to be born in Mississippi and any black child born in Mississippi was already born in prison. It would be the judge, who, sensing the fire in her and wanting no part of the potential public relations disaster of sending this pregnant woman to jail, would back down and suspend her sentence.

Almost from the start her peers had sensed her special capacity to rise to the occasion, and they made her their chairman. It was an honor she desperately wanted to decline. The fact that her friends believed in her and wanted her as a leader had, however, made her fear, if anything, greater than ever, because her recognition was greater: Since she was a leader of the Nashville sit-ins, she became more a marked person than ever before. There were more photographs of her in the local papers, and the television cameramen seemed to look for her when they covered the story, inevitably drawn to her because she was the most glamorous person in the group, slim and striking. Defiance of the white authorities was written all over her face. The fear was concealed within.

Yet every time she and the others left the First Baptist Church, where the workshops had been held and which they also used as a staging area before heading for the lunch counters, and walked the handful of blocks to the heart of the downtown shopping area, Diane Nash could feel the white violence begin to surge around them, the white toughs heckling them and throwing things and screaming cruel racial epithets. Then as they entered the restaurants and tried to take their seats, there would almost always be the violence, the hoodlums pouring coffee on the protesters and trying to extinguish cigarettes on their heads. There were, she was aware, no immunities for her. On February 20, at the time of the second major sit-in, she was in the downtown area, working as a control person—this was before the days of portable phones, and so the control people were important; they were like the communications men in war, the eyes and ears of the headquarters.

The downtown had been crowded on this day, and unusually dangerous too. There were groups of young white marauders looking for blacks on the streets. There had been a picture of Diane in *The Nashville Tennessean* a few days earlier, and one of the roving white marauders had shouted, "There she is! That's Diane Nash! She's the one to get! She's the one to get!" She had quickly slipped away through the crowd, but she was terrified. They knew her face now and they were after her. She was a marked person.

She found a spot where she could get away from everyone and she sat down on the corner. The whites had looked tough, and there were reports that some of them were now carrying knives. She sat on a curbstone and took a fifteen-minute break. She found that she was gasping for air, though she had not run. It was as if the fear had sucked all the oxygen out of her system. She had to decide whether she had the strength to continue her job. Her dilemma was clear: If she could not conquer her own fear, how could she send the others out? And if she could not conquer her fear, would she have to resign not just from the leadership position but from all aspects of the sit-ins? The most important thing she had learned from reading Gandhi during the workshops she had been attending for almost three months was that leaders did not expect others to do things they were not willing to do themselves. That was true for cleaning latrines, and it was true as well for risking their lives.

She knew she had to make a decision and make it quickly. If she failed here, she would have to leave the Movement. She sat for a time, and gradually her ability to breathe came back. She thought about how important the sit-ins had become to her; she realized that this was the most important thing she had ever done, and perhaps more valuable than anything she might ever do again. Overnight, because of the sit-ins, she had felt of value to herself. Therefore she had to go forward—she owed it not just to the others but, in a way she had never felt before, to herself. She would be extremely careful in every decision she made—there would be no recklessness. But she would not turn back. If something terrible was going to happen to her, she decided, let it happen when she was doing something she believed in. She got up and walked back to her job.

1

THE EVENTS WHICH WERE JUST ABOUT TO TAKE PLACE FIRST IN
Nashville and then throughout the Deep South had been set in
motion some three years earlier in February 1957, when two talented
young black ministers, both of them strongly affected by the teachings
of Mohandas Gandhi, had met in Oberlin, Ohio. One of them, Martin
Luther King, Jr., was already world famous, having led the successful
Montgomery bus boycott which had begun in December 1955,
thereby emerging as the best-known leader of a new generation of
black ministers; a year earlier he had been named the head of a new
organization, the Southern Christian Leadership Conference, a group
of young activist black ministers who intended to use the techniques
of Christian nonviolence to challenge segregation throughout the
South. The other minister, Jim Lawson, was unknown not only to the
country at large but to the other leaders of what was already becoming
known as the Movement. Jim Lawson had entered Oberlin College a
few months earlier in order to get his master's degree in religious studies. His more traditional academic and ministerial career had been
interrupted for the past four years, first by nearly a year spent in a federal prison as a conscientious objector, a young black ministerial student who had rejected his government's rationale for the Korean War
and had refused to register for the draft; and then, after he had been
released from the federal penitentiary, by three years studying and
teaching as a Methodist missionary in India.

India had been a rich experience for Jim Lawson and had strengthened his belief in nonviolence as an instrument for social change, to be
used eventually in the emerging civil rights struggle in the United
States. Jim Lawson, son of a distinguished minister, was determined to
be not just a minister but an activist minister, a man who used the

church not merely to comfort the members of his congregation but to spread a social and political gospel as well.

In his last two years overseas Jim Lawson had felt a growing pull to return to the United States, a pull which began the moment he read in the Indian papers of developments in Montgomery, Alabama, where ordinary black citizens, led by a sophisticated, well-educated young minister named Martin Luther King, Jr., were putting nonviolent resistance to the most practical application imaginable. The more Jim Lawson read about the Montgomery bus strike, the more excited he became. The specific issue was the desegregation of the city's bus lines, but Jim Lawson understood immediately that it was not just the bus lines which were being challenged but the entire structure of segregation—in Montgomery and in every other city and town in the South. What was happening in Montgomery, he believed, was merely the first stage of what was going to be a long and difficult struggle. Reading about it in Nagpur, he knew it was time to go home.

What Martin King and his people had done in Montgomery represented a new and critical increment of change in what he viewed as a long historical process of the black struggle for equal rights in America. It was something Jim Lawson had long expected. Back when he had been in college and studying about Gandhi for the first time, he had read about the great Indian leader's meeting with Howard Thurman, probably the most distinguished black minister of his time. Thurman had always been fascinated by what was happening in India. He had written a short book called *Jesus and the Disinherited,* which was a reflection on Christ and racism in America. As their talks were ending Thurman had asked Gandhi what message he should take back to America, and the Indian had said that one of his great regrets was that he had not made nonviolence more visible throughout the world. But perhaps, he had suggested, some American black man would succeed where he had failed, because America offered such a formidable platform for the world. There it sat, Gandhi had said, a powerful modern nation, and yet it had its own domestic colonial oppression within. For the first time, reading about Martin Luther King in Nagpur, Lawson had sensed that this young minister in Montgomery was the black American whose coming Gandhi had first prophesied. (In that sense his views paralleled those of Glenn Smiley, who was to become one of Lawson's foremost mentors in a group called the Fellowship of Reconciliation, and who on meeting King in Montgomery had written of his chance of becoming a "Negro Gandhi."[1]) Gandhi, Lawson came to believe, had shown in those talks with Thurman that he understood America better than America understood itself.

Martin Luther King and the men around him, Lawson believed, symbolized the rise of a new generation of black religious leaders. They were better educated than their predecessors, and more confident than them as well, because they were backed now by the moral authority of the Supreme Court of the United States, which in 1954 had ruled in *Brown* v. *Board of Education.* Theirs was nothing less than an appeal to the nation's white Christian conscience to redress age-old grievances. More, they were using the tactics employed by Gandhi himself in attaining independence for India, the very tactics which Lawson himself believed in.

As Jim Lawson readied himself to leave Nagpur and return to the United States he believed he saw his own future quite clearly. The three years in India had been everything he had wanted, and he had often felt that he was walking in Gandhi's footsteps. But there was also no doubt that because of his time there and his time in prison, he was in danger of falling behind his own schedule for getting both his advanced degrees as well as his pastorate. He would start by getting his master's at Oberlin in Ohio, a famous school with an unusually liberal faculty and a strong department of religion that was not far from his home in Massillon, Ohio. After Oberlin he intended to go on to Yale Divinity School for his doctoral studies. *Then,* properly credentialed, he would go to the South, where he could become an important part of the movement which had sprung up in Montgomery.

By chance, a few months after Jim Lawson had arrived at Oberlin in the fall of 1956, Martin Luther King was invited to speak there. The man behind the invitation was a young professor named Harvey Cox, himself at the beginning of a distinguished theological career and at the time the director of religious activities at Oberlin. Cox had heard King speak in Nashville a year earlier and had immediately decided that he ought to bring this remarkable man to the Oberlin campus. He had scheduled him for three appearances in one day: a noon assembly on "The Montgomery Story"; a second speech on Gandhian techniques, "Justice Without Violence," in the midafternoon; and finally a panel that night on "The New Negro in the New South." Despite (or because of) the fact that Oberlin was an extremely liberal place, there had been some debate over where King should speak; some faculty members were supportive of King's presence, but only as long as he spoke in a specifically religious setting; if too secular a setting were chosen it might imply that the school was inflicting religion on its students. In time a decision was made: King would make two of his three appearances at First Church, a local Congregational church. That seemed to be a worthy compromise and the liberal opposition soon died down. Still, Cox was utterly unprepared for what happened next. All morning chartered buses arrived from Cleveland and other surrounding cities and towns in Ohio, and large numbers of black people had filed into both the chapel and the local church. Clearly the word had gotten out all over Ohio, Cox realized, and he was amused by the irrelevance, indeed the foolishness of the faculty debate to which he had so recently been a party.

For Jim Lawson it was a particularly moving day. He was stunned by the size of the crowd and the emotion that these ordinary people brought to the church. Martin Luther King was everything he had hoped for, a brilliant speaker who was able to reach a vast variety of people. After King's first speech, Cox, who was the campus minister, had given a small informal luncheon for King in a private dining room at the school's cafeteria. Jim Lawson had become something of a favorite of Cox's, and he had been invited to the meal, a not inconsiderable honor for a new graduate student, but Cox was already impressed by the unusual inner force and drive of Jim Lawson and his commitment to nonviolence. He thought these two young men, who were almost exactly the same age—both of them twenty-eight, with Lawson four months older—should meet.

Lawson was impressed on that day by King's simplicity. He was already one of the most famous young men in America, for his face had graced the cover of almost every national magazine, and he could regularly be seen on the nightly fifteen-minute black-and-white network newscasts. Indeed if anything, his international fame was even greater in comparative terms than his fame in America, for the nonwhite world was not only more aware of the universality of his message than many of his fellow Americans but often more receptive to it.

The rest of the world regarded King as a critically important new moral voice, a man with the requisite heroism and inner spiritual strength to go against the grain of racism in his native land.

King was clearly a remarkable speaker, Lawson thought: alternately cool and rational, and then impassioned and emotional. He had been, as he often was, extremely skillful that day in reaching both the university community and the black Baptists who had driven over to hear him. It was not that there was a little for everyone in his speech, Lawson thought; there was a lot for everyone in it. When the speech was over, Jim Lawson had gone to the luncheon and had found to his good fortune that most of the other guests were late, and he had about ten minutes alone with King. Martin King wore his fame and his burden lightly, Jim Lawson thought. He seemed simple and modest and open, far more obsessed by the issues he was confronting than by any idea of personal glory. He traveled without an entourage, a young black man taking on what seemed a Herculean task, armed with nothing but his beliefs and his faith, and his increasing awareness that he had been selected by forces outside his reach for a task far larger than any he had either sought or wanted; that he had been chosen by fate for a position of leadership in a movement that was far more powerful than any one man; and that his voice was something of a gift, a voice that belonged to others but had been granted to him. If this was not something he had sought, then somehow he was resigned to accepting it.

They had talked quickly to each other in a kind of shorthand, two cerebral young black ministers with much in common, both the sons of successful pastors, though of different denominations. They shared comparable backgrounds, mutual ambitions, and strikingly similar beliefs. They had swapped the tiny tidbits of identity as all Americans do as they sought to place each other. Martin King had been to the Boston University School of Theology, which was a Methodist school. Jim Lawson had a good many friends there and spoke of professors at B.U. whom he knew who were close to Martin. They both had been strongly influenced by Howard Thurman. There was, of course, a certain gap between them, one that was both theological and cultural, King being a Baptist and Lawson a Methodist, that being no small difference in black ministerial and political circles.

Lawson spoke of his particular interest in what King and the others had done in Montgomery because of his own personal experiences, first as a prisoner in a federal penitentiary and then as a student of nonviolence in India. As Jim Lawson began to discuss his background, Martin Luther King became very interested, for King had a quick sense that this man, who did not, as so many others did, claim to be a brother, was someone with a very similar vision of the struggle ahead, and a man who had acted upon conscience early in his life, when that kind of action was hardly fashionable. There were not many black ministers, after all, who had gone to prison because of their rejection of the Korean War.

When Lawson mentioned his time in India, King had gotten excited and had spoken about his own vague plans to go there and study. "I'd love to do that someday," he said, but he said it wistfully, in a way which showed that the moment was somehow already past. Then Jim Lawson had spoken of his own plans. "I've always wanted to work in the South and I hope to do it as soon as I've finished all my studies," he said. He said this almost casually, thinking that his time frame was about five years: First he would finish Oberlin, then go on to Yale, and then as a newly minted Yale doctor of divinity, he would venture down to some endangered place in the South. His was the most orderly of timetables. Years later he was quite amused by the casual way in which he had said this. But Martin Luther King was fascinated by the discovery of this kindred soul, who seemed to see politics and religion blended together into an activist gospel that had not merely a larger strategic purpose but tactical goals.

As such King had quickly interrupted him. "Don't wait! Come now!" he had said. "We don't have anyone like you down there. We need you right now. Please don't delay. Come as quickly as you can. We really need you."

There had been no doubting the urgency in King's words, and Jim Lawson had understood immediately what he was saying: Events are exploding, they are ahead of us, we are trying to catch up with them, and we need all the good people we can get to combine politics and theology each day in our activism and somehow not lose our way. We are becoming teachers when we are still so young that we ought to be nothing but students. It was as if he was telling the inner truth of the Movement: Things are happening so fast that we find ourselves in danger of leading by responding. It was not just a request he was making, Lawson thought, it was nothing less than a call. Without thinking, knowing that this conversation had turned from idle chitchat to the most serious dialogue imaginable, Jim Lawson had heard himself saying, "Yes, I understand. I'll arrange my affairs, and I'll come as quickly as I can."

An emergency appendectomy slowed him down slightly and kept him in Ohio longer than anticipated. He had by that time been a member of the Fellowship of Reconciliation for ten years, the Fellowship being a group of activists, primarily with Protestant religious affiliations, who wanted to use the force of Christian love—the love as seen in the life of Jesus Christ, the ability to love one's enemies—in all relationships, be they issues of state, issues of the workplace (labor against management), or issues of the most basic kind in terms of two people trying to get on with each other in a marriage. As a college freshman at Baldwin-Wallace, Jim Lawson had run into A. J. Muste, who was the grand old man of the FOR, a man of great conscience, consuming kindness, and high intellect. Muste had immediately reached out to this hungry, intellectually curious young black student and turned Lawson into something of a protégé.

Lawson called Muste to tell him of his plans to go south. Perhaps, Lawson said, he would relocate in Atlanta and go to Gammon, a black theological seminary there. Muste told Lawson not to rush ahead, that perhaps the FOR could find something for him in the South. In time a call came back to Lawson from Glenn Smiley, then the national field director of the FOR, saying that the Fellowship needed a field secretary in the South—a roving troubleshooter to watch events in this part of the country where events seemed to be speeding up at so surprising a rate. Would Jim Lawson want the job? Yes, he thought to himself, it was exactly what he wanted and it would take him where he wanted to go.

2

THE FIRST ISSUE FOR JIM LAWSON ONCE HE DECIDED TO GO SOUTH WAS, of course, where he would be based. He had casually mentioned Atlanta to Glenn Smiley as the most likely site. Clearly he would have to spend a great deal of time on the road, but the right base was important. Atlanta was the obvious choice, the biggest, richest city in the South, the capital of what was often referred to as the New South, a place where the power of new business opportunities was said to eclipse the power of old hatreds and racial tensions. Atlanta was thought to be new and modern, not only the biggest but seemingly the most forward-looking of the South's cities. Skyscrapers were on the rise, and that almost of itself seemed to prove that the future had arrived, for it would seem obvious that something as new and grand and modern as a skyscraper could not harbor something as old as racial hatred.

Atlanta certainly had some attractions. In terms of the journalistic protection that an enlightened newspaper could offer black activists, *The Atlanta Constitution* boasted the legendary Ralph McGill, a Southern editor known for his courage and decency, a towering figure to a generation of younger Southern journalists coming of age in the years after World War II, who revered him and wanted to be like him. But the truth was that the *Constitution* was viewed by most of the able Southern journalists of that era as something of a joke, quite possibly the most overrated paper in the region, a paper, aside from McGill, which was both timid and penurious, afraid to cover this most important of stories opening up right in front of it. At a meeting of NAACP executives held in Atlanta in 1954, Wallace Westfeldt, the civil rights reporter for *The Nashville Tennessean,* had been surprised to find that once the meeting was over, he was approached by a reporter from the *Constitution* who had missed the entire daylong session and wanted to be filled in on what had happened. Westfeldt discovered the next day that the Atlanta paper gave scant notice of the meeting, a couple of paragraphs, far less than the coverage in his own paper back in Nashville. Throughout the South, where in most cities a small group of white liberals was just beginning to come of age, men and women determined to wrestle with the issue of race, the timidity of the *Constitution* on the issue of race mirrored nothing less than the attitude of all too many of Atlanta's leading businessmen on this issue.

So Glenn Smiley was not so sure about Atlanta. He knew the South well. He had stayed somewhat in the background during the Montgomery bus strike, but he had nonetheless been one of the most important influences in helping to instruct King on the pragmatic, daily use of Gandhi's teachings. Smiley thought Jim Lawson needed a safe haven for his base, a place where his own daily existence would not be at issue and where he would not be buffeted by local racial tensions. Atlanta might be new and progressive commercially, but it was also the capital of a distinctly unreconstructed Deep South state, and the prejudices of Georgia weighed heavily on the social and political climate of the city. The two Georgia senators, Dick Russell and Walter George, had both signed the Southern Manifesto, a declaration of opposition to the Supreme Court decision on *Brown* v. *Board of Education.* Marvin Griffin, the Georgia governor, had been one of the hard-line figures who had visited Little Rock in the summer of 1957 in order to help crowd the then ambivalent governor of Arkansas, Orval Faubus, into resisting the Court-ordered integration of the Little Rock schools, pressuring Faubus to make his ill-fated decision to employ the Arkansas National Guard to block the integration of Little Rock Central High.

Georgia was a state where white supremacist groups, pledged to resist racial change, were extremely powerful and dominated the state's politics. So Glenn Smiley thought Atlanta was a city with a relatively modern physical exterior, a modern mayor, an upbeat commercial booster spirit, and one great journalist (if not a good newspaper). But he also thought it a city where the essential establishment leadership had not yet come to any decision about the city's racial and therefore moral future.

By contrast, Smiley thought, for a variety of reasons Nashville, the capital of Tennessee, was a far better choice. The defeat of the poll tax some ten years earlier had dramatically changed the state's political climate. Blacks voted in large numbers throughout Tennessee as they did not in Georgia. The mayor of Nashville, Ben West, was at the very least moderate, if not actually liberal, a quiet prototype of a new breed of enlightened post–World War II politician just coming to power; as a young state senator he had helped increase black political representation in Nashville. Because of West's leadership in changing the way people voted for city council representation, there were now two blacks on the city council and the local and regional black vote was growing larger and more influential each year. Nashville was a smaller city than Atlanta, true, but because Tennessee was a border state, the enmity of the rest of the state did not poison the atmosphere of Nashville in the way the racial anger of rural Georgia affected the climate of Atlanta.

Tennessee was a border state which sprawled, sliverlike, some five hundred miles from Johnson City in the east to Memphis in the west. Politically, socially, economically, and racially it was considered three separate states, the Grand Divisions as they were called. East Tennessee, the mountainous section east of the Cumberland Plateau, had harbored powerful Unionist sympathies during the Civil War, and at one point Abraham Lincoln had tried to get it to secede from the rest of the state. Back in the fifties it still elected two Republican congressmen, and it had few black residents. Its politics were conservative but slavery, because of the nature of the terrain, was alien and attitudes on race had never hardened. West Tennessee, which lay between the Mississippi and Tennessee rivers, could not have been more different. Much of the land was alluvial soil, and its politics and demographics were not unlike those of the Deep South. And Middle Tennessee, which lay between the Tennessee River and the Cumberland Plateau, was a gentle area of small farms which produced a tempered, albeit modest liberalism. It both helped shape the generally liberal outlook of *The Nashville Tennessean,* the dominant newspaper in the region, and at the same time was affected by it. The sum of these parts was not without its own unique political contradictions, but there was an essential resistance in statewide campaigns to overt racial demagoguery.

Frank Clement, the ambitious young governor of Tennessee, had run as a segregationist in 1954, and when the question of school integration had come up, he had pledged that he would *never* integrate Tennessee's schools. His opponent, former governor Gordon Browning, a much older man and a moderate who had been a critical part of the coalition which had smashed the old conservative and racist Crump machine only a few years earlier, had responded somewhat dryly that he had been around a bit longer than Clement and that Never was a very long time in politics. That was one of the wisest things that Gordon Browning ever said. Shortly thereafter, Frank Clement, as the good ambitious son of a border state, angling for a place as vice president on the Democratic national ticket, had called out the National Guard on the occasion of the first school integration riots in the state. This was in Clinton, a small town in East Tennessee. But unlike Orval Faubus in Arkansas, Clement had used force to protect the right of black children to attend an integrated school. From that time on Clement was considered in some quarters a traitor to the Southern cause, the man who had sent tanks in against his own people. It was not mere political expediency which moved the governor; Frank Clement in his private moments would talk with a handful of reporters he trusted, saying that this—the Supreme Court decision— had been coming for a long time and that it was the right thing to do and that it was time to end the historic injustice of segregation. "I'm not going to say that publicly, of course. All I'm going to say is that we are going to obey the law in this state. And that's enough. But it's overdue and it's the right thing. It's time for all of us to get on with our lives."[1]

Clement was not alone among the state's leading politicians in his stance and his core beliefs. Neither Estes Kefauver nor Albert Gore, the state's two senators, had deigned to sign the Southern Manifesto. At the Democratic convention in 1956, all three of the state's top political figures—Kefauver, Clement, and Gore—had been in some way or another candidates for either the presidency or vice presidency. It was clear to anyone studying the political balance in Tennessee that the pull of national ambition was far more powerful on many of its politicians than was the competing pull of its local segregationists. Harsh demagogic campaigns based primarily on race had consistently failed in Tennessee in the fifties.

That was a plus for Nashville. The racial texture of its daily life seemed less edgy than that of comparable cities in the Deep South, where there was a sense of growing rage on the part of many white elements after the Supreme Court's decision on *Brown*. A white liberal minister named Will Campbell who had come to Nashville in 1956 after being driven out of his job as chaplain of the University of Mississippi was struck by the quantum difference between this city and the mean, ugly quality which he had found everywhere in Mississippi, a state which in its desire to resist integration had effectively restricted freedom of speech and turned the full force of its police and judicial powers against anyone who might surface as a potential integrationist. Mississippi had in every real sense become a totalitarian state. In Nashville, where the varying segregationist organizations were significantly weaker, people who came out publicly for integration enjoyed freedom of speech and were not ostracized from their social groups.

One of the first things Will Campbell did when he came to Nashville was to go to the local NAACP office and join up; as he crossed the street to enter the building which housed the office, he still felt enough of the fear generated by his experience in Mississippi that he instinctively stopped and looked around for possible police informers or cameramen outside, men stationed there to record the doings of the state's enemies. Later, as he left the office, he found himself again looking back over his shoulder to see if anyone was watching him or whether he was being followed or filmed. The Mississippi twitch, he called it. In Mississippi, his superiors had always kept a close watch on him. Because he was rumored to be a secret integrationist, there had been informers everywhere. An Ole Miss student had come by at the end of each day to collect the used carbons from his office so that authorities—Campbell was never sure which ones—would know to whom he had written that day and what he had said.

Nashville was a great center for colleges and for religious education. The Protestant Vatican, some people called it, because it was the headquarters for so many Southern religious groups, their publishing arms, and their sectarian colleges. It was home to Vanderbilt University; Peabody, a large teachers college; and Scarritt, a Methodist college for whites. For blacks it had Fisk, then a great black private college with a distinguished history; Meharry Medical College; Tennessee Agriculture and Industrial College, or A&I as it was then known, which was the largest black school in the state (since blacks could not yet, of course, go to the all-white University of Tennessee at Knoxville); and American Baptist College, a small, deeply impoverished black seminary. This meant that even if the top figures in the white Baptist and Methodist worlds were not necessarily integrationists, and were often quite conservative, there were a large number of younger, more liberal members of those churches who would be teaching or studying in Nashville or working in their religious publishing houses and who might become sympathetic colleagues of Jim Lawson. Besides, Vanderbilt Divinity School, which was a jewel in the crown of an esteemed but extremely conservative Southern university, had just begun to integrate, and it might be an excellent place for Jim Lawson to take his graduate degrees.

Finally, Tennessee, though it did not have any journalist of the awesome stature of the legendary McGill, had a far better and far more aggressive paper, *The Nashville Tennessean,* which might at that moment, along with *The Charlotte* (North Carolina) *Observer,* be one of the two best papers operating in what was the traditional Confederacy. That was not unimportant. Unlike the Atlanta papers, the *Tennessean* had pursued the story of racial change aggressively. It had made a commitment from the start to make its readers aware of the historic confrontation taking place under Court order, and that some form of social change was inevitable.

That decision, and the flinty editorial integrity which drove it, made the *Tennessean* an unusual paper: At a time when most Southern newspapers were surprisingly passive and soft in their news coverage, often content to use wire service stories to report on events which had taken place locally, the *Tennessean* not only supported editorially the right of black children to go to white schools, but it covered the ongoing story with a fearlessness that made it nothing less than a beacon to young journalists in the South. A liberal paper could make a great deal of difference in a city trying to move from an older, segregated order to a new, more liberal, integrated one.

For all of these reasons, the organized segregationist movement in Tennessee was exceptionally weak, and indeed it was part of the enduring embarrassment of Vanderbilt University in those years that one of the centers of organized segregation was its English department, containing men who were part of the old Southern Agrarian movement, most notably a professor named Donald Davidson. The fact that the Vanderbilt English department harbored some of the segregationist leadership seemed to reflect both the weakness and the eccentricity of that leadership.

3

THE BUS TRIP WHICH JAMES LAWSON TOOK IN EARLY 1958 FROM MAS-
sillon, Ohio, to Nashville, Tennessee, was some five hundred miles
and it seemed to last for the better part of a day. To James Morris Lawson, Jr., it was a journey filled with both excitement and anxiety. He
was thrilled by his decision to put aside the academic part of his career
and follow his real calling. After all these years of planning, he was
finally going forth to do battle. But he wondered if he was worthy of
the call. He was a man who believed deeply in the power of Christian
love and nonviolent protest, and he wondered what would happen
once he actually began the long, hard process of challenging age-old
laws and customs. Would he have the inner strength to accept that
part of the South which he could not change, and live at least part of
his daily existence within the South's segregated confines? Or was he
too proud to succeed? He had wanted a job that would take him to
the epicenter of the action, and he had been granted his wish. It was
always a dangerous thing, he mused, to have your wishes granted.

Above all, Jim Lawson, a very proud, outspoken, and independent
young man, a black child of the urban North, was worried about how
he would deal with his own personal encounters with a segregated
world. Just in the last year, after he had returned to the United States
from India, he had been greeted by an ugly incident in Detroit. A
white friend who was just beginning to test racial policies in the North
had, during a trip they had both made to Detroit, suggested that Lawson try to get a haircut in a barbershop in downtown Detroit. The
friend said he had checked it out himself and the proprietor seemed
amenable to the idea; so Jim Lawson had gone in and taken a seat in
one of the barber chairs only to be forcibly evicted from both the chair
and the shop by a very angry white barber. It had been relatively easy

for him to control his anger, but it was also a reminder of how little things had changed even in the Midwest, and how many tests there would be for him still ahead.

The trip to Nashville was not that difficult. Because he went by bus he did not have to worry, as blacks traditionally did, about where to stop and eat and stay overnight on their trips to the South. The bus itself was not segregated. The early part of the trip went easily but as the bus crossed over into Kentucky, as the culture and the local ethos changed more quickly than the landscape, he began to feel his own anxiety rise. The Nashville bus station was segregated, but he was met by Glenn Smiley, who quickly whisked him away, so that he never got caught up in any local racial debate about whether a black man could hire a white taxi or whether he had to wait at a different cabstand until a black cab showed up.

Glenn Smiley seemed to know the city well. Smiley had arranged for him to spend the first few nights at the home of a black dentist in the city, and then it turned out that the dentist had an apartment in town, which he was willing to rent to Jim Lawson for a relatively small sum. That spared him the potentially humiliating task of looking for an apartment and finding out that the ones he wanted were not available to blacks.

At the moment when he arrived in Nashville the pace of integration seemed ominously slow. The high hopes which many blacks had felt just a few years earlier when the Supreme Court had ruled on *Brown* were dissipating in the face of the relentless resistance posed in many Deep South states, and a strategy which seemed to demand that if blacks were going to challenge the existing status quo, then they were going to have to do it school by school, child by child, lawsuit by lawsuit. Black political life in most of the South, particularly the Deep South, was virtually nonexistent. The segregationists completely controlled the machinery of the ruling Democratic party within the Deep South, and they had used that control to exclude blacks from voting; they seemed determined to exhaust emotionally, physically, and financially the forces of integration. If the Supreme Court had spoken, its voice at that moment was essentially a lonely one. The President of the United States, Dwight Eisenhower, had yet to speak out morally on the issue and seemed, if anything, sympathetic to the white power structure in the South; the Congress remained quite conservative, particularly in its Southern-dominated committee leadership; and the American people were still very much on the sidelines.

So far victories for the forces of integration had seemed few, and surprisingly marginal. The largest victory post-*Brown* had been that achieved by Martin Luther King's Montgomery bus boycott. There blacks had, using Gandhian tactics, stayed off the buses and walked to work or carpooled (or forced the middle-class white women for whom they worked as maids to drive over and pick them up each morning). The boycott had been stunningly successful and had brought the local bus line, whose primary customers were black, to its knees. Their protest, the dignified manner in which they had gained their victory, plus the eloquence of their young leader's words had captured the imagination of much of the country. It was their first successful assault upon the national conscience. The question which had been left largely unanswered after Montgomery was whether these same tactics would be applicable elsewhere.

And now here was another black leader, one even more steeped in Gandhian techniques than King, coming to what would prove to be a vulnerable Southern city at precisely the right moment. Lawson saw himself as a teacher, and he was sure that he would not be disappointed in finding large numbers of frustrated young black students eager to learn his techniques. For Jim Lawson was absolutely convinced that what had happened in Montgomery was not a fluke, that it was the first step in a long, enduring process which would inevitably force not merely local communities but the American people to make a larger commitment to justice on the issue of race. He was confident from his own studies that the possibilities of using Gandhian techniques in the American South were almost limitless. His timing, he later decided, was almost perfect. For Nashville was a city which was a major magnet for black college students at a time when their frustration was beginning to smolder. The talent he found around him there, Lawson soon decided, was uncommon, nothing less than the best of a generation of young black students, most of them from the South, many of them burning with an inner rage about the injustices inflicted on them, eager to find some movement to which they could belong. That they would have to go to jail would not, he was sure, deter them any more than the fact that some of them might have to die; he was sure he understood what the depth of their conviction would be, because the depth of his own conviction matched theirs. That he was offering them a course of political activism completely consistent with their primarily Protestant religious backgrounds would help greatly; his confidence, absolutely unshakable, was based on his own certainty that he was doing nothing less than God's work.

Years later, he was struck by one additional bit of good fortune, which he had not thought about when he had begun. That was the increasing power of the media, particularly the coming of television news, which would greatly amplify the moral issues at stake and thereby give ordinary Americans a chance to understand the cruelty of racial injustice in their own country. Because he had been out of the country for several years and because he was too busy and serious a young man to watch television on his own, he hardly knew that something called network television even existed. He had no idea at all what a significant asset it would prove to be in the next few years.

There was, Lawson thought, an almost inexorable quality to his own journey which had brought him to Nashville at this moment. He was thirty when he first arrived and would be thirty-one a little more than a year later, when the sit-ins actually began. This was his cause, and this was how he had always seen himself spending his time and using his considerable talents. He came from a politically committed family. His paternal great-grandfather was an escaped slave who had slipped away from Maryland and made it to Guelph, Ontario, by means of the Underground Railroad. There the Lawson family had settled and there Jim Lawson's father, the first James Morris Lawson, was born in 1884. Family records were incomplete, but there were some pieces of paper recording the family's migration north and an oral history, never transcribed but passed on generation to generation, which contained bits and pieces of one family's American journey. Jim Lawson's great-grandfather appeared to be the first in the family to have taken the name Lawson, apparently in honor of a man who worked on the Underground Railway and had helped the family escape the South.

His was an enterprising, ambitious family with a passion for education and for religion. The senior James Morris Lawson was one of the first black graduates of McGill University, and he had come to America as an AME Zionist minister, first in Massachusetts and then elsewhere in the country. He was an itinerant minister in those days, following the Methodist tradition of country ministers, who arrived in newly settled communities on horseback. There they would settle briefly, start up a church, and then, the church firmly established, ride on to yet another frontier town. Creating powerful religious roots in small rural communities was very much a part of the Wesleyan movement.

The Reverend James Lawson, Sr., was not a man on horseback, but he might as well have been. He had worked in rural Massachusetts, and then in New York State—in Jamestown, Elmira, Rochester, Syracuse, and Ithaca. Early on he had married Philane Cover, a young woman who had been born in Jamaica and had come to America on her own in her late teens because she thought there was no chance to be anything more than a domestic in Jamaica. In America she had started out as a nanny to a white family. There was nothing easy about her life with Jim Lawson's father. James Lawson, Sr., was constantly on the move and so was his family: A child was born in almost every town he preached in—nine children in eight cities. He had spent a slightly longer tour in Sharon, South Carolina, but he had not particularly liked the South Carolina system of justice, and much to the subsequent consternation of his pacifist son, he had carried a gun in those years. His tour of Sharon had ended one day when he watched a group of white men beating up a black boy. Lawson had waded in, stopped the fighting, rescued the boy, and taken him home, where he had found the boy's house locked up and the windows shuttered. The smell of fear was everywhere. Lawson was absolutely sure some members of the family were inside. He had knocked on the door several times without an answer, until finally the door had opened and a woman had stepped out and, without saying anything, not even thank you, had snatched the boy away, pulled him inside, and locked the door again. He decided right then and there that the kind of ministry he wanted to run was hopeless in South Carolina. With that he left the South.

In time he took the pastorate of a black Methodist church in Massillon, Ohio. There for the first time his wife could raise their growing family with some measure of stability. The Reverend James Lawson, Sr. was a transitional figure in the church, both a literalist in terms of the Bible—an old-fashioned man who believed the Bible enjoined against vices like smoking and drinking—and an activist too, who, wherever he went, organized and founded both an NAACP and an Urban League. The senior James Lawson was strong and proud, not a man who believed in nonviolence. The origin of Jim Lawson's belief in that came from his mother.

It was as if there were a dividing line which ran right through the Lawson home. The Lawson children were taught by their father not only to be proud, but to defend themselves against any assaults on them, be they physical or verbal. They were not to turn the other cheek. That was anathema to their mother. If their father was a man who believed in vigorous and instantaneous self-defense, their mother was a woman who believed that nothing was ever settled by the use of force. Sometimes the difference in their attitudes was palpable at the Lawson dinner table. Since they lived among people who thought that any son of a preacher ought to be beaten up, the opportunities to fight were constant, particularly for the rare black child living in a world which was predominantly white. His mother hated these fights.

One day when he was about six Jim Lawson came home for lunch. He was followed by a group of other boys, all white, who insisted that one particular boy could beat Jim up. Up the steps Jim went, into his house. The others boys remained outside jeering. His father, who was home, heard the noise and found out what was causing it. "You better get outside and fight that other boy," his father said, and so Jim Lawson did, fighting the other boy to a draw. His mother watched silently. This was not her way. One fight led to nothing more than another fight. She was sure that as the boys got older the fights would become more serious and more violent.

A few years later, when Jim Lawson was about ten, he happened to come home from school alone. It was his habit to come in the back entrance and sit with his mother in the kitchen. It was one of his favorite moments of the day. There was a chair which he liked to sit in because he could face her and talk to her while she was working in the kitchen, preparing that day's supper, and he could always get her full attention and did not have to share her for these precious moments with his siblings. It was her favorite time of the day too. Here she could talk to her children with some degree of pleasure in the middle of a long and hard day that had no visible respites. On this day she had an errand for him to run on Main Street, and so he took care of it, going the seven blocks from their house to the store and back. On the way back he passed a car parked on Main Street. The car window was down and in it was a young white child, four or five years younger than he, so small that the child could stand up in the backseat of the car. As he passed the car, the child yelled out the window: "Hey, nigger!" Jim Lawson did not hesitate, but immediately went over and reached inside the car window and slapped the child as hard as he could. Then he finished the errand, regained his seat in the kitchen and told the story to his mother, telling it proudly, with a note of triumph as he recounted his victory over this tiny racist.

Philane Lawson was cooking and her back was turned to him as he told the story, and when he finished he heard her voice—she did not turn at first, but her voice was very clear—and she asked, "What good did that do, Jimmy?" Everything in his life, he later remembered, seemed to change at that moment. Everything seemed completely still in the kitchen. He was absolutely surprised by her response. He remained completely silent, wondering what he had done wrong. Then she began to talk to him, telling him how much he was loved, by her and his father and his siblings and by God. "We all love you, Jimmy, and God loves you, and we all believe in you and how good and intelligent you are. We have a good life and you are going to have a good life. I know this, Jimmy. With all that love, what harm does that stupid insult do? It's nothing, Jimmy, it's empty. Just ignorant words from an ignorant child who is gone from your life the moment it was said. That child is gone. You will never see him again. You do not even know his name."

He was stunned. Her words had never seemed more powerful. She was saying that there had to be a better way. She was absolutely right, he decided. It was one of the most critical moments in his life, something, he decided years later, that John Wesley would have called a sanctification experience, a moment when his life seemed to stand still and then change forever. In the future when he spoke of his own conversion to the philosophy of nonviolence, he began with that moment in the kitchen with his mother. For he had made a vow at that moment never, if possible, to hit anyone again. She had been right: There had to be a better way. In his later years, after he became a distinguished pastor and theologian, he regarded this as a *numinous* moment, which comes from a Latin word which means that what had happened was virtually a mystical experience, one so special that it carried with it a

special sense of illumination and enlightenment. It was a moment forever frozen in time for him, and as a grown man, whenever he was
moved to anger in a moment of confrontation, he would remember
those words: *Jimmy, what harm did that stupid insult do? Jimmy, you
are loved.*

Her love, her optimism about human nature, and her belief that
there had to be a better way than responding to hatred with hatred of
your own—a hatred which she feared might end up devouring the
hater—formed his home every bit as much, he later decided, as did his
father's strength and hard work. She was a strong, careful, loving
woman who knew how to maximize the limited amount of money a
black minister in the North made in the thirties and forties. They got
their home from the church, and there was a church salary, probably
no more than $1,000 a year. The black women of that generation, he
believed, were brilliant at many things, none less than making-do,
raising families virtually outside the cash economy. On a tiny salary
Jim Lawson's parents raised their nine children, sent five to college in
an austere American economy, and did it so well that no one ever felt
poor. Philane was a skilled cook, a magical repackager of food, so that
nothing was ever wasted. She was a talented seamstress. By ritual
every December each Lawson child was allowed one new suit of
clothes for Christmas. If in more affluent families new clothes were
taken for granted, this was not true in the Lawson home. There it was
an exciting event: Philane Lawson would somehow in the months
prior to Christmas manage to set aside enough money for the rough
cloth. Then everyone would be measured, and given an early fitting
and then a second fitting, and then eventually would come the trying
on of the clothes and the minor adjustments, all done step by step,
child by child, the little ones first.

They grew a lot of their own food, and they always seemed to eat
well. They had a big backyard and that allowed them not only to grow
vegetables, but to keep chickens as well. It was a family where everyone shared in the chores and everyone accepted responsibility for getting the work done. When Jim Lawson eventually married a woman
named Dorothy Wood and they began a family, he found that he was
more skilled at changing diapers than she was, because he had so
much practice with his younger siblings. During World War II his
father had not only kept his church but had worked for the Eaton Ball

Bearing Company in Massillon. That period, as it was for many black families—black men and women took the jobs which had been left open by white men going off to war—was the most affluent for the Lawsons. Jim's mother, in addition to her other household chores, worked regularly in her home doing alterations for a local dress shop, and there were frequent offers for her to come and work full-time in the downtown store. It was only when the youngest children were in high school that she took such a job. Even in the late fifties, with her family largely grown and her holding the full-time job, she still ran a wonderful home. The first time Dorothy Wood came to Massillon to meet her husband's family, the thing she remembered both then and every other time she visited was that on Saturday, at 4:00 A.M., the wonderful smell of baking bread would fill the house because Philane Lawson had gotten up early and started cooking so that her family would have the best of homemade foods all weekend, full-time downtown job or no. She was, her daughter-in-law decided, a woman full of human richness and a woman who took her own codes seriously; Dorothy Wood Lawson in years to come was impressed by the fact that because Philane Lawson did not believe in gambling, her children, by then grown, accomplished adults, observed her ban on cards and waited until their mother went to bed before playing their harmless card games in her home.

As Jim Lawson came to manhood he had a sense of how hard his mother's life had been. It had been difficult for her as a girl—a life with little opportunity—but she had set out to create against all odds a better life; she had come to this country on her own and married and raised a large and loving family. Most important, she had managed to pass on not merely strength but compassion and a capacity to love to all of her children. She had strengthened them without hardening them. That, her son thought, was truly miraculous. She had not approved of her husband's more combative view of human conduct, yet she had not opposed him openly. Their children had never seen them argue over this point. Instead she was content to offer an alternative, kinder view of human conduct to her children, if they chose to follow it.

When Jim Lawson thought about his family, what he remembered years later was its strength and simplicity. His was, he came to realize, a privileged childhood. Not privileged materially, but privileged in human terms, in his parents' belief that nothing was to be wasted, least of all education. He was the oldest boy, and his parents had had five daughters before he was born. As such he was always a bit spoiled, the black scion of the family. ("Jim," one of his older sisters told him when he was a grown man, "you were always special—you were the first boy—you had all of us [sisters] to love you.") He was good at school. He grew up attending largely white schools, and yet he could remember no prejudice, overt or covert, on the part of his teachers. Instead there were teachers who seemed committed to him, including one who thought he could do better than he was doing because he needed glasses. That was unusual: It went against the prevailing prejudice that glasses were for white people because they read, and not for black people, since they did not do anything which demanded the ability to read.

As he went through high school he was torn by conflicting career pulls. He was, after all, a young star of the black world of Massillon, a bright, studious child from a family much admired in the local black community. There was his father's example, a man of God who loved what he did and whose life seemed extremely valuable. But there were others, members of his father's church, who encouraged him in other careers—the family doctor who pushed him toward medicine, and a friend of the family, head of the Urban League, who wanted him to be a lawyer. But the religious pull was always very strong for him. He admired his father, a devoted church man, a minister who took pride in his work and had no sense of bitterness about his life. The Lawsons' religion was a part of every aspect of their daily life.

He was a good reader from the time he was very young, and his father liked taking him to Bible study classes and asking his young son, then only six years old, "Jimmy, could you read that next paragraph?" His father was a close friend of the Reverend James Lincoln Black, who was the pastor of the St. Paul AME Zion Church in Cleveland, a large black Methodist church in a city where the black population was steadily growing. On occasion they would exchange pulpits, and when Jim Lawson was in the huge, almost cavernous Cleveland church, Black would insist that he sit near the pulpit, and he loved it; he felt the richness of the emotion in that huge room. He sensed in those moments, he said years later, that something extremely powerful was taking place all around him; that the passion in that room, a place where it was safe for black people to release their most private and powerful emotions, was not merely religious but political as well.

It was a memorable experience for him, listening to his father preach. The power in the church when he spoke was real and it seemed to come not from the heavens, but from the people themselves. In time he came to feel that those emotions must not be turned on and off each Sunday. They had to exist for a larger purpose; they were there to be utilized and focused. As such he became a social activist even as a teenager. He intended to use his life for some larger purpose. As he neared the completion of high school there were several scholarships available for college. College was a given: His talent was not to be wasted. You were, he often reflected, using a word the Methodists were fond of, the steward of your own life. That meant that you were supposed to maximize your purpose: You were to be diligent in the service of your life to God, and you were not to be careless with anything, least of all God-given talent and intelligence.

In his last two years in high school, Jim Lawson had begun to tilt more toward the ministry, and when he graduated from high school he had decided to go to Baldwin-Wallace, a United Methodist school in Berea, Ohio. It was a college of about two thousand students, around sixty of them black in those days. He had already visited the campus several times, for he had been active in Methodist youth functions; the Methodists actively recruited talented high school students, particularly young people who might have the gift of religious service.

His political beliefs had been crystallizing while he was still in high school. He knew nothing of the politics of pacifism then, but he knew a good deal about Mohandas Gandhi, whom he had read about in the black press. At first he had seen Gandhi as a secular figure, a political leader in a faraway country whose singular political skill was in gaining his people's independence without the use of force. In addition Lawson's political awakening had been accelerated when he had learned of the use of the atomic bomb while still in high school. The more he read about the event, the darker the shadow over the world, and the more important a course of pacifism seemed to him. In his last years in high school, as a star debater, he often argued the question of whether the coming of the bomb meant that traditional arms were now obsolete.

In this same period he was also making a vast additional discovery: He was finding out that there was a world which existed beyond the rather provincial one described in American newspapers and spoken about on American radio. This other world was one which was non-white, and here people did not so lightly accept the principal division of the world as being between Communist and non-Communist. In this other world, the division was between white and nonwhite, between rich and poor. At the same time his own political dissidence was becoming heightened. When he was sixteen and still in high school, he and a friend, acting entirely on their own and with no parental discussion, had stopped by a local hamburger joint near his school. In the past it had been made abundantly clear that blacks were only partially welcome there—that is, they could come in and order as long as they did not eat inside. On this occasion he and his friend had insisted on service; the proprietor reluctantly served them both, but made it clear that they were not to come back and ask for service again. It was his first sit-in.

Others soon followed. By the time he entered college, he had become, almost without realizing it, both an activist and a political dissenter, wary if not actually scornful of the conventional American political attitudes. He thought that by the late forties America's world-view was dangerously simplistic: It seemed to take a complicated, pluralistic world, where to his mind the single greatest driving force was the desire of nonwhite peoples to rid themselves of colonial rule, and see it instead in terms of Communism and anti-Communism. As far as he was concerned the most powerful force in the world was the combined force of race and poverty as it was manifest now in the Third World. What Gandhi had done in India was the symbolic victory of this great new force, driven as it was by anti-colonial rage. What he heard and read about in terms of colonial oppression overseas seemed to have its own domestic reflection back in the Midwest. At the same time he continued to test white-only restaurants at different Methodist youth meetings in small cities in the Midwest, doing this more often than not on his own and without sponsorship, and finding that attitudes in the region, while rarely burdened by all-out racial hatred, were not that different from those in the South.

Baldwin-Wallace was the perfect school for him, or, as he later said, the person he was in the process of becoming. At Baldwin-Wallace he found kindred spirits who reinforced his own political doubts and his own belief that a great deal had been left out of his high school history books; here he found a core of people, some pacifists, some not, most of them driven by religious beliefs, who thought the same things he did and shared the same doubts he had. The more he read, the more he decided that there was in fact an alternative history to the rather conventional one taught in most American schools and colleges. Not surprisingly the local chapter of the Fellowship of Reconciliation was very strong and Jim Lawson joined it in his freshman year, 1947.

That year the local chapter of the FOR sponsored a visit on campus of A. J. Muste, at the time its executive secretary. He was a formidable figure in pacifist circles, a man of profound religious convictions who had been a political dissenter for much of his life. Muste was a Presbyterian minister who had for a time worked with the labor movement, and had flirted at another period of his life with Communism and agnosticism before becoming a leading figure in the nonviolent Christian liberal left. He was, by the time he arrived on campus to give a series of lectures, one of the most articulate dissenters from mainstream American foreign policy.

A. J. Muste became a critical figure in Jim Lawson's life, a man at once learned and kindly, someone who could unlock a vast history which helped support what Jim Lawson's own political instincts told him was right. Muste helped show the young Lawson a solid intellectual and historical basis to the things he already believed in. He not only discussed the history of contemporary nonviolent opposition to seemingly overwhelming force—telling of the Danish and Norwegian resistance to the Nazis and of Gandhi's leadership in India, giving Lawson a historical background for the things which he believed intuitively—but he also asked the most demanding and challenging questions of this young man. To Lawson it was as if Muste, more than the people empowered in Washington, had a real sense of how strong and powerful America had become in the years right after World War II. Muste spoke of a prosperous, affluent, yet curiously anxious nation, one that had emerged untouched by enemy bombs after a world war which had obliterated so much else in the developed world, but which was terribly uneasy and uncomfortable with all of its newfound wealth and power. Muste, in Lawson's eyes, virtually alone was willing to ask the questions which that new American condition mandated: Who, in this extraordinary moment when the nation's wealth and power are so overwhelming, helps the victor to have any humility? What political form does that humility take?

To Jim Lawson, these were precisely the questions which increasingly had come to bother him. The answer, Muste believed, had to come from the teachings of Jesus Christ, based on Christian love—the ability to love someone who was supposed to be an enemy, at home, in the workplace, or, if necessary, in foreign policy. Love was the most basic law of life, Muste seemed to be saying: You will love the Lord, you will work actively for Him, and thereby, because His belief is love and His life is love, you will end up seeking a concept of greater social justice and a more just (and peaceful) country and planet. Before meeting Muste, Jim Lawson had had an instinctive sense of what he believed in; Muste now gave him form and serious intellectual structure to go with his original beliefs. He brought together the two main parts of Jim Lawson's youthful philosophy—his political dissidence, based as it was to no small degree on race, and his religious convictions, and made them one strand.

He also reached out to him at a personal level. To the young Jim Lawson, Muste was a mythic figure, but he was also a kind, compassionate, and infinitely gentle one, a great man who did not behave like a great man and whose modesty was his most memorable personal quality. From the start he seemed intrigued by this confident young black student. In the brief time that Muste spent on the Baldwin-Wallace campus, they were together constantly. Lawson was quite surprised by his easy access to someone who by all rights should have had so little time for someone so young.

That visit changed Lawson's life, and it was central in the creation of what he was to become, a gentle black middle-class Christian radical. Muste in turn connected him to other figures in the pacifist movement like Jim Farmer and Bayard Rustin and Glenn Smiley. The leadership of both American political parties might be converging into a consensus position which accepted most of the givens of the Cold War, but Jim Lawson was moving to a far more radical position. He found himself, as a college student, in almost complete opposition to all of the accepted norms of American political life. By the time he was a junior, he had already realized that he was probably going to have to go to prison for his beliefs. At eighteen, as a freshman, he had registered for the draft, but he had written down that he was doing this with reservations, that he did not believe in the draft, and as a Christian, he did not know if he could serve in the armed forces. His radicalism was born of religious belief: His Jesus was a modern-day Jesus in modern dress who wrestled with modern questions, where and about what to pray, and whether or not to serve in the military. His Jesus did not fear jail, and if he was a minister he was more likely to be found at the poorest church than at the richest one. His Jesus had said, "Follow me, and live as I live." Jesus, Lawson believed, did not limit His revelations to some moment nearly two thousand years earlier; rather, He was there every day in every daily moral situation.

Because Jim Lawson did not think America was under attack, and indeed because he thought that America was the co-aggressor in the madness of the arms race and the Cold War, he had decided by his junior year that he could not serve in the armed forces. In 1949 he had been sent a second classification form by his draft board, but he had refused to fill it out. By that time the small but vibrant world he was a part of at Baldwin-Wallace was becoming a hotbed of religiously driven dissidence. At first that dissent was something of an abstract issue which did not concern the government too much. But by June 1950, at the end of Jim Lawson's junior year, North Korean forces had crossed the 38th parallel and American troops had intervened in what had become the Korean War. By late November, when American forces had pressed to the banks of the Yalu, Chinese Communist forces had entered the fighting. As that happened, the domestic political debate had inevitably grown far more ugly in the United States; Americans no longer simply feared the Communist Chinese in some theoretical way; we had stumbled into a shooting war with them. Draft calls were up and tolerance of those who considered themselves conscientious objectors went down.

Suddenly the political dissidents whom the country had previously not paid that much attention to were sticking out like sore thumbs. Among them was Jim Lawson, trying to follow his own definition of Christ in modern dress. One weekend in his senior year, knowing in advance that there was a warrant out for his arrest, he turned himself in and was fingerprinted. He was charged with violation of the country's draft laws.

At that moment his post-graduation plans had seemed set: He had been ticketed for a position as a Methodist missionary in Rhodesia, still a British colony, a journey which excited him greatly. But he had also understood long ago that the course he was following would almost surely take him to jail. There were any number of ways he could have avoided jail. He could have easily gotten a deferment as a student by continuing his graduate studies, he could have gotten a ministerial deferment, and he could have tried for a conscientious objector's deferment. He had refused all three options. Lawson had thought long and hard about each, and he had decided that he had no moral right to take a deferment, if he was to act on conscience.

For nothing outraged him more than the concept of the ministerial deferment. To Lawson it was a moral and ethical sellout. As far as he was concerned, the government, by offering deferments to young ministers, was effectively buying off both them and their churches, thereby silencing those who should not be silent. As long as a church could save its own, it would not have to take a moral position on the war, he believed. At one point, as his case was just about to go to trial, his mother, clearly upset by the prospect of her son going off to jail, had asked him plaintively, "Why do you have to go to jail? Why can't you take one of your deferments?"

"Mama," he had answered, "you should never have taught me to believe in Christian love. I learned all this from you. You were the one who objected to my using my fists on the playground. You're the one who taught me to feel this way." After that she never challenged him again about his decision.

He had no illusions about his forthcoming court case. In the past year there had been more CO cases going to the courts; those that might have been dropped in the past were now attracting attention. Of those young men who did not choose to go to war, examples clearly would have to be made and on them judgments would have to be passed. The Fellowship of Reconciliation did not lack for expertise on what happened to draft resisters. After being fingerprinted Jim Lawson made bail and was told he would hear in the spring about his trial, which would almost surely be held in Cleveland. His lawyer, assigned to him by the FOR, warned him that the climate in the country had turned very ugly and Lawson should expect the worst. The trial was held at the end of April 1951, his senior year in college. Representatives of the Methodist Board of Missions argued on his behalf, telling of his forthcoming missionary assignment to Africa, arguing as well that he had acted for reasons of conscience. His court case, he remembered, lasted three days.

During the trial Lawson's lawyer asked for leniency and pointed out that this was a fine young man acting on his most deeply held beliefs. His qualities of leadership both at college and in his local Methodist youth work were exemplary, his supporters pointed out. But the more they praised Jim Lawson, the more irritated the judge became. This young man was a leader, he said, a leader in his church, in his community, and in his college. America could not allow its young leaders to behave like this, at a time when the very security of the country was being tested so cruelly by its sworn enemies. An example had to be set. The judge gave Jim Lawson three years in a federal prison.

That the legal system had come down hard on him did not surprise Jim Lawson. What did surprise him was the response of officials at Baldwin-Wallace. He had gotten excellent grades there, had been active in a wide range of social activities, and he thought that his act of conscience would be looked on, if not with complete admiration, at least with compassion by the authorities there. All of this had transpired in the last few weeks of his senior year. Since by this time he and most of his senior classmates had completed their work, Lawson hoped to get his degree with the class of 1951. But the faculty of the college withheld his degree. They ruled that Lawson would have to come back when his prison term was finished and take his final term over.

It was, Lawson thought, a very deliberate slap in the face, a Methodist college in effect taking the side of the government against a young man who thought he was acting on the highest ideals of the church. In time he discovered that his status as a CO had worked less against him in this instance than his race. He learned that he had angered a number of faculty members whom he had thought of as friends, or at least as people who were not enemies. Aspects of his behavior that he could not even remember had apparently irritated them, and they had neither forgotten nor forgiven. He had made the mistake of believing that he was something of a role model for how a black student should behave at Baldwin-Wallace, integrating himself into as many aspects of college life as possible.

But two somewhat older professors, one the head of the department of religion, the other the head of the department of psychology, had apparently been offended by his conduct on campus. One of them had spoken on several occasions to Lawson, telling him he was a bright and talented student but that he was hurting himself as a person by having so many white friends and participating in so many activities. Instead of being on the debate team and in the student theatrical productions, the professor said, Lawson should not be as aggressive. That was the key word, *aggressive;* the Southern translation of it, he would learn later, was *uppity.* Translated, Lawson believed, it meant: You're bright and able, but you do not know your place.

The other professor was the father of a co-ed, and one night at a dance Lawson had apparently danced with his daughter, a major mistake, it turned out. Other professors argued in his behalf, but to no avail. It was an important lesson for Jim Lawson; here he was at a school which thought of itself as a small bastion against racism, and yet even here it was very easy to hit the trip wire which triggered powerful feelings about race. Years later, as a prominent figure in the civil rights movement and one of the college's most distinguished graduates, Jim Lawson was asked back to receive an honorary degree. The new president of the college asked if there was anything else he could do for him, and Lawson asked that his original degree be listed with the class of 1951, which it was.

He entered prison on April 25, 1951. He went, he believed, exceptionally well prepared for the test ahead. He had talked to a number of FOR people about how to deal with prison and they had all spoken along the same line: Do not let prison define you. Do not let the prison routine control your habits. If you do, if you accept its hierarchy and its schedule and, most important of all, its definition of you as a man, you can quickly become a prisoner in the psychological as well as the physical sense and thus very quickly a diminished man. They have control of the locale, but you can, within that important limitation, still have an existence that you can look forward to and which can intellectually and spiritually transport you beyond the locale.

If they do not have a time for prayer on their schedule, you can create a time. If they do not have a time when you can be with other prisoners to discuss God, you can demand it. If you like sports, you must continue to work out. If you like to read, find books either for pleasure or to expand your education. Be wary of prison food, which is starchy, and can quite quickly add lots of pounds to you and make you slothful, that is, the person they want you to be. In addition, do not limit your sense of service. You can help other convicts: If there are things you know and they do not, you must help them. That is as much a part of your calling as going to prison in the first place. If you are a minister and an educated man and you are sent to prison, you must realize that there are a lot of troubled people there and you can talk to them and help them—you can create your own informal ministry.

Above all, they told Lawson that he must not let prison change his self-definition. The guards hated prisoners and thought they were the scum of the earth. The guards would try and prove that they were part of the highest order in the universe, and that the prisoners were of the lowest order. He was not to let himself be pulled into that mind frame; he had to remember at all times that he was there temporarily, by choice, and by conscience. He was not to answer the contempt of the guards with his own contempt toward them, which was surprisingly easy to do. He was going to jail because he was acting as Jesus would have acted; now that he was in prison, Jim Lawson had to act toward those who hated him the way Jesus would have acted.

He believed he could *endure* in prison, a word he chose very carefully, for it was the word which Jesus had used for experiences like this. To endure meant that he would not only live through it, but would learn from it and grow in strength and wisdom. But before he surrendered himself to the authorities, he had to overcome his own innate wariness of prison, all the things he had heard when he was young about prison being so terrible. He had to shut out the words of all his friends in Massillon and Berea who came up to him before his court case was heard, telling him they hoped that he would not have to go to jail because, as they said, *prison would ruin his reputation.* These people meant well but it was not the kind of support he needed just then. Instead he began to reread Gandhi, for Gandhi was the shining example of how a man could use prison to his own needs.

He entered prison at Mill Point, West Virginia. It was a minimum-security federal prison designed for nonviolent prisoners, an honor camp located in the Appalachian woods. It contained an odd mixture of inmates, a fair number of people like himself who were there because they were conscientious objectors, as well as a considerable number of moonshiners brought in from the surrounding hill country, congenital violators of the nation's distilling laws. Mill Point in 1951 was still a segregated institution, particularly in its dorms. Because a large number of CO's had been sent there over the years, it had a wonderful library in those areas Lawson cared most about, religion and philosophy and ethics.

If Mill Point was not a country club, it was nonetheless not a harsh or brutal place. The day began at 8:00 A.M., so Lawson and the other CO's, or would-be-CO's, met two or three times a week at 6:00 A.M. to discuss political and religious issues, to meditate if need be, to form, in effect, a small ministry within the prison. By meeting regularly, they reinforced the idea that they were not alone. That was important. If one of them was momentarily having a hard time, the others could reach out to him.

Jim Lawson found prison quite bearable; indeed, it was gradually becoming like a rare university of the streets for him. To his surprise he quite liked some of the rougher men, the kind he had never met before, the people from the poorest walks of life, whose lives had always been extremely hard, and who were in prison because life for them was one giant net in which sooner or later they were bound to be caught. He found he could learn as much or more about life from them as from his peers. He stayed busy, he worked in the motor pool as a bookkeeper, an easy job, and he read a great deal. He began to feel strengthened by the experience. He was keeping the faith.

Then it all blew up. In December 1951 President Truman issued an order desegregating all federal institutions. That included Mill Point. There were a number of white prisoners who immediately asked to live in the black dorm: Some were CO's who were integrationists, others were white men who were tired of the overcrowded white dorm and thought there would be more space and privacy in the less crowded black one, and a few whites who wanted to move because they no longer wanted to be in a dorm with the Appalachian moonshiners. A committee was formed to ask the prison officials to expedite the desegregation. At a certain point in the ensuing tension a group of the white Southerners physically forced some of the CO's out of the white dorm, calling them nigger-lovers. Soon the word came back to the motor pool that the white leaders were out to get Jim

Lawson because he was the leader of the would-be integrationists. It was, he later learned, as if his very manner—a black college man among poor whites, his exceedingly careful use of the language— seemed to be an affront to them.

Suddenly the previously quiet prison was engulfed in a racial storm. The white CO's who had wanted to switch dorms were now identified by the white prisoners as nigger-lovers, and had to be quarantined. They were all sent to the hospital ward, and the hospital was placed under guard. A few days later, right before Christmas 1951, some of the white integrationists, as well as Jim Lawson, now perceived as a troublemaker, were all put in a car and transferred to a federal prison in Ashland, Kentucky. Ashland was a much meaner, grimmer place, housing a good many violent criminals who were doing hard time. From the moment he arrived, Jim Lawson was singled out by the warden as the man who caused the Mill Point riot. "We know you're the ringleader," the warden said, "and you better believe that we know how to deal with troublemakers here." Lawson answered that he was not a troublemaker, he was a man of conscience. A heated argument ensued, which the warden won; he gave Jim Lawson a maximum-security cell in a particularly violent cell block.

The maximum-security cell block contained a row of singularly violent criminals, all of them black. This was a new and far more brutal world, one where Lawson was seemingly without protection. Here, in contrast to Mill Point, he was virtually alone, and he could sense the hostility all around him. The one person who might become a friend was a powerfully built black man whose prison name was Liberty. Liberty was a dedicated career robber and mugger. Prison was a part of his life. He would do his time, be let out, return to the streets, mug people, be picked up, and then return to prison. Liberty accepted the dynamic of his life without complaint. They formed an odd couple, the cool, cerebral Lawson with his knowledge of the world of ideas and religion, and Liberty, with his knowledge of the country's meanest streets. "Professor, you've got your profession—it's your church," Liberty once told Lawson, "and I've got mine." What's that? Lawson asked. "Mugging people," he answered. Lawson would argue with him that he had to get a different job, that he was caught in a terrible cycle, but Liberty said it was the only work he knew. "Listen, Professor," Liberty once told him, "my profession is as good as your profession." To him mugging was a career, and he made a good living (until he was caught, which was inevitable).

It was in Ashland that Lawson faced the only true moral and spiritual crisis of his prison career. Not long after he arrived, there was an attempt on the part of a number of the black prisoners to make him a queen—a prison sexual object. The men who came after him were the toughest criminals in the cell block, habitual criminals who had become accustomed to taking their sexual favors where they could find them. Until then Jim Lawson had not felt threatened by any aspect of prison life. But this was different. He had his choice, he was told. He could go along with what they wanted, in which case he would come off lightly, and they would make it pleasurable for him, or they would make it a gang rape.

He thought of it as nothing less than a threat to his very soul. The idea of homosexual rape, either by one or two men or by a gang, was the most repellent thing imaginable to him. For the first time in his life, he was absolutely filled with fear. One night he woke up in his cell—all cells were supposed to be locked—to find one of the most violent men in the cell block just outside his cell, peering down at him. It was like getting a greeting card of what was still to come, a confirmation of their threat that all cell doors could be opened, as well as a not very subtle warning that the guards had been bought off and were in on it. Finally he decided that he would resist. There was a steel chair in his cell and he decided he would use it as a weapon. But his very resistance would be a violent act, violating his personal vow of nonviolence. It would mean he would leave prison having failed to be true to himself. He might spare himself the rape, but he would leave having failed in his sense of Christian duty.

It was at that point Lawson had one of his numinous experiences. It was as if he heard a voice explaining everything to him. Everything which had been so difficult suddenly became clear. The voice told him that he was not there of his own volition or because he had done something wrong. He had not sinned; if anything he was there because he had been sinned against. The voice explained his dilemma to him. "If something terrible happens to you, it's not you causing it, and what happens is not your fault. What happens would be outside your control. You are responsible for only one thing—above all you must not violate your own conscience. If something terrible happens it is because of them, not because of you. It is not about personal choice. That makes it one more thing you have to endure in order to be true to Him. It is part of the test He set out for you." When Jim Lawson heard that voice, his fear fell from him. He would not resort to physical violence to protect himself. He would endure. He prepared himself for the worst. But at almost the same time the threats against him stopped. He always suspected that it was because Liberty had put out the word to leave him alone.

He stayed in Ashland for five months. When he was first sentenced he had been told that he would probably not be paroled and would have to serve his entire term. But much to his surprise, in May 1952 he was paroled. So too within a few months were all five of the other CO's who had been with him at Mill Point. The Korean War was not so much winding down as flattening out. Jim Lawson left prison that May, took the summer off, and returned to Baldwin-Wallace in the fall to get his degree. If he had lost the chance to go to Rhodesia, the Methodist church was offering him something even more attractive, an opportunity to serve in India as a missionary, and India meant a chance to get closer to Gandhi, part of his life's dream.

Lawson was assigned to a Presbyterian college in the British system in the city of Nagpur. The president of Hislop College there, David Moses, an Indian with a Ph.D. from Harvard, already knew a good deal about Lawson, knew of his time in prison, and had requested him. If anything the time spent in prison had made Lawson more attractive to Moses. Among other things, Moses wanted a man of God who was also likely to be a good athletic instructor—he had been impressed by the vitality and democratic nature of American sports, and Jim Lawson had been a good sandlot athlete. Visas for India came through very slowly in those days, and Jim Lawson received his in early 1953 and showed up in Nagpur in April 1953. His tour was supposed to last three years.

It was a wonderful three years, the perfect complement intellectually and spiritually to the fascinating but difficult time in prison. What a journey, he later thought, first Mill Point and then Nagpur. One additional reason he had wanted to go overseas was a desire to de-Americanize himself as much as he could culturally. After all, he thought he wanted to follow in the footsteps of Jesus, and Jesus had not been a contemporary American figure, living in a rich, white, highly industrialized society. He wanted to be able to make decisions on ethical questions which were less derivative of his own American experience.

He loved India. He loved the diversity of color, he was intrigued by the social complexity which came from living in a nonwhite country where the undertow of caste was so powerful, and he loved the ferocious way Indians argued back and forth about everything. Not everyone at Nagpur was pleased with him; some old-timers in the foreign missionary community believed he had gone native and resented it. He got around on a bike when almost all the other missionaries and foreigners had cars. Warned that he dare not eat Indian food lest he become violently and perhaps permanently ill, he largely ate off the economy. On occasion he even wore Indian clothes. In everything he did he had one goal—to try and comprehend the man who had emerged as the most important contemporary political-religious figure for him.

What quite surprised him was the number of influential Indians and missionaries who scorned Gandhi. At first their dissent came as something of a shock, but then gradually Jim Lawson came to believe that based as he was at Hislop, he was operating in what was primarily a Christian religious milieu and therefore he was dealing with what was almost unconscious Christian arrogance. Because Gandhi was a Hindu, there was a certain Christian belief that he represented a lesser religion and therefore was in some way a lesser man spiritually. Many of Lawson's colleagues, particularly the older ones, benign in their attitude toward the locals or not, anti-colonialist or not, he believed, held nonetheless to the belief that Christians had all the answers to all questions and were the most advanced people in the world. Because Christianity was the dominant religion in the most advanced nations, they believed that theirs was clearly the most advanced religion in the world. One manifestation of that was a disdain for anyone who was a Hindu, a religion which in their eyes did not lend itself to success, at least not industrially, materially, or technologically. Even these men of God, sent to foreign nations to spread the word of their own faith, Lawson decided, managed unconsciously to connect the power of religion with their own nation's industrial and military index and sanitary codes. The other thing which surprised him in the missionary circles in which he traveled was the core belief that Gandhi, whatever his accomplishments, had been a troublemaker, an attitude prevalent among the more senior missionaries.

His own admiration for Gandhi's life continued to grow. If Jesus had come back to earth as a nonwhite living under British colonial rule in the late nineteenth century, Lawson sometimes asked himself, how different would he have been from Gandhi? The answer, he believed, the more he studied the riddle of these two men, was not very. Jim Lawson had gone to India as a believer in the Gandhian technique, and his years there strengthened that part of him. When he left he was more than ever the most unusual of hybrids, a black middle-class Christian disciple of a Hindu activist who had so successfully challenged British colonial rule. No other figure in the twentieth century, he came to believe, had emulated the prophetic vision of the Christian and Hebrew religions so clearly. No one else was so close to Jesus.

Jim Lawson was in India in December 1955, when the Montgomery, Alabama, bus boycott began. It was for a variety of reasons very big news in the Indian papers, those printed in English and those printed in the different local languages. It seemed almost from the start to show that his two worlds, the one in America and the one in India, were converging. He was absolutely fascinated by the emergence of Martin Luther King, a man whose background was so much like his own and who seemed to see the struggle ahead in absolutely the same terms as he did. In the spring of 1956 it was time to go home, but he had made a number of African friends while in Nagpur and undertook a long tour of Africa on his way home, where he sensed and was exhilarated by the rising force of anti-colonial feeling. He had just started his studies at Oberlin when he had his meeting with Martin King.

Therefore when he began to teach his seminars in Nashville in the fall of 1959, he had already become an impassioned expert on the subject of race and freedom. He was ready both to teach and to lead a protest. He was as absolutely clear in his mission as he was of his own vision of what America should be. Mild and gentle he might seem, but he was a true radical Christian who feared neither prison nor death. He was not an arrogant man, but of his own mission, and in particular of the validity of Gandhian nonviolence as an instrument of change in the American South, he had no doubts.

He had barely unpacked his bags when he took off for a regional conference sponsored by the Southern Christian Leadership Conference in Columbia, South Carolina. It was a conference arranged by Martin Luther King, and it was his assigned job to teach a workshop each day on nonviolent protest. The first person to greet him when he arrived in Columbia was King. Then and at every subsequent SCLC meeting, the normal morning meeting on strategy would be followed by lunch and then a workshop led by Jim Lawson. King made sure each time that he sat down in the first row. It was his way of saying that these workshops were central to the meeting's purpose.

4

WHEN JIM LAWSON FINALLY BEGAN TO GET SETTLED IN NASHVILLE and started to take inventory of his new city, he was immediately impressed by the fact that he was hardly alone there, that there were a surprising number of other young like-minded black ministers just beginning to surface in Nashville's religious and political life. Later one of the most prominent members of that early core of ministers and students who came together in Nashville, the Reverend C. T. Vivian, said that it was as if God had a master plan, bringing so many uncommon people of such rare strength and vision together in one place at one time. Jim Lawson thought that C.T. was right, that it was a coming together of rare, committed, talented people. But the word he used was different. It was *providential,* he said, a Methodist word which meant that God was working in people and through them to bring them together at a certain time so that certain things could happen which He had wished for.

The Nashville black community was just beginning to emerge as a modern liberal one; that which often limited progress elsewhere in the South, bitter divisions in the black world between an old conservative faction and a new, better educated, more liberal one, did not exist there. Nashville was largely unburdened by the shadow cast by a powerful, extremely conservative black bourgeoisie—that is, black leaders who had become extremely affluent and influential under the aegis of segregation and who, consciously or unconsciously, resented the coming of a new, more aggressive leadership, a leadership which might put their own past gains and hard-won status at risk. Atlanta by contrast had a large, affluent black middle class, primarily commercial in its professions, one which over time had accepted segregation, however reluctantly, and had become, more than it realized, a participant and, in the eyes of younger blacks, a beneficiary of the old order. Throughout the South, to the younger leadership now challenging existing racial mores, some of these older leaders were part of the problem.

In Nashville there was an ascending young group of leaders who had already emerged much in the way that Martin King and Ralph Abernathy had in Montgomery and Fred Shuttlesworth had in Birmingham. The central figure in the Nashville leadership was the Reverend Kelly Miller Smith. He was a counterpart to the other talented, well-educated black leaders now surfacing across the South who, somewhat to the irritation of their elders, had formed the SCLC as a regional political force. In city by city, following the example of King, political leadership was being wielded by ministers, ready and eager to use the white man's Christianity as a weapon against him in the struggle over segregation. Kelly Miller Smith was the pastor of the First Baptist Church, the *black* First Baptist Church, in Nashville.

Smith had been in Nashville for seven years when Jim Lawson arrived, and he was already widely viewed as a rising star in the Baptist ministry. As much as anyone he had been the black community's point man in the often painful, grudging process of helping to negotiate the plan to integrate the city's public schools in 1957, and he commanded great respect among his peers in other cities and among his fellow Nashville ministers. He was a tall, graceful man of exceptional intellect and great engaging human warmth, which he seemed to dispense on all those around him, regardless of color or position. He was well educated—there were degrees from both Morehouse and Howard among his credentials—and yet his roots were in rural Mississippi, for he was born and raised in Mound Bayou, the small all-black town in the Mississippi Delta. Like his good friend Martin Luther King, when he took the pulpit, he readily blended the most sophisticated aspects of the modern social gospel with the cadence of the traditional, small-town black Baptist church.

He was also very handsome, which did not hurt him on either side of the color line in Nashville. The first time that the Reverend Will Campbell, the ubiquitous white liberal minister who had become the National Council of Churches representative in Nashville, saw Kelly Miller Smith was at the convention of black ministers in New Orleans, where the SCLC had been formed. Campbell had looked over and seen one man who seemed to stand apart, tall, with an incandescent smile, a man whom the other ministers almost unconsciously seemed to pay court to. "Who is that incredibly good-looking man?" Will Campbell asked a friend. "Oh, that's the Reverend Kelly Miller Smith of Nashville," his friend had answered.

In 1958 when Jim Lawson arrived in Nashville, Kelly Miller Smith's was the most powerful and influential black church in a black community which was hardly stereotypical. His church was composed of the black elite of the city, but the leading figures were by no means all businessmen. Rather there was a sense of an intelligentsia as well, with faculty members from Fisk, A&I, and Meharry, as well as a large number of people from the different religious publishing houses. In addition, a number of the city's black lawyers belonged (but not, of course, Z. Alexander Looby, the city's reigning black attorney and city councilman, who was born in the British West Indies and was both an Episcopalian and a Republican, which made him very different from all the other black leaders in town).

Kelly Miller Smith had been the critical black player as the city in the past few years had moved cautiously and sluggishly ahead in terms of integration. (*Cautiously* was the right word: In 1963, six years after the school system first integrated and nearly ten years after *Brown,* there were still only 773 blacks in previously all-white schools in Nashville.) Sometimes, he told friends, he thought he was doomed to live a life in which he was always restless with the pace of change, in which every move by the white community seemed too little too late, but which he would be forced to accept because it was better than no movement at all. He had to fight hard, he told them, not to give in to either of the most seductive pulls which went with his job, public rage and private depression. It was not surprising, he sometimes noted, that he struggled with ulcers for most of his adult life.

The integration of the city's schools had begun in September 1957. It was the most hesitant integration imaginable as far as the black leadership of the city was concerned, a grade a year, starting in grade one the first year, and expanding to the second grade in the second year, and the third grade in the third year. The white power structure, quick to congratulate itself in matters such as these, thought it an admirable plan; the black power structure, still finding its way, still unsure of how much leverage and muscle it actually wielded locally, thought it far too slow and too tentative a first step. The Nashville

Plan, as it was called, spoken of with great pride among the leading white liberals in the city's political hierarchy, covertly reflected age-old Southern prejudices. (In the rural South it had not been unusual for black and white children to play together until they reached puberty. Only then, when the more explosive issue of sexual contact surfaced, did separation take place. Therefore, said Cecil Sims, a white establishment lawyer who was a key architect of the Nashville Plan, it was best to let the children come together when they were very young; doing so was less explosive and seemed less likely to violate local custom, and it gave everyone a good deal more breathing room to get ready.)[1]

If white moderate Nashville was delighted with the plan, black Nashville harbored a great deal more doubt. Will Campbell was a member of Kelly Miller Smith's church and had gone with Smith on the night that one of the city's high officials had outlined the plan to white and black parents. It happened to be raining heavily that evening. The cream of Nashville's black leadership was there, and the official had looked out the window and said that it seemed prophetic that it was raining so hard, "because very soon it's going to be raining little nigger babies in our schools." There had been an audible gasp in the room when he said that. Later, when they drove home, Kelly Miller Smith had looked at Will Campbell and just shaken his head.

The integration of the Nashville public school system had not been an abstract issue to Kelly Miller Smith and his wife, Alice. Among the small number of first graders who had been in the first class to integrate the Nashville schools a year earlier was their six-year-old daughter, Joy, the eldest of their four children. Joy Smith was three years old when the Supreme Court had rendered the *Brown* decision, and Kelly and Alice Smith had always assumed that she would gain the benefits of an integrated school system. There had never been any doubt that Joy would be one of the first blacks to enter what was a previously all-white school, for Kelly Miller Smith was not a man to ask others to do what he himself feared to do.

The day before, Smith had prayed not that the day would pass without violence but rather that all of those involved in this momentous day would have the strength to endure, and that his child's first school days would pass happily. As he and his daughter left the house that first morning, he cited this passage of Scripture to his wife: *The Lord is my light and my salvation; whom shall I fear? The Lord is the strength of my life; of whom shall I be afraid?*

Though it was nothing like Little Rock's, Nashville's first day was by no means entirely peaceful. The local segregationists knew the names of the black children and which schools they were attending. Joy, the only black child selected to enter the Clemons Elementary School, walked to class that day holding the hand of her father, and for her it was a painless experience. To be sure there were crowds of white people on the corner yelling slurs, but the teachers and the other children were good to her, and the day passed without incident. That, however, was not true elsewhere in the city. At the Hattie Cotton Elementary School, which had also admitted one black child, someone had planted dynamite, and it went off early on the following day, September 10, destroying a vast wing of the school. It was a quick reminder that even the most cautious venture into the South's future, in a city largely judged to be moderate, and even genteel, always risked a violent outcome.

Balancing the political and racial forces in Nashville, restraining on occasion his own rage, was something Kelly Miller Smith had become involuntarily expert at. The night following the Hattie Cotton explosion he had put his own ambiguity and faith to the test. He had called Will Campbell and asked him to come to a meeting with him. "Oh, Will," Smith had said, "you'll love this—it going to be great fun. For my sins I'm going to be the most conservative man in the room." He was right: It was as if the bombing had touched off all the stored-up rage in the black community. Speaker after speaker got up and denounced the bombing and demanded some kind of reprisal. There was talk of guns and retaliation. For most of the evening, Smith let the meeting go on without challenging the speakers. It was as if he knew that he had to let the rage vent itself. As the rhetoric finally began to subside, Kelly Miller Smith got up and cooled it in his own way. "Now, we can fight them with guns—we can, like some of our brothers here suggest, arm ourselves, except the white people manufacture and sell all the guns, and they have the police force and all the police have guns, and you can guess which side the police will be on. Or we can fight them with knives, except again it's the white people who manufacture and control the sale of knives. So we can do what some of you want, which is to fight them, and we can get a lot of our own people killed. Or we can go forward the way we planned and try to show them the right way." It was Kelly at his best, Campbell thought, shrewdly letting that age-old rage burn itself out, and only then speaking. "Just another day in the Baptist ministry," Smith told Campbell that night as they drove home.

Kelly Miller Smith was not very territorial. He had welcomed Jim Lawson to Nashville on his arrival and had in no way, as might have happened in other cities, let his own ego be at stake. Instead he had made Lawson the social action leader of the local chapter of the Southern Christian Leadership Conference. He encouraged Lawson to start holding workshops as soon as he could and he offered the basement of his church for their meetings. That give Jim Lawson immediate legitimacy. If someone as respected and as influential as Kelly Smith was behind him and offering the full use of his church, then he was no longer an outsider. Not all of Smith's deacons and older parishioners were happy with their pastor's decision, but it was a done deal, and it would mean that it would be easier to get out the word about these meetings.

If, of the older ministers who now began to counsel the younger activists, Kelly Miller Smith was the gentlest and most subtle figure, and Jim Lawson the most cerebral and intellectual, then there was no doubt who the most fiery was. It was the Reverend C. T. Vivian. Cordy Tindell Vivian, C.T. to everyone who knew him, always seemed wired, quick to explode. Like Jim Lawson he had not grown up in the South, being raised in small towns in Illinois, and like Jim Lawson he did not defer to white people, but Jim Lawson did not defer in a quiet, rather low-key way, and C.T. did not defer in an edgy way, which seemed to draw the sharpest of lines, and which seemed to invite additional confrontation. More than any of the other Nashville ministers, he seemed able to provoke the anger, both verbal and physical, of his adversaries. He was intense and outspoken: C.T., his wife, Octavia, once said in a masterpiece of understatement, gave long answers to short questions.

He was both student and minister at that moment, which was important to the young people in the Movement. Here was someone ten or twelve years older than they, a man of the cloth, willing to march with them, share their hardships, and treat them as peers. He had come to Nashville in 1955 to attend American Baptist. In addition to his studies he held two full-time jobs, one as the pastor of a church, the First Community Church at Eighteenth and Knowles (in exchange for his services he was given rent for his house, and had his electricity bill paid as well); he had also taken a job as an editor at the National Baptist Convention, USA, Inc., which was the black Baptist publishing arm, where he was paid a very modest salary, and where he found himself in a constant struggle with the publishing house's more conservative editors, who wanted as little coverage of the rise of Martin Luther King and the new racial protest as possible. Frustrated by their orders to desist and their systematic killing of his articles, he collected all of his clips, interviewed King himself when he came to Nashville, and wrote one final article for the publishing house. It was twenty-four pages long. When it was rejected, Vivian took some of his own money and published it privately and sold it.

His collisions with the segregated side of Nashville life were even more sharply drawn. Almost from the day he had arrived, C. T. Vivian had clashed with the forces of segregation. In the fall of 1956 when he had been there about a year, he boarded a city bus on the outskirts of the town where he lived. The Montgomery strike had already taken place and had been won, and C. T. Vivian was, under no circumstances, a person to ride in the back of a white man's bus. He had taken a seat near the front of the half-filled bus. The driver had turned, walked back to him, and ordered him to the back of the bus. Angry words had been exchanged. Some other white men on the bus had gathered around Vivian and for a moment it looked like they were going to help the driver throw him off the bus. But then the driver looked out the window and realized that they were in the middle of a black neighborhood, and that a crowd was gathering. The driver ordered all the other people off the bus and drove C. T. Vivian to the police station, his prisoner surprisingly eager for the forthcoming confrontation, already planning in his mind the protest which would follow. But the Nashville cops were not sure what the city's policy was. They knew what the policy used to be. They made a few phone calls to city hall and back came the word that the city was almost finished negotiating the end of segregated bus service, that the announcement would be made soon, and that the signs were already coming off some buses. The actual announcement was supposed to come in January 1957. "Damn, but if you'd only done this a year ago we'd have really had you," one of the cops told him. In the end they had packed Vivian into a police car and rather reluctantly driven him home. That angered Octavia Vivian, who had looked out her window to see a new car pulling up and her husband getting out. That man, she thought, mistaking the cop car for a taxi, has absolutely no right to take a cab home. Here we are on the tightest budget in Nashville, already pinching pennies for food, and that man with all his dreams of glory has to ride in some fancy new cab.

For a time the same bus driver would spot C.T. or Octavia Vivian waiting for the bus, and he would speed by them. Then Vivian, accompanied by a witness, hailed the bus, boarded it, and told the driver that they would go to his employer—it was one of several private lines used by the city—and hit the line with a boycott. Suddenly a revolutionary concept became quite clear to the driver: C. T. Vivian wanted the confrontation even more than the driver did. In the past black men had run from any showdown with even so marginal a figure of authority as a bus driver. Not, apparently, anymore. From then on the driver, his face set in a grim, frozen mask, would stop and pick up C. T. Vivian and Octavia Vivian.

For the young students just coming aboard, the combination of the three men—the gentleness of Kelly Miller Smith, the high intellect of Jim Lawson, and the edgy combativeness of C. T. Vivian—was a powerful one; it was one thing to be a mere student and take sustenance from other students; it was another thing to have three such different and uncommon men on your side.

By chance the first connection that Jim Lawson made to the world of black students in Nashville was through a white transfer student at Fisk named Paul LaPrad. Paul LaPrad was from Delphi, Indiana, a small farm town near Lafayette. His people were members of the Church of the Brethren, which was, like the Quakers, a church committed to nonviolence. He had been a student at Manchester College, in North Manchester, Indiana; he had arrived at Fisk after several months touring Europe with a friend, a trip on which he saw more of the sites of Hitler's death camps than he did Parisian nightlife. Somewhat poorer after his visit to Europe, LaPrad had subsequently worked for a year in Chicago to save some money for college, and had decided to study for a time at a black college. He applied to Fisk, which had accepted him. Before he left for Nashville, Paul LaPrad set out to get the name of someone who might help connect him to the kind of community social work he had come to find so rewarding. He had asked one of the local ministers, Julius Belser, if he knew of anyone in Nashville who was interested in Christian nonviolence. "Yes," said Belser, "there's a young graduate student down there named James Lawson who's very bright and very active, and you might want to look him up." It was the only name he took with him when he left for Nashville.

LaPrad arrived in Nashville determined to be a part of something larger than he was, and so he soon looked up Jim Lawson. Lawson mentioned rather casually that he was going to hold workshops on nonviolent action with the eventual object of testing local segregation laws. He wondered if LaPrad knew any Fisk students who might want to attend the workshops. Indeed LaPrad did. He had begun to hang out at the Fisk International Center, and he had made a number of friends there; the conversation among them often swung around to the fact that five years after *Brown,* almost nothing had happened to change the life of most blacks in the South. One of the students who might be interested, he said, was a bright young woman from Chicago named Diane Nash.

Diane Nash was considered the most sophisticated of the early group which came together to study and work with Jim Lawson, at least in the judgment of the other students, in part because she was from the North, in part because she was so beautiful, and in part because, though this was left unsaid, she was so light-skinned (having light skin color in those days had a great deal to do with the perception that she was both beautiful and sophisticated). It was said at the time, and not entirely without merit, that many of the young men who attended the early workshops and then kept going back did so because it was a chance to be near Diane Nash.

Not long after the incident at the state fair when she first confronted segregated rest rooms, Paul LaPrad mentioned Jim Lawson's workshops to Nash. Never in her life, she thought, had she been more interested in political action. She went eagerly to the first session.

5

THE STUDENTS WHO ASSEMBLED IN FRONT OF JIM LAWSON FOR THE early workshops in the fall of 1959 were disappointed at first. They had heard that they were going to be taught by a brilliant and passionate young minister, and perhaps he was, but there were no signs of it in the beginning. He was obviously smart, but he was different even from someone as cerebral and majestic as Kelly Miller Smith. He seemed to lack passion, and when he spoke he was cool and detached. Sometimes when he spoke about the evils of segregation it was as if these terrible things were happening to other people in some distant land, not to them right here in Tennessee. They were all accustomed to spellbinding preachers, men who as they reached the climax of their sermons became louder and more passionate. Lawson was completely different; as he reached a critical point, he became cooler and more careful, and sometimes they had to strain to hear him. Sometimes it seemed as if he were more like a white college professor than a black minister. His meetings, despite the explosive nature of the subject matter, were always low-key. He never, they quickly learned, tried to turn them into an amen chorus. Some of the students, expecting a very different kind of workshop, were more than a little frustrated. They had come to him with their anger and their willingness to act upon it, and again and again he would talk about the power of love. Yet everything he did was quite calculated: Because the journey he was asking them to take was potentially so dangerous, Jim Lawson deliberately did not want to touch the powerful emotional chords within them. He was wary of the power of emotion. Instead what he wanted more than anything else was to let them find within themselves the things he had already discovered within himself.

He in turn looked out at them at those early sessions and saw their uncertainty and he understood their doubts. It was obvious in their faces. They were there to learn, but he sensed at the beginning that they did not really believe in what he was saying, certainly not in all the love-thy-enemy stuff he was talking about. There were just a handful of them in the beginning, and he was acutely aware that they were more conscious of the limits of their numbers than he was. It was part of his considerable strength as a teacher that he could still put himself in their place and that he understood from the beginning exactly what was going on in their minds—their sense of their own vulnerability and their belief that what he was about to ask them to do was quixotic. The fear would come later, he was sure, as they got past stage one. But in stage one he had to impress on them the viability of what he was talking about; he had to convince them that this cause was real and that they could pull it off, young and uncertain though they were individually. He could also sense—indeed, virtually smell—the overwhelming doubt which so obviously existed in their minds. Here he was saying in effect that they could bring down the walls of segregation in the capital of the state of Tennessee, and that they could do it by their faith and their willpower, and by offering themselves up as witnesses against this degrading system.

Therefore when he first met with them regularly in November and December, the most important thing he had to do was change their mind-set, and to prove to them that though their numbers were small, and the forces aligned against them seemingly mighty, they could do it, that the great power was in the righteousness of their idea. That was at the heart of the Gandhian philosophy as he had mutated it to a concept of Christian nonviolence: The might of an idea whose time had come. *Your idea is not small,* he kept emphasizing—it was the first and most basic of their lessons—*and because your idea is not small, your numbers will not be small either.* There would be an inevitable dynamic, he told them. No matter how fearful the task ahead, no matter how cruel the forces of the resistance, it would work to their advantage. Yes, right now at the beginning there were not many of them, and their names were known to no one; if something happened to them right now in this church, no one outside would care very much. But if they acted upon conscience, that would change; if the local authorities, as they were likely to do, lashed out against them, then they would no longer be anonymous. Their names would be known, their deeds spoken of on their campuses, and in the black community in Nashville. It would be known among their friends and peers that they had suffered and paid a price for acting on behalf of others. That would make it harder and harder for others to sit on the sidelines; therefore others would be forced to act, and in turn to take their place.

He was absolutely confident of this, and it became his most basic lesson. He spoke again and again of the awesome power of action which was just in a land where the laws were unjust. If they acted on conscience they would be immediately transformed; they would no longer be a handful of unknown young students who had mounted a bizarre and foolish challenge against powerful, entrenched interests. This was his most crucial lesson: Ordinary people who acted on conscience and took terrible risks were no longer ordinary people. They were by their very actions transformed. They would be heroes, men and women who had been abused and arrested for seeking the most elemental of human rights. The city officials in the end would involuntarily and unconsciously help in their recruiting. That was what Jesus had done in his time, and that was what Gandhi had done, and he illustrated it with stories from the life of both men. Was it just to deny black people such basic human rights? he would ask. Was it fair that their parents had always been treated all their lives as second-class citizens? The answer was obviously no. Therefore, the idea which drove them was extremely powerful, for the greater the injustice, then the greater the force of the idea which opposed it.

Gradually he laid out in front of them a prophecy of the dynamic of their movement which was to prove stunningly accurate. Years later he could remember one early session when he had gone through this vision one more time—their faces had at first reflected a certain predictable doubt—and then he had noticed Diane Nash nodding as he spoke, and he was sure for the first time that he was getting through, that even as he spoke, she could envision what was happening, that they would be the advance guard, they would pay the heaviest price, but in the end, others would follow. If they listened to him, they would not be alone. She was, he decided, his first recruit. Lesson one was taking root. From then on as he spoke, he saw less doubt in their faces.

From the start Diane Nash liked the workshops. They were, whatever else, filled with purpose. There was nothing aimless about them. There she met people her own age who had had comparable painful experiences. They formed an unusual community for the time: They were students, they had arrived in Nashville by and large knowing no one else, and now, as they were drawn to Jim Lawson's workshops, they were not only making friendships but moving toward historic confrontations with the bastions of a segregated America. The more they attended the workshops, the better they knew each other, she thought, and the more they took sustenance from each other.

They were an odd assemblage. There were in the beginning very few Fisk men in the leadership group. That was probably, some of them decided, because the Fisk men were the young stars of the black Nashville student world, privileged, often wealthy young black aristocrats, who felt they were above political protest. One of the original members of the Lawson group, a Fisk graduate student named Marion Barry, thought it was fascinating how sharply the class lines seemed to run through the black college world. The fancier you were, the larger your role in Fisk's powerful fraternity life, the less likely you were to be a part of Jim Lawson's group. Barry himself was poor, perilously close to being a member of the black underclass, and as a graduate student in chemistry, less tied to undergraduate life. He had been drawn to the workshops because his own consciousness had risen dramatically in the past few years, and he had, while a student at LeMoyne College in Memphis, led a daring challenge against a white segregationist member of the school's board of trust; what Barry had done was almost unthinkable in 1958. For him belonging to the Lawson group was the most natural thing he had ever done, although he was by no means sure he believed in nonviolence. It did strike him, however, as being at the very least a shrewd and valuable tactic.

To the degree, in the early days of the workshops, that there was Fisk representation, it came from the women, not the men. Of the men from Fisk who attended, a surprising number turned out to be white exchange students. If Lawson's group lacked Fisk men, it made up for that with a number of students from the American Baptist College, a small and exceedingly poor little black Bible school a few miles away in north Nashville. The American Baptist students liked to hang out at Fisk because it was a far greater center of black social life. Some of the brightest and most ambitious American Baptist students had been brought to Lawson's workshops by Kelly Miller Smith, who was the most popular professor at the seminary.

At first as they began to attend these sessions, the varying students were all a little unsure of themselves. The young men from American Baptist were poor and decidedly rural and the world of Fisk seemed very distant and almost unreachable to them, not the least because of its wealth and because it seemed to be a haven for a large number of very beautiful girls, most of them from what were middle-class or even wealthy homes. In Nashville's proud boast of itself as a great educational center, a city of universities, the city's boosters always mentioned Vanderbilt and Peabody and Scarritt, and on occasion some of the other smaller religiously affiliated white colleges—Belmont for the Baptists, David Lipscomb for the Church of Christ, Trevecca Nazarene for the Nazarene—and even, when they were feeling magnanimous, Fisk and Tennessee A&I, the two most prominent schools for blacks. Never did they get around to mentioning American Baptist. By 1959 it had been in existence for some thirty-five years, supported, very much on the margin, by the exceedingly powerful and wealthy and very white Southern Baptist Convention, a church group which in terms of its attitude on race and integration was not only one of the two or three most influential in the South in those critical years but one of the most conservative. As Bernard Lafayette, one of the three American Baptist students who became leaders in the sit-ins, once noted, describing the schizophrenic roots of his school, "Southern Baptists are *very, very* Southern, and black Baptists are *very, very* black."

This then was an anomaly, a small, separate seminary for poor black Baptist children of the South which was largely underwritten by a white church of the same faith that did not want blacks to worship in the same house. American Baptist was viewed by its sponsoring organization as not unlike some very small seminary for poor blacks in some small and distant country in Africa. It was not an accredited school. The students who attended American Baptist did so more often than not because they had no other choice; if they had even the slightest bit of wealth or connection, they would have ended up somewhere else—Morehouse or Howard or Fisk or A&I or Alabama State. It cost forty-two dollars a term, Lafayette remembered, and most of the students were on some kind of work program, which paid for tuition. It was a place without pretense, without class lines. It often seemed more like an extended family than a college. Everyone ate with everyone else.

But at a time when the black church was becoming the driving force of a larger social revolution taking place in the United States, American Baptist had become a magnet for many of the most talented and passionate young blacks in the country. For young blacks in small towns in the South, dreaming of doing something for their own people, did not in those days dream of going to Harvard or Yale or Stanford Law, they dreamt of going into the Baptist ministry. Therefore the talent and the passion and the innate human strength of the students at American Baptist had nothing to do with the seeming simplicity and relative poverty of the school. It was a place filled with political ferment and passion. Its faculty was gifted and its students, many of them diamonds in the rough, were hungry to learn.

To the students of American Baptist, Fisk sometimes seemed as far away in terms of affluence and privilege as Vanderbilt. Within the black community lines of social classification were if anything more sharply drawn than in the white, based on numerous categories of class and of skin color. Lighter skin was perceived as better than darker skin; lighter-skinned people were judged, in the codes of the era, to be ipso facto more intelligent and more sophisticated than darker-skinned people. When a young black man named Ben Jobe, a graduate of Nashville's Pearl High, had won a scholarship to Fisk, the Jobes' neighbors were sure he would never be able to make it at Fisk. The Jobes were poor. His father did not own a car and walked to work at the railroad yards every day; his mother worked as a domestic; they lived in south Nashville, which was where lower-class black people lived, instead of north Nashville, where the elite came from. More, Jobe was, and this was held against him by other blacks, *very* dark-skinned. So when he had won his scholarship, the neighbors had said it would never work out, that a mistake had been made, that he would never finish such a prestigious school. One particular comment made to his mother by an alleged friend seemed to sum it up, and forty years later Ben Jobe could still remember it, because it was burned into his psyche: *By the time the ink dries on his high school diploma he'll be out of there.*[1]

By the existing categories of that time, Fisk was better than A&I (also known as Tennessee State), which was considered countrier, and where the skins were presumed to be darker; and A&I, in turn, was presumed to be better than American Baptist, which was assumed to be the poorest of the three. Fisk, socially, at least, seemed on occasion like a somewhat smaller black version of a white college, mimicking, it often appeared, the worst, not the best, of white values. At homecoming its light-skinned queens donned mink coats and drove around the campus in shiny new convertibles. The lighter the skin of the contestants, thought Angeline Butler, a Fisk co-ed, the more likely a girl was to become Miss Fisk or the Homecoming Queen, and the better the chance of making one of the top sororities. Fisk then was the center of the black bourgeoisie at exactly the moment when, unbeknownst to these black youths, the challenge to white supremacy was almost involuntarily going to change the existing black order as well.

One thing many of the students liked about Lawson's workshops was that they did not reflect the social order which they had left behind on campus. Wealth, social status, and skin color meant little in the workshops. The only thing valued was the commitment to the cause. Elsewhere the successful young princes of Fisk might look down on the men of American Baptist, the seminarians, the future preachers. But some of the women of Fisk who were part of the workshops thought in fact there was something admirable about these young men from so poor a college. The first time Angeline Butler met John Lewis, a student at American Baptist, she was immediately aware of how shy he was, and of the fact that he had some kind of speech defect. It was as if he stuttered slightly, and had trouble finishing certain words. But she liked him from the start because he was so unlike other college men she knew, who seemed preoccupied with themselves, altogether too proud of their wealth, their status, interested in their weekend pleasures and little else, and who were, she thought, *always* posturing when there were girls around. If John Lewis had been a Fisk man, he would have been the kind of young person you were supposed to look down on, she thought, and certainly wanted to keep out of your fraternity. If you were a young co-ed and you dated him, it might hurt your chances in getting into a good sorority. But there was something strong and good inside him, and he was filled with dreams about what things might one day be, and there was nothing to look down on as far as his dreams for his people were concerned.

John Lewis was the countriest of the original group, which was no small title. He had arrived at American Baptist when he was only seventeen years old. If there had ever been a more rural student arriving at an American college in the second half of the twentieth century than this young man determined to be a minister, who had practiced his spiritual calling by preaching to the chickens he was supposed to take care of on the small family farm in rural Alabama, it would be hard to imagine. John Lewis did chicken births, chicken weddings, chicken baptisms, and chicken funerals; they were in the truest sense his flock. If his country manner was not bad enough upon his arrival, and if he was not poor enough, then in addition his small speech impediment made him seem even more country and inarticulate. The combination was overwhelming. Curtis Murphy, a workshop member who attended A&I and who was himself the product of a small dirt farm in West Tennessee, was stunned the first time he met Lewis. My God, he thought, that boy talks like he has a load of manure in his mouth. Why, he makes me seem like a city boy.

John Lewis had always wanted to go to college; he was a serious boy from an impoverished background in rural Alabama, where ambition was never supposed to be openly manifested other than in dutifully carrying out the harshest physical chores. Yet Lewis was always somehow different, eager to learn and study and get ahead and fulfill his dream of becoming a preacher, a preacher who would in time lead his people to a better life. He had dreamed as a boy of going to the majestic Morehouse, a citadel for young blacks in Atlanta. In his dreams he had seen himself there, a Morehouse man, wearing collegiate clothes, perhaps even smoking a pipe, learning to become the kind of minister-teacher he longed to be, a man modeled on his own personal hero, Martin Luther King, who was, of course, a Morehouse man. But if Morehouse was in his dreams it was not within his financial possibilities. Even Alabama A&M, the large state school for blacks, was too expensive for him. But when he was still in high school, his mother, who worked several days a month at a white Baptist orphanage in nearby Troy as a domestic, had happened to read a journal put out by the Alabama Baptist Convention. It was a journal for and about white Baptists, but there was a story in it which told about a small, inexpensive Baptist theological seminary for blacks in Nashville. The article said that a young black student could go there virtually free on a work-study program. She had shown the article to her son, and John Lewis had written to the school for an application form, filled it out and sent it in, and then a few months later had been accepted.

In September 1957, he had gone to the Troy, Alabama, bus depot, which was, of course, segregated, carrying almost all of his worldly belongings in an old-fashioned army footlocker given him by an uncle who had been in the service. His uncle also gave him a $100 bill, which at the time was the largest amount of money he had ever seen. In some way that he understood quite clearly even then, as he stood there and said good-bye to his adoring family, he was making a complete break with that rural part of his life. Country he might look, country he might seem, but country he did not intend to remain. He was a boy who had always known that there was a larger world out there and had wanted to be a part of it. So when John Lewis boarded that bus to Nashville, he was anxious to say good-bye to farm work, which, in truth, other than preaching to the chickens, he had always hated.

The Nashville bus station, when he arrived there, seemed large and crowded with people who appeared confident and purposeful. It made him acutely aware of how poor and friendless he was; he managed through deft negotiation to find a cab to take him to American Baptist, where even in an atmosphere remarkable for its simplicity and lack of pretense he stood out. That boy is pure hick, thought his closest friend of the period, Bernard Lafayette, a fellow student. Truth to tell, John Lewis was more than a little sensitive about being from rural Alabama, and when people asked him where he was from he would answer Troy, Alabama, but if the person kept staring at him, for Troy was a metropolis of nine thousand people, Lewis would buckle just a little and answer that he came from near Troy, and if the person pushed a little more, he would answer that he was from rural Pike County, which was southeast of Montgomery.

When John Lewis was fourteen, the Supreme Court had rendered its ruling on *Brown* and he had been quite pleased. He believed he was going to go to a white school with white children. It would be a better school with better teachers and newer textbooks. That was the law. He knew what the law was—it was something that everyone had to obey. And then nothing had happened. The law of the United States of America entered his life very slowly; it appeared at first to be noticeably weaker than the law of the state of Alabama and the law of Pike County. So when he had arrived at American Baptist, despite his roots in the literal Baptist church, he was already politicized, and anxious not only to witness some kind of political and social change but to expedite that change.

At first the more socially successful students in Nashville scorned those who were going off to be part of the sit-ins. John Lewis had a powerful and lingering memory of a day when he and a group of other protesters were on their way to a demonstration. As they moved through the Fisk campus, he was first stunned and then saddened to look out and see the rites of fraternity initiation taking place all around him. Almost every male seemed to be part of it—there were young blacks wearing chains around their necks, on all fours, barking like dogs. It was a jarring scene for Lewis: Here he and his colleagues were, in the beginning of what he hoped was a social revolution, risking their lives, and here were these privileged young black men oblivious to the historic change beginning to take place around them, acting out what seemed to Lewis to be their own banal imitations of white fraternity life.

In a way, becoming part of the Movement came easier to the students from American Baptist. They were not part of the black middle class. They had nothing to unlearn. They were for the most part so poor and unsophisticated, one of them once noted, that they even looked on A&I—after all, its very name in those days, Agriculture and Industrial, reflected the intended limits of its opportunities—as the embodiment of everything wealthy and sophisticated.[2]

From the start, two of the most steadfast members of the original Lawson group, John Lewis and Bernard Lafayette, who was only five months younger than John, were from American Baptist, and in time a third American Baptist student, James Bevel, joined the core group. If later some of the more sophisticated Fisk and Meharry students

arrived to give the group some panache, and some A&I people arrived
to help provide more bodies, then nonetheless these three from American Baptist gave the group a quiet, unwavering strength, a foundation
which was based on an unshakable religious faith. They simply could
not be bent and could not be discouraged. Lewis had been first, and
he in turn had brought his close friend Bernard Lafayette to one of the
meetings. A little later, James Bevel somewhat reluctantly joined them.
At the time the growing division among the younger students at
American Baptist was between the social activists, the young followers
of Martin Luther King, and the more traditional literalists. Lewis and
Lafayette were by instinct social activists, and Bevel was by instinct a
literalist. At first he did not particularly like the path they were following, but he also did not want his two closest friends risking their lives
while he sat back and studied at the seminary. Besides, Bevel had a car,
and his two friends pushed him to drive them from the campus to
meetings, a distance of some five miles. So he had started out as their
chauffeur, but he was gradually pulled into the meetings.

It was Kelly Miller Smith who originally made the connection for
Lewis. Smith taught the art of preaching at American Baptist, which
was John Lewis's favorite course. One of the most exciting moments
for Lewis came in his second year at American Baptist when Kelly
praised him lavishly for what was for Lewis the most daring sermon he
had ever tried. It was titled "Is This the One or Should We Look for
Another One?" In it he discussed how they would recognize the Messiah in contemporary life. Lewis had examined the words and deeds
of Christ, trying to find modern parallels for the Messiah. His close
friend, Jim Bevel, had not liked it that much, Lewis thought (thirty-
five years later Bevel remembered not only Lewis's sermon and its
title, but the argument they had after it—he *had* admired it, he
insisted, but he had dissented from a few sections of it). Kelly Miller
Smith was delighted with Lewis's sermon. It was just the type of
spiritual-intellectual byplay he admired, and for him to see something
like this coming from a young man who had had so few educational
and intellectual advantages was stunning. He gave Lewis an *A,* and he
quietly became a champion of this shy, awkward young man who felt
so graceless. Lewis, he sensed, was in some profound way different
from almost any other student he had ever had. He was almost com-

pletely unschooled, and yet desperately eager to make something of himself, and when Smith read his papers, he was touched by the contrast between the rawness in some of the language and spelling and the force of the ideas. More, when Smith corrected Lewis's papers, he would almost always get a note of thanks from the young student— pointing out that no one had ever tried to help him like this before.[3] As the Movement developed and other students came in, some of them exceptionally well educated and extremely verbal, there was on occasion a tendency of some people, both the ministers and some of the students, to make fun of John Lewis because he did not seem particularly articulate, and there were a large number of words which he had a hard time pronouncing. But one person who never made fun of Lewis was Kelly Miller Smith. Every word from him, Kelly told friends, had its own special truth. They might as well be carved in granite if John spoke them. "That young man," he would say, "is pure of heart."

Bernard Lafayette quickly accepted the ideas being put forth by Jim Lawson. Lafayette was one of the rare students at American Baptist who had actually had other educational opportunities. He had been an exceptional student in high school back in Tampa, and because he was such a stand-out student and the editor of the school paper, he had won a full four-year scholarship to Florida A&M. He had visited it, and found it quite grand, infinitely grander certainly than American Baptist. He had also liked the idea of journalism, a profession for which he had often been told he had a natural talent, but in the end he had felt a call to preach. His rational self was somewhat puzzled by his decision to turn down Florida A&M but his spiritual self was sure he had made the right decision, that there was something critical missing in the secular life, as far as he was concerned. Even so he had to earn his way at American Baptist, working simultaneously as a janitor at the school, as a dishwasher in a downtown restaurant, and as a gardener for several black and white families, and as an all-around helper in Kelly Miller Smith's house. "I liked the idea of journalism," he once said, "but I was *moved* by the idea of serving God." As he attended Jim Lawson's seminars he was sure that they were helping to bring both sides of his life together, the religious and the political ones, thereby making him whole.

When Lewis and Lafayette mentioned the workshops to James Bevel, the third member of their little group, Bevel let them know he felt it was a mistake, just one more instance in which, as far as he was concerned, they were straying away from their true purpose at American Baptist, which was to study the teachings of Jesus Christ so that they could better pass them on to their congregations. Bevel was a little bit older, he had already served in the navy, and his religious views were at first quite old-fashioned and conservative. At first Bevel seemed saddened by what was happening to them—they were, he thought, becoming too politically focused. But eventually, as much out of friendship to them and his own idle curiosity, he began showing up at the meetings.

Will Campbell thought the three of them were especially important to the student group, because they had uncommon inner strength. They had spent their entire lives in some way or another being tested by the adversity of the harshest American environment imaginable; the very ability to arrive at the seminary reflected a kind of drive and courage which they themselves did not entirely comprehend. They were young men not easily deterred. There was nothing casual about their respective journeys to Nashville. No wonder, Campbell thought, they proved to be so strong as the struggle continued. So John Lewis and Bernard Lafayette and soon James Bevel were Kelly Miller Smith's gift to Jim Lawson.

The Fisk campus was like a magnet for someone so hungry to learn as Lewis. All kinds of black leaders were always speaking there, like Thurgood Marshall, Roy Wilkins, and Daisy Bates, the hero of the Little Rock school crisis, and other emerging stars of the black protest movement. One day near the end of his first year, he was with a few friends on the Fisk campus and one of them had pointed to an older man walking slowly across the campus. "Do you know who that is?" his friend had asked. Lewis said he had no idea. "That's W. E. B. Du Bois," the friend said, and for Lewis it was a marvelous moment: He was watching a living hero of black American history walking as a rather aged mortal among them. Lewis and his friends had walked over and spoken to him for a few minutes. The great thing about going to school in Nashville, he thought, was that it expanded his vision of his own people and of his country; he found there for the first time the traces of an almost secret history of black life in America, a rich, conflicted, often suppressed,

often ignored history of black men and women fighting white repression over this country's entire history.

IT WAS, THOUGHT JIM LAWSON, AN INTERESTING AMALGAM OF STU-
dents he had brought together. He liked the mix from the start. The
students talked all the time with each other. They would leave one of
Lawson's meetings and sit on the steps of Jubilee Hall at Fisk and just
talk. That they were even thinking of challenging the status quo in
early 1960 marked these young people, in so quiescent an age, as
being dramatically different from the black college norm. For the
mood on most black campuses in those days was curiously tentative.
The old order still held. That was true at Fisk. It was an enormous
struggle just to get a college degree, and there were powerful but
often covert social and economic conventions working on the black
middle class to keep it somewhat in line. There was almost no campus activism in the period immediately after *Brown;* David Levering
Lewis, a 1956 Fisk graduate and later a distinguished historian,
remembered that in the months and years after the Supreme Court
decision, there was a belief that things were going to change now, that
opportunities for young black college graduates to enter a previously
all-white world were going to grow exponentially, and therefore it
was important for Fisk students to show what good citizens they
could be and to be models of decorum. The idea that nothing was
going to happen unless black college students themselves took the
lead in pressing for change had not yet dawned on them. Its first
dawning was in Lawson's workshops.

The great battles that David Lewis and a few of his more politically
inclined friends fought in those years were of a smaller and more traditional nature—trying to curtail the overwhelming power of the fraternities and sororities on the Fisk campus (and to them the unseemly
sight of the freshman pledge classes, shirts on backward, ties tied but
on collars which faced backward, coming into the dining hall in lock-
step and singing fraternity songs) and trying to do away with the Miss
Fisk election, which to them seemed an embarrassing black imitation
of the worst of white college rituals. Lewis had been on the student
council, and he and his friends had won the battle of Miss Fisk and for
a brief time it was suspended, which gave them, Lewis noted years
later, a reputation of having been campus radicals.[4]

The pressures for conformity were extremely powerful at a school like Fisk. The dress codes were quite strict. Women, for example, were required to wear stockings and high heels every day, and only for a few brief hours on the weekend could they wear blue jeans. Nor were men to wear blue jeans or to go around without ties. One rather rebellious undergraduate, Julius Lester, later a professor at the University of Massachusetts, who was a member of the class of 1960, found that one of the deans, Anna Harvin, was furious with him because he continued to wear blue jeans. She not only called him in and upbraided him for his casual attire, she called his parents, who lived in Nashville, to complain to them as well. Lester, who seemed to be gaining a reputation as a campus beatnik, and Dean Harvin had argued somewhat bitterly over the issue of conformity and in time a debate on that subject was scheduled between them. The debate, Lester later recalled, was not the most edifying in the world, but it reflected the times: "Mr. Lester," she had said, "you *must* conform to our rules and dress codes!"

"Dean Harvin," he had answered, "I will not conform."

"Mr. Lester, we are the ones who set the rules."

"Dean Harvin, I will not accept these dress rules; I am here to expand my own social and intellectual possibilities." (Later that spring, just before graduation, Lester, who had learned to play the guitar from Guy Carawan, a traveling folk singer who had joined up with the students and helped supply much of their music, had sat on the corner of the Fisk campus, playing his guitar and singing songs, until he was told by the Fisk authorities that he must stop doing it because he could be heard and seen by people who were driving by in cars, and that his was highly improper behavior for a Fisk man.)[5]

It was this background which made what was happening in the workshops so unusual. Not only were these young people drawn together for a larger social-political cause which demanded that they take action themselves and do things which their parents had not done and probably would not sanction them doing, but they were also, in the process, unburdening themselves of their inner thoughts and pain on the subject of race. That of itself was surprisingly rare, for young black people did not in those days lightly share their deepest feelings about the anguish of segregation. But here, sitting around the Fisk campus after the workshops, they could for the first time unveil their most private hurts. Typically, Angeline Butler had come from Eastover, a little town southeast of Columbia, South Carolina, and she had been humiliated on what was supposed to be one of the happiest days of her life, the day she had left home to go off to college at Fisk. Her father, who was a local black minister, had put her on the bus to go to Nashville, and she had taken a seat right behind the driver. The bus driver had ordered her to the back of the bus, and had told her that he would not move the bus as long as she sat up front. That had been bad enough, but then something worse had happened: Her father saw what was happening and he had boarded the bus and had told her to move. *He had taken the bus driver's side against her! He had taken segregation's side against his own daughter!* She had cried all the way to Nashville. Her first two years at Fisk had been miserable, and she believed that her special misery had started with the humiliation of that bus trip.

These wounds were part of the secret self, the stories they had never told to friends, as if, more often than not in the past, there was a certain guilt attached to the subject, as if it were the fault of the person himself that he or she had been discriminated against, not the fault of a society which erected such powerful barriers limiting black freedom. There was an intensity to these informal social sessions that none of them had ever known before. In the past many of them had heard their parents talk about race and segregation, but they tended to do it when they thought the children were not around. To talk about their treatment as inferior citizens seemed to confirm that they *were* inferior citizens and that the fault was theirs. Better not to discuss it. So gradually it had evolved into the secret subject, something that dominated their lives and yet was rarely addressed. And now here they were, drawn to each other because they were about to confront it, and so they began to talk about this most forbidden subject. The words seemed to pour out. They were not alone. As far as the students were concerned, that was the first great lesson of these workshops. They had all felt the same pain and they all felt the same frustration. The more they talked, the more they were bound to each other. All of them had been hurt in different ways. All of them had been turned down for service at a store, or had gone to a lesser school and used hand-me-down books passed on by white schools, or had witnessed a terrible scene in which one of their parents had been humiliated by a white man. All of them not only bore the same pain, but all of them had bottled up that pain for a long time.

The other thing which was happening, Angeline Butler thought, was that for the first time they were talking openly about what they felt about the future. It was coming up on six years since the Supreme Court had ruled on *Brown* and nothing had happened in any of their lives. *Nothing.* The sense of disillusionment, indeed bitterness, was growing quickly among some of them. What were they going to do after graduation? Go back to South Carolina or Georgia or Alabama and be schoolteachers? That was what their people had always done. Wasn't there anything better? Were they doomed to end up just like their parents or, if anything, more embittered? Maybe the wealthy ones, the men who were truly advantaged financially, could go on to Meharry and become doctors, but even they were probably going to have to practice in segregated communities.

Their lives, they all agreed, were terribly circumscribed. The ceiling seemed to be as low for them as it had been for the generation which had gone to school here just ahead of them. As they spoke, their unwillingness to accept the ceiling placed on them grew. The speed of integration was pathetic. All deliberate speed was no speed at all. Every child who wanted to attend a Southern school was going to need his or her own lawsuit. The law which they had all been taught to respect was not necessarily that powerful a weapon after all, they reluctantly decided.

Two things were happening to them at once, Angeline Butler later noted. The first was obvious: They were gaining the technical skills from the workshops—of how to resist those who attacked them, and how to accept the Gandhian vision of nonviolence—as well as the spiritual understanding that necessarily accompanied the drill. Attacked, they were to turn away from the violence. But equally important, a bond was growing among them. They were not merely rejecting the white world as it existed, they were rejecting that part of the black community which accepted the status quo. Almost without realizing it, they were forming their own community. A college all their own, Angeline Butler later called it. In the process they were becoming each other's friends, and learning to be responsible for one another. It did not matter that the other students at Fisk sometimes made fun of them as they prepared to start the sit-ins. They had each other.

6

As the workshops extended into December 1959, Jim Lawson began to emphasize the second critical concept of Christian nonviolence, which was how these young people should respond to the cruelty, both verbal and physical, which was sure to come from those who would try to block their way. Here he knew that he needed to create a bedrock of inner strength and confidence, and the capacity to turn away from taunts and to know that those who taunted them were revealing not strength and superiority but weakness and fear. If lesson number one had been that their numbers were not small because their idea was powerful, then lesson number two was about shedding the most powerful of all feelings—the shame of being black in a white nation which had chosen, as it suppressed its black citizens, to create a philosophy of shame and vulnerability among the very people whom it had suppressed and exploited, saying in effect that it was the victim's fault for turning out to be the victim. It was bad enough that white people seemed to accept this philosophy, but it was even worse that all too many blacks seemed to accept it as well. He intended to reverse this age-old psychological weight.

So first, before they could accomplish anything else, he had to teach them not just pride in themselves but the capacity, when provoked, to rise above the existing cycle of anger and hatred, to be their better selves. Only then could they create in those who would deny them their rights—and equally important, those other citizens watching the struggle from the sidelines—a sense of respect, and thereby end a devastating cycle of violence. In the process he had to destroy the cruel power of the magic word—*nigger*—used by whites both to undermine them and to create in them a terrible sense of shame, as well as an immediate instinct to lash back.

That was critical to the concept of Christian nonviolence. You are all *someone,* he taught, you are all children of God, you have within you the greatest of qualities, human nobility. The true children of God, he taught them, do not reap anger or violence on others. Nor were those who thought they were superior because they were richer or whiter any closer to God. Quite the reverse. God was in all of them. Those who were going to attack them as they sought their rights were not strong; they were, to the contrary, weak—they would not be doing this if they were truly powerful or confident or well loved. The rage of their enemies was produced by anger and ignorance and fear. They who were about to be abused had to try to understand their own anger and control it. He and the people he was advising needed to end the cycle of violence. They had to start by forgiving their enemies. Just as Jesus and Gandhi would have done.

In his teaching he emphasized the life of Jesus. Jesus, he pointed out, turned away from His tormentors again and again, and triumphed by using the power of His love. Lawson used the Book of Luke in the New Testament, chapter four, verses 16–31, to illustrate this. Jesus is threatened with being thrown over the cliffside. He had coolly looked His accusers in the face and then walked calmly through them. Lawson used the example of John Wesley, attacked by mobs who wanted to rough him up, who deliberately faced down the leader of his opponents, and converted him so that the mob's rage was stilled, and the leader had said, No harm will come to this man. Nonviolent response to violence, nonviolence as a political instrument, he taught them, was the best-kept secret in human history.

His teaching style was surprisingly clinical. He spoke without anger. Intelligence and individual commitment were valuable, but anger could burn out too quickly. Those who were driven by surface anger might lack the staying power of those who were driven by commitment. So Jim Lawson talked instead mostly about the power of love, and among their first assignments was one in which they were supposed to discuss what love was and how it could be used as a tactic in a personal or a political crisis and why people tended instead, when confronted with a seemingly insoluble problem, to turn to their anger. For some of them, anxious to get on with the job, anxious to challenge the white political structure, much of what he was talking about seemed a decided waste of time. But gradually as the seminars and workshops continued, it all began to make sense: They had to come to terms with their own dignity, their own belief in themselves, and their own motivation before they dealt with those who would oppress them. As they accepted themselves, as they accepted that this condition was not their fault, only then would they have the strength to be more tolerant of those who oppressed them. They were to be teachers as well as demonstrators. If they accorded others dignity, there was a great chance in the long run that fair-minded people would accord them theirs. There was a phrase Jim Lawson often used in talking about the kind of community they were working to create, and the first time he used the phrase it simply jumped out at John Lewis: *the beloved community.* It was not a utopia, but it was a place where the barriers between people gradually came down and where the citizenry made a constant effort to address even the most difficult problems of ordinary people. It was above all else an ever idealistic community. It became a permanent part of Lewis's vision of what he believed he was working toward.

In the most primal sense Lawson was trying to end the power of their accusers to destroy with words, particularly the cruelest word of all, *nigger.* He was trying to reverse a social order which had been so psychologically crippling for so long, with its age-old assumption that things white were better than things black, that white people had a better life because they deserved a better life, just as blacks had a poorer life because they were less worthy. They had to value themselves, he would teach them; they had to end that longstanding self-hatred. To do that they had to stop shrinking and being diminished when they heard a word which had in the past so readily paralyzed blacks in the South: *nigger.* They had to learn the most basic lesson of all, that it was a word which defined only those who used it, not those whom it was used against.

So they acted out the scenes of what was to come in their workshops, some of them taking the part of the white resisters who attacked them and beat them and hurled epithets at them. They learned how to get into the fetal position to protect themselves when they were knocked down, and they learned how, when one of their colleagues was knocked down, to use their own bodies as shields. "Nigger!" they would shout at one another as they did their demonstrations in the workshops. "Get out of here, you ugly nigger! Go home to Africa where you belong. Nigger!" They had to learn to hear it, and to immunize themselves to it, to keep going and to feel neither shame nor anger, but just to keep doing what they were doing. Lawson intended to strengthen not so much their quotient of physical courage but their psyches—above all their sense of their own value.

That singularly ugly word still stood in their way. Even in a border state like Tennessee in the late fifties it was still the operative word. Not every white person in Nashville used it, of course. In polite circles, university and religious social groups, the word *Negro* was now on occasion in play, however awkwardly and tentatively, and in certain polite but conservative circles, the euphemism *colored friends* was sometimes used; for people of an older generation, in polite academic and upper-class circles, where the word *nigger* now had too harsh a sound but where the reach to *Negro* was simply too great, the word *Nigra* (or *Nigruh,* a variant spelling—it was a word more often spoken than written out) was used, signifying a compromise of sorts, for it was a bastardized word, one which seemed to start out saying one thing but which in the middle was suddenly but not completely or successfully softened. *Nigra* was a word for those who straddled the issue and wanted things both ways. It meant that the user knew that *nigger* was wrong, and that he was going to make an effort to improve—but not too great an effort.

In terms of psychic power the word had a force all its own. Serious black citizens of Nashville, attending a meeting where it was used, knew that they were being told something, being beaten down and humiliated. Hearing it at a semirespectable meeting was, Kelly Miller Smith once said, like having the wind knocked out of you. As powerful as the word itself was, its adjunct—*nigger-lover*—was equally powerful within the white community, for it was a phrase employed against white people sympathetic to blacks, which ended all arguments and isolated the accused as a do-gooder on social issues and traitorous to the values of his own people. One of the things most reporters on *The Nashville Tennessean* accepted, particularly when they dealt with the local cops, was that they would sooner or later be referred to as nigger-lovers.

Nigger in those days in Nashville was almost a generic word. A killing in the black section of town was known as a *nigger* killing. A black minister, no matter how well educated, was a *nigger* preacher, and that included Martin Luther King and Kelly Miller Smith. A worn-out car which made its way downward onto the city's second-hand car lots was known as a *nigger* car; a dog of many different component breeds was known as a *nigger* dog. A certain kind of popular music was *nigger* music.

They would, Jim Lawson told his students, have to become accustomed to hearing it. Every time they went downtown they would hear it, from the people who attacked them, and they would hear it from people working in the restaurants, and they would hear it, of course, from the cops. So they might as well get used to it right now in these workshops. For the young people there were few lessons harder to learn. When it was all over, they decided that the greatest victory of Jim Lawson's had been to turn what had been a source of shame and weakness into a source of strength.

7

THE MESSAGE WHICH JIM LAWSON WAS EMPHASIZING, THAT THIS WAS something which would transcend selfish interests within both white *and* black communities, appealed to two of the other early sit-in leaders, a young man named Rodney Powell, who was a student at Meharry, the black medical college, and a friend of his, another Meharry medical student, who was a year behind him, named Gloria Johnson. For both of them the Lawson workshops came at exactly the right time; both were graduates of predominantly white Eastern colleges, and both of them had felt completely out of their element at Meharry, utterly miserable until they had joined up with the other students in the Lawson workshops. Rodney Powell had joined first. Until that moment he had done extremely well in all things academic at Meharry and very poorly in all things social. For that reason Rodney Powell thought the sit-ins saved his life; during his years as a medical student they had given him a purpose which he desperately needed, and in time, eventually, a wife. For the first time since he had arrived in Nashville from Philadelphia, he felt a part of something larger than himself. For if the limits of class seemed pervasive at a school like Fisk, then they were, he was sure, even worse at Meharry—for Meharry produced doctors, the superelite of black society. Because there was so much less in the way of opportunity for blacks to be successful in business and the law, doctors in the black world formed, even more than in the white one, a special class; as far as he was concerned Meharry in those days was a conclave of the spoiled and the smug.

Rodney Powell was the child of poor black parents in Philadelphia, and as an honors graduate of St. Joseph's, a Catholic college in that city, had entered Meharry in 1957. He had had other opportunities at respected white medical schools, but he had decided, after the

Supreme Court decision on *Brown,* that his life as an outstanding and lonely black student in a world that was almost exclusively white had been too privileged. Was he being true to himself every day when he went out and worked so hard to meet the standards set by whites? Had his decision to succeed in the white world, he wondered, pulled him away from his essential blackness? Because of these lingering interior doubts, he chose Meharry.

Rodney Powell had come to Nashville therefore as part of a conscious adventure, the purpose of which he did not entirely understand. He was uncertain of what he would find—perhaps a sense of brotherhood among his fellow black medical students as they dealt with the declining symbols of Southern prejudice in the years after the Supreme Court decision; perhaps a reaffirmation of some secret inner black self long buried because of his relentless striving for success and acceptance in so white a world. To his surprise he found no black solidarity at all at Meharry, save that of young black medical students who gathered on the weekend to party as extravagantly as they could at the nearest fraternity house. The only commitment seemed to be to chasing women, not to some worthy social idea.

He had never felt so different before. Even in the most superficial way he felt apart: All the other male students talked incessantly of their success with Fisk and A&I co-eds and he was made uneasy by that kind of talk; it was as if they were the victors and the women the vanquished. They all seemed to place a great priority on their ability to dance, and he did not like to dance at all. They liked a loud and, to him, raucous blues music, and he, having played the violin, preferred classical music. At Meharry he became known early on as a geek because he went to the lab by himself on Saturdays.

He had hated Meharry from the moment he arrived on campus. *Hated it.* As far as he was concerned this was a world in which the worth of everything and everyone seemed to be judged on the most materialistic of terms, one which rewarded whoever had the biggest car, the richest father, and, of course, the lightest skin. What seemed to be important at Meharry was how fancy your clothes were, and how good a dancer you were, rather than what the level of your social conscience was. Nor were its faculty members in those days, he thought, much better, and he sensed a certain bias against students who had attended good Eastern colleges, as if these Easterners might think

they were somehow superior. Some of the faculty members made fun
of his accent, for he spoke in a careful, quite formal way which gave no
clues whatsoever about his ethnicity. "You think you're better than we
are," one student had said to him early on, summing up a feeling of
resentment that he often felt from student and professor alike. The
truth was that he did not so much feel that he was better as he felt that
he was different. First at home and then at St. Joe's, he had developed
a passion for learning as an end in itself. Now he found himself in an
environment where the atmosphere was decidedly anti-intellectual:
The more serious you were and the more you wanted to learn, the less
respected you were.

Given how hard-won his own victories were, how hard it had been
to go to college, he thought constantly of transferring in his first few
months. But there was one faculty member at Meharry who seemed
not only to like him but to reach out to him, a white professor named
Theodore Greene. He was from New England, a Harvard graduate;
he had served as a medical missionary in China for most of his life.
When the Communists had taken over the mainland of China in 1949,
Ted Greene had relocated in America and, in keeping with his missionary principles, had become a faculty member at Meharry. He
understood this young man's loneliness and knew how hard Meharry
could be on him. Along with his wife, Phoebe, Greene brought Rodney Powell into his own world, a relatively rare integrated world in
Nashville where their friends were white and black doctors and ministers, and where the conversation was often about larger social issues.
Still, that did not entirely fill the rather large social void in Rodney
Powell's life and his need for peer friendships, and in his second year
he was still thinking of transferring when he met a student who was in
as much trouble as he was, a young woman from the Boston area
named Gloria Johnson.

Gloria Johnson was a first-year student who had just arrived at
Meharry, choosing it, like Rodney Powell, over other better-known
and more prestigious medical schools because she too wanted more of
a black experience. She was if anything even more lonely, isolated, and
despairing than he was. So when he joined Jim Lawson's workshops
and found solace and *community* there, a sense finally of belonging to
a group, he soon brought Gloria Johnson in as well.

Gloria Johnson of Roxbury, Massachusetts, loved going to the workshops. Like Rodney Powell she thought they—and the idea they embodied of challenging the outdated codes of the South—had helped save her from what she considered the social and intellectual wasteland of life at Meharry. Her dilemma there had been much the same as that of Rodney, who was already something of a legend on the Meharry campus when they met. So exceptional a student was he that the other students often bet on his grades. At Meharry the grades were posted in each course. When the physiology grades were about to be posted, a good deal of betting took place among the students, because physiology was the hardest course of all, the course *everyone* hated. Rodney Powell had never gotten less than a 95 in any course, and now everyone was watching to see how he fared. Some bet conservatively, which was that he would make his 95 or higher as usual, and others, the contrarians, went against the prevailing odds and bet that he would finally slip and fall beneath 95. He got his 95, of course.

The consensus at Meharry was that Rodney Powell was brilliant but weird. But there was a constant debate about him—was he really modest or was he arrogant? Gloria Johnson, long before she met Rodney Powell, knew a great deal about him, this curiously dignified, seemingly unreachable black man, so different from most of the others there. She knew that he liked to go to the lab on his own on Saturday, which was bad enough; but even worse, he listened to classical music on the radio.

She assumed that someone so successful would be quite happy in med school and she had no idea that he was as miserable as she was. At the time she met him Gloria Johnson was sure that choosing Meharry was the worst decision she had ever made in her young life. She had arrived after doing brilliantly on a very demanding track which had taken her to two of New England's best schools, the famed Girls' Latin School in Boston, where she had been one of the top students in her class, and then Mount Holyoke, a prestigious women's college in Massachusetts which she had attended on a full scholarship, and where again she had done very well. She had decided to try Meharry because she, like Rodney Powell, wanted to be part of something larger that emphasized the black experience, and where she could be part of the coming racial desegregation of the South.

She had felt out of place from the first day. She did not think of herself as pretty or socially graceful—but she knew she was a damned good student. But being a good student in those days seemed to matter little at Meharry. She was not, most demonstrably, foxy, and that was the preferred style, it appeared, in female companionship. She was serious and intellectual; after four years at Mount Holyoke she not only spoke fluent French and could not only read poetry in French, but she *liked* to read poetry in French. She had almost no capacity to be different, to throw a switch and become, for an evening at least, a somewhat frivolous black co-ed who giggled and laughed at things she did not think funny and who played up to men she did not like.

She had often cursed the almost whimsical decision that had brought her from a protected and surprisingly comfortable world to Meharry, where she was so out of place. In her senior year at Mount Holyoke she had been part of an informal small group of black students who were struggling to find their place in contemporary American life. The world of black students at the Ivy League and the Seven Sister colleges in those days was small and cloistered: There was a sense that everyone knew everyone else; the handful of Harvard blacks knew the Mount Holyoke blacks, who knew the Dartmouth blacks, who knew the Wellesley blacks. They were well aware of their special dilemma, of being caught between two separate and very different worlds. When they were together they often talked of the complexity of being the rare black student in this privileged white world and of the conflicting pulls on them from the world they were becoming a part of and the world to which they had once belonged. There was a good deal of discussion about how they could find their own true identity—was there a black American identity which was separate from a white identity, and were they prevented from finding it as long as they existed primarily as part of an esteemed and fortunate black chosen few?

She and her black friends had argued constantly about that issue. One of her friends was a bright young student at Harvard named Tom Sowell, who was going off to do graduate work at the University of Chicago, and he encouraged her to go to medical school in Chicago. An early tour at Howard had upset him. He had come away, she sensed, deeply alienated by his experience with the black bourgeoisie. But another of Gloria's black friends, John Barber, was at Yale doing graduate work, and he had been to Morehouse, and he thought his time at Morehouse had been a plus. There for the first time he had felt the stirrings of a new generation of black leaders just coming of age. "The problem with the lily-white schools like the ones we know is that they take you away from the action. They're good schools and they're very pleasant, but the action is going to take place in the South," he had said. "You ought to go to medical school where things are going to happen." Where in the South? she had asked. "Why not Meharry?" he had said. "Me-what?" she asked. So he described Meharry to her, this legendary black medical school which had stood alone for so long as an outpost in an essentially hostile region where the white leadership did not seem to feel that blacks needed medical treatment. Tom Sowell, when she mentioned it to him, was not so sure. Meharry to him sounded like Howard except populated with would-be doctors.

When Gloria Johnson had been twelve she had seen a book which listed scholarships for worthy black students and she had read about something called the Jessie Smith Noyes scholarships, given to blacks who wanted to go to medical school. She had carefully written down all the information on the Noyes fellowships, and stored it away and kept it all those years. Now as a senior in college she wrote to its administrators and they quickly answered back saying they would be glad to fund her four years at any medical school she chose. Gloria Johnson decided to apply to four medical schools, none of them in the East because she had already been to school there. She decided to try the University of Chicago, the University of Illinois, Creighton University, and Meharry. Three weeks after writing to Meharry, she received a letter of acceptance, and with that, the decision was made. She had thought the process of getting into medical school would be a long and torturous one, and now with so little pain and anxiety, she had been accepted at a legendary school which would allow her to find her own inner identity. Because she had so little money she had never visited any of the schools she applied to; there was no small irony there, she later thought, because if she had visited Meharry, she probably would have sensed all the things which eventually bothered her and would have deprived herself of one of the most defining experiences of her life.

Gloria Johnson's first year at Meharry was the most painful year in her young life. She found herself longing for New England and even the small, occasional racist moments that she sometimes encountered there and knew how to deal with. At Meharry, she sensed a wariness bordering on hostility which emanated not merely from other students but, worse, from certain members of the faculty as well. One of the things which particularly distressed her about Meharry was, in those days, the pervasive cheating. It seemed to be ingrained into the very culture of the school. Nor did this cheating involve only students. It also involved some professors, who sold copies of their exams to students for handsome amounts of money, perhaps as much as $250 in a key course, the money to be collected from a large number of eager and acquiescent students. There had been one terrible moment in her first year in a course on fractures when she heard that the instructor had sold the exam to the students. There was a phrase the students had when that happened: *The Eagle is out.* Because some of the other students knew that she refused to cheat, they would come and warn her whenever the Eagle was out so that she could at least defend herself by studying harder than usual. In this case it did not help. She got her mark and it was an *F.* She was stunned; she had never gotten an *F* before in her life. Then she got her exam paper and the grade was an 89. Now she was even more stunned. So she went to see the instructor and asked how, if she had gotten an 89, she could get an *F.* "Because you had the lowest grade in the class," he said. "But it's still an eighty-nine," she protested. "Listen," he said, "if you're too stupid to get the Eagle when it's out, then you deserve an *F.*" He had, she realized, just told her to cheat. She took her complaint to the dean, who was not interested, which convinced her that the school's authorities had come to accept what was going on.

There had been one kind face among the faculty that year, the same Ted Greene who had befriended Rodney Powell. Crushed by her experience with her fractures professor, she had gone to see him. She had started to talk to him about her social problems and now this cheating, and in the middle of it she had burst into tears. Ted Greene had tried to soothe her and then he had picked up the phone and dialed his home number. "Phoebe," he had said to his wife, "do you remember the young girl I spoke to you about, the one from Mount Holyoke? We talked about her, and I told you she was going to need your help sometime this year? Well, she needs you now." So the Greenes had taken her in as they had taken in Rodney Powell.

Then at almost the same time she had gone to a dance at Meharry. She had gone reluctantly, for she always felt out of place at these things, awkward and unattractive, more likely to be rejected than selected. At Meharry's social events easy conversation eluded her. The prevailing talk, she thought, was a combination of braggadocio and bluster. At Meharry, unlike Mount Holyoke, she felt, the men drove the conversation, always it seemed with some kind of sexual innuendo, and the girls played their assigned roles, flirting back on cue.

It was at one of these dances that for the first time she had started talking to the young man about whom she had heard so much, Rodney Powell, and found immediately that he felt the same way about almost everything. Their first bond was that neither could dance. Their backgrounds were, it turned out, oddly similar, as black students from impoverished families in the North, who under fierce parental urging had maximized their lives and ended up with values reflecting the ambitions of the meritocratic white middle class. He had been a serious Boy Scout; she had been an equally serious Girl Scout. Both of them had come to Meharry seeking to explore their blackness. Both of them were bitterly disappointed with what they had found so far. They did more than talk that night; it was as if each had found his or her soul mate, the person each had always been looking for.

Now for the first time at Meharry she had a close friend, someone she could always talk to. Medical school became infinitely more bearable. She stopped thinking of transferring. At first she and Rodney did not date. But they immediately became close friends. About that time she started going out with a Meharry student named Michel Kildare, who was Rodney's best friend, a young man who was also an outsider, having a French mother and a black father from the Caribbean; he was more sophisticated than most of her friends and was himself searching for his identity.

When Rodney heard about the workshops being held by Jim Lawson, he suggested that she come along with him, that this was what they had both come to Nashville for. She went along and was immediately impressed by Jim Lawson. She and Rodney agreed that they would never work together on the exact same team, for fear that if one of them was being hurt by a white assailant, the other might not be able to sustain the vow of nonviolence.

8

THE ONE THING JIM LAWSON AND THE OTHERS WERE UNSURE ABOUT AT first was what their first specific target would be. But then suddenly at one of the workshops, the choice became obvious. They had been sitting around talking about potential targets, and some of the middle-class women who also came to the workshops, most of them from Kelly Miller Smith's church, had begun to talk. "You men don't know anything about the downtown," one of them had said. "You don't shop. You don't know the humiliations that they inflict on us every day." And then suddenly it had become a chorus, as if someone had unleashed all that stored-up black rage. All the women started talking at once: Stores where they had separate rest rooms for blacks. Stores which had no rest rooms for blacks. Stores where they did not treat you like a grown-up and called you Auntie. Stores where they would not let you try on clothes. All of these stores where they took your money, and had restaurants, but would not let you eat at the restaurants.

The stories had poured out. DeLois Wilkinson had told of going to Harveys, one of the two main downtown department stores, with her young son, and going past the Monkey Bar, which was a small restaurant set up in the store specifically for little children and which had a small caged-in area with live monkeys. Her young son had desperately wanted to stop and eat, and she had to tell him again that they did not have time, that they were in too much of a rush. She spoke of how she hated it all, not being able to enjoy the small pleasures of a shopping trip the way that white people did, and worse, having to lie to her son about what she was doing. Someone else told the story of a Fisk biology professor named Mildred Ray who had gone downtown on a summer day with her five-year-old son and had gone to a small juice bar near Fifth Avenue and Church to get an orange juice. The little boy had gotten up on a stool, when the counter man had said very angrily, "Get that nigger kid off that stool!" If you are the mother, the woman said, what do you tell the child at that point? How do you heal the wound? Does it ever heal? Others told of being downtown with their young children when the children needed to go to the bathroom and being unable to use the facilities, and of the children, unable to restrain themselves, wetting their clothes. Everyone had a story. And they were all of a kind—stories that ended with the cruelest kind of humiliation. It was nothing less than an explosion: deep, visceral, and impassioned. They had accepted it for so long, and they had been diminished in the eyes of their children and diminished in their own eyes. Jim Lawson heard it and he knew he had his target.

The downtown lunch counters represented the perfect objective, Lawson believed: They were visible, they were within reach, they seemed to unite the entire black community, and the desire—and right—to use them was something any fair-minded white person in the city would probably sympathize with. It would also allow the black community to employ a potentially powerful weapon, its economic leverage, if need be, to help expedite white conscience. In addition it would almost surely set in motion a story for the local media that had visibility, drama, and the pursuit of justice. What could be more American than wanting to eat at a store where you had just shopped? What could be more un-American than taking people's money for the purchase of clothes but refusing them the right to eat in the store's dining room?

As December 1959 arrived, there was some question as to when they would actually start the sit-ins. Christmas was approaching, and if they so chose they could begin at the Christmas season. In some ways that would be particularly damaging to the stores, which desperately needed Christmas sales to have a successful season. But for the same reason it might backfire. Interfering with someone else's right to shop for Christmas might cause something of a white backlash, and they needed the approval of the larger white population. So they decided to spend December doing reconnaissance of the downtown area, and then make their move after school reopened.

Very quietly, without letting either of the newspapers know, they sent integrated teams to a variety of stores and lunch counters. It was all very low-key and very controlled. The marching orders were quite strict: Everyone in each team was to buy something in each store. Then they were to go to the lunchroom or lunch counter and sit down and order something to eat. They were not to be disputatious. If they were refused service—and they always were—they were as politely as possible to ask why, and they were to ask if someone from management would come and talk to them about the policy. Then they would ask who determined the policy, and whether it was a national or local policy. They were to try to sense the mood and the degree of resistance in each store.

The recon had gone surprisingly well. Reactions had varied greatly store by store. In some cases, at the lunch counters—as at the downtown Greyhound and Trailways terminals—they found segregation was national policy adjusted to local custom. Some places were very hard-line, and the attitude of the store managers cold and hostile; they could sense the seething racism in the answers given. But at a couple of stores, including Harveys, which was the most modern and most important of the department stores, and whose owner, Fred Harvey, was not a Nashvillian, they received surprisingly friendly responses. Greenfield Pitts, a senior executive of Harveys, seemed fair, enlightened, and if anything commercially (and quite possibly morally) bothered by his own store's practice. By contrast, the people at the main rival to Harveys, Cain-Sloan, which was locally owned, seemed much more hard-line. At Cain-Sloan they had been treated coldly, with contempt. They did not know their place, and their place was within a segregated order. The recon taught them that if they made their assault, the resistance would be considerable. There was a wall, but it was not without its vulnerabilities. Christmas came, and the students scattered for the holidays. There was a vague decision made that they would all return sometime in January and the first test would come sometime in February.

They did not get there first. On February 1 four students at the Agricultural and Technical College of North Carolina, in Greensboro, went into a local Woolworth's, bought a few things, and then sat down at the lunch counter and asked to be served. The four, Ezell Blair, Jr. (later Jibreel Khazan), David Richmond, Franklin McCain, and Joseph McNeil, were all freshmen, which reflected something that was to be a constant as the student movement grew throughout the South—the younger the potential volunteer, the more willing he or she was to take risks (while the converse was generally true—the older the students, the more they had a stake in terms of career and career expectations, and the less likely they were to join up). They had been talking about testing the Woolworth's for several weeks, and finally McCain asked the others whether or not they were chicken. They all said no.[1] At the Woolworth's lunch counter that day Ezell Blair asked for a cup of coffee. The waitress said that they did not serve Negroes. Blair pointed to a package which he had bought. "You just finished serving me at a counter only two feet from here." The waitress pointed to the end of the counter where there was a take-out stand where blacks could get their food. "Negroes eat at the other end," she said. "What do you mean?" Blair asked. "This is a public place, isn't it? If it isn't, then why don't you sell membership cards? If you do that, I'll understand that this is a private concern."[2] A black woman working behind the counter, watching the scene, was enraged. "You are stupid, ignorant! You are dumb! That's why we can't get any-where today. You are supposed to eat at the other end,"[3] she shouted.

The local manager, who had earlier on asked his superiors what to do if something like this happened, had been told to do nothing. Perhaps they would eventually get tired and go away. The four remained there for more than an hour until the store closed. When they got back to campus they spoke to the student body president and asked for his help. The next day, instead of four students there were about twenty. Again they were allowed to sit at the counter. Ezell Blair told a reporter that he was doing this because older blacks had become fear-ful and this was the students' way of waking them up. Day after day the demonstrations grew larger. They began to spread to other stores and other cities. In Greensboro local officials asked for a two-week moratorium to see what they could work out.

Douglas Moore, a Methodist minister in Greensboro, had become an adviser to the North Carolina students and he was a friend of Jim Lawson's. Soon after the Greensboro sit-ins had started, he called Lawson to see if the Nashville students would join in. On February 6, five days after the first sit-in in Greensboro, a group of some forty-five students staged a sympathy sit-in in Nashville.

Now finally the question arose of going beyond just a sympathy sit-in on behalf of the Greensboro students and of starting their own drive. Jim Lawson thought the Nashville students were ready for it.

They were, if anything, quite impatient by this time. They had wanted to begin two months earlier, and now some North Carolina students had beaten them to the punch. On the night of February 10 they met at a science building at Fisk. Kelly Miller Smith was still not sure that they were ready to go ahead. If they were to sit in, there had to be sufficient money for lawyers, and money for bail, and the truth was that the local chapter of the SCLC was broke. It had all of $87 in the kitty, Smith reported. He and some of the other ministers wanted to wait until they were a little better prepared for the problems they certainly would face when they were arrested. A lot of money, Smith warned, was going to be burned up in court costs. But the students were restless. There had been too many delays already.

Ironically, the one who seemed to be pushing the hardest to go forward was James Bevel. Bevel was the friend who came to the workshops with John Lewis and Bernard Lafayette, more as their chauffeur than as an active participant. He was theologically more conservative than his two friends, a man of the literal Gospel, and when his two friends had first gone off to attend these workshops, he thought they were going down the wrong road, away from their church and their calling and, worst of all, away from Christ. They more than anything else needed to be *saved,* not politicized. If there was a religious need, it was not so much for political assistance as it was for redemption. Dogmatic and unyielding, John Lewis thought of him. The most bullheaded person in all of Tennessee, thought Bernard Lafayette, who was his roommate. A minister's job, Bevel believed, was to ease the terrible burden of his people at least one day a week. A minister had to make his own life more like that of Christ and thus move his parishioners toward a life like Christ's.

Bevel was older than his two friends. He was from Itta Bena, Mississippi, one of seventeen children. He had already been in the navy, and there was no doubt on the part of anyone who met him that he was brilliant. If he was difficult and didactic, he was always original and creative. He argued with everyone about everything, for there was no subject on earth that James Bevel did not have an opinion on. No one, it was believed, had ever won an argument with Bevel. It was like arguing with a brilliant mule, Bernard Lafayette thought. Bevel would, if need be, change the given. He would even, it sometimes seemed, switch sides so that you ended up arguing his case and he took yours. No one thought of him as an easy colleague. As the student group coalesced, almost every one of the leaders within the group became known by his or her first name: John Lewis became John, Diane Nash was Diane, Bernard Lafayette was Bernard, Marion Barry became Marion, but Jim Bevel was always Bevel, as if identifying someone who was different, and potentially contrary, and potentially brilliant. A student reporting back on a meeting might say *Bevel says,* and that was important because it meant, Here is the information that we got, and here in addition is the source of the information; it might be extraordinarily valuable, and it might be so idiosyncratic as to be worthless.

There was an edginess about Bevel which seemed quite deliberate; it was as if he had placed a sign on himself—that he was a part of this, he would risk his life if need be, and he was their brother, but he was not necessarily their friend. Do not know me too well, he seemed to say: I will keep my distance, I will be part of what moves me and is acceptable to me, but do not make any assumptions about me, for I will make sure that they turn out to be wrong. He was that way at the start of the Movement, a man who always, no matter what the exterior pressures, heard only his own truth. If there was one great advantage that Jim Bevel had over almost all of his peers in the group, it was that he did not care at all what others thought of him, and he *never* sought popularity. That immunity to conventional opinion, which very much reflected the way in which he had been raised, was a considerable source of strength.

James Bevel had arrived in Nashville in early 1957 by a circuitous route. He had grown up in Mississippi, had stayed there when his parents had separated and his mother had moved to Cleveland, and had served briefly in the navy, where he had done well until his own readings about nonviolence made him wary of serving in a military force. When he left the service in 1955 he had returned to Cleveland, where he worked as a bricklayer's helper at a Jones and Laughlin steel mill; he repaired the brick ovens used in the manufacture of steel. He had always planned to go to college, perhaps for engineering, perhaps law school, for he had always done exceptionally well in school. But he also liked working as a bricklayer, and the pay was good. In addition he was trying to make it as a musician, for it was 1955 and black rhythm and blues, until then called race music by white music industry executives, was beginning to make it into the mainstream of American taste. Bevel's life was full: He was working during the daytime and getting a lot of hours and making good money, well more than $100 a week and sometimes, with overtime, $140. But his music was important; everyone who knew him had always remarked on what a beautiful voice he had, and he was also trying to write his own songs. On weekends he would sing at different clubs with two of his brothers, Charles and Victor. They called themselves the Beveleers. He had most of the things he wanted.

When the Beveleers played, which was usually on the weekends, he would usually get home after 1:00 A.M. He was living in the house in Cleveland which had belonged to his mother, who had died recently. On one Sunday morning, having worked late at the Copa Club outside Cleveland, a worthy night of music and drinking, a woman named Beatrice Bates had come by to try and get him to go to church. Mrs. Bates, an extremely religious woman, was a kind of all-purpose family friend and godmother in the period after his mother's death. "I just can't do that," he had answered. "I've been out drinking most of the night, I smell like a gin mill, I haven't really slept, and my clothes are all wrinkled." "Well, in that case," she said, hardly bothered by his excuses, "I'll just sit here and read the Scriptures with you." That, he told her, was unsatisfactory, because she would end up missing church because of him. So he washed up and put on clean clothes and off they went to the Unity Baptist Church. That day the sermon had been from the sixth chapter of the prophet Isaiah. It was the day which changed his life. It was as if he heard the voice of God speaking directly to him and to no one else in that church, and He was saying: *If you do not come with us, who will? If you do not take up the challenge, who will?* With that everything changed.

The voice was like a personal challenge and he could not shake it. It seemed to know something about him, and seemed to come from inside him. It was telling him that he was being too selfish, that even if his own life was going well, what about the world around him, what about all those young black men he saw every day who were not doing as well as he was, who were floundering in their lives, hanging around pool halls and drinking whiskey and Thunderbird wine and doing drugs? It was something that had long bothered him but about which he had done nothing. The voice seemed to be telling him that it was his responsibility—if he did not do something about this, who would? Suddenly the voice was everywhere. He could not shake it. He turned on the water in his house, and the water seemed to be talking to him; he opened the door to his bedroom, and the door seemed to be talking to him. He spoke to his sister about the voice and she told him that it was probably God's way of calling him to be a minister.

He took the voice seriously. It was 1956 and he decided he was not going to be a minister unless he could go to college. By chance that had happened to be a peak work year at the steel mills—the brick furnaces seemed to be falling apart everywhere at the plant—and he got a lot of overtime, sometimes even double time. By January 1957 he had saved more than $1,000, a huge amount of money. He had heard about American Baptist, which was supposed to be a good but not very expensive school. About that time he heard a minister named Joseph Blake, who taught at American Baptist, speak, and he was impressed by his intelligence and his reasoning. Beatrice Bates wrote the people at American Baptist and got the school's catalog for him, and so he applied. There were three questions he wanted answered when he set out for college, he later told friends: How did Moses go into Egypt and get his people out? The second was, How did Solomon know who was lying and who was telling the truth? And the third was elemental: How did Christ raise Himself from the dead?

He arrived there in January 1957, eight months ahead of John Lewis and twenty months ahead of Bernard Lafayette. He was four months past his twentieth birthday, older than the two young men who, when they arrived, were to be his closest friends ("They were only teenagers," he later said of them) but younger than many of the other students, most of whom had not only been in the service but had often worked in the ministry before attending. Almost from the start he became the minister of the small Chestnut Grove Baptist Church in nearby Dickson, Tennessee. He made $50 a week for preaching there, plus the food that the parishioners often brought instead of money. He was at the outset very much of the evangelical tradition. Lewis, he thought, was already a social activist, a disciple of Martin Luther King's activism, while Bernard, not quite as confident about his future as John, was nonetheless edging over in that direction.

At the heart of his calling, Bevel believed, was the need for redemption. Redemption was necessary not just for the members of the congregation but for the minister himself. It was what he was seeking for himself. "I was," he later said of himself, describing that moment, "overwhelmed by my own need for redemption, the need for man to turn his life over to God, and to seek and parallel the life of Christ." That was more important than social activism. Without redemption he could not help others because he could not help himself. He needed to be God-conscious, as did, he believed, the young long-lost black youths of the inner cities.

Bevel believed that he and Lewis and Lafayette were different from most of their colleagues at American Baptist, and the difference was probably generational. The three of them, he thought, were bonded by one thing: All brought a concept of love to their relationship with God. All too many of the others, he believed, came from a tradition of hellfire and damnation and were driven as much by fear as by love. Their God, Bevel thought, was a God quite capable of being angry and letting them and their congregations know of His anger. He did not lightly forgive those who had transgressed. The others were ministers, more often than not, James Bevel decided, because they were terrified of going to hell. By contrast, for Bevel and Lewis and Lafayette, their God was equally alert, equally vigilant, but he offered much more in the way of love and kindness and forgiveness.

At Chestnut Grove Baptist, Bevel was an evangelical minister. He was there to save souls and do battle with the devil. At the start Bevel had been a great whooper and hollerer, John Lewis thought, and when he took a shower they could all hear him practicing his sermons, or singing in what was clearly the most beautiful voice of anyone in the entire school, a voice that seemed to carry through the entire dorm.

Eventually James Bevel swung around in that period. But even before he did there were small signs of the radical underneath the veneer of the traditionalist. He hated greed, and he hated selfishness at the most personal level. At American Baptist, because everyone was so poor, when a package came from home or someone had some money and was able to buy snacks, everyone shared. No one was to hoard a package. They were trying to walk in the footsteps of Christ, and Christ had not hoarded things. But there was one student who did not like to share and that offended Bevel, both personally and spiritually. Was this man who did not share really studying to be a soldier for Christ? This young man had a hot plate, and he was known to go out on his own, buy a dozen eggs, slip off to his room, lock the door, boil the eggs, and eat them by himself, one by one, never sharing. Locking the door at American Baptist was unheard of, for no one had anything to steal, and locking the door to eat without sharing was considered sinful. One day when the student was out, James Bevel managed to get inside his room and he substituted uncooked eggs for the cooked eggs. Bevel and his friends then made off with the student's cooked eggs. Soon the young man tried to eat what he thought were his cooked eggs, with disastrous results. When the student tried to figure out what had happened, he confronted Bevel. "Did you throw out the water after you boiled them?" Bevel asked him. Yes, said the young man, of course he had. "Well, there's your problem," Bevel said. "When you do that, they always turn back." It struck Bernard Lafayette that Bevel's practical jokes reflected his social activism before his preaching did.

When the workshops had first started, Jim Lawson had sensed the doubts among many of the students about nonviolence, but it had showed most clearly on the face of Jim Bevel. At first it was as if Bevel were saying: I'm only here because my friends are here; I'm driving them here, but I don't believe this can work. I don't think the system will allow it. People like you with all your fancy words—you're smart and you've been to good schools, but you don't know the South, my friend; you don't know how hard they're going to come down on you. Bevel made no attempt to hide his skepticism. When Lawson spoke about nonviolence and the need to turn away from those who were violent toward you, Bevel was unimpressed. That guy is saying it because he's afraid, he thought; he's scared to fight back. I don't need lessons from a man like that. But gradually he was pulled in. Nothing was more important to his conversion than Lawson's use of the Gandhian example. The fact that Gandhi was a devotee of Tolstoy's book *The Kingdom of God Is Within You* was critically important. That was the book which had begun the change in Bevel's life when he was in the navy.

Bevel had entered the service in 1954, with what he later saw as completely conventional views, a black son of Mississippi anxious to take on the forces of Communist totalitarianism. But in the navy he had met an older black seaman, who had a Ph.D. but who was serving as a lowly cook. That had puzzled Bevel: Here was a well-educated man who should have worked at an important job but who was content to serve as a mere cook. How was that possible? he had asked. Well, the cook had explained, he thought every man ought to serve his country, but you ought not to kill other people. So this was his compromise. Bevel, still ready to be a warrior in the Cold War, had scoffed at him. The cook had given him a copy of Tolstoy's book.

It had taken him a week to read Tolstoy, but it was an epiphany, the most compelling book on Christianity he had ever read. It was as if there were one immutable law to Christianity, he decided, agreeing with the author—it was that you could not kill people. If you killed others you were not a Christian. There were no exceptions. When Bevel had finished reading it he had decided he had to get out of the navy immediately and he had gone to his commander. He had had an excellent record up until then and the naval officials were bothered by the request of this gifted young man who suddenly wanted out. First they sent him to a psychiatrist. Then they tried to talk to his family. Then they called his family's pastor in Cleveland, the Reverend Henderson Jarmon. "We've got this very bright young man named Bevel who's doing well in the navy, one of our best young people, but now suddenly he says he doesn't want to serve because it violates his conscience." "Well, if he's a Bevel and he says he's not going to serve, then he's not going to serve," Jarmon had answered. "I know that family. I can't tell you what's going on there with that Tolstoy book you mention, but I know those Bevels and they mean what they say." Within a few weeks he was processed out. And now as he listened to Jim Lawson talk about Gandhi, he realized that the same book had also been very important to Gandhi. In fact, Gandhi had named his ashram the Tolstoy Farm.

The different strands in Jim Bevel's life were coming together. Sometimes when he would drop John Lewis off at the workshop at Kelly Miller Smith's church, he would go over to the Nashville Public Library to read. There, somewhat to his surprise, he found a wealth of books on Gandhi. Apparently at the time of Gandhi's death, the Indian government had given gift books of Gandhi's writings to the library of every major city in America. It was a treasure trove for Bevel. He was, he realized, as he went through their remarkably pristine pages, almost surely the first person even to open them. It was an odd feeling, sitting there in this library, surrounded largely by white

Southerners, reading these books which had sat there untouched for more than a decade. The parallels between colonial India and the effectively colonized American South were striking. It was as if he had finally found a key that could unlock doors which had always been closed to him.

For unlike the works of the other prominent liberal theologians which he had been told to study, these books had meaning and an immediacy for him, and they seemed to explain the racist world and nation he found himself caught up in. Bevel had already studied Niebuhr, and Niebuhr was supposed to a great man, but as far as Bevel was concerned, there were too many rationalizations in Niebuhr, and the world which he described seemed vastly different than the one which Bevel was contending with. Men like that might be learned and they might know a great deal about Christianity, but they did not know very much about being a black Christian, he had decided. But it was as if Gandhi spoke to Bevel directly, not about India but about the South, as if Gandhi himself might have grown up in Itta Bena, Mississippi. As he read, and as he listened to Lawson now, his purpose became clear. Thereupon, with the blessing of the librarian, who, he said, encouraged him to share these otherwise virginal books with his friends, he walked out of the library with them and started circulating them among his friends. The Bevel Lending Library, it was called. After all, the books had sat there in the library all these years untouched by human hands. Now he was going to put them to work.

James Bevel began to take Jim Lawson very seriously. No longer was Lawson the man who spoke of nonviolence because he was afraid of physical confrontation: He was a man, like Gandhi, who had been willing to spend time in prison for his beliefs, and he was a man who had given up three years of his life to go on a journey to India to understand what Gandhi had done. Lawson, he decided, was not a fearful phony after all; rather, he was a great teacher, a man who took you beyond the easy emotional response to oppression and pushed you to find your true, better self. Yes, if you had enemies, it was easy to hate them, but what good did hating do? Who was the beneficiary of hate? And didn't you in the end become as much a prisoner of the hatred as the man who hated you? That was what Jim Lawson was teaching them.

Ironically, after the Nashville sympathy sit-in honoring Greens-boro, as they debated among themselves what to do, it was James Bevel who now pushed everyone to go forward. Bevel was not inter-ested in the cautionary doubts of his elders. He was sick and tired of waiting, he said. There had been too much of it. There was always going to be a reason not to go, and it was always going to be a very good reason. "If you asked us to wait until next week, then next week something will come up, and you'd say wait until the next week, and maybe we'd never get our freedom."[4] They had waited in the fall, and that had taken them through Christmas, and they had waited at Christmas because they wanted to be nice, and that had been a *political* not a moral decision, he said. But now Greensboro had happened, and they were obviously far better trained than the Greensboro kids, who had acted not out of training but out of impulse. What more was there to wait for? he asked. Yes, he said, they might not have enough money for bail, but they had not had any money the year before, and it was quite likely that they would not have very much more money in a month or two months or even a year. Nothing was going to change in the unknown, he argued—they did not know what was going to hap-pen, what the level of resistance was going to be, and what the finan-cial hardship would be. But, and this was the most compelling part of his argument, only by acting could they make the unknown of the white resistance become the known. As they acted, the unknown would become the known and they would be able to struggle with their problems one by one. Lewis, listening to him, was impressed by his friend, sensing that there was an original and unshakable quality to his thinking. Of course there was going to be risk, Bevel said, coming up with what was to be the most basic rule of the Movement over the next five years—if there was no risk, then all of this would have been done a long time ago. They were being asked to do it only because there *was* significant risk. By the time Bevel was finished speaking, the argument was effectively over.

9

THE PACE OF AMERICAN LIFE IN FEBRUARY 1960 WAS SIGNIFICANTLY more languid than it was soon to become. Though the nation had been wired for television for much of the previous decade, that medium had not yet taken control of the country's political agenda. The idea of a media society, one driven both politically and socially by the prime purpose of reaching fellow Americans, watching television in their living rooms at six or seven each night, though close at hand, still seemed oddly distant. Demonstrations of any sort, particularly those which seemed to be designed at least in part for television cameras, were still relatively rare. The evening network news shows lasted only fifteen minutes, and were seen on black-and-white screens. Social change came slowly. When people wanted change they addressed their grievances by going through the courts or through the political process; they did not readily go into the streets and become demonstrators. The sight of political demonstrators, particularly black ones, was rare indeed as the new decade began.

On that winter day, February 13, 1960, there was something quite striking about the sight of 124 young people, almost all of them black, all of them well dressed, leaving a black church in downtown Nashville and walking through the streets in the most orderly manner imaginable and going to a number of the city's downtown dime and department stores and quietly taking their places at the luncheon counters. Their posture—it was one of the first things any observer noticed—was absolutely impeccable, for on this day they all stood tall. There was, their body language seemed to say, nothing to be ashamed of in what they were doing. If individually they seemed less than heroic, being ordinary people of ordinary size and seemingly of ordinary human gifts, their dignity and their propriety were palpable.

None had the idea that what they were about to undertake would change their own lives and that they might one day become famous. To the degree that they were reflective, some of them thought about how ordinary a group of students they really were and how great the odds against their success were. As they walked to their appointed stores, they looked past those who had already begun to mock them using words which were age-old in their cruelty. Taunted by local whites, they looked into the distance and did not deign to answer name-calling with name-calling of their own. They represented nothing less than the cream of Southern black students who had decided they had waited too long for change and were now taking things into their own hands. Their sense of purpose was obvious. Anyone taking the time to watch them and then to talk to them would have come away with a sense that something very important had happened that day and that these young people were not easily going to be turned around. If it was not technically the first major act of social and civil disobedience taking place in this new decade, following as it did the protest in Greensboro, it was one of the first, and it and the demonstrations which now followed, wherein people went into the streets to protest their conditions and the perceived lack of justice in their lives, were to mark the new decade as being far different and infinitely more volatile than the rather passive decade which had preceded it.

The white community was stunned. The word spread quickly throughout the white establishment in the city. Phone wires burned up, a message repeated over them again and again: "The niggers have just left a church downtown and are going to the department stores and demanding to be served!" The message was relayed breathlessly, from one office to another, stores to city hall, city hall to police department, local store to headquarters in New York and Chicago, as if this were the first step in a larger, grander apocalyptic scenario which everyone had for so long feared. The news was terrible. What was even worse was that no one knew what to do, other, of course, than to refuse them service, and gradually to start closing down the counters. Instinctively, the decision on what to do tilted to the past rather than to the future; the store owners decided to resist.

The students had caught the white community completely unprepared, and the small marauding bands of white toughs, who would soon become a staple of the downtown confrontations, had yet to materialize. To the degree that there was violence on this day it was verbal—people startled by the presumption of the young blacks instinctively yelling out epithets, middle-aged white waitresses telling young black college students that they did not serve niggers. (Of the 124 participants, most were college students.) When the day was over, the leaders were pleased; they believed it had gone well, and they had not been surprised by the fact that the store owners had immediately closed all the counters and lunchrooms. Although Greensboro had been first, Nashville became in time the city where the student leaders were uniquely well prepared, having, unlike the Greensboro students, studied in workshops for several months. More, the decision of the Nashville merchants to resist was critical: It meant that the Nashville student leaders were to become over a period of four months much more battle-hardened than most of their peers elsewhere.

Nashville turned out to be the ideal experience for the young student leaders. City officials in a more tolerant city might have conceded too readily and thereby deprived them of the chance to develop their leadership skills; city officials in a less tolerant, Deep South city might have crushed them immediately, not only having them arrested, but forcing the heads of all state schools to expel any student participating. If Jim Lawson had wanted perfect laboratory conditions for forging leadership skills among his young acolytes, then it seemed the local officials, political and business, were determined to accommodate him. In Nashville there was just enough resistance to strengthen his young people and test their skills, but not so much that his movement was broken on day one.

To the students themselves, the experience was nothing less than exhilarating. John Lewis had been scared before the first sit-in. There were two things which helped him get through. The first was his absolute certainty that what they were doing was right. The second was that he was not alone. He was with his friends, the closest friends he had ever had in his life. He had sat there in the First Baptist Church right before the sit-in began and had looked around, and he could tell how nervous all of his colleagues in the core group were. Everyone was edgy. Some of them were more silent than usual, and some were noisier than usual. The reality of what they were about to do had finally set in: They were about to go up against the full power of the city of Nashville. Lewis had never thought of himself as being brave, and the others, he was sure, did not think of themselves that way either. What they were doing was not an act of courage, he decided; it was an act of faith on all of their parts. They were certain that they would all be arrested. Certainly some of them might be beaten up, and it was quite possible—Jim Lawson had never tried to minimize the consequences—that some of them might even be killed. All they had was their faith, and they were bound together by that, he thought: faith in Jim Lawson as a teacher; faith in each other, that they would not let one another down at the moment of crisis; faith in what they believed was right; faith, curiously enough, in Nashville, a city they did not know and which had never been particularly generous or kind to them; faith in the country which would, they believed, somehow understand what they were doing and respond generously and support them; and finally, most of all, faith in their God, who would not allow His children to be punished for doing what was so obviously the right thing.

He was afraid, he was aware of the price that might be exacted before it was all over, but he knew that it was also time to move ahead, and he liked the idea that as he entered this dangerous new world, he was not alone; that he was accompanied not only by his closest friends but, equally important, that he was acting on behalf of his God. He did not think of himself as being strong or brave, but he did believe that he had the requisite faith, and now he found in his faith the strength to go forward and do things which in another setting and under different conditions would have terrified him.

10

THE CITY WHICH HAD BEEN STUNNED BY THE VISIT OF 124 BLACK STU-
dents to downtown lunch counters in 1960 was a singularly divided
city. There was a distinctive physical quality to that separation. To the
black community in the neighborhoods around Fisk and Tennessee
A&I, the white world, literally on the other side of the railroad tracks,
was known as Crosstown. It was physically near but, in all real ways,
extremely distant. For along what was largely an east-west axis, there
were railroad tracks which separated the two communities. The city
fathers had seized on that seemingly casual division and arranged it in
a way that quite successfully isolated the heart of the black community
from the surrounding white community. A minimal number of streets
crossed over those tracks from the black world to the white world.
Two main thoroughfares ran along that axis: the outer boundary of
the black world was Jefferson Street; the outer limit of the white world
was Charlotte Avenue. It was not easy to get from the center of the
black community in the Fisk, Meharry, and A&I area to the white
world on the other side of the railroad tracks; and of course, it was
meant to be that way. (The nature of that division was a source of
anger to many blacks in Nashville for the most primal of reasons—
what would happen, black leaders argued, if a pregnant woman was
on her way from South Nashville to Meharry Hospital and was held up
by one of those endless L&N freight trains? It was not until the seventies, as black political power in Nashville increased, that a bridge was
finally built over the tracks at black insistence.) If it was not easy to get
by foot from the center of the black community to the white world so
close by, it was *very* easy to get to the posher areas of west Nashville
and Belle Meade from these same black quarters by *bus*. Once again it
was meant to be this way, for the bus routes, as they had been in count-

less Southern cities, were drawn up to ferry maids to and from middle- and upper-class white homes, where black women could find work.

Other than that, the two worlds were not meant to connect. Separated as they were by geography, by race, by history, more often than not by class, and above all by myth and superstition, they had an extraordinary capacity to misunderstand each other. Little in the way of truth was communicated from one community to the other; the truth of one community, it had been learned long ago, tended to make the other community uneasy. In the mid-fifties, Nelson and Marian Fuson were among the few people in Nashville who tried to bridge these two separate and distinct communities. The Fusons were an anomaly in that time, white liberals, committed Quakers, integrationists, people who quietly lived their values. They were, one friend said, the kind of people who were against the Vietnam War even before there was a Vietnam War. Nelson Fuson was a professor of physics at Fisk; his wife was a member of different civil rights groups in the days and years before there was a Movement. From their religious and professional associations they were unusual in having friends on both sides of the railroad tracks, and on May 17, 1954, the day when the Supreme Court ruled on *Brown,* Marian Fuson had called a white liberal friend of hers named Pauline Haynes about one-thirty in the afternoon to share this transcending bit of news. Pauline Haynes was the wife of Sherwood Haynes, a Vanderbilt physics professor. "Pauline, isn't it wonderful?" Marian Fuson had said, and Ms. Haynes had asked what was wonderful. "The Supreme Court decision on segregation in schools—they ruled nine to nothing against it," Ms. Fuson said. "Oh," said Pauline Haynes, "that explains everything." What does it explain? Marian Fuson asked. "Well, our mother's helper, who's a student at A&I, has been excited all day and she's had the radio on all the time, and she's been making phone calls all morning, but she hasn't said a single thing to me. I kept wondering what she was so excited about," Ms. Haynes answered. Pauline Haynes sounded quite wounded. Amazing, thought Marian Fuson. We live so close to each other, we see each other every day, and yet we live in a world where we might as well be deaf and dumb. These were worlds, Ms. Fuson thought, separated not merely by laws and customs but by their own vast silences, their own unique social inhibitions; even people of goodwill did not know how to talk to each other across the color lines.

The simple truth was that ordinary blacks in Nashville in the late fifties got the worst of everything, particularly jobs. Whites got the good jobs, the good housing, and the good education. Blacks got what was left over. According to the 1960 census, there were 399,743 people in what was greater Nashville. Americans did not move around as readily in those days as they soon would, and 80 percent of the people counted in that census were people born in Tennessee. Roughly 38 percent of the city's population was black. According to the census the median income for the city was $3,816 a year, and almost 40 percent of the population earned under $3,000 a year. Most black families made well under $3,000 a year; an income of $1,500 a year was more along the lines of what an entire black family managed on.

There were 2,432 black college graduates in Nashville in 1960 and they formed the core of an enlightened new black middle class; in addition there were nearly seven thousand high school graduates. In what was perhaps the most revealing statistic for black economic progress, there were 523 black women who were teachers, 756 black women employed as cooks in restaurants or clubs, and 5,454 black women employed as domestics. Anyone knowledgeable about how blacks responded to the census (and the degree to which black people withheld information from the government, because nothing good could come from telling the government anything about how much money you made because it might mean someone would come and want some income tax money) would have estimated that the number of black female domestics was probably two or three times greater, with almost all of the workers being paid off the books and without benefits. A salary of $15 a week for a black domestic who worked all day long, five or six days a week, cooked and cleaned (and took the bus to and from work—probably an extra forty minutes each way), would have been the going rate.

In February 1960, Nashville was a city living largely as it always had, right before the storm which was to come. It was an extremely livable city, albeit somewhat sleepy economically. It was culturally conservative and more than a little smug, and it liked to think of itself in social terms as representing a genteel part of the older South, one where the agrarian values of the past had not been completely brushed aside by the harsher forces of modern materialism and badly needed industrialization. It called itself the Athens of the South, and an exact replica of the Parthenon stood at Twenty-fifth and West End. It was, like many cities in the South, only marginally industrialized and unionized. Well into the fifties an older, essentially local oligarchy still controlled the economy and above all controlled wages, and was resistant to the intrusion of new, more modern economic forces, particularly those which were not locally controlled. When in the early fifties word leaked out that the Ford Motor Company was considering locating a glass plant in Nashville, a powerful cadre of existing Nashville business leaders bitterly opposed it, fearing (quite properly) that it would change forever the economic base of the city and force all competing employers to start paying real wages to their blue-collar workers, wages that might go above a dollar an hour. The white middle class was quite narrow in Nashville in the late fifties; the black middle class, of course, far narrower.

Nashville's segregation was largely of a soft kind, administered, it sometimes seemed, not with the passion of angry racist officials but more as a cultural leftover from the past. The desegregation of the city's schools had begun two and a half years earlier in the fall of 1957. In Nashville the segregated past still lingered, often woven tightly into the fabric of the city's daily life, and as such it was extremely easy for white people to forget that a significant percentage of the city's citizens were denied elemental American rights every day of their lives because of the color of their skin. The segregated quality of life was surprisingly complete: In the unlikely event that a white man and a black man wanted to have lunch together to talk about doing a business deal (unlikely because few white men would have considered black men potential business partners), the only public place they could do it in February 1960 was at the luncheon counter at the Nashville municipal airport, itself only recently integrated.

The city's movie theaters were segregated, and blacks wanting to go to a first-run movie at a downtown theater had to go to a separate box office at the side of the theater and then walk up a narrow staircase also along the side to a separate section in the balcony. Years later, Dr. Matthew Walker, one of the city's foremost black physicians and a man who was particularly helpful to the students in their protest, spoke of going to the movies with his wife. It had been in the winter and his wife had worn her best clothes, and he told of how she had put on her fur wrap and how the two of them, accompanied by a few friends comparably decked out, had been forced into this black-only route to their seats in a segregated world, a back alley venture toward an evening of pleasure, and how painful it had been for both of them, how he had felt his manhood diminished. As he told the story forty years after it happened, he broke into tears.[1]

Faced with the prospect of racial challenge, the white citizens believed that their city could deal with change in an orderly and civilized way. Yet there was more talk about change than there was change. If anything, the city had made more progress politically than it had socially or commercially. Ben West, the talented and ambitious young mayor, was dependent upon black votes for his election. West was a decent and humane man whose own instincts on race were far ahead of the political curve in Nashville. He was a principal beneficiary of the changes wrought by *The Nashville Tennessean* some twenty-five years earlier, when it had fought a long, bitter, and eventually successful fight against the forces of Boss Ed Crump of Memphis and his use of the poll tax to suppress and control black voting. That battle, successfully waged, had opened up a generally liberal era in Tennessee politics.

The effect of the *Tennessean's* prolonged assault upon the poll tax had been both immediate and dramatic in Nashville. In 1939, as the fight was about to begin, there were only 45,000 people registered in Davidson (Nashville) County. By 1948, the year of the paper's great political victory over Ed Crump, that figure had jumped to 79,000, many of them black. In the black community, starting in 1947, there had been a series of major voter registration drives, called Solid Bloc. The success of those drives, much enhanced and encouraged by the *Tennessean,* was considerable: In the fall of 1948, the Fifth Ward in north Nashville, the city's primary black area, had had fewer than seven thousand registered voters. Four years later that figure had more than doubled to sixteen thousand, giving blacks a critical if not quite decisive voice in local politics. Ben West had understood—and encouraged—these changes long before most other politicians in the city. As a young state senator before becoming mayor, he had pushed for the charter reform which allowed local residents to choose their own councilmen, and that in turn had led to the election of black city councilmen. In the 1951 elections both Z. Alexander Looby, a black lawyer who had run for the city council twice before and lost, and Bob

Lillard were elected to the council, the first blacks elected in forty years.

Perhaps equally important, West was by the standards of his day quite liberal on racial issues: He had been willing as early as 1949 to speak openly at the Fisk Race Relations Institute, something that few white politicians were willing to do in those days when if they wanted black votes, the traditional means of seeking them was to do it as covertly as possible, often with the passage of a considerable amount of money under the table to local fixers. In his appearance at the Race Relations Institute, West had openly encouraged blacks to become more involved in politics, again something that was quite daring for the era. West had also increased the number of blacks on the police force and in the fire department, had helped integrate the restaurant at the local airport, and had placed Coyness Ennix, a black lawyer, on the school board. West did this not only because he was smarter than most other politicians and could see the political changes which had an inevitability to them, but also because he was an innately decent man who was clearly made uncomfortable by a citizenry in which one race systematically dominated and exploited another. All of this created an anomaly of its own, for black councilmen like Looby and Lillard had the dubious distinction of being able to sit in and vote on whether certain people in Nashville received licenses to run restaurants where they themselves could not be served.

By all rights the city, essentially one of the most sophisticated in the South, should have been able to deal with the sit-in crisis. It had a liberal mayor and a significant swing bloc of black voters, and the larger and more important of its two papers was not only liberal but had made a serious commitment to deal honorably with both the legal and moral implications of race. The downtown stores themselves were more and more vulnerable to black economic leverage anyway, for though few realized it at the time, the coming of the automobile had marked the essential end of the downtown as the principal white shopping area in the city. Rival suburban shopping areas had sprung up in the satellite communities ringing the city, catering to new, increasingly mobile white middle-class customers, who owned cars. The downtown was disproportionately supported by blacks, who often did not own cars, and shopped there because they were prisoners of the city's bus schedules.

But there was an undertow at work in Nashville as well, an undertow formed in part by the customs of the past and in the most immediate sense by the political fabric of the city. It was important to remember of both Nashville and Tennessee in this era that they were still a one-party area and that their political divisions were not fashioned along the lines of Democrats versus Republicans but existed entirely within the Democratic party itself, which was, of course, badly divided with its own factionalism. Throughout the state, the voices which defined the two factions tended to be that of the state's leading newspapers, often very much at odds with each other. In Nashville that particular factionalism had created divisions which defied normal political rationality. For if on this most compelling issue the modern mayor and the modern paper, the *Tennessean,* took the same position, then it stood to reason that the paper would support the mayor if he incurred any wounds in following his conscience. That certainly would have made life a good deal easier for everyone involved, a liberal paper supporting a liberal mayor and helping to diminish the power of conservative critics. But in the complicated and often bitter division of the day, the liberal paper, the *Tennessean,* and the liberal mayor, Ben West, *hated* each other. They had taken opposing sides in a number of earlier elections, and a remarkable amount of bitterness remained. No amount of mediation on the part of well-meaning self-appointed friends of both could heal this breach.

The paper did not talk to the mayor. The mayor did not talk to the paper. Politically the paper was for many of the things the mayor was for, but it was unalterably, pathologically (and almost inexplicably) opposed to him. By the time the sit-in struggle had arrived, almost no one remembered why the paper and the mayor hated each other, but everyone on both sides remembered that they were supposed to hate the other and that neither side was permitted to give an inch. When Wallace Westfeldt, the *Tennessean*'s skilled civil rights reporter, who was also a stringer for *Time* magazine, would call Ben West on a story, the mayor would ask who he was representing, the *Tennessean* or *Time.* If it was *Time,* they could talk. If it was the paper, Westfeldt could forget it.

It was a split not without serious consequences as the sit-in demonstrations pushed forward. It meant that the most powerful segregationist in Nashville, the true leader of the local resistance, was not, as it was in many Southern cities, a politician or a sheriff or a judge or the head of an all-white segregationist movement; it was a newspaperman, James G. Stahlman, publisher of the extremely conservative *Nashville Banner*. Because the liberal *Tennessean* was sworn to destroy him politically, the liberal Ben West found himself involuntarily dependent on the support of the very conservative Jimmy Stahlman, whose political power was otherwise in significant decline. That greatly reduced West's freedom to maneuver on this issue and meant that as the sit-ins continued he was unusually vulnerable. He needed, in order to survive, the votes of Nashville's black wards, but he was dependent as well on the good wishes of Jimmy Stahlman. From the start, this was an issue on which Stahlman eagerly drew the line. He hated the idea of integration in general, and he particularly hated the idea of young local blacks, led blindly, he was sure, by outside agitators, violating in his mind the rights of private property holders in his city. He knew the box Ben West was in, and he knew he could put the screws to him.

The agent who passed many of Stahlman's warnings on to Ben West was a man named Neil Cunningham, who was ostensibly a *Banner* political reporter but, more than that, a political ambassador from the *Banner* to local and state politicians. Ben West was frequently reminded by Neil Cunningham in the blunt and often colorful language of Jimmy Stahlman that if he buckled on this goddamn issue, he could kiss his goddamn political career good-bye because there wasn't going to be any goddamn newspaper in the goddamn state which would support him or even write his goddamn obituary when it was all goddamn over.[2] There were other warnings which were said to be even harsher.

Though the forces maintaining segregation in 1960 were generally amorphous in Nashville and certainly in decline, there were not a lot of people who wanted to cross Jimmy Stahlman on any issue, least of all one like this, about which he felt so passionately. He was a man capable of personalizing even the smallest dispute with opponents. When he was angry, which was quite often, he let those who had angered him know; when he felt betrayed, which was less often, for few people wanted to cross him, he was exceedingly dangerous. Even those who were nominally his political and business allies tiptoed gently around him, acutely aware that if they committed even a minor infraction in which they were perceived to have inadequately stood their ground alongside him, Stahlman would let them know, often in blaring type and with a choleric choice of words.

He was, in the paternalistic vernacular of the time, Mister Jimmy to his staff and those who coveted his favor. The *Banner* was in every sense his personal instrument. Far more than the *Tennessean,* the *Banner* was a reflection of its editor's interests, his passions, and, perhaps even more important, since the mainstream of American life was taking a direction opposite to most of the things he believed in, his prejudices. He was the most bombastic of men. His editorials thundered out their points. A reader glancing through the *Banner*'s editorials had a sense that when these florid words had been written back in the *Banner* offices, a desk had been pounded and the color of the editorial writer's face had turned to a dark, flushed red. Stahlman's sentences seemed to cry out not for periods at their end but for exclamation points. He was a man of certitudes and his certitudes were enduring; he was not, even those who were fond of him believed, a great listener. His power and influence were not to be underestimated, particularly on the enormously emotional issue of race. If he did not exactly have the capacity to lead, then he most certainly had, on this issue, the capacity to scare and intimidate; he was, those who were both his allies and his enemies thought, the journalist as bully.

He was a volcanic man. Everything with Jimmy Stahlman was potentially explosive. "He was like a stick of dynamite always ready to go off," said Jack Gunter, a *Banner* photographer who often drove Stahlman around, since the publisher preferred being driven by his own people rather than by cabbies, this not merely to save money, but because he could keep himself informed about the inner workings of his paper that way.[3] Everyone who was not his friend was a son of a bitch. Often they were goddamn sons of bitches; goddamn sons of bitches were the kind of people who had to be watched.

If the *Tennessean* had certain sacred cows, the *Banner* too had its own, and there were more of them, and they were, if anything, in some cases far more sacred. Nothing was more sacred than America (an America which was red, white, and blue) and capitalism, an old-fashioned proprietor-dominated capitalism, one, as the Nashville labor lawyer George Barrett once noted, untempered by the power of labor unions, where owners could determine wages without the slightest interference on the part of labor. In his America the greatest of military-political heroes was, of course, Douglas MacArthur, while the greatest villain was George Catlett Marshall. Jimmy Stahlman, as one friend said, was a man who went to his grave sure that George Catlett Marshall had been part of a great Communist conspiracy to bring this country down by turning China over to the Communists.[4]

These were a few of his favorite things: the United States Navy, the Boy Scouts (which he and his brother worked diligently to keep segregated), the Shriners, the Belle Meade country club, the Southern Way of Life, and, of course, perhaps more than anything else, Vanderbilt University, which to him symbolized the best of the old South and its ways. Most things that he loved were in some form or other political, although it should be said that he loved all birds, and whenever the temperature dropped near freezing in Nashville, *Banner* reporters were assigned to go to the lake in Centennial Park and chop the covering ice so the ducks who lived there would not find themselves frozen into the lake's surface and unable to move;[5] in addition it was one of the principal jobs of the city editor of the *Banner* to put what was called a bird box on the front page, reminding the paper's largely white readers to feed the birds. The writer of this box was always known to his colleagues as the Bird Man.

The news executives, of course, knew who was in favor and who was not. Once Larry Brinton, one of the *Banner*'s best reporters, put the name of Glen Ferguson, a local politician, in his story. Out it came. Why? he asked. "Mister Jimmy's mad at him," he was told. A few weeks later Brinton noticed that Ferguson's name had reappeared in another reporter's story. What's happened with Ferguson? Brinton asked. "We ain't mad at him anymore," he was told. Stahlman hired people he thought were conservative and agreed with his policies, and he hired them for about half of what the *Tennessean* paid. His regular editorial meetings were what one staff member called an amen chorus, with different executives vying to agree with what he said with the most enthusiasm. He would outline his ideas, then the others would come in and say on cue, *That's right, Mister Jimmy, that's right.* Once when one of Stahlman's business colleagues named a horse after the publisher, Jimmy Armistead, one of the paper's executives, complimented Stahlman, noting what a singular honor it was. "As a matter of fact I hate the goddamn horse and I hate the son of a bitch who did it," Stahlman said. "You're right, Mister Jimmy," Armistead said. "I never liked him either."[6]

There were certain rituals to working for the *Banner* that reflected the paternalistic nature of the institution. At Thanksgiving every *Banner* reporter got a turkey. Every Christmas there was a small keg of jam for every reporter. Stahlman had a fishing camp in Destin, Florida, and each year when he returned from it, he brought back a huge number of iced fish. All *Banner* reporters were not merely asked to go and pick up the fish if they in fact wanted fish—they were *told* to do so, and there was a check-off system so that if someone did not pick up his fish, the publisher would know who his ungrateful employee was.

The Stahlmans were not Old Nashville—that is, one of the families who were socially successful and wealthy, and whose modern position and privilege in the community more often than not had evolved over multiple generations from a position of landed wealth in the previous century. These families had remained wealthy (although occasionally, if their finances showed some slippage, new blood and wealth were allowed to marry in) and were based in Belle Meade. Everyone knew who the old families of Nashville were, for they seemingly enjoyed that status in perpetuity—it took a very long run of bad financial decisions and poor marriages to let it slip away. By the standards of Old Nashville (people for whom the melting pot and the meritocracy of modern America remained largely alien concepts), the Stahlmans were arrivistes, German immigrants when they arrived and German immigrants still, albeit a century later. Because of that, there was still a lot of scar tissue left over for Jimmy Stahlman, and much of his hyperpatriotism and self-conscious Southernisms was, even his friends thought, a somewhat sad attempt to become part of an elite group which had never completely accepted his family. During World War I, when anti-German feeling was at its height in this country, Luke Lea, then publisher of the *Tennessean,* had hammered away at the fact that the name Stahlman was *German.* (In the years after World War II, Stahlman had led the fight to change the name of a Nashville street called Fatherland to another, less offensive name.)

That explained much about him as a superpatriot and a super-Southerner. It was not by chance that the *Banner* was named the *Banner,* and the real banner, the American flag, forever proudly waved at the top of the paper. Much of his politics came from his sensitivity to the anti-German slurs of his boyhood. He had served with the navy in a noncombat role during World War II, and had risen to the rank of captain, and he liked that rank and the uniform. Long after World War II was over, there were men who called him Captain Stahlman, or better still Captain Jimmy; when he was introduced as a speaker at civic luncheon clubs, enterprising younger men tended to dwell at length on the sterling quality of his wartime military service and his love of country.

Stahlman's German heritage was not the only part of the past he was living down. Even worse than being German, to some old-time Nashville residents the Stahlmans were carpetbaggers who had arrived right after the Union Army and had profited off the bare bones of the postbellum South. "The thing you have to understand about the Stahlmans is that they arrived in Nashville after the Civil War with the railroads, and they were regarded as outsiders and foreigners, German newcomers, and even worse, as carpetbaggers," said John Nixon, a liberal judge in Nashville and the son of a distinguished Vanderbilt political scientist.[7] "That was used against them in political struggles early on, and it stung and hurt and they were very sensitive to it, particularly Jimmy Stahlman. He became in his fervor for things traditionally Southern, like segregation, very much like the convert to Catholicism trying to be more Catholic than the pope."

He hated certain things. He regarded most aspects of change warily. He hated daylight saving time. Part of the reason was that daylight saving time hurt the late edition of the *Banner* in the summer. The *Banner* in those days had four editions, and the last one, which carried the Wall Street closings, locked up at 4:18 P.M. But Wall Street closed at three-thirty, which meant that in the summer the *Banner* missed closing time. That enraged him. Daylight saving time was against God's own natural order, as far as he was concerned. "Battle," he would say to the *Banner*'s city editor, Bob Battle, "you're a farm boy. You know that the cows can't adjust to daylight saving time. Every farm boy knows that!"[8]

The rest of Middle Tennessee might spend the summer living on daylight saving time, but the *Nashville Banner* did not, and every summer, while virtually every other institution in the city switched quite naturally to daylight saving time, the *Banner* held fast to standard time, sending the entire city into total confusion. If Stahlman could not hold the line politically, he could at least try and hold it on the clock. Almost symbolically, since the two papers were housed in the same building and the *Tennessean* favored daylight saving time, the clock in front of the building at 1100 Broadway reflected the schizophrenia of the very differing publishing mind-sets inside: It said, in the midafternoon, 3:00 P.M. on the *Tennessean* side, and 2:00 P.M. on the *Banner* side.

Jimmy Stahlman was a man who liked things the way they were supposed to be. Every day at lunch he had a can of Campbell's tomato soup and four crackers. Nothing less, nothing more. He had set ideas about how a man should dress. He believed black shoes should be worn with a blue suit. That nearly cost the young, ambitious Frank Clement, already known as the boy orator of the state, the support of the *Banner* early in his career. Les Hart, the *Banner*'s political writer, had seen the golden-tongued Clement as a political comer very early on, and Hart had sent Clement's father and unofficial manager, Robert Clement, by to meet Stahlman. If the meeting had gone well politically, it had been a sartorial disaster. For Robert Clement had arrived wearing a blue suit with *brown* shoes. "I don't know about this," Stahlman said later, "I don't know about trusting a son of a bitch who wears brown shoes with a blue suit."[9] A few days later he was still talking about it. "I wanted to tell him how wrong it was," he said, "but I was just too upset to say anything."[10]

He was not so much a conservative as a reactionary. His paper was one of the very few—if not the only—major metropolitan papers in the country that openly endorsed the policies of the far-right John Birch Society in those days. What Jimmy Stahlman did not know he instinctively viewed with alarm. He did not deign to read anything by anyone he disagreed with. He did not lightly consult or listen to people whose views were different from his. If people thought differently than he did, then there was something wrong with them—they were less American than he was. He might think he believed in traditional institutions, but if an institution like the Supreme Court of the United States or the Congress of the United States made decisions he did not like, he felt there was no need to obey whatever law they propagated. The proper thing—the patriotic thing to do—was to attack the institution and ignore the decision. Technically the paper was supposed to be Democratic so that it could be a player in the state's decisive Democratic primaries, but he had never supported a Democratic candidate for the presidency. When a younger colleague once introduced him by saying that he had steadfastly supported every Republican presidential candidate during his years as publisher, Stahlman had quickly and proudly corrected him: "Young man, that is not exactly true. In 1948 I supported the States Rights ticket of Strom Thurmond and Fielding Wright." So he had: He had loved that campaign, men of his own kind running on a separate ticket, with a good chance of taking away enough Southern votes to sabotage Harry Truman and keep the Democrats from winning.

He did not think of himself as a racist, but simply as a man who preferred the existing racial order. Black people were all right, but they had to know their place. Jack Gunter, the photographer, often drove Stahlman to the train station when the publisher went on trips. As they pulled up in front of the entrance, and the black porters moved toward the car, Stahlman liked to pull out a bunch of crisp, fresh ten-dollar bills—a huge tip in those days. "Watch them shuffle for these, Jack," he would say, and as he got out of the car he would hand them out. "Look at them shuffle."[11] Shuffle they did, for ten dollars was probably what a porter working at Union Station made all day if he was lucky. So there it was: He had wanted them to shuffle, and shuffle they did. It was the natural order.

His paper was hated in black Nashville. To the black leadership and the ordinary laypeople of the city it was *the* enemy. "That damn *Banner*" was what they called it. It ignored black success; it refused to recognize any black aspiration for change. What Jimmy Stahlman did not like about the growing black movement for political and social change in the late fifties, and there was much he did not like, he did not print, unless it was to show that all the pressure for racial change came from what were then called outside agitators. For a long time the paper's circulation in the black community was marginal; it devoted one page once a week to black social events, but then when people in the black community found out that the paper did not even circulate the black page to white subscribers, an informal boycott took place, and the paper's black circulation became virtually nonexistent. At that point Jimmy Stahlman decided to hire a black reporter. Later he was immensely proud of this, and he would boast of what he had done, the Southern publisher who had hired the first black reporter in 1950. "There were a lot of goddamn people," he liked to boast, "who did not think we would do it, but by God we did it, and it worked and we showed those sons of bitches!"

His political influence, particularly in certain circles in Nashville, was considerable. Neither he nor the people he was allied with could turn back the clock in some areas, and the coming of the black franchise had steadily diminished the political forces aligned with him, but he was very influential in wielding his power privately in upper-class commercial Nashville, in the world of Belle Meade, and in intimidating those who were his peers. The prime movers and shakers might not particularly like him, and in truth many of them regarded him as something of a live hand grenade; ostensibly they were pledged to segregation as he was pledged to segregation but they feared him, afraid, if they buckled in any situation, he would make them pay. His influence at Vanderbilt, where he was an unusually forceful member of the board, had already shown itself; the authorities there were quite sensitive to Stahlman's power and his alliances with other conservative board members, and it was one of the main reasons why Vanderbilt had done so little to integrate.

He took the sit-ins as a personal challenge. He might not be able to stop blacks from voting and he might not be able to stop the integration of the city's schools, but he had a lot of influence downtown, both with the mayor and with store owners like John Sloan, and he felt the students had crossed a line when they had gone into the local department stores. The *Banner*'s reporters were not, of course, supposed to cover the sit-ins. He hated what was happening and he did not want it in his newspaper. It was all a scam as far he was concerned, and he had no need to cover a scam. He was convinced he knew Nashville's colored people and he knew they were happy in their lives. The last thing they wanted was any kind of integration. All of this was the fault of outside agitators. He gave orders to his reporters and photographers to stay away from the downtown area when the protests were taking place. The penalty was simple—by God he would fire them if his orders were disobeyed. To the degree that the *Banner* was willing to cover these news events, it seemed to be an attempt to show that Jim Lawson was an outsider and a troublemaker manipulating otherwise docile young Southern blacks. The growing power and effect of the sit-in movement locally went unreported in his paper. Stahlman had decided one thing—that Jim Lawson was a sworn enemy.

11

JIM LAWSON WAS SURPRISED BY HOW PLEASANT HIS PERSONAL LIFE HAD turned out to be in Nashville. At first he had been nervous about his ability to control his anger in the face of segregation. But almost from the start, in his work locally and in his travels for the SCLC and the FOR, he had found himself so fully employed and his talents so fully utilized that his only problem was that of time, of being able to take care of all of his responsibilities.

He had not been in Nashville very long when he paid a visit to the offices of his white counterpart, Will Campbell, the field representative of the National Council of Churches. Campbell was a true radical by the standards of the fifties, and he wanted to live as he thought a religious man should live: He had not only joined a black church, that of Kelly Miller Smith, upon his arrival locally, but he had put his money in the city's one black bank, and in addition he had decided to do something which was virtually unheard of—hire a black secretary. Perhaps that was the most radical of his decisions. For in Nashville's downtown business world there was de facto segregation. A white man with a good job had a white secretary; he did not hire a black woman. The rare black man who had need of a secretary would hire a black secretary. But Campbell decided to hire a handsome young woman named Dorothy Wood who was a recent graduate of Tennessee A&I. That did not particularly thrill Dorothy Wood's father, an old-fashioned self-made black man who lived in Charleston in East Tennessee and ran a number of grocery stores there, for he knew well the old-time dodge and how it worked in the South, a white man on occasion hiring a black woman for some job, and then using his economic power to extract sexual favors from her. So before his daughter could accept this job, he ventured forth to Nashville and visited Will Campbell, questioning him about why he wanted to hire Dorothy, and he decided what Campbell sought was spiritual elevation rather than sexual favors, and agreed to his daughter working for this strange Mississippi white man who believed in integration.

When Jim Lawson visited Campbell's office he was much taken with his secretary and soon asked her out. On about their third date he startled her by telling her that he had already spent time in prison. But, he quickly explained, it had been for an act of conscience. She knew from the first time they went out that he was different from all the other young men who had pursued her, that he was driven by a purpose much larger than himself, and that the material things of life, which were so important to most of the young men she knew, meant absolutely nothing to him. In December 1958 they became engaged. As the two young people became increasingly serious about each other, Will Campbell for a time opposed the idea of their marriage and even warned Dorothy against it. It was not that he did not think Jim Lawson a good man—if anything he thought him too good a man. Lawson, Campbell believed, was in the truest sense not only a Christian radical, but he was a moralist warrior. Campbell knew that Lawson was going to be trouble to the day he died because he was so committed and uncompromising. Campbell was by no means sure that Dorothy Wood, whom he thought a gentle and soulful person, could handle the kind of tumultuous life Lawson was sure to lead. "You know, Dorothy," he told her, "often it's harder to be married to a good man than to a bad man." By that he meant that a truly good man like Jim Lawson was bound to challenge the prevailing conventions of society, thereby endangering not only himself but his family as well. He had a powerful moral vision, which he had already followed into prison, and he would surely follow it again.

Dorothy Wood, of course, did not listen to Campbell. A good man was a good man, and Jim Lawson was a very good man: attractive, serious, purposeful. On July 3, 1959, they were married, and in February and March 1960, as Jim Lawson entered one difficult situation after another, Campbell watched the strength in Dorothy Wood Lawson grow and he decided it was not that he had judged Jim Lawson wrong, he had in fact gotten him exactly right; it was simply that he had underestimated the courage and strength in Dorothy.

Almost as soon as he had arrived in Nashville, using his Methodist connections, Lawson had applied to and been accepted at Vanderbilt Divinity School, the second black student to be admitted there. And he was, now that he was married to Dorothy Wood, determined to have a full social life. A few weeks after they were married, Jim Lawson happened to wander by the divinity school bulletin board. There posted for all to see was a notice advertising discounted tickets for the Nashville Symphony. Lawson liked classical music, as did Dorothy. He called and asked her if they wanted inexpensive symphony tickets. "Of course we do," she answered. They had shown up for the first concert of the new season, displayed their tickets to an usher, and he had, looking at *them* but not at their tickets, automatically pointed them to the balcony stairs, where until then a small number of blacks listened in a Jim Crow area. Up they climbed to the balcony, showed their tickets once more to an even more surprised usher, who told them they were supposed to sit downstairs. Down they went to show their tickets to the first usher, who seemed very surprised and not a bit pleased to see them again, but finally escorted them to their seats in an otherwise all-white section. Quietly, and without incident, without even knowing what they were doing, Jim and Dorothy Lawson had integrated the local symphony concert series and War Memorial Auditorium, where the symphony played.

He also integrated other aspects of Vanderbilt life. When blacks were first admitted to the divinity school there had been a gentleman's agreement with the outgoing dean that they were, in effect, to be invisible men, not to be seen and not to be heard, if at all possible, outside of the classroom. They were not supposed to eat in the school cafeteria, and they were most decidedly not supposed to play on intramural athletic teams. But by a fluke a new, quite liberal dean had arrived at the divinity school just as Jim Lawson was being admitted, and the new dean, Robert Nelson, had never gotten the word on the covert limitations placed on black students, and so Lawson had never been warned of his partial status. It became obvious to him that the authorities did not expect him to eat in the student cafeteria, and he could sense their uneasiness when he ate there. In addition he loved athletics, and had been a good playground athlete, and when a notice went up about intramural athletics, he immediately signed up and played for the divinity school team against the other graduate school teams and the undergraduate fraternities. (The divinity school football team, said John Nixon, then playing for the law school, was notoriously dirty.[1])

Eventually Lawson would hear that there had been a drum roll of complaints almost from the start about his aggressiveness as a student, about his eating in the cafeteria and playing intramural athletics. As he played intramural sports, so soon did other blacks. The chancellor's office was passing down warnings to the divinity school dean, but the chancellor and his aides appeared unwilling to do anything directly. Bob Nelson, who was more liberal than the chancellor, had no intention of reining Lawson in, at least not for playing touch football or eating lunch. So high up in the Vanderbilt administration there was already a good deal of grumbling about Jim Lawson, not about his performance as a student but about his audacity as a student. But as happens in these matters, no one bothered to say anything to him, not that it would have made much of a difference. But there was no doubt that he was moving too quickly on sensitive ground.

His schedule in those days was brutal. At first, it seemed, he was always traveling, always on his way to some regional meeting for the FOR or for Martin King and the SCLC. His studies made his schedule even harder. Fortunately his situation was not that different from that of a good many other divinity school students who were practicing ministers, working for their higher degrees while still tending to pastoral duties at small regional churches. The divinity school organized its classes accordingly: Students had from Friday afternoon to early Tuesday morning off, so they could go home and pastor. Tuesday was a heavy day of classes, and then there were classes on Wednesday and Thursday as well, and sometimes Friday morning. In those years Jim Lawson was almost always tired, almost always short on sleep. But his life seemed at that moment unusually complete, exactly the kind of life he had once hoped to lead.

12

AT FIRST THE LOCAL MERCHANTS DECIDED TO TAKE WHAT WAS FOR them the path of least resistance. They would not bend. That was where peer rather than economic pressure pushed them. At the moment it seemed the easier of the two courses. What weighed most heavily on them was the past. That was what they knew and understood—they were Southerners, and Southerners did not give in on things like this, and of course, they also felt the pressure from men like Jimmy Stahlman and a few of his hard-line allies in the business community like John Sloan. To resist was to be manly and strong; to give in was to be different, and to risk being called a nigger-lover. In the first two weeks the sit-ins were largely peaceful, though, despite the large number of cops on hand, by the second major one, there were more incidents. Small groups of angry white youths had become more noticeable in the downtown area, and there were a number of quick strikes against blacks as they sat at counters.

The reaction of the merchants in no way surprised Jim Lawson. But he did not for a moment believe that the situation would remain static. He was sure that sooner or later the forces opposing them would lash back and that there would be some sort of major confrontation which would move the conscience of the white community. That confrontation finally came on Saturday, February 27. Big Saturday, Jim Lawson later called it, because of the violence inflicted on the sit-in protesters and the subsequent arrest of eighty-one students (and the arrest of none of their tormentors), and because of the way the police miraculously, or unmiraculously, managed to disappear from the scene of the violence just as the whites attacked the protesters.

Tensions downtown had been mounting and there had been warnings in advance that something like this was going to happen, that the police were going to let the white youths, the counter-protesters, have a clean shot at the activists. It took place on the fourth major sit-in, counting the early sympathy strike for the Greensboro kids. Saturday was traditionally the big shopping day in the South, in rural towns as well as the cities. It was the day when blacks, their work finally done for the week, poured into the downtown area both to shop and socialize. Anything which slowed down or threatened to limit black spending on a Saturday cut right to the heart of the ability of the stores to survive.

A decision had been made between the merchants and city officials to lash back at the demonstrators. Will Campbell, who was well connected politically, had been told that much of the pressure for this decision came from Jimmy Stahlman and a few of his friends and that he had used his leverage with city officials to let the cops and the white marauders have one good shot at the black activists. The idea behind it was to let the protesters know that there was a price for what they were doing.

Campbell, the resident representative of the National Council of Churches, had picked up from his sources, both political and journalistic, that the city officials were going to pull back the limited protection offered the students up until then (in the earlier demonstrations there had been just enough police presence to keep the angry whites from all-out physical assaults on the demonstrators). Violence against the students was likely to take place, Campbell was told, and in addition there would be a large number of arrests of the black demonstrators. Mayor West, Campbell learned, had been pounded by his conservative supporters like Stahlman to do something about stopping the demonstrators. West had been caught in the middle between a black community which thought he should take the leadership in calling for integrated lunch counters, and a white business and commercial leadership which thought he had been offering the protesters too much protection. Just two days earlier the student leaders had met with Douglas Hosse, the police chief, and had asked for greater protection, specifically requesting one cop in each store. Hosse had answered that his force was not large enough to provide that kind of protection, but he would give the greatest amount of protection he could, and he would enforce the law fairly—any whites causing a disturbance would be arrested. Then as the meeting was breaking up, the chief turned to Curtis Murphy and asked, "Is all this worth a twenty-five-cent hamburger?"

On Saturday morning, February 27, when the student leaders had shown up at First Baptist, which was their staging area, they were very nervous: It was important to show the local officials that their numbers were steadily increasing. Because Lawson did not believe in hierarchical leadership, a central committee decided on all actions, and it was large rather than small. Though in the end a core of about a dozen members were the most committed and made most of the decisions, on occasion as many as forty students would show up for central committee meetings. At first on this day the number of regular students who showed up as volunteers was very small, only thirty or forty. That was especially disappointing: They had wanted at least 100 or 150 demonstrators. The idea that a few weeks into their challenge they might demonstrate weakness instead of strength was disheartening. Because of it the core leaders went downstairs to the basement and debated for more than an hour what their tactics should be, given the seemingly small turnout; whether they should hit a small number of stores with relatively large numbers of students or whether they should disperse into smaller groups and hit as many stores as possible. Those who wanted to hit the maximum number of stores argued that it was important to show the merchants and the city officials that this was not some kind of fad, and that the demonstrations were going to continue, and continue to grow in number. Those who wanted to hit a limited number of stores with a maximum number of protesters argued that this was going to be a dangerous day and that there was a certain security in numbers—the larger the group in one given place, the less likely the white violence was to get out of control.

In the end the leadership decided to hit as many stores as possible, and to try a human wave technique—as one group was arrested, another group would take its place—to let the merchants and the cops know that there would always be more bodies and more people willing to become part of this new cause. Finally the central committee leaders came upstairs and found out that while they had been debating, some three hundred students had shown up and were waiting to start the protest. That's it, Bernard Lafayette thought to himself, God has truly spoken. We have been down there in the basement worrying about whether our call has been heard, and now we have the largest turnout so far. He is hearing us. The debate over strategy, he thought, was finished.

Lafayette was amazed by the young people who showed up that day, almost none of whom had been in any previous sit-ins or had attended any of the training sessions. Most of them did not know the leaders personally, they had not been to any workshops, yet when they were warned that the protest was likely to be violent, no one pulled out. It was, he believed, pure faith on their part. That they had had so little training was somewhat bothersome—some might not know how to respond when attacked, how to go into the fetal self-protecting position, and some might be tempted to meet acts of violence by lashing out themselves. So the veteran leaders quickly gave the newcomers a crash course on nonviolence. The leaders told them what to do, and warned what might happen. The white kids might beat up on them. The cops apparently were not going to offer any protection. Indeed the cops might beat them up at the police station. In all instances they were to look to the group leaders among them for any further instructions. Under no conditions were they to strike back, either physically or verbally. That was the cardinal rule. If they struck back they would undermine the sacrifice of everyone else. When the lessons and warnings were finished, no one withdrew.

Observers, weighted with coins to call back to headquarters, were sent to pay phones strategically located near every store. The observers had all the requisite phone numbers with them—the numbers for the headquarters, the numbers for the white hospital for ambulances for any white kids who were badly beaten, and the numbers for the black funeral homes for any blacks badly beaten, for there were no black ambulances, and it was traditional to use hearses from the funeral homes as ambulances in the black community. Off they went that morning with one mission: The more of them who were arrested by the police, the better; they would move the conscience of the white community by filling the jails. It was the Gandhian way, which they now had come to accept.

Thirty-five years later Paul LaPrad, at the time a twenty-year-old white exchange student from Manchester College in Indiana, remembered February 27, 1960, as the day he had his own moment in history, small and fleeting though it was. But to LaPrad, who had originally helped connect Jim Lawson to some of the other students, it was no small thing. It gave his life exceptional purpose and value. Indeed, he decided years later, everyone ought to have one pure moment in history, one glorious instant which set you apart from everyone else and made you feel that you were not ordinary, that your life was worth something. Most of the other students from that time remembered that the sit-ins took place in February and March, but Paul LaPrad remembered the exact date of his historic moment. It was the day on which he was beaten savagely by the white mob, and even more important, a photo of the assault upon him was taken by a United Press photographer and sent around the country and around the world. Within a few months, his tour of Fisk completed, LaPrad would go back to Indiana and to what was a pleasant, rather commonplace life. And yet on that one day he had been at the cutting edge of history, in a moment captured on film for millions of Americans to see.

Paul LaPrad was the product of, he liked to say, simple country people. They were small-time farmers who had migrated west from Virginia to find only marginal prosperity in Indiana. His father eked out a modest living with two jobs, as the local mail carrier, and as a local pastor for a Church of the Brethren congregation of about seventy people. Essentially his income came from being a mail carrier. He had been a conscientious objector in World War II, and a life of nonviolence was ingrained deeply in him. There had been some degree of local grumbling when he had refused to join the army during World War II, but most people in the community had accepted his decision for what it was, an act of conscience. He did not push his pacifist and antimaterialist beliefs with his family, but it was his hope that his sons would be like him.

His son Paul had registered for the draft when he was eighteen, and had been placed in the 1-AO category, which meant that if called he would serve, but in a noncombatant role, as a medic. In the summer of 1958 on the occasion of the 250th anniversary celebration of his church he had gone to Europe, where he had visited the site of Hitler's concentration camps, which had effected him powerfully and moved him further toward the teachings of Jesus Christ in nonviolence. Man, he decided, simply had to learn to come to peace with his neighbor, and love his enemy as himself; otherwise the consequences were too terrible, particularly in an age of nuclear weapons. When he had returned to Indiana, LaPrad had changed his registration, asking and receiving a straight 1-O, which was the traditional conscientious objector position.

Because most of his meager financial resources had been spent on the trip to Europe, LaPrad decided to take a year off to earn some money. Like many an Indiana farm boy before him he had migrated to Chicago. At first he took a job working for Motorola, which paid well. But it was in a plant allied with the defense industry and so he quit the job and took one which paid a good deal less, working for the city of Chicago as a clerk in the Cook County hospital. He also did some community service work and liked it—he had found the world of the poor to be far more complicated than he expected. It taught him to be wary of generalizations about the poor: Some of them were gentle people, and others from the exact same background might prove extremely dangerous.

Rather than return to Manchester College after his year in Chicago, he decided to attend a black school for a year. How could he think of himself as an educated young Christian when he knew so little about so many other of God's children? he wondered. He applied to three black schools and was delighted when Fisk had accepted him. He arrived at Fisk determined to show that he was hip, and when, in September 1959, he first set foot on campus he was surprised at how formal a place it seemed, how old-fashioned, indeed decorous the dress codes seemed to be. To ensure his reputation for hipness, he had arrived in Nashville sporting a small goatee. He was immediately summoned to the office of Dean William Green. The dean had cast an unsympathetic eye on the meager amount of fuzz on his chin. "Mr. LaPrad, Fisk men don't wear goatees," Dean Green said, and LaPrad had shaved his beard off that day.

LaPrad, because of his connections from Chicago, had been Jim Lawson's first recruit. He was always aware of the limits of his role within the group, that he was a foot soldier, not a leader, and that his role was not to talk at critical junctures in the meetings but to listen. The black kids were intrigued by him. White college kids were supposed to be more sophisticated than black ones, but Paul LaPrad was about as unsophisticated as you could get. He was, they thought, nothing but an Indiana country boy. At first when he talked to them he began by saying, Well, I'm just a farm boy, and they were all a little wary, but then it had turned out that he *was* just a farm boy, and they accepted him at face value.

Paul LaPrad later thought of their group that day as an army, albeit a small army, embarking on what was nothing less than a holy war. What they were challenging seemed so wrong to him, what they were doing—seeking rights which ought to be enjoyed by all Americans— seemed so right, that no price was too great to pay. He had participated in the earlier sit-ins and on February 27 he, like the others, was aware that it was probably going to be rougher than usual because the local hoodlums were supposed to be out and the cops might disappear. He had been assigned to McLellan's, and his memories of the encounter there were at once both sharp and indistinct. The white mob was bigger and noisier on this day and it seemed to be unusually emboldened. There was always, he thought, more hatred aimed at him and the handful of other whites because what they were doing was considered traitorous; they had gone over to the other side. The yells of *nigger-lover* were constant as he walked to his seat. The white women in the mob, he remembered, were as angry and as noisy as the white men. Most ominously, there were no police there, and because of that the mob seemed less restrained, more confident of its right to inflict verbal and physical harm.

He was seated at the counter with two black students, Maxine Walker on one side and Peggy Alexander on the other, when someone came up from behind him and yanked him off the stool. Down he went. People were swinging at him and when he was down he felt someone kicking him. The kicks were sharp, the pain the kind he imagined would come with being stabbed. He moved into the fetal position, trying to protect himself, as they had all been taught to do. It was at that moment, LaPrad lying on the floor trying to cover himself, hands over the back of his head, the crowd of white men and women yelling and jeering at him, that the memorable photo was taken of him.

The violence was over quickly. LaPrad managed to pull himself up and get back on the stool. It was the sheer fury of it all—how quickly and violently they had struck—which stunned him more than anything else. The pain did not last. The blows from the fists of the attackers—he was never sure how many there had been—had glanced off him. No ribs were broken. A few minutes later the police arrived and arrested LaPrad for disturbing the peace. They did not arrest any of his white assailants. Shortly after that Paul LaPrad's draft board took away his 1-O status because he was pledged to nonviolence in order to enjoy that status, and as far as the board was concerned, his actions that day had resulted in violence.

Another hero of that morning was Angeline Butler, a Fisk co-ed. She had been assigned a role as an observer and she was at McLellan's just as the scuffle had broken out and Paul LaPrad had been beaten. She was appalled by the way the white crowd had lashed out at LaPrad, but she was even more upset by the way the store manager was handling the sit-in. The demonstrators had hoped for mass arrests, but the manager was denying them what they wanted most, a jail filled with students. LaPrad had been arrested but his companions had been forced off their seats by the cops and led out of the store without being arrested. LaPrad was being placed in the paddy wagon by himself. It was almost as if the manager knew their game plan. But Angeline Butler noticed that the front door was still open and that the manager seemed to be getting ready to lock it to keep out any more protesters. Without saying anything she signaled to Bernard Lafayette, another team observer, what was happening. She got her hand on the door and opened it, and as she did, an entire new group of students moved in and took their seats at the counter. There they waited for service, which never came. Soon the police came and arrested them, just as they had intended. By the end of the day eighty-one of the demonstrators, seventy-seven black and four white, had been arrested. None of their assailants was arrested.

That Saturday was the first time Diane Nash was arrested. She was seated at a lunch counter, and there was a cop, a rather pleasant one, actually, she decided, and he tried to be nice to her. He politely asked her and her friends to get up and they all refused. "Listen," he said, "if you don't get up you're going to be arrested," as if that were the most terrible warning imaginable, and upon hearing it, surely they would get up. The threat of arrest had probably always worked for him in the past. And these were, after all, well-dressed people, and the last thing well-dressed people would want was to go to jail. But no one moved. "All right, all right," he said, his patience quickly exhausted, "that's it! You've been warned! You're all under arrest!" They all got up, and as soon as they did, a dozen more of their colleagues came into the store and took their seats. The policeman seemed stunned: These young people *wanted* to be arrested. And when *they* got up, others took their places. After he helped arrest the second wave, a third wave took their seats. His face seemed to say it all—were they ever going to stop?

On the way to the jail in the paddy wagon Diane Nash found that her fear was almost suffocating. Sitting there, she tried to turn herself into nothing but an observer, to try and see this as if it were happening to others rather than to herself. At the police station they all waited to be fingerprinted and booked, and they began to take some courage from the fact that they had each other for support, and that their numbers seemed to be getting larger. If there was not strength in numbers, she thought, there was at least some degree of comfort in them.

But she was still frightened. Jail was the unknown, the place about which she had heard such terrible stories. She was, she later realized, as she came to sample other, harsher jails in less hospitable venues, dealing with a psychological block more than anything else, the belief that she was crossing a line which she had been raised since childhood never to cross, to be a good girl and stay out of jail, since only bad girls went to jail. She was deathly afraid of the physical search which was sure to come, and which would be an added indignity, and surely it would be abusive as well. But there was no search. She wondered why. Perhaps there had been too many prisoners that day and the cops had simply lacked the time.

But she found the very act of being fingerprinted humiliating. Even worse was the conversation of the two white male cops who were doing the fingerprinting. They looked at her and saw her light skin and they talked to her as if she were different from the others. Perhaps they thought she was white. They made disparaging remarks about the other blacks, about the way they looked and smelled, and about the thickness of one boy's lips. One of the students said he was a minister and the two cops then made fun of black preachers. They were in some crude way trying to let her know that she had a chance to be like them, a chance to be on their side. To her surprise she felt her fear turn into a growing anger. Who, she thought, were these two white cops to judge her? Who were they to sit there and make fun of her colleagues? Who wanted to be white in the first place? Who were they to judge her and her friends, who had been arrested and put in a filthy Nashville prison just because they had tried to eat a crummy Woolworth's hamburger? And in that instant she understood completely why she was doing this, that this country forced you to make decisions about color that you did not want to make. Suddenly, after all these years she knew how black she was. It was not her idea to judge people on color; it was America and Tennessee and Nashville which had decided to judge her on her color and the color of her friends. She gave them her fingerprints, and walked away from the desk more sure than ever of what she was doing and why she was doing it.

13

ON BIG SATURDAY BERNARD LAFAYETTE HAD FINALLY DECIDED THAT he was worthy of being a warrior in this army. For weeks he had been bothered by private doubts over whether he was truly nonviolent. He had found Jim Lawson a remarkable teacher, but privately he wondered whether he could live up to Lawson's teachings. Was Lawson's advice simply too spiritually demanding for him? At the time he was trying to find his way, as a man, as a minister, and as a political person. True followers of Gandhi were able to rise above the taunts of their adversaries. Would he be able to turn away in the face of the taunts of his enemy, all those white rednecks yelling *nigger*? So far it had been hard. Lafayette was all too aware of his own frailties. He knew there was nothing noble about himself, that he was a person with all too many human weaknesses, above all an instinct to lash back at his attackers. The Bible had asked him to turn the other cheek, and here was Jim Lawson telling him exactly how and when and where he was supposed to do it. Could he sacrifice his own safety—his own manhood—for the ideals which he believed in? What was most difficult about this particular question was that only he would know the inner truth. He knew that he could, if he so chose, fake it, hide his inner hatred and rage, and pretend that he felt love toward these people who were trying to hurt him and his closest friends. But merely hiding his rage would not be good enough. For him to be in the truest sense part of this he would have to feel love. He found almost to his shame that one of the things which bothered him was how he felt about their young white assailants: He did not mind taking their blows, but he did not want them to walk away and think that he had turned the other cheek because he was a sissy.

But on that Saturday he faced the challenge, and decided he was worthy. He was completely unprepared for the moment when he was tested, and he had no time to remember his own internal debate. He was in a group of students walking from the First Baptist Church to the lunch counters, and he was near the end of the line, about three or four people from the end. Suddenly a group of white toughs charged the black line and attacked one of his colleagues from American Baptist, a young man named Solomon Gort. It happened very quickly, with a speed and intensity all its own, and yet at the same time, it seemed to take forever. Years later he could remember almost all the details. The whites had knocked Solomon Gort down, and they were kicking him, and Bernard moved as quickly as he could to get back and protect Solomon, to put his body down on Gort's as they all had been taught. That would make them switch their attention from Solomon to him, and they did, beating and kicking him instead. Just then Jim Lawson walked over. He did not rush over as if to an accident or as if to stop a beating. Instead he walked over very calmly, as if to a long-standing appointment. It was as if he knew all along that Solomon Gort was going to be knocked down and mauled and that Bernard Lafayette was going to try and protect him.

Lawson's arrival shifted the attention of the whites from the fallen Gort and Lafayette to Lawson. The thing about Jim, Bernard remembered, was that he was so utterly self-assured, so confident, as if he were accustomed to dealing with white toughs beating up fallen black demonstrators every day of his life. Jim seemed nonchalant—just another day at the office. The leader of the whites was sporting what was the prevailing uniform of the day for white toughs, black pants, black leather motorcycle jacket, duck's-ass haircut. When he saw Lawson he was enraged by Lawson's coolness and he spat at him. Lawson looked at him and asked him for a handkerchief. The man, stunned, reached in his pocket and handed Lawson a handkerchief, and Lawson wiped the spit off himself as calmly as he could. Then he looked at the man's jacket and started talking to him. Did he have a motorcycle or a hot-rod car? A motorcycle was the answer. Jim asked a technical question or two and the young man started explaining what he had done to customize his bike. Amazingly, Bernard thought, these two men were now talking about the levels of horsepower in motorcycles; a few seconds earlier they had seemed to be sworn ene-mies, one ready to maul the other. By this time both Solomon Gort and Bernard Lafayette were back up on their feet, the line was moving again, and Jim and the young man were still talking about the man's motorcycle. In that brief frightening moment Jim had managed to find a subject which they both shared and had used it in a way that made each of them more human in the eyes of the other. As they walked away Jim waved to the man, and the man remained still, nei-ther accepting the friendship nor, for that matter, rejecting it. It had been a marvelous example of Christian love for Bernard.

The lesson for Bernard Lafayette was obvious: It did not matter what the other person thought of you; it mattered only to do the right thing, to follow your conscience. In that split second of confrontation Jim Lawson had not only conquered his ego, he had forced his enemy in some basic way to try and see him as a man. From then on Bernard Lafayette understood some of the things he had been searching for. He did not need to explain to his enemy why he was doing this. Too much time, he decided, was wasted in this country by people who worried how they looked to others, and too little time spent on simply trying to figure out what was the right thing to do. Christ had not wor-ried about how he looked to others. If you did the right thing, he learned that day, it was all right to be misunderstood. He did not have to shout out that he was doing this as an act of courage, not an act of fear.

14

WHEN JOHN LEWIS WAS ARRESTED THAT SATURDAY HE WAS FULL OF fear, fear of what might happen next. But then as they took him from the downtown store and fingerprinted him, the fear fell from him, and he felt as if a great burden had been lifted from his shoulders. He felt his own strength growing. As the cops arrested his group he had looked at the faces of his friends and had seen the same thing he felt himself. He did not, as he had sometimes feared in the past few months, feel small and vulnerable. He felt empowered, part of something much larger than himself. It was as if he had crossed a great line, one that was both political and psychological; he had gone from being afraid of the white power structure to being emancipated. Is this all there is? he thought as they brought him to jail. Is this all they can do to us?

He had grown up terrified of prison. He had been taught again and again by his family that it was the most shameful of all things to go to jail, that only bad people from bad families went there. And he had been taught as well that terrible things could happen to you if you were arrested for political reasons, that you might disappear and never be seen again. But here they were being arrested, and they all knew that they had not done anything shameful, they had done the right thing, they had been true to their purpose and to their people. Jim Lawson had prepared them well. He had taught them what to expect, what the white cops were likely to do, even what kind of things would most likely be said to them at the police station. Most important of all, they had each other; there was strength not so much in their numbers, although that helped, but in their shared belief. Jail was not crushing; it was, he thought to his amazement, liberating.

Years later he could point out the photos of the very young John Lewis coming out of jail on that day, and note that there it was in his face, the confidence, the dignity. *I had never had that much dignity before,* he said years later. *It was exhilarating—it was something I had earned, the sense of the independence that comes to a free person.*

15

On that Saturday there had been, in the midst of the mass arrests, a quick exchange between Jim Bevel and Diane Nash. Because it was clear that almost everyone was going to land in jail that day, Bevel had told Diane not to get arrested, that they not only needed her as a leader, but they needed a leader who stayed out of jail and who might be able to get back to the different campuses and bring in more, instant recruits. Someone, Bevel had said, had to run this thing, and it could not be run from jail. But Nash, understanding the dynamics within the group, told him that if only one of them was going to manage to stay out of jail, it had to be him. If she were not arrested that day, she said, the others might think that it was because she had been afraid to go to jail. But if it was Bevel who was not arrested—Bevel, who was so self-evidently afraid of no one—there would be no kickback, and no one could later claim that he was a coward. So Diane Nash had been arrested, and Bevel had become in those critical moments the de facto leader, going back to both Fisk and A&I and bringing in more and more young people for the mass arrests they so badly wanted. But what had happened on that day convinced Bevel and the others that they still had to make some adjustments in their leadership group.

Jim Lawson had always favored communal leadership. It was, he thought, the true Gandhian way. He wanted these young people to argue their way through every issue until they found what was their own truth. If they had a hierarchy, if only one or two people at the top were the acknowledged leaders upon whom all the others depended, it would have a number of negative effects: It might convince those at the top that they were more important than they actually were, thereby increasing conflicts over ego and personality; equally important, it might subtract from the sense of importance of many of the others and make them feel their strength came from their leaders and not from themselves; and finally it would convince their white opponents that all they had to do was arrest the leaders to close the protests down.

If anything, as the students began to respond to the forces gathering against them, Lawson was surprised by how well the idea of communal leadership was working. The members of the central committee, often thirty or forty young people, would argue their way through a decision, responding, for example, to Bevel's greater sense of urgency to begin right after the Greensboro sit-in, or deciding on how many different stores they would hit on a given afternoon. They would make sure that everyone had been heard and that everyone was on board before adapting something as policy. It was a long and arduous way to do things, and meetings often went on for three or four hours, but it had its benefits as well: It was inclusionary, and it allowed some people who were not naturally good at public speaking to participate and have their say. It also contributed to an aura of mutual respect.

Yet within the larger group about a dozen young people had gradually begun to surface as leaders. They were, it became obvious, not only the most gifted organizers and best tacticians but the most committed, and finally, the ones most willing to take risks. But Bevel and some of the other leaders were unhappy with the two young men who in the early days of the workshops had somehow emerged as the student leaders: He felt they had been imposed on the others because they had arrived with credentials already proclaiming their leadership ability, rather than gaining the positions by emerging from the workshops as natural leaders. He had a sense that they were of a type, the kind of young men that college administrators liked and deftly pushed forward to students as model student leaders. They were, he thought, very conventional, and very career-oriented, young men who were always looking to their elders for signs of approval. Whoever led this movement, Bevel thought, had to be willing to make mistakes or at least make what the dean of a black college thought was a mistake, a mistake being something which went on your record and could slow down an otherwise bright future. To be successful at this, Bevel believed, you could not consider the consequences of what you were doing. Instead, you had to believe that these actions you were taking were of themselves right and therefore, no matter what else, they *were* the future. Most student leaders, he was sure, would somehow manage to steal a look at the dean of their college to see if they were meeting with his approval. And no dean of a black college in 1960, Bevel thought, was going to approve of what they were doing. He had looked at the two young men who had been the early leaders and he had been absolutely sure that they would not be able to take the pressure, and he was right: The more confrontation there was on the streets of Nashville, the more they buckled. During the early confrontations one of them simply disappeared, and the other did not so much disappear, but seemed to appear primarily at moments when reporters were around.

By the middle of February, Bevel had thought it was time to do what everyone knew had to be done and make Diane Nash the chairman of the central committee. She was the one person who would be acceptable to everyone. She was fearless and selfless. That she was strikingly beautiful did not hurt: "The first time I saw her," Rodney Powell said years later, "it was like looking at Maria from *West Side Story*." Bevel knew that the chairman of the central committee could not be, not this early anyway, Bernard or John or himself. Talented and committed the three of them might be, but he knew that the young men from Fisk and A&I who were being brought into the Movement were not going to let it be run by one of the seminarians. Bevel had no illusions about how young black college students viewed Baptist seminarians—too Christian, too square. "We were against segregation, and they were against segregation," Bevel said years later, "but we were also against a lot of other things they were for, drinking and partying. The three of us," he said, "knew that there was a secret fault line which ran through the group at first and that we were regarded with suspicion by the men."

So now, wanting to replace the two other leaders, he decided to push Diane. She had a capacity to subtract her ego, or as Bernard Lafayette said of her later, "Because she was a woman and not a man, I think Diane never had to go around and do any posturing." Whatever it was that needed to be done, she just did it. She was acceptable to everyone. The men from the traditional colleges liked and respected her, the seminarians liked and respected her. Jim Lawson was intrigued that though she was a Catholic and had begun to doubt some of the tenets of her own faith, she seemed to be finding other spiritual answers in Gandhian nonviolence.

The others were intrigued by her. She was the most fiery of all and yet because of her light skin she had no need to join up—for she could, they knew, always pass as white even, on occasion, when she did not intend to. At the beginning of the sit-ins, wanting to recruit others to join the group, she had once proselytized a young, rather dark-skinned woman named Frankie Henry to come along, and Frankie Henry had listened to Diane and had thought to herself, Hey, Frankie, here is this young girl, and she's *white,* and she's putting her life on the line for people like you in these sit-ins, and so the least you can do is join up with her, because if a white girl like her can do it, maybe you ought to do it too. So Frankie Henry had joined up that day and someone had extinguished a cigarette on her hand, a minor scar she would bear for the rest of her life.

Diane Nash was there, the others decided, because she wanted to be, not because, based on pigmentation, she needed to be. Diane had had a sixth sense that Bevel was going to nominate her for the job, and she had already decided to fight it. Just serving as a soldier in this citizens' army was already taking all of her strength and willpower. She wanted no larger responsibility. She immediately turned it down, saying she was not right for the job, that she was too frightened. But then, one after another, the others got up and challenged her.

The leader had to be a person who made good decisions under terrible pressure. Like it or not, she was that person. Bevel said that they had a right to have a leader they all respected and trusted. Then he made the most telling point of all: They were all there as a part of something larger than themselves and, because of that, they were not free to make decisions based on personal preference. They had to accept jobs based on talent. It was not what they wanted to do; it was what they were obligated to do. But she remained wary; she thought she did not want the responsibility of sending people her own age off to confrontations where they might be beaten or killed. She tried one last time to turn the position down. "I can't take it because I have a serious illness," she said. They had all leaned forward to find out what her secret illness was—amazed that she had functioned so well despite being so sick. "What's the illness?" Bevel asked. "I'm a woman and I have menstrual cramps," she said. "You take the job and we'll cover for you when you can't function," Bevel said. Chairman she had become.

During those extraordinary weeks and months, Diane Nash was quite surprised by the change which had taken place in herself. She had never thought of herself as a political person and, even more, had never thought of herself as a leader. She had grown up on the south side of Chicago in a rather privileged environment. She had even been, although it was not something she liked to boast about at the time, a teenage beauty queen, competing in the local Miss America contest in 1956 as a high school student.

At the time she had been in pursuit of the title of Miss Illinois and performed at the regional contest, sponsored by the Chicago South End Junior Chamber of Commerce. She had sung "Take Back Your Mink," from *Guys and Dolls,* and she had even gone to a costume rental store to rent what she later thought of as a rather impoverished fur piece but which at the time had seemed quite fancy. That night she had worn a flashy, spangled gown, to which she had affixed snaps. At the crucial moment, when she sang "Take back your mink, take back your pearls, take back your gown," she had dramatically pulled at the snaps and the gown had come off, leaving her standing there with nothing on but a leotard. The judgment was that she had done well, had sung nicely, and she was named a runner-up, albeit not the first runner-up.

That Diane Nash, would-be beauty queen, was, she thought later, a very different person from the Diane Nash who finished up her first year at Fisk as the head of the central committee of the sit-in movement. But the old Diane Nash had been the most sheltered of black children; she had lived in a home which downplayed all talk of race, and tried consciously to think of itself as an American home, not a black home.

Diane Nash's family was the most middle class and least radical of black families. It was as if race in America did not really exist because they willed it not to exist. They had made it from Mississippi to Chicago and had enjoyed the first fruits of that migration both economically and politically; if they had not become wealthy, they had generally prospered in the North. Theirs was the most patriotic of families: Her blood father, her stepfather, and two uncles had served in World War II. Her aunt had been a WAC; one of Diane's favorite outfits when she was a child had been a child's WAC uniform given her by her aunt. The Nash family had followed the war news avidly, sitting around the living room listening to the overseas reports on the radio. They had hated the idea of a racist Nazi Germany winning, and they had accepted the idea that America was freer for blacks than it really was.

Her family members were determined to be good Americans, and to show that blacks could be just as loyal as any whites. But the racial hurts were always there. There were, she remembered, all kinds of little incidents which she had turned away from when she was growing up, but which must have been extremely painful for her in some way—otherwise they would not have found their way into so permanent a part of her memory. When she was five she had gone to the parochial school nearby, run by the Sisters of the Blessed Sacrament, an order which taught only blacks and Indians. One of the nuns had said to her rather casually one day, "You *know* that we love God in our order, because we deal with the least of God's people." Some fifty years later she could remember the exact words: *the least of God's people.* As she recalled the words, she was aware in some way of how painful it must have been for her, having a teacher tell her that she was one of the least of God's people. What intrigued her was not only the hurt, but the ability she had showed to suppress it. She had done what everyone in her family did. She buried the incident.

If there was a philosophy to her home it was, she thought, that white people had better things because they worked harder and were better people. That philosophy had been in many ways inculcated in her and others by Carrie Bolton, her maternal grandmother and the most powerful member of her family, a woman who had grown up in Memphis early in this century. Carrie Bolton had gone to work for a white family in Memphis as a maid, learning the domestic ropes at the age of nine. The white family she worked for was extremely cultured—the man of the house was a wealthy doctor—and quite dazzled this young black child. She had loved being in their home, for they lived with such seeming ease and grace, amid so much human kindness and consideration.

The whites were always polite to each other. They all read books, and spoke of interesting subjects, and their conversation was a great deal more refined than that of the servants, who worked in the kitchen or who were maids or laborer-handymen and who were, of course, all black. If you went into the kitchen, she later told her daughter and granddaughter, the talk was always filled with sexual innuendo. The white family seemed to take an interest in Carrie, who was bright and extremely impressionable, and they planted in her mind that most dangerous of all ideas, that she was different from the other blacks. This moved her greatly. Yet it was a destructive idea, one which ran through many black homes, Diane Nash later decided, instilling a sense of shame about being black, and creating an instinct on the part of the victims of racism to blame themselves rather than those who had suppressed them for so long. But to the young black girl growing up in Memphis, what she saw seemed to confirm the most unattractive stereotypes about her own people. As she went north, Carrie Bolton greatly favored the things that whites had and did, and she passed on to her own family that these things, manners and making a good impression on strangers, were very important.

Diane's blood father's name was Leon Nash. He had been born in Canton, Mississippi, and been part of the great trek north, in his case to Chicago, which had taken place between the two world wars. He had gone to college at Tougaloo, and when he went into the service during World War II, he held a clerical job. After his discharge he was able to use the G.I. Bill to study dentistry. Diane's mother had found work during the war as a keypunch operator in a factory, putting information on war bonds, and Diane had been raised during the daytime in the first seven years of her life by Carrie Bolton. When the war was over the marriage of Diane's parents broke up, and her mother, Dorothy Bolton Nash, married John Baker, who was a waiter on a Pullman car. That was considered a prestigious job in the black community, and it made him a member of one of the most powerful black unions in the country. Because his job was so good, Diane's mother did not work after her second marriage.

No matter how American the family wanted to be, there was no escaping the flashes of pain which came from racial incidents. When Diane was fifteen and had just entered high school, she saw an advertisement in the Chicago paper about a charm school for teenagers. The ad had been placed by a modeling agency, clearly on the lookout for potential models. The charm school would run for three or four Saturdays and the girls would be taught how to put on makeup, how to do their hair, and how to walk. Diane was immediately interested and called the number in the ad. The man she talked to was very friendly at first. "Well, you seem like just the kind of young woman we're interested in," he had said. At a certain point he had started taking down information about her, her age and height and weight. But when he asked for her address and she had told him, something clicked, for hers was in a predominantly black section of town. His voice had immediately grown more distant. "My dear, are you by chance colored?" he asked. She had said yes. "Well, dear, we don't have a facility for colored students," he had said. Her pain was quick and bitter.

If part of her grandmother's ethic was that white was significantly better than black, and that it was better, all things considered, to marry a light-skinned man rather than a dark-skinned one, then there was another part of this older woman's teaching which was extremely important in defining the young Diane Nash. For Carrie Bolton absolutely loved her bright young granddaughter and she let her know this every day. This was not an age when people spoke about levels of self-esteem, and yet Carrie Bolton greatly added to Diane's self-esteem. For despite her ambivalent views about being black, she had raised this young child, whom she loved so desperately, to be proud. Every day when Diane was young, Carrie would tell her how precious she was. They had a game they played: Carrie Bolton would take Diane Nash into her arms, and she would say, "You're more precious to me than anything in the world."

"More precious than one hundred dollars?" the child would say.

"That isn't even close," Carrie Bolton would reply.

"Two hundred dollars?" the child would ask.

"Not even close," the old woman would say.

"More precious than five hundred dollars?"

"Not even close."

And in the end it would turn out that Diane Nash was more precious to this older woman *than all the money in the world.* Though it was a game, there was an underlying lesson to it, which was, You are of value and don't ever let anyone mistreat you. That, she was sure, had been in her mind on the day she had encountered the racist signs at the Tennessee State Fair.

16

CURTIS MURPHY HAD BEEN ONE OF THE EIGHTY-ONE DEMONSTRATORS arrested on Big Saturday. Somehow at the police station he had been quickly separated from the other students. It was Murphy's first venture into the black prison world, and it frightened him even more than being arrested. He had been placed in a holding pen with other prisoners, all black, and these were not pleasant young college students from middle-class homes; these were hard-core criminals. There he was in his best clothes—jacket and tie and a handsome topcoat; he knew he was out of place. He was soft and they were tough.

There was one man in particular who scared him, a huge, mean-looking man with very dark skin, perhaps six feet two and 230 pounds, with a great scar on his neck where he had been cut in some violent knife fight, most likely one of many. He had appraised Curtis carefully when he had arrived in jail, and given him a look which seemed to say, Boy, you are candy for the rest of us.

Curtis Murphy did not know very much about jail, but he knew instantly that nothing was going to happen in that holding pen that this man did not sanction—he was the real warden of the jail. Curtis rolled up his coat and tried to make it into a pillow and tried to read. As soon as he did, someone yelled for him to turn off the light, and he was scared by the voice, which sounded tough, and his fear intensified. Just then he heard an even tougher voice, the voice of the black man with the cut on his throat. "Hey, schoolboy," the voice said. This voice scared him even more, and he decided he was truly out of his element. *Schoolboy,* he thought, that about said it all; he was nothing but a little schoolboy in the world of men from the streets.

"Yes," he answered, aware of how shaky and tentative his voice sounded.

"Schoolboy—if you want the light on, you can put it on and keep it on," the tough black man said. "I know why you're in here, schoolboy, and what you're doing, and you can keep the light on all you want, my young friend."

When he heard that Curtis relaxed; it was a curious way of finding out how much support the students had in the community.

Even in those days, when the sit-in leaders were becoming stronger and stronger, more sure of their purpose, more confident that white mobs and the threat of jail could not turn them aside, they were still a distinct minority on campus. If there was any one student who was expert on how hard it had been to bring the average black college student of that era into the sit-in movement, it was Curtis Murphy, whose job it was to work Tennessee A&I, the largest and, as far as he could tell, most politically apathetic of Nashville's black schools.

He had entered the workshops himself almost on a lark. Dorothy Wood Lawson had a younger brother at A&I, a place where they badly needed recruits, but Philip Wood, a somewhat carefree young man, had no desire to be a hero and wanted no part of the sit-ins. As far as he was concerned, the whole idea sounded crazy. But Philip Wood thought that his roommate, Curtis Murphy, might be the perfect candidate. Curtis Murphy, as far as he was concerned, was truly weird: He was weird because he studied so hard and got such good grades in weird engineering courses, and he was weird because he wanted to fly jet airplanes. That made him a perfect match for Philip's new brother-in-law, Jim Lawson. For if Curtis Murphy was weird, then Jim Lawson was even weirder, not only because he was already going to divinity school at the most unattainable of Nashville schools, Vanderbilt, but because he had simultaneously started holding classes on how to challenge segregation in Nashville. So one night right after the Greensboro sit-in, Philip Wood had come back to his room, and had turned to Curtis. "Hey, Rim," he had said, which was current A&I slang for roommate, "you want to go to a meeting tonight?" What kind of meeting? Murphy asked. "Well, my brother-in-law, the one that goes to school over at Vanderbilt, is having these meetings about doing sit-ins here. He asked me to come along, but I'm not doing that—I'm crazy but I'm not that crazy. But I told him I've got a roommate who's really crazy. 'My roommate'll do anything,' I said.

'He's perfect for you.' So I gave them your name. I think you ought to try it—you're just crazy enough for it."

That was how Curtis Murphy came to join the sit-in movement. He had barely noticed the first story in the papers about a group of students in North Carolina who had gone to a local lunch counter and demanded the right to be served. That's interesting, he had thought at the time, but not for a minute did their action seem to have anything to do with him. He was a serious young man who intended to become a pioneer jet pilot. That was the real world for him. What had happened in North Carolina struck him at first as being something of a student prank. But prodded by Philip Wood, he had gone to a workshop, where he had met for the first time the core of the group: John Lewis, Diane Nash, Bernard Lafayette, Rodney Powell, James Bevel, and a young man who had been ahead of him at Booker T. Washington High School in Memphis, Marion Barry. Curtis had intended to attend only one meeting and then go his way, but he was hooked almost from the first moment by the quiet force of Jim Lawson's intellect and personality. But he also knew it was going to be hard to bring in many of his peers from A&I.

From the start Curtis Murphy was well aware of the powerful undertow working against him at Tennessee State, for many of the students came from backgrounds as poor or poorer than his, and a college education was not something lightly placed at risk, particularly when so much of his parents' limited means were invested in his getting a college degree. He had understood from the start that his principal job at A&I, because it was so large a school, was to supply the bodies. But his early efforts at recruiting had been pathetic. Almost no one had seemed interested. He went to old friends and almost without exception they rejected him. He was crazy, they said, he was going to get himself killed, and if they went along with him, he was going to get them killed as well. "Hey, Curtis," said one, "do you really think that those old white men who run this town and this state are going to let a handful of crazy niggers tell them what to do? Curtis, my man, it doesn't work like that."

So, rejected by those he knew best, he went to his crazier friends, those who lived on the wild side, people who would do things simply because they were risky and dangerous. Here too, he failed. They

might take risks at the hands of the college authorities or a rival fraternity, but not at the hands of white folks. Once, when he had stood up
on a chair at the school cafeteria and tried to explain what they were
doing and why they needed volunteers, he had been met by a thundering silence. He had felt terribly lonely at first, and he could almost feel
his hard-won and greatly prized social status on campus slipping away
from him. He had already held student office twice, and in this, his
junior year, he had just barely lost the presidency of the junior class in
what was a close election.

The full nature of what he was trying to do by proselytizing for the
sit-ins in so sleepy an environment came home to him when he tried to
recruit the young man who had beaten him for the class presidency.
The other boy was quite popular and Murphy thought it would be a
significant coup to bring him aboard. "Are you really serious?" the
young man had said. "Why, that's beneath me—that's rabble-
rousing." What then followed was an exceptionally condescending
lecture: This was not the way to go. It could only cause trouble. They
would be breaking the law. White people who might otherwise be
their friends would turn on them. They would not be able to justify it
because what they were doing was illegal. It might irreparably damage
their careers. "I'm going to go to law school," the young man had con-
cluded. "I think you'll be surprised how successful we can be—how
much money we're going to be able to make now." Years later Curtis
Murphy decided that he had, without realizing it, hit a class line
within the black community, that he had tapped into the automatic
response of the black bourgeoisie, people who had done comparatively well for a long time without putting themselves or their status at
risk. But at the time Curtis had felt terribly put down.

The one thing which kept him going was his growing belief that
what they were doing was right. Somehow Jim Lawson had managed
to make a real convert. Others challenged the wisdom of what they
were about to try, but no one had challenged the truth of it.

The more time Curtis spent with the Lawson group, the more
impressed he was with the other young people. He had never before
been with a group of people defined by such a powerful purpose. In
his other friendships he had his partying friends, his wild friends, who
would do anything on a dare, and he had friends who got good marks
and were likely to be successful, the kind his parents would approve

of. As he continued to go to meetings, Curtis began to sense a change in himself: There was more to him than he had ever thought possible before. He was becoming a serious person. At meetings he was able to speak up and say what was on his mind, and when he did people seemed to respect what he said, and the more respect they gave, the more serious he became.

He kept surprising himself. He had always thought of himself as someone who got good marks but was essentially carefree and happy-go-lucky. That was a point of pride with him: Most of the people who got good marks did not know how to have fun, and most of the people who had fun did not get good marks, but he had been able to do both. But this was a new Curtis Murphy, with a purpose that was larger than his own selfish needs. He liked the respect he got from the other sit-in kids. In this new world nothing was decided on popularity. People he had once been fond of—happy-go-lucky, seemingly carefree students much like himself—no longer interested him. When they spoke incessantly of their parties and dances, he thought of them as frivolous. He began to judge the people on campus on a new and unbending scale: Were you with us, or were you still on the sidelines, in which case you were not with us.

He knew he had his work cut out for him, because he knew that most of the students came from homes like his, where a college education was attained at great sacrifice, and where the students were often the first members of their families to go to college. He knew the fears and vulnerabilities of his fellow students, because he knew his own vulnerabilities. If he had one great fear as he continued to work with the group, it was the fact that he was putting his college education at risk, that he might be expelled from A&I and would not be able to go to any other college. Because he knew how much his education meant to his parents, he did not dare tell them what he was doing.

Curtis Murphy always knew he was going to college. Back when he was a little boy, when he had no earthly idea what a college was and for what purpose it existed, when people had asked him what he was going to do when he grew up, he would answer that he was going to college. That had been drummed into him from the very start by his parents. Only college, he had been told repeatedly by his father, would allow him to get off the farm and live a better and richer life. Buck and Lucille Murphy, his parents, had decided on that goal for him long ago. Buck (George Murphy, Jr.) and Lucille (or Duggar, as she was known) were away for most of his early life, trying to earn the limited cash which would keep the extended Murphy family from losing its precious parcel of land, and Curtis had lived with his grandparents, George Murphy, Sr., and Maggie Murphy. He called his grandparents Momma and Poppa, and his parents by their nicknames, Buck and Duggar.

The family land when Curtis was a boy consisted of about 150 acres in Whiteville, in Hardeman County in West Tennessee. Whiteville was a small town in that part of the state, where, because of the nature of the land and the culture which had evolved from a cotton economy, racial demographics and racial attitudes were more like those in a Deep South state than a border state. Owning land was always hard for black people, and almost from the time that Curtis was born, Buck had had to leave the family farm and move around the state taking whatever jobs he could as a construction worker. That meant that Curtis Murphy might as well have been a kid from rural Mississippi or Alabama, and that the ideas which Jim Lawson was preaching were completely alien to the way he had grown up; he knew a world where blacks were completely under the thumb of the ruling whites and where there was a constant threat of white violence hanging in the air. The best that could happen to black folks was that white people did not turn to aimless violence against them. Black people had no legal protection in Hardeman County.

Curtis Murphy had come during the workshops to accept the most elemental concept which Jim Lawson was preaching—that things did not have to be the way they were. That of itself was the first radical thought he had ever entertained. He had always accepted the idea that things were the way they were because they had always been that way and it would be dangerous to try and change them. That he had decided to join a crusade against the status quo still surprised him.

Curtis Murphy had always been good at school. That was lucky because it was the standard against which his father measured him. Buck had made it to the twelfth grade, and there had been some talk of college but he had not gone. But he knew that he had a son who was bright and gifted, and that with his natural abilities, Curtis could rise to a far higher level than he ever had himself. His son's study habits were good because they had to be. Buck would accept nothing less.

When Curtis's sister, who was two and a half years younger, and not as good a student, would bring home *B*'s and *C*'s, her parents were pleased and would give her two dollars as a reward. "But I got straight *A*'s," Curtis once told them, "and you gave me nothing." "That's what you're supposed to get," Buck had answered. For the first eight years of his life Curtis went to school in Whiteville, where the principal was a woman named Elma Motley, sturdy and indomitable, every bit worthy of Buck Murphy's vision for his child. Curtis had dutifully gotten nothing less than straight *A*'s at her little schoolhouse, and had even lived in her home for the first year of high school in order to save himself the three-mile walk to and from school each day.

By the time he was in high school he was smarter than his math teachers, and he had asked for permission to go to a boarding school for gifted black children in North Carolina which some friends of his were planning to attend. But Buck Murphy said that they did not have the money; what little they had was better saved for college. But Memphis, Buck said, had good black schools, and they had relatives there, and Curtis could, if he wanted, live with his kinfolk and attend school there.

So he moved to Memphis and lived with his aunt. He loved living in the big city, and Booker T. Washington High School was not that hard. Years later, after he became an educator himself, Curtis Murphy realized how good a school Booker T. Washington was, the last vestige of the best of an older order, with its great strength being that the teachers there were among the ablest, most ambitious black people in town. Many of them had been on a mission; they knew how hard a life awaited these children outside that school and they were determined to do everything they could to prepare them for some victories, however small they might seem by white standards. He was salutatorian of his class, missing being valedictorian by four tenths of one point, and that, he was sure, only because he had once gotten a *C* in gym back in Whiteville in the ninth grade. Buck Murphy, never one to drop his standards, accepted the news of his son's accomplishment with reservations. "Why weren't you valedictorian?" he asked.

Buck Murphy did not travel the sixty miles to Memphis to attend his son's graduation. "I'll come when you get your college degree," he said. A few years later when Curtis got his bachelor's degree, Buck again did not make the trip. "I'll come when you get your master's degree," he said. When Curtis got his master's degree, Buck still did not show up. "I'll come when you get your Ph.D.," he said. At first Curtis Murphy was disappointed, but then he came to realize that his father simply did not like to leave Whiteville, that he felt comfortable and protected there on the farm, and vulnerable when he left it.

The only question in the Murphy household as Curtis neared graduation had been which college he would attend. Buck did not want him to go to one of the smaller regional black schools in West Tennessee, like Lane in Jackson or LeMoyne in Memphis. Early on Curtis had decided to go to Tennessee A&I, which seemed to him at the time a great university. In reality, of course, it was a minimal-amenities black state school, badly underfinanced when compared with the great state schools of the North or the white universities of the South, like the state university in Knoxville. But at the time he was quite dazzled by its endless, handsome modern dorms; it had seemed a place for young men and women far richer and vastly more sophisticated than he, a simple country boy just off the farm in Whiteville.

To the Murphys of Whiteville, A&I was expensive: It cost about $1,000 a year, which he realized later was probably more than half of the family's cash receipts for a given year. Buck Murphy had already put aside enough money for four years, wary that if he tried to pay the tuition year by year, the elements might interfere—there might be too much or too little rain and a resulting bad cotton crop, and Curtis would be forced to leave school.

Curtis graduated from Booker T. Washington on a Sunday and entered A&I on the following Monday, in the summer of 1956. He was seventeen at the time. Summer school was Buck's idea. He thought his son might as well go off to school right away and start learning. That way he would be better prepared in the fall, when school started. Curtis had never thought of himself as being poor before he reached Tennessee State. He and his family had lived simply, and they had lived off the land, growing and producing almost all their food, but they had never gone without, and he had always owned a Sunday suit. If anything they had been almost wealthy compared with other black people in the area, particularly those blacks who were sharecroppers. But in Nashville, for the first time he had an awareness of money and the power which came with it. The young people there seemed to be from all over the country, and while many had backgrounds like his, some of them seemed to be rich. They had cars, and often the cars were brand-new. Their parents, as far as he could tell, were doctors and lawyers and undertakers and teachers.

He arrived with his proudest possession, his four new suits. Just as he was graduating from high school, a friend who was already at A&I had told him that he needed four suits in order to be a real college man. Everyone on campus, this young man said, had four suits: a blue serge suit, a gray serge suit, a black serge suit, and a brown serge suit. Curtis Murphy had taken his friend seriously and told this to Buck, and Buck had marched him off to a store in Memphis called Weinberg's, where he had in fact bought four serge suits of different colors, for what was by his family's standards an immense amount of money.

He arrived in Nashville two years after the Court had rendered the *Brown* decision. Yet he was decidedly apolitical, and he had absolutely no knowledge of or interest in civil rights. Someone had told him while he was in high school that engineers made a lot of money, and so when he arrived at A&I and he was asked at a freshman registration what he intended to study, he had answered engineering. The man talking to him asked him what kind of engineering. Curtis Murphy had no earthly idea that there were different kinds of engineering, and he had stood there, completely puzzled. "What kind?" the man had repeated. "Electrical, mechanical, or civil?" Electrical sounded fairly good; a man who could do electrical engineering was probably someone a lot of people were going to need. He had no idea at all what a civil or a mechanical engineer did. So he answered electrical engineering, and for the first two years at A&I, that is what he studied.

Clothes had never been important to him before, but clothes were extremely important at Tennessee State. There were all kinds of different factions from all kinds of different places, and they were all, he decided, trying to say something about themselves with their clothes. There were the Birmingham kids, who wore extra-large shoes and then let the shoes curl up at the toes; the Memphis kids, who bought high-waisted pants and then wore them extra high, as if replicating some zoot suit of an earlier age; and the Eastern kids, who wore conservative clothes—sports jackets instead of suits, preferably blue blazers and gray flannel slacks, with jackets cut narrowly at the shoulder instead of flared, and white shirts with collars buttoned down, which he had never seen before.

From the start he had gotten very good marks. Somewhat to his surprise he was perceived as being gregarious and outgoing and he was elected vice president of the freshman class. Buck had given him little in the way of spending money, so he made extra pocket money by selling his own blood. He got eight dollars a pint. You were supposed to wait six weeks before coming back and donating again, but he would be back in three weeks, and the attendants would tell him that it was too early for him to give again, but then they would take the pint anyway and pay him his eight dollars.

The one thing he did not like about studying electrical engineering was that there was no true resident faculty at the school. Instead the course work was taught by professors who were all local practicing electrical engineers, who came by the school after work. That meant a large number of his classes were at night, when everyone else was having a good time, and that his social life was suffering from his so casually announced career choice. In his junior year he switched his major over to math, as much as anything else to improve his social life.

He was, he later noted, a nice, upwardly mobile black kid operating by all the rules in a pleasantly cushioned, somewhat protected, completely segregated society. He felt little of the direct pain of the segregated world in his daily life. He had a vague sense that blacks would now, in this changed society, be able to do things that they had not been able to do before, including, in his case, to fly jet planes. But he had not thought much about the Supreme Court ruling applying to him. Then he joined the Lawson group.

He had been scared on the day of his first sit-in, not so much of being beaten up, but worried and frightened about how he would behave if the girls sitting in with him were attacked by the rednecks. Would he be able to heed Jim Lawson's clear instructions? He accepted the idea of nonviolence, but it was not who he was. In his heart he was still someone who, when anyone, white or black, lashed out at him, fought back. Curtis Murphy was no sissy, and there was a part of him which regarded Jim's tactics as sissified. He understood the basic philosophy, but at first he accepted it as tactical, nothing more.

But there was one crucial change in him. He had begun to realize that he cared deeply about the issues being raised and that the workshops had touched feelings and an inner rage long suppressed in the deepest part of his heart. It was not that he did not know about the injustice of the world in which he had grown up. It was that the entire experience of growing up in a small West Tennessee town was premised first and foremost on learning to bury those emotions so deep within you that they were completely defused. In rural West Tennessee, like Alabama and Mississippi, even the smallest response to white provocation could cost a black man his life. What Jim Lawson was doing was tapping into these feelings. Murphy's grandfather and father had felt the same way, he was sure, but they had been forced to accept the rigid limitations placed on black existence in a small Southern town.

The more he examined how he felt, the more he discovered examples of his secret rage. One summer when he was about ten years old, he had gone into Whiteville on Saturday with all the other children from the area. Work was over on Saturday at noon and everyone went to town to shop and socialize. It was something that he always looked forward to, the chance to be with other kids his age whom he did not see the rest of the week. They would sit among the feed bags in front of the general store and talk and play games. It was a time of laughter and boasting among the children, but one day there had been a scene which had badly frightened Curtis, the kind of scene they had all been warned about since they were babies.

A black man had come into the store and started talking to the white owner. Suddenly the conversation had started to go badly. There was anger in the white man's voice, which was frightening, and a quality of fear in the black man's voice even more terrifying. The black man began to cower and plead, and as he did, the store owner hit the black man as hard as he could and then he kicked him. The black man had cried out in pain. Then he had run out of the store. To a young black child like Curtis Murphy watching all of this, the image of the black man's fear and cowardice had been particularly upsetting, and he had never forgotten the incident. Even as a boy Curtis knew the things that whites could do to blacks and the things blacks could not do to whites, but he had also been taught that at certain times you had to defend yourself. And this man had not even tried to defend himself: He had run from his white attacker. Later that day he asked his father what had happened. It was a sad case, Buck Murphy had answered; the black man was not only a customer in the store, but he was a sharecropper on the land belonging to the store owner. Therefore he was completely beholden to the white man, and no matter how hard he worked, he was bound to be behind financially. The black man had owed the white man some money, and had failed to pay it.

Curtis Murphy had understood both the rules and the built-in limits of social behavior for a black boy in a white community early on. No matter how proud you were, you learned how to defer on the sidewalks and move aside as white people approached. White people always had the right of way. Blacks had to call all white men, even those younger than them, *sir* or *boss.* In addition, black adults were to be known only by their first names; it was part of a subtle, deliberate ritual of dehumanization; they were always to be treated as children. The young black children of Whiteville also knew, as they grew up, which white people were pleasant and easygoing, and not exploitive of the social order, and which ones were hard and mean and squeezed every ounce of leverage they could from it. These were the ones you had to tiptoe around as carefully as possible, because they were not merely unpleasant, they were dangerous, always looking for trouble. Generally these rules were easy to understand, but occasionally something went wrong—a word would be dropped, a voice would sound demanding instead of supplicating, and a local code would therefore be violated.

That had happened to Curtis Murphy when he was fourteen. He had gone to Curry Cooper's grocery store, about six blocks from the black school he attended, after school one day. It was a place where his parents always did their business, and he had liked the store, and he thought of Curry Cooper and Buck Murphy, as being if not friends, men who respected each other, and gave each other the proper mutual deference within the complicated social dynamics of the town. On this particular day the woman behind the counter had asked Curtis what he wanted. He said he wanted to buy some candy, and he pointed at the glass display case near the cash register where the candy was kept, indicating the kind he wanted. "What kind," the woman had asked, "this kind here?"

"Yes," Curtis Murphy had answered.

Just then he felt a powerful hand grabbing his shoulder and shaking him, and heard Curry Cooper's voice saying, "What did you say, boy?"

"I said yes," Curtis Murphy repeated. He had by mistake failed a deference test; his answer should have been, "Yes, ma'am."

"Boy, if you ever say yes to my wife again, I'm going to be forced to slap you."

Curtis Murphy pointed at an old barrel near the front of the store which contained ax handles, and he had said, angry now, "If you slap me I'm going to break every one of those ax handles over your head." Just then an old black man named Gee Price saw what was happening and told him, "Son, be quiet."

Before Curtis Murphy left the store he had told Curry Cooper, "I'm going to tell my father and we'll be back." That night he went home and told his parents what had happened. He was scared, aware that he not only had gotten himself in trouble but that he had in some way jeopardized his father's relationship with Curry Cooper, ended their friendship, such as it was, and started a dangerous chain of events which might in a way he did not entirely understand put his father on a collision course with an important white man. When he told his parents what had happened, they reacted in different ways. His father was hesitant, uneasy about the confrontation which might lie ahead. His mother, by contrast, was furious over what had happened. His parents fought seriously over this for several days, and finally Duggar said that if he did not go to the store, then she would go. That scared Buck; she was far more hot tempered than he.

So several days after the incident, Buck Murphy had taken his son in hand and gone to Curry Cooper's store. It was obvious, in retrospect, Curtis decided, that he had thought this out very carefully, and knew exactly what he was going to do and say. He walked into the store and told Curry Cooper that he wanted to talk to him. They nodded to each other and walked to the back of the store, so that others would not eavesdrop on their conversation and thus make an explosive situation even more dangerous. Buck Murphy began by saying that he and his wife had always raised their son to be polite and never to be rude. Then he asked if Cooper had in fact grabbed his son by the shoulder and shaken him. The owner answered that he had. "Look at him," Buck Murphy had said. "It's not possible for that boy to be this black and for you to be his father. So you don't touch him again. If he does anything wrong, you come to me and I'll discipline him. I promise you that."

It took some fifteen years and his own entrance into adulthood before Curtis Murphy realized how strong, and subtle and shrewd his father had been at that moment. He had confronted a white man who had acted improperly toward his son, and yet he had done it within the acceptable limits of the local culture. He had let Curry Cooper know that Cooper had misbehaved and overstepped the accepted boundaries of the community; most important, he had defused the situation without pushing Cooper too far. Later as he came to understand his father's life, and the limits imposed on both his freedom of speech and freedom of anger by the social contract around him, Curtis Murphy thought his father had handled the situation brilliantly. It was his father's way of letting Curry Cooper apologize without ever having to apologize. Buck Murphy continued to shop in Cooper's store, though it was almost seven years before Curtis Murphy returned to buy anything there.

So as he had joined up with the other sit-in students, he was acting on something deep inside himself, on his own inner truth. He knew his father would not permit him to risk so much, and he knew that he was secretly crossing a generational line. During the first three sit-ins he thought he was one of the lucky ones. No one had ever hit him or punched him or put out a cigarette on the back of his head. He had worried constantly if he could be true to his pledge of nonviolence. His closest call came when a group of white punks started beating C. T. Vivian, who was one of the ministers working with them. They had been sitting in and C.T. had been leading them in prayer when a white youth had rushed over toward Vivian and hit him as hard as he could on the chin. C.T. had gone down momentarily and then gotten back up, and the young white boy, rage etched all over his face, had struck again. Curtis, his own anger now plainly showing on his face, had moved to help out. It was one thing to strike a black student, another thing to strike a minister, a man of God. But Vivian had caught the look on Curtis's face, and he had seen Curtis's hands come up to a boxer's position, and C.T. had said quickly and with surprising force, an order, not a request, "Put your hands in your pockets!" Curtis Murphy had listened to him and put his hands in his pockets, but it had been a close call.

There were times when Curtis Murphy's confidence swung back and forth during that winter, times when he was sure the students' goal was doable. There was a strength and a solidarity among them. They would not be turned around. But there were other times when he felt very much alone. Once, at the height of the crisis, he had gone to a basketball game, and at halftime the school's president, Dr. Walter Davis, had gotten up and made a speech in which he had referred to the sit-ins without ever mentioning them. "Beware of those who would take you down the primrose path when you have so much still ahead of you," the president had said. "Beware of those who want you to do their political work for them. Remember, you're here not for politics, but to study." A friend of Curtis Murphy's, who was sitting next to him, said, "He's talking about *you,* Curtis." And he was, there was no doubt of it, and Curtis Murphy felt wounded, because he had thought of Dr. Davis as a warm, friendly figure who reminded him of his own grandfather.

For a time he felt angry that Dr. Davis had done this, and then years later he realized how shrewd Dr. Davis had been. Of all the black educators in Nashville, he was the most vulnerable, the one man who was directly under the thumb of the state's white authorities; more, the new governor, for whom he effectively worked, Buford Ellington, was not just a rhetorical segregationist, but a man closely allied with the *Banner.* Dr. Davis's speech at the basketball game, Curtis came to understand later, had been his way of acting without acting, of giving the governor what he wanted without betraying his own people. Curtis had waited nervously to be called in to Dr. Davis's office and to be chastised for his leadership, or to be warned that he was missing too many classes. That would have been the easy move, he thought, threatening a good student whose grades were beginning to plummet with expulsion. Years later he realized that Dr. Davis had done so subtle a job of protecting him that he had never even known it was happening.

17

WHAT NO ONE HAD UNDERSTOOD AT FIRST, BUT WAS BECOMING increasingly clear, was that during the sit-ins, a generational fault line was being crossed. The children had quietly and resolutely moved ahead of their parents. Early on in their meetings, even before the first sit-in, there had been a suggestion on the part of some of the more conservative students that no one who did not have a parental release be allowed to sit in. Others, led by Diane Nash, had quickly rejected it. First off, few of their parents would give that permission. But second, she had argued, why go to their parents for permission to do something which they all agreed ought to be done, and which their parents had failed to do? If their parents had failed to do it themselves, then surely they would not let their children go where they had feared to go. Her logic had been devastating, and since most of them knew that the less they told their parents the better, they had agreed to go ahead on their own.

That meant that when they challenged the laws, they were carrying a dual burden—of violating the laws of the city of Nashville, and violating various agreements they had made with their parents as well. All of them in different ways were at some kind of tension point with their parents over their participation. All too typically, Bernard Lafayette had been stunned to get a letter from his mother saying how upset she was with him, that she had not been able to sleep at night because of what he was doing. "What are you fighting for?" she had written. Then she told him he was doing the wrong thing, and that white people would surely help him out someday and he should not fight them. "Remember, God will straighten out everything if you just get in line. You don't have to eat with the white people. You've lived all these years just praying, trusting God. You're not learning your lesson in school. God is nobody to play with. You are just making a disturbance." When he had gotten the letter, he had been saddened and had turned to his friend John Lewis, and pointed out that she was so upset, she had not even given him any affectionate words at the end of the letter. "She just doesn't understand," he told Lewis.

Lafayette decided he would keep going, but that he would simply tell his parents less of what was happening. He was hardly alone. The one other thing which Curtis Murphy had truly feared when he had decided to become one of the leaders was telling his father what he was doing. So at first he told him nothing. By the time the sit-ins had started, his younger sister, Lacie, was a freshman at A&I. He had warned her not to tell anyone back home what he was doing, and for a time she had kept her silence, but then, after the first major confrontation, it had been too much and she had passed on just enough information to alarm them.

The next day Buck Murphy had arrived in Nashville, driven by one of Curtis's cousins because he did not own a car. Buck was obviously frightened by what was happening, but he worked hard to remain calm and not to lose his temper. Interestingly, he was frightened only for his son, not for himself and his wife, as some of the parents were, fearing that the white power structure would lash out, as it often had in the past in the South, at the families of the dissidents, striking at their parents in the small towns where they were so vulnerable. To Buck, the whole idea seemed hopelessly idealistic. "You're crazy," he said; "you've got to stop this. They're never going to let you do these things. I know white people and they won't let you do this. They'll kill you first."

It was the first serious disagreement they had ever had, Curtis thought. The son who had always been obedient was now venturing into the unknown without the approval of a beloved, idolized parent. There was no way that Buck would understand or like what he was doing, Curtis thought. But Buck listened carefully to everything his son said about why he was doing it. "I don't like it," Buck kept repeating when Curtis was finished; "it won't work. You're going to get killed, or at the least thrown out of school." Curtis Murphy knew that Buck wanted a promise right then and there to drop out, so he played his cards carefully. He could not drop out now, he said, because he was a leader, and he had brought others in. He was sure that Buck would understand that a man could not take a position of leadership and then back off. "How much longer are you going to do it?" Buck Murphy asked. Curtis had lied and said he was going to do it only a few more times. Buck, unconvinced by all that he had heard, neither agreed to let him continue, nor did he order him to stop. "It's all crazy," he repeated. Then he shook his head and drove back to Whiteville with his cousin. I've bought a little more time, Curtis thought.

Before they had been arrested on Big Saturday, the students had already decided that they would stay in jail and not come out. That was the true Gandhian way—force not only your adversary but the good citizens of the ruling class to see the price of their oppression. But for Curtis it was an idea which had become less attractive with each day in jail, in part because jail was very unpleasant, and in part because he was sure that Buck was going to find out and he was going to be angry. Curtis's job in jail was to clean out the drainage in the cells, a less than pleasant task, and he was working on it for the second day in a row when he happened to look out the window. There he saw a black man, clearly a country man, wearing his best clothes and ill at ease in the city, walking stiffly toward the courthouse. The man was some distance away but he looked familiar, and as he neared the building it was obvious that he was Buck Murphy. It was a sight which both pleased and scared Curtis, for he was glad to see his father, but he was also far more afraid of dealing with Buck Murphy than he was with the Nashville police. Buck was allowed to meet with his son, and told him it was time to leave, that he had already paid his fine. Curtis argued that he could not leave, that they had made a pact with each other to stay inside, but Buck was insistent—the only way the white officials had been willing to let him talk with his son was if he paid the fine and so he had paid it. That presented Curtis with a moral dilemma, but just then Avon Williams, one of the lawyers for the students, had shown up and said he had posted an appeal bond and they were all free.

Buck was different when they spoke this time, Curtis thought. He was angry at him for having lied—for there was no doubt that Curtis had not told the truth the last time they had talked. But it was also true that in some way he had not only come to understand what his son was doing but to take some pride in it. It was not something that he particularly wanted Curtis to do, and he was scared that Curtis was not going to finish college, but he was, in some way, the son realized, signaling to him that Curtis now had his sanction. "Now, you worry about yourself, boy," Buck had said. "You don't worry about us back in Whiteville. I'll take care of us. No one's going to do anything to hurt us, you can be sure of that." So Buck was at least partially aboard for the first time.

Everyone in Whiteville, it seemed, knew what Curtis had done; the story was big news there. A few days after Curtis's arrest, Buck was walking down a street in Whiteville when a white man he knew yelled over at him, "How's that jailbird son of yours doing?"

"He's doing just fine," Buck had answered.

"Where is he?" the man said, mocking him. "Is he still in the Nashville jail?"

"Wherever he is, I am too," Buck Murphy had answered, and when Curtis heard that story a few days later, he knew that whatever else happened during the sit-ins, he might never again feel so close to his father.

A few days after that, freed from jail, Curtis had returned to Whiteville to see his family, to let them know that he was all right and that he had not changed. His father, clearly very proud of him, had taken him downtown and they had gone into Curry Cooper's store, the first time that Curtis Murphy had been in there since the incident over the candy years ago. Curry Cooper had come over to him and had said, "I don't know what it is you're trying to do up there, but whatever it is, I wish you luck." Curtis Murphy had been moved by that, as had his parents, and he had felt in that moment their admiration and their pride in him.

18

THE GENERATIONAL TENSIONS THAT CURTIS MURPHY WAS DEALING with were not very different in Gloria Johnson's home. On Big Saturday, all the protesters had agreed not to make bail, but Gloria Johnson had been an exception. Her mother did not know she was part of the sit-in movement, and Gloria wanted to keep it that way. She was afraid that if she stayed in jail, there was a great chance that somehow or other her mother would find out, and so after talking about her problem with Rodney Powell, she had asked for and received dispensation to make bail and get back to her studies as soon as possible and to be near the dorm phone in case her mother called.

One of the reasons Gloria Johnson was so nervous was that Elizabeth Johnson's health was failing. She was suffering from congestive heart failure and had had to go into the hospital repeatedly in that period. Gloria was scared that if her mother found out that her daughter was putting her academic career, and indeed her life, at risk, she might die of heart failure.

For her mother was almost pathological in her hatred of Southern racism, and had almost come unraveled when Gloria had announced her intention of going to Meharry. The only serious dispute mother and daughter had ever had was when Gloria, having finished Mount Holyoke with so many other opportunities open to her, had told her mother that she was planning to go to medical school in Nashville. Elizabeth Johnson had simply exploded. *No!* she had shouted. *No! You don't know those people! I do! I know what they do down there— they lynch people. You're the last person in the world who should go down there because you don't know how to keep your mouth shut! They'll kill you! You think you can argue with those people and talk sense to them and make them understand what you believe, but you don't know anything about them! I know you—you'll be up on your soapbox! You'll be killed!*

Gloria Johnson had never seen her mother, a person of singular force and determination and strength, so angry. The vehemence of her response was amazing. The very idea of her daughter's going to medical school in the South seemed to rip aside scar tissue and reveal all the old wounds and memories which remained there from growing up in the South under the heel of white racism earlier in the century. When, that first fall, Gloria had left for medical school in Nashville, she had been stunned by the sadness in her mother's face; what should have been a happy occasion clearly had a major shadow over it.

That meant as she continued the sit-ins she also had to work hard to keep the news from her mother. Gloria Johnson was intrigued by the irony in this: She was sure that she was carrying out the teachings of their home, and doing what her mother would have done had their positions been reversed. But she was also aware of the gap—indeed the chasm in generations—both in her own family and those of her friends who were part of the sit-ins, and that almost all of them were in the same position, part heroic, part traitorous. They were being true to the way they had been raised only by disobeying strict family orders and continuing their role in the demonstrations. In that sense, for her, and for many of the others, it was the hardest thing she had ever done.

Her mother had always been her hero and she did not lightly keep any secret from her. Elizabeth Hendren had come to Boston from Virginia as a young girl filled with the belief that there was a better life in the North, far from the pervasive and crippling racism of the South. She had married when she was still young to Walter William Johnson, an ambitious black man, who seemed able to handle two and sometimes three jobs in order to support his young family. But then when their four children were still very young, he had died in a tragic auto accident; that had left Elizabeth Johnson not only virtually alone in a strange city but pregnant with their fifth child. Others might have been overwhelmed by such a harsh fate and turned inside themselves or at least have returned to their families, but Elizabeth Johnson was determined that she would not return to the South, and that she would raise her children to have a better life than she had ever had and to enjoy the freedoms of the North. She would work as a domestic, so that they would all one day go to college. The great lesson of her life to her children, Gloria Johnson later decided, was her absolute fearlessness in the face of constant adversity.

Somehow she had managed to become one of the early welfare recipients in that era, which was extremely difficult because, her daughter found out years later, not only was welfare relatively new back in the thirties, but only about 3 percent of welfare recipients at the time were black. She not only managed to receive welfare when it was still in its embryonic form, but Mrs. Johnson managed to talk the social worker she dealt with into paying no attention at all to what she considered some of the arbitrary and petty rules which governed it. She was not shy about being in the right if the government was in the wrong. Welfare recipients were not supposed to have any luxuries. Among the forbidden luxuries was a refrigerator. Why, that was absolutely ridiculous, Mrs. Johnson said. She needed a refrigerator, for she was buying food for six people and she needed to buy in quantity, and there were leftovers constantly which could be used for subsequent meals. All right, said the social worker, you can have a refrigerator; just don't talk too much about it.

The rules also forbade welfare recipients from having a telephone, and Mrs. Johnson thought that equally absurd. Here she was, she said, a single parent with five young children. She could not be home every moment. If one of the children got sick and there was a crisis, there would be a pressing need for a phone. As far as she was concerned, it was a potential instrument of emergency, not a luxury. The social worker quickly agreed. Irons and ironing boards were luxuries, according to welfare rules. But how, asked Mrs. Johnson, could she send her children off to school in clean and well-ironed clothes—clothes, she noted, which she made herself—rather than wrinkled ones without an iron? Then there was the matter of a radio. Mrs. Johnson, you're simply not supposed to have a radio, the social worker argued. "But my children need to be educated, they need to know what's going on in the world, and they need some entertainment too; they need to listen to the good things that are on the radio." And so the social worker approved the radio as well.

She was like that in all ways, fierce, courageous, and protective. She was a brilliant shopper who managed to work out her own deals with store owners—she bought the furniture for their home on time, setting the schedule herself, of course, a dollar each week, faithfully paid. She managed to get her children into the best local public schools, and she closely monitored their progress. In time, she had helped guide Gloria, the third of her children and academically the most gifted, to the famed Girls' Latin, one of America's famed elite public schools. It was at Girls' Latin that Gloria had been politicized for the first time and quickly paid the consequences for her politicization. In her senior year she was near the very top of her class, and there was some talk that she might even be first. Certainly she was a lock for the school honor society, which each year took the top 10 percent of the students. But in her last two years in school her own growing political alienation had begun to surface. Oddly enough, it did not begin over the issue of race, fertile though that might have been as a breeding ground for alienation. This, after all, was the fifties, and black issues had not yet emerged at the top of society's agenda.

Instead it was over the issue of the Holocaust and the murder of some six million Jews by the Nazis. To Gloria Johnson, many of whose childhood friends were Jewish, that seemed like the most dangerous possible expression of nationalism, and it made her extremely conscious of any abuse of it. She was already beginning to pull back from organized religion, questioning the existence of God, and now the more she studied this issue, the more wary she became of nationalism. To her the Pledge of Allegiance seemed like an American version of extreme nationalism, and in her junior year she stopped reciting it and standing when it was recited, and she stopped saluting the flag as well. Years later she looked on this as a manifestation of the most normal kind of early social rebellion on the part of a bright, curious child, but at the time it threatened to end her college career before it even began.

During her junior year she had sat in the back row, so when she did not stand for the pledge, no one had noticed. But in her senior year, she was seated in the front row, and when she refused to stand up and salute the flag, the teacher immediately noticed. In addition the school prayer had been replaced with a religious song which was sung each morning, a song which seemed to her perilously close to being a musical prayer. Believing that prayer was private, she had refused to sing. She had refused, she later explained to school authorities, because she had begun to doubt the existence of God. Later, when she was grown up, she was sure that what she had seized on was a proxy issue, and that in truth it was the first surfacing of a deeper, racial alienation on the part of a young black child who was at once increasingly successful in the white world, but also aware of how difficult life was for most blacks in the South, and in the North.

Suddenly Girls' Latin had a crisis. Gloria Johnson, star academic senior, popular and highly respected among her peers, was sent by her homeroom teacher to the guidance counselor, an old-fashioned woman who did not see Gloria's behavior as an early demonstration of individualism by a bright, interesting child. Rather the counselor saw it as a frontal challenge by someone unwilling to play by the rules in an age and in an environment where everyone always played by the rules, particularly the poor and the vulnerable, and where, of course, school authorities held all the power. The guidance counselor immediately took her to the principal, very much a traditionalist himself.

He was obviously outraged: A poor black child to whom so much was being given in this elite school was refusing to be a good American. That was unacceptable. He suspended her for a day and told her to come back to school with her mother. In addition, he warned her of the severe consequences of what she was doing. He would be forced, he said, to write all the colleges to which she applied and where she was hoping to win a scholarship and tell them that she was a nonconformist, taking back what the school had said about her earlier in its recommendations. At the very least she would be likely to lose her scholarships.

She went and spoke to her mother, who even as Gloria was becoming less and less religious was herself becoming more and more so, having left the Baptist church and become a Jehovah's Witness because she did not think the Baptist services sufficiently impassioned. To Elizabeth Johnson, this was a terrible crisis. Her child was on the verge of nothing less than entering the world of her dreams, and now all of their mutual sacrifice was being placed at risk. When mother and daughter spoke it was the most somber of talks. "How seriously do you feel about this?" Mrs. Johnson asked Gloria. "Very seriously," Gloria answered. "I couldn't believe in it more." To Elizabeth Johnson the basic law of life was that all actions had consequences, and the consequences for blacks were often far more severe than for whites, and it was important for a young person to understand this. "Are you prepared to give up college for a couple of years in order to earn the money to go to college in case you don't get a scholarship?" she asked. Yes, said her daughter, she had thought it through, and she knew this was part of the price. "All right," said her mother, "I'll back you up."

Gloria Johnson came to believe that what happened next was her mother's finest hour. Off they went to school, this small black lady who had come to this city virtually as an orphan when she was no more than a child, who had worked hard all her life as nothing grander than a domestic, who had no education and no title, and who received welfare checks and worked at cleaning other people's houses. For years almost all of her energy had been focused on her children's education. Now she was taking with her the most talented student of the five, one whose otherwise exceptional educational opportunities were suddenly in jeopardy, and they were going to meet with a white man who seemed to hold her child's future in his hand. He must in some ways have seemed all-powerful to her. But he was also doing something she thought was wrong, and if her daughter had crossed a line at school, then he had unknowingly crossed a line with Elizabeth Johnson.

It was clear to Gloria years later what the principal of Girls' Latin must have expected, having checked his own records: a scared black woman who was on welfare, and who therefore was dependent and malleable. She would surely understand his power and his mandate that the dependent had fewer rights than the independent; she would help bend this child to his will.

The meeting did not go as he planned. He barely had a chance to speak. From the start, to his surprise, she took over the meeting. She never raised her voice. She told the principal that this meeting would not last very long, at most half an hour. There were a few things that the school had to consider before it pursued the course it was now threatening her child with, she said. "First off, there is a law that says you don't have to salute the flag," she reminded him, "and I don't think you want to punish this child for obeying the law." Second, she asked, since when did the state of Massachusetts force people to pray? "It was always my understanding that this state was founded on the idea of freedom of worship, and the freedom as well not to worship." Then she asked what kind of school he was running, which promoted serious intellectual development among bright, talented young people, and yet the first time a girl showed her intellectual independence, the school tried to punish her? "That is ridiculous for an educator," she said, "and if it becomes known outside this school it will embarrass you greatly, and you know it. If you persist in this course, the consequences will be severe, not just for my child, but for you as well."

Then, she said, there was the final and most important threat he had made that she wanted to deal with: his warning that if Gloria did not change and accommodate, the school would write an additional letter to the colleges that could cost Gloria her scholarships. "You should think a long time about doing that. You have written to these schools saying how well you know her and how well she has done, and of course, she has the grades to prove it, and now at the last minute you want to write again and say you did not really know her that well after six years, and she does not deserve a scholarship after all. If you do that, they will never believe another recommendation from you again. Believe me. They will never take you seriously again." With that the meeting was effectively over. The principal had barely spoken. There was no more talk of withdrawing her recommendations.

He struck back in one other way, however. At the assembly late in the year when they named the nine girls who had been chosen for the honor society, he made sure that Gloria Johnson was not one of them. When a member of the school's administration read out the names of the girls selected, and Gloria's name was not mentioned, there was an audible gasp from some of her classmates. They knew that a girl who might well have been first in her class had been denied a rightful place in the honor society. Gloria was in tears, some classmates were in tears, and some of her teachers were in tears.

When Gloria got home that night she unburdened herself to her mother. Mrs. Johnson took the news calmly. "Let's go for a walk," she said. "We may not have a lot of time left together," her mother had said at the start of the walk, a reference to her heart condition, which appeared to be worsening, "so I want you to remember something that is very important. Remember, Gloria, whatever you do in life, you must not do for the glory of man, for men and women, mere mortals, are fickle. Getting in the honor society is not that important. How well you have done in school is important and I am proud of you for that. All your friends are proud of you. But the things you do in life, you must do for the glory of God, because they are the right things to do. But never for the glory of man as this society offers that kind of glory."

That was the lesson she had learned from her mother when she was young, that you had a right to stand up for the things you believed in, for the things promised by God, even if doing so put at risk an easier and more pleasant path offered by man. That was what she was doing in the sit-ins, standing up for rights which God had promised. Gloria Johnson was intrigued by the irony in her familial dilemma as she made bail that Saturday. She dared not tell Mrs. Johnson what she was doing, for fear of triggering a heart attack. She had to continue to go along with the charade which she herself had created, that she was a good girl who was not going to get into trouble in the South and who was, as she always had in the past, going to concentrate solely on getting good grades. But she was going to continue to sit in and the reason she was going to was that she was her mother's daughter.

19

CURTIS MURPHY BECAME ONE OF THE FIRST TO SENSE THAT THE momentum was changing and swinging to the side of the students. The mass arrests on Big Saturday had not damaged their cause, as the white city leaders had hoped; they had instead helped strengthen that cause. That was more obvious at A&I than anywhere else. If at first it had been very hard for him to turn out troops, then things had dramatically changed after Big Saturday. Suddenly there was a new dynamic: The more that they sat in and were arrested, the more publicity they got—with stories in the *Tennessean* and film clips on the local television stations—the more it became not only the right thing to do, but the popular thing to do. It was as if the city officials of Nashville were determined to do their publicity for them, and the Nashville cops had become their recruiting agents. Suddenly Curtis Murphy found, much to his amazement, that he was becoming a hero on campus, bigger even then the school's football and basketball stars. When he returned to campus after being let out of jail, other students, many of whom he had never spoken to before, came running up to him, wanting to know when the next meeting was going to be held and whether they could join in. He could look around the dining room and see other students pointing him out and talking about him, hearing them say, "That's Curtis Murphy, the sit-in leader; you know, the guy who went to jail." There were girls too who came by his dorm leaving their phone numbers and earrings and even articles of clothing for him. There was a call from students at the University of Wisconsin who wanted to be involved and who wanted a speaker to come to the Madison campus and tell them what was happening. Curtis was sent there, and he was lionized by the Wisconsin students, a greater hero there than he had been at home.

20

KELLY MILLER SMITH WAS WORKING CAREFULLY IN THE BACKGROUND to keep the black community united even as the students pushed ahead on the sit-ins. He was working on two fronts, first to calm the fears among some of the older and more conservative members of his congregation at the First Baptist Church, people worried that the sit-ins were going to put the church itself and the black community in general at risk. He knew the unspoken coda, that the protesters were *young* (and therefore not to be trusted), that they were not local residents, that they would come down here, challenge the laws, and then, when things got ugly, when the whites started to crack down, they would be gone, off to their next lark. Kelly Miller Smith had deflected this natural wariness of an older, more wearied generation with great skill; he had brought the young people into his church, had introduced them to his congregation, and he had lavishly praised what they were doing, outlining the terrible risks they were taking each time they set forth. And he had shrewdly chosen to refer to them not as the students. The *children,* he called them again and again, reminding the congregation that they were very young to be taking such chances, and suggesting as well that they were not alien blacks plunked down carelessly in this place, but the children of ordinary black people just like themselves, and could easily be the children of the congregation. They were the ones taking all the risks, he said, and they were doing it for all the people of Nashville, all the people of the South. Gradually the grumbling died down. The local white officialdom helped greatly. The more it lashed out at the students, the more arrests there were, the more united the community became. By Big Saturday, Smith later said, he had never seen the black community so united.

The second area where he was using all his skills was to make sure that the black economic boycott of the downtown shopping area grew tighter and tighter. No one was exactly sure of the origins of the boycott; some believed it began with a handful of middle-aged black women who had long resented their treatment by the stores, and had moved immediately to back up the sit-ins with a boycott. Later it became part of local legend that four women from Smith's church had been playing bridge, had discussed what the young people were doing, and had decided to make ten calls each that first day, asking their friends not to shop downtown, and asking each friend in addition to make ten more calls. There were others who knew Kelly Miller Smith and knew how committed he was to this cause who thought he himself might have made the first phone call suggesting the boycott to some of the ladies.

Whatever its origin, the boycott had quickly turned into a major success. At black churches, the ministers would get up and ask members of their congregations to stand if they had refused to shop in the downtown area. More often than not the entire congregation would stand up. By the beginning of March the boycott was believed to be around 98 percent effective, a serious dent in the commercial district's profitability. That had always been a critical part of Jim Lawson's game plan, to prove to the white community that the price of segregation was not merely moral, that blacks in postwar America had an expanded economic power which they had never flexed before, and that discrimination of the kind being practiced in the city could cut two ways.

Vivian Henderson, a distinguished economist at Fisk who had studied black purchasing power in Nashville, believed that in the month of March the downtown stores lost something like $250,000, a huge sum for businesses whose profit margins were normally slim. Their overall purchasing power in the city, he estimated, was a staggering $50 million a year. Henderson believed that blacks represented 30 percent of the customers in the downtown area and that black sales represented at least 17 percent of the overall total sales in the area, and quite possibly more. In some stores the black customers comprised as much as 40 percent of the customers. The boycott was a confirmation that the protest now represented the entire community. As the pressure of the boycott continued, a number of downtown merchants had called

Kelly Miller Smith, asking in effect for a separate peace, and wanting to expedite negotiations. The more of these calls he received, the surer he became that time was now on their side. He was aware of the grief the demonstrations were causing the mayor, and aware that the mayor in his heart probably wanted to do the right thing. The question then was for him to do it.

21

THAT THE YOUNG PEOPLE WERE GAINING MOMENTUM, AND THAT THE hard-line counterattack on them on Big Saturday, driven in no small part by pressure from Jimmy Stahlman, had completely failed, and that they were, if anything, stronger than ever with even greater community support was not being reflected in the pages of Stahlman's *Nashville Banner.* Stahlman's editors, responding to his direct orders, still minimized all reporting on the events of the sit-ins, most particularly anything which might reflect on the growing momentum of the movement and its increasingly widespread support in the community. The *Banner* effectively censored all news of the growing economic power of the blacks, and the devastating effect the boycott was having on the merchants. Jimmy Stahlman was simply not going to run news like that in his newspaper. As far as he was concerned, his purpose was not so much to inform as it was to work for his own cause, which was the cause of the South.

That the *Banner* was doing this did not surprise Robert Churchwell, the man who under normal circumstances might have had the assignment of covering the sit-ins, simply because he had the largest number of contacts in the black community. He was the paper's one black reporter, albeit a ghettoized reporter. Jimmy Stahlman liked to boast that he had been a pioneer in hiring a black reporter on his paper, that he had done it when no one thought he would. Churchwell, the man upon whom this singular distinction had been bestowed, a gentle, thoughtful man, was not so sure that it was so wondrous an honor, and in those days he was absolutely appalled by the way the paper he worked for was treating the community of which he was a part. Years later he would talk about how hard and lonely those years had been, being the one black reporter on what he and

many of his friends thought was a racist paper, and when he talked to
a reporter who was writing about his travail, Churchwell said at the
end of the interview, "Whatever else, don't forget the pain." The pain
was of being a half citizen, a man who was never really accepted, and
who worked in the same city room with, but was somehow always
apart from, his colleagues. And who, when he went out into the black
community, was on occasion snubbed by some blacks for being an
Uncle Tom working for a racist paper.

When the sit-ins began Robert Churchwell had an ominous sense
that a terrible collision was about to take place between his paper and
the truth as it existed in black Nashville, and that things had been
building toward this collision for years. He could feel the growing tension in the city room as the *Banner* pulled away from covering one of
the biggest local stories in years. The paper was largely ignoring the
news of the sit-ins, yet railing away at the students on its editorial
page. Though Churchwell went to all of the mass meetings being held
at the First Baptist Church and in some Zen way it could be said that
he covered them, he never actually reported on what was said. From
the start he had had a sense of the true power of the Movement
because in his own heart he knew how passionately he supported
what the students were doing. As he felt himself engaged in their
cause, so, he was sure, did thousands of other blacks. But no one at
the *Banner* was interested in his perceptions. Sadly, he thought his editors believed that if they failed to report about events which they did
not like, then these events in some miraculous way would not have
happened.

There was nothing Churchwell could do, no one he could talk to.
He could not go to editors and suggest stories about the changing
mood in the black community and the growing support for the young
people. Instead, in the way the *Banner* always worked, his editors
were supposed to come to him and tell him what they wanted covered
and how he should write it. It would have been inconceivable for him
to go to Jimmy Stahlman or one of his deputies and try and explain
the mockery the paper was making of itself in the black community.

Not that Robert Churchwell talked intimately to Jimmy Stahlman
in any event. Seemingly they spoke to each other every day; indeed
there was a ritual to their meetings, or more precisely, their nonmeet-
ings. Churchwell was seated at the very back of the *Banner* city room,

and Jimmy Stahlman would enter the room from the rear, moving quickly, his pace, Churchwell sensed, picking up as he neared Churchwell's seat, and then came the words, "Hello, Robert," addressed to his back; Churchwell then returned the greeting— "Good morning, Mister Stahlman"—addressed always to Stahlman's back as the publisher virtually flew by. Those morning encounters, such as they were, seemed to define his status, and he wondered almost every day whether the pain and isolation were worth the job. And then he would be reminded of his obligations and responsibilities—for he and his wife, a schoolteacher, had five children. He was also aware of the lack of alternative jobs open to him. White-collar work for a black man in Nashville, no matter how painful its nature, was extremely rare.

Ironically, it was the *Banner*'s executives who had come to him and asked him to take the job. Their circulation had been down in the early fifties, nearly nonexistent in the black community, and that did not necessarily help with some advertisers, who were increasingly eager for black customers as long as they could be quietly eager about it. The paper did not capitalize the word *Negro*, which was considered a deliberate slight within the black community, and indeed, the word *nigger* often slipped into the paper. In time the *Banner*'s executives had decided that its lack of a black readership was something of a weakness and they had gone to two local black leaders to see what could be done. The two men were Coyness Ennix, a black lawyer who was to become an influential local politician, and L. J. Gunn, who was something of an activist in the black community. The decision had been made to try and hire a black reporter. Coyness Ennix had listened and had said he knew a young man just out of Fisk named Robert Churchwell who wanted to be a writer.

This young man had seemed just the right type. He was from a small town in Middle Tennessee, had served in World War II with the 375th Engineers, had graduated from Fisk with the help of the G.I. Bill, and he had literary aspirations. He had tried for a time to run his own newspaper but that had failed, and he had written for a local black paper called *The Nashville Commentator*. Robert Churchwell liked to think of himself as a writer, and it was his secret ambition not to be a newspaperman but a novelist. When Ennix and Gunn had summoned him and explained what they wanted, Robert Churchwell had immediately rejected the idea. "Hell, no, I'm not working for the damn *Banner,*" he said. To him the *Banner* was an openly racist paper, enthusiastically supporting men like Bilbo and Rankin and Eastland, the virulent Mississippi demagogues. But they had been insistent, and Ennix had said that Churchwell would be like Jackie Robinson. He would be the first. He would open the doors for others. In time Churchwell's resolve had weakened, in no small part because he had no other job, and because he was about to get married. He had been hired in 1950 for $35 a week. Charlie Moss, the executive editor, who seemed to be a pleasant and decent man, apologized because they did not have a desk for him—a lack of space, he said.

So Robert Churchwell became a reporter. At first he worked out of his home and paid for all his own telephone calls and his own taxis, since he did not yet own a car and he needed to get around to different churches. He did not own a typewriter and he did not know how to type, but a friend loaned him one, and he would write his stories in longhand, printing in block letters, and first his sister and then his wife-to-be, Mary, typed his stories for him. Later he learned to type using, like most journalists, the hunt-and-peck method. Eventually he was given a desk in the newsroom. His marching orders were clear: He was to give the *Banner* a pleasant, albeit innocuous presence in the black community, covering social events, Masonic Lodge meetings, church suppers, and award nights at Fisk and Tennessee A&I. He was aware of the limits placed on him, but the job was also a fascinating window through which he could watch the black community function. He felt a gradual acceptance of himself on the part of the black political leadership—as if they too knew the limits placed on him, because they knew the limits placed on all blacks in those days.

From the beginning, a few *Banner* reporters had gone out of their way to be nice to Robert Churchwell. A man named Dick Battle, who covered city hall, had come into Charlie Moss's office on the day that Churchwell was hired and had offered him his hand and his friendship and remained a friend for the next thirty years, defying local tradition. Others, like Jess Safley, the farm editor, and Eddie Jones, the local columnist, had also gone out of their way to be friendly. But, as far as he was concerned, the *Banner* city room remained a place filled with land mines. A few reporters clearly took the *Banner*'s editorial policy more to heart than others, and their dislike of Churchwell seemed almost palpable.

Once he had been given a desk he had integrated the water fountain and the men's room. Yet he never felt a part of the paper. He understood early on that part of the joy of newspapering, why so many bright people did such odd work for so little money, was the collegial aspect of it. These were men playing like boys; they laughed easily together, and they would go out for lunch and for dinner together, as if they were part of some informal but special club. But he was never a part of the club. There were no easy, collegial lunches and no one ever suggested testing the white-only rules at the nearby restaurants where the reporters went each day for lunch. Nor were he and his wife invited to the annual Christmas party, something that bothered him and, in time, other *Banner* reporters.

Perhaps even worse was trying to understand what each of these men thought about race; what, in the end, was in their hearts. Early on, in the first year that he worked inside the office, Les Hart, the political writer, had gone over to the wire ticker and had ripped off some AP copy about the Emmett Till case in Tallahatchie County, Mississippi, where two white men had murdered a young black boy from Chicago. The news had seemed to enrage Hart, and he had gone into a diatribe about mean goddamn racists who would do something like that, and Churchwell had thought to himself, Well, maybe that's one more person who'll be okay, another man who may offer his friendship. But only a few weeks later Hart was writing a story about a black man in Memphis being appointed to a state board. The name of the man apparently escaped him, and he yelled up to Bob Battle, the city editor, "Hey, Bob, what's that nigger's name down in Memphis?" It was the only thing that Robert Churchwell could remember all day: *What's that nigger's name down in Memphis?* It was like someone had stabbed him, as if the secret truth of a man had just slipped out. The city room fell silent with Hart's words. Later that day Hart had rolled over on his chair to apologize, and Churchwell had told him, his own words surprising him, "Les, I don't think I want to hear it today." The last thing he remembered of that day, a day which remained with him for the rest of his life, was Les Hart, about to roll his chair back to his own desk, saying that he had lots of colored friends. Years later, in his seventies, long retired from the *Banner*, Robert Churchwell sat down to write his memoirs and typed the title of his book on the first page: *What's That Nigger's Name?*

There were other, constant reminders of his lesser status. One year there had been a call for a staff meeting in Jimmy Stahlman's office. So Churchwell joined all the others, trooping into the publisher's office with its massive American and Tennessee flags. Stahlman looked around the room, and his eyes seemed to light on Churchwell. He called Charlie Moss over and whispered something to him, and Moss walked over to Churchwell and said, "Robert, this staff meeting is not for you." He had felt humiliated as he walked out of the room, the only reporter excluded. Later he found out that the meeting was about the publisher's fishing lodge in Florida and the fact that all staff members were going to be allowed to use it—all except Robert Churchwell.

Year by year the other *Banner* reporters came first to respect and then to admire Robert Churchwell. He was an intelligent, decent, reserved man with a fine sense of humor for those who cared to discover it. It rankled some of them that he was not allowed to go to the Christmas party. At first the excuse was that the venue, the Colemere Club, was segregated, but that seemed a poor excuse. For a time there was a rumor that Stahlman, in the old, paternalistic tradition, faithfully gave Churchwell $50 each Christmas so he could take his wife and children to a nice Christmas dinner, a story Churchwell said was purely apocryphal. In time, around 1960, Dick Battle went to see Jimmy Stahlman and told him it wasn't right to exclude Churchwell from the party. In fact, Battle said, if Churchwell did not come, he would not attend himself. Stahlman was furious. "Battle, I could fire you right now," he said. "Yes," said Battle, who was one of the *Banner*'s best-connected reporters, "and if you do I'll go across the hall to the *Tennessean,* because I have an offer in my pocket from them right now and it's for fifty dollars a week more than you're paying me."[1] Others might stay away as well, Battle suggested. Finally, the *Banner* Christmas party was integrated.

Those were hard years for Churchwell. He believed that the paper did not really want him to succeed, that Jimmy Stahlman in particular wanted him to fail, and that Stahlman was simply sitting there waiting for him to make a mistake on a large scale, which would show that black people could not be trusted to be reporters. The stress was terrible. Sometimes when he came home at the end of the day, his wife knew, he withdrew inside himself and would not come out and would not talk to the other members of his family. Monday mornings were the worst, because when he went home Friday evening after a full week, the relief was so great that he could barely face Monday morning. He would often spend Sunday night wondering whether he could go back to work. There was a powerful voice within him telling him not to go back; but arguing against it was a more practical voice, which told him he had to go back because he owed it, if not to black people in Nashville, at the very least to his own family.

The worst problem was the psychological one of always being caught between the terrible contradiction of his own identity and the identity of the paper. He knew that the *Nashville Banner* in the most profound sense was hostile to the most important part of his identity as a human being. Most of the black people he dealt with in Nashville, like Kelly Miller Smith, were quite sensitive to his dilemma, and treated him with kindness. But occasionally he encountered tension, as in 1961 when he went to an office at Fisk to interview Roy Wilkins, the executive director of the NAACP. He had interviewed Wilkins many times before, and on this day Wilkins had greeted him pleasantly and then said, "Well, Robert, still with that damn *Banner,* I see." Nor could he be angry with Wilkins—after all, he thought of it as the damn *Banner* himself.

When he faltered on Sunday evening, sure that he could no longer return to his job, it was his wife, Mary, who kept encouraging him to go back. As he began to show signs of what was later diagnosed as clinical depression, she encouraged him to keep going, telling him that he was doing something of far greater value than he realized himself. "It's going to get better," she would tell him. "You'll see, Robert, the worst is over. It's going to get better." In her heart she sometimes wondered if it really would get better, and she wondered why Mr. Stahlman was like that. Did he really believe that black people were subhuman? Did he really feel that negatively about so many other members of the human race?

Nor was it just Robert Churchwell who had a sinking feeling as the protests mounted, and as the *Banner* turned away from covering the sit-ins as a daily news story. A number of the *Banner*'s best reporters were appalled. They were under orders not to cover the protests, and there were specific warnings to staff members. The orders, Larry Brinton, the *Banner*'s top police reporter, remembered, were strict. No *Banner* reporter was to be in the downtown area when demonstrations were taking part. If you were found there, or if someone said you were there, then you would be fired. It was, Brinton thought, all quite demented, "as if we didn't go there and didn't cover it, they [the protesters] would all go away." For a time the *Banner* reporters obeyed the editorial embargo. Then, as the demonstrations continued in full force, the reporters would sneak over, hiding out in cars in nearby buildings as anonymously as they could.[2]

22

In the days immediately after Big Saturday there were two important players in Nashville who were pleased with the way events were going. The first was Jim Lawson, now sure of the dynamic, because of his study of Gandhi, that if a man makes a moral stand against an oppressive regime and the regime lashes out, then his act of itself will surely push others around him to take moral stands. If ten are arrested, Lawson had believed and had taught these young people, fifty more will come the next time, and if fifty are arrested, two hundred more will come. His first lessons for them had been that their numbers would not remain small because the power of their idea was not small. That was what he had predicted would happen, and now it had happened. Not only were more and more students turning out for the protests, but the support of the black community was almost total. The city of Nashville, he believed, was just beginning to realize how strong the will of these young black people was.

The other person delighted with the mass arrests was the man who thought of himself as Lawson's sworn foe, Jimmy Stahlman. He was the driving force of the resistance. To him the arrest of all the students was a singular victory—it had been time to stop mollycoddling these people and strike at them, and by God, the city had finally done that. He was sure that the Movement would come apart now.

If the *Banner* was not covering the story as news, then it was handling it with what later became known as spin. The focus of the spin was the demonization of Jim Lawson. It was as if Stahlman seemed to believe that by going after Lawson in his news pages and editorial pages, he could end the entire protest. The sum of the paper's reporting, noted Will Campbell, the observer from the National Council of Churches, seemed to be saying: None of this is actually happening, so don't take it very seriously, but if by some mistake it *is* happening, it's the fault of this outside agitator.[1] What struck one of his staff members as particularly dangerous was the way in which Stahlman had become fixated on Jim Lawson. Stahlman raged about him constantly. He is not, thought that staff member, cynical about what we're printing—it's much more dangerous than that. He actually *believes* it.

Thus the world which existed in his mind and the world which his paper faithfully reported each day always remained in harmony. That had to be an unusually comforting equation: Stahlman dictated his ideas and prejudices to his paper, then picked up his own paper and had his view of life strengthened by what he read. He did not see the sit-ins as others saw them: Like it or not, the inevitable arrival of a broad-based movement led by young people, who, encouraged by recent Supreme Court decisions, were trying in an age of increasingly modern communications to roll back laws and customs of the past. Rather he saw himself, his city, and his beloved university as victims. They were the victims of pernicious agitators from the North, almost certainly Communists, who were playing mind games on poor, befuddled local blacks, people whom he believed were notoriously easy to manipulate. What had encouraged these students was the weakness of the city fathers and other local officials. Just a lack of good old-fashioned backbone. If the Vanderbilt authorities, Stahlman came to believe, would only stop shielding Lawson, the police would arrest him. Then, presumably, the sit-ins would stop. The issue was becoming, some of the *Banner* people thought, dangerously personalized even for someone as emotional as Stahlman. The publisher hated Lawson. The minister from Ohio was everything he despised: He was black; he was Northern; he had been, it would turn out, in Stahlman's mind a draft dodger; he was an agitator; and, worst of all, he was operating with the protection of one of the most beloved of all institutions, Vanderbilt, and, pure proof that Lawson was as crafty as he was sinister, from its divinity school.

That was particularly painful for Stahlman. Vanderbilt to him was a sacred place. Perhaps only the *Nashville Banner* and the United States Navy were more precious institutions. That Stahlman was so powerful a force locally, that he felt so passionately on the subject of Lawson was to have an enormous effect upon how the Vanderbilt administration behaved in those tumultuous days. Now, as the sit-in leaders seemed momentarily in a stalemate with the local commercial leadership, the crisis moved to its next step and became a crisis at Vanderbilt University.

Vanderbilt at the time was a university trying to break out of some of its regional restraints and limitations, and it had begun to move in the most cautious way imaginable toward integration. To say that the Supreme Court decision on *Brown* had not been welcomed enthusiastically by the Vanderbilt administration and its board of trustees was an understatement. If anything, its reaction had been guarded and grudging, if not actually hostile. If much of the political and economic complexion of Middle Tennessee had been changed by first the coming of the New Deal and then by the breakup of the Crump machine, then the last bastion of the old order in Middle Tennessee was Vanderbilt University.

Vanderbilt in March 1960 was an extremely conservative institution whose board and whose alumni mirrored not so much the region as it was, and might one day become, but as it had always been, where generation after generation of privileged young scions of the South (and their sisters) arrived to become a part of a surprisingly unchanged social order. If the meritocracy was sweeping across much of America in the postwar years, making its first inroads at the nation's great universities, it had not yet begun to touch Vanderbilt, and most particularly it had not touched the Vanderbilt board of trustees, whose most outspoken and volatile member was, of course, James Geddes Stahlman.

Vanderbilt was a school which did not so much want to live in the past as it wanted to perpetuate the past. How conservative the school was—top to bottom—can be seen by the fact that during the 1961–62 academic year, coming up on *eight* years after the *Brown* decision, the undergraduate student body in this privileged university in this border state was still all white, the student senate voted against integration, and a student body referendum favoring integration was defeated. That spring the board of trustees finally and quite belatedly voted to admit black undergraduates. Until then the school's policy was to admit local blacks to graduate schools if there was no comparable black graduate school in the area. It was a policy not merely timid but self-serving, designed to make the school appear significantly more liberal than it was (and thereby not lose the support of the liberal national foundations like Ford and Rockefeller on which it was dependent) without costing the university and key graduate schools the requisite prestige and quite possibly accreditation needed for their future.

From the start Jim Lawson had been different from the handful of other pioneer black graduate students. When Vanderbilt had made its first tentative steps toward integration in its law, divinity, and graduate schools, there had been built-in restrictions. The black students were not to dine in the student cafeteria, they were not to play intramural athletics, they were not to buy tickets that allowed them to sit in the Vanderbilt gym for athletic games, and they were most assuredly not to live in an otherwise white dorm. If at all possible, they were not to use the toilets, which had been white-only until then.[2] Nor were they, if the administration had any choice in the matter, to feel particularly welcome. In 1959 one of the school's deans had received a letter of application from a would-be black Ph.D. candidate. The dean wrote back to warn the young man of the "annoying, embarrassing, or very distasteful" experiences he would probably face as a Vanderbilt graduate student. He would not be able to live on campus, so he would have to find housing in a black residential area. He would, the dean warned, be refused service in restaurants and motels, and he would run into other forms of rejection at the hands of white Nashvillians.[3] Otherwise, it was presumed, he was quite welcome to come.

Harvie Branscomb, the chancellor of Vanderbilt, was sixty-five in 1960. He had come there from Duke in 1947, where he had been the head of the theological school. He had been mildly liberal as a young man, particularly as a young instructor in religious studies at Southern Methodist University, where he had momentarily defied university authorities on the issue of evolution. It was clear in the late fifties that he still thought of himself as a liberal (or at least as liberal as a man with so conservative a board ought to be). Exceptionally sure-footed in almost all of his political moves for the first thirteen years of his tour, he was about to be caught in a massive collision between the white man's religion as he professed it, and the white man's politics as he lived them.

Branscomb's accomplishments until then were not to be scoffed at. He had taken a poor, rather neglected, and quite parochial school and set out to make it an ornament first to the region and then, perhaps, even to the country. In a surprisingly short time he had done an amazing job of bringing Vanderbilt up to speed, and if anything, given his personal connections with different foundations, the future looked even brighter. The divinity school already had the reputation in some quarters of being the best and most liberal in the South, and the law school was also beginning to gain national recognition. If anything, Vanderbilt under Harvie Branscomb by the late fifties seemed something of a split-level institution: It was a university with an exceptional faculty, which was getting ever better, it had quality graduate schools and serious graduate students, and yet it possessed an undergraduate body dominated to an uncommon degree by fraternity and sorority life, and students who seemed to take relatively little interest in the larger academic possibilities around them, most particularly in the life of the mind.

By 1960 Branscomb appeared to be nearing success in something which was extremely close to his heart—breaking or at the very least limiting the power and influence of the school's fraternities and sororities and cutting back on their almost complete domination of campus life. Branscomb did not believe that Vanderbilt could become a great university unless he succeeded here; but ever shrewd and cautious as a politician, he moved guardedly, knowing that if he moved too quickly and too openly he would offend the board and the alumni.

Branscomb had been until then a skilled tightrope walker, an exceptionally successful fund-raiser who had been able to balance the needs and fears of the conservative board and alumni with the increasingly liberal demands of the major national foundations at whose mercy he also lived. In 1960 his power on campus was unchallenged. He ran the university as his personal fiefdom. He was intelligent, decisive, but not particularly likeable, an authoritarian and dominating figure on campus who did not believe that personal popularity was a particularly noteworthy objective. He was an extremely hierarchical man and he knew the precise place in the hierarchy of everyone with whom he dealt. He was not a man who wasted time on amenities. He knew who was smart but powerless, and he knew who was not very smart but powerful, and whose opposition could slow him down and cost him considerable energy.

Race brought him down. It underlined the contradictions between his two constituencies—the liberal one, which was national, and the conservative one, which was regional and local—and it underlined his own generational vulnerability to change. For on race he wanted to have it both ways. He had been born in Alabama in the previous century, and his views on race reflected those of a marginally enlightened establishmentarian from the Deep South from another era. He once told a Vanderbilt graduate student of his first trip to New York, on his way to Oxford as a Rhodes scholar. He had entered a simple, utilitarian restaurant to eat and he had seen a black person eating and he had felt sick. ("Logically I could understand it, but psychologically it [my reaction] was totally irrational," he said.[4]) He did not doubt that there should be racial progress: Harvie Branscomb felt a handful of already educated and talented blacks should make their way as cautiously as possible into white society, each step forward to be approved by the right kind of white people—a jury, say, of Harvie Branscomb and men exactly like him.

Branscomb did not actually say that blacks were inferior, but he wrote one alumnus after the Supreme Court decision on *Brown,* "A large percentage of negroes have certain well known deficiencies. . . ."[5] He was clearly uncomfortable even with the cautious rate of change taking place in America in the mid-fifties, and because he felt resistance in his heart, he also felt entitled to tell Vanderbilt alumni who complained about integration of his own personal doubts. For example, he would tell of an incident in late 1954 which made him, in his own words, "fighting mad." He had visited nearby Fort Campbell, Kentucky, and had seen black ROTC students from Ohio assigned to common barracks along with the white boys from Vanderbilt.[6] It was true that, given his background, he probably did not like the scene, but it was also true that he was signaling to conservative alumni that he was with them on this issue and shared their doubts about the changes taking place in America.

For he was acutely aware of the board's growing nervousness as the pressure to integrate increased from the foundations in the North. He still believed he could balance these two differing and now diverging forces. He wanted no interference from his faculty—which he suspected was likely to be more liberal on this issue than it should be, and therefore likely to cause trouble.

In 1957, an early telltale incident took place which reflected just how conservative the school's administration was, and how little con-

troversy and dissent Branscomb wanted on this issue. A member of
the Vanderbilt Divinity School named Everett Tilson had been one of
the signers of a telegram urging President Eisenhower to come south
to encourage white Southern religious leaders wrestling with the issue
of integration. The story including Tilson's participation had made the
Nashville papers and Branscomb had not been pleased. That spring
when Phil Hyatt, the acting dean of the divinity school, took his proposed budget to Branscomb for approval, the only items which the
chancellor questioned was a $500 raise for Tilson and a promotion
from assistant professor to associate professor. When the dean asked
why, Branscomb had mentioned the item in the paper. Neither was
approved although a year later Hyatt's successor, Bob Nelson, shep-
herded them through.

In 1960 Branscomb seemed unassailable. He seemed able to handle
the world of academe with skill and dispatch and relatively little
protest, and yet he was able to deal with the real world, that of power
and money, or in his case, the wealthiest and most conservative traditionalists in Nashville. Even his admirers came to believe that he did
not sense the larger moral impact of the *Brown* decision on the country (an impact just beginning to be felt in 1960) nor, equally important, did he sense the explosive impact which televised coverage of
this issue would have on the nation. The capacity of television to
amplify the moral aspects of the crises in both Montgomery and Little
Rock was just beginning to be felt. But Harvie Branscomb, like many
men of his class and station in that period, was not a person who
watched very much television. Almost unconsciously he came to think
that men like Jimmy Stahlman and others like him on the board had
real power, while Jim Lawson, no matter what the moral equities of his
position, was powerless. More, he thought that what he was dealing
with was a regional issue on which he would be judged only by his
local constituency. He was to pay a very high price for these two miscalculations.

He knew he had to move forward on race, but he felt it was merely
enough to be a little ahead of the curve, to point out to the foundations, as he frequently did, that Vanderbilt was doing better than
Tulane and that he was changing the school as quickly as he could. He
became very skillful at leveraging his dilemma with each of his separate constituencies, one against the other: He could tell the conserva-

tive board that he needed to move forward just a bit more because otherwise the foundations might cut Vanderbilt off, and he could offer the dilemma posed by his conservative board to the foundations as evidence of why he had not moved faster.

Branscomb's personal and professional ambivalence on race had been obvious since the late forties as the issue gradually moved toward center stage in American life. When Vanderbilt had played Yale in football in 1948, it meant that it played against the great Negro running back of that period, Levi Jackson. Some alumni complained about this seeming outrage. Branscomb's letter trying to appease them was hardly a ringing defense of what had happened: "I don't think any of us enjoyed the experience of playing against Levi Jackson." He had added that a Yale dean had implied to him that he had expected Jackson to flunk out before the Vanderbilt game.[7] There were more bullets to be dodged and they were coming ever closer. In 1949, a black veteran sought admission to the law school. Branscomb brought the issue before the board, which turned down the application. Branscomb wanted to add the phrase that the application could not be accepted "at this time." The board struck that from the wording. When Rufus Harris, the head of Tulane, wrote him in 1952 suggesting that the two schools act together on racial matters—Tulane had a greater problem than Vanderbilt because it had a founding bequest barring blacks—Vanderbilt rejected the request.

In 1953 as national scrutiny of racial issues, particularly in the religious world, heightened, the Vanderbilt Divinity School quietly admitted Joseph Johnson, Jr., a thirty-eight-year-old minister who was president of a black theological school in Jackson, Tennessee. In 1954, after the *Brown* decision, the law school had to move ahead with integration or risk losing its accreditation: One could not aspire to having a great national law school which challenged the ruling of the Supreme Court of the United States. Reluctantly, in the fall of 1956 it admitted its first two black students. In letters to the alumni Branscomb referred to them as "the two boys."

Jim Lawson was the second black admitted to Vanderbilt Divinity School. At the time of the sit-in crisis he was in his third and last year on his way to gaining his master's of divinity. To the conservative members of the Vanderbilt administration, who monitored carefully the progress and attitude of new black students, there was a vague

feeling, even before the sit-ins began, that a mistake of some sort had
been made, that Lawson had turned out to be unnecessarily aggressive and arrogant, and there had already been a good deal of grumbling about him. Yet the irony of all this was that Jim Lawson was
doing exceptionally well at Vanderbilt. He was a very good student,
participating enthusiastically in his classes and enjoying the richness
of the intellectual life around him. What pleased him the most was not
just the excellence of the faculty, but the openness of his fellow students, many of them from the Deep South.

The person apparently most offended by what Jim Lawson was
doing, his failure to tiptoe quietly through Vanderbilt, turned out to
be Harvie Branscomb. As far as Branscomb was concerned, it was all
going too fast. When Branscomb heard about Lawson playing in
intramural football games he was not pleased, for this was integration
at a faster and fuller pace than he wanted, and so he called the new
dean of the divinity school, Robert Nelson. Branscomb was upset, as
he told Nelson, "because a couple of nigras are playing intramural
football and this could cause trouble." The first thing which struck
Nelson was the use of the bastardized racial form. Nelson had heard it
used before by other conservative members of the community trying
to accommodate change, but he was surprised to hear it from the
chancellor. The next thing the chancellor said was, "What are you
going to do about this, Dean Nelson?" That puzzled Nelson and he
asked Branscomb what he meant. "Well, Vanderbilt is doing very well
on race relations," Branscomb said. "I am very proud of the fact that
we are ahead of Tulane on this." Nelson said something to the effect
that there did not seem to be anything dramatically wrong with a student playing in an intramural football game. Branscomb, however,
remained upset. "Suppose one day there's a game," he asked, "and
there's a fight during the game between a white boy and a nigra, and
the local newspaper picks it up. We don't want this in the newspapers." That was the end of it, though Nelson did mention the complaint to Lawson, letting him make the decision whether or not he
wanted to continue playing, which of course he did.

That incident, Nelson reflected, was the first warning. Later he realized there were a few troubling things about Branscomb's call. The
first was that Tulane was the measuring stick, not what was morally
right, nor what the law said. In addition, and this was quite important,

had Harvie Branscomb asked what kind of young man Jim Lawson was or how well he was doing, to which Bob Nelson would have answered that he was in fact a model student, both academically and socially gifted, a student whose presence was enriching the lives of white students. The other thing he sensed was that the hierarchy was at work and he had been more or less assigned to tidy things up. The words which lingered with him were these: *What are you going to do about this, Dean Nelson?*

The paradox was that until the Lawson case, the divinity school represented Branscomb's greatest achievement, a place where he had focused his prime energies. Some authorities already placed it among the top five divinity schools in the country; others believed it might be even better, for its faculty members were young and their abilities at that moment were greater than their reputations. It might also be, arguably, the most liberal divinity school in the South—just ready, it appeared, for a takeoff to true national recognition. Branscomb had managed to get a large grant from the Sealantic Foundation to house the school in a new building to be dedicated that very March. Also paradoxically, Bob Nelson, the new dean, was something of a fair-haired boy, chosen by Branscomb in no small part, it was believed, because he reminded the chancellor of the young Harvie Branscomb. Nelson had been at Vanderbilt three years that fall, and since his arrival in Nashville had been the recipient of an unusual degree of personal warmth from the chancellor; he and his wife were even tended a guest membership in the Belle Meade country club. That was rare and there were colleagues who believed that in some way Nelson had been anointed for even greater things, perhaps to become Branscomb's successor.

Thus all the forces were in play for a terrible collision without anyone realizing it. The sit-ins were growing more formidable every day. Jimmy Stahlman was convinced that the way to break them was to break Lawson, first by denying him the protection of Vanderbilt, and then by having him arrested. Stahlman by then had succeeded, both in his own mind and in his paper, in demonizing Lawson. When he eventually discovered that Lawson had been a conscientious objector during the Korean War, Stahlman became even angrier. (At one point in 1960, livid over Lawson's war record, Stahlman assigned one of his best reporters, a former *Tennessean* city editor named Jack Setters, who had left the morning newspaper in no small part because he was not in sync with its attitude on race, to dig back into Lawson's court case in Ohio. Setters had retraced the events in Ohio and had written his boss a memo saying yes, it appeared that the rumors were true and that Lawson had a nefarious past. But when he was frustrated in his attempts to get documentation on what was supposed to be a radical speech Lawson had given at a religious convocation of young people, Setters wrote Stahlman, "[It] makes me think there's a nigger by the name of Lawson in the woodpile somewhere."[8] If Stahlman had pushed hard earlier on Ben West to do something about the students, he was now working the other end of the equation, the Vanderbilt one.

The effect of Stahlman on the other members of the Vanderbilt board was a pernicious one. He became a board member for life back in 1930. He was regarded as nothing less than the proverbial eight-hundred-pound gorilla. "You haven't really lived," a subsequent chancellor of Vanderbilt named Alec Heard once said a few years later, "unless you've been the head of a university and had Jimmy Stahlman as the senior member of your governing board."[9] At one meeting of the Vanderbilt University Board of Trust, after Stahlman had delivered a particularly passionate diatribe against some modern-ization of the college's codes, another member of the board was asked what he felt about the issue. "I agree with Mr. Stahlman," the member said, "but not so vehemently."[10] If he was not always that bombastic at board meetings, he nonetheless cast a vast shadow over the executive board. On the issue of race he was almost uniquely emotional—here his feelings about race intersected with his love of Vanderbilt. It begot both his anger and his sentimentality. Stahlman became a force that the other, more acquiescent segregationists would prefer not to deal with.

Not all of Stahlman's fellow board members, on this issue, were exactly true blue. They might not necessarily love the idea of the new, integrated future, but they were businessmen and establishmentarians first and foremost; they were not particularly eager to go to war over race. What they loved most was, like most successful men, the status quo. In addition, they feared Jimmy Stahlman. They were all too aware of his capacity to turn violently in his paper on former friends whom he had judged unworthy during some mutual struggle, and they remained wary of his temper. In private they might mock him, and in truth they had never entirely accepted him into the inner social world which he coveted (they might invite him to dinner, but they were often quite relieved if he could not come, one colleague noted). But they did not lightly cross him on an issue about which he felt strongly. Nor was he alone in his passion on this issue; he had a powerful ally on the executive board of Vanderbilt, John Sloan, the extremely conservative head of Cain-Sloan, a man whose defiance of the student protesters seemed in stark contrast to that of officials from the rival store, Harveys.

By this point Stahlman had literally placed himself on a wartime footing in the sit-in struggle. He might not feel the need to let his paper write about what was happening, but he was literally ready to arm himself and his people in case they were attacked. He had become convinced that the sit-in leaders were going to march on the *Banner,* and that they were going to come after him personally. Even worse, he was certain they were going to be armed. Though the demonstrations had all been peaceful, though the entire Movement was built around Christian nonviolence, though so far not one student had struck back at an assailant, in the end, he believed, it would turn into a kind of Armageddon, an Armageddon at Eleventh and Broadway.

If they were going to come, well, by God, Captain James Geddes Stahlman, USN Retired, was not afraid to stand and fight. He would take a few of them with him. One staff member was sent out to buy about ten reconditioned World War II army surplus rifles, along with sufficient ammunition to hold the premises until, presumably, either the 101st Airborne from nearby Fort Campbell, Kentucky, or the Tennessee National Guard arrived. The rifles were assigned to the top editors and loyalists, and were locked in a small closet off Charlie Moss's office. In addition Stahlman sent Larry Brinton out to buy surplus metal army helmets, bulletproof vests, and mace.[11] The army of the *Nashville Banner* was ready to defend the publisher's way of life. A number of *Banner* reporters watching this believed there was a sense of separation from reality which was almost complete. Still, Stahlman had just enough power to intimidate the chancellor of a would-be great university.

The story now unfolded with a certain relentless inevitability. After Big Saturday, Jim Lawson had returned from a brief trip to Chattanooga in time to join a group of some seventy-five black ministers who were meeting with Mayor Ben West. The black ministers were furious over the fact that the Nashville police not only failed to protect the protesters, but had arrested only the protesters and none of their assailants. The meeting, not surprisingly, had been acrimonious. West felt himself cornered. At one point during his debate with the ministers he seemed to be splitting hairs: He suggested that while the students had the right to sit in, they lost that right once the owners closed the lunch counters.

Jim Lawson was hardly the most outspoken or the most heated figure at the meeting—as usual, C. T. Vivian was—but Lawson dissented strenuously on this point: If the stores closed only their lunch counters *without closing down themselves,* he said, they were using the law as a gimmick and it was nothing less than an attempt to stop the sit-ins. That was hard to argue with. There were a number of reporters at the meeting, and the next day both Nashville papers gave different accounts of what had happened and what had been said. The *Banner* portrayed Lawson as the architect of a blanket attempt to get students to break the law (LEADER SAYS HE'LL ADVISE STUDENTS TO BREAK THE LAW). But other accounts quoted Lawson more carefully and more accurately. Later some members of the divinity school faculty believed that the entire crisis could have been settled easily if Harvie Branscomb had only sat down and talked with Jim Lawson for an hour. But that was the last thing Branscomb wanted. He had absolutely no desire to understand the complexity of what Lawson was saying. The less he knew of what Lawson was saying, the better.

Ironically, Branscomb himself had been quite outspoken about his own belief in the right of free men to challenge laws which they believed unjust. Some eight years earlier, giving a series of lectures at the University of Wisconsin, he said: "The second contribution which religion has made to American life has been the insistence upon a law of God which is supreme above all human institutions and man-made legislation. To this divine law man owes final obedience. If the laws of states or governments deviate from this standard they have no more authority, in fact should be disregarded or rejected. This . . . was a fundamental Christian teaching from the beginning. . . ."[12] That, of course, had been a philosophical point made in the abstract, and was very different from the matter of practical university politics, particularly as a conservative board began to breathe down his neck.

Branscomb seized on what Lawson had allegedly said to the mayor as reported by the *Nashville Banner*. It was a fateful decision on his part. There are, in all social crises, moments when the forces of the past collide head-on with the forces of the future. What makes them particularly interesting is that those who are summoned to make critical decisions rarely understand on the eve of the collision that they are dealing with something epic; rather for them it tends to be bureaucratic business as usual. That is what happened to Harvie Branscomb. For thirteen years, going back to the moment when he had been a candidate for the job of chancellor, his sense of political nuance had been inspired. Back then, when he had showed up for a critical interview session with some board members in a quasi-social setting, a board member had offered him a drink. He had shrewdly accepted the drink, realizing that it was a critical test, for some board members worried that he might be a little too pious and prissy for the job. Then when they had asked him about his feelings about college football—a very sensitive subject, for there was fear that Branscomb might be anti-football—he had answered that it was like sin, "we all have it and we all have to make the best of it."[13] Again he had given the perfect answer. Now, however, for the first time, he miscalculated politically and he did it on a grand scale.

He was about to make a political decision based on a moral issue. Branscomb now made an offering of one black graduate student, a seemingly unimportant albeit moral man, to an exceptionally important and politically powerful board member, albeit an unusually reactionary one, a man largely viewed by those who knew him best as an anachronistic, often destructive loose cannon. (The most stunning thing about the entire affair, Jim Lawson said years later, "was the ability of so truly ignorant a man [Stahlman] to hold a great university hostage.")

More, he rushed to judgment on the Lawson case. It was as if this was something he had been waiting for. Years later, commenting on what had happened, in what was for a long time the closest he came to admitting he had made a mistake, Branscomb said that normally on matters this explosive he bought time by bottling the issue up in com-

mittee, thereby defusing it. But this time he pressed ahead with a rare
sense of urgency, creating his own arbitrary deadlines. This stemmed,
thought some who knew him, from a combination of things—his own
irritation with a black student for being ungrateful, as well as his reading of a very angry Jimmy Stahlman and, of course, his ally John Sloan,
a man demonstrably unhappy with the sit-ins.

On Tuesday, March 1, Will Campbell read the *Banner*'s account of
the black ministers' confrontation with the mayor with its implication
that Lawson endorsed unlimited violation of the law, and he knew
immediately that Jimmy Stahlman had put Jim Lawson in play. Campbell called Bob Nelson, the Vanderbilt divinity dean, to warn him that
Lawson had been targeted by the *Banner,* and that this would have
immediate consequences on the Vanderbilt campus. Unlike most of
the people directly connected to the divinity school, Campbell was a
political man as well as a religious one, and he had a shrewd sense of
how the interior establishment politics of Nashville worked. A decision had been made, Campbell warned: Stahlman and his allies were
going to try and take Lawson out.

Nelson went immediately to Lawson's house. There Lawson
explained what had happened, and gave his own view of the law and
the sit-ins. He had already begun to feel frustrated: He was being
made the villain, even though to him the real evil lay in the segregated
nature of the lunch counters. Lawson said he could understand a conservative business institution such as the *Banner* being obtuse about
what he had said to the mayor, but it was another thing for a suppos-
edly modern university to fail to make the distinction, or to fail to even
try to make such a distinction. Nelson went next to his own office,
where he found that he had already been summoned to see
Branscomb. There he got his marching orders: Branscomb wanted
nothing less than for Lawson to recant what he had said about the law
and civil disobedience. Otherwise he would be expelled. Nelson,
whose political skills and whose sense of the stakes at play were to
prove marginal, went to see Lawson and asked for a statement clarify-
ing his position.

Lawson thereupon wrote out a brief statement which suggested
that while he respected the law, the purpose of the sit-ins had been to
call the community's attention to a profound (legally based) injustice.
He did not and would not disavow what the students were doing. He

would not disassociate himself from them; he was their teacher and he believed that they were acting in a noble way. Branscomb, predictably, was far from satisfied; he wanted something stronger and Nelson was assigned to extract it from Lawson. In addition, time was now of the essence, for on Wednesday there would be a luncheon with the executive board. It had been scheduled previously, but it was now likely to center on the Lawson affair. Nelson was to bring the board some kind of answer.

Lawson, at Nelson's request, now wrote a far more elegant letter, defending himself and his rights to act upon his conscience as a Christian, pointing out that although he had great respect for the law, the violence on Big Saturday had been inflicted upon the protesters, not by them, and that their protest was nothing less than a call to the community at large to take notice of a grievous condition. His statement was uncommonly generous, reflecting his gratitude and feeling of personal warmth toward Vanderbilt, and it explained the moral nature of the protest. He believed in the law, he said: "Defiant violation of the law is a contradiction of my entire understanding of the loyalty to Christian nonviolence." Civil disobedience could be considered legitimate, he said, only in "the context of a law or a law enforcement agency which has in reality ceased to be the law, and then the Christian [resists] only in fear and trembling before God." As for the students, if there had been any blood shed that day, he added, "it would have been shed by those seeking to bring a dire social condition to the attention of the community. That these students did so [protest] with love, with forgiveness, and with a bearing of the burden of sin which we all share, is the real work of the Holy Spirit." If the board members had wanted to find the words of a true Christian, they were all there. Lawson's letter contained everything but a disavowal of future civil disobedience at the lunch counters.

Unfortunately, the entire proceeding was by now more court-martial than academic procedure. Nelson was already becoming a compromised figure. On Wednesday he went before the executive board at lunch. It happened to be Ash Wednesday, and he made reference to that, that it was the anniversary of the day when the Lord had gone to His death for breaking the law. It was not, it was later decided by some board members, the most appropriate way to begin the discussion. When Nelson read aloud Lawson's statement and his attempt to justify continued acts of civil disobedience in the future, someone shouted, "There it is!" The entire executive board seemed to agree. The other members, Nelson remembered, were enraged that a student—a black student at that—would set himself up as the judge of which law was binding and which was not.

Nelson tried to defend Lawson, and tried to speak of civil disobedience against the authoritarian rule of the Communists in East Germany by ministers who had been friends of his. But he was suffering from the flu, was exhausted, and was very much on the defensive. Lawson was not allowed to speak for himself. The divinity school faculty members, who were the true judges of Lawson's behavior and who admired him, were in no way allowed to participate in the process. Nelson, sensing the rage in the room and a growing rebellion on the part of his own faculty members, who had not been allowed to participate in this mounting crisis, scribbled a note to Branscomb urging him not to make a decision at the meeting.

Branscomb was furious now, first at Lawson and soon, even more lastingly, at Nelson. He sent Nelson to see Lawson once again. This time he wanted nothing less than a statement of withdrawal, something Lawson had once mentioned in passing to Nelson that he was willing to do. Otherwise, Branscomb told Nelson, Lawson would be expelled the next day. By then Nelson had been completely undermined by events. He had been looking for a middle ground in what was now a war zone which had no middle ground. A large number of faculty members were already rebellious, feeling that they had not been kept informed. Later, after everything collapsed on him, Nelson decided that going to Lawson's house to summon a statement of withdrawal was his first critical mistake, that both for moral and for procedural reasons what he was doing was wrong, and that he should have resigned at the board meeting. But he played the role assigned to him, one which he later bitterly regretted.

He showed up at Lawson's home at about 6:00 P.M. The situation was hopeless, he told Lawson. The board was unalterably opposed to his staying in school. Then he told Lawson that he was hurting the university, in particular, his friends at Vanderbilt, especially the people at the divinity school who were on his side, and who were working for integration. Why, Nelson said, he had already cost the university, which was just starting a fund-raising drive, some $10 million. "Is that what they said in the committee?" Lawson asked incredulously. "Thank God, no," Nelson answered, "it just occurred to me as a probability." Nelson then suggested that Lawson resign. He also told him if he were expelled from Vanderbilt, he would not be able to gain admission to any other divinity school in the country to complete his work. (On this point Nelson was grievously wrong and his thinking showed how little sense he had of the larger political forces at work; almost every major divinity school in the country immediately competed to get Lawson as a student.) Nelson handed him the letter of resignation approved by Branscomb, as yet unsigned. All of this was devastating to Lawson—his one friend was telling him to resign, adding that he had hurt his friends.

At first Lawson seemed willing to go along. He was tired of it all, and tired of the public misrepresentation of his role and his purpose, and he did not want to hurt Nelson. But then Will Campbell, his closest personal friend in the white community, spoke to him over the phone. Campbell heard the exhaustion and depression in Lawson's voice and told him to come over immediately. Will Campbell was shocked to find that Jim Lawson was willing to resign and to give Harvie Branscomb and the Vanderbilt board what they wanted. That struck him as a perfect reflection of his own thesis of what was taking place in the South at that time—that since the *Brown* decision six years earlier, the blacks had been behaving as far better Christians than the whites. As far as he was concerned, Jim Lawson was the only person in the entire scenario behaving with any measure of Christian charity: "Jim, tear the letter up. Don't do their dirty work for them," he said. "If the sons of bitches want to get rid of you, make them fire you. You are not the transgressor, you are the victim. Flush them out for who they are." Campbell had a sense that Dorothy Lawson agreed with him, and indeed she did; she was puzzled and increasingly angered over the fact that in a dispute like this between her husband, who was a man of the cloth and a divinity student, and Branscomb, who was the former head of a divinity school, Branscomb systematically refused any attempt to meet with her husband. Encouraged by Campbell and his wife, Lawson tore up the letter.

On Thursday, March 3, 1960, Harvie Branscomb expelled Jim Lawson from Vanderbilt Divinity School. The meeting in which Branscomb told the divinity school faculty he was expelling Lawson was a bleak one. It was about the law, Branscomb had told the faculty members; there had to be respect for the law. "Everything that Hitler did in Germany was legal," said Langdon Gilkey, a distinguished member of the faculty who had spent much of World War II in a Japanese prison camp, and who would soon end up at the University of Chicago. When Branscomb continued to emphasize his belief that Lawson was going against the rules of Vanderbilt, another faculty member, Gordon Kaufman, rose to say that what Jim Lawson was doing in the sit-ins was carrying out the very same ethical conduct which the faculty members of the divinity school were teaching. "Maybe all of us should withdraw," he said. It was a particularly chilling moment. (Kaufman was soon teaching at Harvard.[14]) It was clear to Branscomb that even at the operative level—let alone the national and international—severe damage had already been done to the school's reputation. The divinity school was no longer the jewel in the crown for Branscomb. Now it was the burr under the saddle.

But Branscomb could not, as the struggle continued, do the one thing most faculty members demanded, readmit Lawson on their terms, for he could not appear in the eyes of his board to be backing down. For many of the board members, just as irate in their own way as the divinity school professors, were perfectly willing to close down the divinity school altogether. Vanderbilt was demonstrably a house divided: Letters offering jobs were already flying back and forth between the deans of the other prominent divinity schools to the Vanderbilt faculty members. As March ended it appeared likely that many of the best-known divinity school faculty members were going to resign. There were reports that a number of the top schools might take the entire faculty en masse.

Jimmy Stahlman was thrilled with Lawson's expulsion. In his mind he had prevailed and right had triumphed. He believed that only the fact that Lawson was a Vanderbilt student had protected him in the past from the police. Now Stahlman kept the pressure up. Not surprisingly, the next day four Nashville policemen walked into Kelly Miller Smith's First Baptist Church and arrested Jim Lawson. That this was no ordinary mission was emphasized by the fact that one of them was Morgan Smith, Sr., a Nashville policeman notorious for his violent nature and his pathological dislike of black people. They handled him as harshly as they could, until finally Dorothy Lawson had shouted at them, "Why do you have to be so rough! Why are you trying to hurt him! Why do you have to do it this way? He isn't resisting!" As they walked out the door with Lawson manacled to them, a photographer captured a telling photo of the event. In the background was the signboard promoting the next sermon by Kelly Miller Smith:

FATHER, FORGIVE THEM.

23

When the police came and handcuffed him at Kelly Miller Smith's church, Jim Lawson felt a vast sense of relief. For the first time since the entire crisis at Vanderbilt had begun, he felt comfortable with himself. He was tired of being caught in the byzantine politics of a white university. Doing what was right for the Movement and taking great risks for something so basic to his spirit was easy. But compromising his beliefs because he liked Bob Nelson and Nelson was caught in some political bind at Vanderbilt was another thing. The politics of Vanderbilt had begun to seem increasingly treacherous, meaner, ironically, than the politics of the city itself. His arrest, he later decided, sardonically, was Stahlman's finest hour.

Nor did he in any way fear jail; after the exhausting events of the past few days he actually found it restful. He did not want anyone to make bail for him, for being inside jail was the preferred tactic at the moment. More than anything else what he wanted once he was in his cell was to sleep. But even that became difficult. His was becoming a cause célèbre. The rest of the country had begun to listen. A faculty committee from the divinity school quickly showed up to bail him out. It seemed to mean a great deal to some of these men, who were his professors, or had been until recently, so after spending part of the night in jail he let them make bail and out he came.

He was amused by the growing uproar taking place at the divinity school. Some faculty members were concerned over the moral issues involved, but it struck him that others were more bothered by the procedural and territorial violations—the fact that a student in good standing with good marks had been expelled and the faculty had not been consulted. Would that they had been equally concerned when young black and white students had been beaten up downtown, he thought; would that they had been marching with the students in the first place. He did not worry about his future. He had never doubted that if he was true to himself and his belief in Christ, there would be a place for him, and soon it was clear, as phone calls and letters poured in, that virtually every divinity school in the country wanted him. He quickly decided to continue his studies for his master's degree at Boston University. His job now was to forgive his enemies. That was as much a part of his life as jail.

24

In early March 1960 Mayor Ben West felt increasingly cornered. He was irritated that the moves he had been pushed into by Jimmy Stahlman were not ones he had wanted to make in the first place, and even worse, he had known even as he was making them that they probably would not work. He, who was smart and nimble and had a very good sense of his city's political future, had been pushed into something by a man he knew was not only bombastic but at war with the future. Thus cornered, he now created a biracial committee to make recommendations on the lunch counters. The students were not particularly optimistic about the possibility of anything positive coming out of the committee. Their leaders did not believe for a minute that a committee was needed to figure out what was the right thing to do; what was needed was for the people who owned or managed these stores simply to get on with it and integrate. Nor were they thrilled that the head of the committee was a man named Madison Sarratt, who was vice chancellor emeritus of Vanderbilt. Though Sarratt had a reputation for being a kindly man, that was largely a white middle-class perception of him; his acts of kindness, as far as they were concerned, had been reserved for privileged white college students. If he had been kind to blacks other, perhaps, than the domestics who worked for him, they had no knowledge of it. Worse, the truth was that he operated under the aegis of Vanderbilt, a university which still refused to admit black undergraduates, and had just expelled Jim Lawson for advising them during the sit-ins.

Madison Sarratt, the students believed, was under the thumb of Jimmy Stahlman, who had emerged as their sworn enemy. Still, the sit-ins had been temporarily suspended while the committee met. The students were sure the white leaders wanted to delay them as much as possible, to cool them down and freeze all demonstrations until exam time. Then presumably they would be too busy to demonstrate. Soon summer would come, the students would be gone, and the protests would be forgotten. In the fall, it would be business as usual downtown.

The members of the central committee met every day and remained on red alert. Their confidence had grown steadily. They had a mounting sense that they were on the winning track and they could laugh about some of the confrontations now, about the befuddled white woman who had panicked when they had staged the sit-in at Harveys on Big Saturday and had rushed from the restaurant to the ladies' room, opened the door, and found two black Fisk co-eds there, and had started screaming, more in dismay than anger, "Oh my God, they're everywhere! They're everywhere!" Even Jack Setters, the veteran *Banner* reporter who was never pleased by any sign of black progress, had walked into Do's Grille, the local restaurant where *Banner* and *Tennessean* reporters lunched, a place not known for its cleanliness, and had said to the proprietress, "Well, if you'd only clean the goddamn place up a little, they might be willing to sit in here too."

What the sit-in leaders were hearing from their friends on the biracial committee was not encouraging. They were being told that the representatives were toying with the idea of a compromise solution: a two-section eating area, one part segregated, another part which would be desegregated. That was unacceptable to them, for a segregated area would be retained. When they heard about it, some two weeks into the cease-fire, the students almost broke the moratorium, but Stephen Wright, the president of Fisk and a member of the committee, pleaded with them for one more week. Late in March, Kelly Miller Smith had finally been called before the biracial committee. "They asked me what would satisfy our community," Smith told reporters that day. "I thought it was quite late for that question."

On March 26, after a three-week break, the students resumed the sit-ins. This time some 120 students ventured into the downtown area. The principal confrontation of the day was at Cain-Sloan's, in no small part because the students believed that John Sloan, the store's owner, was a major roadblock to a settlement. A number of the smaller stores were obviously eager to make a settlement; Greenfield Pitts, an executive at Harveys assigned to deal with the crisis, wanted a deal because it made economic sense, but also, the students had decided from their various meetings with him, because he seemed like a humane man who always treated everyone well. The contrast between their treatment at the two stores was striking. At Harveys the people they met with from top to bottom were always polite, and at Cain-Sloan's they were almost always hostile. When the other store owners, including the Harveys people, suggested a settlement, they were told again and again that John Sloan would block them. There was, they thought, an intriguing strategy at work: If Sloan could push Harveys into a separate settlement, then Harveys would become the store for black people, and Cain-Sloan the one for whites.

So no love was lost between Sloan and the student leadership. John Sloan, in their eyes, did not like black people and he showed it. He was the kind of man, thought C. T. Vivian, who was willing to deal with black people but only if they went around to the back door. When they had their meetings, Vivian and the others could feel his disdain. He was always telling them that even meeting with them was a sign of his goodwill, because his store was not losing any money, something they seriously doubted. "I'm doing just fine without you people," he would say, "and I can keep going as long as you can."[1] On this day the students entered the Iris dining room of Cain-Sloan but did not sit down. The manager was summoned, and said he would not serve them. Then they asked to meet with John Sloan. Sloan soon arrived, and again they could sense the frostiness. "We don't have to serve you, we won't serve you, and I have to say that not only is it the store's policy not to serve you, but as the head of this store I personally believe in the policy," he said. They had all been told to be on their best behavior, but again C. T. Vivian flashed his anger. "We know what you've been doing behind the scenes," Vivian said. "You've set this whole thing back years." As he spoke, Vivian thought, John Sloan seemed if anything to be pleased. A man in a suit and tie with the soul of a redneck sheriff, Vivian thought.

The middle weeks of April found the mayor locked into a no-win situation. The forces against him on both sides were relentless. He was smart enough and acute enough a politician to know that the black community was growing more unified every day and that in any future election he would be judged on this issue alone, and that whatever he had done in the past would have no bearing when he asked blacks for their vote. Nor did he think the average white citizen begrudged the demonstrators what they were demanding. His closest associates thought he wanted the crisis settled on terms satisfactory to the students, but that he wanted the merchants to make that decision themselves.

Will Campbell, watching the byplay, thought it was fascinating that the political system in Nashville seemed to be more modern and less feudal than the social-cultural system, as measured by what had happened at Vanderbilt and the resistance from men like John Sloan. It recalled something Charles Johnson, then the president of Fisk, had said about the gentry in Nashville when the Supreme Court had made its decision on *Brown:* "I'm not worried about ordinary white people in this state," the distinguished black sociologist told a friend at the time. "I'm worried about the Bourbons. In this state they're the ones who are unreconstructed."[2]

In early April the biracial committee handed down its report calling, as expected, for both a segregated and a desegregated section of every dining area. The students immediately rejected it for failing to deal with the moral issue at stake. Now they were working at two levels—renewed sit-ins as well as the boycott—which as Easter approached were taking a considerable toll on the merchants. Week by week they were getting a sense of the growing national interest in and sympathy for what they were doing, an interest reflected by the number of visiting national reporters like Harrison Salisbury, the legendary *New York Times* journalist, who came to interview them.

At first they had liked dealing with the national press, but in time they began to be jaundiced because it took up so much of their time. In early April a young reporter named Richard Whalen arrived on assignment from *Time* magazine to do what was likely to be a cover story on them. But Whalen soon found to his dismay that he could not get any of the students to meet with him. That stunned him—here he was a representative of *Time* with the potential for a cover story in his hip pocket, and the students did not have the time to meet with him. He soon called a local reporter and asked him to intervene on his behalf. The reporter called Diane Nash to argue Whalen's case and to pass on his estimate of the potential value in a *Time* cover, which in the early days of television was still considered a singularly powerful journalistic instrument. She, however, did not seem much impressed by the idea, although it would almost surely feature her. Their sched-ules were very full, she said. Finally, she relented: She and three of the others would see Whalen at 6:00 A.M., right before their regular meet-ing. The reporter relayed her message back to Whalen. "Six A.M.?" Whalen said. "The only time they can meet with me is six A.M.?" He was assured that he had gotten the time right. "They're going to win, aren't they?" he said.[3]

25

THE SIT-INS HAD HARDLY BEEN LOCALIZED IN NASHVILLE. CLEARLY, they were a powerful idea whose time had come. As such there were soon demonstrations taking place throughout the South, at college after college. Nashville had, however, become something of a focal point of the challenge because of the number of colleges involved, and because of the emerging quality of its leadership. In early April, working in connection with Martin Luther King's Southern Christian Leadership Conference, the Nashville group decided to meet with students from all over the South to see if they could coordinate their efforts and come up with the beginning of a national organization with a broad but flexible national agenda. The idea was that some kind of loose student confederation might be formed, perhaps independent of the SCLC, perhaps as a youth adjunct of it. The meeting was scheduled for April 15 and 16 at Shaw University in Raleigh, North Carolina. Most colleges sent two or three students; the Nashville group sent three cars carrying sixteen people. A young black student from Howard University named Hank Thomas had been impressed by the arrival of the Nashville delegation, by far the largest and most impressive of the many groups attending. The Nashville kids had walked in as if they owned the place, he remembered, and he thought of them as the Nashville All-Stars, cool, suave, with a certain deft but clearly discernible swagger. They were already famous; every young black student leader in America had seen them on television and read about them and admired them. Of all the young black students at the Raleigh meeting, they were the most battle hardened. He noticed something else about them as the weekend went on: In addition to the audacity which they exuded, they trusted each other. They not only had a certain exterior camaraderie, but there was a core trust. Either Jim Lawson had managed to teach them how to control their egos, or they had discovered that for themselves, he decided. In the past when he had dealt with various groups of black student leaders, Thomas had been all too aware of the constancy of the inner rivalries and jealousies, but these young people seemed wondrously immune to any of that. He found that he wanted to be like them, and he began to hang out with them in Raleigh, feeling more comfortable with them than with some of his peers from Howard.

Thomas was particularly struck by their confidence. He understood in some way that although they were roughly his same age, they were far ahead of him in their search for some kind of personal emancipation, and that they had already begun the process of breaking through the largely psychological barrier of fear which had imprisoned blacks in the past. It was, he thought, as if the Raleigh meeting was not so much a convention where everyone went to learn, but a seminar where the Nashville kids had come to teach. Besides, he thought, the women in the delegation, Diane Nash, Angeline Butler, and Peggy Alexander, were all beautiful. The three Fisk beauty queens, he thought of them, and he decided in his first day there that he was in love with all of them, but most particularly with Diane Nash. The idea that someone so beautiful could be so committed to the cause to which he was committed moved him greatly. He had found his ideal woman. He did not merely want to be like the Nashville kids, he wanted to be one of them, and after the Raleigh meeting, he wanted to become their partner in this exciting new movement.

The Nashville students, remembered Julian Bond, who was one of the leaders of the other large contingent, the Atlanta group, were not only savvy but markedly independent. Though Jim Lawson was their teacher and he was to be the keynote speaker at the meeting, they in no way deferred to him. "I was very taken by their group personality," Bond said years later, "not just their panache and the confidence they had in each other, but how far they had already gone. Unlike us they had really taken over the leadership of the sit-ins in Nashville. The older ministers there had been very good in giving them their head, and they were making all the critical decisions themselves. By contrast, in Atlanta, because King and his people were so powerful and so dominant, we had never truly taken over our own movement—we were still essentially subservient to the older generation." In addition

Bond, who was to emerge as one of the most talented, articulate, and beloved leaders of the larger student movement, was struck by the differences between his Atlanta group and the Nashville group, and how much they reflected the different characters of the two cities: "Atlanta was a mercantile city, a business city where money always talked, so the activists instinctively tried to use economic power against the establishment, to nickel-dime segregation to death. Nashville, with those church schools, and all that teaching by Jim Lawson, they used nonviolence as their weapon—they were going to love segregation to its death."[1]

The meeting was not without considerable political infighting, which revealed not only present but also future cracks within the black political world. In a way it served as an early dividing line between the fifties and the sixties; in the fifties it was the NAACP, using the courts, which had been the driving force of black protest; in the sixties, with some of the laws already on the books and with television having arrived as a means of reaching a national audience, it would be direct action, as utilized by King's SCLC, and the representatives of the student wing of the Movement coming together here, which would become the most important instrument of change. Many of the students assembling here, already steeped in the techniques of direct action, would rise to the fore of a new, ascending, ever more radical black leadership.

To the students the NAACP was old hat. Jim Lawson had been chosen to be the keynoter, and in addition to a passionate evocation of the powers of nonviolence, he had delivered a devastating denunciation of the NAACP for being too conservative. His speech cut to the great potential chasm of class within the black community; the NAACP, he said, had become the voice of the black bourgeoisie. Its strategy depended too much on the courts. The great resource which the NAACP was neglecting was the growing power of black people to act on their own, to call attention to grievous injustice and act "in a disciplined manner to implement the Constitution."[2] The tensions between the NAACP and the new activists were already considerable. To King's people the NAACP had seemed tired and timid, and Lawson himself had been a frequent critic, thinking the NAACP too polite in its challenge to American society and too accepting of the givens of American political life. In return Roy Wilkins, the executive secretary of the NAACP, had already written Lawson angrily protesting some of the things Lawson had said about the NAACP. But Lawson's speech at Shaw brought the existing tensions out in the open and damaged already bruised feelings. The NAACP, under constant assault from the racist forces in the Deep South, now found itself under assault within what it considered its own house, the world of black politics, where it had for so long dominated. It was no small irony that within three or four years, the same essential charge, that it too was the voice of the black bourgeoisie and that he was too middle-class, would be made against the SCLC and Martin Luther King by the more radical leaders of this new student group.

Among the young people meeting at Shaw, one of the first questions to be answered was whether the new group would be an appendage to King's SCLC or independent. Here the student instinct was for greater independence, and it was greatly aided by Ella Baker of the SCLC staff. She had always been somewhat skeptical of King and what she considered the cult of personality within the SCLC, and she urged the students to keep themselves separate. That jibed with the instincts of most of the veteran student leaders, who had already decided that they did not want to be controlled by the older generation, whether it was their parents, their school authorities, or the local black ministers themselves, no matter how admired they were. They, after all, were charting this new course only because those who had gone before them had not.

There were a number of other questions to be answered. The name of the organization, reflecting Lawson's commitment to nonviolence, was to be the Student Nonviolent Coordinating Committee, SNCC, or Snick, as it was pronounced. Because the two biggest delegations were from Atlanta and Nashville, it became clear that the first head would come from one of these two groups. Somehow an unofficial deal was brokered in which the headquarters would be located in Atlanta, and the first interim chairman would come from the Nashville delegation. Most of the Nashville students thought it would be Diane Nash. She more than any other young person had seemed to capture the imagination of those who admired the student part of the Movement, including the students themselves. But she had always tried to limit any attempt to create a cult of personality around herself, as, typically, when she attempted to dodge the *Time* cover story. On the morning they chose a chairman, she was late to the meeting, arriving after the balloting started; when the results were in, Marion Barry had won.

This surprised some of his Nashville colleagues. Barry had been one of the original Nashville leaders, but he had not been, it was believed, as strong and as forceful a figure as some of the others. But Lewis, Bevel, and Lafayette were seminarians; Rodney Powell was a soon-to-graduate medical student and would not have time to run an organization. And Diane was a woman, and there was some sensitivity to that—the Movement always had a powerful undercurrent of male chauvinism, and it was believed by some of her friends that this worked against her that weekend.

If Marion Barry was not viewed by some of his Nashville peers as a young man who was around for the heavy lifting, in the way that Nash and Lewis and Lafayette were, there was a sense that he was charming and amenable, and quite possibly the most naturally gifted politically among them. He was tall, good looking, with an innate natural ease with all kinds of people. "I used to say," Julian Bond noted some thirty-six years later, "that Marion was in training for being mayor of Washington even then when we first met at Shaw—he was a very good natural pol even back then, consultative, a good listener, very good at sensing who other people were and what they wanted to hear him say." He was twenty-four years old, a graduate student in chemistry at Fisk, and the fact that he was four or five years older than the others seemed important at the time. He not only dressed better and seemed smoother, but he knew how to comport himself. Few of them had done much traveling, just from home to school, but Marion, it was said, had actually visited California.

Marion Barry, Jr., was born in Itta Bena, Mississippi, the son of parents who were both sharecroppers. His mother was Mattie Carr, a young woman born in 1917 near Minter City, in rural Tallahatchie County; her parents had not been married and she had taken her mother's name, Carr, not her father's name, Bailey. She and her mother and her grandmother and some of her uncles had moved from town to town, or more properly, from one plantation to another in the Delta, following the available work, living in small towns like Coahoma, Hillhouse, and Alligator. With her were a brother and sister, the children of different fathers. Years later when she was asked if she had picked cotton as a girl, she answered, "Did I? Did I? Every day. Starting when I was four I went out in the fields with them when they picked, and when I was eight or nine I was picking myself."[3] It was what everyone did; therefore it was what you did as well. "You didn't look back and complain, and you didn't think of doing anything else because no one knew anything else."

She was twelve days short of being seventeen when she married Marion Barry, Sr. They had courted for some six months. He was forty-two, one of the best workers on the plantation, so respected that the white overseer occasionally put him in charge of other workers. Years later she was at something of a loss as to whether she had been in love with him or not. He had been good-looking, admired by almost everyone, and she was virtually a child. After they were first married, she had wanted to go out at night after dinner and play hide-and-seek with his nieces and nephews, but he would summon her to bed. "What does a child know about love and being married?" she said years later.

She did not think her life in Mississippi was hard because she knew nothing better. Every sharecropper knew that there was no chance to get ahead. That was rule one. No matter how hard you worked, there was virtually no money at the end of the year. It was built into the economics of the plantations that blacks would be cheated. If you had $500 left over you were lucky—mostly the white managers took the money you were supposed to have earned and checked it off against what they said you had spent at the commissary, and you were lucky not to come up a couple of hundred dollars short. You were supposed to owe them; they were not supposed to owe you. She and Marion Senior both worked hard but they often argued over money. Because he was her senior, he would try and take the money which was rightfully hers and she would tell the white boss not to give it to him because she knew that he would either drink it up or gamble it away. She always knew when he was going to go out and shoot craps. One time when he had gone by to pick up her $300, a year's wages, he found that the boss had already given it to her. He had turned on her in a fury.

When their son, Marion Junior, was an infant, they would take him in the fields with them, first in a galvanized bucket that they all washed in at home, and then in a sack that they put the cotton in.

Years later her son would tell *The Washington Post* that one of his earliest memories was a "lingering image of riding the tale of a cotton sack down a dark furrow at picking time."[4] Marion Barry, Sr., was, his wife thought, a good worker. He drank a lot, but never during the week, just on the weekend. Then he would gamble too. He did not beat her. Sometimes when he was drunk he wanted to, but because he had been drinking and she was stone-cold sober, she could handle him. In 1943, encouraged by an uncle who had found work across the river in West Helena, Arkansas, she and her family had moved there. Her uncle was doing well, working in a mill, using some of his money to build small houses for black people. But neither she nor her husband liked life in West Helena much. She was working in a café, making a little money; Marion Senior had a menial job at an oil refinery, which he did not like. He missed the rhythm of life in Mississippi. Whatever else, despite the constant hardships of the life there, it was home and it had its own pleasures. She took a less sentimental view; it might be home, but it was also the cotton fields, and there was no way to improve your life or your children's lives when you were a sharecropper in the cotton fields.

At that point the family split up: Accompanied by one of his daughters he went back to Mississippi, and his son never saw him again. Mattie Barry took the five-year-old Marion and grabbed a bus for Memphis, which was the major regional staging point for the final leg of the migration north. Her mother and her other daughter were already in Chicago. She intended to stay in Memphis only a few days; her mother, who was working in a hotel in Chicago as a domestic, was supposed to send her bus tickets. She was still waiting for the tickets to arrive a few days later when she got a job through an uncle who worked at a meat-packing house in Memphis. It was a good time for black women to get work—first the white men and now even the black men were being called into the service, and a lot of industries needed workers.

Hers was not a job for the squeamish. She worked the packing house floor, where they butchered cattle and hogs. Her job was to take a covering cloth and put it over the animal carcasses to absorb the blood. She wore boots, working in what was a constant pool of animal blood. If it was not work which would thrill most young American women of her age, she nonetheless liked it: It was better than the cotton fields, much less physically demanding, and you could make $40 a week, which was a great deal of money for any Southern black, man or woman, in 1943. Besides, there were other benefits. It meant that the family always had meat, because she like others there became adept at slipping meat into her boots.

In time she married a widower named Prince Jones, who was a top butcher at the packing house; between them they ended up with eight children, three of hers, three of his, and two together. Marion was the only boy. Soon after marrying Prince Jones, she left the packing plant and went into domestic work because it allowed her better hours to raise her own children. They lived simply but well. There was always enough meat. Marion Junior was the bright star of her life; when she had been pregnant, she had prayed every day for a boy. When he had been born, she believed it was a sign that God had heard her. He was always an industrious student and very ambitious, always eager to please her, she thought, whether by the part-time jobs he found or the good marks he got in school.

For three years, when Marion was in his early teens, he would work in the spring on nearby Mississippi and Arkansas plantations chopping cotton. That was harder work than picking; you had to get right in there at the root and cut out the weeds. He remembered an old, beaten-up truck which would appear in the black neighborhoods of Memphis at 6:00 A.M. to take the young kids into the fields for ten or eleven hours a day at about thirty cents an hour. He hated every minute of it. He vowed then and there that when he grew up, he would find work where he could use his brain.

He had thought of himself as being ambitious, a go-getter. He had become active in scouting and decided he would become an Eagle Scout. The only problem was the lifesaving requirement, which he considered the toughest of all the requisite merit badges. Black kids did not get many chances to learn to swim, and he was hardly an expert swimmer, and besides, he was tall and skinny, barely weighing 110 pounds. The part of the test he remembered as the most daunting was when he had to rescue a very heavy bag of sand: He had to throw a heavy bag of sand into the water, let it sink, and then dive in and lift it out. By the time he dove in, the bag seemed to weigh more than he did. He kept trying the routine, failing several times before he pulled it off. That made him, he believed, one of the first black Eagle Scouts in Tennessee.

He had always hated the symbols of segregation, which seemed to abound in Memphis, a city, he said years later, where they did not even let you go to the zoo except one day a week, Thursday. He despised the signs over the water fountains and remembered asking his mother what the difference was between colored water and white water. "I don't know, child," his mother had answered, "except that we can't drink white water." Even before he entered high school, Marion Barry had become a veteran of a civil rights skirmish. His initiation had come when he was still a paperboy delivering the two local Scripps-Howard papers, the morning *Commercial Appeal* and the afternoon *Press Scimitar.* In those days the papers offered prizes for entrepreneurial, go-getting young paperboys, the principal reward being an all-expenses-paid trip to New Orleans. When he first read of it, he had been enthused; it had sounded like a great trip. Then he had learned that it was for the white paperboys only. The black paperboys would receive bikes, which most of them already had. So he became the leader of a black paperboy protest. At first the company treated Barry and his friends with disdain; but in those days the routes were not computerized, and only the paperboys really knew who took the paper and who did not. Marion Barry was the first to realize the leverage this gave the paperboys. About a dozen of them refused to turn over their master lists to the company. They were essentially on strike. Eventually management settled: It could not send the black carriers to New Orleans, one official said, because it was segregated, but instead they could go to St. Louis. Marion Barry had not thought of himself as being political when he had started the protest, but he hated being cheated. The subsequent victory, he decided, was sweeter than the trip, and certainly sweeter than getting another bike.

He went to Booker T. Washington High School in Memphis, which was the leading school for blacks in that part of the state. That was in the days when black schools were really *run,* when discipline was total, and when no challenge to a teacher's authority was brooked. The principal, Blair Hunt, roamed the school, walking in and out of classes and in the halls carrying with him at all times a huge bell, which he would personally ring to announce the hourly change of class. His method of disciplining young would-be troublemakers was simple: Whatever the offense, he would simply hit you with the bell. His authority went unquestioned.

Marion Barry did well at Booker T. Washington, and his experiences as a teenager in the cotton fields had made him determined that he was going to go to college. He had heard a good deal about Fisk and Morehouse, and everyone in Memphis knew that being a Morehouse man was special. Morehouse men became doctors and lawyers. Morehouse, of course, was expensive, and though there was enough money for food in the Barry home, there was very little money for college. But Morehouse had a work program, which was attractive to some young men with marginal financial resources. In the summer after senior year in high school, certain select high school graduates could go up to Connecticut to work in the tobacco fields around Simsbury; the money they earned there would be directly applied to their college costs and take care of about 85 percent of the tuition. Marion Barry checked out the program: You were supposed to bring boots, a rain hat, and a raincoat. He spoke with a friend of his who had done it, and he said it was exhausting work. As far as he was concerned, Marion Barry had already spent enough time in the fields. LeMoyne, a local black college, cost only $1,000 a year, and had offered him a scholarship equal to roughly half the tuition. He chose LeMoyne.

The house of Mattie and Prince Jones was hardly a political one. No one subscribed to the *Chicago Defender* or the *Pittsburgh Courier.* Even though both parents worked and Jones had what was considered a good job for a black man, their lives, with eight children in the home, were largely about survival, of having just enough money to pay for the basics of daily life. Politics was a luxury. But Marion Barry, born in 1936, child of the cotton fields, had caught the first wave of the post–World War II change in black life; he graduated from Booker T. Washington in 1954, which was the year of *Brown* and when, particularly with the young, expectations among blacks were beginning to undergo a dramatic change. He was, in some way he did not entirely understand himself, race conscious as the previous generation in his family had never been able to afford to be. He seethed at all racial slights when he was young. He had worked waiting tables at the local American Legion post, a place, as far as he was concerned, which was a citadel of raw racial condescension. He was, he later remembered, always *boy* or *nigger* to the tables of Legionnaires wanting drinks, and he had hated it. He always tried to exact his revenge, either, as he once told *The Washington Post,* by spitting in the food or scamming the drinkers, cheating them on the chits they used to buy drinks, aware that the more they drank, the less they remembered the number of chits used, and by making a deal with the bartender, who would turn the chits into cash—and then split the money with Barry. That was his way of getting even.[5]

All of this had added an edge to him. He might, as a student at LeMoyne, be something of a big man on campus, a member of a popular fraternity, a member of the track team (he was not, he later noted, very good at it, but it was a way of getting a free meal at school every day), but he was also political and he had become the head of the LeMoyne chapter of the NAACP, which in a Deep South city like Memphis in 1957 meant that he was in the political avant-garde. In the late winter of 1958, as he was nearing graduation, the chairman of the LeMoyne Board of Trust, Walter Chandler, argued in federal court against an NAACP suit to integrate the city's bus lines. Memphis was still very much a Deep South city, and if the power of the old Crump machine had been broken statewide, it still held power there. Chandler, a former mayor and former congressman, posts achieved through the auspices of Crump, argued in a way that was singularly offensive to local blacks: The reason for discrimination, he said, was the innate inferiority of black people themselves: "If the NAACP would expend more of its efforts in trying to elevate the Negro morally, mentally, educationally and health-wise, it would be of far more benefit to the race. I have heard it said that the Negro is a second-class citizen. If he is a second-class citizen, it is just because he wants to be, and has applied the label to himself. . . . The Negro is our brother, but he should be treated as a younger brother, and not as an adult."[6]

For young black students, already frustrated by the lack of progress in their lives—four years after *Brown,* Memphis was trying to hold the line on buses, let alone schools—a statement like this, coming from the head of their college's board of trustees, seemed particularly cruel. Barry, as head of the college's NAACP chapter, immediately drafted a stinging rebuke to Chandler. "We feel that it is humiliating and embarrassing that such an obvious demagogue should have [a] direct connection with our college, especially when this institution stresses to its students the importance of fighting for equal rights." Chandler's resignation should be requested immediately, he wrote. "Either that or the LeMoyne faculty should begin teaching the importance of second-class citizenship." An immense furor followed: In the eyes of the conservative Memphis establishment, it was a classic example of a young black man not knowing his place. For a time the board thought of demanding his expulsion, but Hollis Price, the black president, had argued that if Barry were expelled, it might cause an even greater commotion and trigger additional protests. Instead the board produced a statement calling Barry's letter "impertinent, ill-advised, and did not provide facts on which the conclusion it reached was based."[7] A week after his letter was made public, Roy Wilkins, the head of the NAACP, came to Memphis for a previously scheduled appearance and stood with Barry on the stage of the Masonic Temple and said that Barry had the courage of a lion. It had been his first real taste of fame and celebrity, and he had enjoyed it. He was allowed to graduate, which meant that he was free to accept the scholarship he had won to do graduate work in chemistry at Fisk. He entered Fisk in the fall of 1958, and a year later became one of the sit-in leaders.

He had arrived at Fisk thinking he was going to be some kind of scientist, but the pull of the Lawson group was fateful. He was extremely popular within the group, a rare member who could just as readily have been a traditional campus leader. He could jive with those who liked to jive and party at the black fraternity houses, but he was far more politically committed than most other fraternity leaders. Everyone in the group knew how he had stood up to the LeMoyne board. He would tell as well how his draft board had almost made him pay the price for his dissidence. Suddenly, after the LeMoyne incident, his 2-S deferment, which most college students received automatically, was about to be revoked. He had already had problems with the draft board: When he had first appeared before it to get his deferment, one of the members had insisted on calling him *boy,* and he had answered that his name was not Boy, it was Marion Barry, Jr. Then when he had caused trouble at LeMoyne, his draft board had clearly decided to make him pay. So he had quickly gone to Nashville and registered there, and that had helped keep him out of the service.

26

KELLY MILLER SMITH, IRRITATED BY THE SLOW MOVEMENT OF THE mayor's committee, more and more convinced that it was one more white dodge, was nonetheless sure that the students were going to win. The white resistance was crumbling; he could sense that from the personal pleas he received from some of the merchants to do something to end the boycott. The students, by contrast, seemed stronger than ever. Slowly the white business leadership was beginning to understand two things: first, that the students were not going to go away and second, that they now represented the entire black community. As the black protesters continued to march with dignity and the white hoodlums remained a problem (and an embarrassment), he believed, the city's leadership would eventually turn on the white troublemakers.

In the end, he thought with no small amount of amusement, they would do it not for moral reasons but for commercial ones. He had, by dint of his own melancholy struggles with the white establishment, a shrewd sense of how it worked. At first it had been the sit-in protesters who had been the threat to the existing comfortable order, and the anger of the business leadership had been aimed at them; but gradually that was changing, and now it was the white hoods who threatened the daily commercial life of the downtown area, and so the anger would be aimed at them instead. He had seen this scenario before in the South, and he could already sense it happening in Nashville.

The demonstrators, he believed, needed some kind of galvanizing incident. The kind of act, he thought, which forced decent but conventional men to act when they did not want to act, to make a choice when they preferred to remain silent. The danger was that that kind of event—one which might shock the conscience of both communities, white as well as black—might prove to be so violent that lives, most certainly black lives, would be lost. They had been extremely fortunate so far, Smith believed. The violence inflicted on the young people had been quite cruel but largely marginal: cigarettes extinguished on the back of their heads, hot coffee poured on them, and flash beatings, designed not just to inflict pain but also to let the attacker make his own getaway. Smith hoped their luck held.

Early on the morning of April 19, the galvanizing event took place. At 5:30 A.M. someone drove by the home of Z. Alexander Looby, the city's preeminent black lawyer, and tossed a bomb through the window of his home. The bomb was extremely powerful and it almost completely destroyed Looby's home. More than 140 windows in a building at nearby Meharry Medical College were broken, and a number of students suffered cuts from glass shattered in the blast. Amazingly, neither Looby nor his wife was injured. (Looby rebuilt the house, helped by donations from the community. In the reconstructed version, the side of the house which faced the street had no windows. Even with that architectural nod to the possibilities of future violence, Looby was not able to buy insurance for his new home.) The effect of the bombing on the two communities was immediate and defining. It united and mobilized the black community at an even higher level than before, and it struck a death knell to continued white resistance. From then on, Greenfield Pitts of Harveys later said, the deed was done; it deprived those who opposed the desegregation of the lunch counters of their last remaining social and moral legitimacy.

If Kelly Miller Smith had become the symbol of an ascending church-driven black leadership, then Zephaniah Alexander Looby was the prototype of the lonely black leader of the past, a man who had waged the war against racial injustice for the previous thirty years against all odds, pressures, and threats. His personal courage was legendary in both white and black communities. Looby and many of his generation in other cities were lawyers, and their job was to defend the most vulnerable citizens in their region—blacks. These leaders were on the defensive. By contrast, the new generation of men, like Kelly Smith and Jim Lawson, were going on the offensive.

Looby was a revered figure in black Nashville, always known as Mr. Looby. He was sophisticated, erudite, and tough-minded. He had known a lifetime of racism and had never let it dent his inner strength.

When he had appeared in court once, an opposing attorney, according to legend, had complained bitterly of his presence. "I refuse to be
in a courtroom with a nigger," he had said. "I agree with that," Looby
said. "I won't be in with one either." He was from the West Indies,
raised on the tiny and extremely poor island of Dominica; his mother
had died in the childbirth of a sibling when he was six; his father operated a few fishing boats. He was not a boy who liked to fish, nor did he
want to work in the fields. What he loved to do was read, and equally
important, to read the classics. In 1913, when he was fifteen, his father
died, and he signed on as a cabin boy with a whaling ship; when it
docked in New Bedford, Massachusetts, he jumped ship and took on
a series of menial jobs designed to support himself. His one goal was
to gain an education, and eventually he attended Howard, where he
received his bachelor's degree; after that he had gone to Columbia,
where he got his law degree. In 1928 he had arrived in Tennessee,
taught for a time at Fisk, and then went to Memphis to practice law.
There he had immediately discovered that his and Ed Crump's views
of how a black lawyer should operate differed greatly, and he returned
to Nashville. In Nashville and in the surrounding small towns he took
on an endless series of difficult cases where, more often than not, he
defended indigent blacks accused of terrible crimes before juries
which were all white. Sometimes, he said late in his life, you could cut
the hatred in the room with a knife. When the Supreme Court ruled
on *Brown,* he had immediately filed suit in Nashville on behalf of a
black barber named A. Z. Kelley, whose son had been denied access
to a nearby white school. That had started the beginnings of local
school desegregation.

From the start of the sit-ins, Looby had been an early and enthusiastic backer of the students and had represented them in all their
court cases. That had made him somewhat unusual among the generation of black lawyers, almost all of them connected to the NAACP,
who had been fighting the battle in the courts for some twenty or
more years. Other prominent black lawyers such as the legendary
Thurgood Marshall, who had argued almost all of the pioneering civil
rights cases before the Supreme Court, were extremely wary of the
direct-action route now being taken by the ministers and students.
For it meant that blacks were violating the law—and as far as these
older NAACP lawyers were concerned, in recent years the law had

become the black man's best friend. Marshall regarded the sit-ins with great skepticism. He felt there was no need to go forward with direct action. All they needed, he believed, was to take one case to the Supreme Court. That summer at a Fisk Race Relations Institute meeting, Marshall had turned on C. T. Vivian, upbraiding him: "You, sir, are the most dangerous man in all Nashville." (Later that year Marshall apologized to Vivian.)

But Looby was different. Unlike many of his peers, Looby from the start had no doubts about the new direction. He realized how frustrating the legal path was turning out to be for ordinary blacks and he was quite willing to challenge white domination on other fronts. He greatly admired the students, and he liked the pressure they were subjecting city officials and merchants to. To the black community, given Looby's status as a living local legend, the bombing of his house was the most immediate and direct threat imaginable. Only a comparable assault upon Kelly Miller Smith might have affected the black community in the same way. That day the central committee had already scheduled a 6:00 A.M. meeting. Shocked by the news, the members had decided to go for what they hoped would be a massive march. They would neither talk nor sing as they marched; it would be a silent march. They hoped to meet the mayor on the courthouse steps in the early afternoon.

That march became, the students later decided, their finest hour in the Nashville struggle. It was undertaken with great uncertainty, for the news of the Looby bombing had happened too late to make the morning *Tennessean,* and therefore the leadership feared people would not know what had happened. But on this day the word of mouth was formidable. *Everyone* knew what had happened. The response was overwhelming. In the past the largest march had been about four hundred people; this time as the marchers left Tennessee State, there were already some fifteen hundred; by the time they reached the courthouse there were some three to four thousand.

Their faces that day were memorable, reflecting a sense of anger mixed with resolve. The confrontation began even as only half of the marchers had reached the courthouse square. The mayor, whom they had asked to meet them, was standing on top of the courthouse steps as they arrived. He could look directly in front of him and see well more than a thousand black faces, and then he could look out beyond them and see a line of blacks stretching well into the distance. It was a singularly imposing sight: He was looking at nothing less than his political future. If ever a moment of history had imposed itself right in front of a bright, young politician, this was it.

As the crowd waited there for the mayor, one young white man who had become increasingly influential in determining the music that they sang pulled the guitar off his back and began playing a song. The name of the young man was Guy Carawan, and he was an old-fashioned white radical troubadour, a lineal descendant of the famed Woody Guthrie and Pete Seeger. He came equipped with his guitar, a pleasant twangy back-country singing voice, and a knowledge of protest-folk songs of the ages. At the time he was teaching at the famous (and more often than not in terms of the politics of Tennessee, the infamous) Highlander Folk School in East Tennessee, in no small part because Seeger had told him he ought to visit there. At Highlander an old-fashioned radical named Myles Horton conducted leadership courses on integration. It was at Highlander that a Montgomery seamstress named Rosa Parks had taken lessons on civil disobedience just before refusing to give up her seat on a bus in December 1955. The school, located near Monteagle, Tennessee, was a particular target for conservative Tennessee politicians, not that that bothered Horton or Carawan. When Carawan journeyed to Nashville, which he did more and more frequently because of the sit-ins, he always stayed with the Reverend C. T. Vivian, and on this day Vivian had reminded him to bring his guitar, not that Carawan needed much in the way of reminders, for his guitar was always at the ready. The strain he chose, once called "I'll Overcome Someday," was an old black church song. "I'll be all right, I'll be all right some day," it had once gone. "Deep in my heart, I do believe, I will be all right some day. . . . I will see His face, I'll see His face some day. . . ." Some fifteen years earlier, during a strike of black women in the Food and Tobacco Union in Charleston, South Carolina, the song had become politicized, without any subtraction of its essential religiosity and faith.

From the start, their singing had been a critical part of their demonstrations. When they had been arrested, they had instantly become the jail choir, and that had not only given them strength, it had helped bond them together. Typically Candie Anderson, a young white exchange student from Pomona, had written her own version of a Wobbly song called "They Go Wild Over Me" that they had sung from the jail: "Oh the manager, he went wild over me / When I went one afternoon and sat for tea / He was breathin' mighty hard / When his pleas I'd disregard / He went wild, simply wild over me." Their singing often had roots in the past, in the church songs their parents had sung when they were young, which gave them strength as they had set out for their demonstrations. It had reassured them that they were not alone; they had not only one another, but their religion.

On this particular day as they looked to their leaders surrounding the mayor, their music was to become even more important. "We shall overcome," Guy Carawan began to sing as he picked his guitar. "We shall overcome some day . . . Oh deep in my heart, I do believe, that we shall overcome some day." Some of the leaders, like Bevel and Lafayette and Lewis, who had already heard the song at Highlander, took it up immediately. From the first instant they heard it, the young seminarians knew that it was perfect for the Movement; its words, its chords, above all its faith seemed to reflect their determination and resonate to their purpose perfectly. (One reason it fit so well was because they could always add lyrics. Just a few weeks earlier, local law enforcement officers had raided Highlander, forcing its staff to sit in the darkness for several hours before arresting them. Even as they had sat there singing, they had added new words: "We are not afraid, we are not afraid today . . .")

The others who had heard it before but had not sung it during a demonstration took it up. Suddenly the sound seemed to sweep across the courthouse square. Verse followed verse, the sound becoming ever more powerful. "We are not alone," Carawan sang, "we are not alone today . . ." It was a modern spiritual which seemed to have roots in the ages, the perfect song for this particular moment. It was easy to sing; it expressed not just a sense of long-suffering grievance but an optimistic belief that these grievances could and would be corrected. It was religious and gentle, just right for a Gandhian protest, but its force and power were not to be underestimated; it not only emboldened those who were setting out on this dangerous path, but it helped affect and bring in those on the sidelines, those watching television at home who had seen young blacks, immaculately behaved and dressed, beaten up by white thugs or cops, thereupon sing this haunting song. It was an important moment: The students now had their anthem.

Even as the students were singing, C. T. Vivian, standing next to the mayor on the steps, began by reading a prepared statement sharply critical of the mayor for his failure to lead in the past few months. West quite angrily denied that there was a failure of leadership. "I deny your statement and resent to the bottom of my soul the implications of what you have just read," he said. He tried to continue speaking, but Vivian, fiery and wired for the moment, was immediately on top of him. "Prove it, Mayor! Prove the statement is wrong!" The two men began to argue until another minister moved forward to restrain the volatile Vivian.

Angered by Vivian's challenge, West tried to defend himself, and tried to move the subject to safer grounds, the tradition of Christianity in the black church.

"I ask each of you to search your soul and heart—think about being better Christians. We are all Christians together. Let us pray together." As he said that, a Fisk graduate student named Earl Mays yelled out, "What about eating together?" West ignored him and started debating with Vivian again, who asked the mayor if he thought segregation was moral. "No," the mayor said, "it is wrong and immoral to discriminate."

It was at that point that Diane Nash took over the dialogue. Like the others she had been scared that they would have too small a turnout because of the timing. Then she and Rodney Powell had gone to the starting point, and they had seen more than a thousand people already gathered. She had been thrilled, at that moment sure that they were going to win. Now, standing on top of the courthouse steps, facing the mayor, she who had once been so afraid of confrontation with powerful white men could look at Ben West and see how vulnerable he was. He was just another white politician who could not bring himself to do what he knew was the right thing. As she stood there she found that she was tired of all the wasted words, and tired of West behaving like a politician instead of a human being. He was going to recite, she was sure, yet again his I-integrated-the-airport-lunchroom-for-you speech.

This is getting us nowhere, she thought; here we are arguing the past on this day when hoodlums have just tried to kill Mr. Looby. She had not prepared a speech. What she said next, she later noted, came to her like a divine inspiration. Or if not divine inspiration, at least a remembrance of what Jim Lawson had taught them, that they had to get people—those on the sidelines and their enemies alike—to see one another as human beings instead of enemies. So she asked Ben West to use the prestige of his office to end racial segregation. West immediately did. "I appeal to all citizens to end discrimination, to have no bigotry, no bias, no hatred," he said.

"Do you mean that," she pushed ahead, "to include lunch counters?" She had no idea where these words were coming from or where they were taking her.

"Little lady," the mayor answered, "I stopped segregation seven years ago at the airport when I first took office, and there has been no trouble there since." That, he thought, should end it.

But she was too nimble for him. She had one more question. "Then, Mayor, do you recommend that the lunch counters be desegregated?"

"Yes," he found himself saying. She had ambushed him morally, nothing less than that, and then as he realized what he had said, he tried to amend it slightly. "That's up to the store managers, of course." But the deed was done. Finally, after three months they had flushed him out and he had lent his voice to their cause. She had spoken to him not as a politician but as a human being and it had worked. A moment later an A&I student named Cupid Poe asked the mayor if he had just recommended ending eating-facility segregation. "Right, that is absolutely right!" West said. Then the black leaders and the mayor started embracing each other. Diane Nash was thrilled. On this day, she believed, she had been able to behave as a leader should behave, getting everything right, as if by the purest of moral instincts. They had won, she was sure. The next day's *Tennessean* banner headline said it all: INTEGRATE COUNTERS—MAYOR.[1]

Within a few days a plan was worked out and integration of the counters quietly began. It was, Greenfield Pitts of Harveys added, not just the right thing to do commercially, but the right thing to do morally. As for himself, he added, he was tired of all those important and influential white people who went around saying that they knew what black people wanted but who did not deign to talk to black people. It was time, Pitts said, to find out what black people wanted by talking to them openly and listening to them. There had not been a lot of listening taking place in the South in a long time, he said, and it was time for white people to start. It was time, he added, for white people to try and put themselves in the position of black people in the South and understand what their lives were like.

BOOK

2

THE VALLEY
OF THE SHADOW
OF DEATH

27

IT WAS A GREAT VICTORY, JOHN LEWIS THOUGHT, REMEMBERING THE
moment when Diane Nash had faced down Ben West on the courthouse steps, although it was only the first step. Thirty-five years later
Lewis could remember almost everything about that moment. Diane's
performance had been nothing less than brilliant. She had managed to
get the mayor to move past his politics to the very core of his humanity. That was the whole purpose of the Lawson ethic, Lewis thought,
to make people who were nominally your opponents get outside of
their normal vision and see the human dimension wrought by segregation. It was one thing to talk about it in workshops, but Diane, in the
most heated confrontation imaginable, had actually done it.

John Lewis liked this new community which he had become a part
of; it existed not on the basis of geography—of people living in one
town or coming from one particular college—but rather, he believed,
on spirituality, of people brought together by a cause and willing to
sacrifice all their other, more selfish needs for a common good.
Because of it he had a wealth of new friends, and they had become, in
the shared purpose and shared dangers of the past few months, more
than friends, more like family. If anything the pull of his new life in
Nashville was becoming stronger than the pull of his former life in
rural Alabama; he was in some way which would be difficult to
explain to strangers closer to his new friends in the Movement than he
was to most members of his own family. One of the hardest things he
had had to do was tell his mother, when she had asked him to withdraw from the sit-ins, that he was going to continue, that he was acting
not for himself but for all of them, all of the Lewises and all their
neighbors. He understood in some way the change taking place in
him, that he was gradually being pulled into a new, different world

which was both exciting and terrifying. He knew, even as they had won the victory on the issue of lunch counters, that he had found a defining purpose in his life, one which combined his deepest religious convictions with a growing political commitment. The very struggle for lunch counter rights was almost miraculous in the way it had transformed him and his sense of self: In rural Pike County he had barely existed as a person, an almost invisible black child of an almost invisible poor black farmer. He had no voting rights, precious few educational rights, and almost no social rights. But because of what they had just done in Nashville, he was now a proud young man, someone to be reckoned with, a full-fledged American citizen capable of standing and fighting not just for his own rights but for those of others. He very much liked being the new John Lewis, a young man who had been set free within himself. But the real battle, he knew better than most as a child of the rural Deep South, had barely begun. The terrible price of winning, he understood, was that you could not stop now; to the victor went the far greater obligation of carrying the struggle into the Deep South and far greater danger.

It would be hard to imagine a purer product of the Deep South than John Lewis in the spring of 1960. He was so country, so simple, so completely unpretentious that it was easy to underestimate the powerful force, and considerable intelligence, which had always guided him. Over the years, a surprising number of people, white and black alike, would make that mistake, would judge John Lewis by his exterior, by the fact that he did not seem to speak well and stumbled over certain words, only to discover much later that they had completely misread him, that he was a person of singular purpose, unshakable in his beliefs, limitless in his faith, and with sufficient intelligence, at each critical junction in his life, to know the difference between right and wrong and between a good man and a bad man. Nothing deterred him from what he believed was right; he was, when the larger purpose of the cause was at stake, fearless.

No one loved being in Nashville more than he did. He still loved his family, but he went back to Alabama less frequently. He had always hated life on the farm. "I was always," he said later of those years when he was supposed to help out his family with the daily chores, "a complaining child. I complained all the time because I did not want to go out and work in the fields, which we all had to do in order to survive." Nashville set him free because it set his mind free. John, known to his family as Robert (he became John only when he went off to school in Nashville), was by his own admission the laziest of Buddy and Willie Mae Lewis's ten children. From the moment when he had been old enough to start accepting responsibility for even the lightest chores, he had complained, claiming that it was too hot out to pick, too hot even to carry water to the others. His mother would try and explain to him how hard it was on all of them, that they were poor and that therefore everyone had to do his or her share, but it seemed not to dent him. "We're working like slaves out there in the sun. It's like olden times in the Bible. It's like slavery," he would say to his mother, and she would tell him yes, perhaps it seemed like it, but they had no other way of surviving, and they had to eat. They could fast, he answered, and the way he mispronounced the word, it sounded like *feast*.[1]

When the picking season conflicted with the school calendar—at cotton picking time, or peanut picking time—and he, like almost all the children of the black rural South, had to be held out of school for a few days, he would try and sneak off to school instead. "Robert," his mother would say, "you're going to have to stay home from school tomorrow and help pick the peanuts," and he would nod his assent; then, in the morning after breakfast, as the others were getting ready to work, he would slip off from them and when he saw the school bus coming, he would run out and get on, knowing he was disobeying family rules but willing to take the risk involved because he so greatly preferred school. His brothers and sisters would try to warn their parents—"Momma and Daddy, he's got his school clothes on, he's plannin' to go to school"—but his parents were curiously tolerant. This child was different, they decided. They never came down that hard on him, and they did not as others might have, drive off to school to bring him back and punish him. The next day they would simply say, "Robert, we really need you today," and sufficiently chastened, he would return to the fields for the day, though he remained ready to skip the fields on the following day. "Let him go to school," his older brother Edward said. "He's no help out in the fields. All he does is fuss. It's better out there without him." He was the third child of ten. Edward, who was partially deaf, was always irritated with him. If they were chopping cotton Edward stayed on his case: "Come on, catch up,

Robert, you've got to catch up, you're not pulling your load!" Even on their day off, when the other boys would play baseball, he would be by himself reading or practicing at being a preacher. It was, his sister Ore noted, as if he had always been a grown-up, never a child.[2]

He did not like the heat or the hard work or the snakes, which turned up all the time when they plowed the fields. His mind was always elsewhere. He lived a fantasy life in which the primary objective was to get out of Pike County. He and a cousin of his had even decided how they would do it. They were going to saw down one of the great pine trees and cut it into pieces and make a wooden bus and drive away to a place they had heard about called California. What saved him in those days were the chickens. He loved raising them and they became his primary responsibility—his family was delighted that he had finally found something he liked to do, and so he became the chicken man when he was about nine years old. He took his chicken responsibilities very seriously. An electric chicken hatcher cost about $19, as advertised in The Wish Book, which was what the members of the Lewis family called the Sears, Roebuck catalog, because it was filled with all the things they dreamed about. John Lewis wished for nothing else so much, no toy or baseball, as an electric chicken hatcher. Without one he was forced to exploit the sitting hens by switching their eggs so they would be more productive. This, of course, exhausted them and caused the hens to lose weight. His other great passion as a boy was his religion. He became something of a boy preacher when he was about five, after he had been given his first Bible. As a little boy he often went to church on Sunday, and then spent the rest of the week repeating what the preacher had said, forcing the younger children to listen to him. He loved the game of church. He often baptized his sisters' dolls. Soon, with the coming of his chicken duties, he began preaching to the chickens, telling them to lead a good life, not to fight among each other. If a chicken died, he would deliver the chicken eulogy, and then he would bury the chicken in the Lewis chicken cemetery.

He had told his mother early on that he intended to become a preacher, and at first she was a bit skeptical. She told him that people could not just go out and announce that they were going to be preachers, but that God had to call you to be a preacher; but gradually, watching him, seeing how different he was from his brothers and sisters, how he was always with a book, she decided that in some way the Lord had touched her son.[3]

The one thing he disliked about being a chicken man was that he could not trust his parents. Because the Lewis family lived constantly on the edge of survival, and under the continual threat of losing their land, they were always short of cash and were always trading his beloved chickens for food. There was a significant difference of opinion in the Lewis family about the chickens: To him they were pets; to his parents, they were food, or barter. So when a chicken disappeared in the middle of the day, traded off by his parents in exchange for sugar or flour to the man who drove the rolling store (an old bus converted into a store), he protested. As far as he was concerned the chickens were his. His parents, in turn, tried to explain that his chickens were not pets, that they were critical to this poor family's food production, and by bartering them they could help bring other kinds of food to the table. There was a ritual to these disagreements. He would come back from school to find one of his chickens gone and would protest at once, and his mother would explain that the family had to eat. He would then refuse to talk to anyone during dinner.

Sometimes, looking back, he was more than a little embarrassed by his behavior in a family which was so poor and in which everyone had to work so hard. His parents were both hardworking people. In 1944, when he was four, they had achieved a singular success by moving up from being sharecroppers by buying the land they worked. They had bought 110 acres for $300 from a white family named Hickman, who no longer seemed to want or need the land. The buying of the land was a momentous family occasion, and though John was quite young, he could remember the excitement of his parents, their sense of liberation as they moved one step farther from economic servitude on that day. He remembered how his family had packed up all their belongings and moved from the tiny shack they lived in to another home about a mile and a quarter away, to a house which had once been rather stately, a part of a once-grand plantation, with a huge fireplace and high ceilings and a tin roof.

Above all he remembered his father's pride on that day: They were no longer sharecroppers. They were owners now, not tenants. Yet owning the land, they still lived at the mercy of not merely a hostile white power structure, which made black ownership of land a danger-ous venture, but at the mercy of the elements as well. For a drought or too much rain could quickly return them to sharecropping status, even if they worked hard and were careful in their bookkeeping.

The land they bought had not been cared for and they had to clear it. This land was called the New Ground. They raised hogs and cows and chickens, and cotton and peanuts. Willie Mae Lewis was said to pick cotton as fast as most men in Pike County. She could pick one hundred pounds a day easily. But that was not good enough. She and Buddy, her husband, decided that if she could pick 150 or 160 pounds a day, and he could pick 250, then that would give them 400 pounds between them, instead of the 300 which most hardworking black cou-ples were willing to settle for.

In addition to working in the fields, she managed to cook and can food. If she was not cooking or working in the fields, she was sewing for her ten children, whom she raised with endless patience and a con-stancy of love and warmth. Willie Mae Lewis never complained. When he looked back at her life, John Lewis never understood how she made it through the day. She was a Carter, and there were Carters scattered throughout the region. On the small family table there were photos, which showed, among others, her Grandfather Carter, a man who was virtually white. If you had seen him without the other mem-bers of his family in the picture, Lewis thought, you would have thought he *was* a white man. That meant for sure, John Lewis believed, that his mother's great-grandfather had been white. It was a very sensitive subject with her. Though she liked to talk about the past and about her family, it was the one thing about which she remained closed-mouthed. Clearly, he believed, it stirred up all kinds of images of those terrible days on the plantation, when white owners could leverage their way sexually with black women as they wanted.

Willie Mae Lewis was, for her limited station, an invincible person, and a woman of great faith. Her religion was central to her life and the essence of her strength. Once later in her life when one of her ten chil-dren had died, her daughter-in-law Lillian Lewis had tried to console her. "All I know how to do," Willie Mae Lewis had told Lillian, "is pray."[4] That was the source of her strength, praying for a better day, and believing it was coming. Because of that faith she believed things were going to get better. She talked that way all the time: The children had to work hard and study because things were going to get better, and they had better be prepared for the day when they did. She had always wanted to go on in school herself, but had been forced after the eighth grade to go work the fields, and in addition, she had been responsible for raising her younger brothers and sisters, as often happened in black families. The sign of that longing for more education, John believed, was in her handwriting, which was quite beautiful. As a grown man, when he looked at her handwriting, he saw the person she had longed to be. But she had readily transferred her own dream to him.

She had considerable faith in her religion and a greater belief in the power of prayer than in the workings of the American government. That allowed her to believe in the future, and to work as hard as she did. She believed as strongly as her son did in the idea of a college education, which was surely why she allowed him to sneak off to school instead of working the fields. "Once you learn something, Robert, once you get something inside your head, no one can take it away from you," she liked to say. One of her favorite slogans was "Be particular." That was a phrase which applied to all situations: It meant be careful, and be responsible for yourself, and always be well prepared. (Years later, when her son was a senior member of Congress and taking on his archfoe, the conservative Congressman Newt Gingrich, she would often remind him, now a man in his fifties, "Now, Robert, I want you to be particular with that man." That meant he was to be careful in his criticism of Gingrich; any attack had better be factually accurate.)

His mother, he thought, had a very positive vision of what a black child in America could become, even in rural Alabama in the early fifties. His father's vision was in some ways more narrow. Eddie Lewis, who was known as Buddy, was a good man. Like his wife he was hardworking and he never complained. He was not particularly tall, about five-six, but he was proud, and diligent. The amazing thing about him, John Lewis decided years later, was that he went out every day and worked as hard as he did in such difficult conditions. His life was never going to get better, yet he never became depressed. He never turned in anger on his own, as did so many black men caught in a hopeless, brutal grind, taking out their frustrations and disappointments on their own families.

The economic realities his father faced, John realized later, were unrelentingly hard. It was never a question of getting ahead. Rather, it was always a question of trying not to fall too far behind. Everything was about survival. The debt was constant, for feed, for fertilizer, for the animals. He needed to borrow constantly to get the things from the Sears catalog which could get them through one more year. Yet John's memories of his father were of his optimism, his belief that he could raise his family successfully, and his unwillingness to complain about his life or the difficulty of being black.

John's lasting memories as he was growing up were of his parents talking together at night, constantly planning what they could do if the crops were good, if they could only get three tons of peanuts that year instead of two and a half. It was the talk of *if,* for they lived in a world bordered by if's rather than constancies. *If* his mother could pick a little more than even her high norm, say two hundred pounds of cotton a day in the next couple of days, perhaps they could buy another mule. *If* he could pick an extra bale of cotton there might be furniture. *If* they picked an extra five hundred pounds of peanuts there might be more clothes for the children. Everything was ticketed, but everything was always possible. But everything also depended on the vagaries of the great *if.* John's mother watched Buddy's shopping like a hawk, worried that he might become too grandiose when he went into town and buy too much feed or even a new wagon.

John Lewis had been given a Bible when he was five and he had begun preaching to his younger siblings and cousins, lining them up in the family's homemade chairs. All over America other children were playing cowboys and Indians, but John Lewis and his siblings and cousins were playing preacher and congregation. Soon everyone in the family, grown-ups and children, started calling him Preacher. When he was sixteen he preached his first formal sermon. It was at the Macedonia Baptist Church, a Sunday evening sermon after an earlier, morning sermon by the local minister. John wore his best clothes, a dark blue suit, a white shirt, and a blue tie. His mother was nervous. "Are you prepared, Robert?" she kept asking. Everyone in the whole community knew that Robert, this most serious child, Buddy and

Willie Mae's boy, was going to preach a trial sermon. As he stood there preaching from the Old Testament, from Samuel, about a mother praying for a son, he could look out and recognize almost everyone in the congregation. Afterward he was more convinced than ever that this was the right course.

The religion he had grown up with was old-fashioned and literal, and the more emotional the congregation became on a Sunday, the more successful the sermon was judged to be. But even as a teenager his view of the ministry was broadening. In his junior year in high school John Lewis had turned on the radio one Sunday to WRMA, which was the black soul station, to hear the guest sermon. On that particular Sunday the speaker was Martin Luther King, about whom John Lewis had heard so much, but whom he had never heard preach. King's sermon that day was on Paul's letter to the Corinthians. But Martin King was not talking about a letter written thousands of years ago; his was a modern letter, one that could have been written yesterday, about segregation in modern America. John Lewis found the sermon thrilling, and he realized for the first time that religion could be applied toward the cause of social justice. On that day it was as if Dr. King was talking to him alone. With that he began to save clippings about King from the newspapers.

He had been all too aware, of course, of the burden of being black and poor in the South, that the students at the white schools had new books, and the black schools had, at best, old, hand-me-down books if they had any books at all. He knew that white children went to good schools and were driven there in new buses over good roads, and that black children went to poor schools in old, worn-out buses which always seemed to break down, in no small part because they were traveling on unpaved roads. He knew that children at the white schools played sports, and black schools were almost completely without athletic facilities.

He knew all too well the symbols of segregation and racism in nearby Troy: the monument in the courthouse square to Confederate soldiers who died fighting for slavery; the soda fountain, where white children could drink at the counter, and where blacks could order, but had to carry their drinks outside; and the local movie theater, where the whites could sit downstairs, but the blacks had to go upstairs to their small, segregated section. He did not as a boy like going to movies, and even as a grown man that wariness remained, and he instinctively rejected movies as a form of entertainment.

He was by his own account a curious child, "a very nosy child," and he liked listening to the grown-ups talking when they thought there were no children present. Much of that secret talk was about race. Clearly they did not like to tell their worst stories about racism in front of the children. Most of the other children were quite content to accept that rule, but John Lewis was different. He was fascinated by these stories, and he would sneak in and hide under a chair and listen. Sometimes they caught him: "Boy, I see you there—now you get in the other room. We're talking grown-up stuff here." Then they would make him leave the room, but he would continue to listen with his ear to the door. It was only then that they spoke of the pain and danger of the past and the present, and of the bad days of the Klan and the night riders. He had a sense that his father had never witnessed a lynching, but that he had felt the fear of the Klan during his own boyhood. Later, after John had grown up, he realized that in some way he had been preparing for the teaching he had found at American Baptist and for his role in the sit-ins long before he had arrived in Nashville. A commitment on racial issues, he decided, had always been in his heart. Having been a part of the sit-in movement, he had no intention of turning back.

That December in 1960 when he went home for Christmas, John Lewis took his personal protest of segregation a step farther, this time into the Deep South. He and his friend Bernard Lafayette decided to test segregation once more, this time virtually on their own, with a small, highly personal protest, unannounced, and extremely dangerous. For the Supreme Court had just ruled in the *Boynton* v. *Virginia* case banning segregation in interstate travel. Lewis was still angry over the first bus trip he had made from Troy to Nashville when he had arrived at American Baptist. It should have been one of pure pleasure and optimism about the new and better life he was about to lead, but it had soured when he was forced to ride in the back of the bus. The *Boynton* decision meant bus travel, including the bus terminals and waiting rooms and restaurants and rest rooms, could no longer be segregated. It was to prove an important decision, for in a few months it would open the way to a far more audacious challenge to the mores of the Deep South. These two young men volunteered to do their own test of this new decision.

As they prepared to go home for the holidays Lewis and Bernard Lafayette decided to take the same bus and, more important, to ride in the front. They did not sit together. Lafayette got on first and sat right behind the driver, a man not at all pleased by his presence. The driver asked Lafayette to go to the back of the bus. Lafayette just looked straight ahead and said nothing. Now spotting Lewis as well, the driver asked him to go to the back. Lewis did not budge. The driver, his anger obvious, got off the bus as if to get the police. He came back a few minutes later, without the police, apparently rebuffed by them, and all the angrier for his failure. In a moment of rage, the driver released his own seat and slammed it back as far as it could go, as if to nail Lafayette. If it hit my legs, Lafayette thought, it would have broken them. Instead, the driver had merely driven a hole in Lafayette's suitcase.

For both students it was a journey into fear. They were traveling at night and there was no support system behind them, no one back in Nashville monitoring what they were doing. They were very much on their own, testing what might as well have been a law decreed by an invisible governmental institution back in Washington. The bus made what seemed like an interminable number of stops in the small towns lining the route, and at each of them the driver went inside for a few minutes, something no driver had ever done before on any of their previous trips. Both Lafayette and Lewis were sure that he was tipping off the Klan. Each of them was scared for the other. John Lewis had to get off first, and the driver dropped him off on the highway outside of Troy, with no one else in sight. "You watch it now, brother," Lafayette had told him as he got off. "People can disappear out here and never be seen again." But Lewis had already alerted his family to what he was doing, and they picked him up almost immediately.

Bernard Lafayette remembered watching John Lewis's small, stoic figure standing by the roadside as the bus pulled away, and being frightened for his friend, and then being frightened for himself, alone on a bus which was going to stop in all those small Alabama and Florida towns, where the Klan had surely been alerted. He knew what might happen, and his imagination began to run wild. He did not

allow himself to fall asleep that night. Every time the bus pulled into a
small town and stopped and a white person walked toward the bus,
his fears would escalate again. It was so much harder to do this, he
realized, when you were alone, as opposed to when you did it with
your colleagues. It was, they both decided when it was over, the first
Freedom Ride of the post-*Brown* era, though neither of them had
thought of it that way at the time. They had just done it.

It was their first Freedom Ride, and others would soon follow. That
winter John Lewis had received a letter suggesting that he might want
to join a racially integrated group of people who were going to take a
prolonged bus trip through the South in the spring of 1961, testing
facilities in a variety of cities. The trip was being sponsored by CORE,
the Congress of Racial Equality. These rides would test segregation,
not just on the buses, but in the public accommodations themselves—
the restaurants and the rest rooms in the terminals. Freedom Rides,
they were going to be called. They would start innocuously enough in
states like Virginia and North Carolina, but the venues would become
increasingly less innocent, going on to South Carolina, Alabama, and
Mississippi, and ending in New Orleans on May 17, 1961, an auspi-
cious date since it would mark the seventh anniversary of the *Brown*
decision and would show therefore both what had been done and what
had not been accomplished in the intervening years. They seemed like
the logical next step for the Movement, coming after the sit-ins. The
letter said the rides might be dangerous. Well, he had already dealt
with a good deal of danger, and so he filled out the application.

Bernard Lafayette also saw the CORE letter and immediately
wanted to go along. But Bernard was a little younger than John, and
according to the CORE rules, anyone younger than twenty-one had to
have parental approval. The Lafayette family of Tampa, Florida, was
not about to send its only male child up to South Carolina and Alabama and Mississippi to sample previously all-white men's rooms.
Bernard Lafayette, Sr., refused to sign the release. "Boy, you're asking
me to sign your death warrant," he had told his son. They had three
daughters, he reminded him, and only one son, and he did not want
the Lafayette name to die in some unknown Southern bus terminal.
Bernard was disappointed, sure he was going to miss the greatest
opportunity of his life. No one looking at the two of them could tell
whether John was older than he was, he liked to say. But the small for-

mality of parental permission did not bother a young man who became a good friend of both Lewis and Lafayette that summer, Hank Thomas.

Hank Thomas of St. Augustine, Florida, was the product of a dreadfully deprived background in rural Georgia; his blood father had disappeared even before he was born, and as a boy he had watched his stepfather, beaten down by his job at a nearby sawmill, take out his anger in alcohol and then systematically abuse his mother before eventually deserting his family. Years later when he watched the movie *The Color Purple,* Thomas felt he was watching the story of his own life. In the St. Augustine school system he had been a good student, and a good high school football player, and a number of colleges had competed for his athletic talents until in his senior year he had keeled over from sunstroke and his athletic career had come to an end. But he had set his mind on college and had managed to win a scholarship to Howard, where he had always felt like something of an outsider, being neither rich nor connected. Money and status were obviously quite important there. When the Howard gentry sat around talking about what their fathers did, he would answer that his father was in business, which might or might not be true since he had no earthly idea what his father did, never having seen him.

Hank Thomas had been largely without purpose, social or intellectual, at Howard until the sit-ins had broken out, and though in no way until then could he have been considered a student leader, with the coming of the sit-ins he had begun to find an outlet for some of the stored-up resentments he had long harbored. He had enjoyed leading a number of sit-ins in the greater Washington area, and as he did, he began to feel for the first time part of something that mattered.

Hank Thomas had heard of the CORE Freedom Rides from his roommate at Howard, a young man named John Moody, who had been accepted; when John Moody became sick at the last minute, Hank Thomas had simply gone in his place. Unlike Bernard Lafayette, he had no father to block his way, and he simply forged his mother's name and sent in the form. He was tall and he looked older than his nineteen years. He was pleased when he showed up for the four-day training and found that John Lewis, who was one of his heroes, a leader of the famed Nashville group, was one of the other students who was aboard, though in truth he would have been a great deal happier if it had been Diane Nash whom he had met at the Raleigh meeting the year before. John Lewis for his part liked Hank Thomas immediately. He was glad that someone his own age was on the trip, and he was pleased by the fact that Thomas's presence showed that what had happened in Nashville was spreading to other colleges.

They had all arrived in Washington at the end of April. They were to undergo four days of training on the use of nonviolence in social protest. The group was an odd mixture of people, some young, some old, some white, some black, some Quakers, some ministers, plus two rabbis. John Lewis, as a graduate of Jim Lawson's rather demanding seminars, thought the Washington training simplistic, lacking in discipline and rigor. To him the most memorable part of the Washington tour was the dinner they had on their final night. Someone thought it would be a good idea if they all went out to eat together at a local Chinese restaurant. John Lewis of Pike County, who had never been in a Chinese restaurant before, was quite awed. They had sat down at a huge circular table. Then a large number of Chinese waiters had rushed back and forth bringing what seemed like an endless array of dishes. The food was the most exotic he had ever eaten but he was even more impressed by the setting itself—he had never seen so many silver bowls and platters before. At the start of the dinner one of his fellow riders had said, "We better eat well because this may be our last supper."

The Freedom Rides were, for the forces which had been gradually gathering, wanting to challenge the virtual totality of segregation in the Deep South, like stumbling into combat. That they marked the beginning of the long-awaited assault upon the bastions of segregation, however, surprised everyone. CORE was on a comparative scale one of the least-known and seemingly smallest of the different groups pledged to end segregation, and there had been remarkably little pre-ride publicity. Although CORE had put out a small publicity sheet listing the various cities to be visited and tested, the event had barely dented the mind-set of the editors of most national publications. As such the national media at first seemed disinclined to give the rides much publicity. The only reporter assigned to the rides was Simeon Booker, a black reporter for *Ebony*, the black version of *Life*. The same press release had ended up at the Justice Department, where a few people had taken note of the stops in Alabama and Mississippi, and where there was a preliminary sense of trouble in the making.

Almost no one sensed that the rides were to be the beginning of something larger; that their legacy would grow and set a pattern for the next five years; that the forces of integration would now go into the most dangerous part of the country, determined to force the American government to move forward on this issue by raising the issue as prominently as possible and making ordinary Americans aware of what was at stake. In retrospect it is easy to understand the volatility of the ingredients: The forces pledged to integrate had moved forward during the sit-ins with considerable success, and their victories at the lunch counters had served only to convince them, first, that integration could be achieved and that they had the courage to do it, and second, how much farther they still had to go. At the same time, the forces of segregation, already angered by various developments in the past seven years, the increasing access of the integrationists to the national media, and what seemed to them the mounting arrogance of the black leadership, particularly Martin Luther King, were already on a hair trigger, just itching for a fight, particularly, as now was promised, on their own, sacred terrain.

The battle, therefore, was about to be joined, without any participation of the U.S. government, which was at that moment passive and, on the surface at least, largely disinterested. If there was one overriding objective of the varying people about to rally together, in SNCC, the SCLC, and CORE, the three groups which favored activist demonstrations, it was to move events forward in a way which prodded the United States government into active participation.

The federal government in the spring of 1961 had not committed itself in any sense to the side of integration. Not only had Dwight Eisenhower failed to say anything supportive of the Supreme Court's *Brown* decision almost seven years previous, but he had privately signaled his sympathy to the Southern traditionalists, and had referred to his appointment of Earl Warren to head the Court as the biggest damn fool mistake he had made as president. That reflected both generational prejudice and political opportunism, for his White House political operatives were wary of losing the first inroads which the Republican party had made in the South in generations. In addition the FBI, headed by J. Edgar Hoover, was a bulwark of opposition to black progress. Hoover, by generational political instinct, was anti-black. He hated activists like King, tended to see any aspect of social activism as Communist inspired, and more than anything else was skilled at playing to the powerful and extremely conservative Democratic committee chairmen who ran the Congress and determined his handsome budget. Throughout the South, Hoover had implanted a generation of FBI men with Southern roots, men who had been told that their principal job was to get along with the local police officials, who were, of course, often the leaders of the local white resistance. It would be four years before the FBI—acting then only in the most reluctant way—would be much help to those trying to break the alliance of white Southern hate groups and local white police authorities.

As for the Congress of the United States, it was extremely conservative on most social issues (particularly those concerning race), far more so than the country itself. It reflected the darker side of the New Deal coalition, that of diverse ethnic groups and big-city machines in the North married up for combined political benefit to conservative Democrats from one-party states in the South. The Democratic party's congressional face favored the South more than the North, it had a stranglehold on any number of important committees, and the men who held that stranglehold, like Judge Howard Smith of Virginia, were a geriatric sampling who reflected the America of the twenties more than they reflected the forces now at play in the post-war America of the late fifties and early sixties. To the degree that the congressional leaders were aware of these new forces, they were more often than not devoted to slowing them down. They made it clear early on to the new, young president of the United States, John Kennedy, elected as he had been on the narrowest of margins, and far more interested in America's destiny in foreign affairs than in domestic ones, that they would tax him dearly—indeed Pyrrhically—for any changes he might even think of trying to make in terms of bringing integration to the South.

That appeared to be all right with the young president himself. Kennedy as a candidate had not seemed particularly interested in civil rights. It was not an issue which had touched him deeply as a young man; if he did not actually distance himself from it as he began to run in 1959, he did not seem to commit himself to the full nature of what it meant, and of the powerful stirrings of change which had begun to

surface during the Montgomery bus boycott. Like a great many people of that era, he felt that as long as he was not an active racist himself, then he was on the right side of the issue, and that black people
would understand the essential goodness of his heart. In truth, civil
rights activists, those rare white Americans in that era who had committed themselves to working for progress on this issue, made him
uneasy, and he thought of them as do-gooders and zealots. To the
degree that Kennedy was aware of the new forces at play, he saw them
as something to be handled, lest they get in his way and cause
unwanted problems. He had not wanted to be the candidate who
went to the convention in 1960 unable to hold the Southern Democrats in line, he had had no interest in accepting the nomination of a
divided party; one of the reasons he had chosen Lyndon Johnson as
his vice-presidential running mate was because he wanted to keep the
South in line, and it was Johnson's designated responsibility that fall
to work the South and keep it Democratic.

As a professional politician John Kennedy was cool in all things,
and that was particularly true of the race issue. The challenge for the
black groups restless with the pace of racial change in the spring of
1961 was to focus enough moral and political heat on Kennedy to separate him from his coolness. Not surprisingly, blacks saw him as being
distant and uninvolved in their plight; he was in 1961, as far as most of
their leaders were concerned, one more indifferent American politician.

More, while he had welcomed men like Harris Wofford who were
truly committed on race into his campaign, in no small part to help
subvert opponents like Hubert Humphrey during the primary fight
for the nomination, he remained wary of them. They were not cool
and might even bring with them too much of an ideological tilt; Wofford, after all, had been the first white law student at Howard, which
in the early days of the Kennedy administration was not considered an
admirable credential. Given a major confrontation between the interests of black people and the interests of Kennedy, men like Wofford
might prove too committed to the equities of the issue rather than to
John Kennedy. Kennedy did not want Wofford in what would have
been the most logical spot for him, assistant attorney general for civil
rights—he might, in the current phrase, be too soft. Instead Wofford
became a White House staff man assigned to deal with racial issues,

somewhat isolated because of his lack of rapport with his immediate superiors. But when the blacks began to push ever harder for their rights, Kennedy, with some irritation, would refer to them to Wofford as "your constituents."[5]

Not surprisingly John Kennedy had been irritated from the start with the Freedom Riders. As far as he was concerned there was no upside politically. The rides could only cause him problems—and force the federal government into situations into which he had no desire to move. In addition, he believed, the international publicity would surely help the Communists, who were always trying to exploit domestic American racial problems. Even as the Freedom Rides had started and tensions between riders and local segregationists mounted, he was preparing to go to Europe and meet with Khrushchev; thus he saw what these young black people were doing through the prism of his own interests—potentially a major embarrassment to him—rather than through the prism of their interests, their belated attempt to win long-denied rights. The Freedom Riders were, in his words, a pain in the ass.[6]

As for the American people, those ordinary people who lived outside the South, they were at that moment sitting on the fence. Americans liked to think of themselves as being above prejudice, and believing in both simple justice and elemental fair play. They had been delighted more than a decade earlier when Jackie Robinson had made his successful debut in baseball, thereby proving that the American dream worked across the board. But how deep that commitment to justice went in other aspects of life was still in question. Shown specific instances of injustice and brutality, the American people tended to sympathize with the victim. There was no doubt that Martin Luther King, during the Montgomery bus strike, had touched a resonant nerve nationally. But could that feeling be sustained—could those who were leading the Movement affect the national conscience in a way that would move the American political process forward on so broad a scale as to create a committed majority vision? That was the great question. Otherwise it was not an enviable political equation— 10 percent of the population wanting to gain full citizenship, in a system run by geriatric reactionaries. That made the job of the activists both simple and dangerous—they had to lure the beast of segregation to the surface and show to ordinary Americans just exactly how it was that the leadership of the South maintained segregation, not as that leadership constantly claimed, by a genteel partnership with its black citizens, but by the exercise of raw and brutal police powers.

That was the political landscape as the Freedom Rides began: Their force was small and their activism unwanted; almost the entire U. S. government was indifferent, except for those parts, like the FBI, which were openly hostile. The Freedom Rides began on May 4, 1961, some four months after *Boynton*. Two buses were used, one from Trailways and one from Greyhound. At first things did not go badly. Some of the towns no longer had their white-only signs at the rest rooms. In Fredericksburg, Virginia, the signs still existed, but when the Freedom Riders challenged the tradition, with a white rider going into the black men's room and a black rider going into the white men's room, there was no incident. The first bit of real resistance came in Charlottesville, Virginia, when one of the black riders, Charles Person, tried to have his shoes shined at the shoe-shine stand and was refused service. He did not leave the stand and a few minutes later was arrested. A day later the Virginia attorney general dropped the charges, deciding that Person was within his rights under the *Boynton* decision.

Hank Thomas felt his fears evaporating at first. They had hit Richmond, Virginia, which was supposed to be a tough town, with the passions of the Old Confederacy still alive, but Richmond had gone well, there had been a large mass meeting and a good many reporters present. This was turning out to be fun. Richmond had been followed by Charlotte, North Carolina, and Charlotte had been easy. A cakewalk, he had thought to himself. Jim Farmer, the leader of CORE, was on Thomas's bus and he kept saying things were going to get a lot tougher. Well, maybe, Hank Thomas thought, maybe. But he was young and full of the adventure, by far the most talkative of the group, eager to make friends with every other rider. John Lewis, he decided, was almost taciturn by comparison, a young man who was thoughtful, and often seemed to be within himself.

They reached Rock Hill, South Carolina, which was no more than twenty miles from Charlotte, but it was South Carolina, and that was something new for all of them—their first stop in the Deep South. It was John Lewis's turn to do the testing when they got to Rock Hill. Years later it was said of John Lewis, who was probably arrested more than any of the other students, some forty-five times by his own (probably incomplete) account, that he was a magnet for the hatred of white racists, and the joke was that the white mobs would wait until he showed up before they unleashed their violence. When Lewis and an older white man named Albert Bigelow stepped off the bus in Rock Hill, they were immediately beaten.

It was all very quick, Lewis remembered. There had been a group of young white men waiting at the station, and perhaps twenty or thirty of them surged at him. He went down instantly, and felt them swinging at and kicking him very hard. He knew he was bleeding, and he felt a stab of pain in his side, and then suddenly they were gone. Even as he lay on the ground, stunned by the quickness and the ferocity of the attack, he realized that the game was different now and that the protections offered in a border-state city like Nashville were gone; they had now graduated to the real struggle, which was in the Deep South. This was a journey into the unknown and there were no longer any legal or judicial or moral restraints on the people who opposed them. They were going into the valley of the shadow of death, he thought.

Hank Thomas watched the assault upon Lewis with disbelief. He saw the mob gathered and poised to strike, and he watched John Lewis prepare to descend, and he saw the mob start to come at Lewis. Even as Lewis saw it approach, he had continued, absolutely without hesitation, to walk right into the surging mob. That was courage, Thomas remembered thinking, that was what it took to be a real leader in this struggle. John had gone forward without fear as if to accept his fate, the fate of being badly beaten and perhaps killed, the price to be paid for wanting his full rights. The good martyr, Thomas thought, and wondered if he had that same kind of courage. He wondered if he even had the courage to leave the bus, and then it struck him that sometimes you are more afraid *not* to do the things that you are afraid of than of actually doing them. In that moment, as he was supposed to get off the bus, Hank Thomas balanced his two fears and found that his fear of cowardice was even greater than his fear of being beaten. He steadied himself and got off the bus. By that time the local cops had intervened, and the white youths had, as if by some prearranged signal, quickly moved on.

Hank Thomas walked inside the bus terminal, where it was his assignment to test the white men's room. A cop told him he was under arrest. "Can I finish what I'm doing?" Thomas asked. The cop let him finish.

John Lewis was lying in the fetal position in front of the terminal, more stunned by the quickness of the assault than anything else. Someone from Friendship Junior College had come and picked him up, and taken him to the college. There he found a message saying he had been chosen to be a finalist by the American Friends Service Committee for a grant which would send him to Tanganyika (later to be amalgamated with Zanzibar and called Tanzania) for two years. It was something he had rather casually applied for earlier, when some time spent in Africa had seemed unusually attractive, and before he realized how compelling his role in the Movement was becoming. No longer sure that this was still the course he wanted to follow, Lewis flew to Philadelphia, thinking that he would eventually rejoin the riders in Montgomery, Alabama.

Hank Thomas had been arrested and taken to the local jail, where he was kept by himself. He was completely alone—as far as he could tell no one else had been arrested, and the bus with his friends had gone on. He was in jail for several hours, becoming more and more nervous all the time. Then around midnight two cops showed up and let him out of the cell, and ordered him into their car. He was very frightened by then. Images of late-night rides taken by blacks who were never heard from again were much in his mind. "Where are we going?" he asked them. "Well, you wanted to go to the bus station to get out of town, didn't you?" one of them said. "So we're taking you there."

The cops seemed very pleased with themselves; the happier they were, the edgier he became. The bus station itself looked dark, but there was just enough light so that he could see a mob of white youths waiting in the lot. Real good old boys, he thought, waiting there for me. None of this was happening by accident, he knew. "Is the bus station waiting room open?" Thomas asked. No, one of the cops said. Thomas was not sure he wanted to get out, and the cop realized it and tapped his gun—the choice seemed to be the mob or the gun, and so Hank Thomas got out of the car, ready to face the mob. The cops, he remembered, burned rubber getting out of there, and he knew that some kind of deal had been arranged; it was a game and he was the prize.

Just then a car driven by a black man pulled up and the black man yelled to him, "Get in, boy!" He jumped in. The driver was the local head of the NAACP, and he had been alerted by the CORE team the moment Thomas was arrested, and been told to watch both the jail and the bus station. The man drove him to Columbia, South Carolina, where he stayed with friendly blacks. The next day he was driven to Atlanta, where he rejoined the team. The others on the Freedom Ride noticed that he was more somber now, less ebullient. The young man who had been so eager to talk to everyone now seemed to be alone, lost in his thoughts, much older in just one day.

There had been a rally for them in Atlanta. There was more media coverage now because of the assault on Lewis in Rock Hill. More coverage usually meant more protection, but it also meant, the riders all realized, that the Klan and Citizens Council members in the Deep South cities along the route had more time to plan their own receptions. Hank Thomas became even more quiet on the next leg of the ride from Atlanta to Anniston, Alabama. They were going due west from Atlanta, and they were for the first time crossing into the most feared part of the South, Alabama and Mississippi. Anniston was said to be a tough town, a Klan town. They were on the Greyhound bus that day, and Hank remembered that one of the riders had joked that Anniston was so scary that even the greyhound painted on the outside of the bus as a logo was going to get inside when they reached Anniston. There were two FBI agents aboard the bus, but they did not seem very friendly; if anything they seemed wary of the Freedom Riders, who in turn were wary of them. The belief among the Freedom Riders was that given the prurient interests of J. Edgar Hoover, the principal assignment of the agents aboard was to find out if there was even the slightest hint of interracial sex taking place.

They were right not to count on the FBI, which had ample information that they were about to be beaten on arrival in Anniston but did absolutely nothing to protect them. When the Freedom Riders had stopped in Atlanta their leaders had had dinner with Martin Luther King and his top aides. (Jim Farmer later complained quite publicly that King and his aides had taken them to a rather fancy black restaurant in Atlanta, where they had all dined well, and then King and his people had left them with the check.) At the dinner King had taken aside Simeon Booker, the black reporter for *Ebony,* and warned him of the increasingly hostile mood in Alabama. "You will never make it through Alabama," King had told Booker. Booker had tried to respond by laughing at the warning—he would stay close to the rather portly Jim Farmer, because he was sure he could outrun Farmer.[7] King and his people, including King's quite conservative father, knew from their sources in Alabama, which were excellent, that the Klan planned a violent reception for the riders there. If Martin King were aboard the bus, these sources warned, he would be killed.

King's information turned out to be surprisingly exact. The Klan had been waiting for that day in Anniston, and had been given permission by the local law enforcement officials to strike against the Freedom Riders without any fear of arrest. Years later, through various sources—lawsuits against the government, a tell-all book by a paid Klan informer for the FBI—an increasing amount of information was revealed about the activities of the Klan and its connections to Alabama law officers in those days. It became clear that there had been a conspiracy on the part of some local law enforcement officials to let the Klan attack the Freedom Riders. Nor did the FBI, which knew in considerable detail what was going to happen, do anything to protect the riders or to stop their assailants.

Alabama was known at the time among civil rights activists as a Klan state. No one was quite sure why the Klan was so much more active and powerful there than elsewhere—among other things, an organic part, it seemed, of a number of the state's larger police forces. Perhaps part of the reason came from the large number of blue-collar steel workers in the Bessemer-Birmingham area; there the combination of traditional blue-collar class resentments and racial tensions had turned into an unusually ugly mix. Mississippi, by contrast, distinctly less industrialized, was not a Klan state, at least not at that moment. It was a White Citizens Council state, a place where the white establishment figures, top to bottom—judges, politicians, lawyers, ministers, and editors—joined the councils. There, the pressure and fear of economic, political, and above all social ostracism managed to keep the ruling elite, statewide and community by community, in line on the issue of segregation. The difference between the two states seemed to be one of class: The Citizens Council members were white collar—the good people of the state, as they liked to think of themselves—but the Klan members were blue collar, made up, as the Citizens Council people liked to say, of rednecks and pecker-woods, and potentially far more violent in any confrontation.

Sunday, May 14, 1961, was not a date widely celebrated in the civil rights movement, unlike the date on which the *Brown* case had been handed down, and unlike December 1, 1955, which was the day Rosa Parks refused to go to the back of the bus because her feet hurt. But it was an important day as well. It was the day on which the orbital thrust of the Freedom Rides, so innocently conceived a few months earlier, took these vulnerable men and women to Alabama, and the great violent confrontation between integrationists and the angry white mobs in the Deep South that everyone had been expecting for so long finally took place. Therefore it was the day that the Rubicon was crossed. No one had plotted it that way. If anything the Freedom Ride architects themselves seemed to have little sense of how much they had upped the stakes. This was no minor, little venture into sampling hamburgers in different bus stations. This, instead, was a frontal assault on the very nature of the beast of segregation, in the place where it was most powerful.

Later asked by reporters why there had been so little protection of the Freedom Riders in both Anniston and Birmingham on that day, Eugene (Bull) Connor, the Birmingham public safety commissioner, had answered that he did not have enough police available because it was Mother's Day. So it was, though that was hardly the reason. As they crossed into Alabama the Freedom Riders knew something was up: The warnings from King and his people could not have been more serious. The closer they got to Anniston, the quieter the bus became.

As they drove into the city limits, the town too was eerily quiet. No one seemed to be about. The streets were deserted. It reminded Hank Thomas of Western movies he had seen where a showdown was about to take place between the good guys and the bad guys, and where most of the local people were staying home watching from behind closed windows with drawn shades. As the Greyhound pulled into the bus station, Hank Thomas, seated two seats from the front, saw his first signs of life—a mob of people waiting with clubs and iron pipes and baseball bats. There were perhaps 150 people, perhaps two hundred. He did not have time to count.

Thomas was very scared. Two days earlier when he had sat with John Lewis on the bus, John had spoken in the simplest way imaginable of the fact that they had to be ready to die on this trip. He had spoken without emotion or bravado, as if the two of them, the youngest members of the group, should not be on this ride unless they had already arrived at that knowledge and that willingness to sacrifice. Listening to him that day, a young man his own age, Thomas had been deeply impressed, not just by what Lewis said, but the calm, understated manner in which he said it. John Lewis, Hank Thomas had learned, simply did not posture. He made his decision, he chose his course, he accepted the consequences of his decision because he had decided on a greater purpose for his life. That was his great strength. It was impossible to separate religion from politics in his philosophy. If they did not accept the idea of death, then they could not move ahead. Hank Thomas had no doubts about John's commitment, but he had plenty of doubts about his own. For a moment he envied this stolid young man, who seemed to have no need at all to impress other people. On occasion he had felt envy for those who were more talented than he or better looking, but this was something different—the envy of an inner spirituality which turned an ordinary man into a person of unwavering faith. Hank Thomas on that day wondered whether he even believed in nonviolence. Looking at the mob, he was not sure that he could go through with it. But he also knew that he could not back out on the others. This mission, he was aware, might be the last thing he ever did. Why am I here? he had thought. How foolish to be risking your life at nineteen. He thought that he had signed on with a certain false bravado, a boy trying to act like a man.

He remembered the driver yelling to the mob outside with a certain heartiness and pleasure: "Well, boys, here they are. I brought you some niggers and nigger-lovers." Then the mob surged at the bus and started beating on it, trying to smash the windows and slashing the tires. A quick decision was made not to let passengers out in downtown Anniston, and the bus started up, as if to go on to Birmingham. As it pulled out of the station, Thomas watched a bunch of pickup trucks roar ahead of it and another group of trucks and cars follow it—they were caught in a redneck sandwich, he decided, and it was unlikely they would escape. He remembered the absolute fear in the bus and the pleasure of the bus driver, chortling, laughing aloud at what was going to happen. It was all taking place as if in slow motion now. The mob, mobilized in its pickup trucks and cars, would not let the bus go faster than fifteen miles an hour. Five miles outside of Anniston the bus stopped. The tires had been so badly slashed that they were gone. We are not going to die in Anniston, Thomas thought, we are going to die on its outskirts.

The driver pulled over to the side, where the crowd had already gathered around the bus. It was a strange sight, for these white people were surprisingly well dressed, Thomas remembered, wearing jackets and ties, as if they had all just come from church. It struck him that it was both a lynching and a picnic—people in their best clothes, men with their little children perched on their shoulders so they could get a better view, something for the children to remember when they got older. They all looked so nice and ordinary; later, he learned that most of them were Klan members and they had been waiting for a moment like this for several years. But pleasantly dressed or not, there was no doubt of their intention: Hank Thomas looked at them and knew that he was doing nothing less than watching the end of his life.

At first it seemed that the mob wanted to get on the bus and pull the Freedom Riders off. Some of the whites charged forward toward the bus, wielding their clubs, and then started rocking the bus, as if trying to turn it over. When that happened the Freedom Riders decided to lock the door and keep the mob out. Then someone threw a firebomb inside. Almost instantaneously the smoke inside the bus was thick and terrible. Because the upholstery was made of some kind of artificial material, it burned with a dreadful, toxic smell. "Let's roast the niggers!" someone shouted, and others took up the cry. "Roast them!" "Burn them alive!" "Fry the goddamn niggers!" The mob, which only a moment earlier had been trying to get inside the bus, was now determined to keep *them* inside.

For that brief moment, when he was absolutely sure that he was going to die, Hank Thomas tried to decide which way he would rather die, whether he would leave the bus and let the mob beat him to death, or whether he would stay inside and be burned to death. In one quick flash of desperation, he decided to commit suicide, believing that somehow it would mean a less painful death, and for a moment he breathed as deeply as he could of the toxic fumes in order to exchange one terrible form of death for another. But just then one of the gas tanks on the bus exploded, driving the mob back and scattering it. The explosion, it was later decided, probably saved the lives of all the Freedom Riders. It also made up his mind for him, and even as the mob was scattering, he was reacting in the same way. He stumbled off the bus.

Hank Thomas, who had so much wanted to be like the Nashville kids, staggered off the bus and became as much by accident as anything else the first of the young black student protesters on the Freedom Ride to sample the full fury of the two most dreaded states, Alabama and Mississippi. As he landed on the ground, reeling from the fumes, a white man came up to him and asked, "Are you all okay?" He asked this solicitously, and Thomas, relieved to be outside, sensing for the first time someone who might help him, said that he was all right, at which point the man took a baseball bat, which was hidden behind him, and swung at Thomas as hard as he could. Thomas went down immediately. He had a vague sense of the other riders spilling out of the bus and crawling on the ground around him, they like he retching and gasping for air. The heat from the fire in the bus was terrible, but it was keeping the mob at bay. Later, he was not exactly sure of the sequence of events: He heard another explosion, probably, another gas tank blowing, and there was a shower of broken glass, and that drove the mob back farther.

He and the others were saved at that moment by of all people a plainclothes official of the Alabama state police named E. L. Cowling. Ell Cowling had been covertly planted on the bus by Floyd Mann, the Alabama director of public safety, for a variety of reasons: because Mann wanted information on the Freedom Riders, and needed to monitor what they were doing, and because Mann did not trust the local Alabama police authorities because of their ties to the Klan. What was happening was just what Floyd Mann had feared, and at this critical moment Cowling, gun in hand, had stepped forward, shed his disguise, and had driven the mob back. (Little was made of Cowling's rescue at the time; there were no points to be gained in Alabama politics for saving the lives of Freedom Riders.) The trooper positioned himself between the Freedom Riders, who were lying on the ground gasping for air, and the mob. Gradually the mob, still angry, moved back, and eventually an ambulance pulled up. It was a white ambulance and the driver said he would not take black people in it, and so the white Freedom Riders who had already boarded it got off and said they would not go without their black partners. Finally the ambulance was integrated, perhaps, Hank Thomas later thought, a first in Alabama history, and they were taken to a hospital in Anniston.

The people running the hospital offered little respite. They said they would not treat the Freedom Riders, which was in keeping with what Governor John Patterson had said over the radio, that no medical help would be given to outside agitators. But for the first time one of the FBI men proved to be helpful; he told the hospital authorities that they had to give some kind of medical aid to these people. Even as they waited inside the hospital, a mob began to gather outside, its leaders telling the hospital authorities that they would have to turn over the Freedom Riders, or else they would burn the hospital down. Thomas was appalled by the behavior of the hospital authorities. Here were a bunch of patients, some of them elderly and in some form of shock, and the hospital authorities seemed more an extension of the mob than they were of a medical profession which was supposed to treat all needy people. Once again Hank Thomas was sure that he was going to die, be evicted from the hospital and turned over to the mob.

But then the Reverend Fred Shuttlesworth arrived. He was the leading black activist minister in Birmingham, a man legendary for his physical courage, and he had heard what had happened—indeed he was the man who had warned Martin King of the waiting violence in Alabama—and he had organized a caravan of his deacons and of other ministers and driven through the mob to rescue them. Shuttlesworth had told those who were coming with him he had only one simple rule—no one could carry a weapon. If you felt you needed a weapon you could not come. The drive by Shuttlesworth, thought Hank Thomas, was one of the bravest things one man could do for another.

Later that same day, the second bus, this one from Trailways, arrived in Anniston; its passengers were beaten and then, when the bus went on to Birmingham, another mob, which had been waiting for a few hours, attacked them. Jim Peck, one of the CORE leaders, was knocked unconscious, and needed fifty-three stitches to close his wounds. In Birmingham, the original Freedom Riders from both buses now gathered. They were in terrible condition, both physically and emotionally, almost paralyzed by these terrifying events. Some of them were treated at a hospital in Birmingham. After they got out of the hospital, they reassembled and tried to board buses for the continuation of the journey on to Montgomery and the other stops. But no one would drive them. Frustrated, exhausted, unsure of what the federal government was going to do and whether they would be given any protection, they decided to abort the rest of the trip and to fly to New Orleans in time for the final rally, which had been scheduled for May 17.

John Lewis was in Philadelphia completing his interviews for his fellowship to Tanganyika when he heard about what had happened in Anniston and Birmingham. The Philadelphia paper had a dramatic photo of Hank Thomas escaping from the burning bus. Lewis felt an immediate pang of guilt that he had not been there and a sense that he had let his friends down. Interrupting the Freedom Ride to come to Philadelphia had been a mistake, he thought. He feared the Freedom Rides would now end, that these pleasant, gentle people, most of them older and not, he thought, terribly well prepared for the ordeal, would not continue. Lewis was suspicious of the federal government; the Kennedys, he knew, while paying lip service to supporting civil rights, were most decidedly unenthusiastic about the Freedom Rides. They did not want a bunch of integrationists going through the Deep South, causing what was for them political trouble, and forcing John Kennedy to choose between his more liberal and humane impulses and the hard reality of a Democratic party still dependent on the all-white political machinery in the South. What the federal government had wanted in the case of the Freedom Rides was first, for them not to happen, and now that they had happened, for the riders to back off.

Lewis and a number of the other young people in the Nashville group of SNCC immediately decided that this was a critical moment in the Movement. The one thing which they could not do was to allow the violence of the mob to defeat the nonviolence of the protesters. If they had done well so far, then it was a mere beginning. Winning the right to eat at a lunch counter in Nashville was the most limited kind of victory. If they stopped now, their enemies would be even more audacious and dangerous. To stop now would also mean that John

Lewis and his young colleagues did not have the courage of their convictions. More, if they backed off now, so would the federal government.

John Lewis immediately called Diane Nash on the phone, and was
delighted to find that if anything, she felt even more strongly that this
was a fateful moment, one from which they would either go forward
or might, like generations before them, be crushed by the system. The
two of them had decided on the phone that the Freedom Rides had to
go on. They would at the very least use Nashville students to reinforce
the original CORE volunteers. And if the CORE people were going to
back off, then the Nashville students would take over. In the mean-
time Lewis flew back to Nashville.

28

DIANE NASH HAD CROSSED A CERTAIN THRESHOLD OF COMMITMENT herself earlier in 1961. She had been at a steering-committee meeting of SNCC in Atlanta in late January 1961, when she and her friends had heard about the arrests of some students at Friendship Junior College in Rock Hill, South Carolina, for daring to integrate a local lunch counter. Her meeting over, she and a few other SNCC friends had gone to Rock Hill, where they were immediately arrested and sentenced to jail for thirty days. At first that had seemed devastating—thirty days was a long time, and though she had been in jail before, her tours had been brief. But she and the others had decided to keep their vows and not to post bail.

Much to her surprise, those thirty days turned out to be among the best and most peaceful of her life. In jail the women had been separated from the men and had been put in a single room. If you are placed in jail for a political crime, she decided, and you are absolutely sure that you are right and that the jailers are wrong, the pain of jail is marginal. She had plenty of time to talk with the other women, not just the ones arrested with her for political violations, but the local black women who had been arrested for all the normal transgressions that marked small-town black life in the South. That of itself was a healthy lesson for her. She had grown up in a rather rarified world where people were supposed to be either good or bad, and where the bad people went to jail and the good people did not. All her life she had been warned about women like her new cellmates—to stay away from them, as if they carried some highly contagious moral disease. Now, sharing this limited space with them every day, she saw them differently. They were people who did not have much education and they were prone, she was sure, to too much drinking and fighting. But they worried about their children like all the other women she knew, and there was a lack of meanness to them which surprised her. She actually came to like the community of the jail. If these people were not always honest in their lives outside of prison, here inside the jail they were strikingly open and candid about their flaws, and about life in general. There was no posturing. The things that most people she knew in her world were most reticent in talking about—their sexuality, their weaknesses—these women were quite open about.

The food was surprisingly good. Not the prison food, which was bad, nothing but cornbread and buttermilk, but the food which the local people brought to the jail for them. Besides, she discovered a surprising spiritual side to her time there. When she wanted solitude, she had solitude, albeit not in an ideal setting. She had a lot of time to think about what she was doing, and a great deal of time to read. She read Gandhi's autobiography and she read the Acts of the Apostles, and was reassured that they too had been arrested for disturbing the peace. Given the emotional pressures of the past year she found the time for meditation comforting.

One day she woke and realized that she had only four days left to her sentence. The idea of reentering the outside world made her uneasy. The jail life to which she had gradually become accustomed was not unpleasant, and she liked the relaxed social order. On the last day that she was there, she found she had to fight a part of her which did not want to leave. When she returned to Nashville she was spiritually stronger, she thought, more sure of her commitment.

The first decision she made on her return to Nashville was whether or not to go back to college and get her degree, or whether to go to work for the Movement full time. She was wary of college: She was tired of all the reprimands she was getting at Fisk because of her work in the Movement. The more she did in the Movement, the more it seemed to offend the Fisk authorities and she was constantly being threatened and warned by Dean Cheatham, the Fisk dean of women. Once during the sit-ins Dean Cheatham had spoken to a Fisk assembly and said she had been downtown and was pleased to report that there were not many Fisk women involved.

There was no small degree of irony there, Diane Nash believed, for she was doing things in the real world which had true social resonance, and for which important black newspapers and magazines as well as white ones took her seriously, but for which she was scolded by her college administration. She was sure she knew what Dean Cheatham wanted her to become: some nice young girl who mimicked white manners and white values, and who would get her degree and marry some black doctor, and live a black life parallel to the life of the wife of a white doctor. She was struck by the difference between the real world as she saw it as an activist, and the tidier, more antiseptic world which seemed to be taught at Fisk, with what seemed to her its unconscious acceptance of a segregated, evil order.

In the end she decided to drop out of college. College, she thought, was all too much about seeking degrees and titles instead of learning about humanity and ethics. So she became a full-time paid worker for the local branches of both SNCC and the SCLC. She had a tiny office in the black section of town. Her salary was about $25 a week, and there was just enough money for her to rent a room at the YWCA. About that time she was interviewed by *Jet* magazine, and was asked how long she intended to be an activist. "I'll be doing this for the rest of my life," she answered. Back in Nashville and more committed to the Movement, she had been one of the architects of the stand-ins, a difficult assault upon segregation in downtown movie theaters.

When Diane Nash heard the news on the radio about Anniston that Sunday, she had the exact reaction that John Lewis did: If they permitted the Klan to stop the Freedom Rides, they would be sending the wrong signal to their enemies—if you want to stop the Movement, all you have to do is resort to violence. She and her colleagues were riding nothing less than the force of history, she believed; they were going to go forward because they could not afford to go backward. Standing still was a form of going backward. If they backed off now, it would only make it harder for future generations. Someone sooner or later was going to have to do what they were doing. Why not let it be them? Why not now?

Both she and Lewis had come to the same conclusion and made decisions which were to be fateful both for themselves, the student part of the Movement, and within the next five years, the country itself. They had not consciously thought about what to do next, after the sit-in victory. As they prepared for the next step, there was an awareness that they had operated so far, no matter how great the seeming danger, in a protected environment, one which they would leave the moment they crossed over into the Deep South. In Nashville they had been under the partial protection of a liberal mayor; of a police force which, if not exactly sympathetic, had never turned truly ugly; a powerful local newspaper like the *Tennessean,* whose coverage had offered no small amount of protection; and the almost complete absence of organized local segregationist groups. Even the governor, Buford Ellington, who had called himself "an old-fashioned segregationist" when he first announced his candidacy, had not turned out to be much of an opponent; he had done some mild posturing, as much for the benefit of Jimmy Stahlman as anything else, but he had clearly believed that the less done the better. In the words of the *Tennessean*'s top political writer, Wayne Whitt, who covered him in those years, "Buford was not nearly as bad a governor as he had promised to be."[1] But the Deep South would be completely different. There would be no sympathetic local newspapers. The state political machinery, top to bottom, would be allied against them. And there would be, they were already realizing, close connections between the Klan and the police themselves. The only way they were going to be effective, they all realized from the start, was by risking their lives, and making the federal government respond to the cruelty which it was their job to reveal.

Diane Nash had grabbed Rodney Powell and they had set out to round up as many members of the coordinating committee as they could. Jim Bevel was the temporary chairman of the Nashville group, and they had located him at a picnic celebrating the victory recently won in the stand-ins. Bevel had seemed to be in no rush to end the picnic, but she and Powell had pushed him, and finally, he had turned his attention to the issue at hand. Bevel's lack of urgency had irritated her. That was typical Bevel, she thought, both brilliant and selfish, but they got him to schedule a meeting for later that day.

Even as Diane Nash and the Nashville leaders started organizing phase two of the Freedom Rides—one in which a large number of Nashville activists joined in as reinforcements to CORE's initial group—she felt they needed something dramatic to energize the protest and gain more national attention. So she had phoned Martin Luther King in Atlanta and had urged him to become a Freedom Rider. When he seemed to hold back, she and Rodney Powell had decided to drive to Atlanta and to pressure him in person. *That,* they both believed, would do the trick. If Martin Luther King, surrounded by his top people, walked into one of those Alabama bus stations and boarded a bus for Jackson, Mississippi, it would all come to a head: The nation would have to watch, and the federal government would have to come in, as so far it had refused to do. Jim Lawson, watching all this in Nashville, thought that the students were right to want to push forward at this moment. But he also felt that Diane and the others were probably being overly zealous and putting too much pressure on Martin King.

Rodney Powell was eager for the assignment, in no small part because of his frustration with his own lack of participation in the Freedom Rides. Knowing that a lot of his sit-in colleagues were going to go to Birmingham to resume the Freedom Rides, Powell had wanted to join up, but the Meharry authorities had made it clear that if he went, he would probably not get his medical degree. He and Gloria Johnson had long been aware that the Meharry authorities were angry at both of them for their prominent roles as sit-in leaders. A significant number of messages had been passed to them by their few friends on the faculty about the rising anger within the school's administration.

The Meharry administrators, he was told, were apparently taking far too much heat from the school's white trustees every time his or Gloria's name appeared in a newspaper story. Was the course work at Meharry so easy, the authorities there were being asked, that its students could not only do their class and lab work but find time to demonstrate against white businesses? Of all the black schools in Nashville involved so far, Powell and Johnson both believed, the officials at Meharry were the most antagonistic to students participating in the Movement, perhaps because a medical school, with its costly support system, was unusually dependent upon white philanthropy. One dean had personally warned Powell that if he went on the Freedom Ride and was arrested, he would not get his degree. Graduation was only a few days away, and if he was in jail on graduation day, that would be that. Rodney Powell felt a certain contempt for the Meharry authorities: The people who should have been encouraging him in an act of conscience were telling him he was damaging the school. It was one more sign, he thought, that people in the medical world seemed to feel they were apart from social and political obligations which applied to black people.

The scene which unfolded in Atlanta when Powell and Nash had gone to talk to Martin Luther King was one that Rodney Powell long remembered, for he left convinced that he had transgressed in front of the man he admired more than any other living American. He and Nash had arrived at King's home in time for dinner. Coretta Scott King was cooking fried chicken, and the King house, as it often was on Sunday, was filled with people—family, friends, members of the Movement, Martin's inner circle. They had been warned that King and his people were wary of joining the Freedom Ride, but they did not know how wary—that Daddy King had already described it as a death sentence for his son. There were a number of other ministers from the SCLC there, and the subject was, of course, whether Martin should join the Freedom Rides. It was obvious to both Rodney Powell and Diane Nash that none of the men around King wanted him to go, that they considered it far too dangerous. Powell could feel a mounting sense of hostility against them as he and Diane made their pitch.

Because they had the passion of the young, neither let the almost unanimous resistance deter them: They were absolutely convinced that the one sure way to push this forward and guarantee that the entire nation watched would be for Dr. King to come on board. If anything, Nash, who was intense and unbending on occasions like this, was the bad cop and Powell, always so gentle, the soothing, good cop. They said they would not in any way try to minimize the dangers. But they represented the Movement's young people, they added, and they believed that Dr. King had to act and act now.

Back came the arguments why King should not go, made, of course, not by King himself—his own words were always to be saved, and he was in all things to be protected—but by the people around him. There were two reasons for him not to go. The first was technical—he was still out on probation from a 1960 traffic arrest in Georgia. If he was arrested again, he might have to go to jail immediately for another six months. But the real reason was security. More than anyone else he was now the special target, the symbol to the angry white Southerners of an insolent new black leadership; he was the man who more than anyone else was likely to lure out of the shadows some dark-visioned man anxious to be the assassin. He and the others knew that the mood in Alabama and Mississippi had turned even uglier, that the gradual successes being won elsewhere in the past year had greatly increased the mutinous defiance of the hard-line segregationists.

Ralph Abernathy, King's closest friend in the Movement, a virtual brother to the man, had tried to deflect the pressure away from King by speaking for him and by saying that if Martin got on the bus, he would surely die. That was the moment when Nash and Powell were supposed to back off, for Abernathy almost always spoke for King. But they were too young and too impassioned to understand the rules of the game, and they had continued to push forward. Rodney Powell had replied that he spoke for the students in Nashville and that they had thought about this very carefully, because they knew how dangerous a journey it was, but that they were going forward despite the danger, and therefore they did not think that the danger should be a deterrent to Dr. King. Dr. King had to act, had to get on that bus, Rodney Powell said.

Suddenly he realized that he had pushed too far, a mere child telling the leader of the Movement not what he should do, but what he *had* to do. With that he had crossed an uncrossable line. There was a flash of anger, and King himself spoke. "Do not tell me when my time has come!" he had said. "Only God can tell me that! How dare you try and tell me!" The room became completely silent. Powell had wanted to disappear at that moment. And then, Martin Luther King began to talk about what those in the Movement should do after he was killed. He spoke in the most fatalistic of voices: not if he was killed, but *when* he was killed. The room became even more quiet. It was as if his violent death was a given, and the only question was when it would happen.

29

As they prepared to reinforce the Freedom Riders in Alabama, the Nashville students wanted the approval of their older colleagues in the Nashville branch of the SCLC. Part of this was the desire to have the blessing of those men who were their racial and spiritual brothers and who had been their teachers, and part was a good deal more mundane. They had no money of their own—they did no independent fund-raising, and to the degree that their operations demanded money, it had always come in the past through the good offices of the SCLC. They had already tentatively fixed the number of students who were going on the Freedom Rides at about twenty, and it was going to cost a fair amount of money to move twenty people by bus to Birmingham and then on to Jackson and New Orleans. There had to be enough money for the bus tickets, and for a minimal amount of food each day. Lodging was not a problem; black homes could be found. Perhaps even more likely, the riders would be lodged in the local jails. But there was no doubt about the danger involved; even as the Nashville leaders caucused they learned that the beleaguered original CORE riders, badly beaten and in virtual shock in Birmingham, had decided to abort the bus part of the trip and, if possible, to fly to New Orleans. That meant the Nashville group would not just be reinforcements, they would become the focal point of any attempt to continue the rides, and they would be going into a region where the mob seemed out of control.

The older ministers, men like Kelly Miller Smith, were quite ambivalent about the Freedom Rides. There had been some generational tensions before, thought Bernard Lafayette, but now for the first time there was a surprisingly clear division between the students and the ministers who had served as their advisers. If Kelly did not want to tell them not to go, he also did not want to be the man who too readily dispatched them to what might very well be their deaths. Because Kelly was from Mississippi, Lafayette thought, he knew all too well the consequences they faced. "I understand the importance of what you want to do," Kelly Miller Smith had said. "I think some of you are going to die if you go ahead. This is not something to rush into. I want you to think about it more."

Theirs was a long session lasting several hours, and it was Diane Nash and John Lewis who carried the argument for the young people. When the older ministers repeatedly warned of the danger, Diane had said that if they stopped now it surely would be even more dangerous for those setting out the next time. When Kelly said that some of them might die, there had been a moment of silence, and then John Lewis had said, "Yes, we understand that. We understand that that may be the price. But it has to be done." As he said this John Lewis had looked over at Kelly Miller Smith, who was his favorite teacher at American Baptist, the man who had brought him into the Movement, and he thought for an instant that Kelly looked old and tired. That grayness in his face, he thought, came from fear—not fear for himself, but fear for them. This was a man who loved them, and he was terrified of sending them forth to their deaths. He thinks of us as his own children, Lewis had thought, and he cannot bear to send his children to their deaths.

It was at that moment that John Lewis had an epiphany: Not only did their own parents not want them to make the trip, but now the Nashville ministers felt the same way because over the past year they had become the proxy parents of the students. They had all gotten too close to each other. Because they had been through so much together and had come to admire one another so much, human emotions and personal attachments were outweighing what was good for the cause. That was wrong, Lewis believed. We cannot listen to them anymore, he thought, and we cannot listen to them because they love us; it is the same reason that we have to turn away from the advice of our parents, though they too love us. "They've all grown up," Kelly Miller Smith had told Will Campbell the next day. "One day they're children, nervous about going to jail for the first time in Nashville, and the next day they're going off to Birmingham and Jackson, Mississippi. I've watched them for a year, and they've grown up in front of me."

Lewis realized that the scene was like a much sharper replay of some tensions which had surfaced a few months earlier when events had become quite tumultuous during the assault upon Nashville's downtown movie theaters. The attempt to integrate the movie theaters should not have been particularly difficult; the real battle had been won earlier over the lunch counters. But it had turned out to be a surprisingly ugly struggle for several reasons: It was at night, which made things instantly more dangerous; the old Nashville library, which was across the street from Kelly Miller Smith's church, was being torn down, and the bricks from it had provided ammunition for the white attackers; and the police had shown little interest in limiting the violence. Night after night the violence had mounted, and finally Kelly Miller Smith and some of the ministers had decided that it was time to back off slightly and see if they could use their new political power to bring a kind of settlement.

The first glimmerings of a split between the generations had been evidenced at that meeting. Kelly Miller Smith and some of the other ministers wanted a cooling-off period and they spoke repeatedly of how dangerous the stand-ins were becoming. But it also became quite clear that as far as the young people were concerned, the danger was the very object of the exercise, and was what they wanted in order to push things forward. They had come to sense in some intuitive way that the things they wanted to happen would happen only if they reached and crossed a certain danger point. An intuitive philosophy of the students in the Movement was being born: The safer everything was, the less likely that anything important would take place. Changes would come only with risk; the greater the risk, the greater the change. The children were the first to understand that, Will Campbell thought, for they had not yet made the compromises which had been forced on their elders, and they were willing to resist those compromises, if need be, with their lives. They still lived in a world where the truth was absolute.

Campbell had been intrigued by the way the young people had handled the meeting over the stand-ins. Jim Bevel, who was their most brilliant speaker, had argued for continuing them, and he was predictably dazzling. But in the end their anchor had been John Lewis. There was Kelly at his best, a man whom John loved, Campbell knew, saying that the city simply could not take another night of violence, and therefore he was recommending that they take a break, and John Lewis would nod, as if agreeing with Kelly, and then he would say in a voice which had no flex in it, yes, but they were going to march again. There were several exchanges along this line: John Lewis would nod, and then he would say in his own steadfast way that yes, he agreed with them that it was all too dangerous, but they would march again.

Finally Will Campbell spoke. He had always liked John Lewis but he had not thought of him as a leader in the first rank because he did not seem as articulate as Diane Nash and Jim Bevel and some of the others. That early categorization, he was beginning to learn, had been a mistake. He had underestimated Lewis's hold on his peers, which came not from the power of words, but from the power of belief. "John," he had said, "it seems to me that whatever we say, you agree with. We're telling you that it's too dangerous and we have to slow it down, and you agree and say yes, and then you say that you're going to demonstrate again. So what we really have here, John, is your own hubris, your own stubbornness. You know that you shouldn't go ahead, but you insist on doing it anyway. You're refusing to accommodate us because of your pride, which is your own sin." John Lewis had smiled at Will Campbell and had agreed that, yes, Will was right, he *was* a sinner. And then he had added, yes, they were going to march again that night. That was the night Will Campbell had finally realized the leadership of the Nashville wing of the Movement had changed, that the young people had taken over, that a dramatic generational passing of the torch had already taken place, and no one had quite understood it. The first thought Will Campbell had was, They have gone beyond us; the second was that it was the way things were supposed to be. The next day the demonstrations had continued and John Lewis had been arrested. It was his fourth arrest. He was not yet twenty-one.

Now, with the young people wanting to resume the Freedom Rides and go off to Birmingham, that generational line showed again. The SCLC had made out a check for the expenses, around $900, but there was only one signature on the check and in order to be cashed, it had to have two signatures, the second being that of the Reverend John Copeland, a black minister who was the local SCLC treasurer. Copeland, as did some of the other ministers, needed a second job to support his family, and he worked at night for the L&N Railroad; that night the students had searched all over town for him without any success. It was, Bernard Lafayette thought, a deliberate ploy on the part of the older ministers to try and slow down the Freedom Rides. For a moment they were stymied. Then one of them had the inspired idea of going to see a wheeler-dealer who operated out of one of the black nightclubs and who was a big numbers man. Big numbers men always had a lot of cash. They found him, and the numbers man had looked at the check, and he had smiled, a small private smile all his own which went back to an age-old war within the black community between the good blacks, who went to church, and the bad blacks, who worked the night at different gambling joints. Then he had reached in his pocket and taken out a huge bankroll, and peeled off a few large bills. With that the money was available, the check processed by the two faces of the black community, the daytime face and the nighttime face.

For the students the meeting they had held earlier to decide whether or not they were going to continue the Freedom Rides was their most somber ever. They now knew that CORE was going to back off, and they knew that the federal government wanted them to back off—the phrase they would hear again and again was about letting things cool down. "Been cooling down for one hundred years and now it seems like white folks want another one hundred years," James Bevel had said at one point, and they had all agreed. But the dangers were obvious. There was no way you could look at the bus being set on fire in Anniston and not think about death.

Each of them had to make a terrible choice. There were many valid reasons not to go. If they went, there was a strong possibility that some of them would be in jail and would miss their final exams. That had to be considered. Someone spoke about how if they went, they might be letting their parents down. But that was an old argument, decided long ago. There was a strong consensus to go, but they had decided that each of them had to spend some time thinking about what he or she was going to do. Because the stakes were so high, the decision had to be right for each individual.

Bernard Lafayette knew he had come to a point of no return, and that he was making the most fateful decision of his life. After the meeting he spent the evening and much of the early morning talking with his friend Joseph Carter, who was also a student at American Baptist and was considering taking part in the Freedom Rides himself. Joseph Carter was the perfect foil for Lafayette on this decision in the way that Bevel and Lewis were not. Bevel was original and eclectic, a wonderful friend, but he was *Bevel,* maddeningly different from anyone else. He had already irritated some of them by announcing that even though he was acting chairman of the local chapter of SNCC, thereby in charge of deciding who would go on the next segment of the Freedom Rides, he was not going himself, at least not at the beginning because he had a previous commitment to go to New York with a friend, Alonzo Blake, who had just gotten married, to pick up some furniture and move it back to Nashville. To the great annoyance of his other friends, he intended to fulfill that promise. At first Bernard Lafayette was furious with Bevel—here they all were about to set off for Alabama and Mississippi, and Bevel, who was one of the most experienced leaders they had, a born strategist, was not going to come with them because he had to help a friend move furniture. That was pure Bevel, the contrarian as ever. His decision clearly angered most of the others. Bevel, of course, cared not at all what others thought. He had given his word, and that was all that mattered. When the furniture mission was completed, he flew directly to Montgomery, where he became a critical part of the decision making there.

Lafayette might have discussed his decisions with John Lewis, but John, Lafayette knew, had already made up his mind—he was going to go. Nothing could stop him now. But Lafayette was less certain about his own course. That was why Joseph Carter was ideal, careful and thoughtful, a young man with an excellent analytical mind who seemed on occasion more like a lawyer than a ministerial student. Lafayette was in a serious dilemma. He knew his parents would not want him to go. They had already expressed their powerful reservations about what he was doing. There was little evidence that the federal government would protect them—if anything it was clear that the feds were using all the pressure they could muster to get them to stop.

Joe Carter was, Lafayette believed, just a bit more conservative and timid than Lafayette himself. So they stayed up all night and walked the campus together, and in the end Carter, who was the most cautious of all his friends, said they had to go, that they could not stop now. "Bernard," Carter had asked, "are you prepared to die?" That was the only question worth asking and they both knew it. Bernard had pondered the question, and thought of how young he was, and he had pondered the choices and he had said yes. Carter said so too. "There'll be no protection," Lafayette said, "we'll be on our own." Carter agreed.

What they were doing was, Lafayette thought, the logical extension of the nonviolent course which they had chosen. The first step had come in the sit-ins, when he had tested himself to see if he had the strength not to lash back at those who had assaulted him. But this was a further step. Could he die for this cause? To him and to Lewis and a handful of the others, nonviolence was not just a tactic, it had become a way of life. If he died, he would at least die for his beliefs. Blacks, he knew, had died for more than a century at the hands of whites in the South in lonely settings, without witnesses, their deaths never even reported in newspapers. None of those deaths had advanced the cause, but if he and the others died in Alabama on this trip, the nation would know. If the nation was now ready to watch them suffer, then he was ready to sacrifice.

That night he, like nineteen others, made out his will and signed it. It was the most serious thing Bernard had ever done. The wills detailed who would get their limited belongings, their clothes, and their handful of books. It was all very somber. The next day, they handed Diane Nash sealed letters filled with instructions of what to do in the case of their deaths.

Among those wrestling with the issue of a will was a young white student at Fisk named Jim Zwerg. Zwerg was an exchange student from Beloit College in Wisconsin who had barely arrived in Nashville in the early winter of 1961 before he found himself pulled into the movie theater stand-ins. Zwerg, who hoped to become a Congregationalist minister, had watched a stand-in as an observer and had then been invited back to a workshop by John Lewis. At first he thought little of what he saw, but then he had been gradually impressed by the degree to which these young people were driven by their religion and their simple belief in a different, less-prejudiced America, and in particular, he had been moved by the modest yet steadfast nature of John Lewis, who from the start had personally reached out to him. Zwerg had quickly become a regular in the stand-ins and had been beaten badly on one occasion when he had showed up, bought two movie tickets, one for himself and one for a black friend, had entered the theater, and had been coldcocked from behind and knocked unconscious.

The beating did not bother him. Never before had he felt so confident of his purpose, and a phrase used by Kelly Miller Smith had stayed with him—the use of redemptive love to win over adversaries. Never had he felt so deeply the value and purpose of his religion, and never before had the Scriptures seemed so meaningful, indeed so contemporary. But his participation and in particular his decision to go ahead and ride a freedom bus had put him at a tension point with his parents. His father, an Appleton, Wisconsin, dentist, had suffered a number of heart attacks and one small stroke, and his mother believed that if Zwerg boarded the bus, his father would almost certainly die from the shock. That he could not reconcile the objection of the people he loved the most with this act of conscience which meant so much to him caused Jim Zwerg considerable anguish, and the night before he left Nashville he called home one more time trying to explain what he was doing and why. He and his mother had argued for a time and finally his mother hung up on him. He then wrote his parents a long letter trying to explain what he was doing—a letter which was in effect a will, since he was sure he was going to be killed.

30

WHILE THE OTHERS INVADED ALABAMA, DIANE NASH WAS TO REMAIN in Nashville in charge of the headquarters. Among her first tasks was to handle the negotiations with the leaders of the other black groups and to alert them about what the Nashville students intended to do. She had been chosen by the other students to be the coordinator because they felt that no one handled negotiations better than she did, and no one made better decisions in the midst of conflict. But to her it was an unwanted responsibility—she would greatly have preferred to be one of the riders herself, because then your only responsibility was to yourself. But if you were the coordinator you might be sending your closest friends to their deaths. She remembered the most important of Gandhi's lessons: Leaders were not truly leaders unless they were willing to do everything that they asked of others. Was she willing to die at this moment? she wondered. As the others were debating whether to go to Birmingham, she was trying to decide whether she had the courage to get on one of the buses herself, and only when she decided that she had that courage did she accept the job as coordinator on this mission.

Very early on she made one crucial and valuable decision: Even though they had very little money and even the smallest expense was a considerable burden, she installed a second phone line. It was *never* to be used for outgoing calls. It was always to be open. Only their own people in the Deep South knew the number. That way anyone in Alabama or Mississippi who got in trouble would always be able to get through to headquarters.

One of her first jobs was to work things out with Jim Farmer, the head of CORE. Farmer had been on the Freedom Ride at the start, but had left before the Atlanta-Anniston leg because of the death of his father. Now, with his own people pulling out, she had to ask Farmer for permission to take over a CORE project. This was a touchy area. It got into the world of egos and territory, and a surprising number of people on all sides of the Movement were quite territorial. There had been an unspoken agreement among the different civil rights groups not to steal one another's programs. By taking it over, there was the inevitable suggestion that the young SNCC kids were somehow braver and more committed than the CORE people. Her talk with Farmer had been a delicate one, but Farmer had been very good about it. She told him that she and her colleagues had caucused and it appeared that they had about twenty people ready to continue the bus rides. They would assemble in Birmingham. Some of them would arrive in Birmingham by bus, some would arrive by car, and perhaps some would get there by train. Farmer was nervous about what the young people were suggesting, the danger they would face. "It's the most dangerous thing I've ever seen," he told her; "the other side, the Klan, they're well organized and they're working in partnership with the local cops and state troopers." But she persisted and he understood why they were coming in. "Well, you guys have good instincts and you're well trained, so go ahead," he had said. A big hurdle was cleared.

She then called the Reverend Fred Shuttlesworth in Birmingham to let him know they were coming. Shuttlesworth told her that it was going to be terribly dangerous, worse than anything they could imagine. "Young lady, do you know that the Freedom Riders were almost killed here?" he asked her.[1] She said yes, she did. "We're going to come," she said, and he had said yes, he could understand that, and that he would do all he could to help them, but unfortunately he could not offer protection to them because he could not really protect himself and his own people.

She went to a telephone away from her office for her next conversation with Shuttlesworth, and they devised codes they could use, for both of them were sure that their phone lines were already bugged at both ends, probably by both state and federal authorities. For reasons she did not understand, she and Shuttlesworth used chicken nomenclature for their code. One species was a black male, another a black female, another a white male, another a white female.

Diane Nash had become, without even realizing it, the commanding general of the young people. It was as if there were two separate and distinct Diane Nashes, one who had existed before the sit-ins, living her personal life with great shyness, uncertain in all things, and another who had come alive and been empowered because of her entrance into the Movement and her role in a cause larger than herself. Quiet and tentative and surprisingly vulnerable on her own, loathe to speak up for herself, she was, when she operated for the Movement, utterly fearless, unimpressed by power or title, aware only of what she and the others thought was the right thing to do. She would stand up to anyone. Not surprisingly, all kinds of powerful white men, some liberal, some conservative, some who worked for the state government, and some who worked for the feds, disliked her intensely, and thought her incredibly arrogant and unbending.

The decision to go forward made, she called her contacts in the Justice Department to tell them that the Nashville kids were going to continue the ride. The people at Justice were not pleased. It was nothing but unwanted trouble for them; the more the young people exposed themselves to physical risk, the more it pushed the government of the United States into protecting all citizens in all places within the country at the risk of alienating white Southern voters and white Southern politicians, all of whom were Democrats. There was absolutely no political profit in that. Her calls reached Burke Marshall, who thought her stubborn, and who in turn talked to Robert Kennedy, who in turn talked to John Seigenthaler, his personal assistant.

To the degree that there was now a federal presence as these two opposing forces prepared to gather in Alabama for the beginning of one of the early battles of the Deep South, Seigenthaler was it. He was thirty-three years old at the time, about to be thirty-four, a former reporter for the *Tennessean*. He did not have a law degree; indeed, he had barely attended college. He had no troops or cops under his command, and now as he began to work the phones, he had a sense that all hell was about to break loose and no one was ready for it. The irony was that he was on this mission in Alabama largely because he was the only Southerner around Bobby Kennedy; he had already been sent to Alabama to shepherd the first group of Freedom Riders out of Birmingham to New Orleans.

Seigenthaler had been in Washington on Sunday when the incidents at Anniston and Birmingham had taken place, and the attorney general had ordered him to take the next flight to Alabama. By the time he connected with the original Freedom Riders on Monday afternoon, they had left the Birmingham bus station because no one would drive a bus they were on, and gone to the Birmingham airport. There they hoped to board a plane, skipping the Montgomery and Jackson legs, and instead fly directly to New Orleans. He had found them in the Birmingham airport, besieged and terrified, clustered together in a small, despairing group. They were being tormented by the local authorities and by angry whites. Outside the airport a large crowd had gathered and seemed to be threatening to come and take them away. If this was not yet a riot, he thought, it was very close to becoming one. The Freedom Riders themselves seemed to be in a state of shock. They were kindly people, ill prepared for what had happened, and from his years as a reporter on the *Tennessean,* he thought he detected a type—Quakers, people of conscience, pacifists, the people who stand lonely vigils for unpopular causes and do not even seem to know that the cause is unpopular. This was a mission for a special kind of warrior, and despite the inner strength he sensed in them, he did not think they were that kind of warrior. His main job was to shepherd them out of Birmingham to New Orleans.

They seemed among the loneliest people he had ever seen. The food stalls in the airport would not serve them. The other passengers taunted them. To the degree that there were cops present, the cops seemed to be on the side of the mob. The Freedom Riders were unable to go to the rest rooms alone; as such they went in pairs. The vocabulary of the crowd seemed to be limited to two phrases, *niggers* and *nigger-lovers.* All these people wanted to do was to get out of Birmingham, but every time they were booked on a flight there was a bomb threat and the flight would be canceled.

Seigenthaler, acting in the name of the attorney general of the United States, got on the phone with the airline people and told them just to get these people out of there. "You know damn well there's no bomb on these planes, and it's just harassment," he said. Then he gave his plan: Just pick a plane, get the baggage of everyone else on it, then get the Freedom Riders' baggage on it, slip the Freedom Riders on, then at the last minute announce the plane, and from the moment you announce it, don't answer the phone because all you'll do is get a bomb threat. The airline manager had followed his instructions, and finally they had been flown to New Orleans at about 10:45 that night after more than five frightening hours in the airport, where again they were harassed. Cops were everywhere, but were behaving more like rednecks. But Seigenthaler had gotten them out of Birmingham, and things were about to quiet down, or so he thought.

They were not. About 2:00 A.M. on Tuesday, May 16, he was awakened in his motel room in New Orleans by a call from Robert Kennedy, who told him that the Nashville students were about to take over the Freedom Rides and were planning to move on Birmingham, and that it was his job to talk them out of going. Some young woman named Diane Nash, Kennedy said, was in charge. Seigenthaler then talked to Burke Marshall, who was Kennedy's deputy for civil rights, who gave him Nash's phone number. She was being very stubborn, Marshall reported, and did not appear to be a good listener. The prospect of the arrival of more Freedom Riders in Alabama was the last thing the Justice Department needed, Marshall said. Alabama, Seigenthaler agreed, was not just Klan territory, it was now like a hornet's nest, with the segs seething with anger and the state officials sitting it out. "She's from your goddamned city," Marshall told Seigenthaler; "see what you can do to stop them."[2]

From what Seigenthaler had heard about the young, increasingly militant students, he had little hope that they would listen to him. He waited until about 7:00 A.M. and called an old friend of his in Nashville, George Barrett, a labor lawyer who was close to the local activists. He asked Barrett to make a call to Nash to see if he could soften her up. Barrett phoned back a few minutes later to tell Seigenthaler he was wasting his time: The young people were determined to go ahead and they were going to do so despite the uneasiness of the older generation of ministers. Seigenthaler then called Nash. He warned her of how dangerous it was going to be. He had just been in Birmingham and it was about to explode, a city without any restraints, where the cops were actively on the other side. He asked for a temporary halt to the rides. No, she said, no one was going to stop them now. "You're going to get your people killed," he warned. "Then others will follow them," she answered.

Listening to her he had a sense that she and the young people simply could not be moved, and it reminded him of the words of the old hymn: "Just like a tree that's planted near the water, we will not be moved." It was as if he could hear her singing the hymn as he tried to warn her of the dangers ahead. Then he had brought up the possibility of their deaths. "Then others will follow them." And if they too were met by violence? "Then even more will come." Talking to her was, he later reported to his superiors in Washington, like talking to a brick wall.[3] Seigenthaler hung up knowing that his boss in Washington was going to be furious, but he was full of admiration for these young people about to undertake so perilous a journey.

Years later he understood more clearly the collision of political interests which was about to take place, and realized that he himself had been a rare witness to a preliminary skirmish a few weeks earlier when Martin Luther King had visited Robert Kennedy in Washington. It had been, he believed, a fascinating moment in history, a scenario played out by two powerful men, one, Kennedy, the attorney general and at that moment the ultimate pragmatist, and the other, King, the ultimate idealist with just the proper amount of pragmatism built in. It had been a pleasant meeting; each had been respectful if not warm and trusting toward the other. Each understood the other's potential political orbit and political problems. Each had a separate agenda: King, to assault the remaining bastions of segregation and dramatize the evils of it as best he could for the nation to witness; Kennedy, to maintain order, but above all to protect his older brother's political interests. That meant, given the president's awesome burdens in other areas, such as foreign affairs, as little confrontation as possible between civil rights activists and Democratic state officials in the South.

The Kennedys were not segregationists, but the war over race tested the historically divided soul of the Democratic party. It was a badly needed war, as far as King was concerned, but an unwanted one as far as the Kennedys were concerned. Robert Kennedy was reasonably candid—his brother had a Congress dominated in its committees by conservative Southerners, and if that was not bad enough, he had problems with the FBI, whose director, immensely powerful with Congress and an icon to conservatives in both parties, was deeply hostile to civil rights (and to King personally). Kennedy, predictably, said that he was for the things that King wanted, but he needed time. King, for his part, was gently adamant. The white man had been given a great deal of time—it was coming up on one hundred years since the

end of the Civil War. Time had run out on the patience of black people. Our job is to dramatize this evil, King kept repeating. Robert
Kennedy kept talking about the need to use all that energy that King
could now tap into in Southern states to mobilize black people to
vote. He should take all these brilliant young ministers and these
bright, idealistic young sit-in leaders and go out and register voters.
That would, of course, have a duel benefit for the Kennedys: It would
diminish confrontation in the streets, and it would increase black
franchise in the South—poor black people were more likely to vote
for Kennedy in 1964 than Goldwater.

Seigenthaler remembered one exact phrase from his boss, because
the word he used was so old-fashioned. If King and his people went
into states like Alabama and Mississippi and multiplied the number of
black votes, he said, "Men like Jim Eastland would not be so fresh" in
their speeches on race. *Fresh,* thought Seigenthaler, what an odd
word. Some twenty years later he attended a biracial meeting in South
Carolina where the subject was civil rights, and sitting near him was
Strom Thurmond, by then, because of increased black franchise, a
friend of South Carolina's blacks, the same Strom Thurmond who had
run for president in 1948 as a Dixiecrat, and he remembered his boss's
words, and knew that Bob Kennedy had been right. Strom was not so
fresh anymore.

The meeting between Kennedy and King had lasted some forty
minutes. At the end King had said something pleasant—"I know
you'll do the best that you can." But the distance between them,
Seigenthaler remembered, had not narrowed at all. It had been like
the first round in a boxing match between two powerful men, each
circling the other, trying to find out what he was like and what was at
stake. They might be allies on some occasions, and they might just as
likely come up against each other in some terrible unforeseen collision. Now, thrust back into Alabama, into what he suspected was
about to become a raging hell on earth, Seigenthaler understood what
the young people from Nashville were doing. They knew that all
things being equal, Robert Kennedy intended to protect his brother
instead of the civil rights workers. So what the Nashville kids were
doing almost by instinct—knowing that only the ultimate sacrifice
could change the equation from one of all things being equal—was

offering their very lives up so that Robert Kennedy would have no choice; he would have to protect them instead of his brother.

Of all the phone calls Diane Nash made, the ones which irritated her the most were the ones with the representatives of the Department of Justice in Washington. As far as she was concerned, they were treating her with consummate condescension. These Washington officials who enjoyed full citizenship, and could eat wherever they wanted and travel wherever they wanted, were presuming to tell her what was good for her people, which of course reflected only what was good for John Kennedy. She was unmoved by their expressed concern for her cause. She kept repeating that the SNCC volunteers were going to continue the Freedom Rides. One particular Justice official kept telling her that it was too dangerous, that they might be killed. As if her friends who were already making out their wills did not know that! she thought. "We know that we may be killed!" she had told one Justice Department man. "We are more aware of that than you can imagine."

For the young students headed toward Birmingham, the plan was to get there by different means and then assemble at Fred Shuttlesworth's house. They would go by bus and by train, but they would not integrate the buses and trains on their journey to Bull Connor's city. John Lewis, they decided, would be the leader of the bus group. He had been a Freedom Rider, and knew the risk involved.

31

THIRTY-FIVE YEARS LATER JOHN LEWIS REMEMBERED THE EXACT DAY
and moment they left the Nashville bus station heading for Birmingham. It was Wednesday, May 17, 1961—seven years to the day, he
remembered, from the day the Supreme Court had ruled in *Brown*—
and it was 6:30 A.M. There were ten of them, seven men and three
women. John Lewis had no doubts about their course. In the defining
moment of the debate with the ministers he had asked the critical
question: "If not us, then who? If not now, then when? Will there be a
better day for it tomorrow or next year? Will it be less dangerous
then? Will someone else's children have to risk their lives instead of us
risking ours?" No one had been able to argue with that. How would
they ever be able to explain to their own children, he had asked, that
they had started out to protest segregation, had won a battle over
lunch counters in a border state, and then stopped?

Now he was going back to Alabama, the state from which he had
come. He tried not to think about the danger ahead, but rather of
their purpose in taking this journey. He remembered when he had
been a little boy and the family had driven from Pike County to Buf-
falo, New York, and the humiliations of that trip, of how his mother
had been forced to cook all their food in advance because they could
not eat at restaurants and how they had had to go to the bathroom
along the roadside. He had hated the sight of that, of his grown parents being forced to turn the roadside into a rest room. If nothing else,
this was a blow he and his friends were striking against that America.
John Lewis was determined that he was not going to watch his own
children humiliated.

As their bus approached Birmingham, the driver had been flagged
down by a police car, and had pulled over. Bull Connor, the Birming-

ham police commissioner, a mythic figure, if not among local whites, then certainly among the city's blacks, had boarded the bus. At that moment he was, as far as black people in Alabama were concerned, the best known white man in the state. In Nashville, because the political situation was much healthier, the police force did not operate on its own in a lawless and essentially totalitarian way, and the students had barely known the name of the police chief, Douglas Hosse. In Birmingham no one knew the name of the mayor, but everyone knew Bull Connor.

Bull Connor liked it that way. There was nothing subtle about him. He had quite deliberately made himself the symbol of a certain kind of white-black relationship, one in which the raw police power of white people was used as nakedly as need be to keep black people in their place. In Birmingham he *was* the law. What pleased him on a given day was legal; what displeased him the next day was illegal. His fondness for pure physical force appealed to white people in Birmingham: no niceties, no subtleties. "We ain't gonna segregate no niggers and whites together in this town," he had once said in a memorable statement.[1] Bull, it was said in the local vernacular—and it was the principal reason for his political success—knew how to handle niggers. Even his nickname helped: He had originally gotten it as a broadcaster of local baseball games because he was able to kill the long, boring moments of a game by shooting the bull over the air, but now it had a new meaning, someone who used brute force on black people.

His was an elected position and he had held it once before, but had been voted out of office when he had been caught by a political rival in flagrante delicto with his secretary in a hotel. But post-*Brown*, as the tensions over race had escalated sharply, he had staged a political comeback and had been reelected in 1957. Birmingham was his city, and it was a testimonial to his will and his reputation as a hard man that it was generally considered the most segregated city in the Deep South, its police force notoriously hostile to blacks. In racial matters, he was not merely the top cop, he was judge and jury as well. He took no small amount of pride in that. In recent years there had been an increasing number of bombings aimed at blacks who did not seem to know their place, against some who wanted to move, in his opinion, too close to white residential areas, and others like Fred Shuttlesworth, who were leading protest marches or trying to put their children in all-white schools. When one black man had had the audacity to buy a home near a white neighborhood, it was Bull Connor who went out to see him to tell him personally, in unvarnished language, that he and the Birmingham police could not protect him if he did so foolhardy a thing. The translation of that warning was simple: Bull Connor could not and would not protect him from Bull Connor. When Shuttlesworth had surfaced as the Birmingham embodiment of the modern social-activist minister, someone had thrown a packet with sixteen sticks of dynamite at his house, destroying it and part of his church, but in no way dampening Shuttlesworth's remarkable willingness to challenge the existing order. A certain black section of Birmingham where a number of explosions had taken place was known as Dynamite Hill. The failure of the Birmingham police to find the people responsible for any of these bombings had convinced not merely local blacks but federal authorities that if Bull Connor himself was not a member of the Klan, he had very close ties to it.

There were no black cops on Connor's police force in 1961, unlike in other major Southern metropolitan areas. Not everyone in the white establishment was entirely comfortable with the growing power of Bull Connor, and just under the surface there was a significant division among the people of the upper middle class, the business establishment, and Connor himself, but as racial tensions grew in the late fifties, those dissident whites found themselves increasingly intimidated.

That morning as he boarded the bus, Bull Connor's confidence was obvious. He was a man who seemed to swagger even when he was standing still. He stopped at the front of the bus, where Paul Brooks and Jim Zwerg, the former black, the latter white, were sitting in the seats right behind the driver. Though there had been a general agreement that they would not try to integrate either the buses or trains which took them to Birmingham, Zwerg and Brooks had decided to sit next to each other, something which irritated the others. They had been aware of the risk they were taking; Zwerg was sure he was going to be killed, because he had learned the hard way that white boys were the prime target. He and Brooks had spoken on the way down about how beautiful Alabama was at that time of year, how green everything outside seemed. He had pondered the contrast of that, the verdant quality of the countryside, with the darkness of what he was sure his fate was, and was amused by the irony of the thought. Bull Connor, boarding the bus, asked them both to move. They refused. Connor seemed pleased by their refusal. They were in violation of Alabama law, he said, and arrested them. The two of them were taken off the bus. With that, this new group of Freedom Riders had crossed a line with the most powerful racist in Alabama.

Bull Connor stayed on the bus and told the driver to drive to the Birmingham bus station. Once they got there, Connor came back and checked everyone's ticket. The tickets of the SNCC kids read Nashville-Birmingham-Montgomery-Jackson-New Orleans. He separated everyone with one of those tickets from the regular riders. A young white woman named Selyn McCollum, whose assignment was to serve as an observer and report back to Diane Nash, and who was under orders *not* to be arrested, was herded in with the others. "I'm not with these people," she had said, but Bull Connor did not play the game. "Yes, you are," he said, and pointed out that remarkably enough she had the exact same kind of ticket. Even as this was being played out, Connor's people were covering the windows of the bus so that members of the media could not see in.

John Lewis, looking out the window as the bus first pulled into the station, picked up on something which the others had missed, and which was critically important: He saw that there were more reporters waiting than he had ever seen before. That meant what they were trying to do—to catch the attention of the government by catching the attention of the media—was beginning to work. In addition these journalists were, he was sure, from the *national* media, because it was extremely unlikely that many Southern papers would cover an event like this. That was a plus—there was no purpose in offering yourself up to your sworn enemies if no one was watching. Soon they had all been arrested and put in the Birmingham jail. Bull Connor had kept them on the bus for about two hours before arresting them.

By the time John Seigenthaler arrived in Birmingham, Bull Connor had already put Lewis's bus riders in jail. It was Seigenthaler's first assignment to try and talk Bull Connor into releasing the Freedom Riders. That was not going to be easy, he soon discovered. He identified himself to the police commissioner. The first thing that Bull Connor did was to laugh at him. That meant he was laughing not just at Seigenthaler but at the Kennedy Justice Department. The other thing he kept doing was calling Seigenthaler "sonny boy." "Well, sonny boy," he said, "they violated the law, so they're going to have to pay the price. You just tell all your friends up in Washington that." Seigenthaler did not like the idea of these young people being in Bull Connor's jail, and he felt that events were racing forward in an ominous way.

Bull Connor had sent Jim Zwerg and Paul Brooks to jail. Zwerg was to spend most of the next two days in a drunk tank. Connor told the eight others that he was going to take them into protective custody. They were all put in a paddy wagon around 1:00 P.M. on Wednesday, May 17, and taken to the Birmingham jail. The group stayed there that night, and the next day, separated by gender and by race, cut off from everyone else. The one thing they had any control of was their own bodies, and so before they were split up they had decided to go on a hunger strike, which was part of the traditional Gandhian strategy. Then early Friday morning, Bull Connor came in and roused them. It was around 1:00 A.M., Lewis believed, though he could not be sure of the time. Connor was accompanied by a few of his aides, and, Lewis believed, a reporter from one of the Birmingham papers. "I'm going to take you all back to Nashville," he said, and then he put them in a three-car caravan. Seven of them were packed in the cars; Selyn McCollum had apparently already been sent home separately.

John Lewis was in the car with Bull Connor and Catherine Burks, a beautiful young black woman from Tennessee A&I who was part of their group. He was intrigued by the fact that Connor, rather than being the fierce anti-black racist of legend, now seemed if anything quite relaxed and genial. He had taken a liking to Catherine Burks, and the teasing byplay between them was almost surrealistic. Their conversation did not seem like that of a legendary white racist with a dangerous Freedom Rider. Rather it was more like that of an avuncular uncle and favored niece, with slight overtones of flirtation. She seemed to enjoy talking to him—it was easier for her to challenge him, she believed, because she was a young woman and she could get away with saying things that Bull Connor would not accept from the men.[2] Connor told them he was taking them all back to Nashville and would drop them off at their schools. At one point Catherine Burks said they were all hungry because of the hunger strike. When Connor said that he was hungry too, she invited him to join them for breakfast at Fisk.

"You ought to eat with us, you ought to get to know us better," she said. "Well, you know, I might just do that," he said. It was all very low key and pleasant, Bull Connor being a good old boy, Lewis thought. And then the caravan slowed as they came up on a little town near the Tennessee-Alabama border named Ardmore. There on the outskirts of town, the three cars stopped, and probably around 3:00 A.M. Connor ordered them all out and told them they were on their own. "There's the Tennessee line. Cross it and save yourselves a lot of trouble."[3] No longer the good old boy, once again his harder self, Bull Connor started to get back in the car, and Lewis heard Catherine Burks tell him, "We'll be back in Birmingham by the end of the day." Bull Connor laughed as if he thought that was the best joke he had heard in weeks. It was a moment John Lewis loved; the spirit was there among them. She really is fearless, he thought.

They were, of course, absolutely terrified. They were by themselves in the midst of Klan territory. It was, they were sure, a setup: They would disappear into Klan hands at night, and Bull Connor would be able to say that he had taken them all back to the Tennessee border, and he would even have a journalistic witness to his benign role. John Lewis knew how dangerous the game had suddenly become; he was sure that there were already Klansmen, tipped off earlier, who were out looking to pick them up. Rural Alabama was where alien black people—uppity ones like the Freedom Riders—disappeared and were never seen again. No outside media people had witnessed the exchange at the Birmingham jail; it had been done in the dead of night. In Nashville, Diane Nash thought they were still in the Birmingham jail. Only their enemies knew where they were.

But John Lewis knew one thing, that Ardmore was in Alabama and it was poor, which meant that it had to have poor black people living there, who if approached quietly, would help them. Their job was to try and find some black family before any white people found them. They knew they had to get off the highway as quickly as they could because that was the most dangerous place for them.

It was still dark out. No one was allowed to light a cigarette and they spoke in whispers. Finally someone noticed a dilapidated old shack. It seemed to stand apart—there were no other shacks clustered around it as in the black sections of most Alabama villages. No lights were on. "There's got to be black people there," one rider said. Beside the shack was a beat-up pickup truck. For sure, John Lewis thought, black people live here.

They walked to the shack and Lewis knocked on the door. They could hear sounds inside, and then the voice of an old black man, asking what was going on. "We're Freedom Riders, and we're in trouble," Lewis said. What he was doing was in one sense terrible, he knew, bringing the danger of the modern civil rights struggle to the door of the simplest, most vulnerable black people in the South. For people like this, any knock on the door in the middle of the night would be trouble. But he had no choice; he was their leader, responsible for six other lives. The movement inside the door seemed to stop. "We're Freedom Riders. Please let us in," Lewis repeated. "Keep talking loudly," Catherine Burks said. "If we talk loud enough we can wake the woman inside there and she'll let us in." Catherine was sure they had a better chance with the woman of the house—in places like this the men were more directly vulnerable to white society, she believed, and were more readily intimidated.[4] Then they heard a lock turn, and they had a terrible sense that the door was being locked. Lewis could feel his own hope slipping away, and then he heard the man's wife say, "Honey, let those people in."

The man did what he was told. This was the poorest of houses. But amazingly enough these simple, dreadfully poor people had a telephone. The Lord truly works in wondrous ways, Lewis thought. He quickly called the Nashville headquarters, and again was surprised by his luck because Diane Nash was there. First she updated him using their latest codes. "Ten other packages have been shipped by other means." That meant that ten additional Freedom Riders were going by train. Selyn McCollum's father had flown down to pick her up and take her back to Nashville. Zwerg and Brooks had been released from jail, had been tried and convicted of disobeying a police officer, and the two of them had headed to Fred Shuttlesworth's church, eager to continue.

The one thing that Diane needed to know was whether Lewis and his group wanted to come back to Nashville or to go right back to Birmingham. They decided they wanted to go back to Birmingham as quickly as possible. By then it was Friday morning and they were starved—they had not eaten since Wednesday morning. They gave the old man some money and he went out for food. He intrigued Lewis. He was absolutely terrified. His world was being threatened as it had probably never been threatened before. The most dangerous words in Alabama at that moment were *Freedom Rider.* But whatever else on this day, he was going to act like a man. He was also very shrewd. In order to get enough food for so many people, he went to three different stores, so that no one would know how many guests he had.

Diane Nash dispatched a young sit-in leader named Leo Lillard to pick them up. They did not have a lot of cars and so Lillard drove alone. He got there in less than an hour, which amazed them. They all piled in. By then it was late Friday morning. How they ever fit in his car, eight people including the driver, plus their luggage, no one ever knew. They were tired and they were dirty, but they were going back to Birmingham. On the radio all the news reports were about the Freedom Riders, which was gratifying. They heard bulletin after bulletin: Bull Connor had delivered them back to Nashville. That pleased them, they had fooled old Bull, but then a few minutes later there was another bulletin: The Freedom Riders were reliably reported to be on their way back to Birmingham by car. That was not good news, Lewis thought, because they were so obvious a sight for police eyes, crowded in as they were in one car, and in addition it confirmed what they always suspected, that their phones were tapped. But no one spotted them, and when they got back to Birmingham on Friday they teased Catherine Burks that she should call up Bull Connor and tell him she was there so they could still get together for a meal or for a date. There was already a certain sense of victory among them—they had made it back to Birmingham in order to join the Freedom Ride, despite Bull Connor's attempt to dump them like trash on the Tennessee-Alabama border.

They went first to Fred Shuttlesworth's house, and then later they linked up with Bernard Lafayette's group at the bus station. It was midafternoon when they got to the bus station. John Lewis looked over and saw a group of ten other Freedom Riders. There was Bernard and he was wearing what Lewis considered his silly little hat. Bernard thought the hat quite snappy—indeed, it did have a snap brim on it, and clearly he thought he was a man among men when he wore it. John had never entirely shared Bernard's opinion that the hat made him seem older. But he had never been so glad to see Bernard and his goofy little hat. Bernard and his people all looked rested and fresh and were wearing clean clothes, and Lewis and his group were tired and dirty and wearing clothes which they had been living in for almost two days, both in prison and in the Ardmore shack. Now, as the two groups joined up, they all felt a little less alone.

32

JOHN SEIGENTHALER WAS SURPRISED WHEN HE HEARD THAT BULL
Connor had released the Freedom Riders and driven them up to Ardmore. Later he was told by sources that it was because they had taken
over his jail. In the past, the very thought of the Birmingham jail had
silenced and terrified all blacks. But these young people were different. They had not been frightened; they had sung their freedom songs,
and apparently, Seigenthaler was told, the noise and the subsequent
disruption they had caused in Bull Connor's jail had helped earn them
a quick release.

Even as Bull Connor drove his caravan toward Ardmore, early Friday morning Seigenthaler heard that more Freedom Riders were
heading toward Birmingham by train. Robert Kennedy ordered him
to drive down to Montgomery and meet with the governor, John Patterson, and to get Patterson and the state authorities to protect the
Freedom Riders from local police and angry white mobs. That visit to
Montgomery did not mark one of Seigenthaler's happiest days. Rarely
had an American politician's office seemed so hostile a place. Right
behind the governor were three flags, the Confederate, the Alabama,
and the American, giving Seigenthaler the feeling that he might well
be in a foreign land, under a foreign set of laws, and that his legal and
political mandate, that of someone representing the most powerful
law officer in the United States, as well as his brother, the president of
the United States, was totally meaningless here. Still, Seigenthaler's
appearance before Patterson marked a victory for the young people,
for they had finally begun to move the federal government, in the person of this one young man who felt so alone in Montgomery. With
Seigenthaler's visit to Patterson, the feds, in the most tentative and
reluctant way imaginable, were being put into play.

John Seigenthaler received from the governor of Alabama nothing less than a tongue lashing of the first order. John Patterson was in a rage. He reminded Seigenthaler that he was the first Southern governor to have endorsed John Kennedy when Kennedy had announced for the presidency. Well, he could tell Seigenthaler now that it was the biggest damn fool mistake he had ever made in his life. He was sorry as hell he had ever done it. But he was standing his ground now—and the American people loved him for doing it. Not just the people of Alabama, and not just the people of the South—the people of the entire country. He was more popular in the country now than John Kennedy because he had taken a stand for what was right. If no one else in the country had the courage to stand up to the niggers, by God, John Patterson did, and every white man in the country was on his side. He pointed to a pile of telegrams on his desk. There was the proof of his popularity.

Seigenthaler was listening to him and trying to decide how much of this was show, macho theater for the benefit of his cabinet and the Alabama journalists who would hear later in the day how their governor had told off Kennedy's man, and how much was real. Certainly Patterson had played the race card before. In the 1958 election for governor he had appealed to white prejudice even as his opponent, a young state judge named George Wallace, had run more as a populist. (That race was not without its own fateful impact on American politics, for it had led to Wallace's famous vow after his defeat that he never again would be "outniggered."[1]) Gradually Seigenthaler sensed that most of the anger was genuine, that Patterson felt betrayed, that he had expected upon Kennedy's election to be rewarded in some way, befitting a good and loyal Southern Democratic governor who had supported a Democratic winner early on and who therefore expected the president to work on his side. If the new Democratic president did not actually slow down the process of civil rights, then he would at least keep his distance and not expedite the process. Patterson expected it to be, at the least, business as usual: In the past, what went on in a Southern Democratic state, who was allowed to vote and who was not, was none of a Democratic president's business. It was a part of an unspoken, unviolated covenant that went back to the beginnings of the New Deal coalition which had allowed the essentially conservative South to be an uneasy partner with Northern liberals. The Southern Democratic machinery would hold its nose and turn its people out for candidates it felt were far too liberal, and in return the attorney general of the United States would not turn his powers against Democratic state administrations when they kept their local political franchise lily white.

Seigenthaler, listening to Patterson, could just imagine what had happened: Patterson had supported Kennedy early on, had taken a lot of heat at the start because Kennedy was a Northern liberal and a Catholic. Then the long shot had come home, and Patterson had probably done a little boasting about how connected he was in Washington. But all that his connections had gotten him were a bunch of Freedom Riders bearing down on his state. But John Kennedy can't help John Patterson on this one, Seigenthaler thought, on this one he can't even help himself. Here we are, he thought, the young black kids think we are doing far too little, and they're probably right, and the Southern officials think we're doing far too much.

Seigenthaler tried to change the conversation. He knew his main job was to get some sort of guarantee of protection for the young people without provoking Patterson further. What they wanted, he said, was to get these young people safely through Alabama. Make it Mississippi's problem, he suggested, adding that Robert Kennedy was already in negotiations with the Mississippi authorities. We are asking you to protect them, or, Seigenthaler suggested, if you can't protect them, to ask for federal assistance. That seemed to enrage Patterson even more: If federal troops came to Alabama, blood would run in the streets. Seigenthaler saw his opening. "Governor," he reminded Patterson in what was his best moment of the meeting, "blood ran in the streets of Anniston on Sunday." But Patterson continued his tirade against the Freedom Riders: Why, the bus company couldn't even get anyone to drive them. It was all out of control, he said. "There's my public safety commissioner," he added, pointing to a member of his cabinet; "his name's Floyd Mann and he can't protect them. Tell him, Floyd."

Seigenthaler turned to see a rather ordinary-looking man seated near the governor. "Governor," he said, "I'm commissioner of safety. I'm your appointee. If you tell me to protect these people, then I'll protect them." It was, Seigenthaler thought, like a thunderclap. For a moment everything else in the room stopped. Until then, the meeting

had been like a play scripted by John Patterson, but now the script
had been changed, unbeknownst to the playwright himself. Seigenthaler thought it was a critical moment. He could sense the cabinet
members on both sides of Floyd Mann seeming to tilt their bodies
away from him. No one was more startled than Patterson. "Floyd," he
said, "I don't believe you understand what you just said. I said you
couldn't protect them, and you said you can. Can you explain how
you would?"

Floyd Mann was, John Seigenthaler decided, by far the most interesting man he had met so far in Alabama. "I'd put the highway patrol
in front of the bus, a couple cars if need be, and the highway patrol
behind it, and have a helicopter and an airplane overhead, and some
additional highway patrol cars at the ready," Mann said. John Patterson, Seigenthaler noticed, had become silent.

"Can you do it without federal help?" Seigenthaler asked him.

"I can do it without anyone's help," Floyd Mann answered.

John Patterson remained mostly silent as Mann outlined his plan.
The only thing that Patterson insisted on was that he did not want his
people preempting the authority of the local police. That meant that
the highway patrol could escort the Freedom Riders in and out of
cities, but within the city limits the local authorities would be in
charge. Seigenthaler was not that pleased with the addendum, but
there was nothing he could do about it. He was sure that Patterson
was trying to buy himself just a little more distance from what was
going to happen. But Floyd Mann had obviously gone beyond the
rather limited political role John Patterson had intended for him, and
just as clearly he was not, in the modern sense of the word, liberal on
civil rights, for you did not rise in the world of Alabama public safety
with any kind of liberal taint. But he was something different and perhaps even better, Seigenthaler decided, a man who was absolutely
apolitical, a law man, simple and decent. His job was to save lives, not
to ask about the politics or the skin color of those whose lives he was
saving. That kind of simplicity of purpose was refreshing and old-
fashioned, Seigenthaler thought, in a part of the country where law
enforcement had been completely corrupted by a powerful and ever
more dangerous obedience to the politics of race.

There was nothing fancy about Floyd Mann. He was a country boy,
from Alexander City in Tallapoosa County in the eastern part of the

state, the beneficiary of a limited education; he had never gone to college, which was one of his regrets. He often mangled the language—he was wont to say that he could hire twenty-four new troopers despite a budget hold-down because there were going to be a lot of openings through *nutrition* when he meant *attrition*. His friends were often stunned by the Floydisms, the quick, jolting reminders that he had come from the simplest background imaginable, and that words were not his strength. He had grown up in a segregated atmosphere, but been raised by parents who felt that their son ought to be fair in his dealings with all people—and that it was as bad to mistreat a black person as a white person. He had gone into the service in the early days of World War II and served as a tail gunner on a B-17 because he was smaller than the other gunners, and the smallest of the gunners went into the tail; he flew twenty-seven missions, including the first daylight bombing of Berlin. He had known John Patterson since they had both been in the third grade, and the bond between them was very strong.

When the war was over he had gone into police work in Alexander City. He had been known among the black population as "Red Man," a name at once respectful and admiring, because of the color of his hair and the way his skin turned red when the sun was out.[2] He had become the police chief of Opelika in eastern Alabama at thirty, and had reconnected with the Pattersons, John and his father, as they were cleaning up Phenix City from racketeers and gamblers. (Phenix City, across the Alabama border from Columbus, Georgia, and Fort Benning, was a kind of local sin city in those days, and the senior John Patterson had been elected to local and state office largely because he was sworn to clean it up.) Seventeen days after being elected attorney general of Alabama, the senior Patterson had been murdered by some of the hoodlums he had pursued; his son took over his mantle, becoming attorney general, and then in 1959, governor. Floyd Mann became a part of the Patterson political entourage, and when the young John Patterson became governor, he had made Floyd Mann his public safety commissioner.

He was a law man, nothing more, nothing less, he liked to say. Even in Opelika he had gained an enviable reputation as a man who could not be pushed around. When the top figure in the local Phenix City rackets, a man named Hoyt Shepherd, decided to launder some of his money by buying respectable businesses elsewhere, he had bought a motel in Opelika. The ability of men with big money to bend small-town cops was considerable, and Ray Jenkins, a young reporter in Columbus, Georgia, at the time had called Mann to ask about the transaction. "Well," Floyd Mann told Jenkins, "Mr. Shepherd has come to see me, and he has told me that he intended to run a legitimate business, and I simply told him, I know you will, Mr. Shepherd, I know you will run a legitimate business." Small-town cop or not, Jenkins decided, no one would push him around.[3]

Mann's view of police work was, for an Alabama law man in that era, amazingly color blind, and he had been made uneasy by the hate which had begun to swirl through Alabama in the late fifties, and by the rise of the Klan, operating all too often with local cops. The problem with police work, he once told Ray Jenkins, was that by its nature it tended to attract a certain percentage of sadistic people, who enjoyed the job because it legitimized their natural meanness. So, he added, the first thing any good police chief had to do was set the limits for his own people.[4]

Years later Fred Powledge, a reporter who had covered much of the civil rights turmoil, asked Mann what he felt about the political objectives of the Freedom Riders. "I wasn't involved in that," he said. "My purpose was law enforcement, trying to make certain that nothing tragic happened to those people while they were in Alabama."[5] That was why he had planted Ell Cowling on the first bus going into Anniston. He hated the idea of the Klan working in partnership with local cops, and he knew all too well that more of the same might still be in store.

John Seigenthaler called Robert Kennedy and told him that the Alabama authorities had finally come around. The meeting, which was one of the most brutal Seigenthaler ever attended, was over. If it had been painful it was also, he thought, a significant success: The young people, he believed, would be protected.

33

BERNARD LAFAYETTE WAS THE LEADER OF THE GROUP WHICH ARRIVED in Birmingham by train. When they got to Birmingham they went as quickly as they could from the train station to Fred Shuttlesworth's house. Once there he called Diane Nash, and was updated on what was happening to John Lewis and his group, who had started out by bus, been arrested, and dumped on the state border near Ardmore. Told that they were now headed back to Birmingham by car, Lafayette had decided that his group would wait for Lewis and his people at the Birmingham bus station. He was greatly relieved when his friends, tired and dirty, showed up.

Lafayette was impressed by the grandeur of the white waiting room of the Birmingham bus station. All he had ever seen before were the waiting rooms for black folks, which weren't much. White folks surely took good care of themselves in bus stations, he thought, noting the large and spacious lobby, beautiful walls, marble floors: plenty of work here for black folks just to keep it clean. They waited while bus after bus was called, but it was never their bus. As the late afternoon passed into evening, they were joined by the Klan.

Bernard Lafayette had heard stories about the Ku Klux Klan all his life. The Klan was mighty and all-knowing and it devoured black folks, snatched them away in the middle of the night. Its leaders were supposed to know everything that black folks did, even what they were thinking. And here they were, led by Robert Shelton, the Grand Dragon. There was no mistaking that. The Klansmen were supposed to have white robes, but Shelton's distinctive costume set him apart, for his was a black robe with a giant serpent on the back. Bernard and John and their people were bunched together in the waiting room when the Klansmen came by. They all wore boots and they swaggered, and they tried to bump the Freedom Riders and step on their feet, and they threw water from paper cups at them. They did not wear the hoods to their robes. That was a mistake, Lafayette thought, not just because there was more fear in the unknown, in the mystery of the hooded face unseen, of deeds done in secret in the middle of the night, but because the faces were pathetic. Absolutely pathetic, Lafayette thought. The poverty was all over their faces. They were rural, back-country faces of people whose hold on life was pitifully thin. What he saw was acne and neglected dental work. In daylight, without their robes, about the only people these men could scare would be their own wives and children. They might be dangerous, he did not doubt that, but there was nothing *imposing* about them. Truth be told, even their robes looked cheap.

There were a lot of cops with long billy clubs, and within limits they let the Klan have their way. Clearly, he decided, some kind of deal had been reached between Bull Connor and the Klan. Light hassling of the Freedom Riders—a jostle here, a sharp kick there, a cup of water poured on a black student—was permitted, but for the moment, at least, an all-out assault was not. The riders decided they would make one major concession to the Klan: They would not go to the rest rooms alone. If they used the facilities, they would do it in pairs.

The next stop on their itinerary was supposed to be Montgomery. As they sat waiting for their bus to be called, some kind of game, they soon decided, was going on. A bus would be called, they would come out and try to board, and then nothing would happen. Once, they had started to board and they noticed that the driver did not seem very friendly. As they got on, he asked, "How many of you are from the NAACP?" They said that none of them were. "How many of you are from CORE?" he asked. None of them, they said. With that the driver walked off the bus. "I've got only one life to give, and I'm damned well not going to give it to the NAACP and I'm damn well not going to give it to CORE."

They did not trust the federal government, which was supposed to be on their side, but wanted more than anything else for them to go home, the local government, or the bus lines. But now as they pushed forward, they had picked up one new powerful asset, and that was the media. If the Freedom Rides had started with a handful of people willing to risk their lives in order to make witness to segregation, then finally it was beginning to become a front-page story and the nation, through the media, was beginning to take notice. The burning of the bus in Anniston—those graphic photos reflecting the predictable explosion of Deep South violence—had caught the eye of editors everywhere. The Klan in Anniston had done their work for them: The media contingent was large and getting larger, and big hitters from the country's leading papers, and equally important, network reporters, were there too. The students understood the dynamic which they had created immediately: The greater the media coverage, the less room for maneuver the Kennedy administration was going to have. The Kennedys might not be that sensitive to what happened to a handful of blacks trying to integrate bus lines in the South, but they were *very* sensitive to what might happen if millions of ordinary Americans sitting in their living rooms watched black people being beaten on the evening news. Therefore the Freedom Rides were working, John Lewis realized, for they were beginning to ride into the nation's consciousness if not yet its conscience.

For many of the young people, this was their first encounter with the big-time media. Nashville had essentially been a local story, and while from time to time a reporter from a national paper had shown up, the students had been largely isolated from the world of modern communications. Now for the first time they were reaping some of the benefits of entering the big time. The coming of the media did not mean that their journey was going to be any less dangerous—they would soon learn that—but it meant that there were going to be millions of witnesses, and it meant also that they were wired into events as they had never been in the past. For that was something additional about the media which both Lafayette and Lewis were learning even as the scene in the bus station was playing itself out: The people from the media were connected. Some of the reporters in the bus station had colleagues in Washington working the Justice Department and the White House. Others knew what was happening at the state capitol in Montgomery. These reporters were clued in, and they kept passing on what they were hearing to the Freedom Riders, trading information to get information as reporters traditionally do. The bigger the story got, the less darkness the Freedom Riders operated in, the more information they were given. As the reporters were connected, so now were the students.

It was the reporters who told them of a plan that was being hatched in Washington to have the riders board a bus to Montgomery and then, because their tickets said New Orleans, have them taken straight to that Louisiana city. That was a solution designed to make everyone happy, and to ignore the issue which they were challenging in the first place. So they went over and bought another set of tickets, this time only as far as Montgomery. They were well prepared now. If it hadn't been for the reporters, Lafayette thought, the trick might have worked and they might have boarded the wrong bus. What they also began to realize was that the federal government was slowly but steadily being pulled into this crisis, albeit reluctantly. Robert Kennedy was the key figure, caught between what was good for his brother and yet at the same time increasingly aware of an additional responsibility, of trying to do what he thought was morally right. He was, they learned, pushing the bus company to take them to Montgomery. The bus officials were wary. Their drivers were in no way interested in being a part of this. They would drive but only if their supervisors came along. Finally the supervisors agreed to go.

The deal, negotiated between the feds; Floyd Mann, the head of the Alabama state police; and the bus companies called for two officials of Greyhound to sit on the bus on the front seat. As Floyd Mann had suggested, there would be plenty of police protection outside the city limits of both Birmingham and Montgomery. Not only would the riders have state troopers with them between cities but a plane would be flying overhead. There would be no ambush. They would go on Saturday morning.

So Saturday morning, May 20, at about eight-thirty they started boarding the bus to Montgomery. Bernard Lafayette took comfort in the fact that John Lewis was on the bus. If John was on this bus on a day when they might have to die, then this was the right place to be.

In the beginning it was an impressive convoy, sixteen highway patrol cars in front of the bus and sixteen behind it, and a helicopter overhead for reconnaissance, in case anyone intended to blow a bridge or ambush them along the way. Floyd Mann had received assurances from the Montgomery police that they would handle the Freedom Riders once the bus pulled into their city, but those assurances meant little to him. Just to be sure, he had summoned seventy-five additional state troopers and billeted them near the state capitol.

As the bus neared Montgomery, Floyd Mann kept in touch with L. B. Sullivan, the Montgomery police commissioner, who assured him that there were plenty of police in the bus terminal area. Indeed there were, but then just before the bus arrived, as if on signal, they began to disappear.

The drive from Birmingham to Montgomery is some ninety miles. That day it took about two hours. Both John Lewis and Bernard Lafayette knew the route exceptionally well because it was the route both of them took when they traveled to and from school. They had never seen anything like this procession, however. They had their bus, some of the media people had *their* own cars, and then, of course, there was the constant escort: The Birmingham police had taken them to the city limits, the state highway patrolmen picked them up and were taking them to the Montgomery city limits, and the Montgomery cops would meet them there and escort them to the Montgomery bus station.

Montgomery, thought Lafayette as they arrived there, was strange: It was late Saturday morning, virtually the middle of the day, a time when any Southern city was crowded. Yet not a soul was moving. No one was walking on the streets, nor were any cars about. The bus made a big, lazy swing into the station. There was no one there. It was like pulling into a ghost bus station in a ghost town. As they prepared to get off the bus, Bernard Lafayette knew something was wrong.

He stood before the others at the front of the bus, giving them their instructions as they got ready to get off. They were to go in pairs, he reminded them, each of them responsible for the other. Do not lose each other, he said, do not get lost. They were to hold hands if necessary. It would be too easy for someone to disappear. It was the last moment of calm. He had a quick glimpse of media people assembling; they had arrived in rented cars, following the bus most of the way and then speeding ahead at the end in order to be at the station for the moment when the Freedom Riders arrived. Then he had a sense of a mob moving toward the press, where John Lewis was supposed to brief the reporters. Much later they found out there had been a deal between the Klan and the local police officials. The local cops had agreed to give the Klan fifteen minutes to welcome them and work them over, and then, the damage done, the cops were to arrive. Fifteen minutes to have their pleasure.

34

JOHN LEWIS HAD BEEN AN ORIGINAL FREEDOM RIDER, BUT HE HAD NOT been in Anniston or he would have realized that the silence which greeted them in Montgomery was the exact same silence which had greeted the first riders when they had reached Anniston, the terribly unnatural quiet just before the storm. Lewis got off the bus. Because he was a senior Freedom Rider and sit-in leader, he had been chosen as spokesman, and it was his job to brief the media on their arrival in Montgomery. He was instantly surrounded by members of the press. He was still uneasy with the stillness. Lewis had just begun to answer questions from the various reporters when he saw the mob, coming, it seemed, out of nowhere, moving at them quickly and angrily. They went for the journalists first, particularly the photographers.

Lewis was startled by the violence of it. These were men and women who had turned into animals. They had been waiting all morning and the anger had been building. They were beating up reporters and swinging clubs at photographers and wrestling cameras out of their hands. Typically, Herb Kaplow, the NBC correspondent assigned to the story, had felt the raging hostility in the last moments just before the bus arrived. Some local toughs had surrounded him and his crew, and even as the riders descended from the bus, they struck at him and his crew, knocking the camera out of the hands of Moe Levy, his cameraman.[1] Bernard Lafayette, watching the assault on the NBC team, was stunned by the ferocity of the scene. My God, he thought, if they treat the journalists like this, then what are they going to do to us? And then he realized exactly what was happening— they were, in his words, knocking the eyes out of the press corps first, so that there would be as little record as possible of what was about to happen next. He watched one man, whom he later found out worked for *Life,* take pictures and then toss his camera like a football to a colleague in order to preserve some sort of record.

The attackers all seemed to be armed with pipes and clubs and baseball bats. "Stand together. Don't run," Lewis told his people. "Just stand together!" If they were going to be beaten they would be beaten, he thought. If they were going to die, they were going to die, and they had better die together.

One of the things which saved them was the fact that there was a large post office next to the bus terminal, and a bunch of the postal workers, primarily white, saw what was happening and managed to shepherd some of the Freedom Riders into the postal building. All around Lewis, people were sprawled on the ground, some being beaten, some, having already been beaten, just lying there; he had a sense that this must be what a battlefield was like, particularly if in a war where one side has all the weapons and the other has none.

Lewis was fighting for his own life at that moment. The mob, this group of two hundred or three hundred men and women, violent and raging like a group of human hornets, switching from person to person and group to group, had found him and Jim Zwerg, his teammate in the instant buddy system they had created. They were backed up against a wall, and isolated from most of the others. Lewis could not believe the rage. It was obscene, frenzied, accompanied by an odd sound, a communal roar of anger: He had on occasion seen one or two people out of control, but this was different, hundreds of people, all wielding clubs and bats and pieces of pipe. There was not, he remembered, a single policeman in sight.

Jim Zwerg had seen a police patrol car drive away as the bus had pulled into the station, and then he had seen the mob race toward the bus. One of the last things he saw was a television technician trying to handle a boom mike being beaten by a burly white man (later identified as an off-duty Montgomery cop who had taken the day off in order to be in on the fun) who had snatched away the mike and smashed it into the ground. As the mob reached Zwerg, he knelt and started to pray. He was sure he was going to be killed, and in what he believed to be his final prayer on earth, he asked God to give him the strength he needed to be nonviolent in the presence of his enemies, and to love the people who were now beating him. Then he felt a certain sense of peace sweep over him as the mob arrived.[2] Down he went, knocked quickly to the ground, and when he tried to get up someone kicked him violently in the back, so viciously that three vertebrae on his spine were cracked. Someone grabbed his suitcase from him and was hitting him with it. Lewis was appalled by the scene he now witnessed. Zwerg seemed gone to Lewis, surely unconscious, or perhaps in even worse shape. One man was holding him up, at the same time pinning his arms back so that he was defenseless and others could repeatedly hit him. It looked like Zwerg's teeth were being knocked out, one by one, and blood was pouring out of his head. But it was hard to track what was happening to Zwerg, because Lewis himself was fading out: Someone hit him over the head with a wooden crate, and he felt himself blacking out even as he went down. He later remembered the pain, the taste of his own blood, the darkness descending on him, and an eerie sense that this was his final moment on the face of the earth. He had one final thought, and it was that the last thing he was going to see in his life was Jim Zwerg being murdered.

He felt the crowd push in for what surely was going to be the final kill. The mob seemed angrier at Zwerg because he was white, and therefore the traitorous one, the nigger-lover. Lewis thought for a fleeting moment that he was too young to die, and then even in the same instant, he steadied himself, and thought, At least I died in a cause, and at least I was true to myself.

Just then a man walked over and pulled a gun out of a holster, held it up, and said, "There'll be no killing here today." The man, Lewis later learned, was Floyd Mann and he fired two shots, and with that the rage began to subside. But still the struggle went on. After saving Lewis and Zwerg, Mann rushed to stop a group of men from beating a local white cameraman who worked for a television station. One of the men was using a baseball bat, and Floyd Mann walked over to the spot and knelt down by the white attacker, put his gun next to the man's ear, and said, almost softly, just loud enough for the man to hear, "One more swing and you're dead."

Floyd Mann knew in advance what might happen, that the Montgomery police were in cahoots with the Klan and were not to be trusted. Having billeted his own people nearby for that very reason, he had given the order for them to move in the moment he had seen the mob take over. Ray Jenkins, covering that day for the *Alabama*

Journal, remembered the sight: the brutal assault on these young people, and then he had looked down Washington Street and seen the state troopers, all lined up. The cavalry has arrived, he thought, and damn well just in time.[3] Many years later, Floyd Mann said he had never seen craziness like that scene before; his own clothes, he said, had almost been torn off him in the madness. He not only had trouble with the mob, he had trouble with some of his own people, and almost had to relieve one of his top officers. He saved at least three lives, including those of Lewis and Zwerg, and possibly as many as ten. The best thing about Floyd Mann on that fateful day, his friend Bob Ingram thought, was that he did not think he was being a hero, he simply thought he was doing his job the way a good lawman ought to.[4]

35

Two critically important things had happened that day. The first was that for the first time the Freedom Rides had become a national story in the truest sense. It was the quantum jump in violence which did it. The media, particularly the new electronic media, greatly preferred real violence to the suggestion of violence or, as had happened in Nashville, low-level violence. With television increasingly becoming the critical player in the media as the Movement entered the sixties, it was clear that the more *action* a story produced, the better.

That meant that as far as the media was concerned, the Freedom Rides themselves had not been a big story in the beginning, when they seemed to be only about riding on buses and eating in terminals. The transformation had begun in Anniston, when it had all turned violent. Starting on that day, when the Klan had set fire to the bus and beaten the riders, the requisite violence was there. The story had everything: a full-fledged challenge to the citadel of racism, the quiet bravery of the Freedom Riders, the raw anger of the Klan, and the complicity of local authorities.

For the story had changed. It suddenly was producing great footage. Even better, the Freedom Rides had something that every editor loved—they had become a quest which seemed to be mounting in both importance and danger. It not only had drama, and action, good guys and bad guys, it had continuity. Like the Perils of Pauline, it was always to be continued. An equation was being created which now favored the civil rights activists if they had the courage to see the story through, for in every Deep South town, the ingredients were there waiting to be ignited, and there was likely to be a local white police officer anxious to make his bones. All Martin Luther King, still the principal figure of the Movement, had to do was choose the venue, and all the young people in SNCC, whose assignment it was to be the shock troops of this invasion, had to do was risk their lives. The key, the young people and King were learning, was in choosing the right venue. They were still in this embryonic television age, discovering that the right villain was of the essence. And the Deep South contained an endless supply of worthy villains. The capacity to initiate events—that is, to control the pace and schedule of events—had without anyone realizing it, particularly the white leaders of the South, been passed to King and the SNCC kids. They, if they were brave enough, and they turned out to be brave enough, controlled the dynamic now.

The impact of this new dynamic was affecting everyone. One of the first people to realize this was John Kennedy. He had called in Harris Wofford, who was the White House man on civil rights (and whom Kennedy had so far disappointed with his essential inaction), and said with some degree of irritation, "Tell them to call it off! Stop them!" To which Wofford replied, "I don't think anyone's going to stop them right now."[1] In his own mind Kennedy felt he was for civil rights, well ahead of the curve on race (presumably a curve based on what other Irish-Catholic millionaires from Hyannisport felt about race in 1960, which meant among other things that he was probably better on this issue than his father), and he was doing a lot for black people. He had not liked the idea of the Freedom Rides from the start, and as they progressed he became more and more irritable. Didn't liberals and black people, he asked a somewhat startled Wofford, know that he had done more for civil rights than any president in history? "How could any man have done more than I've done?" he asked.[2]

But events were conspiring to change Kennedy. A revolution was taking place. More, it was a revolution that did not merely produce moral consequences, from which he would gladly have stepped aside. Now because of the power of modern media, most particularly television, those events were producing immediate political consequences as well. If Kennedy was cool, he was also very smart and very nimble; if he was not a man to lead a social revolution, he was also most assuredly not a man to get in the way of one either. His most attractive quality as a politician was his modernity. The consequences of what was happening in the South, unwanted though they might be, were for the first time, because of the riots in Montgomery, coming at him faster and faster all the time. Besides, his key adviser on the issue of race was as in all things his brother Robert, the attorney general, less cool and more of a moralist. Robert Kennedy was closer to these events, they were in his domain, and he was slowly and systematically being influenced first practically and then morally by them. He was also a man who tended, as he had in his titanic struggle with Jimmy Hoffa, the Teamsters leader, to personalize issues as his brother did not. That was not without important consequences as the story unfolded.

On that fateful Saturday morning in Montgomery, as the mob had surged at those young people who had gotten off the bus, there had been a dramatic scene at the taxi stand. Two of the young black women, Catherine Burks and Lucretia Collins, had somehow managed to get in a cab driven by a black driver. Two white girls, fellow Freedom Riders who were trying to escape the mob, had also stumbled into the car. The driver had said that he could not drive them because it was against the law to drive integrated groups. "Then get out and I'll drive the car," Catherine Burks said, but the driver had refused to get out and finally, in order to spare the black women, the two whites, Susan Wilbur, a Nashville girl who attended Peabody, the Nashville teachers college, and Sue Herrmann, a Fisk exchange student from Whittier College, got out on their own. As they did they became the focal point of the mob. When she had first gotten off the bus Sue Wilbur had been standing right next to John Lewis and Jim Zwerg and she had watched in horror as the mob attacked them. She was sure that Zwerg had been murdered and Lewis did not seem in much better shape. She and Sue Herrmann had started walking away from the mob after that, and when the taxi rescue had failed, the white mob had managed to isolate the two girls. One hefty white woman had a large, heavy handbag which she was using as a weapon, striking at Wilbur's face; with each blow the Peabody student was becoming dizzier and dizzier. At the same time a young teenage boy was punching her in the back of the head from behind. She did not think she was going to get out of there alive.

Just then John Seigenthaler, Robert Kennedy's personal assistant who had earlier negotiated with John Patterson, drove up in his rental car. He had left his meeting with Patterson and Floyd Mann the day before believing that he was a great negotiator, a man who had helped bring racial peace in our time to Alabama. Confident of his considerable contribution to a better and more brotherly America, he had driven by on this morning to check out the results of his peacemaking. He had reached the bus station in time to watch the mob overrun the helpless Freedom Riders. His eyes swept across the scene and he spotted the mob pummeling the two young white women. By the time he reached them Sue Wilbur seemed close to being out on her feet. "Get in the damn car!" he shouted at her. But she misunderstood what was happening and thought he was a local Montgomery white trying to save her, and she shouted for him to get away, that this wasn't his fight. If she hadn't argued and had gotten in the car immediately, Seigenthaler later decided, they might have gotten away. But her hesitation was fateful.

If it was true as she said that it was not yet his fight, it was about to become his. Even as he was trying to push her into the car, a white man came over and hit him as hard as he could with a lead pipe. Down he went, and the mob, watching him fall to the pavement, momentarily stopped pursuing the girls. That had allowed them to slip away, and Sue Wilbur years later thought there was a very good chance that Seigenthaler had saved her life on that day; at the very least, as the beating took place, he had substituted his body for hers.[3] Even as the man swung, Seigenthaler had been trying to explain to the mob that he was a federal agent. Actually he was a good deal more than that, and this fateful use of a lead pipe on a human skull, for he was knocked unconscious and could easily have been killed or maimed for life, was to effect profoundly the way the government of the United States behaved from then on. For he was the personal representative and closest personal aide of Robert Kennedy, the attorney general of the United States. If Robert Kennedy was in addition to his title the right hand of the president, then John Seigenthaler was the right-hand man of the right-hand man.

On this day, when he was involuntarily welcomed into the civil rights movement, John Seigenthaler was a man of skill and charm and guile, a former reporter on the *Tennessean,* perhaps the most gifted reporter on a paper filled with gifted reporters. He had not been particularly interested in the issue of race, and instead during the late fifties his main interest and some of his most distinguished reporting was in an entirely different area, labor union corruption. He had covered the abuses of the Tennessee Teamsters union and that in turn had connected him to Robert Kennedy, who was the counsel for the Senate Rackets Committee, then pursuing Jimmy Hoffa, the union's head, with a vengeance. Seigenthaler and Kennedy had become close in those years, and closer still from 1958 to 1959, when Seigenthaler had been a Nieman Fellow for a year at Harvard. They had shared the same passion for bringing Hoffa to justice, and as John Kennedy was gearing up for a run at the presidency, Seigenthaler seemed additionally attractive to Robert Kennedy: He was a member of what was by then known as the Irish Mafia, but Seigenthaler was from Tennessee and therefore had an accent which traveled better in certain parts of the country. Above all, he was deemed by Bob Kennedy to be completely trustworthy, a man always in control of his ego.

Seigenthaler had not gone back to Nashville after he had finished his one year at Harvard, but had stayed on with Kennedy to work on his book about the Teamsters, *The Enemy Within,* and once finished, he had gone on to work for the presidential campaign. Of all the people who were in the parking area of the bus station that day as the mob sprawled around looking for targets, the man who had wielded that lead pipe had picked the wrong person to hit. Not only was the television coverage of these events beginning to force the hand of the Kennedys, but from the moment that John Seigenthaler was knocked unconscious, the struggle became infinitely more personal for Robert Kennedy.

John Lewis, looking back years later over what had happened, believed that the beating of Seigenthaler was a turning point. Unlike his older brother, Robert Kennedy was emotional and politics did not exist for him in the abstract—for better or worse, they were a reflection of his own personal experiences. The Klan might just as well have lashed out at Robert Kennedy's own family as John Seigenthaler. Ramsey Clark, then an assistant attorney general, was struck by the dramatic change in his boss from that time on. His attitude toward the segregationists changed overnight to cold anger. It strengthened the commitment of the attorney general, and it began a lifetime of passionate commitment on the part of John Seigenthaler to racial progress in the South.

John Lewis did not know nearly as much about American politics as he was to learn in the ensuing thirty-five years, but he understood in an intuitive way that something historic had happened. The mob had moved not merely against a group of virtually anonymous black youths, and a handful of their equally powerless white friends, it had moved against the government of the United States. Someone asked Lewis years later if he was exhilarated when he heard about Seigenthaler being beaten, and he said no, there was no pleasure in that, in hearing of a man being attacked, but he had nonetheless realized that the protest was working, it was bringing the government in as a player.

John Lewis was in no condition to feel any exhilaration at that moment. He was lying on the ground in the bus depot soaked with his own blood, moving in and out of consciousness, hearing voices coming from some distant place. These voices seemed to be talking about him and whether or not he was still alive. Gradually he sensed that the voices were coming from above him, and as he came to, he realized that he was still lying in the parking area, and people were standing over him trying to decide whether or not he could be moved. The voices belonged to black people from Martin King's Montgomery Improvement Association, who were supposed to have met them in the first place. They were talking about him and Zwerg: *I'll take this one here . . . You better get that one over there to the hospital immediately.* It was as if the people who belonged to these voices had come to claim those left behind on some battlefield.

Lewis was, in his conscious flashes, still sure he was going to die. He had never seen so much blood. At least, he thought, his beliefs had not deserted him. He did not think Jim Zwerg, still lying next to him, was going to make it. Zwerg was suffering from a severe concussion and three cracked vertebrae in his back. In addition, many of his teeth had been damaged, and he had severe internal injuries of his lower abdomen. He was in and out of consciousness for a good deal of the next two days. Later he was surprised to find that he had been interviewed on television, vowing that the Freedom Rides would continue, an interview he had absolutely no memory of giving. He was finished with the Freedom Rides for the time being, if not with the Movement. Zwerg stayed in the Montgomery hospital for five days, and then his local minister flew down from Wisconsin, and asked him to come home because his parents had taken his beating very badly and were in terrible shape. His father had suffered yet another heart attack, and his mother, it seemed, had had something of a breakdown. (Although

Zwerg was eventually able to explain his actions to his mother, he and his father were never able to reconcile their differences over what had happened; his father remained convinced that his son had been manipulated and used by the black leadership, and there was a certain estrangement between them for the rest of his father's life. His inability to convince his father that he had done something he believed in weighed heavily for a time on Zwerg—after all, these were the people who had taught him about Christian love—and during the next year at Beloit he had taken his comfort and solace from alcohol before finding his equilibrium again with the help of a therapist, and going on to Northwestern to study for the ministry.)

John Seigenthaler lay there motionless. A reporter named Dan O. Dowe from the *Alabama Journal* happened to spot his prone body, and had turned to L. B. Sullivan, the local police commissioner (whom the feds later believed was a key figure in the deal which had given the Klan a free shot at the Freedom Riders). "That man is hurt," Dowe had said. "Why don't you call an ambulance for him?"

"He hasn't requested an ambulance," Sullivan answered.[4]

Seigenthaler's hold on rationality was marginal as he came back to consciousness. He had been in Alabama far longer than he had ever intended to be, and he had long since run out of fresh clothes. The day before he had bought some new socks and underwear and he had borrowed the fresh shirt of a colleague from the Justice Department named John Doar who was in Alabama on a different matter. Now as he began to regain consciousness, the thing which bothered him most was that Doar's shirt was completely covered with blood. Doar, he thought, is going to be really pissed off at me. Then a local cop came by. "You ran into some trouble, buddy," the cop said. "Are you all right?" Seigenthaler said he thought he was all right.

"Is there anyone I can call for you?" the cop continued.

"You can call Mr. Kennedy," Seigenthaler said, feeling very frail and realizing he might pass out again.

"Which Mr. Kennedy is that?" the cop asked.

"Either the president or the attorney general," Seigenthaler answered.

"Who the hell are you, anyway?" the cop asked.

"I'm from the Justice Department," Seigenthaler said. Then he passed out.

He woke later in a small private hospital. He had a fractured skull and some broken ribs. The first person in to see him was Floyd Mann. Mann was in tears. He was convinced that he had failed completely, both personally and professionally. What an irony, Seigenthaler thought; the only white official in the state who is behaving with any decency, and he's in tears. Later Seigenthaler talked with Robert Kennedy, who said they were going to flood the place with federal marshalls. The attorney general had asked him what it was like down there and Seigenthaler had suggested he never run for public office in Alabama. Then one of the older doctors who headed the clinic came in. "You're from Nashville originally, aren't you?" he asked Seigenthaler. Seigenthaler said he was.

"Do me a favor, will you?" the doctor said. What was that? Seigenthaler asked.

"Go back to Washington and tell those two boys [the president of the United States and the attorney general of the United States] to stop all this."

Stop all this, Seigenthaler thought. He was in a lot of pain and he had a fracture and a concussion and he was woozy. "I don't think it's the president and the attorney general," he said. "I don't think you can just stop it and turn it off anymore."

When Seigenthaler finally returned to Washington, the first thing that Robert Kennedy placed on his desk were the photos and the FBI records of the two men who had beaten him that morning in Montgomery. Both were active Klansmen. All three assaults in Alabama, the Justice Department had immediately learned, in Anniston, Birmingham, and Montgomery, were the work of the Klan and had the exact same MO—the Klan had been alerted long in advance, it had specific information on where and when the buses were arriving, information relayed directly by friends or fellow Klan members within the police departments. The attorney general was furious with the Klan and he was furious with the FBI as well because there had been two FBI agents watching the scene and they had done nothing to protect Seigenthaler. In that moment the attorney general came to understand why so many of the activists hated Hoover and his organization, and wondered which side it was on and who it intended to protect.

In fact, the Justice Department's eventual knowledge of what had happened in Birmingham was quite precise because, it turned out, there was a paid FBI informer named Gary Thomas Rowe, who was also a Klansman (and quite possibly, a number of high Justice officials thought, a vicious provocateur, a double agent of uncertain and almost always dubious loyalty). Rowe had attended a meeting of Klan officials, including Robert Shelton, Grand Dragon of the Klan in Alabama, with Birmingham police officials, including Bull Connor and one of his top aides, Tom Cook. Connor, the Justice Department believed, was a Klan fellow traveler: He always wanted a veil of respectability, and therefore had Cook as his connection to the Klan. At the meeting Cook had outlined what the exact drill was going to be, what the police were going to allow the Klan to do at the moment the Freedom Riders arrived: "We're going to allow you fifteen minutes. . . . You can beat 'em, bomb 'em, maim 'em, kill 'em, I don't give a ———. There will be absolutely no arrests. You can assure every Klansman in the country that no one will be arrested in Alabama for that fifteen minutes."[5] That had been true for Anniston and for Birmingham also, but in Montgomery, the Justice Department officials later thought, it had been even more violent because the crisis had been building for several days—the white anger had been steadily mounting—and because in Montgomery the local police were operating in the shadow of a segregationist state capitol, with a segregationist governor who had said he was not a baby-sitter. Therefore they had felt even less restrained than the police in Birmingham.[6]

Years later John Seigenthaler reflected on that day and thought it was the day on which the Rubicon had been crossed. He had, he thought with some belated amusement, been an involuntary participant in it. He should have known that the old order was changing when he had made his first call at Robert Kennedy's suggestion to Diane Nash. She had barely bothered to hear him out. Almost anyone else he might have spoken to would have said something about talking to her people and getting back. But not Diane Nash. There was no need to check with her people. They were driven by a kind of belief that was the purest he had ever dealt with. They had done nothing less than offer their lives as the price of their beliefs, and they seemed more than ready to continue with that offering. They were very different from the first group of Freedom Riders he had seen that day in the Birmingham airport, exhausted and shaken after the harassment from the Klan and from Bull Connor's cops. The first group had been composed of pleasant, worthy people utterly unprepared for the terrible test of a city like Birmingham. But these young people were like elite combat troops, well trained, battle ready, completely willing to accept the risks; they were mentally, physically, and psychologically prepared.

He knew relatively little about Jim Lawson's workshops, but he was impressed by the strength and fearlessness of Lawson's students. There was the unbending voice of Diane Nash on the phone, and there was John Lewis leading his Freedom Riders right back to Birmingham after Bull Connor had dumped them on the roadside. No black person, he thought, had ever done that to Bull before. In the past when Bull drove you out of town, you stayed out of town, because his word was law, and the penalty for breaking it was death in some form or other. But they had virtually beaten him back to Birmingham. Even Bobby Kennedy, still primarily concerned with protecting his brother's political interest, but a great admirer of personal courage, told Seigenthaler right after he had been beaten, "My God, they're really fearless, aren't they? They're really willing to die there, aren't they?" The odd thing about their talk, Seigenthaler thought, was that his boss was praising these young people as if they had been Seigenthaler's comrades, and they had all been in this together.[7]

Perhaps the greatest victory of the Freedom Riders that day was not with the government or the media; it was their victory over themselves and their own fears. For they were just beginning the process of breaking down the awful, paralyzing psychic fear which cities like Birmingham and Jackson, Mississippi, had always held for black people, and other blacks, seeing them do it, were emboldened to join them.

36

THESE NEWEST ATTACKS BY THE KLAN IN MONTGOMERY HAD PUT THE Freedom Rides on the map. The children had led the way, and the nation was now watching. Television news was eager to compete with print, eager in its institutional infancy not just to find social and intellectual legitimacy in a great and compelling story, but eager as well to have stories which produced film. As the stakes mounted and the forces came closer to the moment of collision, the media assemblage grew, and as that happened, the government was pulled, however reluctantly, into its unwanted role as the referee.

Everyone was coming to Montgomery. In a way, the best and worst of America were converging on the city. The top leaders of the SCLC were coming to add their prestige and greater visibility to what had started as a children's crusade. Martin King and Ralph Abernathy were on their way from Atlanta. Shuttlesworth was coming. C. T. Vivian, one of the most outspoken of the Nashville ministers, was on his way. Jim Lawson was headed down from Ohio, where he had been visiting his family. In Washington, Robert Kennedy, sensing even greater violence, and knowing what a special target King would make to the already enraged Klansman (and of the devastating international political consequences not just for the Movement but for his brother if the most important leader of the civil rights movement was murdered at home), had asked King not to go to Alabama, and at one point had even asked the wounded Seigenthaler, then in a Montgomery hospital, to call King and suggest he not come, though Seigenthaler was not able to reach King. King himself was equally aware of the danger involved, and it was by no means sure whether or not he would actually go on the Freedom Ride, as many of the younger people, already gathered to map out their next step, wanted him to do.

The men who were arriving were fully aware of the explosive quality of the situation. Jim Lawson told his friend C. T. Vivian that he ought to wear his clerical collar when they got to Montgomery, that it might make it a little less dangerous, and C.T., who did not have a clerical collar, had to borrow one. Octavia Vivian was not that enthusiastic about her husband going to Alabama, but she knew she could not dissuade him. No one was going to slow C.T. down on this one. Octavia Vivian was scared because she thought that C.T. was a man who did not know how to handle himself in the South; there was too much submerged emotion, and he was too likely to explode. He was a nonviolent man who, in his passion, was a singular magnet for violence.

At the same time, the white mob, having tasted blood in three Alabama cities, its own sensibilities offended by this most blatant invasion of its home territory, was growing larger by the hour as angry whites from all over Alabama and other Southern states converged on Montgomery. The white mob's hunger had been whetted by the failure of the local police to act, and by the inflammatory statements of state and local officials. State-sanctioned violence, John Lewis later called what had happened. And coming too, at the demand of Robert Kennedy, were hundreds of U.S. marshalls. When King arrived at the Montgomery airport that Sunday, some fifty marshalls escorted him to Abernathy's house.

Almost all of the Freedom Riders had spent the first night in the hospital; on the second day they met at the home of Richard Harris, a prominent pharmacist who had been a crucial supporter of King's Montgomery Improvement Association in its early days. Harris had a huge, luxurious home—most of the young black students had never seen a home so large, so handsome, and so filled, it seemed, with the best of every kind of food, where there was room for all of them to stay, and where they were being treated as heroes. If they had felt somewhat alone in the past seventy-two hours, they felt less alone now; suddenly Montgomery was the place to be.

Among those headed to Montgomery was Hank Thomas, the young Howard student who had been assaulted in Anniston. He was still reeling from the events at Anniston—his brief, desperate attempt to commit suicide by inhaling fumes inside the bus had had serious consequences (he had inhaled far more smoke than the others, and it had been smoke of a particularly toxic kind). After Anniston, Thomas had gone to New York, where he had stayed in a friend's apartment and tried to recover his health. Mostly what he had done was sleep. Then one day, he had turned on the television set and had watched the news and had heard that the Freedom Rides were going to continue, and what was even more important, the Nashville kids had taken them over. That was perfect, he thought; this was his show and he immediately got on an airplane and flew to Alabama. He walked in and everyone grabbed him and shook his hand, for he was now Hank Thomas, the hero of Anniston, and when Ralph Abernathy had singled him out at their meeting that day he had said, "I'd like you to meet Hank Thomas, this brave young man who will lead our people into Mississippi."

The forces of the army of integration were to gather that Sunday night in the First Baptist Church in Montgomery, which was Ralph Abernathy's church. The other main force, that of the white army of resistance, coming from small towns in Alabama and Mississippi and Georgia, had no single center at which to gather. So it was that large angry groups of whites arrived in the capitol and swirled through its streets, one small group meeting up with another and gradually forming several ever larger and angrier mobs. Estimates placed the mob at well over one thousand people, but no one could estimate its numbers accurately because it was not that organized. In reality there were several mobs moving through the city, some large, some small, some armed with weapons, most armed with only their anger, all driven by rage and rumor—rage over what had happened already and by the reports that even more black people were apparently coming. The rumor buzz was mean and ugly, centering around the fact that the head man himself, Martin Luther King, was back in town and about to take over the leadership. To some of these whites it was an invasion of their most sacred soil. Their great-grandparents had fought for this land once before; now they were ready to fight again. Inevitably they made their way toward the First Baptist Church.

Soon it became clear that the white mob had the blacks—ministers, Freedom Riders, and their supporters—pinned down inside the church. It had become nothing less than a bunker. The one thousand or so people inside the church could not only hear the mob outside, but they could almost feel it. Although they had gathered to celebrate the heroism of the Freedom Riders, now they themselves were in danger of becoming heroes and martyrs, for the great question was whether any of them would get out of the church alive. The Reverend Solomon Seay, leading the service, had told the audience that the Freedom Riders were among them, but that he could not introduce them for fear they might be arrested by the local police. Earlier in the evening cops had worked the inside of the church looking for the riders but had failed to find them because Seay had dressed them up as members of the choir. So there was John Lewis, survivor of the battle of the Montgomery bus station, huge bandage over his entire head and a cap over the bandage, dressed as a member of the choir, singing away. That amused Bernard Lafayette, who remembered that to white people, all black people looked alike. Thank heaven for some aspects of racial prejudice, Lafayette thought as he watched the cops scan the choir, fail to detect John or the others, and then leave the church.

King and his allies had turned the minister's office into a war room. As the sounds of the white mob grew more ominous by the minute, King himself was on the phone pressuring Robert Kennedy to do something, to produce some kind of protection for them since it was clear that the marshalls could not hold the line. To the youthful leaders from SNCC, there was a certain inevitability to the way that King and his people had taken over the moment they arrived, even though they had not been willing to get aboard the original freedom buses. King was the leading figure of the Movement, by now the de facto leader of black political America, the person to whom the media and the white politicians turned in all moments of crisis. When he arrived during a crisis, he became the central figure. Without him, a demonstration tended to be perceived by the government and the media as local; with him it immediately became national. That created a certain ambivalence on the part of others in the Movement, particularly the young. The local people usually wanted him to come into a crisis situation because he had the ability to reach the entire nation, but they also resented the fact that the moment he came in, they lost control and he and his people automatically assumed that all decision making was now theirs.

For even if King himself was not that territorial, then some of his top people were. More, the dynamics at play inevitably ended up making him seem territorial: If the head man in Washington, as far as the Freedom Riders were concerned, was Robert Kennedy, then as far as Robert Kennedy and the media were concerned, his counterpart in Montgomery was Martin Luther King, not Diane Nash, who had come to Montgomery and who, until King's arrival, had been the person the Justice Department dealt with. These were not responsibilities he sought, rather they were responsibilities which sought him. Some of those tensions which would hang much more heavily over the Movement in the near future were just beginning to surface even as King and Robert Kennedy were arguing over what the feds were going to do and whether or not anyone was going to get out of that church alive.

Diane Nash, who was the least territorial of the students—it was part of her particular strength, Bernard Lafayette thought; she was fearless, absolutely committed to the good of the Movement, absolutely without ego, and above all, perhaps because she was a woman, she never postured—found herself increasingly irritated by the way that King and Abernathy and Wyatt Tee Walker had taken over the decision making. Even as she waited in the church, cut out of the fateful Kennedy-King talks, she understood what was happening and why it was happening, why it was Martin Luther King who was going to talk to Bobby Kennedy. But she was also angry over the way it was done, the way she and the other students were being cut out. Her people—the students—were the ones who had pushed forward on the Freedom Rides. They were the ones who by dint of their courage had brought the federal government to the point where in some way or another it was going to have to intervene. But now she was not even being consulted.

She was irritated in addition because from the start, the SCLC people had tried, either directly or indirectly, to slow them down. Now, however, they had come in and taken over as if it was their personal property. Yet neither King nor Abernathy nor Walker had said whether or not they would come aboard for the next leg of the trip. She could literally feel, hear, and smell the white mob pushing ever closer, and yet she was being cut out. "What's going on?" she would ask Abernathy or Wyatt Tee Walker, and they would tell her that everything was being worked out.[1] She knew better, and she resented the fact that consciously or unconsciously, they were condescending to her.

But that was the way things worked. After all, King and his people were older and they were men, and they had dealt with people like Kennedy before. But part of her irritation came from the fact that she knew that she had made all the right decisions so far, that she was an experienced professional now and had been on top of every move, had been able to keep in touch with the people in the field under the worst kind of circumstances. Years later she decided that it was her pre–women's-movement incarnation. Had it happened about fifteen years later, she decided, she would not have stood for it. But then, she also remembered, it was the civil rights movement which had helped spawn the women's movement. Everything in its own time, she later decided.

As the people inside the church wondered whether they were going to die, Seay asked them to sing freedom songs. The closer the mob outside seemed to come to entering the church, the louder the people in the church sang. Everyone was supposed to sing, which was hard for Diane Nash, who was many things, but was not, despite her youthful attempt to sing in the Miss America contest, very much of a singer. In fact, she was one of the worst singers in the entire Movement, she thought. When it was her turn to lead the audience, she could see the people in the audience struggling to follow her. She had looked down at an elderly black woman sitting in the front row, a woman who had clearly sung in church again and again with great gusto, and the woman had given her a quizzical look which seemed to say, Girl, I am doing the best I can, but I cannot follow you. Are you sure this is your calling?

As the mob pushed ever closer, Martin Luther King and Robert Kennedy kept negotiating through the evening. The people inside the church knew they had almost no protection, and King and his people were using all of their skills to keep the crowd from panicking. Privately, in his conversations with the attorney general, his voice was not nearly so soothing. He was quite angry. Kennedy, listening in Washington with a very different agenda, thought him strident. "As long as you're in church," Robert Kennedy said at one point, hoping to find a lighter moment, "you might as well say a prayer for us." King was not amused.[2] Help was needed; his people were in mortal danger.

At the last minute Robert Kennedy decided to call his brother and ask for federal troops. But just as he prepared to call the president, word arrived that Governor Patterson, apparently pushed by Floyd Mann, had declared a state of martial law. Members of the Alabama National Guard, their bayonets fixed, their faces hostile, finally arrived and drove the mob back. The Guardsmen were not friendly to the blacks—far from it, they might as well have been the cousins of the men in the mob which they had just barely and reluctantly managed to disperse.

Inside the church, Seay had announced earlier that everyone there would have to stay the night, that it was simply too dangerous to go home. That dismayed the people inside, who were already exhausted. But by 4:00 A.M. the mob had been sufficiently dispersed so that they could leave. Bernard Lafayette found himself being loaded into a National Guard truck in the early morning. The hatred on the faces of the Alabama Guardsmen was obvious. The Freedom Riders had been told to find places to stay with local people, and while Lafayette was in the back of the truck he asked an older black woman if he could stay with her. "I'm one of the—" he began, about to say "Freedom Riders."

"Hush, child," she said. "Don't be so loud!"

"Can I go home with you?"

"Hush," she said, even more sharply this time. But when the truck got to her house, she beckoned him to come with her. She was absolutely terrified, he thought, as frightened of him as of the mob. Inside her house she pulled down all the shades. She turned on one light so he could find his way around. Lafayette was exhausted, in terrible pain from several broken ribs, but he fell asleep immediately.

37

THE NEXT DAY, MONDAY, MAY 22, IN A SEEMINGLY ENDLESS MEETING about what they were going to do next, some of the tensions between the young SNCC members and older SCLC leadership surfaced again. The more events had caught the imagination of the nation, the more the stakes had gone up. Jim Farmer, the leader of CORE, had arrived, and while the young people respected him, they were quite annoyed by the fact that on reappearing he seemed to be behaving territorially, talking in front of them as if the Freedom Rides were still, in the phrase he kept using, his show. CORE's show it might once have been, but not after Anniston. Here he was talking about it being his show, and yet no one knew whether he was even going to get on the bus to Jackson.

Some of the young Freedom Riders were also irritated by Martin Luther King. Diane Nash had again asked King to ride with them. If he joined up, she said, given the dangers out there, it would be a great example of leadership. In some ways it was a repeat of the conversation which Rodney Powell and she had had with King and his people a few days earlier: He wanted to ride, but he had been advised by the people around him not to go. There was, after all, his probation from that traffic charge in Georgia, he said. That did not move some of the young people, on probation themselves from different arrests but who were going forward on the ride. They kept pushing King. Finally he showed his own edginess. "I think I should choose the time and place of my Golgotha," he answered, referring to the Hebrew name for the hill where Christ was crucified. It was not an image, King discussing himself in Christlike terms, which diminished the growing tension in the room. Finally Wyatt Tee Walker, one of King's closest aides, said that the debate was over. "Look, if Dr. King decides he's not going, that's it. He don't have to have no reason."[1] The young people remained somewhat unhappy. They wanted King to go, and they were sure they knew why he was not going—his fear, a fear which they certainly shared, but they were disappointed by his lack of candor.

The one young activist who thought they were pushing King too hard was Jim Bevel. He thought that the people who were pressuring Dr. King the most were people uncertain of their own commitment, the ones who had not come to terms with the true meaning of nonviolent Christian protest. If the spirit was truly within them, Bevel thought, they would not be worrying so much about what Dr. King was doing, they would be thinking only of what was the right thing for *them* to do. The more certain a person was of the nonviolent spirit, Bevel believed, the less likely he was to politic with others. No one, he thought, had a right to push anyone else toward so dangerous a fate, particularly Martin Luther King, who lived every day with the threat of assassination hanging over him. But even with Bevel's defense many of the young people were dissatisfied with King's answer. John Lewis, who admired King almost without reservation, was disappointed by the way King had explained his reticence about going, though, faithful as ever, he defended him against the others, who were more critical. But it was clear that most of the top people in the SCLC were not coming aboard.

38

Of the original Nashville leadership group, five were aboard the first bus going from Montgomery to Jackson, Mississippi, that historic day, Wednesday, May 24: three of the students, John Lewis, Bernard Lafayette, James Bevel; and two of the ministers, Jim Lawson and C. T. Vivian. Diane Nash had wanted to go too, but the decision was that she had been so skillful at coordinating the rides so far that she should stay in that role, even though there was an awareness that all the roles had changed. Their cause had begun to evolve into an odd, highly original, three-handed board game in which the young people made their move, and then watched as the feds and locals had to jostle each other as they responded.

Hank Thomas, who now thought of himself as a kind of de facto Nashville kid instead of a Howard student, was also on the first bus. He was to become the Nashville group's lifelong friend, retaining his loyalty to them for more than thirty years, eventually attending all their reunions in Tennessee, even as he did not attend reunions at Howard. He had been the first SNCC member assaulted in Anniston and he felt obligated to keep riding.

It had taken every bit of their emotional strength to bring them as far as Alabama, an ability to face the possibility of their own deaths. But Alabama, whatever fears it inspired in black hearts in 1961, had never cast as dark a shadow as Mississippi. Now they intended to go forward, choosing to bring the modern civil rights movement to the most antagonistic state of all, and thereby to challenge more than a century of ingrained fear, created in a state where white men had the full protection of the law, and black men, as they had no political rights, had precious little legal protection either.

Each of the Freedom Riders had his own private Mississippi, even those who had never been there, but who had always known about it in their minds: It was a Mississippi both real and of their imagination, where blacks went to jail for crimes they might or might not have committed and never emerged again, and where black men might be lynched at the whim of a white crowd. It was a Mississippi where the governing party was Democratic, lily-white Democratic, and blacks could not vote; more, in recent years, all the energies of the state had been turned, not to improving what was the nation's weakest state economy or to raising the nation's lowest school test scores, but to preserving absolute and complete racial segregation. The joke in Alabama and Arkansas, both of them also poor and backward, back in those days when there were only forty-eight states, was a simple one: Each time there was some federal census to determine state levels of education and poverty, the people in Alabama and Arkansas would say, "Thank God for Mississippi—otherwise we might be forty-eighth."

Bernard Lafayette had his own Mississippi too. The first thing you thought of when you thought of Mississippi, if you were black, he believed, was of black people hanging from trees with ropes around their necks. He remembered once when there had been a sit-in at one of the hamburger places near Vanderbilt and a young white student had come over and smiled at him in a sinister way and had said, "You wouldn't be doing this if you were in Mississippi." He remembered the absolute silence on this day as they crossed the Alabama line into Mississippi. Two signs greeted them at the state line. The first said WELCOME TO MISSISSIPPI THE MAGNOLIA STATE, and the other—was it a warning?—said PREPARE TO MEET THY GOD. Even the Mississippi National Guard, which met them at the border, seemed different from the Alabama National Guard, he thought. The Alabama National Guard members had gone about their job in a cold and functional way, as if the Freedom Riders were invisible, and they were protecting an empty bus. The Mississippi Guardsmen were different. They were cockier—there was a smugness to them, a certain pleasure in all this, as if they were saying, Just you wait, black boy, you're going to get yours.

John Lewis had not told his family that he was going to be a Freedom Rider. He did not want to scare them and he did not want them telling him he could not go, and so he had decided the best policy was just to go ahead and ride. But after he had been beaten in Montgomery, there had been no way to hide his latest adventure. There had been a story in *The New York Times* (TROY NEGRO IS LINKED TO FREEDOM RIDE), and so he had had to call home. It was not a call he was eager to make, because he was sure he would hear a good deal of anguish at the other end, but his father had been very good about it. Buddy Lewis was proud of his son and was already going around telling his friends, "You hear about this Freedom Rider John Lewis? That's my boy Robert." In rural Alabama that took exceptional courage, he thought.

Years later John Lewis could remember the exact moment when the bus crossed into Mississippi: He felt that he was leaving America, if Alabama could be called America, and going into some foreign land. In Mississippi, he had decided, even before they crossed the state line, the great victory would be simply going there, staying alive, and leaving. But if they were going to die, at least they would die together.

What surprised him almost from the moment they entered Mississippi was that the officials he was dealing with there seemed more sophisticated and significantly more in control than the officers they had dealt with in Alabama. The Mississippi officials, Lewis decided, had thought things out, and had learned from the Alabama experience. They were going to be cool and clinical in their handling of these invaders; they would meet the nonviolence of the Freedom Riders if they could with nonviolence of their own. At least they would when there were photographers and journalists around. Above all, they were not going to allow the Freedom Riders to use Mississippi on this day as a photo opportunity.

C. T. Vivian was sure that someone was going to die. When he had left his wife and five children behind in Nashville to join the others in Montgomery, he had turned to Octavia and told her he was going to Alabama, but he had said nothing about going on to Mississippi. Thirty-five years later she was still angry about that: "I want you to know that my husband never dared tell me he was going to *Mississippi*. Alabama, yes. Mississippi, no!" On the day he left Montgomery for Mississippi, one of his friends called Octavia and reported that he was on the lead bus. Octavia Vivian, then pregnant with their sixth child, was absolutely terrified. She had previously told their children with no small amount of pride of the risk that their father was taking in Alabama, and why he was doing it—for them and their generation. Now she had to go back and tell the children that their father was taking an even graver risk and they might not see him again. The knowledge that he was on his way to Jackson terrified her. C.T. in Mississippi? she thought. C.T. with his hair-trigger temper? Something terrible was bound to happen.

A friend of theirs named Johnetta Hayes, an official in the Nashville NAACP, heard the news about C.T. being on the bus and came by that morning and told Octavia she would be glad to stay with the children if Octavia wanted to go to Mississippi to join C.T. No, said Octavia Vivian, she did not want to go to Mississippi. She was not that happy about C.T. going there, but the risk that the children might lose one parent was too great. There was no point in taking an even greater risk in creating a situation in which they might lose both parents.

C. T. Vivian watched the people along the highway that day, all of them, it seemed, white—if there were any blacks, they must have gone undercover—waving to the troops. The people waving, he thought, seemed pleased and cocky, as if these black invaders had come at last to the right place, where they were going to get what they rightfully deserved, a beating and a jail sentence. C. T. Vivian remembered the officer in charge of the Mississippi National Guard unscrewing the speedometer so that they could break the speed limit—speed seemed to be of the essence to these people. They clearly wanted this trip done as quickly as possible. Vivian wanted them to take a break once they got inside Mississippi. The Freedom Riders had agreed to do that for two reasons: first, so that everyone could go to the bathroom, and second, so they could brief the accompanying press once they had crossed the state line. But the Mississippi Guardsman did not want to stop. They argued sharply and finally the officer said they could make a brief pit stop.

HANK THOMAS THOUGHT HE DESERVED TO BE PICKED AS THE GROUP'S spokesman; he was, after all, one of the original riders and he had been gassed. But Jim Lawson was named spokesman. Thomas boarded the bus that morning torn between the thrill of being a hero for the first time in his life and doing the right thing, knowing with every bone in his body that it was right, yet being desperately afraid once again. He was puzzled about what unknown inner force had compelled him to come back; on the first leg, the one to Anniston, he had been driven by a combination of arrogance and innocence. Then faced with the immediacy of his own death, he had desperately wanted out. Now, unlike the first time, knowing precisely how dangerous it was, something deep within him had made him come back. Thomas too remembered the moment when they had crossed over from Alabama into Mississippi and had switched escorts. "Change of good shepherds," someone on the bus had said. One of the young black riders had opened his window and had put his head outside and said hello to one of the Mississippi Guardsmen, and the soldier had snapped back at him, "Nigger, get your head back inside. You're in Mississippi now." Welcome to the Magnolia State, he thought.

If he was not going to be spokesman, he thought, he could be a song leader. He had a good voice, and the songs were critically important. They had learned that early on. Their music reinforced that feeling of solidarity, and strengthened these young people against the psychic power of fear, which was always there. None of them wanted to lose their hard-won but thin veneer of courage. "I'm a-takin' a ride," he began to sing, "on the Greyhound bus line/ I'm a-ridin' the *front* seat/ To Jackson this time."

Of the older ministers from the SCLC, the men already in their thirties, Jim Lawson had shown the fewest doubts about the decision of the students to resume the Freedom Rides, in no small part because he was probably the most radical of the clergymen. That day the other riders selected him to be their spokesman. To him Mississippi was a foreign country, a place like South Africa, the symbol of everything they were trying to change. It had a brutal economic system which had over the years been mutated into an equally brutal political and social system. Now, long after some of the raw economic impulse for subjugation had declined, when blacks were being replaced on plantations by mechanical cotton pickers, the political and social system remained in place. Mississippi was the citadel of everything he opposed in America; they could not win in the South, he believed, without coming to Mississippi, and they could not come to Mississippi without risking their lives. To fail to assault this state would mark the Movement with a badge of cowardice.

Lawson had one powerful personal image of Mississippi: He had been there two years earlier, as part of a group arriving to do a local workshop with Martin Luther King. At that moment the excitement that Martin King brought with him everywhere in the South was unique. The one exception had been Jackson. Jim Lawson had been stunned by the local response. The hall where King was scheduled to speak had been half empty. A King audience was usually a confident one and more often than not an exuberant one, but not in this case. That night Jim Lawson could literally sense the uneasiness of the people in the audience, the awareness that they probably had been photographed going in or that their names would be given to Mississippi authorities and there would be a price to pay merely for coming out to hear King. Lawson understood that these people sitting nervously in the audience were among the bravest people of Mississippi, and it reminded him that even in the late fifties, several years after the *Brown* decision, and nearly fifteen years after the end of World War II, Mississippi remained the land of their forefathers, the land of intimidation.

So that morning when they took a break on the way from Montgomery to Jackson he had responded to the questions from reporters with a bravado he did not entirely feel. Someone had asked about the protection which they were getting from these federalized National Guard troops. He remembered the sound of his voice as he told the assembled reporters that they did not really want these troops with them, that they felt they had the right to ride anywhere they wanted to in this country whenever and wherever they wanted and that they should not need any protection. Yes, he had said, we will accept it, but we would prefer not to have it. The reporters had looked at him as if he were crazy. He managed, he was sure, to keep a straight face, but he knew that the reporters were right: All of them on that bus desperately wanted the protection. But he was trying to make the larger point that an ordinary American citizen should not need this kind of protection in order to exercise the most basic kind of right within a free society.

Mississippi turned out on that day to be more orderly than Alabama, its officialdom more disciplined. Off the bus they stepped, into
the bus terminal they walked, there was a brief sampling of a racially
segregated room, and then they were arrested. As they moved into the
forbidden all-white waiting room, Captain J. L. Ray of the local police
told them not to stop. "Keep moving, keep moving," he kept telling
them, and when they did not, he put them under arrest. It was almost
as if they were in some weird, Kafka-like delivery system, being shut-
tled through one door to an otherwise segregated waiting room, and
then processed immediately to the paddy wagons. It was almost as if it
had been scripted from both sides, Bernard Lafayette thought; the
activists had their job, which was to violate the segregation statute,
and Captain Ray had his job, which was to arrest them with a minimum of violence. C. T. Vivian was the last to be arrested. He had gone
to the men's room, the white men's room, of course, and by the time
he got back all of the others were already in the paddy wagons. "I'm
with them," he had told Captain Ray, and Captain Ray had smiled
because it was probably the first time a black man had asked to be
arrested in Jackson. There were twenty-seven riders and twenty-seven
arrests.

Diane Nash and Len Holt, a black attorney from Mississippi, had
driven to Jackson on their own to be part of the riders' support system, and to let headquarters know what happened to them. When she
and Holt left Alabama, they had no idea at all what would happen to
the riders when they reached Jackson and whether or not the Mississippi authorities would permit a riot like the one in Montgomery.

Therefore her job on that first day in Jackson was above all else to
gain information without being arrested. Since SNCC and the SCLC
had little base in Mississippi, *she* was, she liked to recall, the support
system, going around with a bunch of change in her pocket, ready to
make collect calls if something happened. Len Holt was much darker
than she; there was no mistaking the fact that he was a black man. So
once they had gotten near the bus station, they decided to split up.
Holt would investigate the black side of the station and she, coming
from another direction, would try and pass as white and check out
what was going on in the white area. They parked about six blocks
from the terminal and she started walking toward the white waiting

room. As she got within three blocks of the station she began to see
more and more cops, until there were two vast lines of them on each
side of the street, each cop about three feet from the next. It was obvious to her that there was not going to be any street violence in Jackson
that day. Since nothing violent was likely to happen, and since her job
was not to get arrested, it was time to get away from there as fast as she
could. But she also knew that if she stopped suddenly and turned
around, the cops might become suspicious and arrest her. Suddenly
she spied a cop who looked younger than the others and considerably
more innocent. In the past she had practiced her white Southern belle
voice, and now she really laid it on.

"Officer, just what is the matter? I've just never seen so many
policemen in my life."

"Oh, miss," he had answered, "it's all right. There's nothing for you
to worry about. It's just those Freedom Riders."

"Fuhreeedom Riders? Oh dear," she had said, quaking just a little
bit.

"It's all right, miss, you'll be okay."

"Well, I declare, I was going to take the bus to Meridian, but I'm
too scared to go there now. I think I'll just wait until tomorrow when
all those terrible people are gone," she had said and turned around.
That gave her cover, and the other cops did not stop her as she left.

The succeeding weeks in Mississippi, when all of her closest associates were in jail, and more and more Freedom Riders were arriving
every day, were among the worst of her life. Mississippi, Diane Nash
decided, was the hardest place in which to operate that she had ever
been. Alabama had been much harder than Tennessee, but even there,
because of the Montgomery bus boycott and Martin Luther King's
local organization and Fred Shuttlesworth's personal heroism in leading the cause in Birmingham, the Movement had a strong foothold, a
very solid logistical base, and a lot of committed workers. But in Mississippi, despite the singular bravery of Medgar Evers, who headed
the local NAACP (which, it was said, put him in a virtual tie with
Shuttlesworth for the title of bravest man in America), there was virtually no infrastructure. She had to have every important local phone
number memorized and she needed a good deal of change in her
purse for calls. In addition, she had to keep moving so that the law
enforcement people would not concentrate on one or two pay phones.

Medgar Evers had proven very helpful; the NAACP's jurisdictional struggles with other black organizations in other places never seemed to bother him, and lonely as he was, he welcomed all allies. She could use his office and phone, but it was the most scrutinized office in Jackson. There were a few faculty members at Tougaloo who were also helpful and who let her use their phones.

She was constantly exhausted by what she was doing, more, she later realized, emotionally than physically. If she made even the smallest mistake, if she was not careful, someone might get killed because of her. The strain of that was terrible. But mostly what she remembered from those days was the loneliness. For most of the first month she was the only one operating regularly outside of jail; the others were first in the local jail, and then in Parchman, the much feared state prison. In Tennessee they had always had each other. Now she lacked the comfort of that special community. Soon the combination of her terrible sense of responsibility and the special loneliness began to wear her down. At the beginning she cried herself to sleep every night. All the people she loved and cared about were completely at risk.

She was like a gypsy moving around Jackson in those days. More people, both white and black now, ministers, college professors, simple, ordinary Americans, offended by what they saw on television, were joining the Freedom Rides every day, buying their one-way tickets for a cameo meeting with Captain Ray and their instant place in the local jails, and it had been her job to keep track of them and make sure that no one got lost, that no one arrived alone or got separated from the others and disappeared into the dark Mississippi night, into a world where no records were ever kept. She was exhausted, frightened, and at times she wondered whether her faith was great enough for her role.

To Jim Bevel on that first day back in Mississippi the most important thing that happened, because he believed so strongly in the idea of redemption, was not that they had survived a terrifying bus trip to Mississippi, or that the Jackson cops had arrested everyone, but that Jim Farmer of CORE had found redemption. That had intrigued Bevel. Farmer was a man of considerable prominence, who had initiated the Freedom Rides and who had, when the Klan had struck, pulled back. In Montgomery, up until the last minute, even as the buses were about to leave for Jackson, Farmer had not intended to go along; his bags were already packed and had been placed in a friend's car. Then, Farmer had walked over to the about-to-depart bus as a genial well-wisher, ready to say good-bye to some of his CORE people. As he did, a young woman from CORE who was already aboard the bus had asked Farmer wistfully if he was coming, and somewhat shamed by her poignant words, he had boarded the bus. To Bevel that was the great moment of the day. Later that first night, when they were all in jail, it was Bevel who had insisted that they were now a congregation, and that Farmer, because he had started the original Freedom Rides, was the head of the congregation.

Bernard Lafayette sensed that his friend Bevel was more at peace inside the Jackson jail than he was outside of it. It was as if Bevel's special brilliance, Lafayette thought, was his ability to reverse the entire social order in Mississippi: What the local authorities thought was legal he knew was illegal; what they thought was orderly, he thought was disorderly. As tensions rose around him, the calmer he became. Perhaps, Lafayette thought, Bevel was almost too good at jail. On the first night during their stay in Mississippi, a group of them sang freedom songs and Bevel started singing a solo. Bevel had a truly beautiful voice, the best voice of any of them, and as he sang, the others in the surrounding cells became quiet, just listening to the sheer beauty of the sound. One of the white prison guards heard the sound and yelled for quiet. But Bevel kept singing. Soon the guard materialized. "I want that radio," the guard said. "No radios allowed in here—you niggers ought to know that."

"You ain't getting the radio," Bevel said, "not this one."

The guard turned menacing and started unlocking the door. Lafayette thought to himself, Why does Bevel always have to be Bevel? Even here in a Mississippi jail with all of us scared to death, Bevel has to push things to the limit. "Bevel, don't do this to us," Lafayette said. Then, Bevel began to sing the same song, "The Lord Is My Shepherd," with that haunting voice. The guard, both moved and angered, turned abruptly and left them.

Jail, Lafayette thought, jail is one thing we really know how to do well. We are experts at it. We know how to behave, how to be a community within jail, how to support each other. They think jail breaks us, but we have come to think jail strengthens us. Why shouldn't we be happy in jail? he thought. We're with our friends and our teachers, men like Lawson and Vivian. There was a Salvation Army Bible in each cell, and Bernard Lafayette had immediately taken John Lewis's Bible and inscribed it as "Presented to John Robert Lewis at the Hinds County Jail, Jackson, Mississippi, by a man from the Salvation Army June 11, 1961." Lewis, both amused and moved by the gesture, kept the Bible with him for the rest of his life.

It was fascinating, thought C. T. Vivian; here were these young people, who by all rights should still be in college studying for final exams, or discussing what dates they were going to have for a weekend, and the thing they had learned to excel at was forming a community of conscience in an alien prison. Jim Lawson, Vivian thought, had done his work well when he had taught these young people. Bevel and Lafayette and Lewis were clearly the most experienced veterans. When one of the Freedom Riders who had never been arrested before was talking about making bail, Bevel, who seemed to live simultaneously in both a modern age and a biblical time, scorned him. "God don't need no bail," he said. When someone else who had never been arrested before complained about the ill-fitting nature of the prison clothes they had been handed by the Mississippi authorities, Bevel seemed irritated. This was not a fashion show; Gandhi, he added, had wrapped a rag around his balls and had brought down the entire British empire.

That Bevel was so bullheaded, Lafayette thought, was often a problem but on occasion it was a considerable asset. Someone had decided that they should all go on a hunger strike. But it was Bevel who had quickly broken the strike, and for a few days some of the other leaders were furious with him. Bevel had opposed the strike from the beginning, thinking it senseless, particularly because as the Fates would have it, there was a giant bakery on the south side of the jail, and when the wind blew from the south it was particularly hard on those trying to fast. He had broken it not for himself, but for one of his friends who had serious stomach problems and would not be able to sustain a strike, and who was too timid to break the strike himself. A hunger strike was stupid anyway, Bevel thought, particularly with so large a group. Some of them who were experienced at this kind of thing might be able to handle it, but a lot of people would not, not with the smell of Wonder Bread there to tantalize them half the time. If anything the strike might have a reverse effect, might make them cranky and force them to turn on each other. So he broke the strike as quickly as he could in order to take the pressure off the more vulnerable members of their group. He knew most of the other leaders were furious with him. It did not bother him at all. Popularity was a concept which never came up with him.

In jail they were interrogated by the police officials. They had discussed beforehand how they would answer questions, whether they would answer by saying "yes, sir" and "no, sir," which was what the Mississippi authorities wanted them to do (or better still, as Bevel told Vivian, here at home in Mississippi the right answer is not "yes, sir" or "no, sir," it is always "yes, suh, boss" and "no, suh, boss"), or whether they would risk the anger of their jailers by simply answering the question without the term of respect. Some of them thought that there was no need to tempt the authorities; after all, they had made their point, they had come to Mississippi, and that alone was standing tall for freedom. Why then provoke the Mississippi authorities on something so minor? There was a debate over this and they decided that they would not use the word *sir,* that it was an important distinction, that using it granted their jailers a legitimacy they did not deserve.

C. T. Vivian was one of the first to be processed, and they could hear what was happening. There were four or five cops in there and they all had billy clubs or blackjacks. C.T. had walked in, and one of the cops had said, "Come in, nigger, get your ass down there," and C.T. had responded by saying, "Hello, how are you?"

"Nigger, you don't talk to us, we talk to you," the cop had said. That had set the tone.

Whenever they asked C.T. a question he would answer yes or no, but he was not subservient and he did not use *sir.* And so they began to hit him on every answer, four or five times for each inadequate response. Normally they were skilled at hitting people without leaving marks, but Vivian was getting on their nerves and one of the cops got too excited and hit him in the head with a leather-covered blackjack. The blood immediately started gushing out. That made them a little nervous, Vivian thought, because the word was out that the feds were supposed to be pouring into Jackson now.

They had brought in a doctor to treat him, and for C. T. Vivian it was one of the most revealing moments on his trip to Mississippi. After all, a doctor is an educated man, a person much higher in the

John Lewis (center, in light suit with vest) on the occasion of his first arrest outside McLellans in February 1960; "I had never" he said, "had that much dignity before." (*Nashville Tennessean* staff photograph)

Almost immediately after his expulsion from Vanderbilt Divinity School, Jim Lawson was arrested at Kelly Miller Smith's church. Note the subject of Reverend Smith's next sermon. (UPI/Corbis-Bettmann)

Paul LaPrad, being stomped in the photo that went around the world and gave him his moment in history. He said sometimes the women hecklers seemed even angrier than the men. (From the collection of Angeline Butler)

Three of the early sit-in demonstrators at an early protest. From left, Marion Barry (hatless in overcoat), next to him Angeline Butler, and next to her Paul LaPrad. (From the collection of Angeline Butler)

Guy Carawan (left) was an old-fashioned troubadour who gave the students "We Shall Overcome," which became their anthem. With him here are Bernard Lafayette (center) and James Bevel. (Thorsten W. Horton)

April 19, 1960. Having gathered at the site of the city's black universities, several thousand protesters approach the courthouse on the day Z. Alexander Looby's home was bombed in Nashville. (Jack Corn, *The Tennessean*)

At the head of the march that day: From left in the first row, C. T. Vivian, Diane Nash, and Bernard Lafayette; in the second row, Paul LaPrad, Jim Lawson (with handkerchief to his face), Curtis Murphy (in striped shirt) and Rodney Powell; in the third row (just behind Lawson's handkerchief) is Gloria Johnson. (Jack Corn, *The Tennessean*)

Just before the fateful confrontation on the steps of the courthouse: Mayor Ben West (in bow tie), C. T. Vivian, Diane Nash, and Curtis Murphy (in striped shirt). (Jack Corn, *The Tennessean*)

The harsh roots of a minister-prophet: James Bevel's family picking cotton in the Delta. From left, his father, Dennis Bevel; his brother, Charles; his sister Floydzella; James at the age of seven, with the sack; and his sister Mary Alice. (From the collection of James Bevel)

The young prince of his grandmother's Baptist church: Bernard Lafayette decked out in a suit at about age ten. (From the collection of Bernard Lafayette)

The congressman as an elementary school student: John Lewis in his Banks school photo. (From the collection of John Lewis)

Rodney Powell at age sixteen, in his first tuxedo, preparing for his first violin concert. (From the collection of Rodney Powell)

Gloria Johnson as a senior at Girls' Latin. (From the collection of Gloria Johnson-Powell)

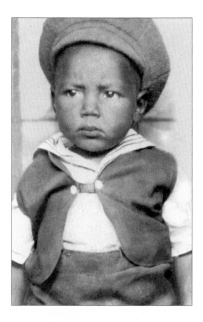

Diane Nash, about three years old, dressed for the Chicago winter. (From the collection of Diane Nash)

Curtis Murphy in his Sunday best at the age of one year. (From the collection of Curtis Murphy)

Diane Nash as she looked the year she arrived at Fisk. (From the collection of Diane Nash)

The revolutionary as schoolboy: Jim Lawson as a senior in high school in Massillon, Ohio, in 1946. (From the collection of James Lawson)

Marion Barry in his Memphis senior yearbook photo. (From the collection of Marion Barry)

MURPHY, CURTIS
Where there is a wrong, there is a remedy.

Curtis Murphy in his senior yearbook photo. (From the collection of Curtis Murphy)

Diane Nash and Jim Bevel on the cover of *Jet* in June 1963: "After being released from jail, mother is in reunion with mate and baby, Sherrilynn," reads the cutline. (*Jet*)

Hank Thomas as a ten-year-old schoolboy in St. Augustine, Florida. (From the collection of Hank Thomas)

On July 3, 1959, Jim Lawson married Dorothy Wood, whom he had met in Nashville. (From the collection of James Lawson)

Rodney Powell and Gloria Johnson-Powell in Ethiopia, 1962. (From the collection of Gloria Johnson-Powell)

John and Lillian Lewis on their wedding day. (From the collection of John Lewis)

Marian Anderson shaking hands with Robert Churchwell of the *Nashville Banner* at Tennessee A&I in February 1957. The author, then all of twenty-two, is to Miss Anderson's left. (From the collection of Robert Churchwell)

The Klan sets fire to the first bus filled with Freedom Riders at Anniston, Alabama. Hank Thomas is standing (in shirtsleeves, back to camera) as the noxious fumes pour out. (UPI/Corbis-Bettmann)

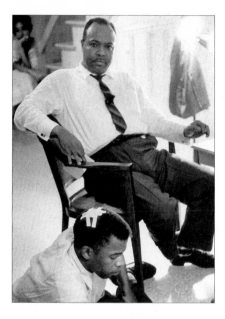

John Lewis after a severe beating in Montgomery, with Jim Farmer (in chair), at the meeting where they vowed to continue the rides. (Bruce Davidson/Magnum Photos, Inc.)

On the ride from Montgomery, Alabama, to Jackson, Mississippi, Jim Lawson with C. T. Vivian (in borrowed clerical collar) telling reporters they did not want national guard protection that day. (UPI/Corbis-Bettmann)

Bernard Lafayette (in aisle seat), next to Rip Patton, looking out at the green fields of Mississippi, as national guardsmen stand by. In the seat behind him is Jim Lawson. (Bruce Davidson/Magnum Photos, Inc.)

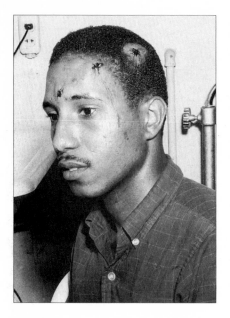

An early casualty in the battle for Selma: Bernard Lafayette after he was badly beaten and almost killed there. (Alex Brown)

John Lewis, newly named as the head of SNCC, speaking at the march on Washington in 1963. (Danny Lyon/Magnum Photos, Inc.)

Jim Bevel (front row, in yarmulke) and Diane Nash at a demonstration in Birmingham in 1963. (Bruce Davidson/ Magnum Photos, Inc.)

John Lewis, alongside Hosea Williams, on the Pettus Bridge in Selma a few moments before the state troopers attacked. (Charles Moore/Black Star)

Alabama State troopers savagely beating John Lewis on the Pettus Bridge a few seconds later; the brutality was more than a century old, but this time a nation was watching. (UPI/Corbis-Bettmann)

The violence on the Pettus bridge was a nail in the coffin of the old order. On the march to Montgomery, Bernard Lafayette is at left, Len Chandler (in flag poncho) is next to him, and Andy Young is in the center, with James Orange to Young's left. In the next row, behind Young, wearing raincoat and carrying knapsack, is John Lewis. (Vernon Merritt III/Black Star)

Memphis 1969: Flanked by his wife, Dorothy, and his son, John, Jim Lawson is on his way to the police station to turn himself in after a warrant for his arrest was sworn in a school-boycott dispute. (Ernest C. Withers/ Panopticon, Inc.)

Bernard and Kate Lafayette today. (From the collection of Bernard Lafayette)

Jim Bevel today. (From the collection of James Bevel)

Curtis Murphy (right) with his wife, Rayna Ristow Murphy, and son, Kevin, at Kevin Murphy's graduation. (From the collection of Curtis Murphy)

Rodney Powell and Bob Eddinger with friends' dogs. (From the collection of Rodney Powell)

Gloria Johnson-Powell (left), with her longtime friend Meg Claytor Woodbury, becomes a doctor again at the Mt. Holyoke graduation, where she was given an honorary degree. (From the collection of Gloria Johnson-Powell)

Another piece of the American dream: Hank Thomas (right) with his wife, Yvonne, and John Melton at the opening of one of his McDonald's restaurants in 1986. (From the collection of Hank Thomas)

normal social hierarchy than these jailers, who to his mind were the lowest of the low, men who took the jobs because they wanted to exercise primitive power over other human beings. The doctor had come in and he was young and pleasant and he seemed to exude none of the normal racism of the region. From the start, he had seemed to treat C. T. Vivian, however cautiously, as a human being. Watching the doctor with the jailers, an amazing thought struck C. T. Vivian: *The doctor was afraid of the jailers.* The doctor had positioned himself between the jailers and Vivian, deftly using his body as a shield so that the jailers could not see what he was doing with his hands. Though he was asking no questions, his eyes were on Vivian's face, and he was delicately using his hands to explore how much damage had been done and how much pain Vivian was in. His hands were asking the questions. It was a telling moment: The doctor in his own way, Vivian thought, was as much a prisoner as Vivian himself was, a successful white prisoner to be sure, but a prisoner nonetheless, afraid of the social order of which he was a part, afraid of these pathetic mean little men who had just inflicted a severe beating on a black prisoner, unable to carry out a normal examination, and afraid of acting like a decent human being. Everyone in this state who is not a complete racist is a prisoner in some way or another, Vivian decided, like it or not, comprehend it or not.

They had spent the first days in local jails, first the Hinds County jail, and then a prison farm at nearby Raymond, but then one day they were taken to Parchman. John Lewis never forgot the trip to Parchman. Every black child in the South knew about Parchman. It was a notoriously brutal place, where everything, it was said, was done at gunpoint. As Mississippi was a harsher place than other Southern states, Parchman was a harsher, crueler prison than other prisons—its local reputation had to be of singular brutality in order to frighten potential prisoners. There was a cruel hierarchy at Parchman; when a convict tried to escape, not only were the prison's dogs sent after him, but black prisoners working as trusties chased him too, aware that if they found him, they would get immediate pardons.[1]

On the day the Freedom Riders were transferred to Parchman the jailers had come for them early in the morning and loaded them in the back of a huge truck. Just like we're cattle, Lewis had thought, like we're not even human beings. They had sung their songs with more intensity than ever on that trip, and then suddenly the truck had jerked to a stop and they had been herded out, still like animals, he thought, with men holding weapons pointing right at them. "Sing your goddamn freedom songs now, niggers, because you sure as hell ain't going to sing them inside," one of the deputies said. "We got real niggers inside here, bad niggers, bad enough to eat you up and spit out the pieces." It was his way of letting them know, Lewis decided, that the easy time in Mississippi was over. Parchman was not even Mississippi, bad as Mississippi was supposed to be; Parchman was worse, a separate, truly evil place created in order to make sure that there was a worse hell than everyday life for blacks in Mississippi. They were marched to a maximum security wing, and he could see the live geese always, he assumed, ready to honk noisily, that were part of the warning system, and the wires. "Those are hot wires, nigger," a guard had said, as if they were contemplating escape.

They had been led into a hallway in the maximum security wing, lined up, and stripped of all their clothes. The guards were all around them, making jokes about the size of the prisoners' genitals. It was all meant to be as dehumanizing as possible, Lewis realized, and it was successful, it *was* dehumanizing. They had been stripped of dignity as well. He hated it for himself, but he hated it even more because men like Jim Lawson and C. T. Vivian, whom he revered, and who were to his mind elegant, distinguished men, men of God, were being subjected to this indignity. Lewis was scared, scared like he had never been before in prison. The debate over whether to say "yes, sir" and "no, sir" was over. He was saying them both. They were walked to a shower, where a guard with a loaded gun watched them. The shower was brief, you were barely in, and someone yelled, "That's enough, nigger," and you were out. Then all facial hair—beards, sideburns, mustaches—was cut off. Then they were walked naked to their cells.

Parchman more than any prison they visited turned out to be the truest test of their faith. Their cells were furnished with tiny bunk beds, rough mattresses, and an old commode. They had a minimal uniform, a pair of green khaki shorts and undershirts labeled MISSIS-SIPPI STATE PENITENTIARY, but no shirts, no pants, no shoes, no socks. John Lewis spent twenty-seven days in Parchman. The only visitor that he could think of that they had was Ross Barnett, the governor, who brought a bunch of his friends to come and stare at them as if they were animals. Lewis was allowed one outgoing letter a week. There was no incoming mail. It was total isolation.

If they were good at prison, so, in a reverse way, were the people who ran Parchman. It was their calling too. From the moment they entered Parchman the riders were rarely together again. The community which had been so strong in other prisons did not exist here: Here it was you and your roommate and the Bible. You could not see out of the cell. There were no other books to read. There was no paper to write on, no pencil to write with, no cigarettes for the smokers. The food was terrible—the Mississippi authorities, Lewis believed, deliberately loaded it with salt to make it as inedible as possible.

Even singing was hard. They had begun to sing their freedom songs the moment they arrived. But the deputy warden ordered them to stop. When they continued to sing, despite his orders, he threatened to take away their mattresses. No one wanted to lose his mattress, terrible and rough though it was. Back and forth the debate went. Eventually they decided to give up their mattresses, and they started to sing again. But then a deputy brought in a fire hose and hosed them down. That was hard—it was wet and cold, and it made their miserable life even worse.

Lewis thought those days in Parchman represented a hard, bitter, glorious time. Although the Mississippi people had been able to keep them from forming the kind of community which they had elsewhere, they had remained essentially undaunted. They had not changed their minds and gone for bail and tried to get out. When it was over, however, when John Lewis had been there twenty-seven days, he thought the day of his departure was a magnificent one. He remembered the drive back to Jackson and the train ride back to Nashville as a time of singular personal triumph. He and the others had done it; they had gone to Mississippi and they had survived. Indeed, in their own minds they had been victorious. They were still alive. They had all been humiliated and subjected to the most degrading experiences imaginable, but it had not dented them. In Jackson and then in Parchman they had truly been in the belly of the beast, the worst beast, he thought, that inhabited America. They were still afraid of Mississippi, they were smart enough to know that it remained dangerous, but they were not so scared that they would not bring the Movement back here again. It was the critical beginning which they had all so badly needed, and which they had so greatly feared. The truth was that most of them were more committed now than when they had gotten on the first bus more than a month ago, and Lewis himself was more sure that in the end, justice could be done, and would be done.

39

JAMES BEVEL HAD HAD NO TREPIDATION ABOUT GETTING ON THE FREE-dom bus in Montgomery and riding to Mississippi, even though he knew Mississippi better than anyone else. The question at the outset, before they had boarded the first bus, was not how safe or unsafe Mississippi was. The question was whether going there was the right thing to do. It was all very simple, he had said. Of course it was unsafe, and because it was unsafe it was the right thing to do. Bevel, thought Lewis, was always good at cutting to the essentials.

It had been an eerie journey for Bevel, coming back to Mississippi, as if he were somehow following an odyssey which was preordained. On the first day when he had been arrested with the others, and the Jackson police officials had brought all the Freedom Riders to the police headquarters, Bevel noted how geared up the Jackson cops were: They seemed to have brought in every typist who worked for the city in order to expedite the paperwork. It was like a mechanized process. They marched in each black prisoner and Captain Ray, who was in charge of the operation, would ask the questions—and the typewriters clicked away rapidly: name, *click, click, click, click;* home-town, *click, click.* Everyone passed through quickly. Then it was Bevel's turn.

Name? "James Luther Bevel." Hometown? Captain Ray had asked. "Itta Bena, Mississippi." Suddenly, as he had given the name of his hometown—a Mississippi boy returning here, knowing what he was getting into—the typewriters had fallen silent. There was a long moment of silence. Then Captain Ray looked at Bevel. "Now, boy," he said, "you ought to know better than to come back here."

He did, of course, know better than to come back. He, like the others, had not even intended to spend the night in Jackson. Originally they were just going to pass through Jackson on their way to New Orleans, sample, as some of them had joked, some of that fine food the Jackson Greyhound bus station was so famous for, and go on their way. It was the state officials of Mississippi, who wanted to prove to their voters that they could stand up to these people, who had decided they should stay there a little longer. But he had known the moment he had gotten on the bus in Montgomery that he was going home, in the strange, terrifying sense that Mississippi was home. From the start he thought of it as a choice: Did he truly believe in what he was doing? Was his motivation pure? To these questions he was confident that the answer was yes.

James Luther Bevel was the thirteenth of seventeen children of Dennis Bevel; of the seventeen his mother, Illie Bevel, bore fourteen of them. The family name had originally been Beverly, but Dennis Bevel had changed it in part because Beverly was a slave name, and in part because he was fascinated by the Old Testament, and by changing it to Bevel he was using part of the Hebrew word for God. The name Beverly had come from a white man named Beverly who was James Bevel's great-grandfather, and who had left some of his land to his mulatto sons, something which was not that unusual a practice in Mississippi; some white plantation owners even arranged a college education for their offspring. Dennis Bevel's share of the family land, some three hundred acres, had been in Humphreys County, an area which was more or less the gateway to the Delta, and Bevel's father had had a hard time holding on to it. Black ownership of good Mississippi land was not easily sustained, for it threatened most whites, and in addition, Dennis Bevel had insisted on sending some of his children to places like Mary Holmes Seminary in West Point and Piney Woods, places which were, James Bevel liked to say, really more like high schools than colleges. That too made many of his neighbors uneasy, for it might stir up a desire for education in other black families.

Because of that, and in addition, according to his son, because Dennis Bevel refused to inform on other black families for the FBI, he was blacklisted, and could not get the requisite loans from the local bank which would allow him to hold on to his land. Certainly given both the vulnerability of so many blacks in Mississippi and the powerful sense of grievance among many of them, informing to police authorities had always been a thriving business. Because Dennis Bevel was considered more intelligent and analytical than other black men in the area, on a couple of occasions, according to James Bevel, the FBI had approached him, wanting information on what was happening among other blacks. He had refused to cooperate. The worst thing a man can do is betray his own kind to people like the FBI, he had told his son.

Dennis Bevel had lost his land in the thirties, a few years before James Bevel was born. It was a catastrophic moment for him: He later came to believe it was responsible for breaking up his family. With the loss of the land, the family's fortunes began to change. In 1946 Illie Bevel left Mississippi and went north to Cleveland. She had custody of the children, but because Dennis Bevel was relatively old by then, James Bevel, then ten, and his younger brother, Charles, stayed on in Mississippi in order to help take care of him.

It was for the young James Bevel a traumatic moment. Suddenly his family, which had always seemed so strong, had broken up. From that breakup came, he said, a deep personal sense of inferiority which lasted a long time. Other kids had two parents, but now he only had one. He could not understand why they had broken up: If he loved them both, and if they loved him, why then could they not love each other? When the divorce took place, he did not so much feel angry as he felt powerless.

Dennis Bevel had gone only as far as eighth grade in school. But his vision of life, James Bevel would later decide, closely paralleled that of James Lawson. He was a serious man of God, though he was technically not a minister. But everyone in that part of the Delta knew about him, and when he preached as a guest minister at various area churches, he often drew larger audiences than the regular ministers. Since he studied the Bible so carefully, his son often wondered why he had not become a preacher himself. "Preaching is not something you choose, not something you volunteer for," he had answered, "it's something you are called to. And I haven't been called to it." He was also a self-taught builder, and the homes he built were considered unusually well built by both whites and blacks.

Dennis Bevel was eccentric, self-educated, well-read, a skillful builder, a lay minister, an extremely competent farmer, a man who behaved by his own codes and had his own carefully thought-out set of beliefs. He was seen by both whites and blacks as being different. Crazy Dennis Bevel, white folks called him. He lived in a bitterly divided, two-tier racist society, and yet it sometimes seemed to his son that he worked skillfully to immunize himself against segregation, creating his own rules so that Mississippi's suffocating racism would crush neither him nor his children. Dennis Bevel thought the idea of segregation, that one race, particularly a race whose vices and weakness he knew all too well and had been born of, was superior to the other was simply insane. If there was nothing he could do about it legally or politically, he tried as best he could to create a code which allowed him and his family to live outside it.

So he designed an existence which intersected with the white world as little as possible and which put his family as little at the mercy of white authorities as possible. Whenever the Bevel family moved from one town in the Delta to another, Dennis Bevel would immediately go into town with his two sons and introduce himself and them to local store owners and the local police. "This is James and this is Charles. They are my sons, and they are under my supervision," he would say. "If there is any trouble in town—if you have any trouble with them—come and see me and I will take care of it. But otherwise I don't want you or anyone else to lay a hand on them."

The thinking behind this was simple enough: If he did not accept the existing codes of Mississippi, then he had to substitute his own codes in their place. This he did, though it often put him at risk. On one occasion his sons were supposed to go to the cotton fields to work for the owner of the land where they had been renting. But that morning they had been told by their father to grind corn for their own chickens. All the other black children had gone on to the field, and a furious owner's son had raged at the two Bevel boys—"You two niggers know damn well you're supposed to be in the fields." That, as far as Dennis Bevel was concerned, was a violation of his own personal code—the boys were under his protection, and only he could administer punishment, whether verbal or physical. When he came home that day and heard the story, he immediately decided to go and talk to the landowner, a man named Alex Perry. Dennis Bevel's own brother cautioned him against doing it—this was, he thought, a suicidal violation of the white-black relationship so crucial to Mississippi farm life. At the very least the Bevels would be expelled from the land. But Dennis Bevel had gone over, and always polite and careful, he had explained his case, why he had requisitioned his own sons to grind corn, and how under what he believed were the agreed rules of the use of his sons' labor, any complaints were to be made to him. Perry had agreed, and the matter had been dropped.

The basis of his codes was his religion: If you believed in Jesus Christ, then you came under the consciousness of God, and therefore no other mere mortal could truly oppress you because under God all men are equal. God, therefore, was within you, and if someone was trying to abuse you based on race, then it was a sign of his own weakness and inferiority and his own distance from God. Because of that, the laws of the state and the conventions of society meant nothing, for Dennis Bevel lived outside them. He believed every day of his life, his son thought, that there was a higher order than that being promulgated by the white authorities of Mississippi, and that he was living an acceptable moral existence under that higher code. The key to his father's own existence and survival, James Bevel said, was his own belief that no one was closer to God than anyone else—least of all someone who thought his skin color and his wealth promoted him to a higher level, and thereby allowed him to act in an ungodly way.

Dennis Bevel was a man who took the ethics of daily life seriously. His sons were not to go around complaining about how other people treated them. Rather they were to pay attention to how they treated others. He did not allow his sons to complain about white people in any generic sense. Complaints had to be specific. White people were both good and bad, like everybody else, he would say. The average white person, he told his boys, did not sit around all day thinking of how to suppress black folks. Most of them were just trying to get through their own hard little lives. They had their own problems too, their bills to be paid, their illnesses, their own fears and shortcomings. Most of them didn't feel very secure or very powerful. Only a few of them, the really dangerous ones, thought much about keeping black people down. But most people, he told his sons, were reasonable, caught like everyone else in things too powerful for them.

He was a man who seemed to move easily between the New and the Old Testament. To Dennis Bevel, and to his son as well, Jesus Christ was a Jew who had clarified Judaism through the use of the New Testament. That was why Dennis Bevel had changed his name to Bevel. It made him God's person, and he thought of himself as being partly Jewish. When his wife had taken their children and gone north, Dennis Bevel had been puzzled, wondering what he had done to God to cause him all this unhappiness.

His religion had more than a little of the mystical to it. When Dennis Bevel had been in his mid-twenties he had not been a religious man; he had instead been a music man, a talented banjo player working the riverboats which went up and down the Mississippi. He played on the boats and one-night stands in the small towns along the river. One night he had been playing in what was then called a barrel house, which was a simple nightclub for black people; on that night the rickety old house had caught fire and the blaze seemed to explode with a deadly force right near the entrance. Dennis Bevel had seen his life about to slip away, and he had prayed desperately to his Lord, offering an instant trade—if the Lord would get him out of there alive and undamaged, he would commit his life to Him. Miraculously, he managed to find a way out. As part of the bargain he never played the banjo again.

Once when James Bevel was about ten, Dennis Bevel was out in the woods cutting trees for firewood. Charles, his younger brother, had managed to slip off and had fallen asleep. By chance he was sleeping in the path of where a mighty tree would land once his father had finished cutting it. When the tree began to fall, Dennis Bevel looked over, saw what was about to happen, saw his young son in harm's way, and he looked up and implored his God: "Don't let that tree hit the boy!" Even as he said this, the tree seemed to hesitate, and Dennis Bevel had screamed at his son to move. The boy jumped aside, and the tree landed just where he had been napping. How did you do that, how did you get the tree to stop? James Bevel asked his father. "A man should live his life in a way that God will obey him," the father answered. That day was a moment of truth for young James Bevel, about God and about his father.

If there had been a second traumatic moment in the young James Bevel's life it had come when he was thirteen and they were living in Leflore County, Mississippi. He had finished school one day and he was on his way home when a big black car had pulled up alongside him and a large black man had gotten out and said in a voice which brooked no dissent, "Son, get in the car!" He had gotten in the car, surprised to find his mother already inside. They had driven to Winona, in central Mississippi, and gone to the bus station there and taken the bus to Nashville and from there to Cleveland, Ohio. Later he understood that the plan had been to take Charles too, except that Charles had been out of school that day because he was sick. It was, James Bevel said some forty years later, nothing less than a kidnapping. He loved his father, who was the ultimate nonviolent man, a man who never laid a hand on him. His mother was different; when she was angry she would periodically whip him. It seemed to him that on that day she had done something over which he had no control and he never forgave her.

He finished his junior high school in Cleveland. In some ways he was lucky. He went for a time to a well-known high school, East Tech, which was a famed feeder school for the auto industry and its ancillary industries. It was a school with a rich tradition—many of its graduates went on to places like Ohio State and Western Reserve. He learned pattern making, which was an important skill for the auto industry, and he was good at it, good at woodworking and making furniture and at printing. After his mother died he returned to Leflore County and graduated from high school there. He was quite sure he was going to go on to college, and he thought of certain black schools, Tennessee A&I or Jackson State. But he decided to go in the navy first, in order to enter college when he was older and had a little more money. Dennis Bevel was appalled by his decision. When James Bevel at seventeen had joined the navy, eager to play his part in the Cold War, Dennis Bevel just shook his head. He was not going to stop his son from his chosen course. If it was what the boy wanted, to be a part of what he thought was the ridiculous Cold War, with all that silly propaganda, then the boy could do it.

Later in his life, the more time James Bevel spent with Jim Lawson, the more Lawson reminded him of his father. The parallels between both men were strong: Neither seemed to worry about being envisioned by local officials as inferior, mostly because it never occurred to them that they might be inferior. Exterior things, the laws of segregation, could not defeat them; their own inner truth, a belief in a just God, sustained them. Both were committed to leading nonviolent lives. When James was a child, Dennis Bevel had been furious when he found out that James had thrown a rock at a friend and had hit him; his son was to go over and apologize immediately. His sons were not to hurt animals. If there was killing, it had to be for food. Lawson's teaching was in a continuum with what his father had always taught. It was as if James Bevel was predestined to return to Mississippi in 1961, at the age of twenty-four, to risk his life in order to end the madness of segregation. Whatever else, he believed that the streets of Jackson were as much his as they were Captain Ray's.

40

CURTIS MURPHY DID NOT GO ON THE FREEDOM RIDES. IT WAS THE most bitter disappointment of his life. In no small part because of that, he became the first of the group's leaders to hit a wall in his personal life. He had made a commitment to his father that when the sit-ins were done, he would go back to school and get his degree. In June 1961, it was time to honor that commitment. When many of the other Nashville leaders moved on to the Freedom Rides, Curtis Murphy had remained largely on the outside.

During the early days of the rides, he had gone by the SNCC office, hoping despite his promise to his father to become a part of them, and wanting to get down to Alabama and Mississippi. But then Diane Nash had quickly put him in charge of the Nashville office and had gone off to Alabama herself. His disappointment was considerable and he felt quite lost. He knew the other kids were dodging parental restraints, but somehow, perhaps because Whiteville was so near Nashville, perhaps because he had pushed it so hard with Buck in the past, he felt unable to deceive his father. He had given his word, and now he had to keep it. But his heart was not in his studies. Getting a degree now meant little to him, although it meant everything to his parents. Grades had once been important, the only clear means of defining who he was. When the sit-ins first started he had intended to be first in his class at A&I. But now the Movement had given him a different definition of self, that of an activist working against injustice.

Back at Tennessee A&I he found himself largely going through the motions. Black fraternity life, which he had once enjoyed, seemed callow and boring. His real friends were the sit-in leaders, and they had gone on to even greater struggles and they were full of the excitement and passion which that kind of life generated. By contrast he was dealing with math courses which now bored him. His grades began to drop immediately. Where he had once made nothing but *A*'s, he was now getting *C*'s. He slept late in the morning and often missed class. He felt older than the other students around him, more like an army veteran who had come back from war than their contemporary.

Later he came to understand that what he had gone through was a profound personal depression, and much later than that, he came to realize that he had not been alone, that many of the young people in the sit-ins eventually went through a comparable experience, although because he had been forced by his father to drop out of the Movement early, he had been the first. The truth was that for all the terror and the fear and the uncertainty of those sit-in days, it had been the most exhilarating and fulfilling experience of his life. Now, back at school, he had returned to a normalcy of being a young man uncertain of and underwhelmed by his future.

He had, somewhat to his own surprise, gotten married while still in college, and the marriage had quickly failed. He had been nineteen years old, going out with a number of different young women, not the least of them Catherine Burks, the beautiful young woman from Birmingham who had challenged Bull Connor, and whom he had met when he and a few friends had created an instant taxi service, ferrying newly arrived black students from the train station to the dorms on their first day of school in Nashville.

He had dated Catherine Burks for a time, and Diane Nash briefly, and then in his junior year he had dated a young woman named Sandra Lillard, the daughter of Bob Lillard, one of the city's leading political figures, a pioneer black on the city council. She was a member of the local black establishment, her family seemed to have both wealth and connections, and there had been something heady about that, of being a part of the Nashville elite. Somehow, very quickly, there had been an engagement and a quick marriage—though there had been no shotgun in the background. On the day of the wedding, his friends had come to pick him up, and they had found him nervous and uneasy, aware that he was in way over his head, about to marry a nice young woman whom he did not know very well, when he had no great desire to get married. They were both very young and they had no concept of the responsibilities involved in getting married. Quite predictably the marriage was over after a few months.

Outside the Movement he replaced his sit-in friends with new friends, but they were too easily impressed by anything he said, and he took little pleasure in their adoration. His parents were thrilled that he had kept his word and was back in school, and though they soon became bothered by the decline in his grades, they had no way of knowing that their son was depressed. In their minds he was one of the luckiest young men imaginable: a child of the cotton fields who was about to finish college, and go on to a life better than theirs. They could not conceive of someone so privileged being lost or unhappy.

He started hanging out at nightclubs around the campus. His favorites were the New Era on Joe Johnson, and Del Morocco on Jefferson. Feeling himself older because of his experiences in the sit-ins, he had begun to pose as a sophisticate. Someone had told him that scotch was the cool drink, the drink which sophisticated (white) people drank, and he began to drink it, both with water, and to his later embarrassment, with milk. Some sophisticate, he thought years later. At night when he hit the clubs, he was with older black men who were part of the city's night world, gamblers and hustlers. He thought they were cool, and because they were cool, he decided that he was cool too. To his surprise, though he was much younger, he was something of a hero to them. He was someone who had stood up to the white establishment and had made it back down. If they only knew, he thought. The real heroes were his friends who had taken the protest a very considerable step further into Alabama and Mississippi while he had remained on the sidelines. Still, he took admiration and respect wherever he could find it in those days. There were always a lot of women around these nightclubs and they seemed to like him. Sometimes, he later reflected, he had as many as four or five women on the string at the same time. Nor were these co-eds. These were foxy women. Only a cool man could handle that many foxy women.

He was hip, he decided. That was his new incarnation. Curtis Murphy, son of a small black landowner in West Tennessee, a man who with his wife had sacrificed much of his life for a son's education, was now an integral and very cool part of Nashville's black nightlife, hanging out with gamblers and pimps. How far he had come, he thought to himself with disgust. He hung out late, until two or three or four in the morning, missed classes, but was sure that as bright as he was, he could coast by. He got up late, usually after ten in the morning, and he stopped taking any course which had early classes. When he finally got up, he who had always been so meticulous about his personal habits was sloppy about himself. He did not brush his teeth. He did not shower. Underneath his cool exterior he was frightened by what was happening, by the lack of ambition, and the growing lethargy in his life. When he returned to Whiteville for visits, he tried to hide what he was doing from his parents. They probably knew better, he later suspected, but there was not much they could do. After all, he had honored his part of the bargain with them by returning to school.

His visits home had turned increasingly painful. Once so pleasant, a time when he could bask in the reflected love and nurturing of two generations of Murphys, these trips had become the most awkward of social occasions. When he returned now, he was filled with self-loathing. The contrast between the physical harshness of their lives, the endless physical labor demanded for them just to stay afloat, and the knowledge of the degree to which both his parents and grandparents had sacrificed for him became a source of embarrassment when he thought of the indolent way in which he was now behaving.

The Murphys had always lived a demanding, spare existence. The central fact of their life was the attempt to hold on to their plot of land, and not slip back into the world of the truly helpless, that of being sharecroppers. Everyone in the family worked hard and everyone sacrificed and a good deal of the sacrifice, Curtis realized, had been, in the long run, aimed at creating a better life for him. There were spartan rules of behavior and spartan rules of work on that farm. The harshness of the culture, the odds against a black man holding on to his own land demanded nothing less. The Murphys asked for no charity, and always took care of their own bills. They anticipated trouble; they stored a certain amount of money aside for those years when the weather might adversely affect the crops. During the worst of the Depression, when Curtis's mother had been a little girl, her father had run off and her family's circumstances had been truly desperate. Yet her mother had gone house to house with her young daughter at the time, asking white people for any kind of work. Not charity, but work. That attitude was ingrained on both sides of the family. Both grandparents let their grandchildren know that no one was to damage the family's reputation. "You don't bring scandal to this house," George Murphy liked to say. That was not a motto, Curtis eventually decided, it was nothing less than an immutable law. Scandal was drinking, using bad language, getting in trouble at school, getting in trouble with the law, and, of course, for a girl, getting pregnant without being married. There was some talk when he was young about a neighboring girl who had gotten pregnant and who had been sent away because she was bad. That was a black mark against the home where she had grown up, and Curtis's parents spoke of her parents with a sense of permanent sadness. The taboo on drinking was not total, it was a taboo about drinking too much. Maggie Murphy, George Murphy liked to say, "made the best lightning in the county." But she made it sparingly, perhaps a gallon at a time. Her grandson would ask her what she was doing, and she would always answer that she was fixing something for medicinal purposes. The whiskey was to be drunk only on Saturday. Sunday belonged to the Lord, but for half a day on Saturday, the time was theirs. Work, miraculously, ceased. Drinking the moonshine with a few friends for a few hours on Saturday was the extent of sin and decadence in their lives.

Everyone in the family had to work hard to hold on to the land. It was a shared family work existence with shared family obligations. George Murphy, Sr., had bought the farm when he was young. Each year had brought some new form of hardship. In order to provide cash for mortgage payments in what was barely for them a cash economy, Buck Murphy and his wife had been forced to leave the farm and to work in places like Clarksville, Tennessee, and Paducah, Kentucky, he taking work as a construction worker, she working as a domestic. If that brought in cash, it also meant leaving their son and their daughter behind with the grandparents. But that kind of sacrifice was inherent, they assumed, in black people's lives. The farm which Buck Murphy took over had been 150 acres. By the time he died it had grown to 300 acres. Because they owned so much land they had three sharecropping families living on it. They had six mules. There was nothing fancy about a mule but they got the job done and they cost very little. It was only later as he started to get slightly ahead of the game, and he expanded his land, that Buck Murphy became one of the first black men in the region to buy a tractor. That too, like owning his land, set him apart as a black success in the area.

From the time when Curtis was five and he took care of the cows, his was a strict upbringing. All grown-ups, even the sharecroppers, were to be called "sir" or "ma'am." No child could talk back to a grown-up. No profanity was allowed. Any use of it would bring an immediate and very hard backhanded whack from his grandmother or grandfather. Sunday was the day of religion. The church, of course, was Baptist. In the morning there was Sunday school, then the church service itself, and then in the evening, there was Baptist Youth. Every black child in the area, it seemed to him, went to church, and every child had to wear his one suit. That suit was not to be worn at any other time except perhaps for funerals or weddings. One of the worst whippings that Curtis Murphy ever got came when he was eight and he had gotten a new suit, and his aunt had sewn his name over the pocket. *Curtis,* it had said, and he had loved the idea of that, a suit with his name on it, and he had refused to take it off. The elders in the family were furious with him. That was frivolous. His grandmother told his mother to take a switch to him, and she did, a peach tree switch, and he saw her coming, ran out of the house barefoot, stepping on a bottle and badly cutting his toe, a wound which did not save him from a world-class licking. He learned early to obey the rigid rules of his home, rules, he soon learned, which extended to school as well. If he misbehaved at school and got a whipping, his parents always knew and gave him an additional whipping.

Gradually as he came to adulthood Curtis Murphy began to understand why finally, in their lives, the ownership of land had been so important to them, as the right to demonstrate had become so important to him when he was at A&I. To his parents, owning land was freedom; to him, being able to act and demonstrate was freedom. In their lifetime, with the lines between the races drawn so sharply and with such finality, a black man was always vulnerable to a white man *except* on his own land. If he was a sharecropper, he was absolutely dependent on the moods, needs, and economic whims of the whites for whom he toiled; if he owned his own land, he was as independent as a black man could possibly become in that age, a man with a fortress of his own to which he could retire, and a man whose own hard work had a chance of eventually being rewarded. Neither George Murphy, Sr., nor his son Buck had ever dared dream of going to school with white people. But Buck Murphy's basic law, like that of his father, was this: If you owned your own land, then you were the master of your own destiny or as close as any black man could be to being his own master. "Every man should have his own piece of dirt. If you do that, if you own it, no other man, no matter what his color, can make you step off it," Buck Murphy liked to say.

Long before he understood the reasons for the primacy of that law, Curtis Murphy had accepted it and the hard work it entailed. Gradually, as he came to manhood, he understood first the economic dynamic behind it, the difference in not being a sharecropper, and then gradually he understood the psychological dynamic which drove it, the respect which came with it, not the least of it, self-respect. Other than his family, the land itself was Buck Murphy's great love. Here he was safe from much of the racial injustice which dominated the region. Years later, when Buck Murphy was dying, he made his son, by then an official in the Chicago school system, promise that no matter what happened, he would never sell the family land. *Never.* It had always given him a kind of emotional reassurance; at the end of a long, grueling day Buck Murphy would often stand there at night looking at his land, saying nothing, just drinking it all in, that he owned this and that he was safe there.

Buck Murphy, Curtis realized, did not believe in an integrated existence for blacks, for he had seen nothing of that in his lifetime, but he believed there was a kind of better life where blacks could work at jobs which demanded the use of their minds instead of their backs, and where they could enjoy some of the good things of life. To get ahead, he told his son again and again, a black man had to be twice as good as a white man and he had to work twice as hard. His children could get ahead only with an education. Without an education, the sad history of black people in America, getting the most menial jobs on the economic ladder, would inevitably continue for yet another generation.

Curtis had remained the dutiful son in his early college years, always doing well in his studies. He was good in his science courses, and because of that he had joined the air force ROTC in his freshman year, fascinated as he was by missiles and jets. Perhaps, he dreamed, he might even be able to fly jet airplanes. The air force was part of the government and the government was supposed to be fair about these things and give blacks a chance. In his sophomore year he took a qual-

ifying exam for advanced AFROTC, and along with one friend from
A&I he qualified. That was the doorway to a glamorous life, he
believed.

By his sophomore year he and his friend were toying with a special
air force program which would allow them to go right into cadet training without finishing college. They passed the requisite tests and
seemed well on their way. The only obstacle for Curtis was his father.
When Curtis finally explained the plan to Buck he had a sudden and
quite accurate sense of what his father was going to say. "I'm all for
it—and I'm on your side. But first you have to graduate from college.
Then you can become a pilot." In this, as in all other things, the
degree had to come first. Buck Murphy was not going to argue the
American past with his son. He might harbor quite a few doubts of his
own about the likelihood of the U.S. government putting his black
son in a jet plane cockpit, but he thought he had an accomplished son,
he knew times were changing, and he was not going to block what the
government of the United States would now permit. But just in case
the jet pilot career did not work out, if Curtis had a degree he could
always get a good white-collar job, one that demanded respect and
was not vulnerable to the weather and soil.

That was the young man whom Jim Lawson had first encountered
in the fall of 1959, talented, popular, and successful. He was an almost
perfect black success story—except that there was something incomplete about it; if he was about to be rewarded materially, then there
was a terrible gap in it spiritually. It was something which Jim Lawson
knew and he shrewdly let Curtis Murphy discover it for himself. His
participation in the sit-ins had put at risk everything his family had
worked so hard to attain for him; Buck's decision, once he had been
arrested, to let him continue was probably the most difficult decision
the father had ever made in his life. It was, because of his father's obvious fear and apprehension, the greatest example of love that a father
could give to a son, Curtis decided.

At least when he had been a part of the sit-ins, even if he had defied
his parents, he had done it for a worthy cause, one that others of his
generation would rally to, and one perhaps that someday his parents
would understand. But now having lost that special sense of purpose
he felt a complete failure. His sense of shame was powerful, and yet he
felt himself unable to change his ways. One sign of his declining self-

esteem, he later decided, were the fights. From being a young man who had always gotten along with everyone, who had seemed to have a natural ability to charm all those around him, he was now edgy and confrontational. There were several fights at the clubs in this period, and suddenly he had emerged not as the easygoing young man of the past, but as a tense, angry young man with a new, volcanic temper. When he was at a nightclub and some stranger said something he did not like, he was immediately ready to fight. Because he didn't like himself, he decided later, he didn't like anyone else around him.

In addition he made sure that he did not see his old friends in the Movement. He made a brief stab at working in the office when all his friends were in Montgomery and then Jackson, but it was simply too painful. The gap between their lives and his was great and getting larger. He thought of them and what they were doing and he was touched by envy for the first time in his life. They were still involved, still making a difference as he was not. He stopped reading the *Tennessean,* which was still covering events faithfully, and he turned away from television when there were stories on about developments in Alabama and Mississippi.

41

EVEN AS CURTIS MURPHY WAS HITTING A WALL IN THE FALL OF 1961, Rodney Powell found his confidence gaining by the day. After graduating from Meharry he had started his internship in pediatrics at the University of Minnesota. Though the other interns were graduates of some of the great medical schools in the country, and among the top students at those schools, he had found that he could more than hold his own with them. He might at first be a step behind them in his medical training, but he was ahead of them in other ways. For he was a graduate not just of Meharry, but of the sit-in struggles of 1960 and 1961. When he told his fellow medical students what he had done in the South, he liked the admiration he saw in their eyes. In some ways he came to realize he was more mature now than most of them, and more confident. He had joined the sit-in group for moral and political reasons, but a side benefit was that it had turned out to be a remarkable leadership course as well. He had tested himself as his classmates had not.

His own personal life had been somewhat volatile in the previous year and a half. For much of the time during the sit-ins he had dated Diane Nash. They had met just as the workshops had begun. She had been seated at the counter at a small luncheonette near the Fisk campus, and the first time he saw her he had been absolutely blinded by her good looks. She was very simply the most beautiful young black woman he had ever seen, the epitome of the modern black co-ed. And even more remarkable, he had thought, she was committed to the cause. Like the rest of us, he had thought, she is angry and alienated.

They had started going out together almost from the start of the sit-ins and they had made an uncommonly attractive couple; Powell's thoughtful, judicious demeanor, his quiet concern that everyone be listened to, and his gentle manner had seemed to balance nicely with the fire in Diane. He seemed to be a young man always ready to listen and she seemed to be a young woman always ready to act. For a time theirs had been a serious relationship; Rodney took pleasure later on in quoting Diane's mother about the two of them, that Rodney liked to go out with Diane because she was the closest thing to a white girl Rodney could date and still be black.

But in the summer of 1960, just before his senior year, he had stopped off in Chicago to visit with Diane and her family, and things had not worked out between them. He thought she was testing him in some way, and she thought that perhaps he was not committed enough for marriage, and when they returned to Nashville they had gone their separate ways. Other members of the leadership group, of course, had wanted to go out with Diane. Before she had become serious with Rodney she had gone out briefly with Curtis Murphy, and the other students had a sense that Jim Bevel was after her, though the idea of Diane and Bevel together did not seem to make much sense to them.

In a way, even before he broke up with Diane, Rodney had been part of an odd threesome. He was going out with Diane, but he spent a good deal of time with Gloria Johnson, who was his medical school colleague, one year behind him, and his closest friend. If he was satisfied with the limits of that relationship—one based on friendship rather than romance—the other students were not sure that Gloria Johnson was. They thought she was very much in love with Rodney, and that her manner varied greatly depending on whether or not he was around. When he was with her, she seemed dramatically happier, almost lighter as a person, no longer the serious, brilliant Mount Holyoke graduate, but someone who was almost girlish; when he was away, or when he was with Diane, she seemed far more somber.

When Rodney Powell had returned to medical school in the fall of 1960 he had felt closer than ever to Gloria Johnson and she, with Diane Nash now subtracted from what she had considered an unwieldy equation, seemed dramatically happier. They had begun to talk not merely of medical school and their mutual loneliness, nor of the sit-ins and the remarkable cast of characters in their group, but now for the first time of more personal things: the possibility of marriage and of raising a family. They would live integrated, activist lives, with white as well as black friends. One day that fall he had proposed to her and she had accepted. Once when Rodney had spoken to Diane of why he was so serious about Gloria she had shown a measure of pique. Diane had asked what was so remarkable about her, and Rodney had listed all of Gloria's remarkable qualities—what a fine person she was, how bright she was, how many intellectual interests they shared, how she had just won a fellowship from the National Institute of Health. "Well, that's fine," Diane had said, "but do you really have to marry Miss NIH?"

The change in Gloria Johnson was almost magical. She had been in love with Rodney since the first time they had met at the Meharry dance. It had been a moment when she was desperately unhappy, and then one night she had met this young black prince, a young man who seemed to make her happier than she had ever been at a social event in her life. That night she had gone back to her dorm and woken up around 4:00 A.M. thinking about Rodney Powell and how nice he was. He reminded her of someone very dear to her, and for a long time she could not think of who it was. She ran through her mind the various boys she had known over the years, a list which was not very long, and the various adults who were friends of her family who had befriended her during her childhood, and she found no one who bore the slightest resemblance to this gentle, thoughtful man.

Then finally it struck her. He seemed like no one so much as Iggilly Wiggilly, her fantasy friend from childhood, with whom she spent so many long hours utterly apart from everyone else. Iggilly Wiggilly was a friend who shared all her thoughts and her pain, who was always on her side and understood her. Her home in Roxbury had had an unusually large closet, and it was there, when things were not going well in the real world, that she would go and spend long hours with this secret fantasy friend. Her mother had been tolerant of time spent with Iggilly Wiggilly, and the fact that Gloria had continued the friendship long after most little children usually outgrow their imaginary friends. It was a sign, Mrs. Johnson had believed, that Gloria was an unusual child, more sensitive than most of her contemporaries, and a child who ought to be allowed to find her own way on her own terms.

In December 1960 Gloria Johnson had called her mother and told her that she was going to get married, and Mrs. Johnson had been excited and had immediately launched into a discussion of wedding plans—a great general summoned to yet another wondrous battle, already marshalling her forces, Gloria thought. "Mom, there's one thing you've forgotten to ask me," she finally told her mother.

"What's that?" asked Mrs. Johnson.

"Who I'm marrying," said her daughter.

They had gotten married on Christmas Eve, 1960, two young attractive black students, handsome, graceful, intelligent, and socially committed. The wedding was in Boston. They had spent a week in New York, and then a few days in Philadelphia, where Gloria had met his parents, charmed by the gentleness of his mother and sensing beneath his father's stricter countenance a kindness as well. Then they had returned to medical school.

Gloria's mother had not met Rodney Powell until the wedding but was thrilled with her daughter's choice. He was everything she hoped her daughter would marry, a professional man, serious, courteous, handsome, and gentle. He was in all ways, as he had been programmed to be, a credit to his race. He took to Mrs. Johnson immediately, and learned how to tease her. When they had first met, she had gone on at length one night about Adam Clayton Powell, the famed New York congressman, who was not a favorite of hers, since among other things she did not approve of his lifestyle, and because he, in her opinion, was far too radical politically. "Are you talking about Uncle Adam?" asked Rodney Powell, who was in fact in no way related to Adam Clayton Powell. For a time Mrs. Johnson was chagrined, and from then on it became something of a family joke that Adam Clayton Powell was Uncle Adam.

Gloria Johnson-Powell could not believe her good fortune. She was not only married to a man she adored and respected, but she was embarking on the kind of life she had always dreamed about, a life full of social value and larger purpose, where she not only would have the respect of the community around her, both black and white, but she would have the daily knowledge of doing something socially useful. The contrast between the way she was starting her married life and the way her parents had started their married lives made her all the more aware of the possibilities of America. For all the cruelty she had witnessed during the sit-ins, she had a sense that the American dream still worked and it was working for her. Her life was the embodiment not

just of her own dreams but of her mother's dreams as well. It was as if
it had all been planned out; she and Rodney had all the advantages
and privileges which her mother and Rodney's parents had sacrificed
so much for.

She had always felt the burden of her mother's ambitions, and of
the life denied her mother, who arrived in the North as a girl hoping
for educational opportunities denied her in the South but, because of
a death in the family, had been forced to work as a domestic while still
a teenager in Boston. Her mother had decided that Gloria and her siblings would lead the life denied her, no small weight for young children. She and her sisters did not think of their mother as Mom or Ma,
but as *Mrs. Johnson,* a kind of family commander; she was the leader,
and they were the Johnson Children. It was by no means easy being a
Johnson Child. There were endless responsibilities. Not only did a
Johnson Child have to do well in school, and behave well socially on
all occasions, but all Johnson Children had to comport themselves
well around the house and accept responsibility for themselves. They
had chores to do during the week, and even more chores on the weekend, cleaning up the kitchen, vacuuming the house. Otherwise Mrs.
Johnson laid a world-class guilt trip on them. If Mrs. Johnson had to
go out and work on a Saturday and the children got up and, being
children, instead of doing their chores got into a pillow fight, and Mrs.
Johnson returned a few hours later to find the house worse than when
she left it, pillows scattered everywhere, she did not spank them or
take away privileges. Instead she talked to the Lord. It was a one-way
conversation as far as the children could tell, but it was always devastating: "Lord, I don't know where I got these lazy children. Now
Lord, you know better than anyone that their father was not a lazy
man, and I am not a lazy woman, and his people weren't lazy, Lord,
and neither were mine. So how, Lord, did I get these children? Their
father worked three jobs, and Lord, I've worked hard every day of my
life. I started when I was a girl and never took a day off. Lord, my people were proud people. If there was a slave revolt they were part of it,
and if there was an Underground Railroad, they worked on it. They
were good people and fearless, and they were *never* lazy, Lord. So why
are my children so lazy, Lord?" The next Saturday when she went out,
the children would busy themselves cleaning up the house, and when
she returned she would talk to the Lord in a different voice: "Lord, I

must be in the wrong house. This house is too clean to be mine." She would then go outside and make a scene of checking the number on the front of the house. "No, it's the right house, it's number four Elbert Street. Now the children who live here, Lord, they must be wonderful children. Thank you for these children, Lord. Thank you for what you have given me."

The weight on Gloria as the most gifted of the five children was the heaviest. Aware that her mother's life was hard, she therefore worked diligently to please her. She was always polite. She never got in trouble. She always got good marks. In a classroom where almost everyone else was white, she always got the best math grades. Years later she became aware of the stress of her childhood; from the start it had been decided that she was the child in the family who seemed likely to go the farthest, not only the most talented academically, but the most dutiful. Her Great-aunt Carrie, a dominating presence in the family who visited their home frequently, had singled Gloria out early on as her favorite because she was so well behaved and did so well in school. In fact she did so well that Aunt Carrie had an unusually revealing phrase for her: "You're Aunt Carrie's Little White Child," her great aunt would say. That meant she was so well behaved and got such good grades that she was as good as a white child. "How's Aunt Carrie's Little White Child?" the older woman would ask whenever she came by the house. Gloria hated it, and her siblings hated it even more, and once when Aunt Carrie came, they had dragged Gloria into the kitchen and held her down, and poured flour all over her, and then brought her into the living room and showed her to Aunt Carrie. "Here's your little white child," they said. Aunt Carrie never called her a little white child after that.

When Gloria was very young, because she was bright and got good grades, it was somehow decided in the family that she was going to be a teacher when she grew up. Her future was all laid out: She was smart, she got good grades, she was going to go to college, and when she finished she was going to be a teacher, because that way she could help her own people and lead them out of the darkness. To a young child that sounded like an immense responsibility—leading other less-fortunate people out of darkness—and Gloria Johnson as a tiny child was not sure she was up to it. But one did not lightly tell Mrs. Johnson that some task she had assigned was too great. But once when Gloria was in kindergarten the teacher had gone around the room asking the children what they were going to be when they grew up, and she had answered that she was going to be a doctor. A little boy in the class said she had to be a nurse instead because she was a girl. But she had stood her ground that day and from then on whenever she was asked what she was going to be, she answered that she was going to be a doctor. It seemed less charged with responsibility than being a teacher.

Because she had done so well in school, she had easily gotten into Girls' Latin, which had been a haven for her. Academic excellence was important—the better student you were, the more you were rewarded with peer respect. No girl was supposed to dumb down, in the great American middle-class tradition. She did very well there, graduating with uncommonly high college board scores, which placed her in the 99th percentile in math and the 90th percentile in English. Although Gloria Johnson had done very well at Latin, her run-in with the school authorities over the Pledge of Allegiance had marked her in the school's hierarchy as something of a troublemaker, and she could feel a certain amount of resistance in her senior year as she prepared to choose a college. The guidance counselor seemed to be pushing her toward Bryn Mawr and away from Mount Holyoke (apparently, Gloria decided, because a favorite student of hers wanted Mount Holyoke, and she was afraid that Gloria might get the acceptance instead of her favorite). She was told by the guidance counselor she could apply to only three schools: Bryn Mawr, Wheaton, and then, as a local fallback school, Simmons. Her chances seemed very good for getting a full scholarship at all three schools. She did not visit any of the schools, because that required money and a trip in a family car, and they had neither, and so she was depending completely on hearsay.

She did not apply to Mount Holyoke, a school which interested her considerably, because of the guidance counselor's instructions, but after the date for applying had passed, and the applications were closed, she received a letter from the dean of admissions of Mount Holyoke asking her to apply. The National Scholarship and Service Fund for Negro Students, it appeared, had not only recommended Gloria Johnson to them, but had forwarded her grades, which were stunning, particularly in math, and had told Mount Holyoke that if the college accepted Gloria, it would help underwrite her college career. It was a group which looked for worthy black students in the South and tried to midwife their way through college, but in Gloria's case her marks were so outstanding that even though she was not from the South, they wanted to sponsor her at Mount Holyoke.

So she had gone off to Mount Holyoke, with roughly one third paid by the NSSFNS, and the rest taken care of by the college itself. The college had been perfect for her, marvelously egalitarian; if most of the girls came from affluent, upper-middle-class homes, they worked hard not to show it. Gloria Johnson had a strong sense that there were other comparable women's colleges in the East where that was not true, and where it was perfectly all right to show off a bit of wealth in your daily or, more particularly, your weekend wardrobe. But at Mount Holyoke the dress code was simple and extremely casual. Scruffy was in. No outsider, looking around the campus, could tell who was rich and who was poor by the way the girls were dressed.

In her senior year, as she prepared to apply to medical school, she faced something of a financial crisis. She planned to apply to four medical schools, and at $75 a shot for an application fee, that was $300, a great deal of money for her. She was still wondering how she might be able to borrow the money when she received a letter from the dean of the college. The letter said that someone at Mount Holyoke who admired her wanted to make an anonymous gift of $500 to pay for her medical school applications. She was to accept the gift in the spirit in which it was given. She was not to know who gave it, and she never did—only that it had been given in the spirit of admiration and respect. She was deeply touched—it was, she thought, the most sensitive and practical gift imaginable. And it saved her life that spring, because she did not want to put any additional pressure on her mother for funds.

From Mount Holyoke she had gone to Meharry and at first it had turned out to be a disaster. But the sit-ins and meeting Rodney had helped save her. In the spring of 1961, she was aware of the fact that she had been living in a pressure cooker for the past ten years of her life, trying constantly to meet the exacting standards of others, feeling that people were always scrutinizing her, as if waiting for her to make a mistake. She had grown up, she realized years later, virtually without an adolescence, without the special grace time permitted the young and which was so critical to childhood—that moment when you were allowed to make mistakes. She had tried to do the most dangerous thing of all, to live a mistake-free childhood. She had always been desperately afraid of getting in trouble and disgracing herself and her family. In college and medical school that might mean losing her scholarship. She did not smoke, and did not drink, and did not dare get pregnant. Even smoking a cigarette might ruin her reputation. Perfect Little Gloria, she thought later, a child who dared not leave the straight and narrow path. Rodney was the first boy she had ever been serious about, and she hoped as she married him that she might be able to have some fun in her life and worry less about meeting other people's expectations. Now, in the fall of 1961, as she entered her last year of medical school, she thought her life was as complete and exciting as she could ever have imagined.

42

RODNEY POWELL HAD DECIDED EARLY ON THAT GLORIA JOHNSON WAS the perfect mate for him. In some ways, he later reflected, they had been raised to be the same person. They shared so much, not the least of it the immense burdens of living up to exacting standards set by impoverished but ambitious black parents who had helped propel their children into a largely white world where they were always going to be walking through mine fields. Both he and Gloria were all too aware that they enjoyed far greater advantages than any other members of their families. The rules of his house seemed to be a carbon of hers. Neither of them, he sometimes thought, had ever been young. A great deal had been given them, but even more was expected of both of them.

Rodney Powell had been raised to work hard, and comport himself well, and to succeed in a world where all the umpires and referees and judges were not only white, but often extremely prejudiced. He had been taught to make himself a living example of what blacks could be, to prove that whatever whites did well, blacks could do as well or better, and in addition, that they could behave with good manners and the proper amount of decorum. He was hardly alone: These same marching orders had been passed on to many a young black child growing up in America in that era.

Like Gloria and so many of his generation, he had been taught that the first and most basic rule was be a credit to your race. In any discussion, that dictum was always followed by a list of black people who had been a credit to their race: George Washington Carver, Marian Anderson, Ralph Bunche, and Jackie Robinson. The second lesson was that it was a very prejudiced world, run by white people, some of whom were fair and some of whom were not, but the only way to get ahead was to work harder than white people at all times. Here there was an implicit warning: In the real world, if anyone is ever fired or laid off work because of a cutback or a momentary decline in the economy, it was the black worker. That was the basic rule of life and it applied to all black people in all work and social situations. The other elemental rule was that the only way he could ever possibly get ahead was through education. Therefore he was supposed to go to college, but that meant winning scholarships, since there was virtually no family money for his education. There was one other lesson, and that was that every door which had been opened for black people had been opened with great difficulty and at a high personal cost, and therefore it was his job to honor and respect those who had been first. However difficult it was now to make progress, it had been even more difficult for those who had gone before him.

His parents were both simple, wildly industrious people. Despite their own constant disappointments and heartbreaks, they had never put their own welfare above that of their children; indeed it was as if they had never even had time to consider their own welfare. His mother, Norma, was very beautiful; by her own reckoning she was part white, part Indian, part black. Her people came from around Savannah, Georgia. Rodney's father, Raymond, a laborer for most of his life, had come from rural Delaware. The two of them had met in Philadelphia when his mother was only fourteen, and his father had pursued her ardently from the start. Her family had opposed their union because she was so young and because he was not an educated man, but in the end they had persisted and had been able to marry. Norma Powell was, Rodney thought, an extremely sensitive, indeed delicate person, with a sensibility that seemed to have little connection to the hardship of her own life. The terrible poverty of her life, Rodney later decided, never wore down her spirit. He had no memory of her ever complaining about her life. Her husband, by contrast, was a man virtually crippled by the harshness of his life. He was a hardworking man, who often carried two jobs in order to provide adequately for his family. Economically, in terms of skills he was at the bottom of the work chain. He knew better than most the truth of his own warnings to his children, that in hard times it was always the black workers who were let go. Jobs came and went for him. Few had even the hint of the most elemental kind of job protection. Sometimes he was a simple laborer, sometimes a chauffeur, sometimes a carpenter. Late in his life he got a particularly good job as a construction worker where, because he was so diligent, in time he ended up in a supervisory capacity.

Raymond Powell was fiercely, indeed unbendingly proud. Even in the fifties, when he was on occasion unemployed, and when there were federal provisions for giving welfare benefits to families, he refused to accept any welfare. Welfare was a disgrace, he believed, and accepting it meant that he had failed his family. There were times, Rodney remembered, when the daily choice in the family on how to use their pathetically small amount of cash came down to whether to spend it on food or on fuel for the kerosene heater in the kitchen, and Norma Powell literally begged him to let them go on welfare, but he steadfastly refused. It would stigmatize him in the eyes of the rest of his family, which was equally stern and unforgiving but somehow had managed to be economically independent. His self-respect as a man was at stake in matters like this, nothing less. He was adamant about this one thing, as he was adamant about few others. On very rare occasions his family went briefly without food because he refused to give in.

Not only did he refuse to accept welfare for his family, but Raymond Powell set sharp limits on what kinds of work his wife could do. He refused to let her work in other people's homes as a domestic. Sometimes she worked as a seamstress taking in other people's clothes, and she did day care for other black families.

After he came to manhood Rodney Powell realized that his family had lived its entire life near the poverty level. And yet except for one or two particularly bad patches, they had always managed to live relatively well. Norma Powell was a shrewd manager of a household, deft at allocating their tiny amounts of savings for the most basic things, every penny committed, nothing ever wasted. Their greatest ambition when the first three of their four children were young was to get out of a rented apartment and have a home of their own. Somehow they had managed to buy their own house, purchasing for around $6,000 a ramshackle home in north Philadelphia in what was still considered a solid, middle-class neighborhood. It was in such poor condition that they had not had to pay anything down. They had fixed it up themselves, Raymond Powell doing the basic carpentry and Norma Powell, his skilled assistant, scraping off the old wallpaper and adding new.

Rodney Powell thought that in some miraculous way his mother was a woman with a triumphant spirit, completely immune to the difficulties of the life around her. The true hardship of the black condition in that era in his family, he thought, was borne by his father. He saw his father as a distant and remote figure, a man exhausted and numbed by both the hardships of his life and by the cruel environment he had been raised in himself; he knew hard work and survival and little else. He had been only marginally loved as a boy, and his ability to love in turn had been sharply curtailed. His own parents had managed against great odds to be small-time landowners in Delaware, fighting constantly to hold on to and to live off their meager acreage. Though Rodney barely knew his maternal grandmother, because she had died when he was very little, he felt he knew her well because his own mother had never really stopped grieving for her, and she had passed on endless stories of her mother's kindness and ability to love. By contrast Rodney knew his paternal grandparents all too well, and he did not like them at all. He had no memory of them ever hugging him or any of his siblings. As a boy, hearing that they were going to visit, the first thing he always felt was fear, for it meant that there were going to be more rules in his own home than usual.

His grandparents had given their own son, if not much love, a powerful sense of accountability and self-sufficiency. Raymond Powell was not a hard man or a bitter man, or at least he never showed any bitterness in front of his family. He was most demonstrably a strict man who hewed faithfully to his own unwavering sense of what was right and what was wrong. When a Powell child did something wrong, there was always a spanking. The spanking was usually done with a belt, around the legs, and about the most ominous words which could be uttered in that household were "I'm going to tell your father." Fortunately, Rodney thought, Raymond Powell was not like some other black men whom Rodney came to know about in later years who took out their disappointment and hardship by abusing their wives and children, lashing out at home because they could not lash out in the workplace, their anger often amplified by the alcohol they turned to. Raymond Powell liked to drink. His drinking was not rage drinking. Rather it was a kind of light, self-anesthetizing drinking after a week of hard work. Norma Powell hated it and it remained a bone of contention between his wife and him, not because he came home drunk but because it absorbed too much of their money. Her bookkeeping was methodical and she could always prove her point: Too much of their limited weekly pay was going to his drinking.

They argued over it constantly, a kind of verbal dance, Norma fussing at him, and Raymond backing off and retreating and trying to get out of the line of her fire. In time they worked out a kind of modus vivendi: Each Friday when he was given his weekly wages in a small brown envelope, he was allowed to take two dollars from his pay and put it in his pocket. The rest of the pay envelope he carefully placed in his shoe, lest he get drunk and continue to drink after his limit was reached. Not that he ever came home angry or difficult. Rather he would return home on Friday evenings with his two-dollar buzz and fall asleep in a chair. If anything, Rodney Powell, as he was growing up, rather looked forward to Friday nights. On other nights his father came home irritable and edgy, unsympathetic to the problems of others in the family. But on Fridays he came home gentler and more relaxed. As a boy Rodney was much closer to his mother. It was only as Rodney Powell, far better credentialed than his father, came to manhood and raised his own family in a far more affluent age that he came to realize how heroic his father had been, keeping the faith, making sure that it was a two-parent household and that they owed nothing to the white man.

It had become very clear early on that of the Powell children, Rodney was the one on whom the family's academic hopes would be invested. From the time he was thirteen, he had started taking after-school jobs, saving his money so that he could create a college fund of his own. In his way he was a kind of black version of the all-American boy, fresh off a Norman Rockwell cover of the *Saturday Evening Post,* a young man who was well behaved, extremely polite, got excellent grades, held down responsible jobs, saved his money, and had a compelling purpose in life. The parents of his white friends were always asking their children why they couldn't be more like Rodney Powell. He was in a Scout troop which was almost exclusively Jewish, and he was extremely popular in that generally liberal climate, probably attending, as he later noted, more bar mitzvahs than any black child in Philadelphia history. He was a credit to his race.

He had always done well in school. There had been one brief blip when he was in the sixth grade when he had slipped and gone into some kind of emotional spin, getting into increasingly serious confrontations at school, in part, he thought, because he was bored. One day he had gotten into a conflict with a teacher who had pushed him physically and he had pushed back. He had crossed a line there, and placed his entire academic career in jeopardy. Suddenly he was being threatened by the school's authorities with a trip to the reform school.

That was something of a wake-up call for him, and he soon straightened himself out and started getting excellent grades again. But a year later the school tried to route him onto the vocational track instead of an academic one. They were doing this despite his record of sterling academic accomplishment, with its one blemish. It was, he later decided, the unconscious racism of the day, which decreed that if you were black, college was not for you. The guidance counselor was a white woman with a fixed, traditional view of who should go to college and who should not. Rodney was, she pointed out, gifted at shop. That was not a talent to be underestimated nor taken for granted, and if Rodney worked hard, and behaved himself, he might be able to have a very good life. When he argued that it was his family's consuming ambition that he go to college, she let him know that he did not know his place. "Your father's a laborer, and you have to understand your limits in life. But don't feel badly—there are some valuable things you can do with your life."

Rodney Powell had tried at first to make the case himself, and he had tried to explain about how good his grades were, that it was not only shop in which he did well, and that he and his family had already begun saving the requisite money for college, but she remained unmoved. "College is not for everyone," she said. But Rodney persisted: In addition to everything else, he understood that academic excellence affected his self-esteem, that good marks proved something important about himself, about what a young black child could do. But as hard as he tried, he could not move her.

Because his people were simple and poorly educated themselves, they felt unable to go to school and make the case for him. But there was a neighboring black family named Crozier which had taken an interest in him. Edna Crozier's own children were grown and though she did domestic work herself, she had a passion for education. She knew Rodney well, and she was quicker to challenge injustice than his somewhat more cautious mother; as such she went to the school to argue in his behalf. There she listened to the litany of reasons why he was not college material, and she answered that much of this was true, his parents were poor, and yes, no one in the family had ever been to college before. But, she said, this was all the more reason to give him the chance. "Look at how good his marks are," she had said. "If he was white and his father was a laborer and he had these exceptional grades, would you be telling him to try the vocational school?" The guidance counselor was equally dogged. "He can't afford it," she said; "there's no hope there. It's the way life is." But Edna Crozier stood her ground and said, "All we ask is that you give him a chance. Why not do that?" She was a strong woman and she carried the day. Rodney was placed on what was called the X track, which was the academic track, and so he went off to an academic high school and continued to hold several jobs in order to save the money for college.

He had gone to high school at John Bartram, becoming the personification of the black overachiever, doing well, getting good grades, and becoming, to his surprise, a student leader. He was shy and reserved, pushed forward for school honors not by his own ambition but by others, because he was best boy, someone who treated everyone well, a young man who seemed dignified and mature beyond his years. It was an odd time for him. He had a sense that he was somewhat different from other boys his age, particularly black kids, and when he boarded a city bus to go off to a violin lesson, sometimes wearing his Boy Scout uniform, other black kids mocked him and yelled at him that he was trying to be white, that he was a faggot, and that worst of all, as far as they were concerned, he thought he was better than they were. As a grown man he would regard that as his first true encounter with the paralyzing quality of black conformity. Rodney Powell was, his mother had already decided, an unusually sensitive child who did not lightly make friends in the neighborhood as her other children did. She sensed that he was a boy who for reasons of his own was somewhat apart, needing his own space, and did not fare well in the rough-and-tumble play of a normal childhood. When there was real confrontation he quickly turned in to himself. He had to share space with his brother in their crowded, small home, and his mother was aware that this was hard on him, that he was a child who needed privacy, that emotionally he kept a great deal in. When the Croziers, who had a larger home, suggested that Rodney come live with them because he would have a room of his own, Norma Powell was quick to accept the offer, knowing that it was good for her son, that he needed to be apart, physically and spiritually. Her own sister argued bitterly against the move, warning that Edna Crozier was trying to steal her son. But Norma Powell was confident of the love of her son and thought this arrangement was better for him. Rodney lived with the Croziers for several years during high school, and it was a sanctuary for him, a house with a room all his own where he could read and play classical music on an early hi-fi system he had built himself, and yet he could visit his own home every day.

He had not thought of himself as being political when he was in high school, but he had done one political thing: He had been elected president of his high school class. In 1953, at the height of the McCarthy years, when all kinds of investigators, national and local, were looking for Communists, particularly in the school system, a science teacher in his school whom he greatly admired had been attacked by a local investigating committee on charges of being a fellow traveler. Rodney had decided to defend the teacher, and along with a few friends he appeared before the local committee which was looking at the issue. It had been a painful experience. Rodney Powell had written what he thought was an eloquent letter defending the man as an exceptional teacher and a true humanist and defending as well freedom of speech in the most ringing and passionate terms. But in the process, referring to the principle of freedom of speech, he had spelled it "principal." The chairman of the committee had mocked him to his face, suggesting that his time might be better spent working on his spelling instead of worrying about what his betters were doing to protect his mind.

The successes in his high school years had not come without pain. When he had run for student body president, he had been pitted against a popular white girl, and he had won, though it was a close race. Then the school principal, whom Rodney had always liked and had always thought of as a friend, had suggested that this year the school choose co-presidents. It was very clear that this was against the bylaws; the school had never had co-presidents before. Rodney was dismayed. But the teacher who was in charge of the election held her ground, and in time he was chosen as the single head of student government.

Still, for a time he had shielded himself from the meaning of what had happened. He knew he had won, and he wondered whether he was the problem, whether the principal knew something about him that he did not know himself, and that he was not up to the job. But gradually he came to accept the truth that the principal had been covertly racist, agreeable and friendly only as long as certain lines were not crossed.

He had gone on to St. Joseph's, a local Jesuit college, as a good, serious, believing Catholic, and had left, somewhat predictably, as a confirmed agnostic. He admired the Jesuits—he thought by and large they were good and generous teachers—and the fact that they demanded that you pursue religion intellectually. But the more he studied and thought about religion, the more doubts he had. In one class a teacher had been talking about Jesus Christ and had made the assumption that Christ was male. Rodney Powell, somewhat to his own surprise, heard his voice asking how they knew for sure that Jesus was male, and that perhaps he might be female with female chromosomes. What he said was considered heresy, though the teacher seemed more perplexed than angry.

His great victory at St. Joe's was to finish the premed course with excellent grades. The premed track was the hardest in the school. The school prided itself on the course, and it prided itself even more that no one who made it through and was permitted by the school to apply to medical school ever failed to get in. That, of course, among other things greatly empowered the school's authorities. They could decide who actually finished this difficult course and who did not. There were, he recalled, about one hundred premeds in his entering class at St. Joe's in the beginning, and only about thirty who finished it and were permitted to apply to medical school. An equation like that guaranteed that it was not a particularly pleasant experience, and he had watched while students whom he thought perfectly adequate and, to his mind at least, potentially very good doctors were squeezed out of the system. In the end he had mixed feelings about St. Joe's; he had been glad to go there, he had done extremely well in a competition with all kinds of other talented young men, almost all of them white, but he had come away feeling that the focus of the school was too narrow, and that he had not been sufficiently encouraged to think on his own. Perhaps, he thought, that was the problem with being a premed;

it separated you from much of the rest of the college experience. But he remembered his graduation day with clarity, particularly the pride and the shyness of his parents. This was their day more than his. They did not know anyone else among the other parents, and they were not entirely at ease in a world where most of the other parents were white and, more often than not, the father had been to college, but their pride was demonstrable. He had, on that June day in 1957, given them a not inconsiderable victory and helped validate their own lives and struggles.

In his freshman year at college, he had heard the news about *Brown v. Board of Education*. Though there was little in the way of course material at St. Joe's focusing on the black experience in America, nonetheless the news had excited him. He had been aware that he had lived his life as a black person in a largely white world. College classmates, well meaning and innocent, would from time to time ask him what it was like to be black, and he had tried to answer, but he was not sure how good his answers were, because he was not sure how much he knew about the true black experience in America. Now as he pondered a choice of medical school, the question of his blackness emerged as an important side issue.

He had thought about Howard and Jefferson, which were black, and Temple and Penn, which were not. He was wait-listed at Jefferson. He had been intrigued by the idea of Howard, the leading black medical school in the land, he believed, but when he had visited it, he had been deeply disappointed. He had already read Edward Franklin Frazier's book, *Black Bourgeoisie,* and it had made him aware of the class lines within the black community. Howard to him seemed to reflect what Frazier had been writing about, a school, he thought, for rich black kids, and he had been turned off. Instead he had decided to go to Meharry in Nashville, which was renowned, he heard, for taking the black students from the Deep South who had no medical school to go to in their own states and giving them this one chance. He liked the idea of that—of a mighty school which reached out to the most deprived and ambitious young men of a subjugated region. In addition, because it was in the South, he would not only get his medical degree there but, he was sure, he could become a part of great events as well. Then he had arrived and decided he had made the biggest mistake of his life. It was only when he had joined the Lawson work-

shops in the fall of 1959 that he had begun to find the larger purpose
which had brought him to Nashville. That Gloria too had found purpose in them made him ever more sure that she was the right person
for him.

Rodney Powell was pleased by the way he and Gloria were starting
out their lives. He loved Gloria: If Diane had been a more exciting figure in his life—intense, beautiful, oddly shy, becoming more confident in the middle of the sit-ins when she got contact lenses for the
first time, then Gloria was a woman for all seasons, smart, steady,
politically committed, a woman who understood his background
because she came from one so similar, and a perfect person to be the
mother of his children. With her he could have what he knew he
always wanted, a family. For if there was one shadow which hung over
the wedding, it was a secret shadow, something which he did not talk
to Gloria Johnson about, his fear that he might be homosexual. Rodney Powell did not want to be gay, and therefore his marriage, in addition to everything else, represented a critical choice in the road ahead,
a step away from a path he feared he might be forced down.

He knew that in the purest sense he was not heterosexual, but he
hoped that he was at least bisexual. He liked girls, but he seemed to
have a significantly stronger sexual pull toward men, and he had
already had several furtive homosexual experiences in Nashville. The
idea of being homosexual was abhorrent to him because the only
homosexuals he knew of in the late fifties were rather campy figures
who seemed to be not only isolated from everyone else, but self-
isolating. They were men with stereotypical mannerisms readily iden-
tifiable to others as homosexual—their walks, the way they moved
their hips like women, and other seemingly exaggerated gestures.
Rodney Powell did not want to be like them; he wanted a real life, not
a life where every day he felt the contempt of others.

He had been extremely careful about his gay experiences in
Nashville. He had a sense of who the homosexual members of his
class were at Fisk and Meharry, and he was extremely wary when he
was around them, because the obvious gays were treated terribly by
the other students—cruelly mocked and completely ostracized. If
anything, he suspected, the black community, because of its own vulnerability to the larger white society and the cruelty inflicted on it over
the years because of skin color, might be even harder than white soci-

ety on anyone who was different from the norm. One of his gay experiences at Fisk had been with a student who was very campy and whose mannerisms were not only effeminate, but quite exaggerated. After that experience Powell had been uneasy about what he had done, and once when he was with some of the other sit-in leaders at the International Student Center on the Fisk campus, the young man had spied him and had waved to him perhaps a little too enthusiastically, and Rodney Powell, quite embarrassed by the recognition, had waved back, a good deal less enthusiastically. Both James Bevel and Bernard Lafayette had been with him at the time, and they had teased him. Later he was convinced that somehow that had been a tip-off to the ever-shrewd, ever-alert Bevel that he might be gay and that Bevel, who wanted to go out with Diane Nash, had used it against him with Diane and had told her that Powell was gay. At one point she had asked him if he was gay and he told her he was not. Years later he was embarrassed by that, his failure to be able to be truthful about something so important to him.

When he had married Gloria he had married a woman whom he loved and who was his best friend, his soul mate, as he referred to her, and who seemed to share his views on almost everything. He had been bitterly disappointed that neither he nor Gloria had been able to go on the Freedom Rides, but the draconian warnings given them by the Meharry dean had been sufficient. Besides, a year earlier Martin Luther King had met with them and some other Meharry students and he had emphasized how important it was that they not jeopardize their careers by their activism because the black community so badly needed socially conscious doctors. He and Gloria intended to use their lives to help others, not to accumulate material wealth. They talked of doing community-service medicine among the poor. By marrying Gloria, he was sure he had made the right choice.

43

WHEN JAMES BEVEL AND BERNARD LAFAYETTE HAD BEEN FINISHING up their tour of Parchman, Bevel had decided that when his time was up, he was not going to leave Mississippi. He was a native Mississippian, this was his home, and he and the others were bothered by the fact that when they had all been arrested for the Freedom Rides, they were all, no matter what their place of birth, perceived by the local officials and the local media as outsiders, because there had been no local blacks arrested. When they had waited in the Jackson jail they had spoken of the need to rectify that, and Bevel had decided to stay on and challenge these age-old laws with local residents. Their recruits would, he had said, have to be young. Very young. Thereupon Bernard Lafayette decided that he could not let Bevel take such a terrible risk by himself and had volunteered to stay on and work with him in Jackson. All they had to do now, as they came out of the ordeal of Parchman, was organize in Jackson itself.

In that sense they were part of the vanguard of a growing assault upon the most bitterly defended citadels of segregation in the South, a broad challenge to the white racist politics of Mississippi, Alabama, and Georgia. If some of the Nashville young people had drawn more of the spotlight than their colleagues in other cities, then they were hardly alone. The impact of first the sit-ins and then the Freedom Rides on young, restless, angry black students across the country was immediate and powerful. The country was clearly entering a new, very different, less passive decade. People who were not empowered seemed less tentative about expressing their grievances. The sympathetic hearing extended to the early Movement activists by a new generation of white reporters, men in their mid-thirties and -forties, many of whom had fought in World War II, had encouraged some in the

Movement; the coming of national television was also speeding up the cycle of protest.

In addition there was the impact of John Kennedy himself, a younger, more modern president, who had said in his inaugural address that he represented a new generation of Americans; he had been brought to the presidency in no small part by television and his own good looks, somewhat against the wishes of the older men in his party's existing political hierarchy. He was arguably the first political product of the new, television-driven popular culture, that is, a culture born of the popular response to what was being witnessed in this new home theater. As both early beneficiary and early product of the new popular culture, Kennedy was acutely aware of its formidable political force and paid careful attention to it, watching the television newscasts each night, unlike most politicians both of the previous generation and even of his own. He was aware, as his political aide Fred Dutton once noted, that even if what was shown on the evening news did not by his definition constitute reality, then nonetheless in millions of homes it was perceived as reality.[1]

By 1961 the protest against racism in the South, particularly the new activist manifestation of it, was in its own way, because it provided action and film for the television broadcasts, becoming part of the popular culture too. As with the Vietnam war soon to follow, it was news received not just as news, but as entertainment as well. Martin Luther King, for example, with little traditional institutional support, was part of the popular culture, with an increasingly broad national appeal, as Roy Wilkins, Thurgood Marshall, and Whitney Young, the more traditional leaders he was supplanting, men who worked through the existing, old-fashioned, institutionally driven hierarchy, were not.

That was part of the line which divided the fifties from the sixties, the age which was past from the age which was emerging: what the camera was interested in. Television coverage was therefore speeding up the cycle of racial protest; millions of other young blacks who had not been part of the first sit-ins and the first Freedom Rides, watching the broadcasts of what was happening across the South, were being pulled into the action too. For a powerful nerve had been touched among black college-age students in the past year. The eagerness with which someone like Hank Thomas, watching and reading about what had happened in Nashville, had joined up reflected something which was taking place across the country. A generation of young impassioned black students had heard a summons not unlike that which had come for many young white American men in the moments after they first heard the news on December 7, 1941, that the Japanese had bombed Pearl Harbor. That had been the call to the best and most impassioned of a generation on an issue of patriotism. This call was not very different. In the summer of 1961, a number of early SNCC leaders whose names were to become legendary in the organization's history—Bob Moses, Charles Jones, Chuck McDew, Bob Zellner, Charles Sherrod, Dion Diamond, and others—had begun to work in Mississippi voter-rights campaigns, first in Greenwood and then in McComb.

Those who went there in the early days did so without illusion. The dangers of working in rural Mississippi and Alabama were limitless. There was no protection from the local racists at all, for those who were supposed to protect you, the state and local police, were agents of the forces of resistance, and in the most infamous lynching soon to come, the murder of three civil rights workers in Neshoba County in 1964, the sheriff and deputy sheriff had been the murderers. In Mississippi these pioneer activists were followed constantly by white men in pickup trucks who seemed to want to nudge them off the highway. Or someone would drive by the house where they were staying and fire a shotgun at their bedroom window.

This assault, which Bevel, Lafayette, and Diane Nash were also helping to lead, was the next step in the larger strategy which had driven the Freedom Rides. The first and most elemental part was to make the federal government pay attention to the inequity of black life in the Deep South. But the second critical part of the strategy was to reach local black people, so long suppressed by local authorities, and encourage them to stand up for their rights, to let them know that these small towns in Mississippi and Alabama were not, as local officials would have had it, separate kingdoms, but were part of the United States of America, and that therefore blacks too enjoyed the rights of American citizens.

As the cause became an ever more impassioned one, SNCC was changing and expanding and drawing in other young men and women of singular talent. Not everyone was quite the same as those of the original Nashville group, with its teaching by Jim Lawson and its bedrock belief in Christian nonviolence. Many of the new leaders were more openly political and less church driven. Some of them were from the North and were therefore more estranged from their religious roots; some simply saw this from the start as a political struggle, not a religious-political one. Even as the Freedom Riders had sat in the different Mississippi jails there had been arguments between some of the Southern traditionalists like Lafayette and some of the new, more politically driven activists like a young Howard student named Stokely Carmichael, who did not take the religious part of the Movement very seriously. These tensions reflected serious divisions within the Movement: In August 1961, there had been a SNCC leadership conference at the Highlander Folk School in Tennessee, where for the first time these sharp divisions between the two factions showed over issues of strategy. The conflict was deep and neither side seemed ready to compromise. The Nashville group and its allies, religiously driven, determined to change the Christian conscience of America, wanted to concentrate on direct action; some of the other, more political people, like Moses and Sherrod and Jones, thought they were engaged in an all-out political battle, and wanted to concentrate on voter registration.

The division was so sharp that for a time it threatened to split the fledgling organization apart. People like Diane Nash and Bevel and Lewis were committed to direct action. Eventually, with Ella Baker of the SCLC serving as a peacemaker, it was decided that there was room for both groups: One faction would work for voter registration, and the other for direct action. It was a wise settlement, particularly since working for voter registration in Mississippi *was* the same as doing direct action. But it was the first sign of a deeper schism within the organization which would surface later.

When Jim Bevel and Bernard Lafayette left Parchman to work the streets of Jackson that summer, they started out at ground zero. They were in the enemy stronghold, virtually without connections; they might just as well have been parachuted behind the lines in Russia and told to recruit dissidents for the CIA, Lafayette thought. The first thing they needed was a place to stay and they found it in the house of a woman named A.M.E. Logan, a woman literally named after a church. She sold cosmetics in the black section of town among Jackson's middle-class black women, her job made considerably easier by the fact that the better downtown stores treated black customers so badly. With that as a base she was relatively immune from the white power establishment. They had met her because she was one of the founders of a group called Women's Power Unlimited, which had been started to help the women arrested in the Freedom Rides to make sure that they had the minimal amenities needed in jail, and then to assist them when they were finally released to get a meal in Jackson and to get a plane ride out of Mississippi.

In the early days Lafayette and Bevel simply worked the streets in the black section of Jackson trying to recruit young people to be activists. In a city where there was such a history of intimidation, they quickly found that the younger the potential volunteer, the better. High school age was better than college, and regrettably, junior-high was sometimes better than high school. They went street by street, door by door, talking to people. Lafayette thought that Bevel was the most intriguing field organizer he had ever seen. If they found kids playing basketball, Bevel might take their basketball and challenge them to a game. Or if they found a bunch of young black kids at a playground, Bevel, an invader on their sacred turf, would challenge them to a fight. That would intrigue the young people, and just as tensions were mounting, Bevel would begin to talk to them. The fight he wanted, it would turn out, was not so much a street rumble but a fight with white people against racism and, even more interesting, it was to be nonviolent. Bevel would say that he and Lafayette were Freedom Riders, which with the very young of Jackson had true resonance. Everyone in Mississippi knew who the Freedom Riders were—they had been excoriated every day in the local newspapers and over the radio. That worked in their favor. Within the black world of Jackson, the more the *Jackson Daily News* and *The Clarion-Ledger* and all of the reigning politicians attacked you, then the more legitimate you were considered. If many of their parents were terrified of the words *Freedom Riders,* then the very young felt differently: Freedom Riders were genuine heroes. Bevel was a natural recruiter, Lafayette thought. He was the more charismatic of the two of them, and he was shrewd as well. They played their own version of good cop-bad cop. Lafayette's role was to make the case for them joining up and becoming activists, while Bevel's was to argue *against* joining up. That only made the possibility of coming aboard more appealing. "Now look at Lafayette there," Bevel would say; "he's from Florida and so he can go home any time he wants if it doesn't work out. All he has to do is get on a bus to Tampa. But you're from Mississippi. They know you here. They're going to come after you. If you come with us, your mother and father might lose their jobs. So you better know what you're getting into." Then he would tell them to sleep on it and come back in the morning. At 6:00 A.M., as a matter of fact. If they could not come at six in the morning, they were not to come at all. "We need commitment and coming at six A.M. will prove it to us," he said.

Becoming an activist in Jackson was, in the physical sense at least, relatively easy. It might take uncommon amounts of courage, but racial lines were drawn so sharply that the young people whom Bevel and Lafayette recruited did not even have to ride a bus to get arrested. All they had to do was walk into the white section of the Greyhound waiting room and they would be picked up. Not all of the black parents of Jackson, Mississippi, were thrilled by what Bevel and Lafayette were doing but the two men, given the odds against them, felt they were making some headway.

Captain Ray of the Jackson police was, of course, omnipresent. They had decided from the start that he was going to know almost everything that they were doing anyway, that his intelligence system, given the availability of informers, would be near perfect. Therefore they ought to be as straightforward as possible with him. In time Bevel and Lafayette worked out an accord with him: If they were going to have a protest they would let him know where and when and what they were going to do, just so things would not get out of control. Their people would show up, his people would show up, the arrests would be made, and Lafayette would even compare his own count of the number of young people arrested with the police count just so that no one slipped through. It was all very orderly at first. Ray appeared to be fascinated by both Bevel and Lafayette, the fact that they did not scare easily, and the fact that they were willing to go door to door. He began to talk to them in a surprisingly friendly manner, and in time they began to develop something of a relationship with him. Ray was a serious churchgoer, and he was also fascinated by the fact that they seemed to be driven by religion, indeed by the same church that he belonged to, the Baptist church. "How're you boys doing?" he would ask, and they would tell him what they were doing was good for the future of Mississippi, and he would laugh. "Well, yes, I believe you boys really believe that," he would say, but he would always listen. Once he offered them both jobs with the Mississippi State Sovereignty Commission, which was the official Mississippi security organization designed to prevent integration of the state, a sort of all-purpose Mississippi version of the FBI and CIA and KGB. He offered a salary of $25,000 and he had promised in addition to make sure they got college scholarships as well. "I don't agree with you boys and what you're doing, and of course we're not going to let you get away with it, but I do admire your dedication," he said.

The accord worked for a time, but then as they began to recruit even younger kids, Captain Ray complained. "You boys have started sending me juveniles, and I can't have that," he said. He was right: Some of the people they were recruiting were now only fourteen years old. Lafayette, whose job it was to go and talk to the parents of all the young people who were volunteering, tended to agree with Captain Ray that these newest warriors were a bit too young. He did not look forward to explaining to frightened local parents why their teenagers were in the Jackson jail. But Bevel took a hard line on this. "He can't tell me what to do and what not to do—I don't care if it is Mississippi or not. These children have a right to be free; they can make these decisions themselves." Lafayette argued that it might be a good idea to back off on this issue. "Bevel," he said, "let's not get hung up on this. They really are very young. We can get these kids in a lot of trouble before they really know the consequences. Their parents are going to be furious." But Bevel refused to back down. "I don't want that man telling me what I can and can't do." So they were soon arrested and charged with contributing to the delinquency of minors. If Captain Ray had on occasion seemed amused by them and their industriousness, now they began to deal with the harder side of the local law.

They spent fourteen days in jail without a trial, all of it in the drunk tank, wearing the same clothes. Even then Bevel treated it as something of a joke. On the first day of their arrest, the jailer had not closed the door of his cell completely, and it had not clicked shut. "Bernard," Bevel told his friend, who was in the adjoining cell, "if we pray really hard I believe the Lord will let us out of here." Lafayette said he doubted it; they were, after all, in Mississippi and he was uncertain of

the Lord's ability to reach into a Jackson jail, but Bevel said he
believed in the power of prayer and he prayed just loud enough so
that Lafayette could hear the low rumble of his words, and then after
waiting awhile, he semi-miraculously appeared in front of Lafayette's
cell, scaring his friend half to death. Other than that it was not much
fun. A lesson was being taught. They were not allowed to bathe, and
they were given the worst food imaginable and a marginal amount of
water. The charges against them were steep: They were facing five separate charges of contributing to the delinquency of a minor, which
meant two years and a $2,000 fine for each charge. But when they
actually came to trial, the Mississippi authorities used only one of the
warrants, holding out the other four in order to ensure added leverage
for the future. All they would have to do is activate the other warrants.
Still, that meant they were each facing two years and $2,000 in fines
each.

Their lawyer, Jack Young, an active local NAACP attorney, plea-
bargained without consulting them and worked out a deal which
would allow their sentences to be suspended. But they would have to
agree to leave town. Bevel and Lafayette wanted no part of that; they
fired Young and decided to defend themselves. Bevel, fearless as ever,
turned on the judge in a rage. He, James Bevel said, was not the person who was corrupting the black children of Mississippi. What was
corrupting them was the system of segregation which denied them
their basic rights as well as decent schools and decent jobs, and their
innate dignity as American citizens. Bevel said he knew that the state
of Mississippi cared not at all what black adults did to black children.
"When was the last time a black person in Mississippi was convicted
for contributing to the delinquency of a black child?" he asked. It was
a telling question. Bevel, Lafayette thought, was brilliant, so brilliant
in fact that Lafayette was terrified: They were in a Mississippi court,
almost alone, having gotten rid of their lawyer, they were dealing with
a judge who was decidedly unsympathetic, and they were looking at at
least two years and, perhaps, if the authorities got tough, ten years.
Yet Bevel was pushing the court. The judge's face seemed to be getting redder by the minute. Watching Bevel that morning, Lafayette
had a sudden insight: In all racial and social situations Bevel instinctively probed for resistance, and the more resistance he found, the
more confident he was that he was on the right track, and the more he

pushed ahead. It was as if the resistance of the white people around him proved to him the truth of what he was trying to do. Therefore, the deeper they went into the heart of the segregationist South, the harder Bevel pushed and probed. Because this particular court represented a classic example of white-only justice, Bevel was determined to challenge this man's very right to judge him. The consequences of what he was doing did not weigh heavily on him.

At that point in the trial Lafayette began to talk, trying to be a counterbalance to Bevel. A new day was coming in Mississippi, he said. What they were trying to do, he said, was be a part of this new day, a time when black children would be better educated and more productive in a new and ever more prosperous society. It was as if they were both preachers, Lafayette thought, and Bevel had been preaching these white Mississippi folks on their way into hell, and he was trying to undo it, and preach them back into heaven. The judge was moved or at least partially moved. He sentenced them to two years each and a $2,000 fine. The sentence was suspended. But if they ever showed up in his court again, he said, he would be merciless.

44

IT WAS IN THE FALL OF 1961 THAT TO THE SURPRISE OF EVERYONE IN the Nashville group, James Bevel and Diane Nash got married. Diane had been the adored beauty of the Movement, and almost everyone had wanted to take her out. Bevel, who already enjoyed a reputation within the group as a considerable womanizer, had gone out with a series of attractive women. As often happened within the larger Nashville group, theirs had been a courtship without a real courtship, the Movement itself being the force which pulled these two uncommon young people together and then held them together.

Talented, committed, both of them increasingly obsessed, Diane Nash and James Bevel had been thrown together for almost a year and a half in the most highly charged atmosphere imaginable. Each day they had focused all of their energy in the most single-minded way on the good of the cause; they had shared the same friends, the same enemies, the same fears; there was a singular intensity to life every day for both of them, for life was always lived on the edge, and the dangers, including prison and, of course, death, were considerable. They were in ways not unlike members of the same infantry unit which has been in combat for well more than a year, in which the bonds of friendship within the unit become stronger than those the members have with any of their family members or previous friends; the longer they have been in combat—or in this case, in the Movement—the greater the sense of separation from the outside world. Being in the Movement was both a uniquely unifying and yet an equally exclusionary experience.

For the two of them, and this was to be true of a large number of Movement marriages, the Movement became the only thing which was real. Their new families were composed of their closest friends in the Movement; their other families had become momentarily, at least, secondary and distant. The only thing they talked about and read about was what had happened that day in the Movement. They did not judge each other on how good or complete the other person was on the normal scale of mating for young Americans; they judged each other on how good each was in the Movement.

That Bevel married Diane stunned everyone, most particularly the other men. Hank Thomas, the Howard student who had long ago decided that he was in love with Diane, was furious and decided that he did not merely dislike Bevel, but that he now hated him. Rodney Powell, by then married to Gloria Johnson and in Washington and preparing to go overseas to Africa in the Peace Corps, was less surprised than most of the others, for he felt that Bevel had always coveted Diane, and that Bevel had tried to undermine him with Diane back when they had first gone out. Rodney admired Bevel, but he did not particularly like him, and he thought for all of Bevel's considerable skills as an activist there was something unnerving about him, as if Bevel cared passionately about the Movement, but cared little about the feelings of the people he worked with in the Movement.

Most of the other men in SNCC did not get it. Diane was beautiful, and Bevel was the last man they might have paired with her. Rodney Powell had made sense as a prince escort; he was tall and graceful with an easygoing charm and palpable dignity. By contrast, Bevel was so unbending and eccentric in his opinions as to almost seem deliberately abrasive. He was in no way authoritarian, he was very good at the communal decision-making process so dear to SNCC, but he somehow managed, because he was so idiosyncratic, so unyielding in his opinions, to seem selfish and disrespectful of the ideas of others. Besides, as far as the other men were concerned, he was not very good-looking. He was not very tall, and his looks were part negroid and part Indian, which in the cosmetic assumptions of that era tended to work against him, not just with whites, but every bit as much with blacks. What the other men did not see about James Bevel was his charismatic quality, which worked with significantly greater effectiveness on women than on men. They missed the sheer intensity of the man, the originality and force of mind when Bevel focused all of his attention on one person. Jim Bevel was not a man to underestimate.

Diane Nash herself had been surprised when she had begun to fall in love with him. Much of it, she later realized, was the isolation and obsessiveness which came with being a part of the Movement. In their world, which was so sealed off from the exterior world, Bevel was fearless, uncompromising, and original. These very same qualities which others saw in her, she saw in him. Gradually, she thought, they had been pulled together by transcending events. Through the Movement they had shared everything, including the risk of death, so now it made sense to share their lives together and get married. After all, they seemed to agree on everything important about life.

Years later, in no small part because theirs had been a tumultuous marriage which did not last that long, Bevel himself would come up with a significantly less romantic version of what had happened. In his version there had been a SNCC meeting and it had been decided that some people had to go into Mississippi to do direct action and he had volunteered. Then, he said, he had told Diane that he did not want to go alone, that not only were you likely to get into conflict with white people in Mississippi if you tried to change the existing order, but that if you were a young black man who had just arrived in a small town and started going out with local black women, the local black men would become jealous. That meant he needed a partner. He liked Diane a lot, they agreed on all things, so he had asked her to come with him, and since in those days couples could not easily live together without marrying, he had asked her to marry him. She had asked to think about it, and the next day she had said yes.

Diane Nash told a very different story: They really had been in love; they had both lived the hothouse Movement existence in a way which excluded almost everyone else from their personal lives. She had come to admire and trust Bevel, thinking him strong and able, and funny in an odd way that not everyone got, and they had fallen in love. The idea of marriage, she said, was his and it was not, as he later claimed, about function. But she quickly consented: They had spent nearly two years together in Nashville finding out that they had a strong spiritual connection. Therefore, falling in love seemed like a logical extension of their lives.

By the time she and Bevel were married they were both working in Mississippi, and so they had little time for a fancy wedding; indeed, if they invited all of their friends to come, it was likely, since almost everyone they knew was an activist working to change the political and social order in Mississippi, that the entire wedding party might be arrested. So they had gone down to the justice of the peace and gotten married in a civil ceremony. They were quite secretive about it, not even telling their best friends. At the time they were sharing a house with Catherine Burks and Paul Brooks, pals from Nashville days; Catherine Burks was the hero of the ride to Ardmore with Bull Connor, and Paul Brooks was a close friend of Bevel's at American Baptist. The four of them were working with each other every day. But on the day of their marriage, Diane and James had said nothing to Paul and Catherine about what they were going to do. On that day Catherine Burks happened to notice that Diane was taking an unusual amount of time getting ready before she went out, putting on her best clothes. Catherine had decided that Diane was going downtown to try and pass as white, something she occasionally did for the Movement, as part of a reconnaissance of otherwise all-white terrain.[1]

Burks and Brooks were surprised by the marriage, as were most of the other people in SNCC. A few nights after the secret ceremony, there had been a SNCC meeting in Greenwood, Mississippi, and about ten members were there sitting around discussing strategy. Late in the evening Bevel had turned to Diane and had said that it was late and time to go to bed, and she had obediently gotten up. Julian Bond, the talented young activist-intellectual, had looked up, and he had seen the famously independent Diane Nash rather dutifully following Bevel out of the room. "Diane and *Bevel?*" Bond began in obvious disbelief.

"They got married last week in Jackson," someone said.

Not Diane and Bevel, Bond replied.[2]

Diane Nash had started her married life living in total fear. Each day when her husband left home she wondered whether she would see him again. All of the people she cared most about in the world, people like Bevel and Bernard and their close friends Catherine and Paul were out on the street risking their lives. It was hard to deal with the normal, instinctive desire to save your own life, she thought; it was even harder to deal with the overpowering fear for the lives of the people you loved and whose daily activities you were coordinating.

45

THEY WERE NOT THE ONLY MEMBERS OF THE NASHVILLE GROUP LIVING
in fear in Mississippi that year. In September Marion Barry, the young
man from Memphis who had, much to everyone's surprise, become
the first head of SNCC, found himself part of a group of SNCC leaders on their way to work in Pike, Amite, and Walthall counties in
southwest Mississippi, a region considered the most dangerous in the
most dangerous state in the union. Even as Bevel, Nash, Lafayette,
Burks, and Brooks had begun to try and create a beachhead in Jackson, other pioneers, led by one of the most extraordinary people in
SNCC, a young man named Bob Moses, were trying to gain a foothold
in this part of the state.

Marion Barry had gotten his master's degree in chemistry from Fisk
in 1960 and immediately received a graduate fellowship at the University of Kansas. But he had been unhappy in Kansas: Not only was it far
from the South, where new civil rights action was steadily on the
increase, but in addition it was a lonely place for a young black man to
be. There were only a handful of other black students on campus. No
one in Lawrence, Kansas, seemed either able or anxious to cut black
hair, and every time Barry and his friends tried to eat at some restaurant near the campus or downtown, they felt the intense hostility not
merely of the ownership but worse, of their fellow students. Nashville
had its problems, Barry had thought, it was only beginning to desegregate, but Nashville, whatever else, contained a separate warm and
welcoming world where black people could hang out among their
own and be themselves. There was nothing like that in Lawrence.
Barry had looked forward to his time away from the South, but to his
surprise, he found that he missed Tennessee. At the end of the year he
decided to transfer to the University of Tennessee in Knoxville. He

was one of the early black students admitted there, the first, he believed, to be a graduate student in the university's department of physical sciences. There were two black law students in the UT law school by then, both of them there by court order, and in addition, the first black students had also entered the education school. Knoxville was, he thought, somewhat behind Nashville on the racial curve, and he soon participated in sit-ins to try to integrate local restaurants and movie theaters.

He was also glad to be back with his colleagues in the SNCC leadership group. He had been an active participant in the summer of 1961 when they had all gathered at Highlander to discuss strategy. There the bitterly divisive argument had taken place over whether to put their prime energies into voter registration or direct action. Marion Barry had been one of the most vocal critics of the voter registration plan, which the Kennedy administration seemed to be pushing. He was, he said, extremely wary of SNCC being pulled into the world of politics. "We don't want to get directly involved with politics, because politics leads to power, and power always corrupts," Barry said. Given what was to come in Marion Barry's own political career, remembered Chuck McDew, who was his successor as head of SNCC and who moderated that heated argument, there was no small irony to those words.[1]

Diane Nash, the leader of the direct-action faction, had immediately wanted to intensify the assault on Mississippi (MOM, it was called, or Move on Mississippi). Thus in September 1961, shortly after the Freedom Rides from Montgomery to Jackson, Marion Barry arrived in McComb, Mississippi, to join the tiny, courageous SNCC team which was trying to establish itself in one of the most hostile of small Southern towns. Most of the others whom he joined up with were working with Bob Moses on his voter registration project, but Barry was going to work a parallel track on direct action. It was a perilous assignment for all of them. McComb and the surrounding region were, even by the cruel standards of Mississippi, considered uniquely mean and dangerous. Initially the harsh rejection of SNCC's first attempts there, and the fact that its leaders were eventually driven out of town, meant that the McComb venture was viewed as something of a defeat for SNCC, although eventually, seen in perspective, the remarkable courage which that first group showed in going in, and the surprisingly eager response of the very young high school students and some of the elders with whom they worked, marked the experience differently. It had showed SNCC leaders that they were wanted even in the most dangerous place imaginable, and it showed as well how eager some local people, particularly the very young, were to challenge the white power structure. In addition, they had begun to flush out the brutality of the local police forces, albeit at a moment when the federal government was not yet ready to protect them.

The venue could not have been more dangerous, or the response of the local hierarchy more threatening. For Pike County, of which McComb was the seat, had some eight thousand adult blacks who should have been able to register to vote. Two hundred were actually registered. Neighboring Amite County, where SNCC was also working, had five thousand adult blacks, of whom one was registered. Unlike the rest of the state, particularly the Delta, which had a certain surface gentility and was the birthplace of the Citizens Councils, in this far poorer region the Klan flourished, and death threats to blacks who challenged the old ways were commonplace. At first both the students and the feds knew the Klan was powerful there; it was only in the next few years, as the federal presence grew and the Klan began to resist, that they discovered how deeply rooted and how closely twined it was with local and state police operations. The region was terribly impoverished; it was, in the words of John Doar, "a place which had not changed in its attitudes on race and its social structure since the early nineteenth century."[2]

The man who was the leader of the McComb voter registration drive, Bob Moses, clearly had his work cut out for him. Moses was a singular figure in the Movement, viewed by most people as being charismatic precisely because he was in every way so uncharismatic. He was, for example, unlike Bevel, who came over to McComb several times to lead mass meetings, in no way a spellbinding speaker. In fact it was often impossible to hear what he said because he spoke so softly, seemed to muffle his words, and his sentences were often separated from each other by what appeared to be long, inexplicable pauses. He was shy, he wore glasses; back at the SNCC Atlanta headquarters, when there was some boring donkey work to be done, such as picketing a recalcitrant store all day long, he was always an eager volunteer. Most of the others, except perhaps for John Lewis, had long ago learned how to minimize their time on the picket lines. Moses had been to an elite Eastern school, Hamilton College, and had come to the Movement because he had read Albert Camus, and decided that it was up to him as a black man to determine his own course, and not to be defined as a victim. At first, because he had also joined an early peace demonstration, before the civil rights movement and the anti-war movement were married up, there was some suspicion among the other SNCC people that he might be a Communist. "One of our group called Moses in during the early days and asked him if he was a Communist and he said he was not," an amused Julian Bond remembered. "Since all of us knew that Communists don't lie, we knew from then on he wasn't a Communist. But we also knew he was different from the rest of us."

Different from the others he most certainly was. Part of his special hold on them, Bond noted, was that he seemed so ethereal, yet he was unlike the other religiously driven people, who were Southern Baptists. "He was very well educated, but he was a great listener. That made him different. Then, he spoke so slowly and softly. You might ask him something, and there would be this long pause—it seemed like five minutes, but it was only a few seconds—and only then would he speak. And he was reserved and we were not, and he did not party and we did, and he did not carouse and we did. No wonder we began to wonder if he was a saint."[3] He was, unlike many of the Northern blacks who by then had begun to come south to join up with SNCC, very good with the local rural people. "By 1961 most of us who were Southerners had become suspicious of a lot of the Northern blacks who were coming down," Marion Barry noted; "there was a barely concealed contempt and condescension on their part, in the way they treated the local people, as if they saw themselves as liberators. They thought they were there to teach us everything and they had little sense of how we lived and the danger of our lives in those small towns. We had a phrase for it then, 'Freedom High,' as if this were all just some big school and they were the teachers and we were the students." Moses was different. He *always* listened to the local people. He was not only educating himself, but letting them know they were worth listening to. Within the Movement, as Julian Bond noted, he was gaining a reputation as a saint, in no small part because he had led his colleagues into McComb.

Moses had arrived in Atlanta in 1960, moved by the sit-ins and anxious to be a part of SNCC. Early on Ella Baker had suggested he take a trip to Mississippi. There he had met Amzie Moore, an NAACP official in Cleveland, in the Delta, and they had talked about the possibility of Moses coming back and setting up a voter registration drive there the next year. When Moses had dutifully returned, it had turned out that the requisite logistical support was missing in Cleveland. But a number of NAACP people living in McComb had heard of the Cleveland project and invited him down to Pike County instead. In July 1961, at almost the exact same time that Bevel and Lafayette and Nash were beginning to work in Jackson, Bob Moses had brought a small group of SNCC people into the even more dangerous town of McComb.

It was a region seething with hatred, where there appeared to be no restraints against white violence. The more that Moses and his handful of followers tried to register voters, the more the tensions grew. Almost from the start there were incidents of violence. On August 29, when Moses tried to register a handful of blacks in the county seat of Amite, the curiously named town of Liberty, he was brutally beaten by a man named Billy Jack Caston. Caston, who seemed to feel he was doing nothing less than his civic duty, was the embodiment of the local power structure. His cousin was the sheriff, and his father-in-law, E. H. Hurst, was the local state representative. Moses, true to his fearless self, pressed charges against his assailant the next day, but Caston's jury quickly acquitted him. It was just one of several terrible beatings administered to SNCC leaders in McComb. There was, thought Chuck McDew, a certain surrealistic quality to the SNCC discussions that summer and fall in McComb: At one point, after one of their group had been beaten and the sheriff himself had taken part in the beating, they had sat for hours talking about whether or not they should go out and make a citizens' arrest of the sheriff. "The question of how we would do this—we had no arms—and where we would take him if we *did* arrest him was not easily answered. Did we take him to Liberty? Did we put him in his own jail? They were great philosophical discussions—Camus would have been proud," McDew said.[4]

Marion Barry had arrived in McComb a few days before Bob Moses's beating, and along with Jim Bevel, who had come over from

Jackson, he was one of the principal speakers at a rally held after the beating: "The attitude of a lot of people is: 'Don't get in trouble.' Let me tell you, Negroes have been in trouble since 1619. . . . How can you get in trouble when you're already in trouble? You're in trouble until you become first-class citizens."[5] McComb seemed to Barry a scary place, a town which was a tinderbox of hatred. The white people were moving around at night in their pickup trucks with their shotguns in the gun racks, and many of the black people, he quickly learned, nonviolent or not, had their own guns, and though by and large they did not take them out of their homes, they were prepared to use them in self-defense. At night, whenever they heard suspicious sounds at home, they turned off all their lights, got their guns, and moved around fully armed. When a car drove up to a house where a SNCC representative was staying, the lights in the house went off immediately; unless the car gave prearranged signals with its headlights, the people inside the house stayed watchful and armed. One night when Barry was off speaking at a meeting with young students, a pickup truck roared by the house he was staying in and shot through the windows, narrowly missing Barry's then roommate, Reggie Robinson, a SNCC worker from Baltimore. Their assailant had used a rifle, Robinson remembered, not a shotgun, and had fired only about four or five shots. Just another night in McComb, he thought.[6]

If it was Moses's job to work the voter registration project, Barry was trying to get some local residents to engage in sit-ins. Four days after Moses's beating, two of Barry's new recruits, Hollis Watkins and Curtis Hayes, had tried to stage a sit-in at the McComb Public Library; about twenty others were supposed to join them but almost all of them backed out. The two were turned away at the library by cops, who thought it might be a target, and instead they went downtown and eventually took two seats at the local Woolworth's counter. The manager quickly appeared, Watkins noted, shaking like a leaf. They asked if the store would serve them. He gave the quintessential Southern answer: "I'll gladly be the second business in town to integrate. But I'm not gonna be the first. No way."[7] They were immediately arrested, and their arrest, and several other comparable incidents, seemed to trigger even more anger among McComb's young people, particularly when Brenda Travis, an audacious fifteen-year-old, was arrested and imprisoned for trying to sit in the white part of the McComb bus terminal. When she was not allowed back to the local black high school, more than one hundred of her fellow students decided to march on the city hall.

The voter registration people happened to be in their downtown office talking about future strategy when they heard the sound of the students marching on city hall. Bob Zellner, the only white member of the SNCC leadership group in McComb, remembered that moment with great clarity. "For those of us sitting inside it was a moment that brought back that great quote from Gandhi—'There go my people, I have to go and run and catch up because I am their leader.' " So Zellner, Moses, and Chuck McDew raced out to join the march and Zellner, on this his first day in McComb, was savagely beaten, singled out because he was the only white.

It was a day on which almost everyone in SNCC seemed either to be beaten or arrested. By chance Barry, the nominal adviser to the students, wasn't there. Unaware that student tensions would explode into a major march, he had told Reggie Robinson to cover for him because he had to go to Jackson for a court hearing on his earlier arrest for being a Freedom Rider (he had been in the third wave of Freedom Riders).[8] Somehow, the fact that on the day Barry's young people had decided to lead a dramatic march it was Zellner who was so badly beaten and Barry who missed the show struck McDew as not entirely out of character, for there was, McDew decided years later, a singular quality to Marion Barry: He possessed immense talent, charm, and great innate political skill, and yet there was a sense that he was something of a surfer as well ("the Teflon don of the Movement," McDew once said of him[9]). That he was not arrested seemed to some of his peers in the leadership fairly typical: He was likable and engaging, sometimes there, but often not.

If Barry was not arrested that day, his own time came soon enough. A few days later he was scheduled to leave McComb to go to New York City for a SNCC fund-raiser. Hollis Watkins and Curtis Hayes, his two young protégés, were supposed to take him to the Jackson airport, but at the last minute they were unable to go. He decided to take the bus, which meant traveling by himself. That was against the most fundamental of SNCC rules—in a place like Mississippi you never traveled alone. *Never.* It was too easy for one person to disappear, there would be no witnesses, and the SNCC people had to assume that all their movements were being monitored at all times by the local sheriffs and the Klan. A SNCC person could board the bus in one town, a telephone call might proceed him, and he might be pulled off the bus in the next town by the Klan.

Barry had boarded the bus in McComb. Jackson was a straight shot right up the highway. The bus was virtually empty when he got on and he took a seat in the middle. Gradually, however, as the bus moved up the highway it began to fill. By the time he reached Brookhaven it was more than two-thirds filled. Then the most dangerous thing imaginable happened: A white man boarded the bus and took a seat across the aisle from Barry. The driver stopped the bus and came back and told Barry he had to move to the back of the bus. What Barry did next was absolute madness: He refused to move. It was stupid and dangerous on his part, he realized seconds later, and very much against SNCC's own rules. But the driver's order had been one push too many on the part of the white world. The bus driver cursed him and went to get the cops. By the time the driver returned, accompanied by the cops, Barry had changed his mind. Brookhaven, he knew, was every bit as tough a town as McComb, a place brimming with rage and fear. Now he faced a night in jail alone, and no one from SNCC would know where he was. If the local cops found out who he was, a SNCC activist who had once headed the entire organization, the price on his head would go up dramatically. The Klan might come and get him in the night. "I'll go to the back of the bus," he said.

"The hell you will, nigger," the cop said; "you're going to jail."

They had taken him to jail that afternoon and he had been even more scared when he saw the jail—the only thing protecting it from any Klan night rider wanting to come and steal a prisoner away was a four-foot wire fence. He had stayed awake all night, cursing his impulse—the stupid false bravado which had gotten him there—sure that even the tiniest of noises now signaled the arrival of Klansmen coming to get him. The next morning he was able to make his one phone call, and then the cops had taken him before a local judge, who said he would let him go if he promised never to return to Brookhaven. At the moment it struck him as being as good a deal as he had ever been offered; his bravado was gone and he had no desire to stay in Brookhaven and even less to return. He took the bus to Jackson and then flew to the New York meeting, sensing that his talent might be more for fund-raising than testing Mississippi jails.

Those weeks that summer and fall in Amite and Pike counties represented the crucible of the Movement experience for many of the young SNCC people. Bevel, Lafayette, and Nash regarded McComb as far scarier than Jackson, where they had at least the semblance of an accord with Captain Ray. Rarely had any of these young people worked such dangerous ground, and rarely had they worked it with so little protection from anyone. The federal government, which had encouraged them to try their hands at voter registration—Robert Kennedy had used his connections with a number of foundations to help fund the effort—was slow to show its power and presence. John Doar did come down, accompanied by a team of Justice Department lawyers, to check out stories of harassment, and in those days the intimidation of Moses and his people and the local people willing to work with him was constant: There were beatings, there was severe verbal harassment, some of it administered at gunpoint, and there were threats that worse things were yet to come. These threats were not received lightly, for the Klan was obviously embedded in the political structure of the two counties. Soon it brought its weight to bear on those local black people brave enough to work with Moses. One of them was a local farmer named Herbert Lee, a man with nine children. He was being threatened by E. H. Hurst, the local state representative and the father-in-law of Billy Jack Caston, the man who had beaten Moses. Therefore he was kin to the sheriff as well. On September 25, 1961, E. H. Hurst murdered Herbert Lee in cold blood. There were a number of witnesses, and one of the most critical, a black man, was intimidated by the sheriff, forced to lie about what he saw, and then when he eventually tried to recant what he said, was murdered as well. John Doar had been looking for Herbert Lee on his last day in Mississippi, but had failed to make the connection; when Doar got back to Washington he learned of Herbert Lee's murder.[10] It was devastating to the Lee family, and devastating as well to Moses and his SNCC colleagues. They had known from the day they arrived that they were putting not only themselves at risk, but those local people they worked with as well, and now one of their principal allies had paid the ultimate price. It was even worse when, at the funeral of Herbert Lee, his widow had come up to Moses and shouted at him, "You killed my husband! You killed my husband!" It was an idea which Moses was all too aware of, something that bothered him terribly; he had begun a process which jeopardized others as well as himself.

McComb represented, the SNCC people agreed, just the beginning of the struggle, both on their part and on the part of the people who opposed them. The young people liked and admired John Doar but they were bitterly disappointed by the failure of both the Kennedy Justice Department in particular and the federal government in general to support them. Doar understood their disappointment but he understood as well why his superiors were not yet ready to commit to a battle here. If the federal government were pulled in at this point in this hate-infested region, he believed it would be pitted against not just a large number of angry segregationists, but the entire state and local police structure. That was a struggle it was by no means prepared for. One day, Doar thought, there might be an all-out battle, a modern Gettysburg, but this was not the time or the place for it.[11] And that, he noted many years later, was a decision made before they found out how complete the Klan penetration of all the local law enforcement bodies really was. It was a battle which was surely coming, Doar believed, and it would come sooner rather than later.[12]

46

BERNARD LAFAYETTE, HAVING WORKED IN JACKSON, MISSISSIPPI, AS part of the pioneer SNCC group, finally decided to head back to Nashville in the spring of 1962 to continue his education. He had not yet gotten his degree from American Baptist, but now like John Lewis he transferred to Fisk, pulled there by the lure of a degree from an accredited college. He went with a full scholarship, and with a commitment that his credits from ABC would be accepted by Fisk. But he soon found himself bored in class, unable to concentrate on his studies, missing the excitement generated by the Movement, and anxious to be back on the front line. Locally, his friends in the Nashville SNCC chapter were engaged in what seemed to him like a series of minor skirmishes, and he began to miss the larger battles of the past, the ones which demanded total commitment.

Of all the original Nashville group, Lafayette was the easiest to underestimate. If everything about his close partner, James Bevel, seemed designed to make others, particularly white people, as uncomfortable as possible, then everything about Lafayette was the opposite; he seemed to put other people, no matter what their backgrounds, at ease. Socially he was relaxed and nimble. If he was at war with the segregated environment, then he was in no way at war with himself. He did not, on the surface at least, have the fire of Diane Nash, the obvious intensity of Bevel, and the singular steadfast, rock-of-ages quality of Lewis. On the surface he appeared almost carefree. But the commitment was there, and it was deep and it was driven by religious faith. Little Gandhi, an impressed Jim Farmer had nicknamed him after they had spent a few days in a Mississippi prison together. It was Lafayette who, when some of the other Freedom Riders had been reluctant to give up their mattresses for the right to sing freedom songs in Parchman, had argued in favor of surrendering the mattresses. Mattresses were *things,* he had argued, one more way that the authorities retained power over them. If need be, you had to will yourself to overcome the dependency upon comforts. Lafayette had willed himself to find the contour of his body in the concrete of the jail cell, so that it would eventually feel comfortable, and finally it became true, he did create the contour of his body in concrete, at least in his mind. Though it was nothing more than an illusion, it had allowed him to sleep in Parchman.

At the end of the summer of 1962, too restless to return to school, Lafayette made his way to the SNCC headquarters in Atlanta to see if they had an assignment which interested him. He was offered a chance to work with Bob Moses and some of his people, then still operating in Mississippi, but he declined because he wanted a project all his own. At that point it appeared that all of the best assignments had been taken. But Jim Forman, who was the executive secretary of SNCC, found one slot which was still open. It was a place where the previous SNCC field workers had run into a stone wall. As soon as they had arrived in town they had been arrested. Why, they had never even made it into the white community, Forman added. "Where is it?" Lafayette asked. "Selma, Alabama," Forman answered. Because of the iron-handed way in which the segregationists ran the town, Forman said, they had virtually crossed Selma off their list of projects. But Forman had heard from people in the civil rights division of the Justice Department that they thought Selma a particularly good place to target because it was almost a textbook example of how the white power structure denied black people the vote. The Justice Department, the SNCC people knew, intended to give Selma a very hard look. If the Justice Department was going to go into Selma, then SNCC was too.

Lafayette knew something about Selma, which was the capital of the Alabama Black Belt, a ten-county region named for the richness and darkness of its soil rather than the racial balance of its population; given what was effectively a neo-slave economy, however, it could as easily have reflected the population balance as well. It was in all things racial—fear, prejudice, and suppression of black people—the Alabama equivalent of the Mississippi Delta. Yet its ethos demanded that everyone white claim that it was, nonetheless, a black paradise.

"Selma," the director of the Dallas County Chamber of Commerce had told Harris Wofford, then a young law student in 1952 who had arrived in Selma to research a paper, "is nigger heaven." (In that case, said Amelia Boynton, a rare local black activist, "then God keep me out of heaven.")[1] For a variety of historical reasons, the region was disproportionately powerful in Alabama politics. In the years after the Civil War the Alabama plantation owners had still been able to vote their ex-slaves: In many instances the newly freed slaves were still working for their former owners, and on election day the planters would round them up and bring them into town and vote them. But then at the turn of the century, there had been a significant change, as the white backlash to the Reconstruction period gained momentum. Blacks, it was decided, had to be disenfranchised. But in disenfranchising blacks these racial architects might also diminish the political leverage of the planters and of the region itself, and there had to be some compensation for that. So a compromise had been worked out, the Black Belt was apportioned within Alabama politics in a way which compensated the owners for the loss of their slave votes. If the Black Belt did not necessarily control the governor's office, it held the key to the Alabama legislature. This made Selma and the Black Belt the key to taking on all of Alabama, Lafayette thought: If you crossed out Selma and Dallas County, of which it was the seat, and the Black Belt in general, you might as well cross out Alabama. Lafayette told Forman he would take the assignment.

In Selma, he quickly discovered, the local whites had already organized a powerful Citizens Council, which existed in near-combat readiness. They were, they claimed, above all else determined to keep the races pure. Lafayette, like many of his colleagues, had always been amused by the idea of racial purity as espoused by Southern leaders. There was no such thing. There were not a lot of pure black people around, he thought, and it was not because black people had wanted to go around mixing up the gene pool. His own family had its own complicated racial blend. His father was of Cuban and Bahamian ancestry with a fair amount of white blood thrown in. His paternal great-grandfather had been a French officer in the Cuban army who had been killed in the Spanish-American War. The real family name was La Farque, not Lafayette, but his father had eventually changed it on his birth certificate because Lafayette was a name which Americans seemed more willing to accept, and more able to spell. The La Farque-Lafayettes, with their blood already well mixed, had migrated to the United States after the death of Bernard's great-grandfather, and his grandfather had settled for a time in Key West earlier in the century. On his mother's side, his people were former slaves from the islands off the South Carolina coast. They seemed significantly more African than most American blacks he knew, largely, he believed, because they had been more isolated from the mainstream of American black life, and therefore had retained more of their old-world ways. The juju was very powerful with them, he thought.

His family had eventually moved north from Key West to Tampa. Bernard Lafayette, Sr., seemed able to handle all different kinds of jobs. He worked as a baker and in the steel mills and as a cabinet-maker. Bernard's mother, Verdell, worked in a hotel supervising the maid service. Because of his father's jobs Bernard had moved around a good deal as a boy and had even lived in Philadelphia for two years when he was young. In Tampa he had been considered both the best boy and the smartest boy around. He not only got the best grades, but he was the pride of the local Baptist church, which was central to the black community's social life. His maternal grandmother, Rozelia Forrester, had virtually founded it, and whenever there was a church event, Bernard Lafayette had been at the center of it. If there was a parade, he marched at the head dressed in his best clothes and wearing a little crown. When there was a Tom Thumb wedding for the young people, he would wear his white suit and play the part of the minister. On Mother's Day, when only one member of the church's youth organization was allowed to make a speech in honor of motherhood, it was usually Bernard Lafayette. He was a little prince as long, he thought somewhat sardonically, as he stayed in the black section of town.

His father had lived a life with virtually no economic rights, always vulnerable to white bosses. He wanted his own children to be strong and proud, and his frequent edicts to them reflected something of the schizophrenia of the black Southern condition: "Now, always stand up for your rights, and don't let anyone walk over you and don't ever be afraid," Bernard Lafayette, Sr. would tell them, and then quickly add, "and don't get in any trouble with white folks." That was the most basic lesson of all for a black kid in Tampa in the early fifties. There were certain codes of the street that you had to learn: If Bernard was downtown he had to walk deftly on the sidewalk, always careful not to bump any white kid, particularly a white girl, because even the most innocent contact might cause very serious trouble. In addition it was important to be careful of where and how you looked at people, and not to seem to stare at any white kid for too long, for staring appeared to be something of an unofficial misdemeanor for blacks. If a white boy wanted trouble, all he had to say was, "What are you looking at, boy?" and you could get trapped, because if you answered "nothing," then he might move in quickly and ask, "Oh, you think I'm nothing, do you, nigger?"

Every black family had to learn how to handle difficult situations. Once, when he was about eight years old, Bernard had been on his way home from school, idly playing with a crushed Carnation milk can, kicking it as if it were a football. Two white men were walking a few yards ahead of him, and he had given it one very good kick and it had hit one of them in the head. Both men had immediately chased after him. He had taken off for home and had gotten there a few steps ahead of the men, grateful that the screen door was unlatched. His grandmother was home and understood the situation immediately, latching the door behind him, and then, as the raging white men had come to the doorstep, she turned on Bernard with a ferocity he had never seen in her before: "I'm going to kill you, boy! How many times have I told you not to do that! I'm going to give this boy a spanking he'll never forget! This boy ain't ever going to give no one no problems after this!" She had gone on like that, Tomming away brilliantly, but never, of course, unlatching the door, so that the men had seemed almost embarrassed for the trouble they were causing. When they finally left, she had turned to him and roared with laughter.

When he was nine he had moved north because his father had taken a job working in the Philadelphia shipyards. The codes in the North were very different, he quickly learned, as were the schools. Instead of being the brightest little boy in the class, he was suddenly in danger of being someone who was held back. His adjustment to the Philadelphia school system was extremely painful, and for a time he had lost some of his considerable confidence. He was unaccustomed to struggling with class work, and he was unaccustomed as well to being the joke of others because he pronounced words differently. His sin was that he spoke with an accent which was Southern, country, and black. When he came to school each day and said good morning to his teacher, the way you were supposed to at a black school in the South, the other kids made fun of his drawl and of his manners.

But in Philadelphia he had gone to school with kids from all different kinds of ethnic groups. The friendships he eventually made there had run across racial lines. In addition there were white teachers who had spotted his eagerness and his native intelligence and had volunteered to tutor him on the weekends. Soon his grades had improved. He was impressed by the more relaxed social order in Philadelphia. In Florida, when he spoke to a teacher, he had had to be far more obedient, saying "yes, ma'am" and "no, ma'am," but in Philadelphia, a simple yes or no was sufficient. With the help of the tutoring he began to do well. At the end of the sixth grade, when it was time to graduate from elementary school, he had been selected to be the graduation speaker. The runner-up was a white girl whom he thought of as a bit of a Goody Two-shoes, a favorite of some of the teachers. He was thrilled; it had been a considerable victory. His speech, "Living and Working Together," had reflected his belief in the integrated world he had become a part of, and he spoke optimistically about an American future in which everyone worked together despite racial and religious differences.

In Philadelphia, for the first time he had felt like a real American. That had been a striking revelation to him. In Florida he had felt that he was somehow outside the reach of the country, and that the patriotic songs about America which they sang in school did not include him. He and his friends knew all too well that they were the descendants of slaves, and that local laws specifically excluded them from full citizenship. But in Philadelphia he sang songs like "America the Beautiful" with gusto. Eventually his family moved back to Tampa, but the years in Philadelphia were important: There, for the first time in his life, he had felt a sense of wholeness. In addition, when he had joined up with the others in SNCC, he had never doubted that he was as good as white people.

Just before he set out for Selma, Bernard Lafayette had gotten married to a talented, fearless organizer whom he had met while working in Jackson. She was Colia Liddell, a member of a strong Jackson, Mississippi, family. She had gone to Tougaloo College in Jackson, and had worked for a time as a special assistant to Medgar Evers, the courageous young black man who ran the NAACP office in Mississippi. They had met briefly in Mississippi and then again in Chicago, at a major SNCC fund-raiser, a "Gospel for Freedom" night. She was somewhat wary of this small Alabama city where she would start her married life. "Bernard told me that Selma would be easy," she said years later. "That was not exactly what I would call the truth."[2]

Life in Selma did not start auspiciously for her. When they checked into the Torch Motel in February 1963, there were already two Justice Department officers there trying to talk both of them into leaving town because it was so dangerous. The agents used all kinds of enticements, including an offer from one agent, she remembered, to get both of them into Columbia University with scholarships. So much for the welcome from the United States government, she thought; so much for its ability to keep them from harm's way. Besides, there was a river which ran right through the center of town, and that frightened her; rivers conjured up images of midnight lynchings and of black bodies, secretly thrown into the water, floating away. Bernard, she remembered, had known of her river phobia but had said nothing about the fact that the Alabama River ran right through Selma.

Near the end of 1962 Bernard Lafayette had gone to Selma ahead of his wife and by the time of her arrival he had a very good sense of how dangerous it was going to be. He had set out, driving an old 1948 Chevrolet which Julian Bond, who seemed to be in charge of these things at SNCC, had procured for him. All the other SNCC people, Lafayette remembered, had wanted bigger, fancier cars, but Bond had warned against it. A big, fancy car called the attention of the police to the owner, he pointed out. The advantage of the old Chevy was that it was like a tank, for it had heavy metal doors and very small windows. "It's hard for them to get a very good shot at you in this one. That's why you want it," Bond had said. These new cars that everyone wants, Bond had added, aren't nearly as good for what you need. Amazingly, Lafayette thought after he had arrived in Selma, Julian had been right; the Chevy *was* quite a bit like a tank, and it was going to be hard for someone to get that good a shot at him.

On the way to Selma from Atlanta he had stopped at Tuskegee University and used its library to do a quick study on Dallas County. He had studied the number of lynchings and the demographics of the county, and he had learned everything he could about the white political apparatus. It was a city with its own sense of disappointment and bitterness, he decided—it had been the capital of Alabama in earlier times, but after some political chicanery, the capital had been moved to Montgomery. The population of Dallas County was almost equally divided between whites and blacks, about fifteen thousand each. All of the whites, as far as he could tell, were registered to vote, and almost none of the blacks were. The amount of white anger, he knew, was far greater than the norm, even in Alabama; during the Freedom Rides a year earlier, even when the bus had been given the protection of the Alabama National Guard, there had been talk of how dangerous Selma was, and on the leg of the ride from Montgomery to Jackson, Mississippi, there had been a decision to bypass Selma. It was said that an angry mob of 2,500 people was waiting at the bus station for them, despite the escort.

In Selma the local white people, he came to believe, were particularly proud and edgy. Theirs was, he decided, the pride of poor people still living in the past. The white men of Dallas County had thought of themselves as volunteers as far back as the Civil War, men quicker to answer the call of the South than other Alabamans. Even now a strong populist chord seemed to run through the poor whites in the region. Sheriff Jim Clark had created what he called his posse, white men who signed on as deputies for one reason only, to hold the line against integration. Apparently the men in the posse felt it was their duty to ride off to try and stop any attempt at integration in the South. Many had gone to Montgomery at the height of the Freedom Rides crisis, and it was said that some five hundred had driven over to Oxford, Mississippi, to join the mob which had tried to prevent the integration of the University of Mississippi.

Selma was centrally located in the Black Belt, the rare small city in what was an essentially rural area. Bernard Lafayette was sure that if SNCC succeeded here, if they could gain even a toehold, they would eventually be able to expand into the surrounding rural counties. He also knew, as everyone who had to deal with Selma knew, that it was going to be particularly difficult because Jim Clark was in a class with Bull Connor, albeit with less varnish, because unlike Connor, he operated in a small town, where there were even fewer restraints on him. He was known as the toughest small-town law man in the region, and his meanness, his need to swagger when the issue of race was at stake, had made him something of a symbol for the entire area. Selma had advertised, in no small part because of the dominating presence of Jim Clark, that it was going to draw the line against any racial change. Here they intended to make their stand. When the Supreme Court had ruled on *Brown,* ten local blacks had immediately signed a petition to integrate the schools; the white hierarchy, using its real might, its unchallenged economic power over blacks, had squeezed so hard that nine of them had immediately removed their names from the petition. Only one, a local postal worker, whose employer was the federal government, left his name on. The postal worker did not, as Bernard Lafayette mused, have to fear for his job—only for his life.

Lafayette had been warned by friends not to go, that in Selma the white people were too mean and the black people were too scared. Certainly his first recon of the town tended to confirm that opinion: The black people were fearful, both repressed, he thought, and depressed. His reputation as a Freedom Rider had preceded him, and at first it was not an asset in the black community. Most of the local people wanted nothing to do with him.

It had been a hallmark of Selma that whenever the local blacks had any kind of meeting—it did not necessarily even have to be a political one—Jim Clark would show up just to let them know he was watching them, and that they were not to step out of line. When Lafayette walked down the street the black people knew he was the new Freedom Rider in town, and they would not even look him in the eye. Even the local ministers would not associate with him or talk to him, and some of them attacked him in their sermons, talking about this outsider who had come to their town only to cause trouble and would soon be gone. The only thing he was going to do down here, they said, was get them all put in jail. When he tried to recruit at a local black high school, he was ordered off the premises by the school's black principal, who personally threatened to call Jim Clark.

Finding a place to live was hard, but one local teacher, a brave soul, he thought, was willing to rent him a room. A very few people there were his natural allies, including Amelia Boynton, an uncommonly brave woman who was a black home-economics extension agent. She was a Tuskegee graduate and had become the modern black matriarch of the community. Her husband, Sam, also a Tuskegee graduate, had arrived there some thirty years earlier as an agricultural extension agent assigned to work with black farmers, and they had both become active in early voter registration drives. Their son Bruce Boynton was the Boynton of *Boynton* v. *Virginia*. He had been on his way home from Howard Law School in 1958 when he had tried to have a hamburger in a previously all-white café in the Richmond bus terminal. The Boynton case had led to the Supreme Court decision which desegregated bus and train travel in December 1960.

At first as Lafayette tried to organize the town, he felt like the carrier of a plague. But he had arrived well prepared for the coldness and hostility he found. Before he had arrived in Selma he had stopped off to visit with Rufus Lewis, a legendary figure in central Alabama, a strong, blunt, rough-hewn man who was a funeral director in Montgomery and had been the football coach at Alabama A&M, as well as leader in the early days of the Montgomery bus boycott. Even more important, Lewis had been a shrewd and skilled player in earlier voter registration drives in the Montgomery area, and Lafayette had heard that he was extremely knowledgeable about how to register people in a hostile rural environment, when the most powerful force in the community might well be the deadening quality of all those years of accumulated fear.

Rufus Lewis had been as good as advertised, perhaps even better. Because he had former football players in every county, he knew the region uncommonly well and had contacts everywhere. Lewis told him to base in Dallas County and branch out gradually.

Everything he said reflected the difficulties of working among the oppressed; what he passed on seemed, Lafayette decided later, like a summation of the cumulative black political wisdom gained working against all odds in this country. Go in as quietly as you can, Lewis had warned. Be low-key. Don't go in with a lot of fanfare, don't call a lot of attention to yourself. Above all, try not to provoke the white people because the more you do that, the more they will turn the screws on the black people before you even get started. Find a black contact person whom you've been told about and who has the respect of the other people in the community. Have a meeting at the home of your contact person. Don't make the first meeting too large—that might attract too much attention. Five or six people would be the perfect number. If your early meetings are larger there will be too many cars parked in front, and the police will become suspicious. Besides, if you

bring in too many people too quickly, you increase the chances that
one of them is an informer. The more immune the people are to the
pressure of the white community in the early organizational days, the
better. If you handle it right in the beginning with just five or six people, in time they would bring their friends.

Lafayette was to talk at first not so much about voting rights as
about citizenship, and then, gradually, about constitutional rights, and
why people in the black community had to move ahead, not just for
themselves, but on behalf of those who were to come after, Lewis said.
He was to talk about their children's lives—to remind them that they
had an obligation on behalf of the young. If Lafayette did this well,
and did not bluster, if he listened to them as much as he talked to
them, then, said Lewis, at each meeting there would almost surely be
two and perhaps three people who would be willing to become
involved. They would thereupon be willing to hold comparable meetings at their homes, and use their influence with their friends. That
way his influence would constantly be expanding, and in that way as
well, he would be quietly growing roots into the community without
the danger of a mass meeting, which might backfire and trigger a violent backlash among the whites. In addition he would subtly be blend-
ing into the landscape; he would bear less and less the taint of
someone from the outside, who might disappear whenever it suited
him.

Bernard, Rufus Lewis emphasized, had to create an atmosphere
where the local people felt free to unburden themselves of all the
anger which was stored up in them. That rage, no matter how deeply
and carefully suppressed, would be his greatest asset. The more they
spoke out in front of their friends, then the more, however unconsciously, they would be committing themselves to his cause. If they did
this, came forward and poured out their anger, then common dignity
demanded they act on their words, and Lafayette would have a
recruit.

It was very important for Lafayette to get a feel for these people, for
their hopes, and above all their fears, for fear was what governed their
lives, more than hope. He was to try and comprehend the limits of
their lives, and he had to make them prepare themselves for the
reprisals which were sure to come.

Listening to Lewis, Bernard Lafayette was intrigued: It was as if he was hearing a familiar story, one which reminded him of nothing so much as the way in which his maternal grandmother had organized the New Hope Baptist Church in Tampa. She had begun her organizational work by holding small Bible circles in the Lafayette living room. Looking back at those meetings, he later decided they had been what were eventually known as support groups—the women would come and talk to each other about their marriages, their financial problems, their problems with their children. They were not, he thought, people with enough money for psychiatrists, nor would they have felt comfortable talking to some stranger about the intimate details of their lives. But they spoke willingly in intimate detail in these small meetings under the auspices of their church. His grandmother was, he realized, a brilliant organizer. She would start with Circle One, which met on Monday, and then she created Circle Two, which met Tuesday, and then Circle Three for Wednesday. Gradually, she had organized a brand-new church. What she had done with her church was what Rufus Lewis had outlined for Bernard in Selma; and it made him aware that the roots of modern black political organization rested, like so much else, in the black Baptist church.

The one advantage he had in Selma was that he was dealing with zero expectations. Those who had gone before him had failed; they had not registered a single person in their drives, and had never broken through the terrifying wall of black fear. As Lafayette began his meetings, there were a handful of people who were helpful who had been part of the old Dallas County Voters League, which was the old Boynton-driven group, but which had slipped in its effectiveness under the resurgence of white segregationist fervor since *Brown*. There were a handful of others who helped: James Chestnut, the black lawyer, and Reverend Lewis Lloyd Anderson, a pastor of the Tabernacle Baptist Church, who was far ahead of his deacons on civil rights issues. One of his most valuable helpers was a woman named Marie Foster, who was strong and committed. She was a dental hygienist who worked for her brother, so there was no way that the white leadership could pressure her economically. As best he could he tried to work through people who were protected, retirees who had some Social Security protection, people whose businesses were immune to white pressure, retired military people, and independent farmers.

Gradually he had a sense that he and Colia were both making progress. Lafayette had already learned in Jackson that if he and the other Freedom Riders scared the older generation, then they impressed young blacks who were still in high school, and he worked the local schools extensively, trying to get recruits, aware that if he got young people involved, some of the parents might be angry, but others would come along, ashamed to lag behind their children. He had used every trick he could. He had virtually baited the local ministers to come aboard. In order to embarrass some of the more sophisticated black people of Selma into committing themselves, he worked the surrounding rural areas, where he found a number of surprisingly tough, gritty independent black farmers, men who could, in some instances, barely read or write. He brought them into his camp and had them speak at meetings, in order to shame the better-educated people of Selma.

The Boyntons were critically important to him. Sam Boynton was incapacitated by the time of Bernard's arrival, his health failing badly, but he was still a respected man in the community. Sometimes Lafayette would sit with Boynton at night, and when he did he occasionally felt a small squeeze of his hand, which Lafayette regarded as an act of transference, a spiritual thing, as if Boynton's passion for voter registration was personally being passed to him. When Sam Boynton died, Lafayette seized the moment, using the occasion to hold his first mass meeting. It would be both memorial service for Boynton and a de facto political meeting to honor his work in voter registration. Lewis Anderson, the one local minister who came to his support, made the Tabernacle Baptist Church available. Anderson's deacons were furious, and when they tried to stop him, Anderson said he would hold the service *outside* the church and use a loudspeaker to tell the crowd that the deacons were too scared to open the church. Jim Forman was brought in to be the featured speaker.

What was slowly happening in Selma was symbolic of what was happening in the larger civil rights struggle in all kinds of small towns in the Deep South. The tide was turning; local people were beginning to overcome the most limiting of all forces, their own fear. If Jim Clark's crude and often brutal violations of elemental justice had made Selma a particularly difficult town in which to operate in the past, then now, slowly, those same qualities, soon to be placed under the withering scrutiny of the national press, would tend to work against the white segregationists. What had once made Jim Clark an asset to his cause—his ego, his need to posture, his unveiled contempt for black people, his willingness to violate their rights as openly as he wanted—was now to make him a liability. He had always spoken about Selma being a showpiece of the South; so it was to be. Jim Clark was to be an ornament to the cause, but in the end, not as he had expected, an ornament to his allies.

When Lafayette scheduled the first mass meeting to honor Sam Boynton, Jim Clark acted quite predictably and made the first of what was to be a series of significant miscalculations. He turned out a large number of his deputies and tried to block the entrance to the service. His deputies set up barriers all around the church. In front he placed armed men from his posse, many of them waving wooden bats. The bats were particularly deadly; they had been made at a local furniture factory as table legs, and therefore were extra long. In addition, they had been somewhat refined as weapons: The local practice among the posse members was to drill a hole in the business end and insert a steel rod, so that it would be even heavier and more lethal. It was all about bullying: The bats were not often used, but their very size made them a considerable asset in the art of intimidation. Watching it all, Bernard Lafayette understood that Clark was bullying these people as he and others before him had bullied them for years, and he remembered something from the lessons learned in the school yards of both Philadelphia and Tampa—that the biggest bullies were often, once the macho veneer was challenged, the easiest people to take on, for their bluster as well as their courage tended to disappear quickly.

That night Clark had lined his people up outside the church, taking pictures of everyone trying to enter. It was classic Deep South intimidation; the blacks could enter but there would be a price. Then, just as the service began, Clark and a few of his deputies stomped into the church with a court order from Judge James Hare, a local circuit judge, who if anything seemed to be the man in charge of running Clark. Hare's order said the sheriff and his men had the right to be there, in order to maintain public safety. Later, as the meeting was breaking up, Clark's deputies went around whacking the cars belonging to the blacks, smashing their taillights. The next day a number of black drivers were ticketed for not having taillights on their cars when they drove around town.

All of this proved a tactical mistake of the first order. Coming as it did at a memorial service for a man who was revered for taking chances, it had been a violation of traditionally drawn and accepted racial lines within the community. Colia Liddell Lafayette, with her own shrewd assessment of small-town black life in the Deep South, thought it was the moment that the tide began to turn in Selma, and that many other events which soon followed flowed from that night when Clark had pushed too hard one time too many, and had tried to humiliate these simple people in a matter of what was for them elemental self-respect. The lesson learned, she thought, was not about integration; it was more basic, about whether a man could stand up and act like a man.

Because Sam Boynton had been braver than most, Jim Clark's bullying had enraged both those who attended the service and those who had not. Perhaps 350 black people made it into the church, and a comparable number were not able to get through Clark's barriers. "It had rained that night," Colia Lafayette remembered, "and we were not sure anyone would turn out, and then we got there and there were black people as far as the eye could see—it was as if you had never seen so many black people in all your life." Inside, with Clark and a few of his deputies as self-invited guests, Jim Forman had given an audacious speech—a speech on behalf of all the blacks who had waited too long for too little in the way of their rights. It was time to end the wait, he said, and the way they could do it was to go out and register to vote. The crowd, angered rather than intimidated by the sheriff, began to cheer Forman and to punctuate his words with its own amens. Later, when a conservative minister named C. L. Hunter had given what was a rebuttal—saying that much of the black man's problems were of his own making, that he had to raise his own moral standard before thinking of voting—the crowd had sat in stony silence.

Not only were the lines being drawn, but the escalating nature of the events was forcing many of the local people to declare themselves; it was becoming harder and harder because of the choices being forced on them by both Jim Clark and Bernard Lafayette to stay on the sidelines. Clark was unwittingly playing into the hands of his sworn enemies, and creating an ever-smaller neutral zone. After the rally in honor of Sam Boynton, Lafayette decided it was going to be easier to have mass meetings. That also meant, because he was out in the open now, that it was surely going to become more dangerous for him personally. He was right: After the next mass meeting Lafayette was arrested. He was driving home afterward when the sheriff's deputies pulled him over. He was charged with vagrancy. He had been scared that night that they would plant drugs or a weapon in the car. That was one of his constant fears—of going to prison on a trumped-up charge.

From the day he arrived in Selma, Bernard Lafayette had known he was a marked man. From the start he accepted the possibility, indeed the likelihood of his death there. The valley of the shadow of death, he, like John Lewis, sometimes thought of it. He was aware of his powerlessness: If they were going to kill him, there was little that he could do to stop them. What was he going to do, he thought to himself, go downtown and ask for police protection from the sheriff's office? Yet he dared not let fear become his dominating impulse, for it would be visible immediately to all the others. After he had been in Selma about three months the local paper ran a story about him, telling who he was and what he intended to do and where he lived. As if to mark a bull's-eye on him, he thought: Come and get the Freedom Rider. Whenever he drove around town, he always paid close attention to his rearview mirror, and he always drove slowly so they could not arrest him for speeding.

Colia Lafayette was scared too; because she was from Mississippi, she had known when she started to work for Medgar Evers that she was leaving the safety zone behind and offering her life to a cause, but there was something about the way they were being monitored in Selma which was very frightening. It was not just the way their car was often followed, nor the fact that when things happened to them and they complained to the feds, the information always seemed to be passed to the local officials. The most frightening thing of all was the personal nature of some of their phone calls. These were not merely obscene and threatening calls, in which Colia would be told she was a black bitch and that she would never see Bernard again. Certainly there were plenty of those calls. Rather, there was an intimacy to other calls which was unnerving. Because they had no money, they regularly used a code for their long-distance calls to SNCC headquarters in Atlanta. Colia Lafayette would pick up the phone and, using a coded name, place a collect call to herself at headquarters. That was a signal that, at least for one more day, everything was all right. But when she did, placing the call under a pseudonym, the local Selma operator would cut in and say, "I know who you are—you're Colia Lafayette, and I know *where* you are too."[3]

Both of them understood that the more successful Bernard was with his organizing, the more dangerous it would become for them in Selma. On the night of June 12, 1963, Bernard Lafayette was coming home from a mass meeting when they finally moved on him. He lived in a small building which had been divided up into apartments, located in an area near where the two sections of the town, black and white, started to go their separate ways. It was about ten o'clock at night, a late hour in a small Southern town, and an unusually dark night. As he pulled up into his driveway, however, he could see two white men across the street having trouble with their car. The hood was up and they were bending over the engine, peering in. Lafayette was getting his papers out of his car when he heard footsteps behind him. His first thought was, Here it is, I am going to die here. But if nothing else he wanted to see his assailant. So he turned just in time to see a huge white man in a T-shirt, its sleeves rolled up; a real Southern good old boy, who would probably weigh in at nothing less than 270 pounds. "Buddy," the man said, "how much do you charge for a push?" Lafayette felt a huge sigh of relief, and he said he would do it for free. Theirs was a pink and white '57 Chevy, a perfect good old boy car. He drove up behind it, and as he did he noticed that the two men were still conferring. Then the big man came and told him he had better get out and take a look. "What's the matter, aren't the bumper guards matching?" Lafayette asked.

That seemed odd—the bumpers ought to match and they looked like they matched. But he got out of his car and went forward and bent over, and when he did the big man smashed him as hard as he could on the top of his head with a gun. Lafayette went down but did not lose unconsciousness. When he tried to get up, the man hit him again. He managed to get up again, and then the man hit him a third time. The third was the worst of all, a deep gash, and he knew blood was pouring out. He was sure they were going to kill him now. He had been beaten before, but this time was different. The other beatings had been random, but this one seemed to be aimed precisely at him, as if there was a master plan to it. By the third lick Lafayette could barely make out the man hitting him because there was so much blood in his eyes, but he could see that the man was backing up now, and Lafayette was sure he was doing it in order to have room to shoot him; as that happened Lafayette yelled to a black neighbor of his, and the neighbor came out on the porch with a shotgun. Lafayette shouted at his neighbor not to shoot, somehow aware, though he was losing consciousness from the beatings, that given Selma's judicial system, if there were any shots fired by blacks, he himself would be put away on charges of murder. He was barely conscious, but he had a vague glimmer of his neighbor on the porch with the shotgun and the two white men beginning to run to their car. He was never sure why they had not killed him outright; perhaps, he thought, he had thrown off their plan by offering the push for free.

Later as he pieced together information—what he knew firsthand from the beating and what the Justice Department officials eventually told him from their files—he was sure that it had been a deliberate, calculated plan to murder him. They had intended, he believed, to knock him out, abduct him from the neighborhood, and then kill him. That night he was taken to a hospital and was kept overnight. He had eleven stitches, and the doctors told him, given the number of times he was hit, that he was very lucky indeed. That happened to be the same night that Medgar Evers was murdered in Mississippi; Lafayette was later told by people in the FBI office in Mobile that the assault on him and the murder of Evers were both part of a three-state conspiracy which had been hatched by the Klan in New Orleans, and that the third victim was to have been a CORE activist in Louisiana who was out of town that night.

By chance, Colia Lafayette was not in Selma that night either. A few weeks earlier she had joined other activists in the Birmingham protests and she had been badly beaten when Bull Connor's cops had turned the fire hoses on protesters there. She was pregnant at the time. Normally she thought of herself as a good athlete, someone with a track star's speed, but on that day she had been wearing little shoes with high heels ("I've never had on a pair since," she said years later) and because of the heels she had not been able to get away quickly enough. She had been badly bruised, with some internal injuries, and she and Bernard had decided that she ought to go home to Jackson and rest. So she was in Jackson when he was beaten, and at first all she knew about the events of that terrible night was that Medgar Evers, who was a close friend, had been murdered. She was devastated by the news, and her family and friends decided to wait several days before telling her that her husband had been badly beaten as well, and probably the object of a murder plot.

In Selma the day after the beating, James Chestnut, the black lawyer, ran into Bernard Lafayette on the street. The young activist looked terrible. His face was bruised, his eyes were swollen, and there was blood all over his shirt. Chestnut told him to go home and get cleaned up and change his shirt. "No way," Lafayette had answered. "This is the symbol we need."[4] He knew that Jim Clark expected him to run after the beating, so he was more determined than ever to stay. So he kept on his bloody shirt and made himself as visible as he could downtown. He knew the black community was watching him. The most powerful argument used against SNCC organizers like himself had always been that they were outsiders, that they would stir things up, and then at the first sign of trouble they would flee, leaving the local people more vulnerable than ever. So he intensified his schedule, making himself and his wound as visible as possible. Chestnut thought the beating was a defining moment for Selma. It not only helped prove Lafayette's own legitimacy but it shamed local black people—someone from the outside was willing to take greater risks than they were in the struggle for their rights. From then on, he believed, Lafayette's efforts steadily gained momentum.

Lafayette's meetings were getting bigger. The confidence of the local blacks was building. The crude way in which Jim Clark had responded to Lafayette's work—all the blacks in town assumed that Clark was behind the beating or at least was a partner to what happened—was working to the advantage of the protesters. Other speakers came in for Lafayette's meetings—Jim Bevel, Ella Baker from the SCLC. The meetings were part modern political protest and part old-fashioned religious revival; those who had gone downtown to try and register, whether they had been successful or not, would stand, and the others applauded them.

It almost did not matter, Lafayette decided, that when they went to the courthouse they were always turned away. The most important thing was no longer the reaction of the white authorities; the most important thing he was accomplishing in Selma was to break the barrier of fear among the blacks, which had paralyzed the community for so long; to show that all their goals were achievable, that the more risks they took, the bolder they would become, and that sooner or later, the feds were going to have to pay attention. For what Lafayette and those who came after him were doing here and in comparable Deep South communities was trying to prove to the local black people that they were not alone, that they were part of something larger, which was going on all over the South, that the nation was beginning to watch, and that sooner or later they were going to win. It had been Lafayette's job to teach them, as Jim Lawson had once taught him, that the requisite strength would not come from the outside, it had to come from within.

That fall when school was about to reopen back in Nashville, Lafayette, pleased with the exceptional beginning he had helped forge in Selma, and with other SNCC volunteers now ready to follow him there, had returned to Fisk to continue his work for a degree; he had created the beginning of a movement in Selma, and he had forced the local ministers to become more active. Within both SNCC and the SCLC there was a sense that he and the people he had worked through had achieved a considerable victory—they had forged a beachhead in one of the most dangerous places of all.

The other important thing he had done was confirm, however involuntarily, something the leaders of both SNCC and the SCLC had begun to suspect, that Selma was one of the toughest of all cities in the Deep South, a showpiece of segregation as far as whites were concerned, and therefore, because of its size, and because of the crude, violent nature of its sheriff, and his almost Pavlovian response to black protest, it would eventually be the perfect setting for a major protest, which would be both showdown and showplace in the struggle in the Deep South.

What had struck Bernard Lafayette most about Jim Clark—and he had many opportunities to watch him—was that his ego was always involved. For him, it was as if his racism were a calling. Clark had begun to see himself as the one man who could stop the Movement, as if even the leadership in Birmingham and Montgomery were soft compared with him. He had, Lafayette decided, begun to believe his own myth. Men like Clark did not listen to other voices, and they were dangerous, in the end, not just to their enemies but to their allies as well. They did not know when to stop. For the clock was beginning to tick. The violence inflicted on those trying to push for civil rights was slowly beginning to change the White House. On June 19, 1963, a week after the murder of Medgar Evers (and the vicious assault on Bernard Lafayette), John Kennedy proposed a broad civil rights bill.

47

AT ALMOST THE SAME TIME THAT BERNARD LAFAYETTE WAS SOMEWHAT quietly beginning to create the base for the Movement in Selma, some ninety-five miles away his close friend Jim Bevel was finally surfacing as one of the most important and most original SCLC strategists in the perilous Movement assault upon Birmingham. Bevel and Diane Nash formed one of the most imposing and unlikely teams in the Movement. On occasion, some of their colleagues thought, it was easier to dismiss what Bevel was saying than it was what Diane was proposing. If he was obviously brilliant, then it was also possible, because of the almost mystical way in which he always spoke, to think of him as something of a flake. With Diane that was not the case. She was not only relentless in her commitment to what she believed in, but she was often terrifyingly logical as well.

By 1962 Bevel was working full time for SCLC, and Diane seemed to alternate between the SCLC and SNCC. In April 1963, the SCLC had decided to make a major move on Birmingham, the bastion of Bull Connor, and thereby not only the most segregated big city in the South, but largely viewed by most Movement leaders as the most dangerous one as well. In Mississippi it seemed that the small, rural towns were particularly dangerous; in Alabama, by consensus, because of Connor, it was the big city.

At the moment that King and his immediate staff decided to move on Birmingham, it was by no means clear that the Movement was going forward in the relentless and unbroken progression which would eventually end up not merely changing the conscience of the nation, but producing in a very short period two critical pieces of legislation. To the contrary, despite other victories, and a growing willingness of young people to commit themselves in the Deep South, the

Movement seemed stalled. The previous major SCLC assault, a year earlier in Albany, Georgia, was widely regarded as a fiasco, King's biggest and most public defeat. The Albany officials, led by a shrewd local police chief named Laurie Pritchett, had been far more subtle in dealing with King and his people than a number of his previous opponents, and had failed to provide the media with the requisite cartoon-like villain, so critical to any Movement victory. The SCLC challenge had not been particularly well thought out, and the local white leadership had managed to exploit existing weaknesses and divisions within the black leadership. In the end the Movement assault had foundered badly. The failure in Albany had also heightened tensions between the older SCLC officials and some of the younger SNCC kids who had been pioneers in Albany. The effort had ended not only in defeat for King, but in a particularly angry session in which a number of the SNCC people, reflecting not only the growing degree of alienation within SNCC but more traditional institutional rivalries and jealousies as well, had quite savagely unburdened themselves of their grievances to King himself, doing it in the most personal way imaginable.

Therefore as he and the other SCLC leaders set out for Birmingham in the spring of 1963, they faced what they believed was a make-or-break experience. They believed that they could not endure two major defeats in a row. That made Birmingham a particularly intriguing site for a major battle. King and his aides would be assaulting the single most difficult big city in the South. In addition to any local gains they might make, they hoped to create a well-televised morality play, which the nation would watch and which would help them in their lobbying in Washington. Nothing about it would be easy, however. Despite the exemplary courage of Fred Shuttlesworth, there was little sense of what the local black community would do when pressed to come forward and join up with these activists. Generations of violent repression had left the local black community divided, wary of taking chances, and extremely cautious about committing itself to the kind of audacious protest which King and his people were leading.

Their strategy was still evolving. From the defeat at Albany on, the print reporters covering King believed that he was becoming ever more aware of the importance of television cameras in amplifying the Movement message, and that Albany had taught them with a certain finality the importance not only of what they were doing locally, but of the greater importance of what the rest of the nation perceived each day. Certainly there had been an awareness of television's power before, but after Albany it changed, as Karl Fleming of *Newsweek* noted; the role of television had become far more important and it seemed to be built into each day's schedule—indeed the schedule seemed to be crafted as much for the possibilities it offered for the evening newscasts as it did for its effect on the local white power structure.[1] Fleming was right: In the planning session for Birmingham, which had been held in Dorchester, Georgia, Andy Young, who was the resident SCLC expert on dealing with the white media, had emphasized the need for a new kind of daily message, one that was visual and which would dramatize the purpose of the campaign each day. It was the coming, they all realized later on, of something historic in American public life—the sound bite. Each day's message did not have to be long—only sixty seconds, Young said, because that was all network television wanted. King had immediately seized on Young's idea, recalling some of the favorite words of Dr. Benjamin Mays, the president of Morehouse when King had been a student: "One tiny little minute /just sixty seconds in it /I can't refuse it /I dare not abuse it /It's up to me to use it." From then on whenever Young would remind them of the importance of the television image they wanted to send out that day, King would say, "One tiny little minute, just sixty seconds in it."[2]

Their timing, therefore, was remarkable, for the nation was just beginning to undergo what was to be a profound change in the transmission of information: Because of the coming of television, events were no longer covered merely by the press, they were covered by the *media;* more important, we were going from the use of words to define events, to the coming of *images* to define them. And these particular images, which were being transmitted from the South with the most modern of instruments of communication passing on the brutality of century-old hatreds with stunning immediacy, were to stand as the most important early use of televised images in the country's journalistic history.

In Birmingham they intended not just to break the heart of the segregationist resistance there. In addition, King and his fellow strategists hoped that the campaign might move the Kennedy administration, ever cautious, to come forward with a broad civil rights bill which would among other things outlaw discrimination in all aspects of public accommodations. The stakes in Birmingham therefore were extremely high.

One reason why Birmingham was so important, of course, was Bull Connor. He was not only hard on black people, but the local white community was afraid of him as well. It was a city where there was a history of violent acts inflicted on black activists and where federal officials believed there was a direct tie-in between the police force and the people who were responsible for these systematic acts of violence. Therefore the Movement leaders both needed and feared Connor. To succeed in Birmingham, they would have to force Connor to lash out, but that greatly heightened the danger there. Often in his meetings with his staff as they prepared for the forthcoming campaign, King would say that he thought some of them would not make it out of Birmingham alive. Because the campaign now loomed so important to the future of the Movement, and because Albany had revealed serious weakness in preparation, the SCLC battle plan this time was exceptionally detailed.

The timing was critical. Connor, still police commissioner, was engaged in a runoff election for mayor with a moderate named Albert Boutwell, and there was a decision that they would start the broad-based campaign once the election (which Connor would lose) was over. Jim Lawson was brought in from his church in Memphis to give a series of workshops, where he taught the essentials of nonviolent protest. They intended to strike at the downtown department stores, trying to get them to desegregate their lunch counters, and to begin to hire black sales help, and they wanted as well to create a local mechanism which would mediate racial grievances in the future. But well planned or not, the original drive in that city sputtered. King and his people had wanted to fill the jails with their people; they had hoped to have as many as one thousand demonstrators a day arrested, many of them, it was hoped, willing to stay in jail for five or six days. But in the beginning the Birmingham merchants danced away from the SCLC game plan. The large department stores did not serve the sit-in customers, but they responded coolly, and there was little violence. The early demonstrations were not particularly vigorous. Many of the city's black ministers were quite conservative, or at the very least cautious, by no means eager to see King come in and triumph on their territory, and were hardly supportive. The local black weekly newspaper editor was for a variety of reasons anti-King and the white Birmingham newspapers did all they could to marginalize what King was doing. The local black population seemed quite wary at first. On the first day of the demonstrations only twenty-one people were arrested; after eight days, only 150 people were in jail. It was going so badly, Jim Bevel later said, that they were sending the same people back to jail again and again, but having them dress in different clothes in order to make it seem like they were different people and that the Movement's base was broader than it was.[3]

When the Birmingham push started, Bevel and Diane Nash were spending most of their time in the Mississippi Delta, trying to register blacks to vote in primaries. They had come over briefly before the first demonstrations to help Jim Lawson with some workshops on nonviolence, and had then returned to the Delta. But when the Birmingham campaign seemed to be stalled, King sent out a call for Bevel. He knew that he needed Bevel and his unique talents; the ugly confrontation with the SNCC people in Albany had already made Bevel, his own personal, somewhat radical link to the younger, more alienated people in the Movement, more valuable to him than ever. Listening to Bevel, King often heard what these young blacks were saying and thinking before these ideas became fashionable.

But their relationship was by no means easy or even: King was at once enthralled by but wary of Bevel; he was fascinated by the originality of the younger man's mind, and by the strength of his moral-political convictions. But, thought Andy Young, the SCLC aide among whose many jobs it was to serve as a buffer between King and Bevel, King was also quite frightened of Bevel and a little intimidated by him as well. King, constantly buffeted from all sides, did not like it when anyone pushed him, and Bevel, in his constant certainty that his own vision was the truest one, always seemed to be pushing him. Again and again Bevel would propose his beliefs to King, and King would neither agree nor disagree; instead he would remain noncommittal, slip away from Bevel, and then tell Young that it was his job to deal with Bevel: "Now, Andy, Jim is right on a lot of what he says here, but you have to help him to see the complexity and the context of the issue."[4] Bevel's truths were a constant problem to the others because they were absolute; he did not seem burdened by the immediacy of the consequences of what he was proposing. If a certain course was the right course, then they should follow it no matter what the price, no matter what the consequences.

Bevel had become an SCLC staff member the year before, but it was during the Birmingham struggle, Andy Young thought, that he began to surface as a critical strategist, quite possibly, in Young's opinion, the most brilliant and original thinker in the SCLC. He often strongly disagreed with his peers and the general path the SCLC was taking. For some time he, like many of the other SNCC people who had ridden the early freedom buses and had done pioneer work in Mississippi, believed that it was time to forego traditional direct-action protests and concentrate on voter registration. That was the bitter lesson of the Deep South.

He and Diane and Bernard Lafayette might early on during the intense internal debate within SNCC have favored direct action over voter registration as the way to go, but they had learned the reality of the Deep South in Mississippi. In that sense Alabama and Mississippi were different from border states, as Lafayette noted, and different even from cities like Atlanta, where the vote was guaranteed. In the Deep South, the direct action which the authorities hated the most was the attempt to register voters. Everything else was peripheral: Attempts to integrate lunch counters were virtually pointless. That was why Lafayette had gladly gone into Selma, and that was why Bevel and Nash were willing to come back and help in the Birmingham drive. Bevel had already been pushing for them to concentrate on voter's rights, and to do it in Alabama. He dissented strongly from what he believed was the general Movement view that poor blacks would not rally to a voter campaign, because the concept of voting was too abstract for them, whereas something like a lunch counter was more dramatic and rewarding. He thought that innately patronizing and that it would not be that hard to connect, even for ordinary field workers, the lack of fair treatment they received from local officials with their lack of electoral power.

Bevel was hardly an easy colleague for the other SCLC leaders, most of them a few years older than he was, men who tended to regard him as something of a live hand grenade. Sensitivity to the feelings of others was not necessarily his strong point. During the Albany campaign, largely run by Wyatt Tee Walker, he had disagreed often and loudly about Walker's more hierarchical techniques, complaining that Walker was running the campaign the way a general ran an army, and that a movement could not be run as if it were a military operation; it had to operate more on consent.

There was no doubt that Bevel was a man with a special vision all his own. Even his trademark yarmulke seemed to signify it. By 1961, he had taken to wearing a yarmulke at all times. He did it in part because he wanted to honor the Old Testament prophets like Jeremiah and Ezekiel, whose strengths and truths he so greatly admired, and he did it as well because he thought of himself as being part Jewish. That is, he did not see how you could separate Judaism from Christianity; he did not see how anyone could be a Christian without being a Jew, or a Jew without being a Christian. He had begun wearing the yarmulke by instinct and then his friend Candie Carawan, a white Fisk transfer student who had married Guy Carawan, had sent him five hand-knitted yarmulkes which her parents had bought in the Middle East. At first they kept falling off his head. But then he tried shaving his skull and from then on the yarmulkes fit snugly. The effect of both the yarmulke and the shaved head was in some ways to sharpen the image of Bevel as the prophet, a biblical man who bore the teachings of the Old Testament with him at all times. Cross him, and you crossed all the other prophets. (Early on he had also started wearing old-fashioned country overalls as part of his own permanent protest of segregation—he did it in honor of all those black people who had been forced into poverty by racism.) Too, his rhetoric added to that image: He always seemed to see contemporary events in historic biblical terms. If he spoke of what had happened that day during some kind of protest downtown, it was as if his words came from the Old Testament, and he was describing a confrontation which had taken place nearly two thousand years earlier in the Holy Land. Nor did it seem to the others that he qualified his words by adding on at the end, "This is what I think." Rather, his sentences seemed to end with the phrase "Thus sayeth the Lord."[5] The others often called him, not unkindly, the Prophet.

More, he was in his own way a great bureaucratic infighter. In addition to the force of his personality, he seemed unusually deft at putting his opponents on the defensive, and making them seem timid about whatever question was at issue. At times like these Martin King liked to sit on the sidelines and let his other people argue it out with Bevel; but those who argued with him were always in danger of sounding like Uncle Toms at the end of a meeting. Because Bevel seemed to deal in absolutes, he had the capacity to make more pragmatic men, particularly men like King, who had roots in the Protestant ministry, feel guilty because he spoke a kind of biblical truth and they did not. King, forced by the rather pragmatic politics of the Movement to become something of a centrist moralist, a leader trying at all times to balance his different black constituencies, and trying at the same time to maximize his effectiveness with white America, regarded Bevel's truths with some degree of caution. Almost everyone else in the top leadership of the SCLC could be controlled, but Bevel was Bevel, an original, a man above all else who could not be controlled.

When Bevel arrived in Birmingham on April 12, on the day that Martin Luther King was arrested there, he gave a rousing sermon at the Sixteenth Street Baptist Church in which he said Birmingham was sick, Bull Connor was sick, the white people of the city were all sick, and more, the local black people were sick too, because they accepted the rule of sick white people and did not fight back. "The Negro has been sitting here dead for three hundred years," he said; "it is time he got up and walked."[6] And that was just for starters.

Bevel had decided that the only way to make the Birmingham campaign work was to turn it into a children's crusade. There were a number of reasons for that: First, he decided that the black world of Birmingham represented far too fragmented a community for King and his people to work with. Except for a handful of churches, most of the black ministers were not with them, at least not at first, and King nominally depended on a church-driven base. That was not surprising in so hostile a Deep South city, he believed, where it was easy to intimidate adults whose jobs often made them dependent upon the white world. But students were another thing. If you started with the high schools, you could incorporate an existing, well-defined, strong community—for these young people had been going to school together for nine or ten years. Besides, in places like Birmingham, the children were the only people left who were at least partially free. He had learned that two years ago in Jackson, Mississippi. There, despite all the pressures they were working against, Bevel had been impressed by the willingness of young people—children, really—to take a risk and to go ahead of their parents. Now faced with a stalled campaign in Birmingham, he believed that the only way they were going to have a mass base would be to start organizing among the high school students. And if need be, after that junior high, and if need be, elementary school kids. So here as he had in Jackson, he went to the children, and with the aid of a few others, he began to work the schools. They were not allowed inside the schools, but they set up their workshops at nearby churches and they shrewdly enlisted student leaders and athletic stars as their early recruiters. One of Bevel's top organizers was a young man named James Orange, who had been a high school football star only a few years earlier in Birmingham, and he had given them excellent entrée to these student leaders and athletes. Again, as in Jackson, Bevel found young black kids eager to come aboard, and eager, he believed, to make a real commitment. His workshops quickly flourished.

Soon a debate raged within SCLC circles: What should be the minimum age for a demonstrator? Some traditionalists thought they ought to be college age at the very least. Others felt the cut-off should be high school students. At one point King teased Bevel about using people so young and reminded him of the charges still pending against him in Jackson for contributing to the delinquency of a minor. There must be at least eighty counts, King said. That, answered Bevel, was the problem. He hadn't gotten enough young people. There should have been eight thousand counts. If he had gotten eight thousand kids, they wouldn't have bothered him.[7] King finally agreed to use high school kids. For a time they set an age limit of fourteen. But Bevel pushed for an even lower age limit; it was pointless, he said, to limit the right of black children to protest against segregation. This might be the best chance they ever had to challenge it, and the terrible truth was—and everyone in the room knew it, he said—that these children were going to have to spend their entire lives struggling against racism in some form or another. It already affected and damaged them, no matter how young they were, he argued; it was already a poison in their systems. It was time to stop the age-old custom in black homes of trying to shield black children from something for which there was, finally, no shield. Was anyone in this room, he asked, really going to sit here and tell him that the disease of racism was not already shaping the lives of these children and limiting their place in

America? Why not let them be involved—it was their lives, after all, that were already being damaged. King was wary—there was already considerable criticism of him for accepting high-school-age volunteers. But Bevel, shrewd and forceful as ever, responded with a compelling argument: If a child was old enough to belong to a church—to accept Christ as the guiding force in his or her life, obviously a decision of considerable permanence and consequence, then he or she was old enough to march for freedom. These children had professed their faith in Christ when they were five or six and no one had said they were too young, he argued; now let them live that faith. Or had they been too young to choose Christ? Neither he nor Martin Luther King had a right to stop these children from acting on their own faith. Nor did the parents have a right to stop their children. It was a brilliant argument, particularly because it was made by one Baptist preacher to another. King, facing what more and more seemed to be defeat in Birmingham unless the pace picked up, finally, reluctantly agreed. With that the Birmingham push became a children's crusade, and a stunningly successful one.

It was Bevel at his most original. Back when they had worked Jackson two years earlier, Bernard Lafayette, himself an accomplished recruiter, had been struck by how deftly Bevel had worked the young people, how skillful he had been at reaching something important inside them. He did not, Lafayette thought, speak down to them; instead he let them discover what they felt about things, what they believed in. There had been one memorable moment in Jackson when Bevel had cooled a minor riot; it had happened when some black teenagers had become enraged by an incident of white violence and had wanted to retaliate. Apparently some white hoodlums had assaulted a black girl, bound her to the hood of their car with wire, and had then driven through the black neighborhood, showing off their victim. Bevel had arrived just as the black teenagers were about to retaliate. They were going to go out, they had said, and kill them a white boy. Who? Bevel had asked, which white boy? The person who had committed this act? Were they going to kill anyone in particular? No. Did they have the names and addresses? he asked. No. Well, suppose the person they assaulted was innocent? Suppose it was a doctor driving to the black neighborhood to help a black person who was sick? "Suppose it's a white doctor visiting your own mama if she's sick?" he said. Was that going to help anyone? "I'm tired of that kind of courage," he had said, "courage in the dark. All the cowards in the world have courage in the dark. All these white hoodlums, all they have is courage in the dark. You're going to be just like them. Why don't you show your courage in the light of day? Why don't you take your courage—if you're that brave—and join me and fight segregation? Come and sit in with us. That takes courage, and we'll do it downtown in the middle of the day when all the cops are watching. Or does that take too much courage for you?" He had not only calmed them down and ended the idea of vengeance, but he had gotten five or six recruits that night.[8]

Now here, as he put together his army of children, there was ample evidence of that talent again. On the first day of the new protest, which began on May 2, wave after wave of children left the various churches, catching the Birmingham authorities completely unprepared. They easily filled all the city's paddy wagons. Soon the police had to use school buses to transport these youthful law breakers to jail. On the first day more than six hundred children were arrested, and in succeeding days it often seemed that one thousand or more young people a day were being jailed. In all, it was estimated that a total of ten thousand children went to jail, filling the prisons as they had promised earlier on, and eventually, because there was no room in jail, they were trucked to an instant outdoor prison, the converted state fairgrounds. The use of children caught the Birmingham authorities completely by surprise. Soon Bull Connor had his people turn high-velocity fire hoses on the children and use police dogs to assault them. All these scenes were captured in their full cruelty by the national media. Birmingham became, to the rest of the nation, not so much a city but an image, and a devastating one at that, where white cops could use maximum force on children trying to exercise constitutional rights. The pressure on the white leadership to deal with King and the local black leaders grew, and finally the Birmingham whites accommodated. Lunch counters would be integrated, blacks could be hired to work in stores, and the city would go ahead with planned integration of its schools in the fall. That which had loomed as a major defeat for King had turned into a stunning victory.

It did not, of course, make Jim Bevel any easier to work with, for Jim Bevel never worried much about making friends within the Movement; Wyatt Tee Walker, who was his nominal superior in running the campaign and who was a significantly more hierarchical man, was constantly enraged by the fact that he could not control Bevel and that Bevel seemed to operate with complete autonomy. Despite their success on the streets, Walker was constantly pushing King to fire Bevel.

It was during Birmingham that more and more of the top leadership in the SCLC began to believe, as did so many of the SNCC kids, that a traditional civil rights bill was not enough, that there had to be a voting rights bill as well. As long as they could not dent the political process locally, they were going to be vulnerable to the local political, judicial, and police systems, constantly needing the feds to protect them. It was nice to have the federal government looking out for your interests, but true, long-term justice could only come locally, when blacks had the franchise and when public officials had to respond to their needs. More and more Bevel was pushing this, and typically, he saw a biblical mandate to it. His phrasing—since one of his strengths was that he was both earthy and prophetic at the same time, managing to blend the roughest kind of street language with his own biblical vision—was that all this bullshit about literacy tests and poll taxes had to end; the right to vote was given to all human beings, brought forth as they were in the image of their creator, and that in any free society no child of God had the right to sit in judgment on any other child of God and deny him the right to vote. Only the godless would do that. The origins of the right to vote, in Bevel's view, were not in some English documents written hundred of years earlier and passed down over the centuries; rather that right existed in the very concept of genesis itself, and if there was any doubt about that, he was glad to remind people of the Declaration of Independence. "We hold these truths to be self evident, that all men are created equal, *that they are endowed by their Creator with certain unalienable rights.*" In that way, both he and his friend Bernard Lafayette, operating at the same time in two very different, very tough Alabama cities, had arrived at the same conclusion—that in order to open up the Deep South, where the political franchise was still largely denied, the final critical strike had to be on the issue of voting rights.

To Bevel the success they were achieving with the Birmingham students was just the beginning. If the nation was starting to watch, then they dared not stop in Birmingham. He wanted to take all these young people, who were so eager to be a part of the Movement, and make them a part of a larger march, a children's march to Washington. He was disgusted with the lack of support they had gotten from the federal government; he knew that an extremely nervous Kennedy administration had lobbied hard with King against using the children, and he wanted to teach the administration a lesson, to treat John Kennedy the way they might treat George Wallace. He was sure, Bevel told Andy Young, that ten thousand or more children would join them in such a march. They would just walk out there to old Highway 11 and head northeast toward Chattanooga and go straight on to Washington. They could eat and camp along the way. It would be like Gandhi's march, protesting the salt tax in 1930. The nation would be enthralled because it was *children* doing it. The *entire nation* would have to watch.

When people arguing against Bevel's idea spoke of the potential for violence, it did not seem to dissuade him: Violence, he pointed out, was already being done to these children every day in other ways, and no one was paying attention. At least this way the nation would have to look at what was being done to its black children. Martin Luther King was not so sure that, given feverish Klan anger, a children's march through the very heart of Klan territory was that good an idea. If children were killed in a march like that, not only would violence have been done, but he thought a lot of middle-class Americans would blame the Movement leadership for having put them at risk. But given the power of contemporary television cameras, some aspects of Bevel's march intrigued him and he stored the idea away. A few weeks later when Bayard Rustin began to talk to him about a modern version of an old Philip Randolph idea, a march on Washington which reflected black anger and solidarity, the concept was already germinating in his head because of Bevel's suggestion. Randolph, one of the grand old men of the black world, the leader of the railroad porters, had dreamed of such a march since the early days of World War II.(Bevel, years later, was furious that first the idea of the march was toned down and made, in his mind, far too genteel, and second, that it was credited to Philip Randolph, when he felt everyone should know that it was his idea. Randolph, he thought, was one more sacred cow in the black community.[9])

48

IT WAS JOHN LEWIS, ODDLY ENOUGH, WHO WAS ABLE TO SENSE MORE than most of his peers in SNCC the changing nature of the struggle in the Deep South, and the steadily changing role of the federal government as the escalating struggle forced it to the side of these young activist warriors. One key benchmark, he decided, was the murder of Medgar Evers in June 1963. It had enraged President Kennedy: When it had happened, John Kennedy had finally, in the eyes of Lewis, begun the process of committing himself to their cause. Up until then he had either tried to avoid the issue or, failing that, to straddle it. But on the night of Evers's death, Kennedy had taken a fateful step forward: He had asked ordinary white Americans to put themselves in the place of black Americans. To Lewis it was the first great speech by Kennedy as president; now for the first time, Lewis believed, the president had showed that he understood that this was as much as anything else a defining moral issue for the entire nation. Kennedy was learning how hard it was to be neutral when racists were beating up and murdering blacks trying to enjoy the basic rights of citizenship. It meant that the bitter price of the past two years—of going into the Deep South and placing their own bodies on the line—had begun to have its desired effect.

In addition Kennedy had asked for the nation's top black leaders to meet with him in Washington on June 21, nine days after Evers's murder. Among those invited were the traditional leaders, A. Philip Randolph, Whitney Young, Martin Luther King, Roy Wilkins, and James Farmer. The invitation also included the head of SNCC, who happened to be John Lewis of Pike County, Alabama, elected to that position almost by chance seven days earlier. That Lewis was now headed for a summit meeting with the great figures of the Movement and the president of the United States surprised not merely the other top people in SNCC but Lewis himself. His election was regarded by some SNCC people as a bit of a fluke. He had not sought the office, had not particularly wanted it, and had not even thought he was the best choice for it. But at the time, having returned to Nashville from Parchman more committed than ever to being in the Movement, he happened to be the head of the local SNCC chapter, which by dint of its constant assaults on two recalcitrant restaurants in Nashville, Crosskeys and Morrison's, was virtually the only major urban SNCC chapter still engaged in daily local protests. His election had not seemed very important at the time, and some people were already saying that he was taking over just as SNCC's glory days were done. Glory, of course, never mattered very much to him anyway. When he was elected, he was all too aware that some of the more forceful and more sophisticated people who were moving into the SNCC leadership class looked down on him. Many of these people were from the North, they were urban and better educated, and certainly more verbal than he, and they were dramatically different from the Southern, church-oriented leaders who had come out of Nashville and other Southern cities and whose strengths Lewis as much as anyone embodied. But their condescension never bothered him; white people had condescended to him and his family for years, and it was not so different when black people did it now. He felt comfortable in himself, reaffirmed in his purpose every day by each beating and each arrest. Besides, he knew he was *of* the rural black South in the truest sense; he could anticipate how ordinary black people would respond to every new situation, because it was the way in which he and members of his family would respond.

When he had left Parchman prison in 1961, John Lewis was more certain than ever that he had found the right path. He had overcome his own personal fears and he, like the others, had survived the daily humiliations inflicted on them in Parchman. He regarded surviving Parchman as a singular victory. He had found strength in one thing he had learned—the more you challenged these age-old forces, the less you feared them, and the less imposing they seemed to be. The first thing he had done on his return to Nashville was to transfer from American Baptist to Fisk. It was in some ways emotionally hard to do—he loved American Baptist and the friendships he had made there—but Fisk was an accredited four-year college, and American Baptist was not, and Lewis wanted an accredited degree. With the help of Martin Luther King and the SCLC he had won a scholarship to Fisk. In September 1961, ten of the young people who had been on the Freedom Rides were honored in a ceremony at the old Ryman Auditorium, the home of the Grand Ole Opry. All ten were awarded scholarships. It was the first time there had been any kind of reward for doing what they were doing, other than the internal rewards. That fall when he entered Fisk, he was quite dazzled by the beauty of it and the sense of history which it represented. There he was, John Lewis staying in DuBois Hall, named after the famed black leader, walking on this campus where so many distinguished black leaders had been before him. He had dreamed once when he was a boy of becoming a Morehouse man; now he was on his way to becoming something just as worthy, a Fisk man.

He was barely twenty-three, the leader of a major civil rights group, and he was going to meet the president along with a number of very distinguished black men, some of whom had always been his boyhood heroes. Yet he was innocent in all things, save his role in the Movement. In this he was sophisticated and possessed a hard-won knowledge born of constant arrests and frequent beatings and overheated meetings called in moments of crisis. At SNCC meetings, when the subject matter went outside issues of the Movement, however, he remained silent rather than speak and show his ignorance. Above all, he did not want to talk and make a mistake. It was part of John Lewis's strength that he never pretended to know what he did not know or to be someone who he was not.

As he arrived in Washington, John Lewis neither owned a car nor knew how to drive one. (He was more than forty when he learned how to drive and he was almost fifty before he bought his first new car.) He had almost no life outside the Movement. He and the other full-time SNCC people, he realized much later, had lived those years in a narrow but completely focused way. They made almost no money, and his salary from SNCC was around $25 a week; years later he wondered how he had lived on it, and the answer was simple: Other than the rent for his apartment, he existed on virtually nothing. When he had to fly somewhere, SNCC paid for the ticket, and locally there was usually someone to drive all of them around. If he needed a place to stay, he would stay at someone's house. Usually there would be some sort of communal meal, served by the wife of a minister or some local woman active in the Movement, who would turn out to be good cooks. He owned little in the way of clothes, one or two suits for his public appearances, and enough shirts so that he could drop two of them off at the dry cleaner at a time.

For a time he hung out in Atlanta with Don Harris, who was from a middle-class black family and had gone to Rutgers and seemed gentle and poised, and Julian Bond, scion of a prominent family of black educators, and by consensus the most elegant of the young men in the Movement. They had worked hard at teasing him out of his shyness. There was a game they played, the game of prosecutor, and Julian Bond was very good at playing the prosecutor and asking questions ("Do you know the aforementioned Miss Smith?" he would ask, using the name of a woman in the Movement, and Lewis would answer that he did, and then Bond would ask, "And do you know her carnally?" at which point Lewis would get too flustered to play). "Mr. Chairman," Bond called Lewis, with great affection.

They had pushed him to take an occasional drink as a way of relaxing. His tolerance for alcohol was marginal; with John, Julian Bond once noted, if you poured beer in a glass, and then poured it out and poured water in and he drank it, he might get drunk.[1] But he finally learned to take a drink of scotch and water, which was what Don Harris drank. To do it he first had to overcome his religious beliefs that what he was doing was sinful. In the summer he had learned to drink gin and tonic, although here he had to be careful because to him it tasted like a soft drink.

As he had headed to Washington in the summer of 1963, he was thrilled, not so much to be with the president, for despite his recent speech, Lewis felt the jury was still out on Kennedy, but to be with the other black leaders, most particularly A. Philip Randolph, a truly mythical figure to blacks of John Lewis's generation, and of course, Martin Luther King. But being with Mr. Randolph—John Lewis was unable to think of him as anything but *Mister* Randolph—was special because when Lewis had been a young boy back in Pike County, he had singled out Mr. Randolph as his personal hero and had cut out every article about him from the *Pittsburgh Courier* and put it in his own personal scrapbook of black history. The local high school subscribed to the *Courier,* and when it was two weeks old, students were allowed to cut it up and save photos and articles. Other young people might clip out photos of their favorite baseball players; John Lewis clipped out photos of black political leaders. He had more photos of Philip Randolph than he did of anyone else, even Martin Luther King.

John Lewis thought there was something singular about A. Philip Randolph, who had given his whole life to this struggle, in an era much more hostile and dangerous, and had never been beaten down as a man. He had never faltered in his commitment, never surrendered an iota of his pride or dignity. To John Lewis, A. Philip Randolph was nothing less than the modern incarnation of Frederick Douglass. In another era, one with less prejudice, Lewis thought, he might have been a governor or senator or ambassador.

Now that he was in Mr. Randolph's presence, he was moved by the simple elegance of the man. Randolph had a great voice, one worthy of Paul Robeson, Lewis thought, and he had unusually elegant enunciation, something that Lewis was all too painfully aware he lacked himself. When Randolph spoke the sound was so beautiful that he might as well have been singing. "Mr. President," Randolph said, "the masses are restless." (To Lewis, loving his pronunciation, it sounded like Mr. Randolph was saying "the mahsses are restless.") "We are going to march on Washington." It was the first that Lewis had ever heard of a march on Washington, but he immediately liked the idea; he was not sure that Randolph had spoken to anyone else about it, though it was possible that he had mentioned it to Dr. King before the meeting. But the idea was now in play.

John Kennedy, Lewis noticed, was not at all sure that he liked the idea of a march. It was the first time Lewis had seen the president up close, and he could tell that he was uneasy with this meeting and uneasy being with all these black men. You could tell that from his body language, from the sense of the distance—he seemed almost physically to be withdrawing from his visitors. By no means was it a meeting he wanted to have. "Mr. Randolph," the president said, "if you bring all these people to Washington, won't that bring violence and a great deal of disorder?" And then Randolph had assured the president. "Mr. President, this will be an orderly, peaceful, nonviolent demonstration." The president did not seem greatly reassured. "I think we have some problems here," he said and quickly left the meeting, turning it over to Robert Kennedy and Lyndon Johnson.

The black leaders had soon left the White House and A. Philip Randolph had spoken to the reporters waiting outside, saying that they had had a very good meeting and that there would be a march on Washington. John Lewis had studied the president closely. During the election of 1960 he had been wary of both candidates; he thought there was nothing particularly attractive about Richard Nixon but he had remained skeptical of John Kennedy. But if he had sensed Kennedy's cautiousness in the meeting, then he had also sensed something else, that the president was better than he had expected, that he was listening, and that he exuded a sense of openness and fairness. What the black leaders wanted and what the president wanted were hardly the same thing, but John Lewis was struck by the degree to which John Kennedy paid attention.

The black leadership met eleven days later on July 2 in New York at the Roosevelt Hotel. Lewis was fascinated by the dynamics within the group. Randolph was the senior man, obviously very close, almost paternally close, to Martin Luther King, and obviously as well very much at ease with Jim Farmer. These were the men who were the architects of direct action. Roy Wilkins and Whitney Young were more apart, cooler with the others; they were the black ambassadors to the white political and business world, the men who had more day-to-day dealings with the white political, legal, and economic establishment. Inevitably they were warier of direct action, which put them in immediate conflict with the people they often had to deal with. In addition, tensions within the civil rights world were rising: The NAACP people were increasingly irritated by their belief that they had not only fought the battle longer and harder than anyone else, but the fact that increasingly, it was King and his colleagues in the upstart SCLC, and even the young people in SNCC, who seemed to be grabbing all the headlines now.

In Wilkins's view King and the others were becoming famous, but were doing little in the way of heavy lifting. Those tensions showed at this meeting; even before King arrived, Wilkins had shocked Lewis by

speaking openly of how naive he thought King was politically—
words, Lewis immediately understood, which were aimed at him as
well. Then after King arrived Wilkins started baiting King, trying to
get him to name *anything* he had ever desegregated. Wilkins pushed
and pushed and finally King answered, "Well, I guess about the only
thing I've desegregated is a few human hearts."[2] It was, Lewis
thought, a masterly delineation of the difference in the respective purposes of the two major groups.

Lewis was acutely aware of Wilkins's coolness toward him and
some of the others, a coolness which bordered on condescension.
(Indeed, Wilkins once told an FBI contact that Lewis was a poor and
inarticulate Negro.[3]) King had shown up with Ralph Abernathy, his
close friend and deputy; Lewis had shown up with Jim Forman; and
Bayard Rustin had come at Randolph's invitation. But Wilkins did not
want them there. Principals only, he had said, and for a time things got
a little tense, and finally the deputies had to leave. That was just the
beginning of the tensions. Randolph and King wanted Bayard Rustin
as the march's principal organizer. Rustin was a venerable warrior who
had worked with them in the past, but Wilkins was wary because of
Rustin's left-wing associations when he was young and because he was
gay, something, because it had showed up on the occasional police
blotter, that the white conservative world might seize on, and something which in particular would offend J. Edgar Hoover. They had
decided Randolph would be in charge of the march, that Rustin
would be the principal organizer, but that he would stay somewhat in
the background.

The concept of the march was a singular personal triumph for Randolph, who had always dreamt of a great march on the capital city;
indeed, back in 1941 he had called for one, and had reluctantly canceled it only at the last minute after some shrewd negotiating with a
very unhappy Franklin Roosevelt. The quid pro quo had been that the
march would be dropped, and in return Roosevelt would desegregate
the munitions industry, then about to go into a boom because of the
gathering war clouds. Now the group running the 1963 march began
to expand: Catholic, Protestant, and Jewish clergymen were added,
along with Walter Reuther, the symbolic labor leader. As the group
increased and became more inclusionary, the politics of it became
more complicated; the bigger it was, inevitably the more centrist it

became, and the more it seemed to have an unofficial (if not wildly enthusiastic) White House sanction.

That meant ever greater pressure to keep the rhetoric within bounds; inevitably it placed John Lewis at the center of a storm. Because SNCC was the most radical of the attending organizations, the one with roots among the poorest people in the Deep South, and because many of its field workers were both embattled and angry, John Lewis's speech was certain to be the most controversial. Not only had he himself spent the past three years in and out of jails and been regularly beaten by white mobs and authorities, but some of his closest friends were in jail even as he was getting ready to speak. Three of them had been arrested in Americus, Georgia, on a remarkable charge—insurrection against the state of Georgia. When that had happened, when they had been arrested for trying to exercise their basic rights, the federal government had been completely silent. "Which side," he asked, "is the federal government on?"

As he worked on his speech, other members of SNCC joined in, adding their personal touches; they were, after all, the real foot soldiers of the Movement, and if their elders, like Wilkins, Young, and even King, were the ones who eventually had to negotiate any settlement with the white power establishments in Washington and New York, they were the ones risking their lives and sampling the true face of the Democratic party as it ruled in the Deep South. Gradually the anger of SNCC began to emerge in Lewis's speech, most particularly when his colleague Jim Forman added a memorable line: "We will march through the South, through the heart of Dixie, the way Sherman did. We shall pursue our own 'scorched earth' policy and burn Jim Crow to the ground, nonviolently. We shall crack the South into a thousand pieces and put them back together in the image of a democracy." The speech was nothing less than a plaintive call from the leaders of the young generation, who had led the way into the Deep South and now wanted help. That put the SNCC people into immediate conflict with the older, more traditional leaders like Wilkins, who saw this march as a benchmark of progress and wanted no controversy.

Lewis's speech, the older leaders decided, was something of a problem because it was critical of the Kennedy administration. Years later he was amused by all the fuss over what seemed in retrospect, given what was yet to come, the mildest kind of criticism of the government.

He had objected to the Kennedy civil rights bill then being put together and said they could not support it because there was nothing in it which would protect the young and the old in their peaceful, nonviolent protests. There was nothing to be proud of on this day, he planned to say, because there were a lot of people unable to attend because they could not afford the trip, because they received starvation wages. Because a few days earlier he had seen a photo of a black man in Rhodesia holding a sign saying ONE MAN, ONE VOTE; that cry in Africa must be theirs in America too.

His speech was finished the night before, copies were circulated, and the word came back very quickly that among others, the Kennedys were quite unhappy with it. Certainly the Catholic archbishop of Washington, Patrick O'Boyle, was offended by the tone. O'Boyle, a generally liberal man, took particular exception to the line about Sherman. He would not give the invocation if that phrase remained in. Lewis and some of the other SNCC people thought Cardinal O'Boyle was not merely voicing his own opinions but, consciously or not, carrying water for the Kennedys, with whom he was quite close. Certainly Burke Marshall, in the civil rights division of Justice, was upset by the tone because he thought the speech not sufficiently supportive of what the Kennedys were doing in civil rights.[4]

Some of the exchanges between Lewis and Roy Wilkins were quite heated; Lewis could tell that Wilkins did not take him seriously, and thought he was too young and too naive to be playing so important a role at this epic event. Therefore Wilkins was quite tough in demanding changes in the speech. Lewis, for his part, was sure that he and SNCC spoke for the poorest and most vulnerable in the society. "This is my speech," Lewis kept saying during many of those skirmishes, "and it represents the people we work with."

"You are going to anger and insult the people who are already for us," Wilkins said; "you are going to set us back and we are here to move ahead."

Wilkins believed, not without reason, that he knew how to deal with white legislators as these young men did not, how to cut the best deal available. That had been his life's work. "You are not going to help us get a civil rights bill," he said.

"We're not here to support a civil rights bill," Lewis answered. "This march is much broader than that."

The differences between them were age old: It was as if the best of two very different generations of black Americans were shouting at each other at that moment.

Roy Wilkins, pragmatic, battle weary, experienced at this kind of byplay and at the legislative process, thought it a major mistake to speak against a civil rights bill at a march designed, as far as he was concerned, to pass it. Some of the others, including Eugene Carson Blake, a white minister who had been arrested in a civil rights demonstration, objected to Lewis's use of the word *masses,* and some objected to his use of the word *revolution,* when he had suggested that nothing less than a revolution was taking place. The political vocabulary which existed in America during the fifties had been notably timid, particularly when it came to words like *revolution,* which might seem to have a connection to the Communist lexicon. But A. Philip Randolph, who emerged as the principal mediator in all this, was not offended by the two words, and *revolution* and *masses* stayed. "There's nothing wrong with using the word *masses,* and there's nothing wrong with using the word *revolution,*" Randolph said. "I use them myself sometimes."

Those words spared, the battle shifted to the Sherman's march reference. Again Blake led the attackers, with Martin Luther King on his side. To King, who knew and admired and sensed the gentle side of Lewis, the phrase did not sound right. "John, I know you and that doesn't sound like you," King said. He was right as usual, Lewis thought; the phrase was Jim Forman's. So the reference to Sherman came out—too incendiary. It was decided that Lewis would endorse the civil rights bill (that was good manners) but he could say he did so with reservations (that was most assuredly the truth). "John," Randolph said as he pushed Lewis to accept a compromise on supporting the civil rights legislation, "we've come this far for the sake of unity— let's stick together a little longer." They worked on the speech right up until the last minute.

Suddenly Lewis found himself up on the podium, looking out and seeing people as far as the eye could see, the mass of humanity, old people and young people, black people and white people. And there was A. Philip Randolph, his great personal hero, the most elegant man he had ever met, introducing him, saying, "I now present to you young John Lewis." That was thrilling enough, to feel that he was in some way, even if it was only as a representative of a generation, part of a long line of black leaders, and that he had been acknowledged by so great a man. He was aware that day as he spoke of who his constituents were and how fragile their lives were. All the others who spoke that day, he believed, spoke for people who had in some way or another gotten at least partial citizenship; he spoke for those who in almost all ways were still close to being the children of slavery.

To his own amazement, when he started to speak he was not at all nervous, and he looked over to the side and saw the SNCC people all gathered together in one pocket, some of them wearing overalls; when he looked over, they cheered, and he felt the confidence surge through him. He spoke at length about morality in politics as it affected black people, who seemed to have no political home, about the fate of ideas too long compromised by racist realities. Men who built their careers on moral principles were all too rare in American politics, he said. "What political leader can stand up and say, 'My party is the party of principles'? For the party of Kennedy is also the party of Eastland. The party of Javits is also the party of Goldwater. Where is *our* party? Where is the political party [which] will make it unnecessary to march on Washington? Where is the political party [which] will make it unnecessary to march in the streets of Birmingham?" And he ended by saying that everyone was telling blacks to be patient, but patience had become a dirty word for them; they had been patient far too long. "We want our freedom," he said, "and we want it now." Then he finished and like everyone else, he listened in awe to the majestic words of Martin Luther King.

Later that day he called home to his family. By then the Lewises of Pike County had a television set, but somehow no one had managed to watch this great moment. John Lewis told them that hundreds of thousands of people were there, and that seemed to please them. He said that Dr. King had given a wonderful speech and that reassured them. Whenever possible, in the past two years, when he had been in constant trouble with the police, he tried to associate Dr. King with what he was doing, telling his parents that Dr. King had been there too. That always made them feel better, because Dr. King was their special hero, and if their young son Robert was with Dr. King, then he must be all right, even if his going to jail still managed to make them nervous.

Years later he would come to understand one additional thing about the march on Washington, not just the size of it, not just how peaceful and orderly it had been, not that it had been the site of one of Dr. King's greatest speeches. As events flowed forward, he realized that Roy Wilkins, if he had been more moderate about the civil rights bill than Lewis, had been intuitively right about something else—that it was important not to blow the relationship with the Kennedys on this day, for it was the day on which, in some final way, with the entire nation watching on television, the civil rights movement was married to the Kennedy administration and thus to the federal government of the United States.

John Lewis's friend James Bevel, whom many in the SCLC and SNCC credited with having come up with the original idea of the march, even if it was a very different kind of march, did not go to Washington that day. At the last minute Martin Luther King had realized that in all the preparation for Washington, Andy Young and James Bevel, both of whom had been critical players in Birmingham, were still down there, and he called Young and told him to come to Washington and to bring Bevel as well. But Bevel wanted no part of the march. It was his way or no way. As far as he was concerned, it was nothing but a damn sellout. "If you're going on a real march, call me," he told Young, "but not if you're just going up there for some damn picnic on the Capitol lawn. I don't want any part of no bullshit picnic."[5]

49

CURTIS MURPHY, FIGHTING OFF THE THROES OF A DEPRESSION WITH-
out even realizing he was in a depression, found himself listlessly looking for work in Chicago in the fall of 1963. At almost the same time
that Bernard Lafayette had finished putting together the beginning of
a movement in Selma, in June 1963 Murphy had graduated from Tennessee State, sadly, without honors. His college graduation, which had
meant so much to his parents, was surprisingly empty for him; he had
achieved their goals but he felt completely at loose ends. His other,
earlier dreams, of being a black fighter pilot or an officer in the space
program, had gradually unraveled, and his grades for the past two
years had not been very good. He had no earthly idea what he wanted
to do. By obeying his father and dropping out of the Movement, he
had lost his sense of purpose.

While still in college and needing a job to help pay for his nightlife,
for he could not bring himself to spend Buck's hard-earned money in
nightclubs, he had called Bob Lillard, who had briefly been his father-
in-law, and who was well connected politically. Lillard had fixed him
up with a job as a juvenile probation officer. Curtis Murphy treated it
as a sinecure. He often did not show up for meetings, and his only
apparent skill was in coming up with excuses to justify his constant
absences. In six months he was gone from the job, quitting just before
he was to be fired.

Restless in Nashville, unsure of what he wanted to do, Murphy set
out for Chicago. An aunt of his lived there. In Chicago his pattern of
behavior did not improve noticeably, for it was a city with more
nightlife and far greater temptations than Nashville. He quickly
became a man of the streets, staying out until 4:00 A.M., drinking nine,
ten, a dozen scotches a night. His aunt was not thrilled. Curtis soon

found himself even more at loose ends, without any plans. Somewhat desperate about his future, he went down to the board of education and applied for a job as a math teacher.

Teaching was something he was confident he could do, although at first he had little enthusiasm for it. But, he had the requisite credits, something for which he could thank his father. Back when Curtis was a student and very confident of his future in the jet and space age, the ever-cautious Buck Murphy had kept pushing teaching to him as a possible profession, and had urged him to take teaching courses. It was a good job, Buck had argued, it paid reasonably well, it had social value—black schoolteachers could do a lot of good among their own people—and it was a hell of a lot easier than working in the fields chopping cotton. Buck had not wanted to throw water on his son's ambition, but he was wary of just how many black jet pilots and black space scientists there were going to be in this brave new world. Every young black man ought to have a dream, Buck argued, but it was a sad fact of life that Curtis had to be prepared to see his dreams collapse. Buck reminded him that he did not have to major in education. But he ought, Buck suggested, to be ready for the day when they came and told him they were not taking any more black jet pilots or any more black scientists in the space program because they already had one of each. "I know you're doing something I never did, and I know you know more about your life than I do," Buck had said. "But just in case that jet plane doesn't come through, you might think of having teaching credits. They're always going to need black teachers." They argued often about this, and though Buck had never won the argument, he won the war, because Curtis had quietly signed up for the requisite number of courses.

The people at the Chicago board of education were intrigued by his application, for Tennessee A&I was a reputable school, and here was a young man with brilliant math grades, or at least brilliant math grades early on. They were equally intrigued by the gap in his record, and the period in which he went from A's to C's and D's, and he had explained that he had been a leader in the sit-ins in that period, and they seemed, he thought, to admire that as much as they did the A's. He got the job. As he walked away from the board office that day, he realized Buck Murphy was a wise and shrewd man, wiser and shrewder than even Curtis had ever realized.

He was assigned to the Simeon Vocational Public High School, which was at that moment something of a wasteland, being in reality an old Kroger warehouse then being converted into a school. It still had portable walls when he arrived. The city officials did not seem to care very much about the school, he decided, and they had assigned nothing but the youngest, least-connected teachers there. But that had turned out to be a plus. If he was not sure that he wanted to be a teacher, he was surprised by how much he liked the camaraderie of his fellow schoolteachers. They all seemed to be on a mission, and because of that they reminded him of his young sit-in colleagues. They were optimistic at that moment as he was not, they had a purpose as he no longer did, and they seemed full of ambition as he did not. If he was not yet one of them, he liked being with them. He was living something of a dual life, hanging out with them after school, but still hitting the clubs, drinking a good deal more than he should. One of his new colleagues was a young teacher named Rayna Ristow, all of twenty, a very quiet, white Catholic girl from Chicago; Curtis found that he liked to tease her, because she was so shy, and when he did, she would immediately begin to blush.

In her first days at Simeon, just out of Chicago Teachers College, she had been, she later recalled, desperately innocent. He had picked up on that immediately. In those days she still lived at home and her mother made her lunch every day; her mother, Rayna Ristow noted, was quite frugal and lunch consisted of a half sandwich and a piece of fruit. That first week her lunch had disappeared every day from the desk where she stored it. She had no idea where it went until on the last day of the week, a beaming Curtis Murphy had come over to her. "Miss Ristow," he said, "do you think you could get your mother to make a whole sandwich for a change?" He would tease her each morning, telling her what nice legs she had, and she would try to remain above it, and then he would tease her even more: "Come on, Miss Ristow, you know you want to go out with me—so when is it going to be?" In time they started dating. Years later, he decided, he had not been particularly nice to her in that period, mainly because he was still at war with himself, combative and drinking too much. But Rayna Ristow liked him from the start and decided he was made of separate, conflicting parts, one part sensitive and sweet, and one part deeply embittered. He was obviously unhappy with himself, and busy taking out that disappointment on others. She suggested that he see a psychiatrist, and he went to one for a few visits, although he was underwhelmed by the idea of spending his money on some doctor who would tell him what was wrong with himself, when he knew nothing was wrong.

Though he liked teaching and sensed that he had a gift for it, he also thought it was something of a comedown from his prospective life as a jet pilot and his thrilling days as a sit-in leader. When his first school year was over, he was still restless and still somewhat dissatisfied with his station as a teacher. He resigned his position with the school and headed back to a familiar place, Tennessee. He first visited Whiteville, where his family, informed by his wary aunt about his behavior, knew that something was seriously wrong with him, that he was in some way which they could not possibly understand at once educated, privileged, but lost. He knew he had become a puzzle to his father. "Son, there are just some things in life that you have to work out for yourself," Buck Murphy told him, while Duggar, unable to understand or comprehend what he was going through, the greater complexity of life that his greater advantages had led him to, told him to do what she always did when she reached a moment of crisis, which was to pray for guidance and help.

Whiteville had not worked out well. He felt furtive around his parents. He began to think of becoming a lawyer. Back in Nashville he again called Bob Lillard and told him that he wanted to go to law school, and Lillard made a few phone calls and told him that there was a place for him at Cumberland Law School, a night law school in Nashville where Tennessee's poor and ambitious young men and women had gone for years. Going to law school pleased Curtis. This was a profession well suited to him as a combat veteran of the Movement. Lawyers helped their own people, made deals, and in the process they became rich.

He was one of three black students at Cumberland in a class of about thirty. By all rights he should have done well in law school. Any success at Cumberland could put him right back at the center of the civil rights action. But once again he floundered. He could barely concentrate on the work. He was showing up in class without having done any of his homework, something that he could pull off in college, but which was a major mistake at law school, and particularly a law school for poor but hungry young men and women who saw this as their one chance to break out of rural poverty. Time after time he made a fool of himself in class. If his self-esteem had been low for the past two years, it bottomed out now. He realized that he was getting a rare break, a young Southern black going to a once segregated law school, and he was blowing it. His grandmother was paying for law school, and that fall she was dying, which made his failure even more painful. When in November she died, he seized on it as the excuse to drop out of law school. The Cumberland authorities did not try to dissuade him, and soon he was on his way back to Chicago to see if he could become a teacher again.

By the time he returned to Chicago, he was desperate. The school board there was less than sympathetic to him. Because he had resigned from his last teaching tour, he was told that he would have to be completely recertified before he could teach again. It was the lowest moment of his life; he was cocky on the outside and absolutely despairing on the inside. Years later, after he had put his life back together, slowly and carefully, accommodating some of his expectations to his realities, he realized that he had been in a profound depression from the moment he had obeyed his father by walking away from the sit-in movement. It had been not only the most compelling experience of his life, but it had been the most fun. Walking away, he realized, was the hardest thing he would probably ever have to do, and he had been the first of the leaders to have to do it. Replacing a life so full with an ordinary life, one replete with the mundane and boring minutiae of daily existence, was much harder than he could have imagined; worse, it was done without any counseling.

There was no school for former activists or revolutionaries where they told you how to get on with the rest of your life, and taught you how to become middle class again, he thought. As the years passed and he heard about some of his friends from those days who had come on hard times, he was sure he knew what had happened—it had been a very difficult experience to come down from. He had been among the first, he realized, who had to return to so ordinary a life, the first to learn how hard it was to be middle class.

50

As some of the first group of leaders had followed the Movement right onto the Freedom Ride buses, others were beginning to follow their careers, careers deeply influenced by their time in Lawson's workshops. Gloria Johnson, now Gloria Johnson-Powell, who wanted to specialize in child psychiatry, had returned to Meharry for her last year in the fall of 1961. The first few months of their marriage were very hard; Rodney was in Minneapolis serving his one-year internship in pediatric medicine at the University of Minnesota. Gloria was back in Nashville and they had very little money to spend commuting back and forth. Even as school had started that fall she was already pregnant with their first child. In addition her schedule was uncommonly full: She was carrying a complete course load and finishing up her medical studies, sitting in at different protest sites, primarily movie houses and churches, and working on a study on the effects of school integration in Nashville four years earlier, which eventually became a small book called *Black Monday's Children*.

On one occasion Gloria and Meg Claytor Woodbury, who was also black and was also pregnant, a friend of hers at Mount Holyoke, decided that they would have dinner at a small but reputedly pleasant restaurant in the downtown area. They had decided to do it with the approval of the other leaders—it would take the protest one more step forward, for this was solely a restaurant, not a department store, and they could not use the excuse that they had bought other goods and then stopped to eat. It was a bitter evening for both of them. One of the waitresses had come over and said that they did not serve niggers, and when they still did not leave, she returned and poured milk on both of them, and when they still did not leave, she returned one more time and poured hot tea on them. Then, as if to top it off, one of the other employees went in the kitchen and returned with a container of Ajax and poured it on both of them. Then the police came and arrested them both. It was a moment when Gloria Johnson felt an overpowering sense of sadness, not about herself, or about the others who were protesting with her, but instead about the city and the country. Here were the two of them, she thought, graduates of an uncommonly good college, now on their way to becoming doctors, trying to order simple meals in what was not a very fancy restaurant, and being abused and then arrested for it. She wept that day, for her country, not for herself.

For her it was an exhausting but exhilarating year; on occasion when she felt too overloaded, friends helped her take notes in courses, and somehow she managed to make it through. April Powell, the first of her and Rodney's three children, was born on April 18, 1962. The doctors had told Gloria the baby would arrive two weeks later and the early birth had caught Rodney and Gloria by surprise. Rodney had been on call in Minneapolis but had managed to arrive the next day. April Powell was, her parents decided, the youngest sit-in person of all, because she had sat in at a restaurant while still in her mother's womb.

In June, Gloria Johnson graduated from Meharry. Her mother came down for the graduation. Gloria Johnson-Powell had never seen her mother so animated in her life. This was as much her victory as her daughter's; perhaps, Gloria decided years later, given the level of sacrifice, the houses cleaned for white people, the laundry done at home for white people, the need to be both parents in a single-parent home, even more hers. Mrs. Johnson cried most of the weekend, but these were tears of happiness. Gloria had taken her medical degree in her married name, Gloria Johnson-Powell, and at one point Mrs. Johnson had said that it would have been nice to have taken it in her maiden name, but even that she said quite mildly, and there was little sense of rebuke. Mrs. Johnson was impressed by everyone she met and everything she saw in Nashville. She, who had repeatedly warned her daughter against crossing the Mason-Dixon line, had changed her mind. This was a new and different South from the one she had known as a girl. Whenever they met a classmate of Gloria's, Mrs. Johnson would say what a fine young man or woman he or she was, and when they spoke to a Meharry professor, Mrs. Johnson would always say how distinguished he seemed. Why, she said, she had met nothing but high-quality people in Nashville, black men and women all of whom were educated and learned. These were the kind of people who were going to change this country. If she had just known how excellent these black Southern schools were, she said, she would have sent Gloria's two sisters there, and indeed, because of the trip, Gloria's younger brother, Billy, eventually went to Tennessee State.

Rodney Powell was confident about their future. He and Gloria shared the same vision of how they would use their talents, always in some larger way for public service. When he finished his internship in Minnesota at the end of June 1962, Rodney still owed a two-year military obligation because of his draft deferments, and he decided to do it as many young doctors did in those days, by serving with the U. S. Public Health Service, his tour being at the National Institute of Neurological Diseases and Blindness in Bethesda, in the field of pediatric neuropathology. This put him under the auspices of the National Institute of Health. Gloria would join him for her internship in psychiatry at St. Elizabeth's. Everything seemed to be on track; they would go through life not just as a couple, but as a team, one fashioned in the new, awakening spirit of greater social responsibility in medicine.

In the fall of 1962 they were starting out their new jobs in Washington when the Peace Corps, a little more than a year in existence, started raiding the NIH for doctors. One of the first people they went after was Rodney Powell, and they wanted him to go to Africa. It was an irresistible offer. There was no more magical phrase for young, idealistic Americans in 1961 and 1962—at the beginning of the Kennedy years, when the young president had asked his fellow countrymen what they could do for their country—than that of *Peace Corps;* for young blacks who had already spent some time in the Movement, the idea of serving in the Peace Corps in Africa was doubly attractive. It seemed to offer everything; service and sacrifice, learning and exploring all at the same time.

For the Powells it was the professional offer which they would have invented for themselves. It seemed to confirm the greater societal change taking place around them in the United States; instead of going against the grain as they had in the past, now, in the new ethos demanded by the Peace Corps, they felt they were about to be *creden-*

tialed members in the vanguard of the new order. They were assigned to Ethiopia. Gloria would have to put her internship temporarily on hold, but that seemed a small price to pay for so exciting a challenge. The only downer was that almost everyone they knew in the medical world—particularly people older than they—warned against it. It would slow down their career tracks, and put them behind schedule. That was odd, Rodney Powell thought; all he and Gloria could think of was the adventure and the possibilities inherent in the choice, and the only thing most of their senior mentors could think of was the effect on their careers. The world of medicine seemed to both of them at that moment oddly isolated from the world they had become part of. In August 1962 they set out for Addis Ababa. Back in Boston, Mrs. Johnson had mixed feelings about their choice. She did not mind them going off, but she hated the idea of her new grandchild living in a land with so much disease. She wanted them to leave April Powell with her.

Rodney and Gloria Powell had decided that this trip would be part of the same larger search for self that had brought them first to Meharry, although this time it was a chance to explore the continent from which their ancestors had come. There were to be three hundred American volunteers in Ethiopia; Rodney Powell was one of three doctors serving them. A generation later they would *both* have gone as professionals; in this case, Gloria went as a spouse, putting her own career on hold in the technical sense, though working every day at two desperately understaffed hospitals. She was practicing more medicine and making more agonizing decisions about life and death in those years than she might have in ten years back home.

For both of them going to Africa was a fateful decision. They had already been, without realizing it, on journeys which make the traditional practice of medicine, that is, a handsome practice with a nice group of colleagues with considerable financial rewards, most unlikely. For them, social obligations dictated professional choices. For Rodney Powell, what he discovered in Africa—the overwhelming, devastating degree of disease, malnutrition, and poor medical practice—meant that he could never again think of having a traditional medical practice; he would move to a broader concept of preventive medicine, and inevitably to a career in public health.

He was moved by Africa, by the social acceptance that both of them found there and by the desperate need for minimal medical and health services as well. If there were cultural and on occasion class differences between him and the people he dealt with, if both the tribalism and the superstition he ran into were exhausting, then he also loved the fact that skin color seemed to mean so little. That which he provided was desperately needed; that which he was, a black American, seemed not to matter at all. He was thrilled by the dimension of freedom which came with shedding what he felt was the American obsession with skin color. In their years there, and then later after he returned to America, he thought seriously of becoming an expatriate and living permanently in Africa, although he decided in the end that, despite his misgivings, he was hopelessly American.

If he was frustrated in his two years in Africa, it was by the thrust of the medical and health practices in these pathetically poor countries, Ethiopia and Tanganyika, in which he served. Though both countries had tiny medical budgets, local officials were trying to create a kind of elite medical care system, not unlike that of Europe and America, which might serve a small percentage of the people, instead of using their tragically limited resources to create a broad-based public health care system, much of it preventive, much of it rurally based, and virtually all of it aimed at malnutrition and elemental disease control. He and Gloria were also appalled at the degree to which the local officials they met and many of the doctors they knew modeled themselves on their Caucasian counterparts, even, it seemed, down to smoking pipes—a practice which to Rodney seemed an unconscious symbol of having become a part of the governing medical elite. What he found in Africa was a deep and instinctive resistance to most of his ideas; success seemed to be success only if it followed a Western model and had Western trappings.

The problems of Africa they faced were so overwhelming that the events in the American South seemed momentarily distant; there were not a lot of newspapers to read, and it was hard to keep up with news back home. They were both aware of what was happening now in the mounting challenge in the Deep South, and that many of their old colleagues were leading the way. Rodney and Gloria had been part of one small protest. It was early July 1963, a few weeks after the murder of

Medgar Evers, an event which had shaken both of them. The local Tanganyikan Peace Corps director had asked Rodney if he planned to attend the picnic which the American ambassador traditionally gave on July 4. No, he answered, he did not think he would go. Why not? the director asked. Powell answered that he did not feel like celebrating Independence Day—he did not feel that independent at the moment. He mentioned it casually to a few other American blacks, and they too decided not to attend.

By chance someone working for the British Broadcasting Corporation picked up the story and used it, saying the American embassy picnic was being boycotted by some blacks. The American ambassador called in Powell and ordered him to hold a press conference and announce that there would be no boycott. Powell refused. "Sir," he said, "it is not a boycott, it is in no way organized, it is merely a personal statement. Nor is it a statement against my country. It is simply the way I feel." The ambassador pushed him a little further. "I could send you home," he said. "If you do that," Powell answered, "there *will* be a boycott, and no American blacks will be there, and there will be damn few Africans either." Eventually the ambassador pulled back; there was no need to create an issue when there was none.

For Gloria Johnson-Powell, Africa was a stunning ongoing lesson in poverty, superstition, and ignorance, much of it tribally based. The poverty and ignorance were overwhelming. She rotated her service at two different hospitals in Addis Ababa. One was a pediatric clinic; when she arrived in the morning she would find a line of three hundred to four hundred children already waiting. They all seemed to be suffering from severe malnutrition; flies clustered around their eyes, their bellies were swollen. It was a horrifying daily image, made all the worse by the fact that there was barely enough penicillin and glucose for three or at most four of the children each day. At other places in Ethiopia, she knew, the nurses would water down the wonder drugs (on occasion using contaminated water) in order to try and save more children. That, she thought, was the wrong way to go.

The best that she could do was to practice her own form of triage. That meant concentrating on those children who had the best chance to live. So she did not dilute the drugs. Instead she would pick out a handful of the healthiest children each day and use the drugs on them. There was no time for sentiment. The harsh reality was that the others were not going to make it anyway. She hated doing this, starting her day by playing God, looking at all those poor, suffering children with the coldest and least sentimental of eyes. So many had wrinkled skin and jaundiced eyes. The contrast between the lives of these children and the life of her own young daughter was dramatic and painful. When she went home at the end of the day, she was profoundly depressed.

The child mortality figures were terrible, 50 percent of the children under five years old, she believed, though statistics were at best erratic. Tuberculosis was so prevalent that the government did not even want to address it because this one disease could drain away the entire health budget. When she was first there she was intrigued by one phenomenon, young children arriving at the clinic in a kind of unisex outfit, a simple gunnysack, which had brought wheat or some other foreign food into the country. They all, both boys and girls, had a small tuft of hair on their heads. She was puzzled why they were dressed this way, for it was often cold in Addis Ababa, and the parents were dressed warmly, but not the children. She was puzzled as well by the peculiar hairdo, because she could never tell, unless she lifted up the sack, whether a child was a boy or a girl. Finally, using two interpreters, she got her answer. The heads had been shaved so there would be no lice, and the small tuft of hair was there so that if they died, God could come down and lift them away to heaven more easily by grabbing on to it. Hearing this explanation, she went home that day and wept. As for other clothes, there was so little money in most families that no clothes were to be bought until the children reached five years old, at which point it was fairly clear that they were going to live and were worth investing in.

In addition to her other responsibilities she operated several times a week in one clinic on endless cases of women who had been disfigured by primitive female circumcision rites. All of this was exhausting and depressing. During her time in Africa, there was one terrifying truth: The patients she was able to treat lived; the ones she could not get to, or lacked medicine to treat, died. That was the hard part—there were so many people, particularly children, who were beyond any help and who were going to die even though they were not beyond the reach of contemporary medical skills, just the finances to support it.

Rodney Powell too was ambivalent in the end about Africa. He felt a more natural sense of acceptance than he had ever felt in America. He was a foreigner, he was black, and he was godlike because he brought a desperately needed service. In the other part of his personal struggle, coming to terms with his sexuality, he remained wary. He sensed, particularly in Ethiopia, a strong religious and cultural bias against homosexuality, and in those years he found that he had to suppress whatever desires he had for men. This was not always easy, because in Africa physical affection among men—within proscribed limits—was far more open, and he often found himself at dinners where strikingly handsome Ethiopian men would embrace him warmly, and he would force himself to remember that there was a definite borderline to this kind of contact. But in general he had been fascinated and enriched by his two years there. He and Gloria had loved being of value. One night at a party at the home of the minister of education in Tanganyika, an evening where there had been a wondrous assemblage of local people and foreigners, the minister had interrupted the normal chitchat and had turned to his guests and said, "These are the people we need, people like the Powells. People like this. When they go out to our small villages they not only contribute their great abilities as doctors, but they show our people what black people can become. Your country must send us more Powells."

Rarely had both of them felt so complete, so validated. But there was also the sinking feeling they both had, the longer they were there, that they were part of a small elite, connected to another smaller elite; that for all the talk of a new, modern, awakening continent, these were countries mired not just in poverty and ignorance, but in the unyielding grasp of a cruel tribalism. They were depressed by their failure to penetrate the dark and often inhumane superstition generated by that tribalism.

51

JOHN LEWIS WAS IN NASHVILLE WHEN HE GOT THE NEWS OF JOHN Kennedy's assassination. He had gone back there for a court date which was connected to one of his many arrests, this one for trying to sit in at the B&W cafeteria in 1962. When the trial was over, he had gone back to the Fisk campus, and was in a car ready to go to the airport when he heard what had happened in Dallas. Lewis had gradually and almost grudgingly come to admire Kennedy. Yes, he was a politician, and yes, he was a cool politician at that, for there was not a lot of emotion to him. He did not lightly show which side he was on, and he was not like many other white people, who once they came aboard did so with a complete emotional commitment. Kennedy, by contrast, even when he decided in their favor, always seemed to keep a certain distance, as if by becoming too emotional and engaged he might lose his cherished rationality, and thereby diminish his political possibilities. But, Lewis thought, the best thing about him was that he was someone who always listened. He had measured every situation as carefully as he could—what was the minimum he had to do situation by situation. But he listened and he was in his own way always fair. He was no immediate convert to the black cause. But if you were black and you were dealing with him, there was one big plus, Lewis thought: He was never wedded to the past.

Lewis kept to his normal schedule that day, giving a speech at the University of Illinois at Urbana, and from there catching another plane to speak to the steelworkers in Detroit; he remembered a certain depression, being alone on the airplanes that day; he eventually ended up back in Washington, where he was supposed to attend a conference at Howard that had been scheduled right after the march. The title, ironically, was "Where Do We Go from Here?" That was now a better question than ever. He was scheduled to speak along with Jim Forman and Bayard Rustin. The conference was canceled, but he met with a group of SNCC people in Washington; he suggested that they, with the Kennedy family's permission, should go to Arlington and hold a vigil for the president. To his disappointment most of his SNCC colleagues vehemently objected. The degree of their animosity surprised him, as did the difference in the way he saw the slain president compared with the way they saw him. To most of them John Kennedy was just another white politician who had moved too slowly; he got no points for his own change or for the fact that during his presidency the Justice Department had moved steadily until it was virtually embracing the black challenge in the South. The idea of an Arlington service was quickly dropped. John Lewis believed the anger he had tapped into was a reflection of a different, more radical, more alienated set of leaders coming forth in SNCC.

52

AFTER JIM LAWSON RECEIVED HIS MASTER'S DEGREE IN THEOLOGY from Boston University in August 1960, he had expected to be assigned to a church in Nashville, and he believed there had been some kind of promise made to that end. Instead he was sent to a somewhat rundown church in Shelbyville, Tennessee, a small town about fifty miles south of Nashville. At first Lawson was somewhat disappointed; Shelbyville was not only small, it was in a rural county, and serious challenges to local racial practices seemed unlikely. Being there, he feared, would pull him away from the action in Nashville, in which he had played so influential a role. For a time Lawson considered rejecting the appointment and going on and getting his doctoral degree from B.U. But then his supervisors made it clear that the appointment was in no way punishment for his political activities, and that his time in Shelbyville would not be very long. So he accepted his appointment at the Green Chapel Methodist Church and in time he and Dorothy were glad that he did.

He sensed a certain wariness among many of the parishioners; he was the famous, or because of the *Banner,* the infamous James Lawson, and there was surely, he knew, a question in their minds whether he might be too radical for this small, quiet town, and whether he was going to come in and start some protests more worthy of a big city which would get them all in trouble. But he had not entered the ministry just to be a part of the new political wave, he had entered it to minister to all the needs of his people, and he found his time in Shelbyville to be uncommonly valuable. He liked being a minister even when it was uneventful; he took pleasure and sustenance from the routine and the mundane. The church itself was in terrible physical condition. He immediately started a campaign for a new building; being one of the least hierarchical of men, he appointed the entire congregation to the building committee.

In the slightly less than two years he spent in Shelbyville, they built a brand-new church, start to finish. In time he came to take a particular pride in his pastoring there, not the least of which came from his knowledge that he had overcome so many doubts about himself in their minds. He liked his duties, enjoyed the people, and enjoyed watching the process of conversion as those more conservative members of the church gradually accepted him, and even began to enjoy the fact that the notorious Reverend James Lawson was their pastor.

In June of 1962 he was appointed to take over the Centenary Methodist Church in Memphis, which was the largest black Methodist church in the mid-South: It had over eleven hundred members. It was at once an exciting and yet somewhat daunting assignment. Memphis was an anomaly, a Deep South city in a border state; it was in some ways the reverse of Atlanta, where the city was modern and the encompassing state was reactionary. Tennessee was generally liberal, but Memphis itself and the immediate surrounding area were politically and socially very conservative. Memphis was only two hundred miles west of Nashville, but it seemed infinitely deeper into the Bible Belt to Jim Lawson. The basic religious beliefs and teachings he found there were more pervasively fundamentalist, far more geared to a literal interpretation of the Bible. It was a city, he thought, far more resistant to diverse ideas, be they political or religious. In Memphis if an idea was different, alien, or radical, it was in danger of being tagged, in the vernacular of the time, as communistic. If Jim Lawson went on a local radio show and tried to discuss political issues with local ministers or local officials, he often found that he had run into a wall—We do things here this way, they always seemed to be saying, because we've always done them this way. And more, we intend to keep on doing them this way. Almost nothing in Memphis, he discovered, had changed in the eight years since the *Brown* decision; it was still almost completely segregated. If Boss Ed Crump's power over the rest of Tennessee had been broken some sixteen years ago, the remains of the Crump machine were still powerful in Memphis and Shelby County. Nashville had been largely segregated when Lawson had first arrived, but it had not been a very passionate kind of segregation; the segregation he found in Memphis was much more deeply ingrained, the local political leadership far more passionately committed on the issue of race. In Memphis, the economic lifeblood had traditionally been the production, selling, and financing of cotton. As the economics were essentially plantation economics, so were its politics plantation politics; in the past Ed Crump had run the modern political version of the plantation; now his legatees were trying to hold on to the past.

Memphis was the true capital of the Mississippi Delta, and the shadow of the politics of Mississippi, East Arkansas, and West Tennessee fell heavily on the city. Its leading paper, the *Commercial Appeal,* was powerful not only in Memphis but extremely influential in the tristate area. It seemed very nervous about offending local sensibilities on race, and its reporters appeared to tread lightly in this area. Its news coverage of the black challenge on race was far less aggressive and less sympathetic than that of the *Tennessean,* and the *Commercial's* editorial page reflected considerable affection for the old order. When Jim Lawson arrived there the schools had not yet been desegregated, the restaurants had not yet been desegregated, and the parks had not yet been desegregated. At his first meeting with a number of the city's leading officials, Lawson came away if not depressed, at the very least disappointed; they were, he thought, extremely conservative men who, because they opposed violence and were not actually Klansmen or in the Citizens Councils, thought of themselves as moderates.

Within the black community he found far greater timidity than in Nashville. It was an NAACP town, he decided, which to his mind made it a conservative town, one where the existing black leadership frowned on direct action, and therefore frowned on him. There was no Memphis equivalent of Kelly Miller Smith or Fred Shuttlesworth, no modern young black minister who played a critical part in setting the new black political agenda, and who could become a rallying point for other young ministers. Of the several hundred black ministers who had churches in Memphis, only a tiny handful, he was shocked to learn, had any kind of theological training. Some of the older black ministers in Memphis and the surrounding region, men who reflected the older order, clearly did not like him and his agenda. The black leadership was exhausted by years and years of trying to coexist with the intense institutional racism all around them.

As in Shelbyville he found a great many reservations about himself among his parishioners. He was not from the South and he did not, to use the euphemism, know their ways, which meant that he did not understand the long, historic process through which they had been so thoroughly intimidated. His activist reputation from Nashville had preceded him, and to many older members of the church that was threatening of itself. Would he put them and their small but hard-won lives too much at risk? He was still young then, only thirty-three when he arrived. *The boy,* some of the older members of the church called him when he was not around. The boy, some of them had predicted, was not going to last a year in this town. He was, they added, too Northern, too educated, and too fancy. Gradually those feelings about him receded. His own respect for some of the older members of the church grew as they told him about the earlier days of their church back in the thirties, when the Klan had threatened to burn it down, and the men of the church had stood guard throughout the night, taking shifts in order to fend off the Klan.

To the degree they could in a city which was so racially divided, the Lawsons tried to lead integrated lives. The local housing was completely segregated and they had to live in a black section of town. Though there was less social ease than in Nashville, they did have a few white friends both in the clergy and in the academic world. The first of their three sons had been born just before they moved to Memphis, and Jim Lawson had taken him to parks and swimming pools in Nashville, and now in Memphis he started taking John Lawson to the small children's park right by the Memphis Zoo. The zoo was still segregated, and the most odious of signs (NO COLORED PEOPLE ALLOWED IN ZOO TODAY) still hung there, but Jim Lawson never gave it a thought. He and John went every day and John played in the tunnels and on the swings. Sometimes white people gave them both hard looks, but no one ever said or did anything. So as he had once desegregated the Nashville Symphony, he and John Lawson, just one year old, now desegregated the park by the Memphis Zoo.

John Lawson did this oblivious to his role in history. He was a little boy and each day at first he played mostly with his father, but there were often other little boys his age there, white, of course, and by instinct he would play with them. He seemed oblivious to skin color, as did, as far as his father could tell, the little white boys. Jim Lawson became fascinated by his son's adventures as a racial pioneer. Kids, he realized, longed to play with other kids and it was the most natural thing in the world. But every two or three days there would be an adult who would watch the same scene and become horrified by the racial byplay and grab the white child and take off. Sometimes it was a mother, sometimes a father, but the scene would be similar—the little white child would be dragging his feet and asking why he couldn't continue playing. Jim Lawson was intrigued by these scenes and he started to read up on the subject. He did not worry about his son: John Lawson was loved and his self-esteem would not be damaged. But what about the white children? What would run through their minds? They had clearly enjoyed playing with this other boy, his skin color had seemed to make no difference, and the little black child had done nothing harmful to them. But obviously something was wrong: Their father—or mother—was pulling them away from an encounter which had been fun. Did, Lawson wondered, the white child come away with some inner sense that the problem was him? Perhaps the white kids would think they were not good enough, or worthy enough, or strong enough to play with this black child. Damage, he became more convinced than ever before, was being done on both sides of the racial ledger.

When John Lawson was in the third grade he transferred to the Memphis State Campus Elementary School, a special public school for bright kids run by Memphis State University. There too he was once again a pioneer: If he was not the first black in the school, he was the first black child in his class, and years later he was amused by the photos of himself in those years, which almost always showed him as the lone black among a number of white children. At the Campus Elementary School he found an exceptionally welcoming atmosphere; his third-grade teacher, Miss Mary Anderson, had let him—and the other kids—know from the first day that this was going to work, that John was very bright, and she pushed him from the start to excel.

The school offered a considerably more humane environment than the city around it; early in the year when the children were playing in the school yard, one child called John a nigger, and the rest of the class immediately ganged up on the offender. Later that day Miss Anderson told an amused Dorothy Lawson that she did not think John had a great problem with self-esteem in situations like this.

"Why, what happened?" Dorothy Lawson asked.

"Well, after the incident, John came up to me and said, 'Miss Anderson, you need to teach these kids something about anthropology.' "

That night John Lawson told his parents what had happened and they told him that he had to meet with the other boy and ask why he had done it. So the next day Miss Anderson brokered a peace conference, the two boys shook hands, and in time the boy became one of John Lawson's closest friends, and his parents became friends of Jim and Dorothy Lawson. Memphis was not perfect, Jim Lawson thought, far from it, but even here he could sense some new beginnings.

53

THE YEARS 1963 AND 1964 SAW A CONSTANT ESCALATION OF THE struggle both in Alabama and Mississippi at a terribly high price to the activists. Starting with the Freedom Rides, the pace of the challenge to the Deep South had picked up steadily and the strategy by the middle of 1963 was slowly crystallizing. If the first stage had been a broad and not necessarily well-focused assault on the very nature of segregation, meant not merely to challenge it but to call the nation's attention to it, that focus was now beginning to sharpen, and there was a consensus that significant progress would only come when the activists could make a breakthrough politically—therefore they needed a voting rights act. It was all very well to call the nation's attention to the evils of segregation, it was believed, and they were doing that with significant skill. But to bring real change, they needed to have some control or at least some influence on the local political machinery, and that would only come with gaining the vote.

The very act of trying to gain even a toehold in Mississippi had demanded the highest degree of courage on the part of everyone involved. SNCC pioneers like Bevel, Moses, Lafayette, Nash, Sherrod, McDew, and Jones had reached into small Deep South towns and touched any number of ordinary blacks, who had then begun to come forward themselves. Years later Diane Nash would recall with great pleasure the tiny meetings which she and Jim Bevel had spoken at in rural Mississippi in 1962 and 1963, in the very heart of the Delta. The terror had been everywhere, the local whites audaciously riding around, displaying their weapons openly, ostentatiously circling the small rural churches where their meetings on voter registration were being held. But they had been undaunted: They had encouraged local people to come forward and become involved in voter registration, and Diane Nash remembered with particular pride one meeting in Ruleville, Sunflower County, at which both Bevel and Jim Forman had spoken and she had done much of the organizing. One of the people who had come forward was Fannie Lou Hamer, a simple woman of incandescent humanity who was to become a legend in the Movement. It had been a special night, and years later Bevel could remember what he had said. He had challenged them to vote because it was the Christian thing to do—how could they think of themselves as Christians if they did not vote, because after all, they had been created in the image of their God. He had quoted the parable of Jesus talking to the Jews; they could look out and see the clouds above and divine what the weather was going to be, but they were unable to look out and divine the equally clear moral and ethical signs around them. If they were good Christians, they would come forward and fight for the right to vote because it had been given to them by their God and could not be taken away by a bunch of white friends of Jim Eastland, the Mississippi senator who was the de facto political leader of the Delta, sitting around down at the courthouse in Indianola. Ms. Hamer had listened to Bevel talk about how they could vote out white officers of the law who mistreated them and his words made great sense to her. After all, right there in Ruleville the night policeman was the brother of J. W. Milam, one of the two men who had murdered Emmett Till. If they had helped bring Fannie Lou Hamer into the Movement, then she herself would become a powerful figure who helped bring others in, and whose voice, in 1964 during the Democratic convention, would be one of the most effective in portraying the complete racism of Mississippi's political process.

Because in the Deep South voter registration drives *had* turned out to be the same thing as direct action, gradually a certain strategy had emerged to demonstrate to the rest of the country the ways in which blacks were denied the vote in Mississippi and Alabama, and therefore to undermine the legitimacy by which the political process worked in the South. If the officials running the Democratic party in Mississippi would not register blacks, then these brave young people would create a parallel political party, the Freedom Democratic Party, and register black people themselves, and they would eventually hold a shadow election all their own. By doing so they would show that there were hundreds of thousands of blacks denied the franchise in Mississippi alone. In the process the SNCC leaders ended up going into every small town in Mississippi. That greatly escalated the risks. In June 1964, at the very start of a vast assault on Mississippi's electoral process by white and black college students from all over the country, three young activists were killed just outside the town of Philadelphia. Two of them, Andrew Goodman and Mickey Schwerner, were white, and one, James Chaney, was black. The cruelty of that murder, the fact that three young Americans had been murdered simply because they were helping other Americans in the exercise of their most basic rights, shocked the nation, and particularly the new president of the United States, Lyndon Johnson.

Although born in Texas, Johnson, in no small part because of the murderous way in which white Southerners had responded to the push for integration, was becoming, unlike his cooler predecessor, something of a genuine activist for the black cause. Part populist, Lyndon Johnson had always hated old-fashioned, overt racial prejudice; his aides would recall his visceral anger and contempt when the three young men were killed, and his determination to find their killers. The conflicts within the Democratic party were self-evident in Johnson himself. On the occasion of the passage of the 1964 Civil Rights Bill, Johnson would speak with great passion about the humiliations vested on his own black family retainers when they were forced to drive home from Washington to Texas, unable to eat at a restaurant or stay at a motel. His anger that any American citizen was deprived of the vote was elemental. But he was also a Southerner and a Democrat, and the contradictions between what he thought was right morally and what was good for his party were obvious and painful for him.

There had always been a grim awareness that the course that the SNCC people were following would be effective only in the cost of blood, that only by taking the gravest of risks and unveiling the violence just beneath the surface would the nation know and care; now that price had been paid. Not surprisingly, the nation seemed able to identify with the death of three young people, two of them white college students, more readily than it could with the death of some otherwise faceless older black person, like Herbert Lee in southwest Mississippi. That the additional publicity and national rage resulted from the fact that two of the three victims were young, white college students rather than anonymous elderly black residents, however, was one more bitter pill for many of the young SNCC activists.

The murders were a terrible, shameful national moment, but they played an important role in moving the process ahead one more critical notch. Lyndon Johnson, able to use the murder of Kennedy as an added lever, was already pushing ahead on what would become the Civil Rights Bill of 1964; within a month of the murder of the three young men in Mississippi (and a month before their bodies were found), Johnson would sign that bill into law.

In addition there was one additional benefit from the mounting pressure that these young people were applying to the federal government. As they squeezed the Justice Department and the White House, so the president in turn began to squeeze J. Edgar Hoover. That meant Hoover, despite his own hatred of King and most of the Movement people, was slowly beginning to move the FBI into a more activist role in the Deep South. To some degree he was responding to a constant bombardment of criticism from people in the civil rights division of the Justice Department, in part he sensed something of a change in Congress itself, and most certainly he understood the commitment the new president himself now wanted in this area. In the past the FBI had always been viewed as being in some kind of partnership with the local Southern lawmen, and its agents. Knowing that violence was going to be inflicted on demonstrators, its agents had on occasion sat back and watched the violence take place. But now that alliance of federal and local good old boys was about to break down. On July 10, 1964, a week after the Civil Rights Bill was signed, J. Edgar Hoover, his top aides, and a handful of trusted reporters flew to Jackson, Mississippi, for the dedication of a new FBI office. He did this at the specific suggestion (some might think of it as an order) of the president of the United States, who wanted to give as clear a message as he could to lawmen in the South: They themselves were now at risk if they were either accomplices or fellow travelers when violence was inflicted on black people and civil rights workers.

Hoover's political ties to the Southern segregationist leaders in Congress had been very close in the past. They had always been the core of his support, had always speeded his wondrously generous budgets through Congress, and it was to them that he had always fed his choicest bits of gossip, whether about people in the Movement like King or the Kennedys themselves. But Hoover accepted the mission to Jackson because, whatever else he might be, he was a superb bureaucrat, and it was clearly part of a larger, unspoken pact with Johnson. It came at a moment when liberal pressures to get rid of him had been mounting steadily, in no small part because of the growing power of the Movement itself and because the FBI had done so little to help these new activists. If anything, the rapidly changing pace of this new social revolution had underscored the fact that Hoover was increasingly out of touch with the American political center, and was becoming, for the first time in his life, something of a political liability. There had been increased talk when Johnson had assumed the presidency that he might get rid of Hoover, and reports of his imminent departure had leaked out of the White House press office on several occasions. Johnson in the end had decided to keep him on. ("Well, it's probably better to have him inside the tent pissing out, then outside pissing in," he said in one memorable aside.[1]) But there was a price to this extended tenure: Like it or not, Hoover was being told by Johnson to throw the resources of the FBI against the Klan and the white resistance in the South, or find that he was no longer the head of the Bureau. He could come aboard on the issue of race, or he could get out. That was the unspoken deal. "That day," reminisced veteran civil rights reporter Karl Fleming, who covered Hoover at the groundbreaking ceremony in Jackson, "was one of the most unhappy in J. Edgar Hoover's life, and one of the happiest in the life of Mississippi."[2]

If it was not the most publicized event of 1964, it was nonetheless one of the most important, and it completed the slow commitment of the executive branch of the federal government to the side of the activists, a process which had begun with the last-minute, reluctant protection offered the Freedom Riders only three years earlier. The last holdout had finally come over; from then on the Bureau, which had spent so much of its energy pursuing Martin Luther King and his allies and which had in the past been in bed with local white lawmen (and thereby often the Klan and the Citizens Councils), was going to use the same energy against the Ku Klux Klan.

By the end of 1964 the leaders of the Movement realized that they had made immense progress, but they still needed one crucial breakthrough. The Civil Rights Bill of 1964 had been a major step forward. But it was more of a public accommodations act than anything else, and it did not help them where they most needed help, in opening up the black political franchise in the Deep South. They were becoming both exhausted and embittered by the ability of Southern officials to nickel-and-dime them, making it appear that they would need a lawsuit for every black who wanted to vote in every small town in the South.

In November 1964, just after he had returned from Norway, where he had received the Nobel prize, Martin Luther King met with Lyndon Johnson and told the president that what they wanted now was a strong voting rights act. But Johnson shook his head. He had just helped pass the Civil Rights Act, he said, and that had been a considerable victory, something he had achieved despite the resistance of powerful conservatives in Congress. But a voting rights act, he said, could not be done. Not now, anyway. The country wasn't ready. The votes weren't there in Congress. It was too much of a reach. He wanted to do it, but he needed the votes of the Southern congressmen for the Great Society.[3] But it was a warm meeting (King had arrived with his wife and his parents), and Johnson assured him of his essential support. In fact, as the meeting was breaking up, the president had in effect encouraged the nation's top demonstrator to continue his work in creating the political conditions for additional legislation. He pulled King toward him, gave him a Johnsonian body squeeze, and then said, "Now, Dr. King, you go out there and make it possible for me to do the right thing."[4]

When King left Johnson he was momentarily disappointed, but then he talked to friends and told them that they would push ahead for the voting rights bill themselves. "We'll write it for them," he said, "and we'll do it in Selma."[5] He meant that they would escalate the drive in the South, and that in turn would help force Johnson's hand. There was a certain inevitability to this moment as they began to zero in on Selma. Early on, almost four years earlier when the Freedom Rides had first taken them into the Deep South, there had been no single, detailed strategy, but nonetheless they had all been building toward a showpiece battle in a showplace city on a defining issue for some time. No one, when they were just beginning to coalesce, had listed a series of different cities and different issues which they would challenge city by city, year by year, or suggested that in about four years they would end up concentrating on voters rights and do it in Selma, Alabama. But that was the way it had worked out. In some ways the Movement had been born with the *Brown* decision, and certainly there were all kinds of critical increments along the way—the violence of the Emmett Till murder, the real beginnings of nonviolent protest with the Montgomery bus boycott, and then in the past four years, the increasing pace of the assault on the Deep South. The path had not always been straight, their challenge not always massive or successful. Sometimes they had faltered. Sometimes the price of what they were doing staggered even those who were the architects of the struggle, as in September 1963 on a Sunday morning when white segregationists, believed to be Klansmen, had exploded a bomb in Birmingham's Sixteenth Street Baptist Church, killing four young black girls. Sometimes when there had been a massive campaign in one place, the spotlight had suddenly and involuntarily shifted elsewhere, to focus, for example, on the bittersweet attempt to register one black student at the University of Mississippi. That alone, in the fall of 1962, had required some three thousand federal troops. Sometimes it had been a massive assault on a major bastion of segregation, like the attempt to challenge the customs (and the soul) of a dangerous, completely segregated city like Birmingham in 1963. Sometimes they had been stalemated, and their strategy, for a variety of reasons, had failed, as in Albany, Georgia. Some of the SCLC leaders, like Andy Young and Jim Bevel, had opposed going into St. Augustine, Florida, the Movement stop which had followed Birmingham. Bevel in particular had wanted to keep the focus on Alabama, and he had already wanted to focus it on the issue of voting rights. But for all the division and debate within, some of it quite heated, and some of it stunningly personal, the Movement had not faltered. Its leadership's greatest achievement was in portraying to ordinary Americans the divided soul of the country. But now, as they began to hone in on Selma, the very forces that made it so attractive as a showpiece battle also guaranteed that the struggle would be a bitter one.

By the fall of 1964, Selma had become more of a fortress than a small city: It was manned by angry, dedicated, well-armed segregationists determined to hold on to the past, even as a growing army of shrewd, talented, battle-hardened black activists began to circle it. If

Bernard Lafayette had made considerable progress in creating the base of a movement in Selma a year and a half earlier, then in the intervening months the local forces had carefully marshalled the forces of resistance. Here the lines were drawn with finality. Some four years earlier, when a comparable move to register voters in McComb, Mississippi, had been swiftly beaten back, John Doar, the point man for the Justice Department, had decided that it was too early for a decisive battle, what he eventually would call a Gettysburg, where the forces of the civil rights movement would take on the forces of segregation. Neither the activists nor the federal government, he had believed earlier, was prepared to deal with the entrenched power of the white segregationists gathered against them. But now, a relatively short period later, all that had changed, he believed. To the outside observer there were at least two armies gathering at Selma, the forces of the integrationists, and the forces of reaction, and potentially a third, the forces of the media. To Doar, who more than anyone else in the federal government had worked the Deep South on voter registration cases, the army of the integrationists was actually broken up into three separate groups, which were all working for the same thing: the SCLC, led by King, the SNCC kids, and the field workers from the civil rights division of the Justice Department, who for several years had been carefully documenting the exclusion of black voters in this region.

Each of these three forces had been operating both separately and yet, in some larger way, in partnership with the others over the previous five years, Doar thought. Now their joint efforts had brought them together for the showdown in a city which he viewed as perfect in every respect for this final push. It was a larger town than most in what was a predominantly rural area, and it was in Alabama, not Mississippi, which was better because the Mississippi electoral injustices and violations, based as they were on interpretation of different laws, were harder to calibrate, whereas the Alabama voting requirements were more narrowly drawn. There was no doubt that the Selma officials in some way were making their decisions based on race, and though thousands of Alabama voting application forms, some approved, some disapproved, had already been sent to the FBI, the Bureau people had claimed that they did not have the manpower to go through them, and to decide whether or not race was a cause. But in much of the Black Belt, the Justice Department field people had discovered, the argument being used against the potential black voters was that they consistently filled out their applications improperly; they seemed unable to sign their names at the requisite number of places on the applications. At that point, a young lawyer in the civil rights division named Bud Sather, after going through literally thousands of applications on microfilm, broke the code of how it was done. On all the ballots which were filled out correctly, he noticed, there was a tiny mark—in truth often nothing but a dot made by a pencil—at the different points where the voter was required to sign. On almost all the others, there was no pencil mark, and the applicant had failed to sign there, and had been rejected. That meant, he was sure, the registrars were aiding white voters on how to fill out the applications (often, he discovered, writing in answers for them in a handwriting much better and more legible than that of the applicant) and yet, just as obviously, remaining silent when blacks filled out their applications. After Sather discovered the pencil dots, it was not hard to prove that in every instance the people who received the pencil-dot guidance were white and the people who did not and therefore did not know where to sign were black. It was, thought Doar, a thrilling breakthrough and it meant they were closing in on the legal basis of their case. Everything was beginning to knit tighter and tighter in Selma.[6]

Equally important, as these two forces gathered for their confrontation in Selma, the entire nation was finally watching at home on network television. All the events of the last five years, since the moment when the bus carrying the first Freedom Riders had been set on fire in Anniston, had led to this moment. Certainly the leaders of the Movement had understood from the start the benefits which accrued to them because of the power of this new instrument, even if their adversaries, the white sheriffs, who reflected the political order of another era, did not. Network television had dramatically affected not merely the pace but the very nature of social change in America. This was not, as it was beamed into millions of American homes, a mere political struggle; it was nothing less than a continuing morality play. Small-town sheriffs might still use physical force to crush their opponents now, and the next morning they might still be congratulated by their peers at the local café for, by God, being man enough to stand up for what was right, but now, as their actions were caught on film, the rest of the nation had a very different idea of what was right, and what God's judgment on all of this might be. The rest of the nation was increasingly repelled by the course of these events.

The timing of the leaders in the Movement had been exceptional. In the beginning, the rise of the Movement had coincided with the country's being wired for national television. But by the early sixties that link was becoming ever more intense and more intimate. In the fall of 1963 the two dominant national news shows—the *CBS Evening News* with Walter Cronkite, and the Huntley-Brinkley show on NBC—had doubled in length, from fifteen to thirty minutes, a change of considerable import for what was happening in the Movement. With the doubling of the size of the shows, there was an ever greater need for film, which meant an ever greater need for confrontation, which the SCLC leadership was ready and eager to provide. And with the Vietnam War still to enter the American consciousness, the dominating national story—the story which all ambitious and talented reporters wanted to cover, which day in and day out provided the most consistently exciting film clips—was that of the South. In addition, by the mid-sixties, color television was coming into more and more homes, giving the events even greater force.

The scenes relayed from the Deep South into ordinary American homes each night had become among the most memorable and shocking of the era; it was as if millions of Americans could sit home and watch—often in the presence of their children—a struggle to attain the basic rights of democratic citizenship in some strange, primitive foreign land. Only, the foreign land was the American South. There was a cumulative effect to this coverage, and it had been building for several years: The sight of police dogs and fire hoses turned on black demonstrators in Birmingham had moved the conscience of the nation. Back in June 1963, when Martin Luther King had visited John Kennedy in the White House, the president had suggested with a touch of irony that King ought to thank Bull Connor for his help. There had been a stunned silence for a moment, and then Kennedy had added, "After all, he's done more for civil rights than any of us."[7] By early 1965, there was an almost hypnotic effect to the coverage of the South. By the time the two forces were ready to do battle in Selma, the entire nation was not just watching the struggle, it was, because of the miraculous nature of this new instrument, slowly becoming engaged in the struggle.

In Selma, in the past two years, as the blacks had felt increasingly emboldened to challenge voting restrictions, the white backlash had intensified. It was as if the local white leadership had decided that Selma should be the symbol of the entire South's resistance. If they could hold the line here, they seemed to be saying, then others could and should hold the line elsewhere. Shortly after the passage of the Civil Rights Bill of 1964, a number of local blacks had tried to go to a Selma movie theater and sit in the main section. Some of them had been attacked by local whites. The police offered them no protection. At virtually the same time several others had tried to eat in a downtown Selma restaurant and had been arrested. A few days later, after John Lewis led a group of about fifty would-be voters to the courthouse in order to register them, they were met by Jim Clark, who used electric cattle prods on them and then arrested them.

Clearly, the first law of physics seemed to apply to politics as well: For every action, there was an equal reaction. Because there had been some progress on the part of Bernard Lafayette and his early group in organizing a stronger group of protesters, the local white leadership had pushed back even harder. James Hare, the local circuit judge, and a central figure in the local white resistance, had issued an injunction, one of marginal constitutionality, against any more demonstrations. Under the terms of his writ, if two blacks stood on the steps of a church together, they could be arrested. That was Selma as 1964 ended.

The Movement leadership had found the right battleground to demonstrate the need for a voting rights bill. In addition to being one of the worst areas in the Deep South, Selma was relatively convenient to Montgomery, about an hour away, which meant that the network television reporters could always get their daily stories out on time.[8] But what was even more attractive about Selma and Dallas County was the compelling figure of Sheriff Jim Clark; if Bull Connor had helped them move the conscience of the nation in Birmingham in 1963, then in Selma there was Jim Clark ready to play the most important of all roles in this next drama, that of the villain.

There was a certain irony to Jim Clark's emergence as the villainous poster boy of Selma and the Deep South. He was not from Dallas County originally, but had come there to raise cattle and had failed in that calling. When the previous sheriff of Dallas County had died suddenly, Governor Jim Folsom, a man who on the Richter scale of Alabama politics was considered quite liberal on race, and who was distantly related to Clark, had appointed him sheriff. That had angered many local residents—a sheriff was not supposed to be an outsider. Then when the race for the office was finally held, Clark was pitted against a man who was to be his longtime rival in Dallas County, Wilson Baker. Both of course were segregationists—every man running for every sheriff's office in Alabama was a segregationist, pledged above all else to upholding what was called the Southern way of life. Though in the next few years Baker was to gain a reputation as by far the more moderate of the two, a civilized man who wanted to limit violence and deal with King and his people, in the beginning he was considered the more vocal segregationist. During their campaign Baker had visited a Klan meeting, where a photograph had been taken of him and published in the local paper. Though there were not a lot of Catholic, Jewish, and black voters in Dallas County there were enough to make a difference in a close primary and that was considered the difference in the race; Jim Clark, seemingly the more moderate candidate, had won the election.[9] It was a race not unlike that first governor's race between George Wallace and John Patterson, in which Wallace was deemed the more moderate of the two candidates, something Wallace prophetically vowed would never happen again. Almost from the moment Clark took office, the pressure against Alabama to integrate different institutions grew, and Clark, like almost every elected official, began to define himself first and foremost as a man who would hold the line on race. More, he came to like and believe in the role. It created a considerable amount of press attention, and this otherwise quite ordinary failed man began to like the limelight and his new role as defender of the faith. It was, at least at first, with him, people who knew him thought, as much about ego as it was about political ideology.[10] He liked being the law, and he liked even more being the center of media attention. It was better than being a failed cattleman. Clark's own vision of his political future was becoming grander by the day: Being sheriff of Dallas County was hardly enough. He had started to entertain thoughts of running for governor when George Wallace's term was up, since Wallace could not succeed himself.

He intended to make his statewide reputation by holding back Martin Luther King and his advancing army. Soon it appeared that he had an irresistible impulse to lash out at any black man or woman who tried to stand up to him and to change the segregated order. In other Southern towns and cities, all kinds of public officials, who felt much the same way about the new black leadership, had learned, however reluctantly and grudgingly, to restrain themselves, to mouth semi-moderate platitudes in these days of ever more intense journalistic scrutiny. They had learned, as one of them said, that "every nigger protester seemed to come equipped with a cameraman from the Nigger Broadcasting Company (NBC), The Communist Broadcasting System (CBS) or the Asshole Broadcasting Company (ABC)."[11] They had learned to hold the line but to try and muzzle their own hatred.

That was not true of Jim Clark; he liked what he was doing and he saw political profit in it. He had become a stereotype of the Southern sheriff of the past, mean and angry and, most important of all for King and the SCLC, absolutely without restraint; he wore his hatred and his rage on his sleeve. Even the reporters who covered the civil rights movement over a long period thought Clark was unusually harsh, a man who seemed to reveal far more hatred than the somewhat more sophisticated Bull Connor. He had the almost unique ability to make old-time prejudice visible to an entire nation. He did not understand that he was fighting a war in which there could be no victories, that it was at best a prolonged, potentially exhausting delaying action, and that the less that he and his allies were in the public eye and the less they said the better.

Laurie Pritchett, the police chief of Albany, Georgia, infinitely more subtle in his dealings with protesters, wary of any billy club hitting a black head when a reporter or photographer was around, had been a problem for those in the Movement. Jim Clark, by contrast, was perfect. With his greater ambition had come a new military look; he sometimes wore a helmet liner, which, as the mayor of Selma noted, recalled visions of George Patton, although John Nixon, then a Justice Department field officer, thought he looked more like a second-tier Latin American dictator. Then there was a jacket patterned after the one Dwight Eisenhower had worn in World War II. Every move of his seemed to bear the mark of the bully. He once sought out Karl

Fleming of *Newsweek,* who had recently written a piece about him strongly implying that Clark was a racist. The sheriff had shoved a shotgun in Fleming's belly and threatened to kill him. He was not angry, it turned out, with Fleming's suggestion of racism, which he appeared not to mind at all, but instead that the reporter had quoted the sheriff as using the word *git* for *get.* "I ain't never said *git,*" he told him, jabbing away with the shotgun.[12] It was, thought Bernard Lafayette, who had tangled with Clark often, as if he were trying to play John Wayne in a movie where the Duke was a white segregationist sworn to uphold the good America and the black protesters were the bad guys trying to tear it down. His sense of casting, Lafayette thought, might be somewhat out of date.

Clark, aided and abetted by James Hare, the local judge, who really ran the town, regarded the Movement as a personal affront—and seemed to take confirmation of his own existence from his ability to intimidate, berate, and if need be, physically abuse the demonstrators. It had become for him nothing less than a compulsion or, perhaps even more accurately, an addiction. It defined not just his status but his integrity. To do less, to stand less tall in the face of this affront was to be less of a man. He was not a man who understood that what Southern sheriffs had done in the past—taken justice into their own hands whenever they wanted, as brutally as they wanted—had been done in an age when there were no national witnesses around, and that it could not be so readily done in this new age because men like King had learned to bring their witnesses with them, not just witnesses from the Justice Department but, perhaps even more important, witnesses from the national media, including television cameramen. Jim Clark, as the journalist Karl Fleming noted, was not very good at understanding the degree to which technology had clamped a new ceiling on the ability of Southern lawmen to brutalize blacks.[13]

In the white councils of Selma there was a constant struggle between the two separate segregationist camps. On one side were Hare and Clark; the other was the more cautious and less provocative group led by Joseph Smitherman, the mayor, newly elected because younger people in the business establishment now believed that Clark was out of control, and Wilson Baker, Smitherman's choice for public safety director (or de facto police chief). Baker, once considered more of a committed segregationist than Clark, had emerged now as smarter and shrewder than his old rival and less emotionally involved in the struggle. He wanted to minimize any move toward integration but wanted to resist in a cool, understated fashion with as few photographs in the Northern papers as possible, a kind of Laurie Pritchett of Selma. "I'm not for integration," Baker liked to say, "but I can understand what they're doing and why—hell, if I were a nigger I'd be right out there with them."[14]

It was the SCLC-SNCC bet that Smitherman and Baker would not be able to restrain Jim Clark. Their entire operation in Selma was premised on their ability to provoke Clark; to that end they had come up with a detailed plan for an ever-escalating confrontation, which the rest of the nation would be able to watch in its living rooms. As King and his aides prepared for the assault on Selma, he had a surprisingly complete plan already on hand. The plan had its roots in a proposal that Diane Nash and James Bevel had come up with in the fall of 1963, after they heard of the bombs which had killed four young black girls in a Birmingham church one Sunday morning. They had received the news while working in a voter registration project in Edenton, North Carolina. Though by that time both Bevel and Nash thought of themselves as relatively immune to the violence which the Movement had touched off in the Deep South, this was particularly chilling, perhaps because their own daughter was one year old at the time. Whatever else, Diane had thought, children in a church on a Sunday morning should be spared—there ought to be immunity for them. The couple had sat all afternoon trying to figure out what the right response was. For the first time, their own faith in nonviolence wavered. Their pain that these innocent children had been murdered was terrible; even worse was their knowledge that the bombing had been in some way provoked by the coming of the Movement to Birmingham, and that therefore part of the responsibility was, however just their larger cause, theirs. There was no escaping that, Nash thought: Because they had helped bring the Movement and thus danger to Birmingham, four little girls were dead, and four families had been torn asunder. That meant, she believed, that she could not just walk away from what had happened. They pondered the possibility of violent retaliation: Both of them were sure that with the right contacts, they could find out who had done the bombing—these things, they believed, were not great secrets in certain white communities, particularly if enough money were offered around. So that was response number one, find out who did it, and make sure that they were taken out. To their surprise they both thought a long time about the viability of following that course. The other response was to create a structure which would guarantee that something like this never happened again, a new political structure in Alabama in which blacks would become politically empowered, and violent whites would have to fear the local police force for the first time. In the end the compelling question for her was, what did they owe their God at this moment? And so she found herself promising God that she would try to change Alabama, so that something like this would never happen again. With that, they sat down and drew up a plan for a massive campaign aimed at changing the political face of Alabama, so that blacks would have a chance to vote for the governor, for the legislature, and above all for sheriffs and mayors. They intended, if need be, to do nothing less than close down the state. Bevel and Nash decided that they wanted the SCLC to move on this immediately, and since Bevel was already committed to the Edenton project, she had gone to Atlanta to meet with Martin Luther King. If he did not accept their proposal, she thought, they could at least provoke an SCLC meeting where the leadership would be forced to take some other course of action.

Martin Luther King had not seemed very enthusiastic about their plan at first. He was polite and kind, as he always was with her, but it was obvious from the moment that she started talking that he thought it was far-fetched and unrealistic. He seemed to be saying, Get real, Diane,[15] she remembered. He told her he was planning to see President Kennedy, to go over with him what the president thought they should do. This did not impress her, she did not have much faith in the federal government, and she suggested that they have an SCLC meeting so that he could bring Kennedy the results of that meeting. But that wasn't what he wanted either. Rejected by King, Bevel and Nash decided that Bevel would go to rural Alabama and start the program himself. He might be in the strict sense defying SCLC orders by going into Alabama without permission, but the SCLC was a loosely organized institution, everyone had considerable freedom, and if they did not fire him, then he was free to start working on voters rights there.

That was what he did. No one fired him. The greater sacrifice at first, she thought, was in some ways hers. There she was, living on the outskirts of Atlanta, with little money and a toddler who was a year old and another child on the way, and she had given Bevel their family car so he could travel in Alabama while she tried to take care of and feed her family while riding public buses. Soon, however, they were both living in a small apartment in Birmingham. Bevel was beginning to work on voter registration there and in smaller towns, in the beginning of what he saw as a voter-consciousness, God-consciousness campaign. They were creating a network of people in these different towns, recruiting staff, and starting voter education programs.

THE STRUGGLE IN ALABAMA HAD ESCALATED IN THE LATE FALL OF 1963 with each side assaulting the other with varying injunctions. Thanks to the rulings by a conservative federal district judge, Daniel Thomas, a man responsible for the southern district of Alabama, who seemed openly hostile to any attempt to expand black franchise, the legal struggle against segregation had been momentarily neutralized and Judge Hare's injunction, dubious though it was, momentarily upheld. "The litigation method of correction," noted John Doar, the Justice Department's top man in the field, "has been tried harder here than anywhere in the South."[16] That some kind of terrible and perhaps bloody confrontation lay ahead was obvious now that King and the SCLC had singled out Selma for their big push. The people of Selma were, as the mayor, Joseph Smitherman, later realized, almost pitifully ill prepared for the sheer force of the Movement about to descend on them. It was at the high-water mark of its dynamism, aided by its ability to enlist the innate sympathy of journalists on questions which seemed so elemental to a free society. How pathetically ill matched, how far behind the curve the people of Selma were in this confrontation is suggested by this story. Knowing that King's people were soon to arrive, Smitherman had called in a handful of local black leaders and had suggested the following scenario. They would call on him and demand that he pave some streets in the black section of town, which, unlike those in the white section, were unpaved. He would reject their demand. Much would be written about his refusal. Then, under the mounting pressure from them and other black leaders, he would reverse himself and give in. That would give them the victory which would keep King from needing to come to town.[17]

Wilson Baker, fearing the consequences of the coming confrontation, that Clark could not be controlled or restrained, had flown to Washington in the late fall of 1964 to meet with Burke Marshall at the Justice Department. There he had asked Marshall to plead with King and the other black leaders for restraint—to go elsewhere, or to delay their assault. Marshall had called King on the phone while Baker was in his office, talked to him for about twenty minutes, and then told Baker that King and the SCLC had too much invested in Selma to back off at that moment.[18]

Their campaign was intricately scheduled. In mid-December 1964, a group of local black leaders formally invited Martin Luther King and the SCLC to come to Selma and start a major voter registration drive. On January 2, 1965, on schedule, Martin Luther King had arrived for the first time and had spoken at the Brown Chapel of the AME Church. There he had said that if he and his colleagues could not reach Governor George Wallace and the Alabama legislature to rectify this injustice of the ballot, "then we will seek to arouse the federal government by marching by the thousands to the places of registration. . . ." Both armies were in place, and were beginning to skirmish.

In the curious political structure of Selma, the face which most of America saw on television was that of Jim Clark, but the controlling figure, the man who really ran the town, and who ran Clark, was the local circuit judge, James Hare, a man superior to Clark by birth, by social position, by law, and by the general assumption of the town's hierarchy. It was presumed within the town that Jim Clark did no damage that James Hare, an Episcopalian and a planter, did not want done, and that Clark would go no farther than Hare wanted him to go at all times in handling blacks. "Judge Hare," the local black lawyer James Chestnut once noted, "was a sort of 1960s version of the plantation owner. Jim Clark was his overseer, the lower class white man who ran the fields and controlled the slaves."[19]

Hare was driven by his own obsessive racial passions. His feelings, some local blacks like Chestnut thought, were not that of true hatred, because in his own way, reflecting the feudal era just passing, Hare thought he liked black people, as long as they stayed in their place. Hare thought of himself as an intellectual and boasted that he was an authority on Africa, on black America, and, of course, on the anthropology of race. His beliefs were, to him, highly intellectual, based on wide readings, though largely of books carefully selected because the writers agreed with him. Many were in fact books by men long since repudiated in their fields.

Hare fancied himself an expert on the tribes of Africa, which ones were industrious and intelligent, and which ones were not, and he liked to hold forth, particularly in front of Northern reporters and Justice Department officials, on his views, claiming that he could look at local black people and tell by their physical characteristics from which tribe they were descended. The problem with Dallas County, he liked to say, was that the shipments containing most of their slaves had come from two of the most backward tribes of Africa. "Our problem," he liked to say, "was that we just got a bad boatload of slaves." Within Justice Department circles, as the young aide John Nixon noted, this was known as "the bad boatload theory of segregation."[20] There was no real hope for these people, Hare would say. "You will not be able to domesticate them any more than you can get a zebra to pull a plow, or an Apache to pick cotton."[21]

There was more than a little touch of madness to him, those who dealt with him thought, as if he were some figure who had stumbled out of the pages of William Faulkner into a modern, high-voltage racial conflict. He once held forth to John Nixon on the sad plight of blacks who had left the South. He himself, he said, had visited his brother, who was a doctor up north, and his brother had brought by a black man who was a doctor. A fine, intelligent person, Hare said; why, if he had stayed in the South, he might have risen very high in the plantation order, might have been given a position right under the overseer, could have been someone *important.*

If there was a new and more modern young business group beginning to come to the fore in Selma and anxious to make some kind of deal with the SCLC and at least minimize potential violence, Hare wanted no part of it. He saw himself as a man representing his ancestors, holding the line against these intruders.

Clark was his man. On occasion he was willing to humiliate the sheriff in front of others, just to let everyone knew who was boss.

"You have to draw that man a picture," he would sometimes say of Clark. For the new mayor, Joe Smitherman, who was not part of the old, Hare-controlled group, he had little but contempt. Smitherman was a poor white, a former washing-machine salesman, a man who had never been to college. "That man has never seen the inside of a university, and wouldn't know what to do if you took him to one," Hare said.[22]

JOHN LEWIS REMEMBERED HIS FIRST ENCOUNTER WITH JIM CLARK DURing the stepped-up 1965 offensive. It came on January 18, 1965. Representatives of the SCLC and SNCC had taken turns leading the people who wanted to register to the courthouse, doing it on the first and third Mondays of each month, which were the days specified for registration. On that day it had been Lewis's turn to lead. There were about one hundred people there, mostly elderly black women and a few elderly black men. And there was Jim Clark, the man who had come at them with cattle prods just a few months earlier. He was a man, thought John Lewis, who tried to make himself as menacing as possible. There was the button which said NEVER in huge letters which he always wore on his jacket. Sometimes he wore a business suit, and sometimes his uniform, the most dandied-up uniform that Lewis and the others had ever seen, all braid and frills.

Clark loved to carry his gun and his nightstick, and was very good at signaling how badly he wanted to use both of them. His look even by the standards of Deep South sheriffs was hard and mean. "It was primarily designed," John Lewis once said, "to show you that if you were black you were subhuman, and therefore you ought to fear him, and that there were no restraints on him because he was the law. Therefore what he did was legal no matter what it was, and what you did was illegal no matter what it was. It was as if he was his own portable Constitution." At first, Lewis had thought, it was the black people of Selma who were afraid of him; then gradually he came to realize it was all the people of Selma, whites as well as blacks, who feared Jim Clark.

On January 18, the day on which John Lewis led the march, Jim Clark wore a gun and carried both a nightstick and an electric cattle prod. Rarely had John Lewis seen a man, even a Southern sheriff, handle a weapon so lovingly as Clark handled the cattle prod. "John Lewis," he called out in his loudest voice, "you're an outside agitator, and that's the lowest form of humanity there is." John Lewis was not quite twenty-five but he was not afraid of Jim Clark and all his braid, all his weapons, and he answered, "Sheriff, I may be an agitator, but I'm not an outside agitator. I grew up only ninety miles from here, and we're going to stay here until these people can vote."

Then Jim Clark moved to his specialty, the intimidation of poor blacks. He walked the line of would-be voters, pointing his nightstick at each of them. "I know you . . . what are you doing here? You know you have no business being here." It was, Lewis thought, as if he was saying to each of them that he knew everything about them—their names, where they lived, who they worked for—and that he was going to get them. His inspection of Lewis's troops finished, he walked back down the line, looked directly at Lewis, and said, "You're all under arrest."

On a subsequent occasion, Lewis brought his people to the courthouse, only to find their way blocked by Clark. The sheriff ordered them to go back, but Lewis stood up to him. The courthouse, Lewis said, was a public place and they had a right to go inside. "We will not be turned around," he said.

"Did you hear what I said?" Clark asked. "Turn around and go back." He seemed closer to an explosion than ever, some people thought, after Lewis's defiance.

"Did you hear what *I* said?" Lewis answered. "We are *not* going back." And he stood his ground. Finally Clark, in some irritation, backed down and told them to go on in. Watching the scene, James Chestnut was amazed: the mighty Jim Clark *backing down* in front of this young boy? He had been sure that Clark was going to beat John Lewis on that day, and yet he had backed down. Chestnut had thought to himself, he later wrote, that it was a moment when his eyes had opened. "To hell with [Judge] Hare. . . . I have spied your nakedness. All my life I believed that white people could and would draw the lines whenever and wherever it wanted." Now for the first time he was not so sure. A revolution was taking place in the minds of the local people.[23]

The SCLC people believed, as January passed, that the drive was going well, if slightly behind schedule. The entire black community now seemed to be committed to the drive. In late January, 105 black schoolteachers marched to the courthouse to protest voting registration procedures. That was an important benchmark—it meant that some of the most vulnerable people in the city were willing to risk their jobs for the cause, and it also meant that the protesters had control of the schools; not surprisingly, the following week there were mass marches on the courthouse by schoolchildren and then by other local groups long intimidated by Clark in the past. Most critically, Clark was playing his role just as they had expected. It was time, they decided, to up the ante slightly, to bring Dr. King in and have him be arrested, albeit preferably by the saner and significantly less brutal Wilson Baker rather than Jim Clark. On February 1, Martin Luther King and Ralph Abernathy were arrested almost as if by script by Baker. Both went to jail and for a time stayed there. Four days later a full-page ad ran in *The New York Times,* headlined in giant type: A Letter from MARTIN LUTHER KING from a Selma, Alabama jail. In giant capital letters it said: THIS IS SELMA, ALABAMA. THERE ARE MORE NEGROES IN JAIL WITH ME THAN THERE ARE ON THE VOTING ROLLS. Clearly the pace was quickening every day.

54

JAMES LUTHER BEVEL THOUGHT THERE WAS SOMETHING ALMOST IRRE-
sistible about Selma. To Bevel Selma was ideal because it was so
authentic. In other cities, the white people knew how to hide their
ways, and their feelings, but in Selma it was all so naked. He had come
there first in 1963, when Bernard Lafayette had invited him, and had
returned periodically. In 1964 he had spent a good deal of time working in rural Alabama and Selma while lobbying his superiors in the
SCLC, particularly Martin Luther King, to make a major effort in the
state.

The local white officials of Selma hated Bevel, who by then was on
the staff of the SCLC. Somehow he seemed to draw a special kind of
venom from them. It was as if his manner made it more personal, a
look he had about him which somehow dared them to act against him.
Sometimes in those days, because as an ex-farmboy he was accustomed to an early start, he would get up just as dawn was breaking and
ride a bicycle around town, a lonely black figure, yarmulke as ever on
his head, riding down the streets of the most explosive small city in
America, doing this as part of his own ritual of morning meditation.
To the Selma authorities it was both infuriating and somewhat frightening, his disdain for their power, and what they perceived as the
hard, unflinching look on his face. What could be more arrogant, or,
as they said in those days, uppity?

Bernard Lafayette would periodically get a tip from a local black
who worked at the jail that they were going to try and arrest Reverend
Bevels, as they called him, and since Bevel, in addition to his bike riding, was wont to drive around the area without a valid driver's license,
Lafayette, who often served as Bevel's ambassador to the rest of the
world, and the rest of the world's ambassador to Bevel, would try and

convince his friend to let someone else do the driving. That, of course, enraged Bevel, who would say that he was not going to let these white people tell him what he could and could not do, and Lafayette would argue that there was a difference between a local law stopping black people from registering to vote and a local law which insisted on a valid driver's license for all people, black or white.

By the end of 1964, as the lines were ever more sharply drawn in Selma, Andy Young and some of the other SCLC people, on the advice of the Justice Department, momentarily negotiated what was called an appearance book, which verified that the blacks who had come to the courthouse had indeed showed up, and would be processed in the order in which they had arrived. It was, Bevel thought, a compromise and a bad one at that. To him and many of the other people working in the field in Selma, it diluted the force of the Movement, which was becoming stronger all the time. On February 8, Bevel took about fifty demonstrators into town and refused to have anything to do with the appearance book. He was showing that they would continue to force the issue. They wanted the registrar's office open all the time, nothing less. He wanted maximum confrontation.

As Bevel and his group were leaving the courthouse on that February day, they ran into Jim Clark. Clark hated Bevel, and on this morning he blew it. He started poking Bevel in the stomach with his billy club. "You're making a mockery out of justice," he shouted at Bevel. Bevel tried to respond by talking about his constitutional right to come there, and Clark, not pleased by a hated black preacher explaining the Constitution of the United States to him, became angrier, jabbing him again and again. Then at Clark's order, about five of his deputies grabbed Bevel and pulled him from the others and started beating him. They took him to jail, beating him all the way. On the way to jail Bevel moved in and out of consciousness. Before he passed out, he had a vague memory of being in an elevator on his way to jail with about five burly deputies leaning into him and whacking him with their nightsticks, hitting him as hard as they could. His only protection was the fact that there were so many of them that they could not get the full swings they wanted.

Before he got to his cell he passed out a second time. When he regained consciousness he found himself alone in a cell, soaking wet—they had sprayed him with cold water, and then they had opened the windows wide so that he would freeze. At the very least pneumonia would set in. He was not sure whether or not he was dying—that seemed to take too much focus and awareness; later he was sure that he had gone in and out of consciousness several times. Ironically, what saved him was the terrible condition of his marriage.

Diane Nash was exhausted by him, and by what seemed to her his constant womanizing—it was, thought some of his friends, truly a constant on his part, something which he apparently perceived as part of his ministerial duties. Even his philosophy now called for greater sexual freedom, for he had gradually decided that one of the most powerful forces of conservativism in America was that part of the Puritan ethic that enforced or pretended to enforce monogamy. Since monogamy was to him the most unnatural of existences, he decided that all too many people, particularly the white men who controlled the political life of America, were pinched up sexually. The more open America's people were sexually, the more natural their sex lives, then the freer and more open America's politics. Traditional marriage seemed to him a block to personal sexual freedom. Thus what he practiced sexually was what he believed theologically and politically. All of this had worn Diane Nash down over the past few years. She had gone to court in Birmingham determined to start the process of divorce, and a representative of her lawyer had come to serve Bevel with the papers, had insisted on seeing him, and had arrived on the day of the beating to find the man named in the suit lying in a cell in soaking-wet clothes, barely conscious. He immediately reported Bevel's condition to SCLC officers. It was typical of Bevel, his friends thought, that his life might have been saved by someone carrying a divorce decree because he had been unfaithful to his wife. His friends managed to get him out of jail, and in a few days he was back leading demonstrations again.

As events progressed in Selma, the SCLC people felt they were orchestrating the resistance almost perfectly. The temperature was steadily going up. Nothing reflected that more than an incident on February 16 involving the Reverend C. T. Vivian. Vivian had come over from Atlanta, where he now worked for the SCLC, and he led about twenty-five demonstrators to the courthouse. There Jim Clark blocked their entrance. In volatility, if nothing else, Clark and Vivian were a match for each other, and soon they were engaged in a heated argument, almost all of it captured dramatically by national television. The subject was Jim Clark's role in history. Vivian turned to Clark's deputies, who were blocking his and his people's way, and said, "There were those who followed Hitler like you blindly follow this Sheriff Clark, who didn't think their day would come, but they were pulled into a courtroom one day and were given death sentences. You're not that bad a racist but you're a racist in the same way that Hitler was a racist and you're blindly following a man down a road that's going to bring you into a federal court. . . ." For a moment it looked like Jim Clark, in what was for him a memorable display of self-restraint, was going to turn away from Vivian. Several of his deputies seemed to be restraining him. But even as Clark began to turn away, Vivian, not a man who lightly gave a world-class racist the last word or the last gesture, said, "You can turn your back on me, but you can't turn your back on justice." That was too much. Black agitators did not get the last word with Jim Clark, and the sheriff wheeled and hit Vivian as hard as he could, sending him careening down the steps. (Apparently he hit him so hard that Clark broke a bone in his left hand.) Vivian, blood pouring from his head, got up, somewhat shaken. He was anxious to rally his followers, who had scattered with the outburst of violence. Vivian had always thrilled to the words of Winston Churchill, summoning the British people in their darkest hour to resist Hitler's Germany, and now he found himself drawing on them. "What kind of people do you think we are that we can be bowed and broken by your violence?" he asked. "What kind of people are *you*?" he asked Clark and his deputies. "What do you tell your children at night? What do you tell your wives at night?" But Jim Clark had had enough of a history lesson. "Arrest this man," he shouted to his deputies. "Arrest him now!" It was high-class drama, and much of the nation was able to see it that night on television; the noose around the white authorities of Selma was tightening.

The incident was not only captured on national television; it also helped lead to a set of circumstances which eventually created the historic march from Selma to Montgomery. For as the conflict had escalated in Selma, tensions had spread to other counties in the region. Different SCLC people had been sent out not just to organize in the smaller communities, but to hold mass meetings there. On the night of February 18, two days after his confrontation with Jim Clark, C. T.

Vivian spoke at a black church in Marion, in nearby Perry County. Then Vivian led a group of black protesters to the local courthouse. A decision had already been made in Perry County to call in the state troopers to crush the demonstration and to arrest its leaders. (Octavia Vivian was later told by the Justice Department that the violent assault upon the demonstrators in Marion that night had been aimed primarily at her husband because of his confrontation with Clark in Selma. She was also told that the state troopers were looking to kill C.T. that night.[1]) As Vivian led his people toward the courthouse, he suddenly saw a wall of state troopers blocking his path. Just then, as if on signal, all the town's streetlights went out, and the troopers charged the protesters. A number of the protesters and reporters covering the demonstration were injured, including Richard Valeriani of NBC, who was hit in the head with an ax handle. One of the protesters, a young black man named Jimmie Lee Jackson, tried to run away from the scene, and made his way to a nearby café. But a state trooper followed Jackson and his mother into the café. There, as Jimmie Lee Jackson tried to shield his mother from the trooper, the trooper shot him in the stomach in what some black witnesses thought was cold blood. Jackson was immediately taken to a nearby hospital, but the chances of his surviving were considered slight. In fact, he had eight days to live.

The next night James Bevel and Bernard Lafayette went to Jimmie Lee Jackson's house to meet with his family. Lafayette, who had over the past four years become all too expert a witness on rural black poverty, thought he had never seen poverty quite like this. The family lived in a shack without running water and without electricity. Inside the home there was a sad little table and a few chairs. Outside, open sewage ran in a stream in the backyard. The young man who hovered on the edge of death and who would die in a few days had been the sole male wage earner in the family. This was the home of the poorest kind of people in America, Lafayette knew, the kind of people who were so poor and rural that they barely showed up on the national census statistics. Worse, they had just become a great deal poorer. The only other male in the family was the grandfather, an elderly man named Cage Lee. "I wish they had taken me instead of the boy," he kept repeating. On the way to the Lee-Jackson house, Bevel had talked to Lafayette about this being the moment to do something dramatic. That night he asked the old man if he thought the demonstrations should continue and the old man said, "Oh yes, Reverend Bevel, of course they should." Would he be willing to continue demonstrating? Bevel asked. "I've got nothing to lose now, Reverend Bevel—they've taken all I have. We've got to keep going now."

"Well, Mr. Lee," Bevel said, "I was thinking we might try to march again, and I wondered if you would be willing to walk at the head of the march with me."

"Oh yes, Reverend Bevel, I'll walk with you," the old man answered.

Lafayette thought Bevel was thinking about continuing the demonstrations in Marion, but later that night when they were driving back to Selma, Bevel started talking to him about wanting to go to Montgomery to talk to the governor: "But I want to take my time before I talk to the governor," he said. "I want to think about what I'm going to say. I want to get it just right." How about, he suggested, a march from Selma to Montgomery, from one of the toughest cities in the South, one run by Jim Clark, to the capital of one of the toughest states in the South, one run by George Wallace? Not bad, thought Lafayette; there was a certain symmetry of evil in a journey from one city to the other.

The next day there was a mass meeting in Selma, one seething with anger, and Bevel went before the crowd and said, "I've got something to say to the governor about Jimmie Lee Jackson. Because we don't really know all that happened. So I've got a lot of questions for Governor Wallace about what happened. Now, sometimes when you talk to someone, you just call him up on the phone, and sometimes you send him a letter, but I want to say this to him personally, and I want to take my time to get what I say right, so I thought I would walk to Montgomery and tell the governor in person. Mr. Cage Lee has said he's willing to walk with me."

Already people in the audience were shouting, "Let's go see the governor."

"How many of you," Bevel asked the crowd, "will walk with us?" Everyone in the room was standing and cheering, and Bevel turned to Lafayette and said, "Looks like we got us a march."

They were, they sensed, closing in on victory. The political pressure driven by media coverage was affecting both parties. Where in the past the Justice Department, all too aware by now of the power of the

Dixiecrats in Congress, had thought of a constitutional amendment as a way of gaining the franchise for blacks in these areas, the political climate on Capitol Hill was changing rapidly, under the press of televised events, and Johnson was now telling his close friends that he thought he could get a bill through Congress. Indeed, events were beginning to move ahead of his own schedule: On both sides of the aisle, younger congressmen were now introducing bills of their own to simplify voting procedures in America, and to offer protection to black voters.

55

THE MARCH ON MONTGOMERY WAS SET FOR SUNDAY, MARCH 7.
Whether the young people from SNCC would be a part of it suddenly
became a serious issue. The night before the march the SNCC leadership debated whether or not to participate during a long, explosive
meeting in the basement of the Frazier's Cafe Society in Atlanta, a
meeting which went on well into the morning. John Lewis, almost
alone among the SNCC leaders, argued in favor of the march. Most of
his colleagues opposed the idea. The politics of SNCC had been
changing dramatically in the past year and a half, he thought, and the
rift between the SCLC and SNCC was becoming more obvious all the
time. The relatively mild rift which had existed on that day in 1961
when the young people had challenged Martin Luther King and many
of his closest aides to join them on the bus ride to Jackson had become
a chasm. The lines were sharply drawn and they were generational,
geographical, and cultural. King and his people were still trying to
influence the governmental process in Washington, while many of the
young SNCC people, ever more embittered by the events of the last
four years, seemed to have completely written off the governmental
process as it existed. Some of them were now talking about revolutionary tactics. They argued that night that if there was a march, then
the SCLC people would come in, take it over at least momentarily,
there would be a great deal of excitement, King and his people would
give a lot of orders and get a lot of credit and publicity, the local people would get their hopes up, and then the SCLC leaders would
depart and leave them hanging there. The payback in a place like this,
they argued, would be too harsh; the locals would be visited by Jim
Clark and they would at the very least lose their jobs.

Lewis believed that the rift also reflected the larger split within SNCC which had been developing for the past three years between the increasingly radical and somewhat more political people in the organization and the old guard, the Southerners, who were more religiously driven. The people coming to the fore in SNCC now were not only more alienated from the government, they were, and this reflected a dramatic change, more alienated from the religion of their parents as well. He and Lafayette and Bevel, who was by then a paid SCLC staff member, had been typical of the old guard of SNCC, but the new voices, many of them Northern ones, were far angrier. He understood what was happening, but he did not sympathize with the new, more alienated tone: Black rage, under the force of events, he now understood, was coming ever closer to the surface, and it seemed to be more fashionable politically than the religious values he and the others professed.

It struck Lewis that night that SNCC had changed, and that he and the others in SNCC with whom he had been so close were now very much a minority within the organization. Clearly his voice was a lonely one that night. The meeting was disheartening for him; he felt very much alone in what should have been in effect his own house. If he marched the next day it would be as an individual and not as the chairman of SNCC. In effect he was defying one organization, SNCC, of which he was the head, and representing another whose board he was on, the SCLC. The power of the Southerners within SNCC, for Lewis tended to see the division as essentially a Northern-Southern one, was on the decline; on the rise were the Northerners, who tended to be better educated, more articulate, and a good deal angrier.

Some of the division came from the vast difference in their backgrounds. The commitment of the Southerners had started with a religious impulse, and their politics had more often than not been cloaked in deep religious conviction. If they were prone to rhetoric, it was often low-key and, as in Bevel's and Lafayette's case, likely to be biblical rather than purely political. Some of the difference, Lewis believed, was the Southerners' greater knowledge of the local terrain, and of just how much progress was attainable in these small towns at a given time. But he was also aware that the rising level of anger and alienation reflected the cumulative response to the violence inflicted on them in the months and years since 1960; so many SNCC field people had been beaten and arrested and harassed and shot at and seen the local people they were working with abused. Two additional factors had heightened their anger: first, the fact that the government and the national media tended to pay a good deal more attention when the violence was inflicted on white field workers rather than on blacks; and second, that the government and the media tended to pay attention only after Dr. King arrived. The SNCC people were the ones putting their lives on the line, but King and the SCLC always seemed to get the credit. Many of them seethed with resentment over that.

Lewis also sensed that the commitment to nonviolence was wearing thin among many of his peers. Some of them who had been very idealistic at the start were, after four or five years of harsh confrontation, beatings, and long days and nights spent in miserable Deep South jails, becoming increasingly radical, if not cynical. They did not see the headway they were making, only the opposition which they had triggered, a death-throes, last-ditch opposition, he believed. The irony, Lewis thought, was that this radicalization of SNCC was taking place after so much success, and precisely, he believed, at the moment when they were moving toward the greatest success of all, a voting rights bill. Yet it appeared that many of his peers did not see themselves as being successful; they saw only the strength of the forces aligned against them and their own defeats. Nor did they understand the degree to which they had systematically bent the U.S. government and Justice Department and now even the FBI to their will, until at this point the Justice Department was virtually a parallel instrument working alongside them in their cause. Lewis saw this all as a singular success for the SNCC field people: Their bravery and audacity, so well orchestrated through the media, had changed the attitude of the past two presidents as well as the American people. Yet many of his colleagues still saw these governmental officials, whom Lewis now viewed as de facto allies, as being sworn enemies.

All of that anger had been obvious in the furious discussion that night at Frazier's. The tonal quality of the debate had gradually changed over the years. It was not that Southern blacks lacked anger, but, he believed, they had grown up with a certain tempering quality of patience. "We were rooted in those communities and their churches," Lewis said some thirty years later, "and we had an understanding of how far you could go, one step at a time. Sometimes I think the Northerners thought they could just come down South and just liberate the natives. Those of us who had been born and raised there had a better understanding of how long a struggle it was going to be."

In the debate at Frazier's most of their anger seemed aimed at Martin Luther King. Some of the resentments were legitimate, and even many of the Southerners who admired Dr. King shared some of them; it was the SNCC people who were the shock troops, who were putting their lives on the line in all these tiny towns, but it was King who seemed to reap the glory and the fame (and it was the SCLC, for this was a particular point of contention, which got the lion's share of the money which flowed in after the young people had been beaten up). After the signing of the Civil Rights Bill of 1964, when a group of the black leaders had posed with Lyndon Johnson at the White House, John Lewis had stood behind Martin Luther King. Later Jim Forman had criticized him for it. "Don't be standing behind him the next time," Forman had said; "you've got to stand in front of him next time." That had seemed frivolous to Lewis; to him Martin Luther King was the leader of the Movement and should be in the front row. Period.

Lewis thought the entire debate begged the main question of their purpose and, even more important, the essential strategy they had employed from the start. The truth of the Movement had always been that Martin Luther King was the Movement's leader; he had caught the imagination of ordinary, middle-class white Americans, and of the national media.

From the start they had all adapted, for the most pragmatic of reasons, to the needs and norms of American society and particularly of the American media, which in turn reacted to the needs of the American people. King had positioned himself brilliantly in trying to appeal to white America, in trying to reach, as Andy Young once said, the white, nominally conservative elderly ladies in Iowa who voted for Bourke Hickenlooper, a conservative Iowa Republican.[1] If they could reach people like that, they had reached the nation. The American people seemed to want a symbolic figure, which meant that the media needed a symbolic leader. The blunt truth was that where John Lewis or James Forman or other SNCC people went did not matter that much to the national media, unless perhaps they were badly beaten or killed, and there happened to be excellent photos of the beating. But where Martin Luther King went *The New York Times* and *Time* and *Newsweek* and the three networks followed. As for the idea put forward by some SNCC dissenters that the march was betraying the local people, it was the people of Selma, and the Black Belt, who wanted the march.

At the end of the meeting in Atlanta, John Lewis told them he was going to march anyway, as an individual. He knew in some way he was defying his own organization and that there would probably eventually be trouble because of it, but he did not think they should come this far, put in so much work, and then pull back just as they were about to taste victory. Around 3:00 A.M. the meeting broke up and Lewis, with two other friends, Wilson Brown and Bob Mants, got into a car and drove to Selma. They arrived a few hours later, absolutely exhausted, got out their sleeping bags, slept for a few hours, and then got up and went to a meeting at the Brown Chapel of the AME Church. There were a fair number of the SCLC people already there, Hosea Williams, Andy Young, as well as Bevel and Lafayette. The crowd of local people was large and eager to march. The SCLC leaders quickly broke the crowd down into small groups and gave them instant training on nonviolence and what was likely to happen to them that day. Then the leaders flipped to see who would actually lead the march, and Hosea Williams was chosen to be a leader. They asked John Lewis to march alongside Hosea, which he was glad to do.

As they gathered at the church that afternoon, they were aware that it was likely to be a very difficult day. There had been serious warnings, particularly from Wilson Baker, the more restrained local police official, passed on first to the feds and then the SCLC leadership that Jim Clark and Al Lingo, who was George Wallace's choice as the head of the Alabama state troopers, who did not seem to share Floyd Mann's view of the sanctity of black life, were not going to be restrained, that they were going to lash out as violently as they could. But that all went with the territory, and they were also aware that their plan was working and that the proof of it was the size of the media contingent by now on hand. For watching them, albeit kept at a certain distance by local officials, were numerous photographers all armed with telephoto lenses. That meant that the country would be able to watch what happened from just off the side of the Edmund Pettus Bridge.

John Lewis had brought very little in the way of personal belongings to Selma, just a knapsack with the necessities for what appeared to be another sure night in an Alabama jail: in this case, a book by the political scientist Clinton Rossiter called *The American Presidency* and another book by Thomas Merton, and, of course, the requisite toothbrush and toothpaste, which he had learned Alabama jails did not supply to their visitors. There were two things you always wanted to be able to do in a Southern jail, brush your teeth and read.

Bloody Sunday, it was later called, Sunday, March 7, 1965. It started quietly enough. The crowd was large, perhaps six hundred or seven hundred people, almost all of them local. They moved toward the Edmund Pettus Bridge quietly and orderly. But for weeks and months, the two armies had been gathering and now they were finally going to meet in full-scale conflict. If the demonstrators were well organized, then so too were the whites. For Jim Clark had been busy as well; he had issued an order for all white men over the age of twenty-one to meet at the courthouse that day to be deputized as part of his posse. The marchers were aware that the whites had put together an unusually large police force. Selma that day, to John Lewis, who had been through so many confrontations, had felt like a ghost town. There was almost no traffic on the streets, nor were there any pedestrians. Other than the whites who had enlisted in Clark's posse, the white population of Selma seemed to have disappeared, intuitively aware that the best place to be was at home behind closed doors.

The demonstrators walked the six blocks from the church to the Edmund Pettus Bridge over the Alabama River; they did so cautiously, as John Lewis was absolutely certain that they were moving toward a fateful confrontation. As they started over the bridge everything around them was absolutely still. Lewis and Hosea Williams moved slowly to the apex of the bridge and then Lewis looked out and saw what appeared to him like a vast sea of blue in front of him—a sea of Alabama state troopers. He had, he remembered, been in many marches, starting five years earlier in Nashville, but so far this was perhaps the most peaceful and orderly he had ever been in. Most of the other marches had featured young college students, more rebellious than their parents and elders. But this march was composed of older, traditionally dutiful rural people who had been suppressed politically all their lives, and the very act of marching that day was for many of them their first act of dissidence and, he was certain, the bravest thing they had done in their entire lives. Their audacity was in their presence, and they were very quiet, absolutely aware of the risk required with every step. No one had to tell them to be orderly.

Lewis and Hosea Williams kept walking, coming to within speaking range of the police now. It was like staring at row on row of an opposing army which was just waiting to attack, Lewis thought: first the rows of troopers in blue, and then the rows of deputies in their khaki uniforms, and then, moving back and forth among them, some men from Jim Clark's posse on horseback. "I am Major John Cloud of the Alabama state troopers," the leader of the other army announced on a bullhorn, "and this is an unlawful march and it will not be allowed to continue. It would be detrimental to your safety to continue the march. You are ordered to disperse, go home or to your church. This march will not continue. You have two minutes." Williams asked Major Cloud if they could speak with him. Cloud answered that they had nothing to talk about. "Troopers," he ordered, "advance!" Some fifty or so troopers started moving toward the assembled demonstrators.

On the bridge Hosea Williams turned to John Lewis. "John," he asked, "can you swim?"

"No," Lewis answered, "can you?"

"No," said Williams.

The two leaders told their people to kneel and pray. "I think they're going to use gas," Williams said. Lewis remembered the moment before the confrontation very clearly: It was completely quiet, oddly peaceful. There was not even the hint of a breeze.

After Major Cloud gave his command, the state troopers charged the protesters on the bridge, lashing out with their clubs, throwing tear gas at them. The protesters had just started to kneel and pray, and their heads were particularly vulnerable to the sticks. As the troopers began their assault, Lewis saw the protesters tumbling backward at once like a giant row of dominoes. It was a stunningly violent moment: lawmen employed by the state of Alabama striking out with their clubs at the protesters, unrestrained mass violence administered amid clouds of tear gas so thick that suddenly it was almost impossible to see. Lewis was hit hard on his head. The tear gas was terrible, the pain immediate, and he felt himself slipping out of consciousness.

There are, because of the presence of the media by the side of the Pettus Bridge, two powerful, permanent images of John Lewis on that day. The first of these is of him walking alongside Hosea Williams, looking very small, oddly vulnerable, his tiny knapsack strapped on his back, obviously aware of the violence which awaits all of them. He and Williams are moving forward to meet this danger with what seems like the tiniest footsteps known to man. Never, it seemed, had marchers gone forward to their objective so slowly but so surely, and with greater certainty of how harsh a fate awaited them, and rarely had the leader of a major march looked so small and vulnerable. The other photo, captured by still photographers, is of him, still kneeling on the ground on the bridge after his attempt to pray, trying to protect his head, while a burly state trooper crashes a club down on his head.

That instant, the trooper poised with the club well behind his back after a full windup, marked the exact instant that for the second time John Lewis saw his own death. I am going to die, he thought, this is my last demonstration, just let me die here. He thought how odd it was to die in your own country so near to where you were born while exercising your constitutional rights. The last image he had before he blacked out was a terrible one: armed men of the law slashing away with their nightsticks in full fury against defenseless black people, most of them either kneeling in prayer or huddling down, trying to protect themselves.

It had been nothing less than state-sponsored mayhem that day, the state of Alabama using its full force to beat and intimidate its poorest citizens, and thereby keep them from being able to participate in the political process. Yet it was the most short-lived of segregationist victories, for yes, they had succeeded momentarily in stopping the march, and they had driven back the terrified demonstrators, many of them beaten and wounded. But Clark and Lingo had unwittingly succeeded in playing the parts scripted for them by Martin Luther King;

they had called national attention to black grievances in rural Alabama. For it had been America at its absolute ugliest: The fury of it— matching the violence of Klansmen assaulting the Freedom Riders in Montgomery and Birmingham—stunned even experienced civil rights reporters and demonstrators. Veteran reporters who had been covering the civil rights struggle for almost a decade were shocked by the scene; they had, after all, seen a great deal of violence over the years, incidents when a lawman had turned viciously on protesting blacks and had punched out a demonstrator, and they were aware of what the Philadelphia, Mississippi, sheriff's office had done to the three young men in 1964 in the darkness of the Neshoba County night. But the scale and the intensity of this, taking place as it did in broad daylight, stunned them.

Lewis was hit so hard that his skull was fractured; he woke up much later in Good Samaritan, the Catholic hospital in Selma. He never knew how he got back to the church and from there to the hospital. Martin Luther King and Ralph Abernathy immediately came to visit him. "We'll make it to Montgomery, John," Dr. King was saying; "they're not going to stop us now." The next day the doctors were still talking about keeping him in the hospital for several days' observation, but there was work to be done, and John Lewis checked himself out and walked over to the Brown Chapel of the AME Church. There was a small house next to it used as an additional headquarters, and Lewis walked up to the top step and began to give an impromptu press conference, unusually fiery and impassioned for him, vowing that the march would continue, that there would be more marchers now, and that they could not be turned back. His head was wrapped so thickly in bandages that it looked like he was wearing a white football helmet, thought Arlie Schardt of *Time* magazine. Because Schardt knew he had suffered a severe concussion, he feared Lewis might keel over, and he quietly mounted the steps to be near him just in case he fainted. That young man, thought Schardt later, is the most indomitable person I have ever met.[2]

There had been television coverage of the violence on the bridge and the footage was simply staggering, given the vulnerability and the poverty of the demonstrators, and the uniformed might of the Alabama troopers. It was not an image of their own country that many Americans took pleasure in. By chance that night ABC was broadcast-

ing the movie *Judgment at Nuremburg,* and network executives cut in
to show the footage from Selma. The juxtaposition of the scenes from
the movie with the scenes from Selma was haunting. "The difference
between barbarity now and in other times is that now everybody sees
it on television," the writer Russell Baker noted a few years later.
"Television sits in the living room corner ready to show us the
absolute worst at the touch of a switch."[3] The images were devastating
for the white community of Selma. "I did not understand how big it
was," Joseph Smitherman later said, speaking for a generation of
white public officials who had involuntarily gotten in the way of the
Movement, "until I saw it on television."[4] He added, "They picked
Selma just like a movie producer would pick a set."[5] King had chosen
his villain brilliantly. To Jim Clark, the inconceivable had happened:
King had been the puppeteer, Clark the puppet.

In the wake of the violence Martin Luther King sent out telegrams
to clergymen all over the country asking them to join him in a subsequent major march from Selma to Montgomery on Tuesday, March 9.
Several hundred clergymen from all over the country, many of them
white, now descended on Selma. There was still a restraining order
against the march, and the SCLC immediately challenged it in court.
By the time the second march was to begin on Tuesday, district judge
Frank Johnson had not yet ruled, and because the SCLC had never
violated a federal injunction, the march they held on that day was
more than a little artificial: King led his people over the Pettus Bridge,
and there, facing the troopers, they knelt, prayed, and then, as if by
signal, they returned to their church.

That night an incident took place which turned out to be one more
nail in the coffin of local segregation. Three of the white ministers
who had rallied to King's call, and who had stayed on after the
abortive Tuesday morning march, went to dinner in the black section
of town. They were unfamiliar with the town, and when they finished
dinner, they by chance made a wrong turn on their way home, and
ended up walking past the Silver Moon Cafe, a notorious white segregationist hangout. Three whites spotted them and set after them with
clubs. One of the whites caught the Reverend James Reeb, a Unitarian
minister from Boston, before he could react and hit him full on the
head. His condition, by the time he arrived at a Birmingham hospital,
was critical. He had two days to live.

One galvanizing event seemed to follow another. The SCLC leadership was still trying to gain permission for the march on Montgomery, and John Lewis was one of the people brought before federal district judge Frank Johnson to testify. Not only did Lewis testify about how he had been beaten on Bloody Sunday, but the lawyers for the SCLC showed Judge Johnson the CBS film clips of the nightmarish scene on the bridge. Lewis kept his eye on Johnson as the film clips of his beating were shown, and he watched first disgust and then rage on the judge's face. "I want a recess," Johnson said, and Lewis sensed the anger in his voice. Shortly thereafter, he returned to the courtroom and lifted the injunction against the march.

With that everyone, it appeared, was on the way to Selma. "We became the march capital of the world," Mayor Smitherman later said.[6] To Lewis the Selma march, when it finally took place, was like a holy crusade. Perhaps ten thousand people showed up, some famous, many of them simply ordinary people who wanted to march on behalf of a better country. John Lewis remembered the song from that day: "Pick 'em up, lay 'em down, all the way from Selma town/Pick 'em up, lay 'em down, all the way from Selma town."

It was a decisive moment. On March 11, 1965, some four months after King had told his SCLC colleagues that they would take the initiative for the voter's rights bill and do it in Selma, Lyndon Johnson went before the American people on national television. "I speak tonight for the dignity of man and the destiny of democracy," he began. It was, he said, "wrong—deadly wrong—to deny any of your fellow Americans the right to vote in this country." At certain moments, he said, like Lexington and Concord, and Appomattox, "history and fate meet at a single time and a single place to shape a turning point in man's unending search for freedom." So it was that past week in Selma, he said. Then he announced that he was going to introduce a strong voter's rights act to Congress. "We *shall* overcome," Johnson said. (Russell Baker, *The New York Times* columnist, hearing the slogan of the marchers now on the lips of the president of the United States, knew that in some way one phase of the civil rights struggle was over, taken over by the federal government.[7])

John Lewis watched Johnson's speech that night in Selma, along with Martin Luther King, in the home of Marie Foster, who had long been one of the heroes of the Selma group. The move on the Deep South had taken four years, bracketed, ironically, by John Lewis's two severe beatings, the first one as a Freedom Rider in Montgomery in 1961, the second in Selma in 1965, both of them taking place not far from the Alabama farm where he had grown up. When the president said he was going to introduce voting rights legislation, King started to cry; they were, Lewis knew, tears of joy, for he felt them himself, tears which reflected all the pain and suffering which had taken place in those years to reach this great victory, one which they hoped would now unlock justice in the Deep South. One man, one vote; we have it now, Lewis thought. They were going to get rid of everything that he hated about Alabama and Mississippi—the literacy tests, the poll tax, the hundreds of cruel ways in which blacks were suppressed, first and foremost by denying them the vote.

It was one of the most emotional nights of his life: He had been doing this now almost five years, he had almost lost his life twice, and in the past fourteen months, after nearly a decade of assault, they had won these two great victories, first the Civil Rights Act of 1964, and now the Voting Rights Act of 1965, both at a terrible price, but great victories nonetheless. The way was clear. The resistance that was normally so strong in both the House and the Senate had been undermined by what the entire country had watched. By August the voting rights bill eventually went through the House by a vote of 328–74, and through the Senate by a vote of 79–18. (On the night of the passage of the Voting Rights Act of 1965, Bill Moyers visited Lyndon Johnson at the end of the day in his bedroom, expecting to find the president exhilarated by such a singular legislative and human triumph. Instead he found Johnson quite depressed. What was wrong? Moyers asked. "I think we've just handed the South over to the Republican party for the rest of our lives," he said, both gloomily and prophetically.[8])

When the bill was signed, on August 6, 1965, John Lewis was one of the leaders called to the White House for the signing. That morning Lyndon Johnson summoned both Lewis and James Farmer of CORE to a small office off the Oval Office and spoke to them about what a great victory it was, and what he had done for them, for Johnson always let people know their exact amount of indebtedness. Then he told them what they owed him, that their job now was to go out there and get their people, all those black folks, registered. "I want you to grab them by the balls like you'd grab a bull," he said. John Lewis was stunned; he was pleased to have the victory, but he did not exactly see himself going into small Southern towns and grabbing black farmers by their genitals.

BOOK

3

COMING HOME

56

SHORTLY AFTER THE VOTING RIGHTS ACT WAS PASSED, THE PRESIDENT of the United States summoned the leaders of the various civil rights organizations to the White House to discuss what the next step should be. Nothing showed how completely the government had changed its position in the past five years than this request, which seemed to imply not merely the fullest cooperation of the federal government in pressing for equal rights, but indeed, its leadership as the senior member of a newly forged partnership. The SNCC leadership immediately voted to boycott the meeting, but John Lewis decided to attend anyway; as far as he was concerned this was what they had fought for for so long, moving the government and the Justice Department to active participation on the part of poor, disenfranchised blacks. To abstain from the meeting was to abstain from the responsibility in following up their victory. He thought there was a certain sadness in all this; they had started just a few years ago when the wall had seemed almost insurmountable, and in five years of continual struggle they had made gains which were beyond everyone's imagination and expectation. But now that they were at the pinnacle of success, after they had achieved these remarkable victories, they were not only divided, but it was as if they had lost sight of their own objectives. The closer we are to victory, the lower the wall which we have to climb over, he thought, the more divided and petty we have become. He had always believed in an integrated community, both black and white, politically and economically just, where the barriers between his children and those of white people might be ever smaller. It was the beloved community which Jim Lawson had spoken of, and he refused to turn away from it; it was a place where everyone was equal, and where love was more powerful than fear. It was a vision which fewer and fewer of his colleagues believed in.

Instead, black nationalism was increasingly on the rise, and it surfaced in SNCC long before it surfaced in other mainstream black organizations. Even in the early sixties there had always been a strong undertow of it. Within a year of SNCC's founding there had been talk of making it a predominantly black organization; whites in the end had been let in, but there had always been a sensitivity to letting them play too large a part in SNCC's decision making. That tension had heightened during the great debate over the 1964 Mississippi summer challenge, and whether or not they needed upper-middle-class white college kids from the nation's best schools to join them as volunteers. The decision had been made that yes, they needed them, but it had been a painful one, a concession they believed they made only because of the prejudices of a white country and a white media. The experience had served only to exacerbate some interior tensions, and there had always been a smoldering resentment over the fact that part of the reason why the Philadelphia, Mississippi, murders had caused such national attention was that two of the three victims were white.

Now, after the Voting Rights Bill of 1965 had been passed, there was more talk of separateness within SNCC, more talk of going a more radical way. The nature of politics in America was changing anyway in the mid-sixties, particularly among the young. Radical rhetoric was on the rise. The very nature of the civil rights movement, and the self-portrait of America which the demonstrators had helped create, had served to radicalize many young people; the sheer affluence of the country allowed them as they graduated from college to concentrate less on the immediacy of getting a job, and more on the day's burning political issues; the war in Vietnam was slowly and steadily being escalated and was becoming of itself a powerful radicalizing force; and the television cameras now rewarded those who went into the streets, as they did not reward those who filed legal briefs. All of that seemed to accelerate and intensify the dynamic of dissent. The debate which was only beginning to take place elsewhere in the country, in the most formative way, had been taking place for some time and with far greater fervor within SNCC, an organization which would later be seen as one of the driving forces of the sixties.

As all of this happened John Lewis, as a classic, old-fashioned integrationist, was meeting increased challenge within his own organization. Among the criticisms made against him now was that he not only was too close to the SCLC and Dr. King, he was too close to white people and was too much of an integrationist. To Lewis the concept of friendship, including friendships which cut across racial lines, was a crucial part of what they had been doing. He would not be, he thought, someone who railed against the racial lines drawn by whites while drawing lines of his own. That was un-Christian, and it would not bring a better day, he thought; if he did that it would turn victory into defeat. The right to have friendships based on choice was, he thought, as basic as any other right. Freedom of choice and association should not be dictated by anyone, either white Mississippi sheriffs or angry black radicals. Earlier, just as these lines were being more sharply drawn, he had attended a SNCC meeting at Fisk and afterward he and his friend Danny Lyon, who was white and who was for a time the official SNCC photographer, had wandered over to a meeting of black nationalists which was taking place on the Fisk campus. When they tried to enter, Lyon was told he was not welcome (although as he later noted, he had taken many of the photographs in the SNCC brochures being given away there). Lewis, Lyon knew, badly wanted to go in, but when his white friend was rejected, he turned and walked away himself.[1]

Lewis had known for some time that he was on a collision course with others in the group. Certainly in the inner leadership council he was increasingly isolated, but he thought he had strong ties among the field workers. He was, he believed, generally strong with the Southerners, albeit weak with the Northerners. On May 8, 1966, when SNCC came to choose its officers for the coming year, Lewis thought he would be reelected, and in fact he was. But it had been a long and contentious meeting and near the end, after he had been reelected, a young man named Worth Long came in and challenged the results. They had failed to meet SNCC's prescribed rules, Long said, an odd charge for a group which had always prided itself on its flexibility and lack of rigidity. The election was thrown out, Stokely Carmichael was put up in nomination against Lewis, and a bitter debate ensued. During the debate it was said of Carmichael that he would kick ass, as

Lewis had not, and the ass to be kicked, it appeared, was that of Lyndon Johnson. Of John Lewis, Stokely Carmichael said, he was too much like Martin Luther King. It was late at night, many of Lewis's supporters, thinking their man had won, had already gone to bed, and Carmichael was elected.

To Lewis it seemed more a coup than an election, something which had been set up earlier and carefully orchestrated. He was deeply wounded; the assault against him had seemed terribly personal, coming as it did in an organization which he had been part of from day one, and to which he had given so much. The next night he went over to the home of Arlie Schardt, a *Time* reporter who had covered him for several years. Schardt had never seen Lewis so disheartened. He was stunned by what had happened. He had known that there were forces determined to bring him down, but it had never occurred to Lewis that his opponents could mount a coup. But, Schardt thought, he did not seem so much bitter as saddened and wary of the future. The Movement as they had known it, Lewis was sure, would now begin to unravel. The rhetoric would be more intense, he thought, and it would be easier to vent long-suppressed black anger. But the Movement, dependent as it was on white support and on true human connection, he believed, would come apart at an accelerating rate. They needed the help of *everyone* to make this thing work, and now it was going to be harder. They would be farther than ever from the beloved community.[2]

Seven months later there was another SNCC meeting—and this time (there was always some uncertainty about what had actually happened) whites, including Bob Zellner, who had been one of the organization's early heroes, almost murdered by a mob on his first day on the job in McComb, Mississippi, were essentially expelled from SNCC. The move did not surprise John Lewis. But he was very unhappy that the organization of which he had been a founding member was moving into positions of black nationalism and heightened rhetoric. As for the rhetoric, it might sound good and might bring a great immediate release in terms of long-suppressed anger, a momentary sense of psychic gratification and pleasure, but he believed that in the end it would lead only to greater political isolation at a time when all too many blacks were isolated from the good things in American life.

57

JIM LAWSON HAD WATCHED THESE SAME CHANGES IN SNCC WITH A certain sadness. More than most he could understand the frustrations and the bitterness among many of the more radical young people, for he had counseled these young people and seen some of them begin to wear out emotionally right in front of him. He had first noticed the changing mood in SNCC after the Freedom Rides in the summer of 1961. He and most of the other Nashville people had returned to the Tennessee capital, where they had launched a series of sit-ins aimed at integrating certain chain restaurants and getting blacks hired at supermarket chain stores. Stokely Carmichael and Dion Diamond, two of the young men whom the Nashville leaders had met for the first time in Parchman, had come through Nashville on their way back east, and they had gladly joined in the protests. But they had brought a new and troubling dimension to their picketing, Lawson thought. Instead of picketing in a quiet, peaceful way, never arguing with those who hurled verbal abuse at them, Diamond and Carmichael had seemed to delight in confronting their attackers. They were verbal, cocky, and quite combative. Some of the local black protesters were quite upset—it was almost, they thought, as if the two young men were deliberately trying to provoke their enemies. There was a certain swagger to these two new recruits which visibly changed the nature of the protest.

Some of the central committee members immediately asked Lawson to talk with Carmichael and Diamond and to get them to back off a bit. He did, trying to explain that Christian nonviolence was not just a physical thing, it was emotional and spiritual and psychological as well, and that violence could be done verbally as well as physically, and that they, whether they realized it or not (and he was sure they realized it), were in some way escalating the potential for violence by their behavior. They agreed to accept his suggestions, but it was clear they did not believe in the superior ethos of nonviolence. Rather, because they were in Nashville and it was the turf of the nonviolent leaders, they agreed to accept the local restraints. But it was obvious to Lawson that Stokely Carmichael and others who agreed with him represented a new force in SNCC, more militant and more aggressive, its anger much closer to the surface. Carmichael, thought Lawson, was immensely gifted and winning, bright and verbal, with an abundance of charm and wit. More, he was absolutely fearless. But as far as Lawson was concerned, he was the harbinger of a new and angrier force: To him nonviolence was a tactic, nothing more, and at best a limited one. In no way was it a way of life.

What fascinated Carmichael, it was obvious, was nothing less than the idea of revolution and the use of violence to achieve a revolution. He had talked about it a great deal when they had all been in prison in Mississippi, about what the Mau Mau had done in Kenya and elsewhere in Africa. Nonviolence might have worked in a limited way so far in the United States, he seemed to be saying, but it was going to take brute force to make any significant change in race relations in America. Lawson both liked Carmichael and was made very uneasy by him. He found the young man extremely bright and quite charismatic, as quick a study as Lawson had met in the Movement, a born leader, one of those gifted young people who seems to have an unerring instinct for the emotions of his constituents at any given moment. The other young people turned to him almost instinctively for leadership, and he never seemed at a loss for words or ideas. He and Diamond left Nashville shortly afterward, and Lawson was both impressed and somewhat melancholy over what had taken place; it was, he thought, a sign of what was to come.

If the scene in Nashville had been the first glimpse Lawson had had of the changing nature of SNCC, then Lawson had ample time to watch its new face on subsequent occasions. The clearest example came in the spring of 1966, when Lawson was a personal witness to the most striking demonstration of the new, radicalized anger among the young people who were replacing those he had once tutored. The occasion was the Meredith march through Mississippi. James Meredith, the courageous and prickly young man who had earlier integrated the University of Mississippi, had decided to hold his own one-man walk against fear in Mississippi. He intended to walk from Memphis to Jackson; the march would last sixteen days, and it would cover some 220 miles. On the second day of the march, June 6, he was shot and seriously wounded by a sniper. Meredith had been taken to Bowld, a Memphis hospital, that first night. Martin Luther King and other civil rights leaders had immediately been in touch with Jim Lawson, using him as their point man in Memphis. They had asked him to put together a broader march which would replace the original one-man march.

That march had seen an almost daily struggle between the old, more traditional, nonviolent forces and the new, angrier face of SNCC reflected by Carmichael. All the top leaders were going to be on this march, but from the start, Lawson knew, Carmichael was trying to drive out both Whitney Young of the Urban League and Roy Wilkins of the NAACP—by being as personally insulting as possible to both of them. His idea was that, by driving them away, he could reduce the conservative forces working against Martin Luther King and thereby move King to the left. He succeeded very quickly in the limited sense—both Young and Wilkins had no need to stand around and be insulted by younger black leaders and both quickly returned to New York.

Almost from the start there was a different tone to this march, a new dimension of anger among many of the younger marchers. On the first day, when a Mississippi state trooper tried to block them from marching on the highway, there was an edgy confrontation. King and the others argued with the highway patrolman—they had been allowed to march down the highway on the way to Montgomery. But, the patrolman answered, they had had a permit then and they lacked one now. Suddenly there was some shoving on the part of the police, and when Lawson looked over, Stokely Carmichael seemed to be shoving back. Lawson had a feeling that Carmichael was out of control, although whether deliberately out of control, he could not tell. What made it worse was that one young highway patrolman seemed extremely nervous, his hand was shaking, and he seemed to be itching to go for his gun. What saved the moment, Lawson believed, was that

Carmichael's arms had already been locked together with King's as part of the solidarity which they had traditionally exhibited while marching, and King quickly tightened his hold on Carmichael in order to restrain him. But it was a signal of what was to come.

The march was supposed to end in Jackson, and there had been talk of holding a major rally there; King had wanted Bayard Rustin to organize the Jackson rally, but Rustin was already wary of coming aboard, sure that Carmichael intended to use the rally for his own purposes, as a forum for black nationalism. For it was on this march that Carmichael first used the cry of black power. They reached Greenwood, a particularly tough Mississippi town where SNCC had done a lot of early voting rights organizing and where Carmichael was well known. They set up camp on the grounds of a black school, and the local police official told them they would have to leave. Carmichael refused, and he was taken off to jail for a few hours. The next day at a rally in Greenwood, Carmichael went to the speaker's platform and gave a particularly impassioned speech. He talked about burning down every courthouse in Mississippi so they could all start over again from scratch. The black people of Mississippi ought to demand black power, he said. There was an immediate resonance to what he said. "We want," he shouted, "black power." The crowd quickly took it up.

"What do we want?" he shouted. "Black power," the crowd chanted.[1]

The lines had been drawn. The new ideology was clearly that of black separatism. In the past the white reporters covering the Movement had been a critical part of the Movement's success, but now Carmichael announced that he and other SNCC officials would no longer talk to white reporters. In addition, Carmichael, until then something of a favorite of reporters on the civil rights beat because he was so bright and charming, and known to them in the general informality of the time and place as Stokely, announced that from then on he would be addressed only as Mr. Carmichael. (When Arlie Schardt of *Time* magazine called SNCC headquarters the next week to find out how to cover Carmichael under the new rules prohibiting contact with white reporters, the latter said it was all right to meet once in a while despite Schardt's white skin and they went out for a long working dinner.[2]) Already on the march there had been signs that the mood was changing: Some of the younger people had wanted to exclude whites from marching, and there had been an incident when a number of the marchers had gotten quite drunk and no one had been able to get them under control. That of itself made it different from the mass marches in the past, where the quality of self-discipline had been impeccable. All of this was precisely what King and Lawson and others had feared. Nothing, they feared, would alienate the white middle class, which the Movement needed for political and financial support, more quickly than a cry of black power. It might have a certain legitimacy, for certainly black people had a right to power too, and certainly black people had enjoyed far too little power throughout American history, but the sound of it to ordinary whites after a decade in which the rhetoric had been based on Christian charity seemed ominous and threatening to white ears. When Carmichael and others had chanted "black power," Hosea Williams and some of King's people had tried to answer with their own chant, "freedom now."

Jim Lawson was appalled by what was happening. He knew that Carmichael had shrewdly programmed all of this. As far as he was concerned, it was a somewhat cynical attempt by Carmichael to steal King's march—there would be no march and no national press coverage if Martin Luther King were not a part of it—and use it as a forum for his own ideas. One night Lawson and Carmichael had a fierce confrontation. The decisions on the march and a rough outline of what they were going to say, Lawson argued, had all been agreed on and it had been a communal decision. But despite that, Carmichael had been systematically exploiting the march for his own needs. If Lawson was angry, King was oddly philosophical. When Carmichael admitted quite openly what he was doing, King said, "Well, Stokely, I've been used before."[3]

Nonviolence, Carmichael said, had taken them as far as they could go. But Lawson said that was not true—Carmichael, he felt, simply had not studied nonviolence. If he had studied it, he would know that a wise leader always has options. The other thing, which he and others argued, was that the alternative to nonviolence was violence, and they would not only inevitably lose that battle, but they would lose the support and sympathy of the vast majority of Americans in the process. But Carmichael was both adamant and confident. Things were going his way.

The words they exchanged were very hard, and the positions they represented polar opposites. Jim Lawson left the meeting as angry as he had ever been with someone in the Movement. Black power was a legitimate concept, Lawson thought, but it was something they should be talking about in their internal debates. At this point, used as a slogan, it would only antagonize the vast majority of white Americans.

Here they were at the apex of their success, he believed, with a leader in Martin King whom the country respected and the world revered. Unlike 1960, when they had no support from the president, and no support from Congress, they now had all three branches of government on their side. Ordinary white citizens, people who were not particularly political, were on their side. They had won victory after victory, and now Stokely Carmichael was telling them their philosophy was wrong and that their time had already passed. He was offering them a slogan which sounded separatist and threatening to white people, and would allow whites to pull back from their support of the Movement and return to more comfortable positions of essential indifference. The rhetoric, Lawson thought, seemed terribly short range. If they moved over from nonviolence to violence, Lawson knew which side would win: He knew which side had more guns and which side had the greater police powers. The radicals might feel good for a few days, but nothing very much would happen. How long, he wondered, would Southern lawmen allow young black men to parade around in their small towns armed with rifles? Not very long. Why do Americans, even black Americans, he thought, always want to take the shortcut? The march had turned into something of a triumph for Stokely, Lawson thought; he had become an instant national celebrity, but it was mostly a triumph of the ego. Lawson feared that the Meredith march might become a turning point in the Movement, that one era was ending and another beginning.

The other thing which Jim Lawson had begun to notice at the same time was that many of the young people whom he had dealt with for the past five years were beginning to wear out. The signs of exhaustion among many of them were more and more obvious. It had been particularly noticeable in 1966 when the SCLC, after considerable internal debate, had decided to make its first attempt to organize in the North, selecting Chicago as the target city and concentrating on the terrible quality of inner-city housing as its primary issue. The campaign in Chicago had been a difficult and often dispiriting one, particularly for some of the young people whose previous experience was in the South. The symptoms, Lawson thought, were those of burnout, or battlefield fatigue. These young people had moved from their normal college and post-college years into a kind of constant wartime footing. They had put in heartbreakingly long hours—some of them for five years, without any respite. They knew nothing of what most people thought of as a normal day. In Chicago, challenging a powerful, well-entrenched big-city machine run by Mayor Richard Daley, a surprisingly supple politician, one who rarely presented them with the kind of target they had enjoyed in the South, they had barely been able to get traction. Instead they had encountered white resistance of a different kind, as well as considerable resistance on the part of entrenched black leaders, who were significantly more conservative than King and his people, and who were not about to share their hard-won political territory with these newcomers from the South. In addition, they encountered a lethargy in the black community which they had never encountered before in the South. There, they had battled fear and intimidation; now in Chicago, they were struggling for the first time with a certain black weariness based on apathy and indifference and a kind of historic psychological exhaustion. Because of that, the Chicago experience had proven particularly disheartening and had been damaging psychically to many of them: They were making this most passionate of efforts, and in many instances no one even seemed to care.

Their disappointment was palpable. These were young people who had had no other lives save the Movement. Their only friends were in the Movement. Therefore, when things went poorly in the Movement as they did in Chicago, where they put in long hours and got marginal results, it was particularly hard on them. In their lives everything both good and bad which took place, every victory, every defeat (of which there were many in Chicago), seemed greatly magnified. They had little in their personal lives to balance against the reverses of their professional lives, for they had no personal lives.

The behavior on the part of some was increasingly erratic. The highs were higher than in the past, and there were certain moments,

Lawson realized, when some of them felt invincible. Then the next day when it would turn out that nothing had changed in this vast, complicated city, the lows would be dramatically lower. Now for the first time a degree of cynicism was beginning to appear among some of the young people. Some of them were starting to drink more. Some of them were slipping into what would years later could clearly be seen as depression. Internal arguments, based on differing political views as well as personality differences, were now becoming more intense and more personal. For the first time Jim Lawson was beginning to hear complaints from some of the women about what would soon be called male chauvinism. Martin Luther King was acutely aware of the erosion among some of their best young people, and he had asked Jim Lawson to come to Chicago regularly as a kind of counselor or therapist for them. King asked Lawson not to participate in any of the Chicago programs. His job was simply to be there for the young people, to listen to them, and to talk through their problems with them. Lawson was alarmed by what he found: They had no idea at all that this had happened, no idea that they were living on the very edge. He thought that a number of them were near the breaking point after five and six years of steady political combat, and he worried about them turning from young moralist warriors to casualties of the war long before their time. The person that King and Lawson and a number of others worried about the most was James Bevel.

58

THEIR OLD FRIENDS HAD WATCHED THE GRADUAL DISSOLUTION OF THE
Diane Nash-Jim Bevel marriage without surprise, but with a growing
sadness. Most of them had been surprised by the marriage in the first
place, and had never thought that it would last very long. Even those
who admired him thought of Bevel as a womanizer, someone who like
ministers in the past seemed to believe that part of pastoring to his
flock was being intimate with women in his congregation. Marriage
had not changed his habits, and it had been bitterly frustrating for
Diane in their early years together. For the others, there was a sense of
resignation: *Well, that's Bevel and that is the way he is.* From the start
he had been that way, for his friends could remember him telling
young women who were joining up with the Movement in the early
days that the Movement demanded a full commitment, that they had
to give their *bodies* to it, and there had been no doubt what giving
their bodies meant. He was the man who, talking to his followers
about the meaning of Jesus' phrase "the water of life," would ask
them if they knew what the water of life was, and when they did not,
would explain that it was sperm. With Bevel, religion, freedom, sexuality, and mysticism were on occasion all mixed together.

But he and Diane had had two children and that meant Diane
Nash's world was going to have to change. He might be a prophet but
prophets were rarely encumbered by the realities of middle-class life,
nor did they always worry about traditional, earthly responsibilities.
("I was the sole support of our family," Diane Nash once wrote of
those years in the late sixties with no small amount of edge, "because
my former husband, the children's father, decided that he did not
want to hold a job and he contributed nothing to our income. . . . Per-
suasion, having friends talk to him, etc., had failed utterly."[1]) When

she had served him with divorce papers while he was in jail in Selma—
cold and badly beaten by Jim Clark's people—it had probably helped
save his life, but it had also been a signal that the marriage was almost
surely finished.

Relatively soon after that, Diane moved to Chicago, her hometown,
just as King was making his first attempt to organize in the North.
Bevel, who within the SCLC circles had been one of the strongest
advocates of the Chicago effort, followed her there not long afterward, and both of them tried to reconcile their differences, but the
damage was too great and there seemed little chance that Bevel was
going to change his ways. That meant that she was a young black
woman who thought of herself as a professional activist who was starting out her life with two young children. She was not, in the traditional American career pattern, credentialed, for she had decided not
to finish college and she had no means of support. She was brilliant at
what she did in the Movement, but whether she could make a career
out of it was another thing. Had she gone ahead with her education
she would have made a simply stunning lawyer, her peers in the Movement thought, and it was a time, when due to the efforts of people like
herself, the opportunities in colleges and graduate schools were
beginning to open up exponentially for young black men and women.
But she was not sure that she wanted to go to law school any more
than she had wanted to finish college.

No one who knew Diane Nash doubted her inner strength. Her
friends were impressed that she did not look back and curse her fate.
She and Bevel, she liked to say, had made a very good team, they had
worked well together, and that had made a difference in both Mississippi and Alabama in those critical years. She was particularly proud
of the work they had done helping to prepare for the battle of Selma;
she and Bevel had jointly won the Rosa Parks award of the SCLC, the
organization's highest honor, for their work there. Years later the marriage with Bevel was not something she liked to talk about, and when
questioned, she said she had asked Bevel for a divorce relatively early
on because it was a choice of divorcing him or killing him.[2] But even
in the more difficult times she never doubted the value of what they
had done together.

Jim Lawson was intrigued by her own highly idiosyncratic form of
spiritual progress. If she had strayed from her original Catholic faith,

it had been replaced, he believed, by a faith and a spirituality of such strength on the subject of nonviolence that she had not been left rudderless, and she was therefore constant in her sense of self, and equally constant in her sense of purpose. She knew exactly what she wanted to do with the rest of her life: She was going to raise her two children and find work as best she could in jobs which, if at all possible, were connected to her political beliefs. Above all, she was not going to give in to self-pity, or let her children down.

By contrast, his close friends worried a good deal about Bevel. He had always been eccentric but now he seemed more eccentric than ever. The story soon spread among Movement people that Bevel had almost been arrested by a Chicago cop because he had been wandering the streets of a particularly bad neighborhood early in the morning while engaged in a violent argument. What made the story interesting was the fact that he was talking and arguing with himself. The Chicago cop had asked him what he was doing. "I'm talking to myself," Bevel had answered. But why? the puzzled cop had asked. "Because Socrates, Aristotle, and Plato are all dead," Bevel was said to have answered.[3]

He had always seemed significantly more idiosyncratic and less anchored than some of his colleagues, like Bernard Lafayette or John Lewis. The signs of burnout seemed more noticeable with him earlier on than with anyone else: moments of almost euphoric and grandiose highs when he thought everything possible, and then comparable lows. He seemed more mystical, more apart from the normal definitions of traditional Christian theology, becoming something of a guru with certain small groups of followers, almost as if he were a cult leader and they were members of the cult, with relationships which were far too intimate for anyone's good. Bevel, his friends had long since decided, was someone who operated on his own and had to operate on his own. He was uncompromising in his political beliefs, and equally uncompromising in his personal actions. No one could change his behavior. If one of the senior members of the SCLC tried to tell him to curtail his personal excesses, he was likely to detail the more private excesses of his colleagues. The difference, he would say, was he behaved this way openly and the others were covert in their extracurricular activities.[4] Year after year, he seemed to become ever more radical. (Once, during a confrontation in Alabama, Bevel had been arguing with John Doar. The subject was the economic injustice which had resulted from some two centuries of white domination of blacks. "If you've got two pairs of shoes in your closet," Bevel had told a somewhat surprised Doar, "one of them belongs to me."[5])

His special value to King was that he was younger, more radical, and more outspoken than most of the other top SCLC people, and therefore he could spot developing issues earlier than most. On no issue had this proven more true than Vietnam. For suddenly that which had been a domestic movement aimed at a nonviolent assault upon the barriers of segregation was encountering a new issue, one which was both domestic and international, and which might put King and the Movement in direct conflict with the president of the United States. The American military commitment to Vietnam began to deepen in 1965 as Lyndon Johnson sent the first American combat units and began massive systematic bombing of North Vietnam. By 1966 it became clear that there would be virtually no ceiling on the number of American troops going there, that this was going to be a very big war in a very small country. No one pushed an ambivalent Martin Luther King, the great and shrewd centrist of the Movement, into coming out against the war more than James Bevel did. For King the politics of the equation he faced were all too clear: He was a man of nonviolence, and the war was terrifyingly violent, a high-technology war being inflicted on a nonwhite peasant nation by the most advanced society in the world, and it was, as far as King was concerned, of dubious geopolitical value. He was the leading international voice of nonviolence, by then the clear lineal descendant of Gandhi. All of that called for him to condemn the war. But to condemn it would surely mean a complete break from President Lyndon Johnson, who was, arguably, more committed to the black cause than any modern American president. More, Johnson was now gearing up for the Great Society, which might have profound implications for poor blacks living outside the reach of the American economy. Johnson would be unforgiving of any break on this issue, and so would, for a time, at least, a large body of centrist, middle-class American whites. Martin Luther King was suddenly faced, as he rarely had been during the pure civil rights days, with a choice between his pragmatic self and his moral sense.

But for Bevel the choice was clear. Vietnam had begun to obsess him as the war escalated. To Bevel it was obviously sinful. The most basic teaching in his life had come from the Tolstoy book *The Kingdom of God Is Within You,* and that book had been a powerful plea against killing. It was not one of the virtues, it was the *only* virtue, Bevel believed. And now here was the United States systematically escalating a high-technology war in a foreign land against people of another color. It was, as far as he was concerned, unspeakably brutal and it was racist.

Years later Bevel would say that he did not think of himself as a prophet, though there was no doubt on occasion he heard voices telling him what to do, and this was one of those occasions. For one morning in Chicago in 1966, when he was doing the children's laundry in the basement laundry room, piling the infant Douglass Bevel's clean diapers on top of the drying machine, a voice spoke to him and told him to stop the war. The voice was very emphatic and it seemed to brook no dissent. "James Bevel," it said, "your brothers and sisters are dying in Vietnam." What was worse, the voice added, was that Bevel was preaching nonviolence in the South, but not in Vietnam. The voice reminded him that it was hardly forthright to tell young black people not to respond by throwing rocks at their oppressors in the South when at the same time the president of the United States was hurling deadly missiles at Asian peasants. Bevel protested to this intruder that he had always preached against violence and fought the good fight in the South, but that he had needed a base camp in the North to come home to where he could rest. If he came out against the war, there would be no place to hide and rest. But the voice was not interested in his evasions and said that his answer was completely inadequate, that he had to take a position against the war. "I can't answer your prayers here in this country," the voice said, "if you are killing people in Vietnam."[6] Those were words he did not for a moment doubt.

So he set out to find Dr. King, who was at that moment secluded in Jamaica, finishing up a book. Bevel borrowed the money for a ticket to Jamaica from a friend in the Movement and flew there. King's hideout was supposed to be secret, but Bevel talked to a number of cabdrivers at the airport, asking how to find Luther King, which was what they called him down there, and one immediately drove him to King's villa. He walked up to the house where King was staying and where a very surprised Reverend Bernard Lee, King's personal assistant, asked him how he had found them. There he lobbied King relentlessly, saying all the things which King knew to be true, that he could not be the leader of the nonviolent movement in America and remain silent on the war. His constituency was first and foremost moral; he dared not lose his special niche, becoming instead of a unique international moral leader, just another black politician. (King's fears, of course, were completely justified; the moment he turned on Vietnam, becoming for a time Lyndon Johnson's most important critic on the war, Johnson, the president who had committed himself more than any American president since Lincoln to the cause of racial justice, began referring to King in private as a "goddamned nigger preacher." There were few surprises with a man like Lyndon Johnson—you were for him when it counted, or you were against him when it counted.[7]) It was a decisive moment. King had been leaning that way himself, and so the decision made, Bevel would momentarily leave the SCLC and go to New York to work on their anti-war moratorium to be held in early 1967. Bevel had again played the role carved out for him by King; he had pushed King to do the things that King knew he ought to do, despite the more traditional restraints of society. Don't speak as the head of the SCLC and don't be political, Bevel told him on the eve of his first major speech on the war; speak as a preacher, a man of God, and make it moral.

In time Bevel became *the* SCLC's man on the war, setting up arrangements for the moratorium in New York; just to be sure that Bevel did not go too far and end up being too provocative, Bernard Lafayette was detailed to go to New York and work with him. His colleagues in the SCLC were particularly wary of one of Bevel's prime ideas—he wanted to send a boatload of prominent Americans who opposed the war to North Vietnam. Once the boat arrived there, these people would take their places in Hanoi itself and along the dikes in the rice paddies so that America would dare not bomb without killing its own people. Martin King did not think it a particularly practical idea. It was exactly the kind of Bevel proposal that he wanted Lafayette to be on guard against.

59

MARION BARRY WAS, IT HAD BECOME OBVIOUS, MORE POLITICALLY driven than most of his Nashville colleagues, though by no means more politically driven than many of the people just beginning to join up with SNCC. Among his peers Barry was thought of as immensely charming, quite supple, able to get on with a vast variety of different people, but not known for his affection for taking on menial tasks. He had a compelling desire to be liked, and that became a skill in dealing with a wide variety of people who did not seem to get on well with each other, but who found him easy to deal with. In that first summer of 1960, right after SNCC had been formed and some of the earliest victories achieved, it was Marion Barry who had been chosen by the other SNCC leaders to go out to both the Republican and Democratic conventions and appear before the platform committees; he was chosen because he was considered the most sophisticated, the most traveled, and in part the most able to talk to white politicians. Years later he would say of nonviolence, which to many of his peers was virtually a way of life, that it was always a tactic with him, never a belief.[1]

He was tall and quite handsome, and he had a natural ease and style which impressed not only his colleagues in SNCC but the white politicians and journalists he met in those early days. He seemed above all else likeable. From the very start, like all good politicians, he was a quick study, as seemingly comfortable with white officials as with blacks. Whatever anger he felt in his heart never seemed to show. He seemed as much as anyone in the early days of the Movement to project a certain exterior sweetness. Clothes were important to him and he dressed with more style and more sophistication than most of his colleagues ("More collegiate than ministerial, and ministerial, of course, was the prevailing Nashville dress code in those days," Julian

Bond once noted[2]). But the mark of the true poverty of the Deep
South was on him both in interior and exterior ways: His friend Bob
Zellner remembered that Barry had obviously not had good dental
care as a boy and had poor teeth and was extremely sensitive about it.
Because of that, Zellner remembered, when he spoke he would cup
his hand partly over his mouth so that a listener would not see his
teeth.

Gradually it was decided that he was better suited to be an ambassador from SNCC to the outside white liberal world, that is, a speaker
and fund-raiser, than he was to be a front-line soldier, and in 1965 he
was sent to Washington to be SNCC's top fund-raiser and leading
political representative. It was a moment when SNCC's people were at
the height of their reputations within the Movement; they had carried
the struggle into the Deep South for five very dangerous years of constant risk, and the Voting Rights Bill had just been passed. But if
SNCC's representatives, like Moses, Lewis, Bevel, Nash, and Sherrod,
were much admired and respected by the veteran reporters who covered the civil rights beat, then unlike Martin Luther King, and a handful of his close aides, they did not yet have national reputations or the
political leverage which went with those reputations. Their reputations and their fame were still in the making. In addition, the nation's
capital was something of virgin territory as far as the Movement was
concerned.

Washington in 1965 was a political and social anomaly: It was a very
black city of marginal indigenous political consciousness. It was not a
border-state city like Nashville or Charlotte, where the battles against
legal and political segregation had recently been joined and won and
where a formidable local black leadership was just coming of age; nor
was it a Deep South city, where a white minority held complete political and economic power and was going to give it up only with the
greatest reluctance and where every increment of black gain would
come only after Pyrrhic battles. Rather Washington was a special case,
a city where a vast racial divide existed but went largely unrecognized
because all kinds of other issues were preeminent locally. America's
survival in the Cold War, not America's capacity to solve century-old
racial divisions and make itself whole, was perceived as the most serious business on the national agenda in 1965.

Washington was a politically neutered city. Black people could live with some considerable degree of comfort, they could even attain middle-class status, but they could not vote and they could not govern. It was, in terms of racial awareness, well behind the curve of the rest of the country, yet many of its young white residents, albeit highly political and by the mid-sixties predominantly New Deal and post–New Deal liberal, did not see that. Although both political parties were endorsing an essentially liberal agenda on racial and economic matters, there was an almost complete absence of progress in local racial matters. Since the early days of the New Deal, white Washington had been a magnet for bright young men and women who were political activists, and who wanted to use the federal government as an instrument of positive social policy. That migration of liberal activists to the capital had if anything intensified during the sixties with the coming of the Kennedy-Johnson administrations. In some ways the city's liberalism was curiously Janus-faced; although these young, highly political people had sympathized with the Movement, they had arrived in town eager to fry far bigger fish and to be involved in the larger issues of statecraft rather than what were perceived as some small, local disputes about schools, housing, and openness of facilities. There was little awareness on their part of what was taking place racially in the city itself. Few of these politically committed activists, when they read the morning papers, even bothered to read the metro sections of the *Post* and the *Star.*

In Washington there was a quite sophisticated old-fashioned, deeply rooted, and generally conservative black middle class, its own battles extremely hard won in the face of a conservative political structure. But it was oddly powerless. Local people could not even elect their own mayor. The city was run by conservative and essentially hostile Southern congressmen, the last powerful vestige of the Dixiecrat majority which had been so influential in Congress for so long. In any true sense Washington was like a colonial city where a distant, foreign, essentially hostile government of people of another race exercised their power and their prejudices.

The profound changes which had been taking place in the country for almost a decade and the escalating pace if not of change then at least of critical challenge to the old order had not yet dented the capital. Though there was a major revolution taking place in sports, the Washington Redskins did not sign their first black player until 1962, and even then only after considerable personal pressure was put on George Preston Marshall, the team owner, by Robert Kennedy, the attorney general of the United States. In Washington finding decent desegregated housing was as much a problem as it might have been in Atlanta, and it was believed that at the start of the Kennedy administration the young president had offered Ralph Bunche, the distinguished black civil servant, a high-level job in his administration but that Bunche had turned it down out of hand because he had no taste for trying to find the kind of housing he needed in the capital. Even the Justice Department, which had become the leading edge first of the Kennedy administration and then of the Johnson administration in pushing for obedience to the law and bringing racial change nationally, was still almost completely white in the upper and middle echelons in 1963.

In Washington the people who were committed to that era's liberal activism used their energies on a grand scale—the national picture, not the sad local one. The city's top journalists, those high in the Washington pecking order, covered national political and international stories; they did not cover local racial stories, nor indeed for the most part did they even cover the national racial stories. If anything, in the curious journalistic ethos of the time, on occasion they tended to look down slightly on some of the reporters who had covered the South, suspecting that they might be too politically committed and not adequately cool, a bit too engaged. "We were," said Karl Fleming of *Newsweek,* one of the journalistic heroes of that period, "somewhat looked down on by the big-time reporters in Washington, who often thought the same way that the powerful people in Washington thought, that we were a distraction and might be making trouble for the powerful people they covered who were doing great things in foreign policy." The men who had covered Tallahatchie County, Mississippi, and the riots in Little Rock, and the bus boycott in Montgomery were not by any means the same ones who went with John Kennedy and Lyndon Johnson on Air Force One.

Washington seemed to the black activists who had been in the front line in places like Alabama and Mississippi more tuned to the past than to the future. There was a relatively small, old-fashioned black bourgeoisie which had operated side by side with the white power structure for years, getting by far the shorter end of the stick in all things. It was a community which had its own institutions and social structure. Middle-class blacks lived in what was called the Gold Coast, a well-groomed neighborhood which ran from west of Sixteenth, south of the Carter Barron Amphitheatre, east of Rock Creek Park, and north of Upshur. Right above it was another, smaller, wealthier black community known as the Platinum Coast. The Gold Coast contained blacks who had tended to live in Washington for several generations: They were doctors, lawyers, college professors. Because black salaries in those days were significantly smaller than those of whites, the black middle class tended to be made up of two-income families, with wives who were schoolteachers or medical technicians. It was, in its own way, quite snobbish. Dunbar was its high school, Howard its university. These were people whose path to a modestly comfortable lifestyle had been hard indeed; they had endured more than their share of racial insults and humiliations from a largely grudging and ungenerous white world. Having fought so hard for their place in an unsympathetic white world, this community was predictably conservative. "My first wife's grandmother," the black writer and activist Roger Wilkins once noted, "said there were three kinds of folks, white folks, niggers, and Washington niggers," meaning by the latter the black Washington elite, who thought they were better than other black people.[3]

Yet the demography of the city had been changing dramatically in the fifties and early sixties with precious little recognition on the part of the city's or the nation's leadership, white or black. The vast migration to the North of poor blacks from the rural South had already changed Washington; for many poor blacks moving from Virginia, the Carolinas, and Florida, Washington was the first urban stop on the great trek north. As such in Washington there was a community within a community, one made up of the poorest of the poor. Bamas, they were called, and the term was pejorative; they were named after the state of Alabama, and a Bama was any child of the Deep South who, migrating north, had stopped off to live in Washington, without in any real sense finding a true home. These were raw, country blacks, their only skill their capacity to perform physical labor, no longer valued by their old employers back home.

They had been driven off the land by the coming of new technology, principally the mechanical cotton picker. Precious little thought had been given to their future. They were in flight now, rootless, even when they took up what seemed like temporary residence in some unwelcoming city in the North. They had been deprived for generations of even the most elemental tools of education, and now they were arriving in the Northern cities just as the entry-level industrial jobs were drying up. In terms of the social change it was to represent, that migration was perhaps the most underreported American social phenomenon of the midcentury; it marked the arrival, before anyone could so define it, of the coming of what was to be known as the urban underclass. These were the children of neo-slavery, the barest step away from plantation life. In the eyes of the older black community of Washington, they were an embarrassment: They were noisy, they used poor English, they lived their social life out on the street, they had poor social habits and bad hygiene.

This was the volatile demographic mix to which Marion Barry and a number of other young black activists from SNCC were drawn in the mid-sixties. Washington was the seat of the federal government, and the federal government, it was just beginning to turn out, was wealthy, and unlike state governments, particularly state governments in the South, it had begun, in the past five or six years, to show that it was a friend of blacks. So the capital was in its heart a very black city where there were almost no indigenous manifestations of black political influence or leadership. The federal government was essentially very white; the city rooms of the two great papers (and the newsrooms of the national bureaus of the great national newspapers and networks) had only the daintiest representation of black reporters. Yet in ways that many of the young black leaders who had apprenticed in SNCC did not fully understand, because they were still in their own political apprenticeship, Washington was the place to be: The old political order was about to collapse, and yet no one in power had given much thought to what might replace it. Washington in 1965 was a political-economic-social cauldron just waiting to boil over.

Marion Barry arrived in Washington when he was twenty-nine, attractive and facile and ambitious; he could if he so chose wear either his Ivy League clothes, a sign of his willingness to be amenable to a power structure if it was amenable to him, or his African dashiki, a sign that his alienation matched that of the angriest, most militant young blacks on the streets. He was young and winning and brave, and he represented—and wore in effect on his chest—the battle ribbons that the best and most courageous young black students of his generation had just earned in the South by challenging and in some cases changing its laws. He bore their proxy as he arrived in Washington.

He had a visceral instinct for what was just beginning to happen around him, the new possibilities that were starting to open up. He sensed that the city was about to change, and a number of young local activists, who were quickly drawn to him, reinforced his own instincts. The city was filled with this new, raw black political energy, much of it unfocused, all of it untapped. Someone was going to have to be the beneficiary of all this, and it might as well be him.

In December 1965, just a few months after arriving in Washington, Barry had become the leader of a surprisingly successful boycott, protesting a five-cent increase in the bus fare from 20 cents to 25 cents. Some 75,000 people had observed the boycott on that day. That was victory number one; soon he was a leader in what was called the Free D.C. movement. Home rule was an issue of rising local importance; Lyndon Johnson was all for it—it made sense in a liberal era to give the franchise to people in the nation's capital—but the old order, led by the conservative Washington Board of Trade, had helped undermine the cause, saying that businessmen in Washington did not believe in home rule, and thereby supplying powerful ammunition to the conservative Southern congressmen on the Hill who controlled the city's political life. Barry quickly became one of the leaders in trying to isolate the Washington merchants who opposed home rule. He did this with more than a touch of the bully boy; he and a few others would walk into a store and set an arbitrary and often very high figure of what they thought the merchant, more often than not white, ought to pay to their pro–home rule cause. It made a number of the more traditional black leaders who had been his allies uneasy, and some of them dropped out. Some critics thought what he was doing constituted extortion, and there was some consideration of bringing racketeering charges against him, but none of the merchants would bring a complaint.

But the entire Free D.C. movement signified his arrival as a new kind of leader in Washington, attractive, charismatic, good with the press in applying in the capital some of the political and social pressures which had worked so well for the Movement in the South. By the mid-sixties a number of talented young reporters were just coming of age in Washington, restlessly waiting their turn before they were given national and foreign assignments, and therefore covering local rather than national events. They liked Barry and sensed that as much as anyone in the city, he represented and articulated what ordinary blacks felt, the rage just under the surface. They were an early source of his power as he began to make a name for himself. There was, noted Bob Kaiser, later one of the *Post*'s most distinguished foreign correspondents, and eventually its managing editor, a sense of excitement that he gave off from the start—a certain optimism, a belief that things could be made better.[4] In the fall of 1966, a *Washington Post* survey of the black community trying to rate leaders who had "done the most for the Negro community," a curiously outmoded concept and term, showed that Marion Barry was now fifth. All the others were longtime Washington leaders. He had been in town only sixteen months.

He was just beginning to sense his potential as a politician. Even before he had arrived, a young local black man named Carroll Harvey, who believed that the old order was about to collapse, had been looking for a new, fresh political leader who could reach out to the poorest people in the city, the Bamas. Harvey quickly spotted Barry as a comer and began to take him under his wing, sensing that Barry had a natural political touch and the ability to reach the people whom no one else seemed to be able to reach. He pushed Barry to think not just of being part of a movement as SNCC's man, but of getting ready to run on his own as a Washington-based politician. By chance those were exactly the same thoughts running through Barry's mind. His skill on the streets—he had among other things sponsored a series of block parties for young blacks—in turn helped him with the media. He seemed to represent something important: That which had been taking place in the South, the coming of a powerful social challenge to historic inequities, and a challenge led by talented young blacks, was finally reaching Washington. There was his natural charm, and the capacity to seem angry at one moment and conciliatory and gentle the next, adjusting his mood, his rhetoric, his clothing, and seemingly his entire self to the occasion. There had been one night in 1967, at the time that other Northern cities were burning and when Washington had come perilously near to exploding, that only the efforts of Barry and his friend Carroll Harvey, working the streets all night and trying to calm everyone down, had kept the city from being torched.

"The Situationist," the talented young writer David Remnick once titled an article about him, picking up on something Barry himself had once said when early in his career he was asked if he had mellowed from his days when he had first appeared on the Washington scene as an angry street activist: "I'm a situationist. I do what is necessary for the situation." Mary Treadwell, the second of his four wives, a woman whom he met in those early Washington days and who was generally considered to be much tougher and much stronger than he was, later said that Barry was always destined to be either an actor or a politician because he always adapted to the scenery around him. The real Marion Barry was, she told friends, a chameleon.[5]

If he was on the rise in Washington political circles, his legend was ensured by an incident which took place on the night of March 30, 1967.[6] It was near midnight and he was walking across the street at Thirteenth and U in a hard-core black neighborhood known as Little Shaw. He was with two women, and when he started crossing the street, he was jaywalking. Just then two white cops pulled up in a car. The two women immediately backed off, but Barry kept walking. "Hey, you," said one of the cops, "can't you tell the color of a street-light?"

"Fuck you," answered Marion Barry, "and fuck the light too."

In a way his instinct was pure: If there was one thing which enraged all blacks in every city in America, it was the sense that they were constantly hassled by cops in their own neighborhoods for all kinds of minor things, and that white people in white neighborhoods were never hassled for comparable—and often far greater—transgressions. It was then and it remained thirty years later one of the great trigger points of black anger. What was implicit in what happened that night was this: Cops were white and were all powerful and could do whatever they wanted whenever they wanted, and blacks, even in their own neighborhoods and territory, even in the most casual of movements, were powerless and had no rights. If you were black, you were always suspect.

The cop, a young man named Tommy Tague, said something which implied that Barry must have a lot of money because this was going to cost him five dollars. Tague also referred to him as "boy." "Bullshit, motherfucker," Barry answered. There were more words, angry now on both sides. Asked to show some identification, Barry refused; he did not need to show any white cops any goddamn thing, he said. His two friends had gone to the nearby SNCC headquarters and a crowd of blacks was beginning to gather just as Tague and his partner started to put Barry under arrest. The two cops quickly called for backup. It was an incendiary moment in a neighborhood always ready to explode. Soon there were a dozen cops standing alongside Tague. A scuffle broke out. Barry was apparently beaten. At one point Barry swung at Tague and kicked him. Then Barry decked another officer. Finally he was cuffed and taken to headquarters, where he was booked and released on $1,015 bail.

He was an instant hero in the black community, where almost every black longed to do what he had done, and where the Washington police had long been regarded as nothing less than the military extension of the existing semicolonial rule. Almost all contact with white cops was bitterly resented by Washington's blacks; in turn any challenge to the intense racism of the police force was bitterly resented by the cops. In the mid-sixties a young reporter for *The Washington Post* named Bob Kaiser was covering a mugging near Capitol Hill and was stunned to have a cop turn on him and say, "This only happened because of the nigger-loving *Washington Post*."[7] His confrontation with Tague had been an incident which had begun with one provocation too many, and Barry had responded with a certain elemental anger, as if he were a black Everyman. There was a press conference the next day, at which his wounds from the beating were put on display by his lawyers. In June, when Barry went on trial for destruction of government property, there was a sense of the tides shifting, of the new temper of the times. If anything it was Tommy Tague, the cop who had arrested him, and the entire Washington police force who seemed to be on trial that day. Marion Barry had great character witnesses, including Bishop Paul Moore, the head of the city's Episcopal diocese and one of the country's most engaged liberal clergymen, who called Barry a man of peace. The sitting judge, Tague later noted, asked him more questions than he did Barry. "He put me on trial," the cop later said. A jury of ten blacks and two whites deliberated for two hours and acquitted Barry. Carroll Harvey had been right: Marion Barry was by his nature brilliant on the streets, and his response to Tague that night had been visceral. Years later Tague noted with some irony, "I made Marion Barry."[8]

60

PROBABLY THE HIGH-WATER MARK FOR THE MOVEMENT IN TERMS OF achievement had been the breakthrough which had come with the Civil Rights Act of 1964, and then the Voting Rights Act of 1965. Those two pieces of legislation were the culmination of an enormously successful, remarkably swift assault on the foundations of legal and political segregation in the Deep South, victories which were critical to the future of the political system in the South and in the nation. Southern blacks were now enfranchised, and future Southern politicians would have to tread more carefully on the subject of race. But the immense damage done to an entire race of people by some two hundred years of slavery and neo-slavery remained. There was an immediacy of benefit for those blacks who were right on the cusp of becoming middle class—all kinds of doors were now beginning to open. But for many others, burdened as they were by the crippling results of American racial history—the poverty, the lack of education, and the larger psychic hopelessness which had existed in the past—the openings which these changes created often seemed beyond their grasp. Much of the hard work was still ahead.

The principal enemy clearly was a kind of numbing poverty, one in which all the enemies of social progress thrived: poor diet, unchecked disease, desperately limited education and job opportunities, all of it culminating in emotional despair and inner rage. Men like Martin Luther King and Jim Lawson had recognized relatively early on that this was going to be their next major challenge, and King knew that this would be a far harder enemy to rally the nation against than the more obvious problems caused by legal and political racism. This particular legacy of racism was insidious: It was woven into the fabric of the society, it existed across the nation, without geographical boundaries, and there was no easy modern villain to blame it on, no Bull Connor or Jim Clark to be its poster boy. A terrible school in an inner city could not be turned around by assaulting an overworked white school principal, who himself was just as overwhelmed by the social pathology he faced as were the children.

Martin Luther King had decided early on to try and dramatize the struggle against this most difficult foe with the Poor People's campaign, which was to begin in all kinds of small towns and large cities in late April 1968 and end in Washington. But even before they could finalize plans for the Poor People's march, an incident took place in Memphis which seemed to symbolize the kind of frustration that black workers had to deal with all over the South, and throughout the country as well. On February 12, 1968, a group of black sanitation workers had gone on what was seemingly a wildcat strike, since in the most literal sense they did not even belong to a recognized union. But if it was a wildcat strike, it was one which had been produced by years and years of economic frustration and limitless grievance based on race—poor pay, cripplingly unfair labor practices, such as benefits for whites which were not applicable to blacks. The strike was in no way orchestrated; it was nothing less than an explosion of the most powerful kind of long-repressed anger. As Jim Lawson, who became the principal adviser to the strikers, noted years later, when garbagemen go on strike and they've thought it through, they do it in the summer, when the garbage rots and stinks and they have maximum leverage, not in the dead of winter, when the cold weather works against them. But one of the long-standing grievances was the fact that if the weather was bad, black workers, unlike their white supervisors, were not paid. That meant that they were always desperate to work, no matter how bad the weather; the fact that a number of black workers had been sent home during a rainstorm when white supervisors drew a full day's pay had been just one of the galvanizing forces which had produced this strike.

On February 1, 1968, there had been a terrible storm in Memphis. The rain had been heavy. Some twenty-one workers had been sent home that day without pay. At the same time two relatively new workers, Echol Cole and Robert Walker, had been working inside one of the city's older, clunkier garbage trucks, one which happened to have a mashing system inside. It was said later that both of them were inside the truck when the tragedy took place, seeking shelter from the storm, wanting some protection. Apparently the electrical apparatus in the truck shorted out and somehow triggered the compressor mechanism, catching the two men unprepared inside the truck. Tragically there was no button inside which they could push to stop the crusher. Appalled witnesses had watched as the machine literally seemed to devour the two men. Their monstrous death became the final catalytic agent for the strike. It seemed to symbolize the total lack of leverage the workers had in determining their work conditions, and the absolute indecency and indignity of their economic condition. Even worse, their superiors seemed largely unmoved by the entire incident. Neither man had any worker's compensation. Neither had any life insurance. The city paid the two men's families their requisite back pay, plus an additional one month's salary, and then $500 each toward burial expenses. But city officials made it clear that they were doing this out of their own goodness, not because they were legally obligated to. The other black garbagemen had exploded with rage. Winter or not, they had walked off the job.

They had no real union, for they were not recognized by any international union. They had been trying for six years to get some kind of local recognition, always without success. They were the poorest of the poor, Jim Lawson thought. They had no benefits at all, no protection when they retired or if they were hurt. The city bought them one uniform when they came to work. Any future, replacement clothes they bought themselves. They had no place to clean up, to try and remove the stench of the garbage from their bodies at the end of the day. Worst of all was the double standard of who got paid and who did not in foul weather. "White men worked shine, rain, sleet, or snow. Them supervisors just sit there till four o'clock and then get up and go home ever since I been here. This is not the way to do things. It just been going on," said L. C. Reed, a veteran black sanitation worker.[1]

There was no chance for promotion, for there were, of course, no black supervisors. When Lawson had first been brought into their ranks he was absolutely astonished to find out how little they were paid. They lived in the city, but even the most senior of them made only about $1.70 an hour, and a good many of them made as little as $1.27 an hour. Few made as much as $70 a week, a salary that even then was at the poverty level in Memphis. Even by the relatively harsh and ungenerous standards of Shelby County, they were among the worst-paid black men in the community, and they performed work which ranked among the meanest of jobs. Some of them, Lawson was stunned to find out, lived in shacks, paying $10 a month in mortgage fees in order to be home owners.

In all the time they had been pushing for some kind of redress, they had gotten nothing from the city fathers, least of all respect. Though their strike was about wages, Lawson thought, it was also about dignity and respect, about wanting—and demanding—that their basic protest be listened to. One of the first things that flowered when they finally went on strike were buttons which said I AM A MAN. Inevitably among the people they had turned to was Jim Lawson, already acknowledged as one of the most liberal and articulate local activists. He soon became a critical adviser to their strike.

If their conditions defied elemental economic decency and justice, the newly elected mayor of Memphis, Henry Loeb, did not see it that way. Loeb was a big, beefy man, scion of a wealthy family which had made its fortune in the laundry business, a man of singular personal rectitude, but regrettably one of limited empathy for those less fortunate than he. From the start he seemed to see the strike not on its merits and the legitimacy of the grievances of these scorned workers, but as a personal affront. These men were not part of a recognized union, therefore the strike was illegal, therefore he would not listen to them. Worse, because he had only recently served as public works commissioner, he seemed to think that he knew them, understood them well, and most surprising of all, was their friend. "I know these people, I've dealt with them all my life," he would say to Lawson. "I understand them because they worked for me." Amazing, Lawson thought, this man spoke the very same words which plantation owners had used about their black field hands in another era; the plantations were gone now, but the attitudes still remained. Henry Loeb, Lawson thought, might as well be the old-time plantation manager talking about how well he knew his niggers.

From the start, perhaps because Memphis seemed to be such a bastion of old-fashioned segregation, perhaps because he was surrounded by so many people who seemed to see the strike as he did, perhaps because of the singularly powerful daily paper, the *Commer-*

cial Appeal, which also seemed to despise the strike and the strikers and seemed unwilling to cover the forces behind it, Loeb and the people around him underestimated the fury which had driven men so vulnerable to take an action that was for them so risky. Loeb had thought only a small percentage of the men would go out. Instead 930 of 1,100 sanitation workers, and 214 of the 230 construction men who worked in sewers and drains, walked out.[2] The mayor also thought it would be easy to recruit new workers, but to a surprising degree other local blacks honored the strike and would not work as scabs. Loeb thought the locals were being manipulated and pushed by the international union. If anything the reverse was true; the local workers were far ahead of the international union, which at first had to play catch-up. In part because Memphis, like all Deep South cities in that era, liked to think that it enjoyed good race relations, Loeb steadfastly refused to accept the fact that the driving force behind the strike was not just traditional labor issues, but a cumulative sense of racial rage. Loeb, who was considered by his peers handsome and imposing and in his own way honorable, but not necessarily the brightest or most nimble man ever to serve in public office in Memphis, quickly drew a line. His integrity was at stake. "I promise you the garbage is going to be picked up," he said. "Bet on it!"[3] Over the two months the strike lasted, all sorts of other people, outside labor leaders, local white civic and religious leaders, offered their good offices to try and find a solution, but Loeb was unbending. A black boycott of the downtown area followed, a boycott, reflecting the difference between Nashville and Memphis, only partially successful. Some local city commissioners moved behind the scenes to work out a settlement; at one point an agreement seemed to have been worked out, for a compromise appeared possible on one of the more divisive issues, that of dues collection. But when the *Commercial Appeal* ran a headline suggesting that Loeb might compromise on the issue, the mayor exploded and scuttled all attempts to find common ground.

Almost from the beginning, when he became an adviser to the garbagemen, Lawson drew the heat of most of the Memphis establishment. It was a time when there were constant threats against him over the phone; every morning, the phone would ring at his home and Dorothy Lawson would pick it up, and some anonymous caller would say that he hoped she had kissed her husband good-bye that morning because she was never going to see him again. Lawson was aware of the bitter resentment of the top people in the police and at city hall as he became the leading counselor to the strikers. He was, as far as the city leadership was concerned, the enemy incarnate, a man who was inciting others to break the law, no matter how unjust the law. Years later Jerry Wurf, the head of the international union which was trying to connect with the garbage workers, said, "What Lawson never understood was the degree to which he was hated in Memphis—far out of proportion . . . They feared Lawson for the most interesting of all reasons—and I am indulging in psychiatry—they feared him because he was a totally moral man, and totally moral men you can't manipulate and you can't buy and you can't hustle . . . and that's why they hung the label of super-radical on him."[4]

As the implications of the strike grew, Lawson stayed in very close touch with Martin Luther King, and asked King, already gearing up for the Poor People's campaign, to come over to Memphis and take part in a march. That would help focus national attention on an issue which seemed to be local, but which Lawson and others were convinced was just the tip of the iceberg of a true national dilemma, historic political-social subjugation which had turned into second-class economic citizenship. King seemed ready to help, but the main question was one of timing, for he was already desperately overloaded, under more pressure from more different forces than ever before. The pressure seemed to come from every direction: from the radicalization now taking place in other parts of the black community and the rise of black nationalism, particularly in the North; from the fact that his assault upon Chicago had been largely unsuccessful; from the need to make the upcoming Poor People's campaign a success; from the fact that his speeches against the Vietnam War in the past year had made him a target of white leaders, who believed that a black leader had no right to speak out on foreign policy; and now as in the past, from some of the more conservative leaders in the black community who had always opposed him, but now had a new weapon to use against him: that he was putting the black community at risk by taking on Lyndon Johnson.

Yet King told Lawson that a strike of this kind was exactly the kind of thing they should be supporting in this phase of the Movement. On March 17, 1968, a little more than a month after the strike had begun,

King flew into Memphis for the first time to speak to a rally at the Mason Temple, the largest indoor building available to blacks. The rally was a major success. People started arriving in the late afternoon, all the seats were taken long before the announced starting time, and yet thousands more kept filing in, crowded now, standing shoulder to shoulder. At the airport, where Lawson had gone to pick up King, he had greeted the leader with a solemn face. "Martin, I have to apologize to you. I thought we would draw ten thousand people . . ." he had begun. King's face had fallen. ". . . but it now looks like it's twenty-five thousand," Lawson had finished. His crowd estimate, it was said, was more than a little optimistic; the crowd was probably closer to fifteen thousand, still a marvelous show of support.

The Memphis meeting, Lawson thought, had a positive effect on King, who had been under so much pressure lately. Huge cardboard buckets were passed around for donations and were quickly filled up. King was in good form and the crowd was responsive. "You know what?" he asked rhetorically. "You may have to escalate the struggle a bit. If they keep refusing and they will not recognize the union and will not agree for a checkoff of the collection of dues, I tell you what you ought to demand . . . a general work stoppage in the city of Memphis. And you let that day come and not a Negro in this city will go to any job downtown, not a Negro in domestic service will go to anybody else's kitchen, black students will not go to anybody's school."[5] Even as he was urging a general strike, his people were negotiating with the Memphis leadership about whether he would come back and lead a march. King told his audience that he was in charge of the Poor People's campaign, but he would return to Memphis to lead a march which would itself become the beginning of the Washington demonstration. This major march was scheduled for Friday, March 22. There would also be a work stoppage, and no black children would attend school. But on the evening of the twenty-first, and well into the morning of the twenty-second, a freak snowstorm struck Memphis. Some twelve inches fell on a city unusually ill prepared for snow, and the march was cancelled. The organizers decided to postpone the march for six days, to Thursday, March 28.

The march turned into a disaster. Not everyone, it turned out, had the same agenda; some factions within the black community were very angry, and the local nonviolent leadership was not as deeply rooted as it was in other Southern cities. In addition, perhaps, the march that day reflected the fact that one era was already beginning to come to a close, that the black community was more divided than it had been some ten years earlier, and that the new black nationalism, manifested by young black leaders, was surfacing even here in the South.

Everything went wrong. King's plane arrived late; the marchers, waiting impatiently to begin, became restless; there were not enough walkie-talkies for the leadership to stay in touch with different factions. Within Memphis there were black youth gangs which did not feel they had been given enough respect by Lawson and the other older leaders, and whose agenda was significantly different from that of the senior leadership. (Some young people carried placards that day, quite different from the old, traditional ones, which said I AM A MAN. These new signs said things like LOEB EAT SHIT and FUCK YOU MAYOR LOEB.) Some of the high school students who had come aboard that day seemed to think of the march not so much as a demonstration of strength and solidarity for black workers, but as a chance to frolic and perhaps tear up the town. The local police seemed undermanned and ill prepared for the size of the group and their anger.

The march was supposed to start at 10:00 A.M. but was delayed by King's late arrival. The crowd, already restless, was fueled by rumors that the cops had injured and perhaps killed a black youth who had wanted to join the march. Finally, with King at the head, the march began, but it had barely started when some marchers near the rear veered off and began rampaging through the downtown area, smashing windows and looting stores. What had been planned as a show of nonviolent solidarity was ending in violent chaos. When Lawson decided to call off the march, it had gone, as the historian Joan Beifuss noted, only seven blocks and lasted twenty-five minutes.[6] Before it was over, some two hundred buildings had their windows knocked out, the downtown area around Beale Street had been looted, and police had shot and killed one teenage looter. The moment the rioting had started, King's aides had hustled him away from the march and back to his room at a local motel. It was to be Martin King's last march.

King was disappointed and depressed, if not embittered, but he knew they had to undo what had happened, and he agreed to return and lead one last march, originally scheduled for Friday, April 5.

When he came back he and his people were fighting a local injunction prohibiting them from any kind of demonstration in Memphis. He checked into the Lorraine Motel in downtown Memphis and worked on his plans for the Poor People's campaign while his lawyers fought the injunction. On Wednesday night he went to the Mason Temple and gave what would be his last speech, one with an oddly prophetic peroration: "Well, I don't know what will happen now. We've got some difficult days ahead. But it doesn't matter with me now because I've been to the mountaintop. And I don't mind. Like anybody I would like to live a long life. Longevity has its place. But I'm not concerned about that now. I just want to do God's will. And He's allowed me to go up to the mountain, and I've looked over and I've seen the Promised Land. I may not get there with you. But I want you to know tonight that we as a people will get to the Promised Land. So I'm happy tonight. I'm not worried about anything. I'm not fearing any man. Mine eyes have seen the glory of the coming of the Lord."

Thursday, Martin Luther King spent much of the day waiting to hear if they would be granted a release from the injunction, and he was pleased later in the day when word came back that Judge Bailey Brown had approved the idea of a tightly proscribed march for Monday, details still to be worked out. Then that night he was shot and killed at his motel by a sniper. The Memphis sanitation workers' strike was settled, on terms largely satisfactory to the workers, a week later.

61

On that fateful April day in Memphis, Martin Luther King, under so much pressure from so many fronts, needing to work on the forthcoming campaign and yet lead the garbagemen's march in Memphis at the same time, had brought much of his staff with him from Atlanta to Memphis, so that they could work on their plans before and immediately after the march. Among them was Bernard Lafayette.

At that moment there was something of a gypsy quality to Lafayette's life. He had evolved into one of the quiet leaders of the Movement, but he was also anxious to get on with his life and come up with more traditional credentials. But whenever he had started to go back to school to finish his course of study, something would happen; either he would become restless outside the Movement, or there would be an impassioned telephone call from Dr. King himself summoning him back for some special assignment. During the sixties, he had gone from American Baptist to Fisk, dropped out for a time to concentrate on his Movement responsibilities, and then gone back to Fisk. Some ten years after he had first entered college, he had yet to pick up his undergraduate career. The last interruption had come when in 1967 King had asked him to work with (and help control) Jim Bevel as they prepared the Vietnam moratorium.

He was called to Chicago in 1966. That done, in 1967 he had moved to Boston to work for a community organization that was serving as a kind of clearinghouse for social organizations in the city, and determined which funds should go to which projects. Then in late December he had been called back to the SCLC by Martin Luther King to work on the Poor People's campaign. His assignment was to work with local groups throughout the country, deciding what kind of presentation they would make in Washington.

He arrived in Memphis ahead of the others, on April 4. There was supposed to be a meeting in Washington on the Poor People's march later in the day, and so Lafayette flew out of Memphis in the morning, expecting to meet with King and the rest of the staff in Washington a few hours later. Lafayette arrived at National Airport, expecting Walter Fauntroy, their local point man, would meet him, and was surprised that there was no one there for him. As he looked for Fauntroy or some other contact he heard the buzz of a rumor, that Dr. King had been shot in Memphis. He immediately called the SCLC office in Washington, where no one seemed to know very much about what had happened; he reached over in the phone bank to the phone next to him, called the AP office, identified himself, and, working two phones at once, received all the terrible details, relaying them at the same time to the SCLC office. He then called Atlanta, to see what they wanted him to do, and he was told there was no point in going back to Memphis, that President Johnson was sending a plane to take Dr. King's body to Atlanta, and that he might as well come back to Atlanta.

The first thing he thought of was that it might not be a localized assassination, and that perhaps whoever had murdered King was going to go after all of the SCLC leadership, perhaps Ralph and Andy, and Hosea and Bevel and Jesse Jackson, a rising young star in the Movement, and even himself. And for the rest of the day he moved around uneasily, constantly looking behind him, fearing that an assassin's bullet might strike at any minute. Gradually he came to realize it was only Dr. King who had been marked for death, and he began to think of what this meant. The most obvious thing was that a singular era was over. It had begun in December 1955 in Montgomery, and it had lasted for twelve and a half years; the amount of change had been dramatic. Theirs had been a definable historic force unleashed in what was now, regrettably, a definable period, he believed. The Movement had been predominantly black, although its aims were integrationist. Led as it was by black Southern ministers, it was religious, nonviolent, and marvelously and often clumsily democratic. It was ecumenical and above all, for people had often lost sight of this, it was optimistic. It was broad based, and it had constantly had one aim, to appeal to the conscience of America. It was, he decided, probably over; at least the part of it driven primarily by a religious force.

He had given almost ten years of his own short life to it. The thing he had to think about now was what he was going to do with the rest of his life. If the Movement as he had known it was over, then he would have to retool himself, and come up with some kind of credential which would allow him to be an activist and yet earn a living. He decided to stay on in Atlanta and work with Ralph Abernathy for the rest of 1968, but he remembered that particular period as a sad and dispiriting time, one tinged always with a feeling not so much of what they were accomplishing, but of what might have been, and the constant awareness that the man who had helped bring them together was gone.

He also knew that even without the murder of Dr. King, it was time for some kind of personal reckoning: He was twenty-eight now, and he needed some sort of professional focus. The truth was not so much that his personal life was adrift as that, like so many of the young people, he did not have a personal life; there had never been a dividing line between his professional life and his personal life. His marriage to Colia Liddell had rather quickly produced two children, James Lafayette, born in 1964 and named after his friend James Forman, and Bernard Lafayette III, born in 1965. But the marriage had come apart relatively soon thereafter. He greatly admired Colia, who was strong and completely fearless, but in his mind their marriage had been all too typical of Movement liaisons, driven not by the kind of love which lasts for years and years, if not a lifetime, but by the immediacy of commitment to an issue. They were two bright young people fighting the same battles at the same time, and mistaking the community of the Movement for the community of marriage.

Colia Lafayette believed, and to some degree Bernard agreed, that one of the things which had begun to work against their marriage was their profound political differences. These were differences which reflected some of the same divisions just beginning to surface throughout the black community in those days. By the definitions which white Americans used to define the black community, Bernard was more traditional in his politics and she was significantly more radical. She was determined to be part of the black power movement. He was a true apostle of nonviolence; she, like others in her family, was by no means sure that she was nonviolent. He was an integrationist; she had always been a pan-Africanist, her heroes men like Paul Robeson and W. E. B. Du Bois, and she thought of herself as someone held as a prisoner of war in America, a black woman whose ancestors had been captured and taken against their will to a foreign country. Long before it was fashionable in black America, her parents had had a strong sense of their African roots, and she knew that her father's people came from the Sudan and her mother's from Africa and that her name, Colia, was a deft Americanization of a tribal name, the Koli, from the old world. In her home she had always been known as Colie, the letter *a* in her name never being pronounced. It was not by chance that she had taken one of the most dangerous jobs in Mississippi as a young woman, working for Medgar Evers.

Bernard's politics were also very much an offshoot of his own ancestry, and his religious faith, she thought, reflected his belief in the powers of redemption and assimilation. He had a belief in the eventual goodness of America, which she and her family did not share. It struck him sometimes that their arguments were very much like those he had had in the Jackson, Mississippi, jail with Stokely Carmichael, when the two of them would debate long into the night about the respective merits of nonviolence and violence. Those arguments might have been fun with Stokely, but it was different when they began to be a dominating part of his domestic life. By 1967 he and Colia were ready to go their separate ways, she to New York, where she wanted to work, he to Boston.

By the end of 1967 Lafayette, somewhat at loose ends, decided to see if he could go to law school, because he thought lawyers would be valuable in the next phase of the struggle. Lawyers, he believed, would take the gains won in the past decade and maximize them. He decided to get all of his credits, those early from ABC, those gained later at Fisk, and have them transferred to ABC, and to take his degree from there. Then he pondered where he ought to go for his law degree. He had all kinds of connections in Atlanta, but he was wary of Atlanta, for if he stayed there, he would never do any studying. Instead, his old SCLC pals would always be calling him for some emergency duties.

So he decided to move back to Boston, a city he liked, and to try Boston University Law School. Boston boasted an added attraction, a young black woman named Kate Bulls, with whom he suspected he was falling in love. She was an activist herself, from an influential black family in Tuskegee, Alabama (her father was an entrepreneur who among other things had run the Propeller Club, where the famed black Tuskegee airmen had gone to relax). She had gone to college at Tufts and was, at the time Bernard met her, running an early day care center in Cambridge for KLH, a company that made hi-fi equipment. She was impressed by him: He seemed an uncommon young man—he had the belief and the courage to be one of the leaders in the Movement, had been through the worst of some terrifying years, and yet unlike so many others from that period, he seemed to have an ability to enjoy life, to put the Movement aside at the end of the day and laugh and talk about other things. He was as a person, she decided, much stronger than he seemed, remarkably supple of personality. Even in the worst of times, and the months after Dr. King's death were in some ways for him the worst of times, he remained essentially optimistic. The only time she had seen him lose his natural ebullience was during those days right after Martin Luther King was assassinated, when he would call her from Atlanta. She would listen carefully to the receiver, but he was unable to talk, and all she could hear were his tears.

In November 1969 he married Kate Bulls in the Howard Thurman Room in the chapel at Boston University, named for the great hero of his old teacher Jim Lawson. James Bevel was his best man; Kate Lafayette, who did not know Bevel well, thought him impressive, clearly a talented man who seemed to take pleasure in shocking others. With that Lafayette plunged into his law studies. He was pleased with the focus and direction of his new life. There was only one problem: He did not like law school. He found it terribly boring. Part of his problem, he was sure, was the difficulty of coming down from the excitement of the Movement and a commitment which had always offered an immediacy of action, and part of it was dealing with the innate drudgery of the early days of a law student's career. But the last thing he had expected to be was bored. The only time he was excited was when President Nixon had ordered American forces into Cambodia and he had been a leader in the campus protests against the idea of an expanded war.

He was quickly learning that this was not the life for him. He liked to be out socializing with people and he was stuck in a library with all these fat books, lonely and uninvolved. He and Kate were living in Cambridge; they owned two cars and about the only thing he was doing at that moment, she decided, was accumulating a record number of parking tickets from the Cambridge police. By chance in those days he had met through Kate a man named Dr. Chester Pierce, who was a black psychiatrist and educator then teaching at Harvard, and who took an interest in him. Chester Pierce was intrigued by the young civil rights activists, several of whom he had met. He was aware of the pitfalls which lay just ahead for some of them as they faced the next stage of their careers and the hard time they might find adjusting to a more normal life.

To Dr. Pierce, there was no doubt that though Bernard Lafayette was not by any means one of the most famous of the young leaders, he had done as much or more than some who were better known. Yet the ease of his manner, his lack of ego, and his seeming lack of intensity belied both his courage and his obvious religious faith. It was also clear to Pierce that this was a critical make-or-break moment in his life, that Lafayette was floundering and might, without realizing it, be entering a period of depression. It did not surprise Pierce that an intense, quite inflexible program like that facing a first-year law student might be exactly the wrong thing for him. By contrast Pierce thought the Harvard School of Education might be perfect for Lafayette: It was flexible; it allowed its students, many of whom were a little older, to reflect on their lives, to catch their breath for a moment, and to redefine, if necessary, their career purpose, and above all to take their existing strengths and knowledge and get some career value from them. That was in contrast to most law schools, which almost deliberately stripped away a person's past achievements, as part of a deliberate professional remake. The danger for Bernard Lafayette, and others like him at times like these, Pierce feared, was that they would drop out and lose confidence in themselves. They would begin to feel that they were not capable of transferring their obvious leadership abilities to more traditional situations. Truly gifted people might slip into failure. Chester Pierce thought that was an unthinkable alternative, all that immense talent wasted. Given American society as it existed, he thought, blacks did not need to be credentialed, they needed to be *super*-credentialed.[1] So he pushed Bernard Lafayette to try for the Harvard School of Education.

His suggestion made sense to both Bernard and Kate Lafayette. The Lafayette apartment was quite near the Ed School and Kate suggested that her husband might be able to solve a number of their problems—get rid of his car, which was starting to cost them a fortune in parking tickets, get out of law school, which was clearly not the right path—by following Pierce's suggestion. He could walk to class, and the school offered a career in something which he liked and might be good at, teaching. So in the late summer of 1970 he had walked over to the School of Education, aware that it was far too late to apply, but anxious to discuss the possibility of future admission. To his surprise the school had a number of openings for the coming academic year; several young people who had won scholarships had decided at the last minute not to attend. If his curriculum vitae was not exactly a traditional one—after all, to the outsider it seemed that he had logged more time in jail than in classes—it had by 1970, with the changing temper of the times, become a very attractive one and, boosted not inconsiderably by Chester Pierce's recommendation, he was given a handsome scholarship to the Harvard School of Education. There he soon emerged not just as a student, but with the new and quite desperate need to have more black students, he found himself working almost immediately in the admissions office. In due time he got both a master's and, in 1974, a doctoral degree. He was not only pleased by his new success, but amused by it: Bernard Lafayette of Tampa, Florida, who had barely been able to patch together an undergraduate career over some ten years, who had entered one of the poorest schools in the country, American Baptist, now had both a master's and a doctorate from Harvard and had been invited to be a teaching fellow there. He was *Doctor* Bernard Lafayette. His dissertation had been about how and why the peace movement and nonviolence could and should be taught in schools and colleges.

62

JOHN LEWIS TOOK HIS POLITICAL DEFEAT WITHIN SNCC VERY HARD. IT seemed both personal and political. He had been charged with being too pious, too close to Martin Luther King, and too much of an integrationist. He had still believed in an interracial democracy, but that was not a particularly hip or cool idea at that moment. In 1967, nearly a decade after he had first entered American Baptist, he received two degrees, one from Fisk in philosophy, the other in religion from American Baptist. He had not really completed all his Fisk studies, but he had written a long paper on the civil rights movement, and there was a general feeling in the Fisk administration that he had not so much written the paper as he had lived it. He was twenty-seven years old and he was finally a college graduate.

He needed a job after SNCC, and a man named Les Dunbar of the Southern Regional Council, who was a leading foundation figure in pushing black voting rights in the South, helped find him a job with the Field Foundation. The job took him to New York, where he rented a tiny apartment on West Twenty-first Street. He was paid about $10,000 a year, which was a stunning amount of money for him. But he always felt like a foreigner in New York City, very much alone; his principal memory of that time was of getting the vast Sunday edition of *The New York Times* early on Saturday night and sitting alone in his room with a six-pack of beer, drinking and reading the paper, and missing his friends in the South. He was, he was discovering, a Southern boy, comfortable with the texture of life back home, the gentle, easygoing quality of the friendships there, and he was equally uncomfortable with the harder, sharper-edged quality of life in the North. He soon went back to the South to work as a community organizer.

In 1968 he went to work for Robert Kennedy's presidential campaign. Robert Kennedy was a politician who seemed to be growing constantly in stature. Lewis had never seen a white politician whom he had so admired; as far as Lewis was concerned, Kennedy was good and getting better on the two vital issues of that period, civil rights (or race relations) and Vietnam. Lewis went to work for Kennedy in Indiana, where his job was to try and get out the black vote in cities like South Bend and Indianapolis. On the night in April 1968 that Martin Luther King was murdered, John Lewis felt himself go cold, as if someone had turned off part of his own human mechanism. He had a vague memory of a large rally being scheduled for Robert Kennedy in downtown Indianapolis, and of a good deal of discussion being held about whether or not Kennedy should speak; the candidate, against the wishes of many of his advisers, some of whom thought it would be too dangerous, had gone ahead and spoken and had given the best speech of his campaign.

Dr. King's murder was devastating to Lewis. He had known King's strengths and weaknesses and idolized him. When he first learned of the murder, to the degree he could entertain rational thoughts, he thought not so much about himself as about the Movement—*where does the Movement go from here?* The answer, he decided, was that they still had Robert Kennedy, and so he should continue to work for him. Lewis managed to scrounge a ride back to Atlanta the following day, and his assignment in Atlanta was one which made him proud— he was to shepherd different members of the Kennedy family over to the King home. He was a witness that night, he decided, to a special kind of dignity on the part of the representatives of these two families.

From Atlanta he went out west to campaign for Robert Kennedy, then locked in a fierce race for the Democratic nomination with Eugene McCarthy. Lewis spoke in Oregon and then often in California, where he was teamed with Cesar Chavez, the leader of the migrant workers. Although their initial assignment was essentially ethnic, Chavez to work Latinos, Lewis to work blacks, their responsibilities soon changed, in no small part because there was still something of a white liberal tilt in favor of McCarthy, who had made the challenge against Lyndon Johnson ahead of Kennedy. Both Lewis and Chavez were soon assigned to work white liberal meetings and caucuses, and to validate Kennedy's claim to pluralistic, multiethnic liber-

alism by their very support of him. John Lewis was quietly proud of
his own role at that moment—he was not only the Movement representative in Robert Kennedy's campaign, but American politics had
changed so much in so short a time that a person with his background,
someone whom they might have hidden only eight years ago, had now
become an ornament to the campaign, someone to be brought forth to
elite *white* audiences instead of black ones.

He was impressed by the ever-larger crowds Kennedy was drawing
in California, sure that he would take California and the nomination.
On the night of the primary Lewis was among a handful of people
allowed in the fifth-floor room at the Ambassador Hotel with the candidate to watch the election returns, which were generally favorable.
Kennedy teased him that night. "I'm very disappointed in you, John,"
he said, "you let me down—more Mexican Americans turned out and
voted than blacks today." Late in the evening, his victory a certainty,
Robert Kennedy told Lewis and a number of others that he would go
downstairs to make his acceptance speech but that they should stay in
the room, and he would return soon and celebrate with them. He
never did. Instead they watched his assassination in the hotel room.

Now Bobby Kennedy, like Martin King, was gone. To whom would
they turn? he wondered. Never had John Lewis felt so lost. For the
next few weeks he was in something of a daze. He managed to get a
flight back to Atlanta, and he wept the entire time aboard the plane.
He wondered if there was any purpose to politics anymore if all the
best young men were going to be murdered. And he wondered about
the purpose of his own life.

It was about that time that he became serious about a young black
woman named Lillian Miles then living in Atlanta. Later Lillian would
joke that she got him at the right moment, a rare moment of complete
weakness on his part, because until then he had been married to the
Movement and to his work. She was a serious young woman originally
from Los Angeles, a librarian by trade, with a specialty in black literature, both American and African; she had done her undergraduate
work at Cal State-Los Angeles and her graduate work in library science at USC. She had spent three years with the Peace Corps in Nige-
ria. Her own people were from rural Kentucky, and they had brought
with them to California stories and memories of the brutality of life
in the South. Therefore the young people of her own generation who

were willing to risk their lives to overturn the cruel system of the past were the very model of the modern black hero to her. She already knew a good deal about John Lewis when they met; she had seen him often enough on television and read about him and his colleagues often enough in the newspapers. They met at a dinner party in Atlanta on New Year's Eve 1967. He is, she thought, the simplest of heroes. He was unassuming and shy and he had, she thought, absolutely no idea of his importance in American society. He had liked her immediately. She was attractive, interesting, and quite outspoken; she had challenged an executive of the SCLC at the dinner party because she had a sense that there was a shortfall between the money being raised in Los Angeles for the SCLC and the money that the organization reported it had raised. She had stayed on his mind afterward, in no small part because he had been so much at ease talking to her, something quite rare for him. But he did not have much time to think about her because he spent most of 1968 working for Robert Kennedy.

He was too shy to ask her out on a date, but he got around his shyness by devising his own strategy to meet her—he would give himself a birthday party and invite a number of his friends, and then quite casually call and include her. That way his intentions would not seem so obvious. He did not think of himself as being very good with women. He had fallen in love once before, in Americus, Georgia, but the young woman had not been in love with him. Now he was determined to be bold. It was the first real dinner party he had ever given and it took all his courage to invite her. He remembered that she had showed up in a green dress with lots of peace symbols on it and that impressed him even more. Later, after they had started seeing each other seriously, he had remarked about the dress and how favorably impressed he had been with the political commitment it seemed to signify, and Lillian Miles, not nearly as political a person as he had thought, had replied that she did not realize that the designs were peace symbols.

She seemed in all ways the perfect woman for him. She was intelligent and kind and she was a member of the Ebenezer Baptist Church, which was Dr. King's church. She had a car and he did not. His close friend Bernard Lafayette said that John should marry her for that reason alone: He, after all, did not even drive. One of her favorite restaurants in Atlanta was a pleasant one at the airport and John was always going to and from the airport: They seemed to date in those days under the constant shadow of Delta Airlines when she either dropped him off or picked him up. John Lewis was quite surprised by how verbal he became with her; it was as if he had finally found someone who allowed him to be free of his often paralyzing shyness. His friends, both black and white, were much amused by him in this period: Here was John Lewis, already a true American hero in their eyes, and he was absolutely bedazzled by the fact that this attractive, talented young woman—he would talk to them endlessly about how good-looking she was, and how intellectual she was—was in love with him. Rarely had his innocence shown through so brightly. Gradually he began to feel more confident about himself as a person—not just as someone who was good at the Movement, but as someone who had other dimensions. Though he was away a good deal in 1968 because of the campaign, their relationship deepened. When Robert Kennedy was killed in early June she realized just how shattered he was. She took her entire vacation in the month of August and instead of travelling or visiting her family she stayed in Atlanta in order to be with him every single day. They were married on December 21, 1968.

When he had returned to the South he had worked for the Southern Regional Council, organizing cooperatives and credit unions in small Southern towns, and then in 1970 Vernon Jordan, who was the head of the Voter Education Project, was named the head of the United Negro College Fund, and Lewis was appointed to take his place in voter registration. The Voter Educational Project was designed to work in eleven Southern states and to push blacks to use the provisions of the Voting Rights Act. That turned out to be one of the most thrilling experiences of his life, particularly given the anguish he and so many of his friends had been subjected to while fighting for the very right to vote in these same Southern towns. It was reward time, he thought, like taking a victory lap in a stadium after running the twenty-six miles of a marathon. He and a few others who worked with him—more often than not his friend Julian Bond—would go into Mississippi or Alabama, and they would over a few days hit ten or twelve counties, where they would have well-publicized rallies at which they taught rural blacks how to vote. They brought in as guest speakers people like Coretta King and Douglas Wilder, already a rising star in Virginia politics. The crowds were big, rarely less than five hundred people and often as many as one thousand. Posters were put up in each town announcing the forthcoming rallies, and the poster had his name and Julian's on it. It showed a black hand picking cotton, and it said that hands which had once picked cotton could now pick their elected officials.

What he noticed was that this was already a different South. In town after town where the sheriffs and the local police had always hassled them and tried to intimidate them in the past, there was now a dramatically changed attitude. The local sheriffs were now helpful, and sometimes they were asked if they wanted a police escort into town. In Belzoni, Mississippi, a notoriously hard town in the past, they held their rally and near the end the local sheriff came in and asked to speak to the assembled black people. Near tears, he told them how much he liked being sheriff, that he thought he was a good sheriff, and that he wanted their votes. For Lewis and Bond that particular moment was unusually sweet. It was, Lewis thought, the beginning of a different world, and it had happened much sooner than he thought. John Lewis thought he had never enjoyed a job more in his life.

He thought he had no illusions about himself. He did not think of himself as attractive or graceful or very articulate, but he knew he was always willing to work hard, and that he was willing to make a complete commitment on the things which mattered to him. He did not go halfway. What he said he would do, he always did. That had always been the source of his strength. Others were more attractive, and others were more verbal. He was the plowboy. He was comfortable with that role; he had no need to be anything else. He thought he would be involved in politics for most of his life, but he did not see himself as running for office. Others would make better candidates, notably Julian Bond, who was one of his two or three closest friends, and who was witty, articulate, and dazzlingly attractive. As Lewis examined himself coldly and saw his own limitations, and his own singular lack of charisma, he saw Julian as the prototype of the new generation of black leaders who would run for office.

In the fall of 1968, after Bobby Kennedy's murder, Lewis urged Julian Bond, already a state senator with a national reputation, to run for the Atlanta congressional seat. "Some of us have said many times that after the death of Martin Luther King and Robert Kennedy, you arose as the political leader of many," he wrote his old friend. "Your presence filled a vacuum, and you became the hope of millions who had previously identified with these two great men. Julian, you have an obligation to the youth of today to use your influence to let them know that there are some basic changes that can be made through the machinery of politics." Even if Bond did not win this time, Lewis suggested, he would establish himself as the black candidate for the future and would eventually win. Bond decided against making the race.

Lewis also showed his letter to Andy Young, equally attractive, the SCLC leader who had been one of King's closest advisers. That year, 1970, pushed by both Lewis and Bond, Young made the race in a district in which roughly 30 percent of the voters were black. He lost the first time, but two years later after redistricting had increased the black percentage to 38 and included young white middle-class voters from the Emory University community, Young won, one of two blacks elected to Congress from the South since 1901. Young won again in 1974 and 1976. After the 1976 victory, Jimmy Carter, who had been elected president, asked him to be the American ambassador to the United Nations. Young accepted the offer. Lewis, like a good many of Young's friends, thought it was a mistake, that the United Nations job was more about ceremony than policy, and that it would pull Young, who had the opportunity and the talents to be a gifted and influential legislator, away from a fast track in Congress and a chance to emerge very quickly in the leadership ranks. Accepting the offer would take him from a job of influence and security and place him in one of the most vulnerable and least influential jobs in the government. Lewis argued against Young taking it, to no avail.

When Andy Young left Congress at Carter's request, Lewis decided to try a run at Young's old seat, and made the runoff, but lost to Wyche Fowler. In the process Lewis's respect for Fowler, his white liberal Democratic opponent, grew and they became good friends. In 1977 Lewis was appointed by Jimmy Carter as associate director of Action, which was the domestic peace corps. He and Lillian looked for a house in Washington and found one, on Logan Circle, a large house which cost $99,000, a figure which to a boy from rural Alabama seemed like all the money in the world. They bought the house anyway, he and Lillian moved, but he found that he missed the South. In

1980 he returned to Atlanta to run for the city council; he was running against an incumbent who was a heavy favorite, but he won with 69.8 percent of the vote. The next time he ran he received 90 percent. He was glad to be back in Atlanta, and somewhat to his surprise he liked being in elective politics and found that he was good at it. He believed his strength lay in constituent service; he was good, he decided, at doing small things, and at paying attention to the concerns of ordinary people, no matter how small those concerns. In addition, at a time when there were increasing divisions between black and white communities in both the North and the South, he still found it relatively easy to have friends in both communities.

He remained an integrationist. His own heroism had given him an uncommon immunity against any insidious charge of being soft on white America. On occasion when there were blacks who were critical of him in this area and who claimed that he was insufficiently radical, it would usually turn out that they had done less and taken far fewer risks during the most dangerous years of the Movement. Black-separatist rhetoric was steadily escalating but his own religious convictions demanded that he treat everyone well, and see the good in all those around him. Everyone, it seemed, knew that John Lewis had a good heart, and that time and again he had risked his life for the cause.

63

Hank Thomas, the Howard student who was brought into the Movement in no small part because of the Nashville kids, and who was almost killed in Anniston in 1961 when the Greyhound bus was set on fire, stayed with the Movement for a time, going to work for CORE as a full-time field worker. That tour was cut short in Birmingham in 1963 when he tried to work on voter registration projects there, only to find that he was being shadowed everywhere by Bull Connor's police. Wherever he tried to spend the night—first at a black motel, then later at the homes of two black families friendly to the Movement—the Birmingham police seemed to have advance notice, and had already told the owners if they let him spend the night they would be arrested themselves for violation of the city's Jim Crow laws. Told by friends that there was a warrant out for his arrest, he left Birmingham in the middle of the night and went back to Washington. He returned to Howard as a student, where somewhat to his surprise and very much to his pleasure he found that he was something of a celebrity because of his civil rights activities. He had gotten married while in Birmingham, a marriage, he reflected later on, very much of the young, and if nothing else it increased the financial pressure on him.

While at Howard, Thomas, like a number of other civil rights activists, began to feel increasing pressure from his draft board back home. Rarely, he thought, had white people, other than the Klan in Alabama and the Birmingham police, been so solicitous of his whereabouts as the St. Augustine draft board was now being. He was convinced, as were others like him, that a number of white Southern draft boards, under prodding by the FBI, were singling out young civil rights activists, aware that they were often away from their colleges for extended periods of time, and thereby risking their deferments. In the middle of 1963, sure that an induction notice was going to be the next missive he would receive from his board, Thomas decided to volunteer for the army. If he was drafted as a black man, he reasoned, he would end up as an infantryman. He wanted to serve in the army, stay out of danger, and come back whole. He was fairly confident about his chances, since there was no real war going on, only a minor conflict in a place called Vietnam, where about seventeen thousand Americans were serving in advisory and support capacities and where, as he made his decision to volunteer, fewer than one hundred had died. By volunteering, he decided, he would have some choice over his branch of service, and he would be able to avoid combat. Unlike white kids his age, he had no one to mentor him, and so he signed up to be a medic. He was sure that if there was ever a war he would be quite safe, working in some secure hospital back near headquarters. The friendly, genial sergeant at the recruiting office confirmed that his was an amazingly shrewd choice.

His luck, as it had been that day in Anniston three years earlier, remained imperfect. Almost as soon as he finished his basic training the war in Vietnam started intensifying, and in the middle of 1965 Lyndon Johnson decided to send the first American combat troops to Vietnam. Among them was the First Cav, an elite unit which was to fight with legendary bravery in Vietnam. Among the medics of the First Cav was Spec/4 Henry Thomas. Having joined the army in a way designed to minimize any participation in combat, he had in some comic-opera way found himself among the infinitesimally tiny handful of Americans destined to participate in some of the most savage action in the Vietnam War.

His Vietnam was bitter and lethal. He was with a formidable American combat unit posted in the central highlands, where it did battle with elite units of North Vietnamese regulars. Only by chance and the fact that the helicopter he was on got lost did he miss the famed battle of the Ia Drang Valley, a fierce, bloody, defining early battle of the war; he arrived on location only when the battle was finally over. His remembrance of the Ia Drang was of bagging the bodies of the KIA, and collecting the dog tags. His memories of Vietnam were framed by the pain of dealing with the dead, the dying, and the wounded. He was twenty-two when he arrived in-country. He thought he had done all of the growing up he needed as an activist in Anniston and Birmingham; now he was learning he had only begun to understand man's full potential for violence.

A few weeks after the Battle of the Ia Drang he got malaria and was sent to an army hospital in Japan to recuperate. His recuperation was slow, and it was only in March 1966 that he returned to Vietnam. One day shortly after his return he was on a seemingly routine patrol in the area around An Khe. The unit he was with was moving through an old burial ground when it was hit hard by NVA fire. People were yelling *medic!*—the losses were heavy that day—when suddenly he felt something hit his hand. The odd thing was that for a time he felt no pain, and he busied himself trying to get to other members of the unit who were down. His ability to help them out was limited, however, because he seemed to have no control over his right hand. Finally he looked down and saw the bones of his hand sticking out. At almost the same time he felt a terrible stab of pain coming from it. He wondered if he was going to bleed to death in some ancient Vietnamese burial ground.

Then the medevac chopper arrived and picked him up, and as the chopper struggled to gain altitude and get out of the area, he was stunned by the irony of his situation and the curious thought which was running through his mind: He was a young black man denied normal American freedoms in his native state who had ended up in Vietnam; but in the end, to his own amazement, he *had* been lucky, for he was a soldier of the technologically superior side in this war. He was almost certainly going to live. Truly bad luck belonged more often than not to the soldiers of the other side, and if he were one of them he might well have bled to death in that burial ground. If perhaps he had been a little unlucky as an American black, he decided, there were others who were *very* unlucky. He was sure, however, that he had permanently lost the use of his hand.

The wound had put a certain ceiling on his military career. Before he was hit, Thomas had decided to become a chopper pilot, which might have led to a professional military career with significant benefits, and he had managed to qualify for pilot training. But now, thanks to the marksmanship of the NVA, he had lost sufficient use of his hand to be unable to enter helicopter training. He was sent to army hospitals first at Clark Field and then back to Walter Reed, outside

Washington. Though three knuckles on his right hand had been shattered, the doctors there did an exceptional job in restoring most of the use of his hand. It was at Walter Reed that he began to read seriously about Vietnam for the first time, becoming significantly more dovish as he did.

He also became acutely aware of the vast differences between the post-army plans of the whites in his sick bay and the blacks. There were sixteen grunts in the ward, mixed quite evenly by race. In fact, it was one of the most integrated environments he had ever been in, and he was aware of the bitter irony of that, of how hard-won this integrated little community was. In some ways theirs was a shared existence, for they all had common problems, frustrations, and enemies, the chief enemy being the system itself. If their conversations seemed balanced and oddly without the normal racial divisions when they talked about the war or the army system, or their girlfriends, there was one moment when the integrated quality of their group disappeared. That was when the whites would talk about their post-army plans.

All of the whites, it seemed, had plans to have their own businesses, and they would talk about how they were going to go back to whatever small town it was they had come from and use the benefits they received from the government to open some auto repair business or small trucking and delivery business that they had always dreamed of. As they spoke of these plans, the blacks in the ward became absolutely silent, because as Thomas remembered, none of them had anything in the way of post-army plans and certainly none of them was thinking of opening a business of his own. It was a devastating insight: The whites, having served their country, having made their way out of those small towns where they had been raised, having survived the terrors of Vietnam, felt they were entitled to a better post-military life; the blacks thought their lives were not going to get any better when they left here, and might in fact turn out to be worse than life in the military. Hank Thomas had looked around the room and he had decided that he was as bright as anyone there, white or black: He had had three years of a good college; he was sure, because of his civil rights days, that he had leadership qualities, and he believed that he had done as much for his country as these white boys had done. He decided right then and there that one day he was damn well going to own a business too.

While he had been recovering at Walter Reed he had worked at night at a nearby McDonald's. He needed the money; he was married with one child. Because he had a cast on his hand he could do only a limited number of jobs there. His specialty was toasting the hamburger buns. But he was fascinated by the energy of the place. He had never seen so many customers rushing in and out of a business establishment, and he had never seen so much money changing hands so quickly. He decided that one day he was going to get into a franchise food business.

64

BACK IN CHICAGO, WORKING AS A TEACHER, CURTIS MURPHY HAD slowly begun to piece his life together. The terrible late-night carousing which had marked his earlier tours of Nashville and Chicago seemed to be over. He found that he liked teaching; it was not just a job, it was a job which he believed in. The person who had helped him the most was Rayna Ristow, the young teacher whom he had teased when he had first started out at the Simeon School. Eventually he had asked her out. At first she had said no, she could not go out with him because he was black. When he pushed a little harder, she had asked him if he knew of any interracial couples, and he had thought for a moment and said that no, he did not. But he had persisted, and they had eventually started dating. With that his life began to change. For the first time in his life, he decided, he had found someone he could open up to without fear. It became a great source of relief to him, the ability to relax and to talk with someone whom he trusted absolutely and to whom he could pour out all his doubts and fears, above all how lonely he felt—all the things he had kept in for so long.

He found that he was very much in love with her, but that though she liked him very much, she was wary of a serious relationship, let alone marriage. She was white and Catholic and came from an extremely sheltered background; her ancestors were Germans and Poles, people who were not regarded as avid integrationists. The Ristow family lived in Oak Lawn, which as far as Curtis was concerned was a bastion of white prejudice. When Rayna finally started dating Curtis, she was living at home, and so she started seeing him covertly, knowing that her parents would not approve, allegedly going off to meet girlfriends and then joining up with him. At first she saw their dates as something of a lark, because his sense of humor was so good and because he was simply more fun to be with than any boy she had ever been with before. But then gradually they began to be serious.

When she finally told her parents about Curtis and how serious they were and that they were planning to get married, Ramond and Esther Ristow were predictably upset. We're sure he's very nice, went their argument, but we're looking out for your best interests. Or as Rayna Ristow remembered, "They were really thinking, 'You're too stupid to be afraid of all the things you should be afraid of.' " Her father told her he would disavow her, and leave her one dollar in his will—which he said would prevent her from challenging the will. "Fine," she answered, "I'll just give the dollar to Curtis. I don't need your money." When late in their courtship Curtis would arrive to pick her up for dates, he would not get out of the car and go into the house. In all the time they were dating, Curtis Murphy had never met her parents. To him courting her became very much like being back in the sit-ins; it was a political experience as well as an emotional one.

Back in Whiteville, Buck Murphy was equally wary about what was happening. Curtis had told him that he planned to marry a white teacher whom he had met. Marrying a white girl, as far as Buck was concerned, could be trouble, big trouble, and it would certainly create a much harder life for his son. He doubted that his son and this young women were up to it. So one day without telling anyone, Buck Murphy got on the train in Memphis and came to Chicago and at his request—it was more a demand than a request—all three of them went out to dinner. After dinner they adjourned to one of the lounges where Curtis liked to hang out. At a certain point in the evening, Buck simply waved Curtis away from the table and then he proceeded to tell Rayna everything he could which reflected either weaknesses or flaws in Curtis's character: how many girls he had had in the past, how he had slipped in his studies, of his tendency to be careless and not push himself to the maximum of his abilities. Each time he listed a new indictment, Rayna would nod and say yes, she knew all about that. "How did you know it?" Buck would ask and she would answer that Curtis had already told her about it. Nothing he said that night could shake her or faze her. This young lady was, he decided, not at all flighty; she was steadfast, she was straight, and even more remarkably, he realized, his son, usually so unwilling to venture anything about his private life, had told her everything about himself. They had a level of trust unusual for young people, white or black or white *and* black, he decided. If she wanted him, Buck Murphy decided, she was going to get him, and she was getting him warts and all. The next day as he was about to board the train back to Tennessee, Buck went to a pay phone and called his son at work and told him he had found a fine young woman.

In April 1966 they were married in a civil ceremony in Chicago, just the two of them, with no witnesses or friends present. Spurned by her family, they had taken a tiny, one-bedroom apartment in the southeast section of Chicago. The day she had moved out, she was later told by others in her family, her father broke down and wept. In her own way she was completely confident of her choice. She did not think of herself as a pioneer, someone drawn to a man because she liked the idea of testing parental prohibitions. Rather she loved her parents, had little desire to disobey them, but she had an uncommon faith in her choice. She loved Curtis: She thought of him not so much as black or white, but as someone gentle and intelligent, filled with the rarest of gifts, both the gift of kindness and the gift of laughter. Rayna's older brother had met Curtis earlier and had liked him, and now as the family seemed to be on the verge of pulling apart, he worked to form a bridge between the generations. Soon Rayna's mother visited the young couple at their apartment. Rayna was her only daughter and Esther Ristow was determined not to lose her. Only Ramond Ristow remained a holdout. A year into their marriage he had yet to meet his son-in-law, yet to visit his daughter.

The first break in Ramond Ristow's resistance came a year later. Ironically, though he was not yet talking to his son-in-law, nor to his daughter, he was clearly thinking of their long-term welfare. Ramond Ristow owned a small house on South Morgan, where his mother was living, and he had been thinking of selling it and moving his mother into a small house much nearer his own home in Oak Lawn. On his own he decided that perhaps he could upgrade the young couple's housing; he decided they would take over the South Morgan house, and instead of paying rent, their money would go against the mortgage. In time the house would become theirs. The offer was relayed to Rayna, who relayed it to her husband. Curtis Murphy was immediately intrigued because he remembered his father's passion for land

and for property ownership—a man had to have his land, Buck always said. Ristow worked out a plan where he would carry the mortgage for eight years but then the balance of the mortgage would have to be taken over by Curtis and Rayna. There would be no down payment from them. It was a very generous deal and it was a sign, Rayna Ristow Murphy thought, that her father was coming around. That Christmas the family gathered at Rayna's brother's house, and this time it had been decided that everyone would come together.

Rayna told her husband that her father would be there. Was that all right? she asked. It would be just fine, Curtis Murphy said, for he was not about to stand in the way of this family's love for one another. It was an oddly formal first meeting. Ramond Ristow walked in and shook his son-in-law's hand and said, "Hello, Mr. Murphy, how are you?" Curtis answered in kind, "Mr. Ristow, how are you?" and with that it was done and they could begin to discover if they liked each other as human beings. With that began a relationship based on mutual respect.

Curtis and Rayna Murphy had decided that being an interracial couple was not going to be a problem because they were not going to let it be a problem. They would, they both decided, work harder at their marriage because they had to work harder. Because so many friends had tried to warn them off, tried to tell them they were making a mistake, they were not about to let the marriage fail, not about to prove all those who had warned against it right. Curtis Murphy thought he was lucky because Rayna was so strong and single-minded, a person who knew her own truth, what was real and what was not real in life, and did not let other people's opinion of them affect what she felt; she in turn felt lucky as well, for Curtis was ebullient and immensely likeable, a man of constant optimism who, however strongly he felt about his own racial pride and identity, did not make judgments on others based on race, but accepted people as they were. In addition they were lucky, they decided, because they were sur- rounded by bright young friends who more often than not were teach- ers and who did not worry greatly about things like this. On occasion when they went out to dinner with a friend who had never been with them before, they noticed the effect on the friend. "Rayna," one of her friends once said after dinner with them, "did you notice how every- one in the restaurant was staring at you and Curtis?" No, she said, she had not noticed, because she and Curtis were so accustomed to being stared at that they no longer paid very much attention.

Curtis and his father-in-law grew close. Years later, Esther Ristow told her daughter that the amazing thing about their two husbands was how similar they were. Ramond Ristow, it turned out, was a generous and good-hearted man, one willing to get on with the future and forget the past. The Murphys of Whiteville accepted Rayna Murphy quickly and absolutely; she was married to the young scion of the family, and she was amused by the fact that whenever they visited Tennessee, it was the cause for a singular homecoming celebration. Curtis liked to drive at night and they tended to arrive around 3:00 or 4:00 A.M., often to find seven or eight members of the Murphy clan waiting for them; Duggar would then fix a meal for everyone and the next day there would be a major barbecue. Curtis was the hero of the family, the beloved son, and Rayna was amused when she was told, again and again by family members, cousins and aunts, that while she was completely accepted by them, that *Maggie* Murphy—Curtis's grandmother who had raised him and, they all believed, spoiled him hopelessly—would never have accepted her, not because she was white, but because she was a woman, and Maggie Murphy was not about to share her love for this wondrous young man with any other woman.

What also came to amuse both of them was the mutual warmth and respect of the two sets of parents for each other. In some ways the world of the Ristows of Chicago was, other than the constancy of hard work, as far from the world of the Murphys of Whiteville as it was possible to be. Yet both sets of parents came to be good friends, supportive of each other and of this marriage, determined to add their strength and their love to that of the young people. Each year when Ramond and Esther Ristow drove South for their annual winter vacation on the Alabama coast, they stopped off in Whiteville to visit with Buck and Duggar Murphy, and major family celebrations were held. Comparably, when the Murphys came to Chicago, they visited and dined with the senior Ristows.

Rayna and Curtis Murphy tried hard to have a child but they were not able to. After about five years of trying they decided to adopt. In those days it was not easy to adopt an interracial baby and the process took some time, but then in June 1972, the woman helping them with the adoption heard from a friend about an interracial baby. When they went to pick the baby up, they were both struck by how beautiful he was. He was, by contemporary American racial definition, black, but he was very light-skinned and he had as a baby an unusual amount of hair, which was straight. For a quick moment Rayna, seeing the baby, was uneasy. "Is he too white for you?" she asked her husband. "No! No! No!" he answered and then added, "How can you even think that?"

Curtis Murphy found that he had a talent, that he was good at teaching, and even better at administration. By the late sixties he was teaching at Farragut, a predominantly black and Hispanic school on the west side of the city; he taught there three years before the principal called him in and asked him if he might think of becoming a counselor, because he seemed to have an unusual ability to talk with young people. In time he started working on his master's degree at Loyola, because in order to be a principal or an assistant principal you had to have a degree in supervision or administration.

He began to notice that while many of the teachers he knew were black, most of the supervisory jobs seemed to go to whites; by 1972 he had his master's, and had started working on his doctorate. He was also doing some interning at schools in the suburbs and at one point was offered a principal's job in a predominantly white community. The problem, he decided, was that he was being offered only a one-year contract, and the support on the local school board was thin, a 4–3 majority to begin with, and the switch of only one vote could bring him down. He opted to stay in the Chicago school system, overloaded by politics and social decay though it was. Dr. Mel Heller of Loyola, who had been his sponsor, and had pushed him to take the job in the suburbs, thinking that it was a good thing for the community to have a black principal and one day a black superintendent, thought he was crazy for making that particular choice.

In 1973 an assistant principalship opened up at a new school on the south side of Chicago, George Washington Carver, located at 131st and Doty. Curtis Murphy applied for it and got it, thinking he would be there two or three years, perhaps five at the most. He was, by the late seventies, still working on his Ph.D. He was also preparing to take the principal's exam. To pass, an applicant needed a composite score of 80 and Curtis Murphy got a 79. The list of those who passed was published, and it both surprised and did not surprise Murphy and some of his black contemporaries who took it that the names of those who passed were almost exclusively white. A few months later he took it again, and again he got a score of 79. There were reports that the test was not straight, that there was a good deal of racial politics about the way in which the results were scored, but oddly enough, it no longer bothered Curtis Murphy that much. He liked being at Carver. He liked working every day with the kids.

He and Rayna had lived for eight years in the small house on South Morgan which her father had offered them. In time the house was paid for, but with the addition of Kevin, their son, they needed more space, and they decided to move to the suburbs. They found a house in Glenwood, a pleasant and modest racially mixed suburb on the south side of town, not that far from where they both worked. The house was almost within their price range. But the finances represented a fairly complicated deal, particularly for schoolteachers, whose sources of cash were limited. They would have to sell the house on South Morgan, a deal which, if they wanted to get full value, might take several months to complete, and they needed to move as quickly as they could to get the Glenwood house. Even so, even if everything worked out, they were likely to fall a little short on the Glenwood house. The asking price was $52,000. But Buck Murphy had always told his son that if he ever needed money for land, he was to call him, and so Curtis called Whiteville and explained his problem, and Buck told him and Rayna to come on down to Whiteville and they would talk to the white banker there.

By that time Buck Murphy not only owned three hundred acres of land, having expanded his holdings, but it was all paid for, and the value, for some of it was cotton land and some timberland, was probably, in mid-seventies dollars, Curtis estimated, around $250,000. Not bad for a self-made man who was a dirt farmer, Curtis thought. He and Rayna flew down to Whiteville and when they first arrived at the bank, Buck spoke alone with Robert Bass, the president of the bank, for a few minutes, and then Curtis and Rayna were summoned in, and Buck left the room. "Your dad says you need a couple thousand," Robert Bass said.

"Well," said Curtis, "not just a couple thousand. Actually, eight thousand."

With that Bass called Buck Murphy back into the room. "Buck, they don't need a couple thousand—*they want eight thousand!*"

"Whatever they need, let them have," Buck Murphy said.

So Robert Bass drew up the papers, the collateral being Buck's land, and gave Curtis a cashier's check for $8,000. "Now, son," Bass said, "you be careful with that cashier's check—it's just like money if you lose it." It was, Curtis thought, a wonderful moment for his father, to sit there as a black man in this white man's bank, and be able to say to a white banker, *give them what they need.* Perhaps, he thought, it was the proudest moment of his father's life.

His father, he thought, was in his own way a wealthy man. But he hated to show it. He liked to wear, even for business occasions, his worst clothes: old shoes, sometimes with knotted old laces, and a rope as a belt for his pants. Oddly enough, Curtis thought, Buck had a lot of good clothes. He just didn't like to wear them. He had five handsome, brand-new suits in his closet which he had bought and which looked good on him. They still had their price tags on them. He loved good shoes and he had several spanking-new pairs, all yet to be worn. He had at least a dozen brand-new shirts still in their cellophane wrapping. Duggar raged at him over this. "You look like a bum," she would say. It never bothered him. "Always keep them guessing," he would say, "always keep them guessing." Wealthy or not, he never changed, refusing to wear his good clothes, but always bringing them out to show visitors to his house. Curtis came to believe that he did this because he had learned as a young man that a black man who had wealth was more likely to cause jealousy than a black man who seemed poor. That, Curtis was sure, was where the phrase about keeping them guessing came from. He was not about to call attention to his wealth and his material success and make people think he was a black man who was getting out of line.

65

In 1964, Rodney and Gloria Powell had returned to the United States too late to be a part of the Mississippi summer program in which so many of their former colleagues had begun to challenge the state's segregated laws and electoral processes. Their second child, Allison, had been born in Dar es Salaam in September 1963. The delivery had been extremely difficult, because the doctor was incompetent and botched the job; Gloria was in labor for more than a day and a half. The delivery had exhausted her, another reminder of how difficult life in Africa could be. After two years in Africa, they were ready to go home.

After the hardships of Africa there was something reassuring about life back in the United States. Mrs. Johnson was thrilled to have them back and immediately wanted to take her grandchildren out to buy them presents. Aware of how little money she had, they had tried to protest, but she had insisted—it would be her great pleasure and besides, she said, she would be able to use her new credit cards. *Credit cards?* they said, dubiously, because in 1964 only the relatively affluent had credit cards. The idea of Mrs. Johnson, the most careful shopper of all time, a woman who would eye a couch for months and then buy it after the Christmas sale was over, when the store wanted to get rid of it—cutting her own deal of $5 down and $2 a week, which she hand delivered herself to the store—now armed with credit cards was something of a leap. But she had reached in her purse and held them up. The credit card companies had come to her and said that she had such a good record as a customer with no debt, they had wanted her to have these cards, and she had signed up for them. Of course, she had yet to use them. Now she wanted to try them out. They, both doctors, neither with credit cards, were once again amazed by her.

In the summer of 1964 it was time to get on with their careers, at least to get over the mandatory hurdles—his residency, her internship. Experienced Gloria might be, as a participant for two years in the most primitive practice of medicine imaginable, when she had virtually played God in deciding which African children would live and which would die, but still, she needed to be credentialed. Somewhat to their surprise, both Rodney and Gloria were beginning to realize that they were in demand, that the type of commitment they had once made only because it had seemed the right thing to do was becoming more fashionable. Rodney Powell took up his pediatric training at the University of Minnesota as a resident, while Gloria was accepted at nearby St. Barnabas Hospital as an intern.

Rodney Powell faced a new set of problems there, chief among them trying to be heard and understood by professional peers who had no earthly comprehension of what he had just witnessed in the poorest continent in the world. If trying to break through the medical mind-set in Africa was hard, he was surprised upon his return to find that it was equally hard in America. He had brought with him his slides from Africa, which in the most devastating way showed the dynamics of starvation and disease. His presentation portrayed an endless cycle of malnutrition: of parents who suffered from malnutrition trying to raise children, who inevitably suffered from it as well. There was no need for the diet to be so bad, he pointed out; these countries were poor, but they were not that poor. But local practices, many of them tribally dictated, meant that most mothers were not using the right weaning foods, and that in addition, again because of tribal customs, the children were the last to be fed in most families. More of this cruel crisis, he reported, was a result of ignorance and custom and superstition rather than pure poverty. Because children were often breast fed for two years they suffered from both a terrible protein deficiency and an amino acid deficiency. This was a problem, he believed, over much of the continent.

The response to his talks from other American doctors was surprisingly cool. What he wanted was to change the entire thrust of medical and public health care toward a greater emphasis on preventive medicine and to break the dreadful cycle which took so many lives. They had first of all, he said, to dent the traditional psyche of the typical African village. He was talking from firsthand knowledge of this disastrous system, yet the response among his medical colleagues seemed remarkably unsympathetic: *Well, this is all very interesting, Dr. Powell, but where is your research? What is your database? How much of this have you worked in a lab and what lab test results do you have for us?* My God, he thought, I've been overwhelmed by it every day for two years and they are treating me as if I'm a fool because I did not go out there with test tubes and research papers and statisticians. My database, he thought, is right there in the slides, children who are dying today and those about to die tomorrow. He felt distanced from most of his colleagues, many of them decent and valuable; we are not just talking about a separate continent, he thought, we might as well be standing on separate planets as we do it.

Gloria Powell was, upon her return, as experienced an intern as St. Barnabas had ever seen. But even here in Minnesota there was always the question of race. Early in her tour, there was a heavy snowstorm, and the regular doctor was not able to get to the hospital to perform the delivery of a child. At the last moment Gloria Johnson-Powell was pressed into service. The pregnant white patient seemed unimpressed by her skills because she was unimpressed by her color. "My room is like Grand Central Station," she complained to the attending white nurse; "first you send the janitor in to fix the radiator while I'm trying to rest. That's bad enough. But now," the woman added, pointing to Dr. Powell, "you've sent the maid in."

"Dr. Powell is here to deliver your baby," the nurse corrected.

The woman was terribly embarrassed and had started apologizing. "It's all right," Gloria Johnson-Powell said. "My mother was a maid— it's honest work."

In 1964 a colleague of Rodney's named Robert Ulstrom was named head of pediatrics at UCLA and asked Rodney to come with him as his chief resident. That was a prized position. Phone calls were made on behalf of Gloria. Would there be a place for her at UCLA as well? Yes, she would become a resident in psychiatry at the school's Neuropsychiatric Institute. That made her, she believed, the first minority person trained in psychiatry at UCLA Medical School.

But again the question of race seemed to be a part of her everyday life. There she was, a young black woman in a white uniform, and so the first assumption on the part of almost every layperson in the hospital was always going to be that she was a nurse. Sometimes there would be patients—and even more frequently the families of patients—who were furious because a black doctor was treating a loved one. Several complaints were lodged, based, as far as her superiors could tell, on race alone. Her boss, Dr. Tom Ungerleider, was very good in backing her. Whenever there were complaints, he would answer that he did not make assignments based on race, he assigned based on competence, but if they did not like his selections they could go to another hospital.

On the surface everything seemed to be going well. Their third child and first boy, Daniel, was born in 1966. They were financially well off: To their surprise, even though neither was trying to maximize their talents financially, they had more money than they had ever expected to have and more than they needed. Because both of them worked, Rodney's parents came out to live with them, and to serve as full-time baby-sitters. Rodney and Gloria were amused by the fact that though they lived in a series of very nice houses in the rather posh west side of Los Angeles, Raymond Powell was made uneasy by the affluence around him in the stores—the fancier the trappings in a supermarket, the more certain he was that the prices were too high. No supermarket, he firmly believed, should have a carpet on its floor, and when he spotted one, he was sure that it was a sign that prices were being jacked up. As such he would drive sixty and seventy miles a day to simpler stores in other parts of the city to do his shopping because he believed that these were honest and also, they sensed, because he probably felt more comfortable in them. An enormously skilled home repairman himself, he was sure that all tradesmen in the Los Angeles area had some kind of scam going, and when a repairman of any kind came to the Powell home, Raymond Powell would shadow him for the entire visit, carefully checking not just the work but with his eye on his watch as well to make sure that the work was good and the bill was honest. Rodney, it turned out, was a spectacular real estate man, able to buy property and then trade up to a better piece of property; they had steadily improved their housing in those years, eventually ending up with a pleasant house in Bel Air.

It was curious, he thought; both he and Gloria had started out as outsiders, particularly within the medical world, but because of the way things had changed, the increased awareness of the political issues which touched on issues of health, and the heightened need for diversity in medical programs—that is, more black faces on the faculty—there were always offers for both of them. In 1967 he went to work for the California Department of Health as chief of child health care, a job which he loved, and that in turn produced a job in 1968 as the director of the Watts Neighborhood Health Center. On the surface it was just the kind of job he wanted, the idea on a domestic level of trying to put in operation the kind of broad-based community public health program he had always envisioned for Africa. He had jumped at the chance. It was after the 1965 Watts riot, and the nation's attention was now focused on a newly perceived crisis, that of underclass blacks, particularly black men, in the nation's urban ghettos. What he envisioned was a full-service clinic, one which offered not just some transitory, minimalist medical attention, but instead gave continuing service in terms of medical, dental, and even psychological care, a center which in some way might help form the spine of an otherwise fragile and increasingly dispirited community.

In some ways he was quite proud of what he created there. The forces pulling down the black community, the terrible statistics of modern black urban life were horrendous, but he believed that he had created a strong staff and a purposeful center, one that was heroically trying to offer primary medical care to thousands of extremely vulnerable people and thus to fight off the downward spiral of the community. But there was an undertow there, and he soon felt himself under increasing suspicion in his job, not for what he did—there seemed to be a broad-based consensus that he was very good at his work—but for who he was. It was, he decided, as if they were all a flock of birds and he was the one bird which was different, and the other birds wanted to pluck the feathers of the outcast. Some of it was because he was insufficiently hierarchical. But it was other things as well. The way he dressed, they believed, was far too informal for a doctor. There was also the problem of his car, which was not grand enough. At first he had driven a new Mustang, which he had parked in the director's slot in the parking lot, alongside all the Cadillacs and Mercedes-Benzes. There had been some complaints. But then he had given the Mustang to his father for his long shopping jaunts around the city, and bought a small, used Falcon for himself. Doctors were supposed to drive big cars. The head of security for the center was offended, and wanted to have Powell's car towed away because it did not seem to belong with the more important cars of the other important people.

But he knew that most of the doubts reflected suspicions about his sexuality. All the old memories from his childhood and from Meharry when he had always felt so different were now recalled. It was known that when he listened to music in his office after hours, he listened to classical music, not rock. His dress was different, more informal than that expected of a doctor in that era. He spoke differently; his tone was gentle, almost soft. He did not swagger, and he did not put sexual pressure on the nurses of the staff. After his first year there, he was aware that he was being scrutinized, that there was a whispering campaign going on about his sexuality. Some people were suggesting that he was gay, which he found disheartening. It was not his work which was being debated, it was his private life. Because he now lived in Bel Air, there were also some complaints against him because he did not live in the neighborhood. The black community, he decided, because it was so vulnerable to the white community, was particularly unsparing in applying its own conventions against those who might differ from the accepted norm. Among other things, he believed, this made it unusually homophobic, because homosexuals were different, and vulnerable, and presumed to be weaker.

In addition he knew he was witnessing the rise of separatism within the black community. The tone of the ongoing racial debate within the black community, he believed, had turned more ominous because of the black power movement. "Black is beautiful" was the new phrase, and he understood the validity of it, the desperate need to take some measure of pride from what had for so long been a source of shame, and the need to reject old, negative feelings about being black and thus being a lesser person. But there was a corollary to this which Rodney Powell found extremely disturbing, and that was that all blacks, including black professionals, were somehow supposed to cast off their white friends and segregate themselves; only blacks could be their friends and only blacks were worthy of trust. It was exactly what he had fought against for almost a decade, and the danger, he believed, was that it was going to put them all back where they had started, with a racial fault line running through the two very separate, very divided worlds. He was an integrationist. He hated racism in all forms. His friends had always been both white and black, and he was as comfortable in some white circles as in black ones. He gave his trust to those who had earned it, and the idea of discriminating against some people because of their color appalled him.

There was an ugly confrontation at the Watts center in April 1968 after Martin Luther King was killed, and it gave him a whiff of what was to come. As soon as the news of King's murder had flashed across the nation's television screens, Powell summoned his top staff people. He made a few phone calls to friends in the city who were politically connected, and learned, not to his surprise, that there was talk of another riot taking place in Watts. If that turned out to be true, then they had to be ready and he wanted everyone on hand. All days off were cancelled. In addition they needed enough food on hand to feed the staff and the volunteers. They had to be prepared to act like a field hospital during combat, he said, and they had better be prepared to practice triage.

What stunned him was the response of some members of his staff. Would the hospital treat whites who were brought in? Should they treat police injured in this forthcoming riot? Some said quite angrily that they had no intention of treating any cops. To his surprise this was not an isolated opinion, but one shared by a large number of staff members. He knew all the historic reasons for distrusting the LAPD, but this was something different. He argued his staff members down—they were the only hospital in the entire neighborhood, and they were going to do their job, which was to treat all people according to need. If doctors were not blind to the race of their patients, particularly in emergency situations, who would be? he asked. But winning the argument was only a small victory; the fact that the argument had taken place at all and that the case for ignoring white victims was made so forcefully was disheartening. The post-assassination riot did not take place, but a few days later he pondered what had happened, and he thought that arguing with his staff over whether a hospital could be used for the larger good of humanity at the time of the death of Martin Luther King, of all people, had been as unpleasant as anything he had engaged in during his life.

Rodney Powell could understand both the anger and the newfound pride which drove the new separatism. He had felt enough pain over the color of his skin himself as both doctor and man. He knew that even when you were successful, as he was, there were small, daily,

seemingly invisible racial slaps in the face, of strangers making snap
judgments about him based not on his individuality but solely on his
color. Therefore it had to be much worse for ordinary blacks less privileged than he. But he had a sense that there was a corollary to this
new ethos, that it was not only about pride, but had a dangerous
potential for justification and rationalization built in as well—that
blacks were not responsible for what they did because history had
treated them cruelly. He feared the decline of any standard that people had been held to in the past. There might be, he sensed, a loss of
distinction between what was right and what was wrong, as far as
black actions were concerned. That was a very different code than the
one which he had grown up with, which in a harsher and more preju-
dicial climate demanded something equally terrible, that blacks perform better than whites to show that they were a credit to their race.

At the same time he was increasingly aware that his personal life
was in crisis, that he was leading an external life which did not connect to his internal life. Privately he had come to the conclusion that
his hopes that he was bisexual were doomed, and that he had to
accept the fact that he was gay; as such he was beginning to lead,
covertly at least, a double life. He loved his wife and his children, he
adored the idea of his family, but he was increasingly aware of his own
emotional incompleteness. He felt himself in a terrible quandary,
aware that he was involuntarily inflicting pain on the person he loved
most, Gloria.

For her part, Gloria Johnson-Powell knew that something was very
wrong in their marriage. She was, she knew, unsophisticated and
innocent in all things sexual at the time of her wedding. She loved
Rodney desperately, and in the early years of their marriage, things
had seemed to work. If, as she sometimes suspected, there was an
absence of passion in their marriage, then she had no way to compare
it with any other relationship, and so at first she assumed that other
marriages were like this. Besides, in those early years the camaraderie
of their great adventure had helped to bind them together. Then there
had been the arrival of their three children, and Rodney was obviously
a wonderful and loving father. There was much to share, much to talk
about. They almost never argued.

To their friends, first in Africa, then in Minnesota and California,
they seemed like a perfect couple, two young people who were always

in step with each other. But gradually Gloria realized that something was missing, that they were more friends than lovers, more like brother and sister than husband and wife. Because she loved him so much, because he was so kind, and because she was so inexperienced in matters sexual, she thought at first the fault was hers. They were both very respectful of each other's privacy. She was, she thought, black or not, a New England girl, a child of Boston and Mount Holyoke, and New England girls did not lightly intrude on the privacy of their husbands. Though she had a few close friends, she had no one, female or male, to talk to about her problem, because in those days it was not something women talked about. What made it even harder was the fact that everyone in those years was telling her how lucky she was, what a wonderful, kind man Rodney was, yet she felt empty of heart.

The Watts years were hard for her. He was becoming more withdrawn. The silences between them were growing greater and greater. Worse, in those years he seemed to be growing increasingly irritable, his movements harder to fathom. It struck Gloria that he was closer to his mother than he was to her. Sometimes he would come home, have dinner with his family, and then, without saying anything, he would go out on his own. Later she assumed that he had been making the rounds of gay bars, and that he had been having a harder time trying to suppress his secret life; in truth he was not, but he was spending most of his time alone in his separate apartment trying to figure out the ethical guidelines for the rest of his life, trying to balance his love and responsibilities as a husband and father with the powerful emotional drive which pulled him to a different kind of sexuality.

How to handle his life professionally was comparatively easy. Rodney had learned something at the Watts center, which was that he should stay out of large bureaucracies, where there were always going to be power plays; when there were power plays, people who were different were always vulnerable, and he was clearly different. Therefore, despite the fact that he was beginning to receive feelers about increasingly important jobs in different parts of the country, he could cross off the possibility of holding a big, powerful job in an important institution. Instead, he would settle for doing his own work in his own way. His personal life was not that simple. He thought of Gloria as his best friend and admired and loved her, but there were significant emotional limits to that love, and it had ended up incomplete for both of them. He loved his family, and he was reluctant to give up his children.

Then one day in 1970, he was sitting in the home they had traded up to in Pacific Palisades, reading an article in the *Los Angeles Times* about a gay couple in Santa Barbara: Both men had been married with children in their previous incarnations and they were raising one of the children from the two families. One man's ex-wife was quoted as saying that she was very comfortable with the arrangement because her ex-husband was by far the more nurturing parent, and therefore it was better for their child. Why can't I do that, Rodney Powell had thought, why can't that be me? It was time, he decided, to stop fooling himself and others and be who he was. If he was true to himself, somehow things would sort themselves out. He was tired of pretending to be something else for the comfort of strangers. What other people thought, what tags they put on you did not matter, unless in the process they changed you. It was time for him to be honest with himself and with his wife.

In late 1970 they were both offered prize positions at the University of Minnesota. It was perhaps the low point of their lives. Just after they moved he decided to come out to her. "I have something to tell you," he began. He was gay, he said. Then he started to cry. It went on for hours. She held his hands and he talked about the confusion of his life. He told her he had known or at least sensed that he was gay as far back as high school, that he had hated the idea of being gay, but that he thought by marrying her he could get beyond it. She had been his redemption: She was centered, balanced, loving, and seemed to want the same things in life as he did. She would be able to save him. Except that even her love and the wonderful family they had created had not turned out to be enough. She asked him what he wanted to do, and he answered that he simply did not know. That night she was more aware of his pain than of her own. She thought her job was to help him in some way. She did not think to ask him at the time why he had never told her about this before. Later, when she was able to bring herself to push him on the question, his answer was that he had been in such confusion and denial.

All the explanations for the emotional void in their lives were now before her. She had been leading a life which was doomed to be incomplete, and he was leading a life which was in most ways covert. (At almost the same time he had told his mother that he was gay and she answered that she knew that. How did she know? he asked, for he had never told her. "Oh, mothers always know things like that," Norma Powell had answered.) Only now could Gloria understand why he seemed so unhappy, when by all rights his life seemed to be so rich.

In Minneapolis they were both offered attractive positions, he as a full professor and she in the department of psychiatry. Her salary had not been set, and when she went for her final interview, the man who spoke with her said that since her husband was going to make a very good salary, $40,000 a year, she would not need as much and would be paid $15,000. She was appalled. Even in a great university in something as sophisticated as the department of psychiatry, they pull stuff like this, she thought. She looked at him and started whistling "The Star-Spangled Banner." "You're right," he said, quite embarrassed, and he thereupon offered her $28,000, which was the proper salary for that slot. That made her, she was later told, the highest-paid woman at the University of Minnesota at the time, a place where there was a major class-action suit going on against the university by a number of women.

If they thought that Minnesota held answers for their private dilemma, they were wrong. For a time Rodney Powell took a separate apartment, joining his family every night for dinner, and then going off to his other, secret world. But their lives were still unsettled, their larger problem unresolved. Then, Rodney got an offer from the Agency for International Development, AID, which was in charge of foreign aid, to go to Uganda. He thought it would be a good family move; they had done well in Africa in the past. Gloria was not so sure; she was finishing up a book, she had her first full academic appointment, their children were getting older, and her marriage seemed very shaky. It did not seem an ideal time to move to a distant continent; rather it seemed a good time for her to build her own curriculum vitae. Unsure that it was the right move, she decided to go with him anyway. Uganda turned out to be in all ways a disaster.

They arrived at the height of the Idi Amin terror. Not long after they got there, the dean of the medical school, who was a personal friend, was murdered, along with his family, by Amin's people. Gloria protested vehemently to the American authorities. The American ambassador at the time seemed unappreciative of her letter of protest and asked Rodney Powell why he could not control her. "Clearly, sir, you have not met my wife," he answered. The position of the American embassy at that particular moment seemed to be that the genocidal devastation which Amin was inflicting upon his people was not in fact taking place. Rodney spoke with an embassy official and outlined his own personal knowledge of brutal murders taking place, and the official answered, "It is our official position that this is not happening." He was being told something, to go along with the line or resign. Clearly it was time for them to go. If anything, they were growing even further apart as a couple in Uganda. As they were leaving Rodney told her of an offer he had to head a medical school in West Africa. No, she said, this family was not going to West Africa, it was going back to Los Angeles. April was getting ready for the seventh grade, the marriage was in serious trouble, and if it broke up, she needed a baseline job to protect herself and their children.

Things did not improve in Los Angeles. Rodney Powell took a job with Kaiser Permanente, which he did not particularly like. The distance between them continued to grow. Rodney seemed to lead more of a separate life. He had moved out of the house and into a nearby apartment building. Gloria's own sense of family seemed increasingly fragile. Her sister Barbara was suffering from a severe kidney illness; her mother, after years of battling poor health, seemed worn out by her struggles and the prognosis for her was not good. In the late summer of 1976, Mrs. Johnson suffered a stroke in Montreal, and Gloria flew out to see her. When her mother was able to talk with her, Gloria mentioned that she and Rodney were separating. "I don't want to hear anything negative about Rodney," Mrs. Johnson said, "he's very dear to me. I love him more than some of my own children." When Gloria returned to Los Angeles, she was met at the airport by Rodney, who told her he was taking a new job which sounded exciting, one where he would be based in Hawaii and where he would work with American doctors who wanted to serve in the rural Third World. It seemed like the right opportunity to him. She agreed.

But her world was collapsing. Her sister was dying, her mother was dying, and she had to solidify her own career and stabilize life for her three children. Yet her mother, ever frailer, remained an emotional rock of strength. She often let Gloria know how proud she was of her success. "Your father and I hoped that our children would have a better life, but we never dreamed that we would be able to have a child like you." Sometimes, she wondered why all of this was happening to her. In October 1976, her mother died.

She felt lonelier than ever. People whom she had thought of as good friends had slipped away from her with the breakup of their marriage, closer, as often happens in these matters, to Rodney than to her. She was lonelier than she realized, and nearer the breaking point. Rodney was now based in Hawaii, and although he was flying back and forth regularly so that he could see the children, the burdens of modern life seemed to fall heavily on her, and she lacked an adequate support system. She was seeing a psychiatrist, a man who did not seem to have great empathy for her problems and seemed to feel that she was a superstoic person who could handle all of her problems without breaking a sweat. When, sensing that she was in a serious depression, she had asked her psychiatrist for an antidepressant, he had said no, that he wanted her to feel the fullness of her depression.

One weekend Rodney flew in, and the two of them, along with Daniel, went skiing and had a good time. Then on the way back he became morose and unreachable again. When he left to return to Hawaii, she went upstairs and took an overdose of sleeping pills. She came perilously close to dying. By chance her brother was staying in their guest cottage at the time. There had been a number of phone calls for her, and she was not picking up the phone, so he wandered over to the main house and found her passed out. The EKG they did on her was so flat that the doctors were sure she was gone. She woke up in a hospital in a deep fog. Rodney was there. Because she had some previously scheduled oral surgery, she thought she had woken up in the dentist's chair. "Why did you let me have this surgery?" she asked him.

"Gloria, don't you know why you're here?" he asked.

"To have oral surgery," she answered.

So then he told her of her suicide attempt. At first she did not believe him. She had never thought about suicide and she had never thought of herself as suicidal. But she had reached her breaking point. She was, she thought, very lucky to be alive.

66

JIM LAWSON STAYED IN MEMPHIS SIX MORE YEARS BEFORE IN 1974 accepting the job as pastor of the Holman Methodist Church in Los Angeles. Before he went west, he returned to Vanderbilt in 1972 on a one-year fellowship. He did not go there to work toward a degree, but it gave him a badly needed sabbatical from his church, and Vanderbilt had made overtures in the ensuing ten years about healing the breach and reaching out to him. Though there was a good deal of serious rumbling within certain quarters of the Vanderbilt board about his return, in the end there was no administrative opposition to his coming back, and he ended up having an extremely pleasant year, and renewing old acquaintances. But the murder of Martin Luther King still weighed heavily on him. His grief over the death of the man who was his friend and who he thought was the most important world leader since Gandhi was overwhelming. If Lawson was, by dint of being a Methodist, not quite a true member of King's inner group, then he was close to most of the people who were, and he was intellectually very close to King himself; they were by background—sons of prominent preachers, privileged with exceptional educations, which put them at a level above many of their peers—intellectually comfortable with each other. The literal part of the Baptist doctrine, that of immersion, one of the things which might have separated them, seemed to mean little to King. "Now, Jim, when you come over here to Ebenezer, we're going to have to dunk you under the water," King had once told him. Then he had paused for a minute. "If I don't, the deacons here will get on me." In recent years they had shared the same belief about the growing importance of taking on the issue of poverty in America, and they had both believed that Vietnam cast a dark shadow on the soul of their country. He and Martin, he thought, had shared the same wavelength, almost always, it seemed, coming out at the exact same position on so many issues, their thinking and their politics so much the same. There had been a time in the sixties when Lawson would be thinking of how the Movement was changing, of the new pressures being brought to bear on the leadership by black nationalists, and of what they should do in response; then he would talk to King and would often find that Martin had been thinking along the same lines.

After King's murder Jim Lawson had worked not to let his grief show in public, fearing if he openly revealed it, this would not help those in his congregation, who were struggling with their own emotions. Only his wife, Dorothy, was privy to the moments when he would think of Martin Luther King, and what had happened, and then burst into tears. She alone knew the signs of when his grief was particularly heavy: He would not be able to sleep, and he would get up in the middle of the night and read in the Bible about the prophets, or do some writing. There were times after King's murder when his grief was so great he wondered whether he could go on—there had been so much killing: John Kennedy and Robert Kennedy and Martin King and Malcolm X. If Malcolm had first come to prominence as a prophet of separatism among the dispossessed and exhausted blacks of the Northern ghetto, seemingly the polar opposite of men like King and Lawson, then near the end of his life, Lawson believed Malcolm had been moving toward a more ecumenical position, one nearer Martin's, even as Martin, concerned with the plight of the unemployed blacks in Northern cities, had moved in his own way nearer Malcolm. That many murders killed hope, he believed, and they killed idealism and they tore the political fabric of the nation, always fragile, apart.

Jim Lawson had watched the beginning of Lyndon Johnson's poverty program with some degree of optimism in the late sixties; it was the assault upon the economic structure of racism which he had always felt was necessary to change American society. But the War on Poverty, he soon came to believe, was a victim of the Vietnam War, of limited resources and of a president whose commitment to reaching out to the most vulnerable citizens had been badly compromised by the war, and who was becoming a leader under siege.

By 1974 Lawson was finally ready to go to Los Angeles and take a church there; his bishop had been pushing him for some time to go to

California but he had resisted, thinking that there was always more to do in Memphis. Finally, Dorothy Lawson suggested that he go out to California by himself and take a look. He did and immediately sensed the new challenge ahead, and knew that it was time to go, after almost sixteen wildly pressurized years in the South. Holman Methodist in Los Angeles was a large middle-class congregation; the members were a reflection of a black community undergoing the full stress of urban existence in modern American society. If some of the challenges of being a pastor in Los Angeles were not as stark as those in Memphis and Nashville, they were as complex, often more subtle, and on occasion more exhausting.

He watched the unfolding court process surrounding Martin Luther King's convicted killer, James Earl Ray, with fascination, and like a number of other SCLC leaders, he visited Ray in prison. There he and Ray formed the beginning of, if not a friendship, some kind of association. He became absolutely convinced that the murder of King represented a conspiracy, and that Ray was an unlikely principal in it. He was, Lawson believed, surely a part of it, but hardly the major figure, hardly the kingpin or architect. James Earl Ray seemed to him a classic kind of poor white drifter, poorly educated, lacking not just the dedication and passion to kill someone like Martin Luther King, but equally important, the intelligence and skill and the wherewithal to escape as he did from Memphis, make his way to Canada, manage somehow to come up with a forged passport there, and eventually make his way to England and then to the Continent. That seemed to require skills and resources, financial and otherwise, beyond Ray's normal capabilities. Lawson did not believe that Ray was telling the entire truth when he now spoke about what had happened in April 1968, although the more Lawson spoke with Ray the more convinced he became that much of what he said about the events preceding the assassination was true. Lawson, like others in the SCLC, was bitterly skeptical of the U.S. government's role in the King killing; no American institution had labored longer and harder and with less constitutional authority to destroy Martin Luther King's reputation in his lifetime than the FBI, and the fact that these very same people—as far as Jim Lawson was concerned, these apostles of hatred—were now charged with finding his friend's murderer left a bitter taste. What the government now proclaimed as the truth, the totality of James Earl

Ray's guilt, Lawson perceived as a series of at best smaller and hopelessly inadequate truths.

In his prison visits with Ray, Jim Lawson had come to know not just the prisoner but his fiancée, Anna, as well, and one day in the mid-seventies he got a call from Ray asking if he would marry them in a prison wedding. The call came just as the Lawson family was about to sit down to dinner. The idea was not without its pain—he was being asked to marry the man convicted of murdering the man he loved and revered more than any American leader. He had no doubt that there had been some degree of participation in these events on Ray's part. As the Lawson family sat down to eat that night, he explained to his family what the call had been about and what he had been asked to do. Then he asked his family members what they thought he ought to do. "Well," said his son John, then seventeen, his head bent over the table, his face already into his food, not even bothering to look up, "if you believe all that stuff you've been preaching all these years, then you'll do it." John was right, Jim Lawson thought; if you believe in the doctrine of nonviolence and forgiveness, then you will do it; indeed, he thought, if Martin King were alive and able, he would have done it too.

In Los Angeles he felt his life was rich and full. Dorothy taught school, and they raised three sons and educated them well. John, the oldest, who had integrated the public parks of Memphis when he was a toddler, in time went off to Oberlin and then Howard Law School, and became a public defender in Los Angeles. Seth, the middle son, would go to the University of Colorado at Boulder, and Morris (James Morris Lawson III) went to Pfeiffer College as an undergraduate, took a graduate degree from Iliff School of Theology in Denver, and was thinking of going into social work.

The crisis of race in America had not abated. Though his sons all were able to attend exceptional schools, nonetheless each of them had been forced in different ways to deal with racism at school, not the harsh, total racism that Lawson and others of his generation had dealt with in the South, but a softer, more nuanced kind. "Fifteenth-generation racism," Jim Lawson called it. He thought for all the subtle racism they encountered, however, his children's lives were richer and their sense of expectations higher than those of young blacks in his generation.

As an old integrationist, he was deeply unhappy with the move toward separatism which seemed increasingly in fashion among black students on the nation's major campuses in the eighties and nineties; it seemed to him to erect unnecessary barriers, after a difficult struggle when so many in his generation had worked so hard to bring them down. It might momentarily make some young people feel more secure, but it essentially defeated the idea of a broad-based, pluralistic university, where young people on both sides of the racial divide could get beyond their prejudices and myths and come to know one another. He was particularly critical of prominent universities which allowed black students to have all-black dorms. One of the worst things which that produced, he thought, was a powerful peer pressure that worked against the right of individual black students to choose all their friends, white or black, as they wanted, and pushed them toward having only black friends. Whatever the immediate benefit in terms of psychic pleasure of young blacks being only with other blacks, he thought, the long-range results would be terribly negative, for in a variety of ways it cut them off from the fullest promise of America. He thought of it as a considerable step backward.

When he looked back he was sometimes amazed by how much they had accomplished in so short a time back in those heady days in the sixties. Martin Luther King, Lawson believed, was the American black leader whose coming Gandhi himself had prophesied to Howard Thurman years earlier, for Gandhi had spoken of an American black man who would some day surface in this country to become an international symbol of nonviolence, using the vastly superior platform of the world's richest, most developed country to reach the rest of the world. What none of them had understood, particularly himself, Lawson later realized, was how remarkable their timing had been, that King had arrived on the national stage at precisely the moment of the surfacing of a great new national media instrument, television. That had been a bonus that few of the leaders had expected when they had started out. At the time he had not been aware of their good fortune.

67

MARION BARRY'S POLITICAL CAREER IN WASHINGTON TURNED OUT TO be meteoric, befitting a city where the existing political structure was imploding, taking with it all existing concepts of who was entitled to ˙rule and who was fit to rule. In Washington, an old black order which had never had a chance to govern was about to be bypassed. Barry had surged forward in what was to turn out to be perilously close to a political vacuum. His timing was impeccable; he was surfacing as a new breed of black activist, a man of the streets, at precisely the time that the old semicolonial order was breaking down, and when the liberal white establishment had become desperately aware that the inner cities of all the nation's urban centers were tinderboxes. Harlem had burned in 1964, Watts had been the scene of a violent riot in Los Angeles in 1965; it was obvious that there were no immunities anymore, and that every city in the North had a black ghetto filled with rage. Washington would be no exception.

Lyndon Johnson was above all else determined that there not be a riot in the nation's capital, not while he was president anyway. In this new, changed, and suddenly explosive climate of the post-Watts and post-Harlem riots, a riot in the capital was judged the most immediate of threats, a humiliation in front of the entire world at the height of the Cold War. That meant that Willard Wirtz, Johnson's secretary of labor, who had become the head of Johnson's War on Poverty, was suddenly looking for young black people who had legitimacy in the ghettos, who could reach other angry black youths and bring them into a system which in the past had always scorned them. It was the most natural instinct of that still liberal era. Johnson and Wirtz wanted to do good; they also wanted to keep America's cities, particularly the nation's capital, from burning. The people they selected as their instruments were to be, in terms of the larger social contract, a kind of black firemen. One of the first they found was Marion Barry, one of the few people who had emerged in Washington with any kind of legitimacy.

Willard Wirtz believed that the crisis was essentially economic—that if young blacks had jobs, they would gradually become part of the system. He was also aware that what had happened in other cities could easily happen right there in the city which contained the federal government, and that any kind of minor incident might set off a devastating riot. In May 1967 an incident with that potential took place: A nineteen-year-old black youth named Clarence Brooker entered a store in the northeast section of Washington, bought some cookies, paid for them, and got in an argument with the store clerk. The clerk called the police. A cop arrived, and he and Brooker got in an argument; Brooker threw the remainder of the bag of cookies on the ground, and the cop tried to arrest Brooker for throwing trash. When the cop tried to overpower the black youth, Brooker got away, the cop chased him and caught him, and they began to struggle again. Finally the cop pulled his revolver and the gun went off. Brooker said he was shot. At first no one noticed any blood on him. Other cops arrived and decided to book Brooker. Only later did they realize he had been shot. That night Brooker died in a Washington hospital of massive internal bleeding. It was the kind of incident which was all too common in black ghettos; it was also the kind of incident which could now spark a massive riot.

Marion Barry immediately understood that this was the kind of defining incident he had been looking for, and he set out to make contact with Brooker's closest pal, a young man named Rufus "Catfish" Mayfield. Mayfield was something of a street hustler, albeit one with middle-class roots. Barry quickly found Mayfield, and a connection was made; soon they were each other's new best friends. There was a certain quid pro quo at work; Mayfield knew the streets and the young blacks who worked them far better than Barry, and Barry, from his days in the Movement, knew the uses of politics, how to take incidents and amplify them politically through the media, far better than Mayfield. That summer the grand jury did not indict any of the cops involved in the death of Brooker. But Mayfield and Barry had become a team, and Barry, who had testified in the Brooker case for several hours, became, because of his new association with Mayfield, even more of a local political and media figure. He was now a man who seemed to know and represent those young people who otherwise seemed unreachable. He was a man to be reckoned with.

All of this helped convince Carroll Harvey, the local black man who had been looking for a new kind of black leader, that Barry was his man. At the time Harvey was working in the local office of a community renewal organization and he was dismayed by the quality and the ineffectiveness of the existing black leadership, and how out of touch it was with ordinary black life. Marion Barry seemed to be exactly what Harvey had been looking for. Harvey himself was a graduate of Howard, and by dint of being the son of a cop, he was also middle class. He was all too aware of the importance of the ghetto's powerful, formidable boundaries of class, and equally aware of his own inability, as a child of the black middle class, to break through it and reach the children of true urban poverty. But Barry, now aligned with Catfish Mayfield, was a Bama from the Mississippi Delta who had even picked cotton as a boy and had been part of that first great wave of SNCC youths who had challenged Deep South cops. He had credibility on the streets in no small part because he had responded instinctively to being harassed and had fought back when Tommy Tague hassled him. He was, thought Harvey, a natural-born politician; in his short time in Washington he seemed to be surfacing as the gatekeeper between traditional white Washington and the alienated black youths of the city. To reach them, if they could be reached, Harvey sensed, the white world now had to go through Marion Barry.

Marion Barry, thought Carroll Harvey, had been in a leadership class for five years without knowing it, for SNCC had been among other things a great leadership training course. Against all odds those young people had taken on a powerful existing order, they had quickly gone beyond the older generation counseling them, and they had in those critical five years made life-and-death decisions under terrible, crisis conditions.

The rules had changed, Harvey now told Barry. After Congress had passed the Voting Rights Act and after Johnson's "We *Shall* Overcome" speech, Harvey emphasized, it was an entirely new ballgame. The young people who had been storming the barricades were now going to have their chance to enter politics and to lead the new order. "You don't need SNCC anymore. It's time to get out of it. We're going to be inside the system now," Harvey told him. "We're going to need our own politicians now, and you can be one of our first. It's going to happen very soon. There are going to be elections in this city and the person who wins is not going to be some upper-class black, not someone with a silver spoon in his mouth—it's going to be someone from the streets. Marion, it can be yours if you want it."[1] It was not very hard to convince Barry, Harvey noted, for he had no doubts that what he was telling Marion Barry was exactly what Barry himself had been thinking for quite a while. Years later Harvey noted that Barry had been hustling him from the start. But, he added, the hustling had been two-way: "God knows I needed him—we needed each other. It was a conscious decision to try and break the city's prevailing caste system." Soon Harvey had Barry on a community service payroll at $50 a day as a consultant. Even their nicknames reflected the attempt to take on the streets: Harvey was known as the Godfather, Barry as the Cooler.[2]

The Brooker case had seemed to underline how volatile Washington was. Willard Wirtz knew he had to have some connection to the ghetto. A meeting between Wirtz and Barry and Harvey was soon held. Barry and Harvey told Wirtz they had a program for these street kids, which of course they did not, so with a few friends they sat down one weekend and drew up a program. Largely Harvey's idea, it was called PRIDE, an independent company which would hire teenagers to clean up the ghetto's filthy streets. Wirtz, with few other choices and a president breathing down his neck, went for it. PRIDE would get $250,000 for a pilot project of five weeks. Mayfield was the street leader, but Barry was the big winner in the eyes of the local community, the man who gave PRIDE its public face and spoke at its different press conferences. In the beginning PRIDE seemed to work; streets which had been filthy *were* cleaned up. A few weeks later the funding was made more permanent, and an additional $1.5 million was found.

There was a simple dynamic which Carroll Harvey had sensed before many others: The more the rawness of this new black community was revealed, the more long-suppressed anger finally began to surface, then the more likely the community was to bypass the existing, rather moderate leadership from the past and turn to leaders from the streets. When in 1968 after the murder of Martin Luther King there were massive riots in Washington and some of the ghetto burned, it was one more sign to the white community and in particular to the white liberal establishment not just how desperate conditions were in the black neighborhoods, but in addition, how out of touch the traditional leadership was. For Carroll Harvey and a few other close friends who had become Barry's closest counselors, the only question in the beginning was which office Barry would run for first, and when. Three years later, in 1971, he got his chance: He would run for the school board. It was a very important local election. Given the lack of other elective offices open for Washington residents, it had considerable visibility in the black community and it would be an ideal stepping-stone for future city council and mayoral races.

Still, for all of his natural ability there were qualities about Barry which bothered some of his old friends and some of his new allies in Washington. There had always been a problem with his drinking; more than others in the Movement, he had been a heavy drinker and there were occasions when he started to drink and he simply did not stop. And there was the womanizing. In Movement circles, perhaps because of the constant physical danger, perhaps because of the excitement of the cause, perhaps because the cause itself challenged existing mores, there had always been considerably more sexual freedom than in the society at large, and one of the perks for some of the leaders had been the availability of women. Asked what the position of women in the Movement should be, Stokely Carmichael had once answered, "Prone."[3] But Barry's activities seemed to go beyond even that level and had bothered a number of his contemporaries. There was a sense that he was relentless, indeed ruthless, in his pursuit of women, almost pathological. As early as 1964 there had been a serious complaint against him lodged in the SNCC files by one white SNCC staffer who said he had assaulted her, a complaint which was quite unusual in those days, for young women did not lightly dispute sexual aggression on the part of the men they knew. A special SNCC meeting had been called to discuss the incident. A year later Barry apparently pushed too far with another young woman, who later wrote, in a letter which somehow reached SNCC's offices, of how he had put his "filthy hands" on her: "You use people, take advantage of them and never give one thought that you might be destroying them in the process. . . . You have betrayed my trust and dishonored me," she wrote.[4]

As he became more successful politically, something of a rising star in Washington, as his circle constantly expanded into the black and white middle class, he continued to hit on a vast variety of women he met. The womanizing was constant, something which a succession of his wives tried to come to terms with for as long as they could. Nothing, it seemed, was going to stop him from it; it was as if in his mind this was his just compensation for his victories, the reward that politicians, both white and black alike, had always taken as part of the spoils, and in his case, his due for all the pain inflicted on him earlier in his life. Sometimes the signals which went out and came back were confused: What some of these women thought was a commitment to an issue too often turned out to be, as far as Barry was concerned, a sign that they were sexually interested in him. The results of these misunderstandings were not always pleasant.

What bothered some of his close friends was that he seemed to be acting this out so openly and carelessly, as if he were utterly immune to any of the considerable consequences of his behavior. Beyond the sheer lack of morality of what he was doing, some of his colleagues were worried by what it showed about him emotionally, as if the need for sex was a reflection not of strength within, not of a certain macho quality, as some people in those days seemed to think, but was rather behavior born of insecurity and incompleteness, reflecting a need to be constantly, if only momentarily, validated and, at the very least, a total lack of discipline. What, they wondered, was so desperately missing in him as a person that he put so much energy into his womanizing and took so much affirmation from it? His first marriage, which had begun when he was still a graduate student at the University of Tennessee, had broken up rather quickly, and by the late sixties, he was living with but had not yet married the woman who was eventually to be the second of his four wives, and his partner in PRIDE, Mary Treadwell.

Mary Treadwell was a formidable person, strong and unbending, the child of the black middle class, daughter of a builder in Kentucky. She was in the beginning of their relationship very much Marion Barry's equal political partner. Most of their early friends and associates thought that she was more willing to make hard decisions than he, an impression which she tended to reinforce on occasion during moments of crisis in PRIDE by saying such things as "Shut up and sit down, you no-dick motherfucker." Marion, it was believed, was the good cop in their team in the early days, the easygoing, occasionally deferential front man who did not like to say no to anyone; Treadwell was the bad cop, tough and often confrontational, far more willing to alienate anyone if she thought she was in the right. Of Marion Barry, Thornell Page, one of his early advisers, once said, it was better to be his enemy than his friend, because in his insecurity he courted his enemies, as if sensing that they somehow understood his real weaknesses, and he therefore badly wanted their acceptance; in turn, he neglected his friends, inevitably taking them for granted.

There was also, some of his friends like Harvey thought, for all of the charm, a constant problem of self-esteem with Barry, as if deep in his heart he actually did suffer from being a Bama, and he really did believe that the people he dealt with, the black upper class and the white middle class, were better than he was. On occasion an evening which Harvey had thought a success would weigh heavily on Barry, not because the evening had not gone well politically for him, but because someone might have done or said something which Barry took as a put-down, a reminder that he was, in the end, rising political star or not, a Bama. Harvey, who knew the upper-class black world better than he, and who knew how empty many of these people's lives were, would have to take him aside and console him: The people who had insulted Barry might have more money and better houses, and maybe they thought they had better manners, but they had not done as much for their people as Marion Barry had. But Barry seemed, for all of his talent and all of his early success, a man without a real center. The desire to be liked by all different kinds of people, which made him almost chameleonlike, might help him as a politician running for office, some of his friends thought, but it might also work against him once in office.

By the late sixties he had emerged as one of two or three leading figures among the new generation of Washington's black leaders. No one else on the ascent so clearly represented a complete break from those who had preceded him. When in 1971, in the beginning of the almost glacial breakdown of the city's old, colonial politics—that is, rule by conservative Southern congressmen—the district was given a nonvoting congressional seat, it was clear to Barry's friends that he wanted a shot at it, but in the end he deferred to Walter Fauntroy, a more senior figure emerging out of the same essential coalition of people. Instead Barry's first race was for the school board. A number of white and black liberals, dissatisfied with the quality of the city's schools, wanted him to take on Anita Allen, an upper-middle-class woman who seemed to be the prototype of the older black middle class. She was the perfect target for him: older, more conservative, light-skinned, and traditionalist, and she had been considered by some of her colleagues a difficult member of the board. To the leaders of the newer forces just beginning to coalesce in Washington, she was a representative of the old, established guard, which they deemed tired, co-opted, and inadequate; by contrast, Barry was perceived as forerunner of the new order, bold, modern, even, perhaps, radical, and very much in touch. The election, however, was not going to be a street election; the voters were largely middle class. Thornell Page taught Barry to modify his radical street incarnation, to get rid of the dashiki ("We're not electing an African king") and stop using the word *motherfucker* in every sentence. He would run as a school reformer. Like the school systems in all too many inner cities, the District schools reflected the exploding demographic crisis of the inner city. The white and black middle-class students of another era were rapidly being replaced by black underclass kids, the city's tax base was becoming weaker all the time, and the schools in general reflected a generally deteriorating social order.

To Allen, Barry was a carpetbagger, an arriviste in a town where you were supposed to wait your turn in the black community for a long time. Nor was she amused by the change in his style of clothing and rhetoric; she was not fooled, she said, by someone who had "suddenly shed his dashiki and donned an Edwardian suit to become a member of the Establishment."[5] But the times were changing. Barry, backed by an interesting white-black liberal coalition, ran as the candidate of moderation and reform and won easily, getting 58 percent of the vote in a four-person race.

He quickly became the president of the board. There he was, smooth, politically deft, and in any real sense largely uninvolved. Though the schools were in obvious jeopardy, it was clear to many of the people around him that the schools were hardly at the top of his agenda; his own political future took precedence, and he was not about to make any powerful enemies, who might oppose his political ascent, when he could use this position to make influential friends, who might aid in campaigns yet to be run. He exhibited, those more involved with the school system thought, an absence of passion for the schools and for the children who attended them. Though there were a number of battles that he could have fought, he did not deign to get involved. His tour, though a great many black children were at risk, was passive.

At one point Kenneth Clark, the distinguished sociologist, had come up with a radical plan to remake the District's deteriorating schools. It was designed to jump-start the kids and give them a kind of educational basic training, which would compensate for what was otherwise clearly a considerable vulnerability, based on terrible social and cultural deprivation. Clark had suggested devoting the first three years of elementary school entirely to the study of math and English as a means of getting these children up to speed quickly; geography and other subjects would simply have to wait. Clark believed that if their basic skills in math and English improved, they would soon do well in other subjects. It was a radical idea, one which seemed to have a good deal of merit for a school system with so many vulnerable children. But it was opposed by the teachers union, a powerful black union, and it would have taken a good deal of effort on the part of the board to push it through; Barry stood aside and gave it a bye.[6]

The school board was merely a launchpad. It was obvious now that what people like Carroll Harvey had been saying for some time was about to come true, that the politics of Washington were changing, that the opposition to home rule was weakening all the time, and that Barry had a very good chance to be one of the first beneficiaries of the new order. One aide remembered that the key staff assignment at every meeting in Barry's school board years was that of the name taker; an aide came equipped with a large notebook and his job was to get as many names and addresses of potential voters as possible for the mailing list—the making of Marion Barry's future files.

The likelihood of home rule seemed to be increasing all the time, particularly as conservative Republicans, reeling from the scandals of Watergate and the fact that Spiro Agnew, the vice president, had taken bribes while in office, saw their ability to stop it limited. Curiously enough the fact that the city was right on the verge of getting home rule might have saved Barry's political career at a critical junction. In

1973, when he was still the head of the school board and when the home rule issue was at a make-or-break stage, Barry had been involved in an ugly sexual incident which was eventually suppressed. He had met a socially prominent young black woman at a political reception and followed her home after the party to talk about a school project important to her. When it was time for him to leave, he refused to go, grabbed her, and sexually assaulted her. It had been an ugly scene: She screamed for help, neighbors heard the noise and called the police, who soon arrived. The woman, wanting to protect her own privacy, and in addition fearing that any report of the incident would give Congress one more excuse to deny the city home rule, denied that anything had happened (Barry hid in the bedroom while the cops were at the door) and decided against pressing charges. If there were no charges, then the assault had not taken place. As such, though informed circles in Washington were eventually full of gossip about what had happened, the incident was never reported; if it had been, it might have ended Barry's career early on because it would have severed his connection to the white liberal wards, which were a source of his early support. (In 1994, as Barry was beginning his return to politics after a term in prison, a talented reporter named Tom Sherwood, who had covered Barry first at *The Washington Post* and then at WRC-TV, was, with his co-author Harry Jaffe, about to publish a devastating book on Barry's decline and fall, called *Dream City.* Sherwood thought he owed Barry the courtesy of letting him know the book was coming out, and what he thought was the worst thing in it—their reporting on the sexual assault which had taken place in 1973. "What did I do," a puzzled Barry asked Sherwood, "beat her up?" No, said Sherwood, and he described rather precisely what had taken place. "When was it?" Barry then asked.

"Nineteen seventy-three," Sherwood said.

"That's twenty years ago," a relieved Barry answered. "No one will care about it."[7]

In May 1974, Washington, D.C., finally got home rule; when that happened, Marion Barry ran for the at-large seat on the city council. From the start, those who dealt with him there thought, it was clear that he thought of the council as just a pit stop and that unlike most of the other members, his vision of the future did not end with a council seat; he was always thinking in larger terms, of being mayor in the age of home rule. He was always thinking future, not present, as a young black reporter from *The Washington Post* named LaBarbara Bowman soon discovered. She dropped by to talk with him soon after his election to the council and found him in an open and candid mood. "I have a choice of going on either the finance committee or the budget committee," he told her, "and I'm going to take finance—it's a much better springboard. On the budget committee all you'll be doing is telling people how little money you have—essentially telling them no. But the financial committee will put me in contact with the powerful people in this city who have money and who need things done. They'll have to come through me. In the end that will help connect me to financial backers."[8] She was startled by the exchange; until then, she had seen only the rather idealistic side of his political face. It was, she decided later, an early lesson on how politics really works.

On the council he quickly set out to solidify his connections with Washington's business interests; he would show that though he had emerged as the radical voice of the new generation, he could also make his share of deals. In particular he set out to signal this to Washington's real estate men. It is impossible to underestimate the importance of the real estate interests in Washington's political-economic order. Because it is a city which lacks almost all other industries save government and journalism and lobbying, because its population is constantly shifting, depending on who wins a national election, the business of real estate is far more important in Washington than it is in most cities. Washington offers unusual real estate opportunities also because of its unusually volatile mix: the poorest of the poor living virtually alongside the very center of the federal government, which, unlike institutions in the private sector, cannot readily move to the suburbs. A rising politician in Washington, black or white, who wants continued access to money has, first and foremost, to come to terms with the real estate lobby.

Shortly after taking over the finance committee Barry got his first real test. A bill arrived there designed to tax the city's worst real estate speculators; these were sleazy operators who preyed on the poor, coming in and buying up rundown houses, often in poor neighborhoods, and getting them, of course, at rock-bottom prices. The neighborhoods in question often bordered gentrified neighborhoods, so the possibility of future profits was considerable, and it made this

kind of speculation a particularly good bet. Sometimes the speculators performed limited repairs before greatly jacking up the prices;
sometimes, when the practice was at its most brutal, they performed
no repairs at all. Houses which the speculator had bought for $20,000
might be lightly touched up, a veneer of repairs worth $3,000 or per-
haps $4,000 made; then they would be sold for a profit of 100 to 200
percent. It was predatory speculation at its worst. Of the many abuses
against the poorest people in the city by the sleekest, this practice
seemed one of the most obvious and cruelest: Often the victims were
poor, black working-class families who would get a loan, buy a vacant
house in a depressed area, the mortgage rate would be rather high, the
family would somehow fail to meet it, and the speculators would come
in and take over the property at a bargain price. A local councilman
named David Clarke came up with a bill to limit the practice by slap-
ping a massive tax on the speculators. It was, in effect, like a special
capital gains tax for real estate operators designed to protect the inner
city.

The local real estate lobby was most unhappy with the Clarke bill—
it not only threatened what had become a wondrous, low-risk, high-
profit game, but it might also set a precedent, and signify a willingness
of the community to protect itself against other instances of exploita-
tion. The best chance to stop the bill, it was decided, was in the
finance committee—once it went before the general council, public
pressure on its behalf would be overwhelming. A black lawyer who
had known Barry well and had been one of his early advisers was sent
to meet with Barry and to talk him into killing the bill. It was, for the
black lawyer, one of the most embarrassing of missions, one so insidious and unsavory that the more senior partner in his firm who normally would have done it had passed. The black lawyer went off to see
Barry and to his astonishment, his old friend was absolutely willing to
go along: The bill would be bottled up and thus killed; the speculation
could continue. There seemed to be no shame involved.

The signal had been given; a terrible practice, built on the sorrow of
the poor, could continue, but the real estate lobby—and other business lobbies soon to come—must know that they owed Barry, and that
they had to go through him for what they wanted. He would be real
estate's man, forging in those early days highly profitable, both to him
and even more so to them, professional connections which were to

last much of his career. An authentic black radical he might still appear to ordinary black citizens, but the old-fashioned power brokers of the city now knew he was something else, a hungry politician who would deal with moneyed interests. It was the first of many telltale signs of what his real interest was, his former friends thought.

In 1978 he was elected mayor of Washington. He had done well in the streets, and there was a certain panache to him in those days: He brought a charismatic quality to an otherwise backward political community. The Gold Coast people hated him and everything he stood for, often as not, it appeared then, for the wrong reasons: He was an embarrassment to them, someone who seemed to mock the long, arduous process of becoming middle class, and seemed to flaunt the customs and manners and speech of the streets to white and black worlds alike. Why, that man can't even talk properly, they said of him.[9]

If the black middle class remained more than a little wary of him, ironically, his reputation as a man of the streets helped him with some white liberal voters, who took him at face value. His powerful desire to be liked had been converted into a basic skill in handling the media, particularly the younger white journalists covering him. Unlike most of the other people on the city council, Barry, in no small part because of his years in the South, understood the power of the media, and he always had time to sit and chat, to give working reporters a sense of the issues at stake, and to seem, in those days, surprisingly open and engaged by issues. When LaBarbara Bowman and another *Washington Post* reporter who had covered him won fellowships, respectively, to Harvard and Stanford for a year in the late seventies, and the *Post* threw a small party in their honor, there was Marion Barry, dropping by to schmooze and be a part of the scene, something in those easier days which still seemed like a friendly thing to do. In the three-way race for mayor, Barry had trailed at first, but he had been by far the best campaigner, and in the end, he had the editorial backing of the most important institution in the city, *The Washington Post.* He had met with the editors of the *Post* on two occasions and had been at his best, and the *Post* had come through for him ("Our strong belief is that it should be Marion Barry"); the paper was, it said, appalled that his work in PRIDE with the city's street youth should be used as an argument against him in the campaign. If anything, it was the strongest argument for him, the endorsement said. The editors of the

Post might not have been in close touch with the reality of black life in their own city, but theirs was a powerful endorsement, and it helped swing Ward 3, which was the white liberal inner-city enclave. On its votes he became the second mayor in the age of home rule. In a three-way race where his two opponents were believed to have divided the same essential constituency, he won by only 1,400 votes over the runner-up and by some 3,000 votes over the candidate in third place. It was something that members of Washington's black middle class never let their white friends forget, that at the crucial point in Marion Barry's ascent, when his career had hung in the balance, it was white middle-class votes, not black ones, which had carried him into the mayor's job.

It would be hard to underestimate, the veteran *Post* reporter and editor Milton Coleman said years later, the sense of excitement among young black activists of his generation when Marion Barry began his career as mayor of Washington, D.C. This was not merely one more of the many American cities which now had a black mayor; this was Washington, the nation's capital, a showcase to the world. More, many of the other black men rising to power seemed to have come from a traditional urban political framework, which just happened, because of the exodus to the suburbs, to be turning blacker all the time, whereas this was a man who came from *the Movement,* an activist and a radical. "We're going to show everyone that black people can really run something," said Ivanhoe Donaldson, probably the most politically skilled of the Barry inner circle, a man who earlier on had run Andy Young's successful race for Congress in Atlanta.[10] For young blacks of Coleman's age, and Coleman was thirty-three when Barry took office, he thought, it was not unlike the moment for the World War II generation of white Americans when John Kennedy was inaugurated, a sense that the torch had been passed generationally.[11] Later, long after everything went sour, there remained a belief among people who had supported Marion Barry early in his career, but who had moved on as his personal and professional behavior became ever more intolerable, that his first term as mayor had been a good one, full of idealism and optimism. To a considerable degree that was true: In the beginning, because Washington was both the nation's capital and a very black city, his administration was a beacon for all kinds of talented black professional administrators, many of them with national reputations. This, after all, was to be the first great experiment nationally, and a highly visible one at that.

The mayor himself seemed pleasant and accessible in those early days, skilled at being the front man for the new administration, a likeable, easygoing man with great natural charm, comfortable with all different kinds of people, a man who knew when to play the race card and when not to, when to come in his dashiki and when to wear his three-piece pinstripe suit. The administration's hammer was his friend Ivanhoe Donaldson, also a SNCC veteran, and part of the younger, more militant group which had gradually emerged from SNCC. Donaldson, son of a New York cop, intensely political, smart, tough, and cocky, seemed to be the perfect counterpart to the rather more laid-back Barry. Donaldson handled the real interior politics of the administration, made the hard decisions, and tried to bend a normally reluctant bureaucracy to his will. There were many people who thought Marion Barry was more likeable than Ivanhoe Donaldson, but few who thought he was smarter, tougher, or more decisive than his close friend. Their offices were at opposite ends of a long corridor. Once Milton Coleman, himself something of a pioneer figure as a black man in what had until recently been an almost exclusively white world, went by to talk with Herbert Reid, one of Barry's early mentors and now his legal adviser. Coleman asked how the mayor was doing. "Which one," Reed asked, "the one at this end of the hall [Barry] or the one at the other end of the hall [Donaldson]?"

In Washington under Marion Barry, it became gradually clear, it was going to be business as usual, with one significant difference: Black people for the first time were going to be in charge of patronage. The city was going to buy from black suppliers. Within limits no one begrudged that. White political machines had taken their share (and more) of their cities' treasuries for more than a century, rewarding their friends and punishing, if need be, their enemies, so now it was only fair that blacks have a chance at their share of the spoils. But it was one thing to take their fair share at the trough and it was quite another thing, when black children were already dangerously at risk, to make the city's school system a critical part of the trough. Almost from the start, Barry and Donaldson cut their political pals in on almost everything, including an important share of the school con-

tracts. A man named Vincent Reed was the superintendent of the
school system at the time; he was a rather conservative, old-fashioned
black man, and, faced with murderous budgets, he had always gone
with low bids for school expenses.

The Barry administration quickly stopped that. Suddenly the
school system was under orders to buy from black suppliers who were
Barry pals. Overnight the school system, which had been buying
cereal for its students at $8.00 a carton, was paying $13.50 a carton.
The cost of fuel oil to heat the schools—a major expense—also went
up some 25 percent. The reason was that Barry and Donaldson had
cut in a black supplier who was a friend and financial supporter. A
black, Barry-friendly trash-collecting service was hired, again at a high
price; among its many considerable weaknesses was the fact that it did
not own any Dumpsters, so the trash often piled up around the
schools, and rats, always a problem in situations like this, became a
greater threat than ever.[12] Reed found himself in a constant struggle
with Barry. He knew from his past experience in St. Louis that it was
the fate of school superintendents to struggle with mayors over budgets, superintendents always wanting more, mayors always offering
less. He had no illusion about how hard Barry's problems were: This
was a poor city with immense social problems, which were growing
greater by the day. But what was taking place was something he never
would have expected: a young, allegedly modern black mayor, only
forty-three years old, representing, it was presumed, the new black
political activism, making things harder for already deprived black
children in order to take care of his business cronies. Reed did not
care what color skin these cronies had.

Their battles were endless. Reed was no novice to this kind of struggle, and he would tell Barry that he knew the political score, that mayors had to take care of their friends, that was an age-old game, and
that every mayor had a right to survival, to think of his next term. But
making crude political deals at the expense of schoolchildren was
something he had never seen before. "Marion," Reed would say, "it's
the *children.*" Barry would say that black businessmen were crucial to
the success of the city and were at the top of his agenda. "Come on,
Marion," Reed would answer, "you're taking it from the stomachs of
kids." Barry would again talk about the need for black entrepreneurs.

"Marion," Reed would say, *it's kids who are at stake. It's kids who are the losers every time you do this.*"

"I'm interested in the kids," Barry would answer. "I care about them."

"Show me," Reed would say; "don't tell me, Marion, show me." And then Barry would once again deliver his lecture about black entrepreneurs, how long black businesses had been suppressed in this city, and Reed would wonder why it was that black entrepreneurs had to charge so much more than white entrepreneurs for food for black children. Reed never dented Barry, but he never changed his tune, and when these sessions were over, his final words were always the same, like a mantra: *Marion, it's the kids.*[13] Within a year of Barry taking over, Reed left the job as superintendent. Years later, when some of Marion Barry's one-time colleagues, men who had once been allies but who had turned against him in disillusionment, looked at what had happened, they saw the struggle with Reed as the most ominous of the many early signals of what was to come. It brought back the words of Julian Bond about the young man he had met early in the sixties: Marion, said Bond, was always about Marion.[14] He was, some of them later decided, the first of a new breed they had not yet encountered, a me-first civil rights leader.

His old friends, watching in subsequent years the tragic decline not just of a man but, far more important, of the city he seemed determined to take with him, wondered how inevitable it had all been. Most of them thought the first term had been a good one. He still seemed quite idealistic, and he had brought in good people. There was some degree of optimism that at least some of the city's problems could be dealt with. But gradually, sometime early in his second term, which began in 1983, that optimism began to dwindle, and the mayor seemed to lose his sense of purpose. Soon the question arose: Had there ever been an agenda which was larger than himself? No one was sure. One reason he was so good at the political game, some of his friends thought, was because so little of it really meant anything to him; he was largely free of causes, save his own. His agenda was always primarily about himself and always in the most immediate sense: He did by instinct that which most immediately served his purpose on a given day. That was why he had called himself a situationist. There was no long-term view of politics, just what was the best tactical move at the moment.

Although in the beginning a critical part of his support had come from the white middle class, white liberals were disillusioned early on. For a brief time in the middle of Barry's career, he seemed to make amends with a newly created black middle class, in no small part by loading the city's payroll and fattening the bureaucracy, adding to the base of what was becoming a powerful, well-financed political machine. Then as his disgrace continued and his fall from respectability became more and more obvious, the core of his support came from poor blacks, many of whom liked him precisely because of their dislike of the people now so critical of him in the white and black establishments. No one, it seemed, could have been so fortunate in his choice of critics and enemies. Barry's covert view of politics seemed to be that white politicians had been doing this for years, therefore why shouldn't black politicians do it as well, a view which unfortunately struck a note of considerable resonance within some black wards.

There was also a sense of Barry's continuing personal deterioration in these years. There had always been a lack of discipline to his personal life, an increasingly chaotic quality to it. There was a good deal of late-night carousing, a need for alcohol, which he did not handle particularly well, and in addition, a constant need for sexual fulfillment. As he had risen to ever higher positions he had been emboldened in his sense of personal entitlement, as if he now saw himself above both personal reproach and political accountability, a view greatly strengthened by the way he was systematically tightening his personal control over the top of the city's police bureaucracy. In addition, he had become more attractive in certain circles to women now, a figure of power, the showcase black mayor of the nation's capital. It was not just that he hit on women: His old colleagues in the press corps would watch with amazement at political dinners when, the dinner over, women would on occasion hit on him. Early in his term as mayor his staff had had to tell him no, he could no longer use the city's official business credit cards for his one-night stands at hotels, nor what seemed to be his trademark means of saying thank you, a dozen roses sent to the lady in question the next morning, that it was all too easy to trace, and he had to find a different modus operandi.[15]

He was often out on the town into the early mornings. In May 1988, his car collided with that of a radio reporter near the Mall at about 3:30 A.M. That raised questions about what he was doing up at that hour. "There's no mystery. . . ." he had answered. "I'm a night owl."[16] From then on he began to call himself the Night Owl Mayor, operating late at night, moving through a netherworld of clubs and bars. Somewhere in the middle of his first term, the sightings began. This was years before he would go on a national television show and, with what might for him have seemed a brief glimpse of penitence, talk of being addicted to sex. One of the first important sightings took place at a cheap nightclub called This Is It? a strip joint on Fourteenth Street notorious for watered-down drinks, readily available drugs, extremely hospitable women, and a generally tawdry atmosphere. Barry had shown up there in December 1981 to attend the club's Christmas party. This Is It? seemed to be a place of flexible moral codes: Washington detectives checking out the case were told that sexual favors had been dispensed to Barry under the table, and narcotics indulged in above the table. What made the case even more interesting—and a symbol of what was to come—was the fact that the reports from the local detectives on what had happened that night made their way to the feds. Because Barry's control over the top level of his city's police department was becoming tighter all the time, not only had the local police done nothing, but Fred Raines, the head of the police department's intelligence unit, had passed three separate reports to officials in the U.S. Attorney's office, a clear signal that Raines believed that his own department had by then been corrupted. Not longer after, Raines was forced out of his job by the local police chief, a Barry pal.

It was an early sign of how bad things already were: This Is It? was, of course, a place where no city official had any business showing up, least of all the mayor. Barry's excuse was as bad as the sighting itself— he had personally gone by to pick up a campaign contribution. When Richard Cohen, the *Washington Post* columnist, wrote a column saying that Barry's being there gave the wrong signal to every cop in the city, Cohen's phone as well as the phones of a number of other *Post* writers and editors began to ring off the hook as all sorts of people checked in with sightings of Barry in other establishments of equally dubious reputation.[17] Most of the people doing the reporting seemed to be irate middle-class blacks. In these calls the mayor was said to be out of control, drinking too much, using drugs, and hitting on women. The women, as Milton Coleman was learning, were said to be getting younger and younger, and the mayoral limo was reported to be parked on occasion outside the dorms of Howard students.[18]

There were also reports that he was using cocaine, though this was extremely hard to prove, and he swore to friend and critic alike that he was clean. A friend of Cohen's, who knew something about the drug world, happened to see Barry on a plane, knocking down cognac after cognac. Cognac, the friend told the columnist, was something often used by cocaine aficionados to balance the effects of the drug. If not everything about him could be printed, soon the word was out that his drug use was on the rise. Where he had once sought alcohol, he now sought cocaine, a dangerous escalation in itself; even worse, crack cocaine, a singularly addictive form of cocaine, was just coming into play. His behavior was increasingly erratic, and the cause of it hardly a secret. In 1983 he was rushed to a Washington hospital for what a doctor who treated him called a cocaine overdose. The mayor's office listed the cause of the hospitalization as a hernia attack, and the reports on the incident were quashed, handed over to the police department's internal affairs division, a place where a Barry appointee had already corrupted the processes.

PRIDE, his original community organization, was rife with scandal. In the mid-eighties the feds moved against Mary Treadwell, Barry's former wife, for serious abuses in PRIDE. She, and others, were charged with taking thousands of dollars ticketed for low-income housing and using it for their own personal needs. She was eventually convicted on charges of conspiracy and sentenced to three years in jail. The U.S. Attorney who pushed the case noted at the time of sentencing that she had remained unrepentant, without "an iota of remorse." At year later she began her prison sentence. In the *Post* Richard Cohen wrote a column which noted that Ms. Treadwell drove a Mercedes and lived in the Watergate. Perhaps, he added, she had told the mayor that she was driving a Dodge and that the Watergate was a ghetto address.

Barry was arriving at work later and later in the morning, and though he seemed to have a remarkable capacity to play hard and yet function the next day, his attention span was becoming shorter; both his megalomania and on occasion his self-pity seemed to be greater. His trips to the bathroom were more frequent, his ties to moneyed influence more naked, his personal misbehavior more brazen. The *Post,* bombarded as it was by constant sightings of the mayor in places where he should not have been at hours when he should have been home, was caught in a terrible dilemma for a serious, old-fashioned paper. It editors believed that a public official had a right to a private life; the problem now was that those two lives, private and public, might be inseparable, and that the chaos of his private life was spilling over into his public life, making him beholden to people no politician should be beholden to. Crack cocaine, ferociously addictive, made drug use ever more dangerous. His suppliers, it was rumored then and it would become clear later, were men and women who worked in this late-night netherworld. His security detail was reportedly being used to connect him to the women he was involved with, who were also his sources of drugs. At the same time there was a sense that the city itself was unraveling, that services were declining, and that the city finances were in trouble.

The *Post* was taking off on a long study on the city finances, to be entitled "Running on Empty." But at the same time the paper's editors, jarred by all these sightings, were trying to do another special report on what he actually did and where he went in the wee hours of the morning. Several journalists were semidiscreetly stationed near all his principal watering holes, and were reporting back to the city desk by mobile phones. Well after midnight, the crack team followed him to a motel on Capitol Hill. While others waited outside, the phone rang at the *Post* for Art Brisbane, the editor in charge of the team. It was Marion Barry calling, and for a moment Brisbane was appalled—perhaps the mayor had picked up on the paper's sleuths and was calling in to complain. What a humiliation that would be! But no, it was just the mayor calling a little late to answer some questions for the other major *Post* takeout, the one on the city's finances. The entire journalistic enterprise, as Brisbane noted, brought back little in the way of details, but made the varying editors involved feel that they had become part of something sleazy in the process.[19]

There was a growing sense early in his second term that Barry's personal life and his conduct as mayor were now of the same piece—

chaotic, arrogant, undisciplined, and finally completely corrupt; that as long as his own primal needs—for narcotics and sexual favors— were fulfilled, nothing else really mattered to him, certainly not governance in a city where the living conditions were steadily becoming more desperate. It all seemed to be about immediate gratification: Everything was about himself, and about nothing else, thought Tom Sherwood, who had covered him for so long; even his carousing, which was now on the increase, was singularly narcissistic. "He was so self-absorbed that if he was having sex, I think in any real sense he was having sex with himself."[20] Not surprisingly, the city itself seemed to be increasingly in jeopardy. Its finances were considered more and more corrupt. Early in Barry's second term Alvin Frost, one of the city's top financial managers, a young black man with a Harvard MBA, became completely disillusioned with the city's financial dealings. He eventually resigned in anger and frustration. But before he quit, on one occasion Frost changed the password to a finance computer, and refused to share the new password with his colleagues. He also wrote Barry a devastating farewell note:

> The press devotes considerable attention to what you've done since your activist days as a college student and your work with SNCC. I believe that the real story goes back to your very early days and holds important clues to your psychological development. . . . The combination of poverty, race, loss of father, etc. . . . created very conflicting drives of insecurity and vulnerability with your ambition and aggressiveness. At bottom you have always been an opportunist, willing and prepared to take advantage of anything and anyone to achieve your own personal need for power, control and acceptance. Isn't it frightening to be so powerful and yet so insecure?[21]

To make matters even worse, his personal decline seemed to coincide with the political demise of Ivanhoe Donaldson. To the degree that the administration early on had reflected a sense of toughness of mind, it had come from Donaldson. But Donaldson, the Hoe, to insiders, had his own troubles. For a number of years, he had been living beyond his means, dressing in expensive suits, driving a Mercedes, and eating at high-priced restaurants. He was living the kind of life which political fixers are traditionally entitled to *after* they leave office, and can become lobbyists and cash in on their contacts. Almost from the start of the administration he had been quietly embezzling funds, writing checks to various people over whom he had power, and demanding as much as 80 percent of the money in kickbacks. He pleaded guilty of embezzling almost $200,000 worth of city funds in December 1985 and was sentenced to a maximum of seven years in prison. It was one more dispiriting moment for the city: First Mary Treadwell had gone to jail, and now Ivanhoe Donaldson. Not only did it cast the darkest kind of moral shadow over the administration, the mayor's closest aide caught in the crudest kind of shakedown, but it removed from Barry's side his pillar, the one man smart enough and tough enough to make unpleasant decisions, the kind the mayor himself, who liked to make people feel good about themselves, was loathe to make.

Years later, when his career became a study in both farce and tragedy, his old friends would still talk about him when they had known him in those early days, young and talented and facile, a great, quick study. Of his innate talents they had no doubt: He understood every political equation in front of him—particularly the politics of race—and he knew a terrible truth: that when things went badly as far as the white community was concerned, viewing him through its white middle-class codes, that it did not necessarily hurt him in some parts of the black community; indeed it might help a black politician who represented a community long suppressed and largely united in its sense of grievance. Behavior which the white community wanted punished, he understood, was behavior which the black community might therefore reward.

For if he learned nothing else, he had learned how to play the race card. He might be a failure as a mayor—the city's services might have declined dramatically, its schools become a tragic joke, the crime on the streets worse than ever, causing the city to be known as the murder capital of the world—but if the white people were against him, then ipso facto, despite the fact that his was a city filled with talented black people, he was a black hero, a sure thing politically. To vote against him was to vote for the white man. He who had once helped challenge men like Jim Clark and George Wallace and Bull Connor had become the black political equivalent of them, a man who used race to obliterate all his other shortcomings. The more incompetent he was as mayor, the more secure his new base was. Mayor-for-life, the *Washington City Paper,* a local paper, called him. Race, not patriotism, in modern America had become on both sides of the color line the last refuge of the scoundrel. He had become a figure of shame to many of those people who had first rallied around him. It was the saddest of sad stories, said his old friend Carroll Harvey, who had once helped talk him into a political life. John Lewis made the traditional black leadership of Washington smile with pride, Carroll Harvey said, and Marion simply made them sad.

68

By the late sixties Diane Nash was living in Chicago, a single mother trying to raise two young children. She and James Bevel were divorced in 1968. At the time of the divorce Sherrilyn Bevel, the child almost born in a Jackson, Mississippi, jail, was six, and Douglass Bevel was four. James Bevel did very little to help out with their children. For a brief few months he contributed some financial help, but then he moved out of the state, and the payments stopped. The lawyers she contacted told her then it would not be worth the time and money pursuing a man who no longer lived in Illinois, because it just wasn't going to happen, he wasn't going to help out voluntarily, and under the existing laws of child support, they would not be able to force him to pay. As far as she could tell from talking to Bevel, his rationale seemed to be that he was doing important things in the Movement, both in civil rights and on Vietnam, that he didn't care about money himself, and therefore it was her responsibility to make her own way with the children. She was, she soon decided, going to have to raise two children absolutely on her own.

She did not have a college degree and she had no intention of getting one. As far as she was concerned, education was a great part of the problem in this country. Here was a country with millions of college-educated people, many of them with Ph.D.'s in economics, and yet the country was barely able to dent poverty. As such, she had decided to go through life without the normal educational credentials which were so vital in American society. She was in all ways still a radical. In 1966 she was part of a small group of American women who went to North Vietnam for a month, and she was impressed by what she saw there, the resistance to a war which seemed to her immoral and racist, as well as the resilience of the ordinary Vietnamese people.

She was also something of a feminist before it became fashionable. Rather late in her life she discovered a diary from her days as a freshman at Howard, and she was surprised to find a note she had made to herself—someone, she had written down, had told her that if she did not stop talking about women's rights, she was never going to have any boyfriends.

She had to have a job to support herself and her family. But having a job and raising two children inevitably put severe limits on her political activities. Hers was going to be a life without luxuries, indeed one which was a struggle for the amenities of life. She soon realized that she could spend the limited amount of time away from work with her children, or she could be a part of the Movement. But she could not do both. It was not going to be a great personal victory, she thought, if she gave herself over to the Movement and her two children became casualties of her absence, and were caught like so many others in the downward pull of the inner cities.

She did not worry too much about finding work. She knew she was able and professional; if she could help run an invading army of black activists challenging the full police powers of several Southern states, she could hold a job in an office in Chicago. She might not get paid her full worth but there would always be jobs. The economics of her life, she realized early on, were always going to be hard. But she was smart and tough, and she quickly learned to be a great family budgeter. With the marriage to Bevel breaking up, she had found a small house in a rough section in the South Side of Chicago on Prairie Avenue. It was in a hard-core, low-income area, which was the only reason she could afford it. It was hardly ideal for her kids. The local schools would not be very good. But her game plan was to live there for a little while, help teach the children at home to compensate for any loss at school, and then eventually sell the house in a few years when they were a little older, and move to a better neighborhood with better schools. Besides, she could get the house for $3,500 with a downpayment of only $500. It was a single-family dwelling that had been converted into apartments and she quickly reconverted it back into its earlier incarnation. Friends helped her with some of the work and she became surprisingly skilled at being a plasterer and doing other house repairs.

Yet her responsibilities often seemed overwhelming. On occasion, she later recalled, she was scared that she would fail in her new mission as a single parent, facing life with two tiny children and almost no financial resources. "There was a part of me that was terrified I couldn't do it," she said years later, "and there was a part of me that told myself, *Yes, you can do it, because you have to do it! Because your kids have to eat.*" One of the things which now irritated her was the fact that when she and Bevel had worked together in the Movement, when she was Diane Bevel and they had done joint programs, Bevel, as the man, and as the more visible member of the team, had gotten most of the credit for what they had done. That had not bothered her at the time, for the mission itself had always been more important than the glory, or perhaps more properly, the mission itself had been the glory, but now that she was out trying to support her family, it had become a factor. By her estimates Bevel's earning power was about three and a half times hers.

In time she sold her house for a profit and moved to a better house in a better section in Hyde Park and her children went to the Whitney Young High School. It was a very good magnet school. Financially, things were always, if not hard, extremely demanding, indeed exacting. Every purchase had to be carefully monitored. There was no room for miscalculation, only so much for housing, so much for food, and so much for clothes. They were budgeted, she said, "to the final penny." Any additional cost threw the entire financial system out of line. If one of the children got sick, they were all squeezed that much harder in the succeeding weeks. If Douglass wanted a baseball glove, and it cost $20, it might throw the normal budget off for several weeks.

It was hard, she thought, to raise children without a father in the house, and it was, she came to believe, particularly hard on Douglass. When he was a little boy she sometimes could hear him and his friends talking in the innocent language of the very young about what manhood was all about. The more she listened to them, the more it became clear that in their eyes it was about being an outlaw. Being a man at the age of six, she decided, after listening to them, meant crossing the street in the middle of the block, not on the corner, and certainly not waiting for red lights. She had a sense then that men who fathered children did not know how hard it was on their children to grow up without them, without someone there to teach them what being a man was all about. The absence of a father, she thought, worked differently on the children of each sex: With the girls, she believed, it raised questions about relating to men, and whether they could trust them; with boys it was more primal, about their own identity, and about how to grow up and become a serious, responsible man.

Finding jobs was not that hard. She knew even if she did not have a degree she was intelligent and competent. One of her first jobs was working for *Muhammad Speaks,* the weekly Muslim newspaper, and she was amused at the irony of that, because she was not a Muslim. But she enjoyed working there. She liked the man she worked for, Richard Durham, very much, and she held all sorts of jobs at once—copy editor, proofreader, general librarian, photo librarian. One of the things she particularly enjoyed about the job was its hours. Because it was a weekly, her superiors did not want too much news early in the week, because it would be old by the time the paper came out. That gave her a couple of days when she could go to her children's school and tutor other kids in reading, something she was fond of doing. She had found that she had a talent for that, for she had taught her own children to read when they were four, using techniques shared by Jean Young, Andy Young's wife, labeling all the objects in their home, and letting these everyday objects become the key to learning to read.

That job was followed by one at Western Union, where she was hired, she was sure, because the managers thought she was white. There she noticed very quickly that the managerial floor on which she worked was almost exclusively white and that the black workers, most of them women, seemed to hit a ceiling and to hit it on lower floors. That meant they were denied access to the bulletin board on which the openings for better in-house jobs were being posted. Ever political, she became instrumental in working with the other black women in the company and telling them where they could learn about better jobs within Western Union. Sure that she would soon be fired for her political activities, she quickly located another job.

She had other jobs she liked. One was at the Chicago Center for Black Religious Studies, and in time she found work in a community service organization. There, among other duties, she checked up on problems poor people were having with their landlords. These cases were at the core of urban life. Poor people, who lived vulnerable, powerless lives, and whose daily existence reflected a constant struggle for basic survival, had difficulty getting enough heat in their apartments during the winter, or having some minimal security in their apartment buildings. She often dealt with landlords who managed to make money off these buildings but who steadfastly refused to make even the most minimal improvements. It was a situation which seemed to bring out the worst in everyone. Apartments were often left vacant, and people would come in and steal a sink, which was bad enough, but then not even bother to cap the pipe, which meant that the entire building would eventually be soaked by the flow of water.

Nothing she did ever quite equaled the sheer sense of fulfillment she had gotten in those early days of the civil rights movement. One of the things about the Movement which she missed desperately as she grew older was not just the sense of purpose which they had all brought to the cause, but that of their selflessness. All their egos had been suppressed. When someone had been driven by ego, the others had quickly intervened. When she was young she had taken that selflessness for granted, and assumed that she would find it in other institutions. She had assumed that in other social service organizations devoted to a larger community good, she would find it again, but that had not turned out to be true. Later, working in other pro bono organizations, she had found that they were far more bureaucratic, driven more, it sometimes seemed, by the needs of the people who were running the organizations than the people they were supposed to help, and that there was a great deal of feathering of nests and of self-promotion.

Altogether too many of her new colleagues were like ordinary people doing ordinary jobs. In one social service organization she worked for, some of the people had joined the board largely because, as far as she could tell, they wanted to get ahead socially. In another she had been dismayed to find that what her superiors wanted was skillful paperwork: Instead of having her go out and work with people in the community, they seemed primarily interested in having her complete reports on time. At one point she had gone to her boss and complained to him about the fact that she was spending far too little time with people in the community. "You'd probably be satisfied if I never went out and did any real community work and just got all my reports done on time, wouldn't you?" she said. "You're absolutely right," he answered. She found it hard to compare that kind of indifference with the uncommon commitment she had known in the early days of the Movement. Now that she was older, she often wondered if the Movement had attracted exceptional people, or whether instead had been a magnet for ordinary people who had been transformed into uncommon people because of their cause. Perhaps, she thought, it was a little of both.

If her life had been hard, then by the mid-nineties, Diane Nash found that she was proud of what she had done, and how she had raised her two children. Both Sherrilyn and Douglass went to college, Sherrilyn to the University of Illinois at Urbana and Douglass to Earlham, a fine Quaker school in Indiana, and though neither finished college, she felt good about the opportunity she had given them. By 1987 she was a grandmother. Sherrilyn was married with two children, living in Atlanta and trying to be a writer, and Douglass was working as a musician in Las Vegas.

In 1989 after they had both left the house Diane Nash went back to school at Chicago State. Certainly not for a degree—her hostility toward credentialed education was as strong as ever—but she felt she needed courses in science and math to understand the world around her a little better. By chance there was a student protest taking place that year over a charge being automatically applied to all students for a health insurance program. The charge seemed quite large—almost $400 a person—yet it seemed to bring the most minimal of benefits. Ever the activist, Diane Nash soon became one of the leaders of the protest, and she and her allies eventually managed to have the charge withdrawn.

Diane Nash still needed to support herself and she worked at several jobs, doing some lecturing about the Movement at colleges, and working in real estate as well. She discovered that she was very good at being a real estate investigator, at going to the city's various legal centers and checking out pieces of real estate and finding out if there were any judgments or liens against them. She thought she had a natural touch for real estate deals, and she hoped to reach a point where she could buy pieces of property which were not in good condition, rehab them, and then sell them.

To her surprise—and it was a pleasant surprise—she also found that as the years passed she had become something of a figure in history. She felt blessed by that, by the fact that she had been at the right place at the right time and done the right thing. Had this not happened, had she not been in Nashville in the fall of 1959 and joined the Lawson seminars, she thought she might have been a far lesser person. Not only were people continuing to reexamine the civil rights movement, but there was, because of the rise of the women's movement, a new interest in feminist history, and she stood at a place where two separate forces of history seemed to intersect. Periodically someone would talk to her about making a documentary film about her life. She found that she felt good about what she had done and the life she had lived. Thinking back to the young girl she had been in those early days, a young Fisk co-ed scared to death of the possibilities of violence, her hands soaked with sweat just thinking of the confrontation ahead, she was impressed by the courage and vision of that person. She had acted in those days on pure instinct, not because it had been the fashionable or popular thing to do, but as she came to study the choices, the *only* thing she could do.

For a long time after their divorce she was angry at James Bevel. Though he was supposed to be a man of God, she believed that he had always done what he wanted to do. She faulted him for what she saw as his selfishness. She admired what he had done as an activist for his people, his bravery and his intelligence, but that, she felt, did not excuse, as he seemed to think it did, his failure to accept personal responsibility for his own children. She had been forced to be both father and mother to them; because of that she had had less chance to be a mother, and less chance to make true career choices in her own life. Gradually over the years that anger waned. It was a mistake, she decided, to have taken what Bevel had done so personally; Bevel, she thought, was just being Bevel. There were no great surprises in his behavior. Nor had anyone forced her to marry him. There had been, she thought, millions of other men out there and she had chosen him, so the choice had been as much about her as it had been about him. Still, Bevel remained something of a sensitive subject, her friends learned, and if in later years she was invited to a symposium which dealt with those early years of the Movement, she did on occasion call the sponsors and ask whether the Reverend James Bevel had been invited to that conference and was going to attend.

69

In 1963, Kelly Miller Smith, the black minister who had played so crucial a role in holding the original Nashville activist coalition together, and who had helped give Jim Lawson so much freedom in the early days of the Nashville movement, decided to accept the pastorate of Antioch Baptist Church in Cleveland. He did it with no small amount of misgiving. He loved Nashville, he loved his church and his congregation; he was, for better or worse, a critical part of the fabric of that city, his affection for it in no way diminished by his knowledge of its frailties. He was at that moment the rarest of black men in America, a leader in two communities, and he had become expert about the strengths and vulnerabilities of both races. Among white people his intelligence, fairness, and decency had slowly permitted even the most recalcitrant conservatives to understand what a strong, generous, and valuable citizen he was. In Nashville there was no part of him which was underutilized.

But there was in the black church, as in almost every other organization, a hierarchical tradition with a ladder to greater success and prestige: Bigger churches in bigger cities were better than smaller churches in smaller cities. The great stars of the black Baptist church were by tradition supposed to end up in the North at large, prestigious churches. Nashville, therefore, was supposed to be a way station; it had brought him only partway up the ladder. He had started at a small church in Mississippi, he had been a powerful force in Nashville, and now a big church in Cleveland was calling.

It was a terrible dilemma, he told friends. He had always assumed that he would some day go on to a larger church up north, but now that the call had come, he did not seem to have much taste for it.

Nashville had become not only his home but a place where to an uncommon degree he felt complete. Still, he was in his forties and if he did not go now, there might never be a comparable offer, and he might always go around wondering why he had not pushed himself to his outer career limit. Besides, there was a certain macho quality to the progression—there were all these other black ministers, he told his friends, who would tease him at conferences, saying yes, he was a big star in Nashville, but Nashville was small, and his church was small, and he ought to try a big church, one with a congregation of two thousand or three thousand people. That was the big time, they would say.

It had happened very quickly. He had given a guest sermon at the Cleveland church, and they had liked him and immediately made him an offer. It was almost, he said later, as if he had been ambushed. He had been unprepared for the immediacy of the pressure. Back home in Nashville, he had talked it over with his closest friends in the Sunday night group, the tiny band of pals and conspirators from his congregation who gathered with him every Sunday, and who knew that he loved to have his Sunday night drink, his Courvoisier, and never told the other members of the church about it. His friends all said he was crazy, that he had everything he wanted in Nashville, that the men who had been teasing him were wrong, and more important, outdated; that things had changed because of the Movement and the action was more in the South than in the North; that each city in the South now seemed to have a distinguished minister with a national voice. The old order, in which fame and distinction resided in the North, had been reversed. Worse, a big city like Cleveland was likely to be filled with powerful, entrenched, quite conservative cliques wary of letting a new minister become too independent.

But it was a challenge he could not resist and he took the job. It was a disaster from the start. It was a big church where he was supposed to deputize others to perform a great many of the small, highly personal pastoral responsibilities which he had done in the past himself. In Nashville, as his friend Dorothy Webster later noted, when people were sick they had tended to call Kelly before they called their doctor. In Nashville, whenever someone was sick or someone had died, he had always paid a personal call. Now in Cleveland, he found himself being waved off by other church officers, who told him that he was not to worry about it, that things like this were not his responsibility. But to him these duties were at the very heart of being a minister.

The day he decided to leave Cleveland, he later told Bernard Lafayette, he had gone by to pick up his paycheck. It was at lunchtime and he was very busy, with a number of other things to do, and there had been a line of employees waiting to get their checks, and because he was in a hurry he had gone to the head of the line. But the cashier, the man writing the checks, had waved him to the back of the line. That had done it. Kelly Miller Smith was not a hierarchical man, he was a man who believed that all people had a right to feel that they were equally important in their needs, but there were times when you were pressured because you had exceptional responsibilities, and anyone who knew him understood that if he cut in line there was a very good reason for it. This particular incident, he later said, was like being told, You may be our preacher, but this is not your church. Perhaps he might be able to win the political-bureaucratic struggle for the heart and soul of this church in a number of years, but he did not intend to wait that long. He made a few calls back to Nashville, and soon he went back to the First Baptist Church. He had been gone four months. Later, when a friend asked him when it was that he realized that he had made a mistake in going to Cleveland, he had answered, "When I got there and was unpacking the moving van and I felt homesick."[1]

Kelly Miller Smith could have, had he chosen, pointed with pride to the progress which had been achieved in Nashville: the steady integration of schools, the victories in the lunch counter and movie theater struggles, the gradual opening of broader opportunities for employment for black people in a number of otherwise all-white businesses, the gradual integration of the city's white colleges, and the increased black political power on the local scene. In time he himself was named an assistant dean at Vanderbilt Divinity School, a position he held in addition to his church and other responsibilities. But in truth he found the process of integration of the city's schools and of the city itself maddeningly slow. The degree to which race was woven into the fabric of the city's daily life, because of the existing economic and class structure, made every bit of progress extremely difficult. The burden of the past was very heavy, he, like so many others, was in the process of finding out. He worried to the day he died that so much of the change they had wrought might be more cosmetic than real.

For the shadow of race in Nashville, like that in other American cities, often seemed overwhelming. By the seventies there were constant battles to save prized black institutions such as the famous Pearl High, which was once the very backbone of the black community and which now, in a new, integrated Nashville, was deemed to be of little value (since white students, it was assumed by the predominantly white city fathers, should not have to go to a formerly all-black school). There were always the small things which pulled at Kelly Miller Smith, small things which were not small. He wanted to make even in smaller ways the city more complete, and one of his objectives had always been to temper the almost total segregation of the city's churches. He had once suggested combining his church with the white First Baptist Church and had not gotten much of a reply from its minister; when he had pushed a little harder the white minister had finally written back that there were too few good churches downtown, not too many, and that had been that. On another occasion he arranged for his church's choir to sing at the same white church, aware that his choir was exceptional and believing that the formidable pull of its music, even if it was only momentary, might lift members of the other church above their normal prejudices and leave them with some greater sense of kinship. But it had turned out to be a disaster instead of a celebration. The black choir had gone over there, primed to do its best, to find that only the white pastor and the church officials and the ushers and a very few members of the congregation had shown up from the white church. What might have been an exercise in brotherhood was, for most members of the choir, singing with all their hearts to so many empty seats, one of bitterness instead.

Kelly Miller Smith was ambivalent about his role at Vanderbilt. He not only wanted the job but he badly needed it. His church, reflecting many black churches in the South in that era, paid him a modest salary with marginal retirement benefits (later, because of his own experience, those benefits were greatly improved). He taught at American Baptist but that was for very little money. So with four children all needing to be educated, the Vanderbilt job was essential. Technically it advanced the black cause, and it was supposed to be personally prestigious for him. His title was assistant dean and lecturer on the black church. His job was not only to teach the history of the black church to students but to represent Vanderbilt Divinity School to the black churches locally and nationally.

But he never felt particularly wanted at Vanderbilt and he came to feel that he was there as much for window dressing as he was because there was a complete acceptance of him and of his mission. At Vanderbilt, he was, he would tell close friends, dean in charge of niggers, using the phrase his old friend Vivian Henderson, the economist, had coined for show window jobs like this in the early years of integration. Vanderbilt was still Vanderbilt, he would tell friends; some of the faculty members were very good, and some of the students were wonderful. But it was still a conservative school with a conservative past and a conservative board determined to ensure that the past still lived. The divinity school dean, Walter Harrelson, was a member of Smith's church, having joined it as an act of protest against the segregated nature of Nashville's white churches, and he thought Harrelson a good man in a difficult position.

At the most personal level he felt only partially connected. Though he was by that point one of the most distinguished black ministers in the country, he never got tenure at Vanderbilt. Nor for that matter did he even get a three-year or a five-year administrative appointment, which Vanderbilt could readily have provided if it so chose, and which would have given him additional status and diminished his annual sense of anxiety about his immediate future there. Instead his contract was done annually, and at the last moment; because of that he felt they were signaling to him how low he was on their list of priorities. It left this accomplished, talented man, self-evidently an ornament to his city and to the university, with a constant feeling of vulnerability. The budget he worked with was quite small, a little bit of money for his own travel and enough to cover two conferences a year. It was a time when all universities were coming under increasing financial pressures, and the divinity school budget always seemed to run on the margin.

He always had, he confided in friends, a feeling that if the numbers got a little harder at the divinity school, he would be the first to go. Though technically he was a member of the faculty and an assistant dean and therefore had a right to vote on faculty issues, he never exercised that vote because he did not feel that he was enough a part of the school. He gave courses on the black church and one of the constant irritants for him was the fact that the black students at Vanderbilt Divinity School took courses on the white church, but the white students did not so readily take courses on the black church. That, he thought, was the old racism in modern academic form: Blacks needed to understand whites but whites did not need to understand blacks. In many ways he believed that Vanderbilt had never really changed. There might be a moderately liberal chancellor in Alec Heard and a moderately liberal dean in Walter Harrelson, but it was a conservative school down to its bones.

He remained a man of consummate social grace and kindness, an affirming man who always seemed to make the people he had just been with feel better about themselves. Because he was so enchanting and warm, because so much of his uncommon energy went into his personal relationships with those around him, it was sometimes easy to underestimate how angry he was. Sometimes the anger would show. On occasion he would have lunch with Peter Paris, his young black colleague at Vanderbilt Divinity School, and they would talk in a kind of code about some of the people around them, men who on the surface appeared to be for the things they were for, but who, when the pressure mounted, were always on the other side. Then and only then would his true anger surface, as Kelly Miller Smith spoke in devastating terms about how certain people tended to say one thing and do another when it counted, and believed that they could still fool black people while doing it.

The death of Martin Luther King was a bitter wound for him. But he resented it greatly when he read references to King in newspapers and articles which called him a "slain civil rights leader." King was first and foremost, Smith believed, a man of the church; not a secular man assaulting America's laws, but to his mind, a man of God assaulting the very godlessness of those laws. It was an important distinction. That made King, in Smith's words, "a martyred prophet who was killed for doing what prophets do. He was not simply working for human rights and against the efforts of oppression, the struggle was against evil. . . . It was against sin. . . . The message of Martin Luther King must be underscored: *the effort to abolish oppression is a work of God, and those who do it are truly God's people.*"[2]

By the seventies, he was, in Peter Paris's phrase, a somewhat saddened integrationist. The longer he struggled in Nashville, the more
victories that were gained, the more he saw the limits of each victory.
In addition he was trying to deal with the full force of an increasingly
radicalized black community at a time which reflected both rising
expectations and, not surprisingly, rising anger as well. Those forces
put the role of a traditional integrationist very much at risk. He still
believed in the ideal of integration, in the concept of a just society,
where all doors were open equally to all people and where people
could choose their friends as they wanted to. Black people did not
need to assimilate, he believed, they could follow their own proud
path if they so chose, but they should also be able to enjoy the cultural
pluralism of so rich a community and a nation and not be crowded off
into the poorer corners and ghettos at they had for so many years in
the country's history.

Smith was aware, in addition to the changing black mood, not only
of the coming of black nationalism, but of the theological implications
of that rise. By the seventies, a black minister named James Cone at
Union Theological Seminary had begun to give what was essentially a
theological explanation for the concept of black power and was
becoming increasingly influential with young black ministers. Cone
was the father of what became known as black theology, which
seemed on the surface at least to reflect a kind of post-integrationist
separatism, and there was at that time considerable resonance with his
work among younger men in the black church. Cone saw himself as a
follower of both Martin Luther King *and* Malcolm X; in his teachings,
blended with the traditional view of integration and nonviolence
espoused by men like King and Kelly Miller Smith, there was also a far
more alienated vision of America reflecting Malcolm's sense of apart-
ness. If King had reflected the optimism of those churchgoers in the
South about the eventual coming of a better day, Malcolm had
reflected the deep estrangement of those blacks who had made the
migration to the Northern cities and who were mired in a faceless
racism as powerful and unrelenting as that of the South, most of it not
so much political and legal as economic, and eventually social and
psychological.

Cone's view soon became quite intriguing to Kelly Miller Smith. It
seemed to provide some role for the church during an increasingly

radical moment on how to deal with an ever-more-alienated new constituency. Cone had written of the need for black people to gain their freedom throughout the world by any means possible. That was somewhat disturbing to Kelly Miller Smith, who was a nonviolent man to his core, and who was wary of the apocalyptic possibilities if American blacks began to resort to violence and if their leaders endorsed it. He wrestled with the issues posed by Cone, and gradually, with some reservations, began to embrace black theology, his close friend Peter Paris thought. He found the issue of nonviolence, particularly as it was to be manifested in struggles of liberation, a fascinating one. The Jesus he had always believed in was a surprisingly radical one, a constant spiritual and political dissenter in his day. But if Kelly Miller Smith was a man of nonviolence, he also understood that there were some parts of the world, like South Africa, where the government was so oppressive that it gave its protesters no alternative other than violence. These were hard issues for him, and he thought some of them came without easy solution. But by the early seventies he had started signing off on some of his professional letters with the Latin phrase *post liberatem pax,* which meant "after the liberation, peace."

Even in his personal life there were now some shadows from the profound changes taking place in the black community. His adored second daughter, Adena, decided in December 1974 to marry a young black man originally named Michael Wright. She had gone to Spelman; he was a young man from Detroit who had gone to Morehouse. Just before they were married they both decided to become Muslims. Adena said that she was not giving up her Christianity, but she was adding Islam to her beliefs. But her decision was devastating to Kelly, for the marriage to Michael Wright, now Mateen Wright, in a Muslim ceremony was the most personal of rejections. Kelly Miller Smith tried to compromise, suggesting that in part of the ceremony she acknowledge her Christian heritage. But as Mateen Wright noted years later, in his own youthful intensity and his own newness to Islam, he had refused to compromise and indulge his new father-in-law. ("It was my arrogance—Kelly was quite good about being willing to compromise with a new force," Wright, a doctor, said years later.[3]) As it had been a rejection of Smith's faith, in his eyes, it had been a rejection of himself as well. The wedding was held in the Smith house, but it was extremely painful to Kelly Miller Smith, and he refused to attend the ceremony, saying that as a Christian he could not be present. At the last minute his son Kelly Miller Smith, Jr., who was also a minister, had to go and bring him in for the reception. His friends were intrigued by the contradictions in his behavior, the fact that he seemed anxious to show both his love for his daughter and his displeasure over the ceremony at the same time. It was one of the rare times his friends had seen this graceful, charming man, who seemed to handle all social situations so well and who was so skilled at telling them how to handle the crises in *their* lives, completely lose his cool and become unable, finally, to handle one of the most personal rituals of all, the marriage of his daughter.

By the early eighties his health began to fail. He had suffered from diabetes, and he had suffered as well from ulcers; it soon became clear that the illness this time was more serious, that he was suffering from stomach cancer. He was working desperately hard to finish a book based on the Lyman Beecher lectures which he had given at Yale. Serious minister and theologian that he was, he had never published very much, just the occasional sermon, for he was not a man of the written word. His passion was using words in conversation and from the pulpit, his connections always human and direct. He would work on his weekly sermons alone on Saturday, but normally he did not like to be alone, and in the past when he was supposed to be working on some article, he always found a way to do something else, to pick up the phone and talk to people. He was a man of uncommon discipline, for he had disciplined himself in many ways all his life, not the least of which was his ability to rein in his anger and to be his more generous self in the face of constant white prejudice, but the discipline of pure intellectual achievement, writing an abstract article for some journal while sitting by himself in a room, was essentially alien to him.

His friend Peter Paris was working with him on his book, which would be called *Social Crisis Preaching,* because Smith did not want it to be merely a black minister's book and thereby be ghettoized. It was something of a race against time to finish it before he died. When Paris went on a trip to Africa in the summer of 1983, his congregation, aware of Kelly's failing health and the close friendship of these two men, gave Paris several hundred dollars so that he could call Kelly every few days and report on what he had seen in Africa. Those calls from Africa to Nashville seemed to give him particular pleasure.

As Kelly Miller Smith was dying, Will Campbell, his old friend and ally in countless crises of the fifties and sixties, went by the hospital to visit him one last time. It was late May of 1984 and Kelly Miller Smith had only a few days to live. They had been comrades in arms for some thirty years, sometimes pastor and parishioner, sometimes just friends. Kelly Miller Smith, more than any man Will Campbell had ever known, seemed to have the strength of the just, and the ability to make other people behave better than they intended to. He had, in Campbell's eyes, always exuded spiritual strength. It was not easy for Campbell to watch him now, tired and frail, and for the first time perhaps a little depressed. He had a television set in his hospital room and was watching a sitcom about a black family. There was a sadness about him now, Campbell thought. "They still don't respect us," he said and pointed to the television set. Campbell asked what he meant and Kelly Miller Smith spoke of this show and others like it on television alleged to depict black life. "They're still making fun of us—we're still comic strip figures to them."

70

The longer he served on the Atlanta city council, the more confident John Lewis became that he could have a full career in elective politics, and that he could eventually run for higher office. He had a strong sense of his constituents' needs and he did not hesitate to represent them against powerful forces, even former President Carter. In 1982 Carter and his allies were pushing to create a major artery to go right through the middle of a poor black neighborhood in order to serve the soon-to-be-built Carter Center. Lewis decided to oppose the change, a decision which greatly irritated the former president, and created for the first time a rift between Lewis and Andy Young, a traditional ally of his within the Movement. (Carter was not amused by Lewis's opposition; he subsequently accused Lewis not only of being a secret ally of the Kennedys but, in an unusual phone call to Lewis's house, of not loving him enough.[1])

In the fall of 1985 there were rumors that Wyche Fowler was going to leave his House seat and run for the Senate. That meant the House seat which Lewis had urged both Julian Bond and Andy Young to seek would once again be open. John Lewis called his old friend Bond and they met over lunch to talk of their mutual plans. Lewis asked Bond what he was going to do, and Bond said he was going to run for the congressional seat. Bond in turn asked Lewis what *he* was going to do, and Lewis said he was going to run for Congress too. "I'll see you on the campaign trail," Lewis told him. They were two old, very close friends, they had shared much over twenty-five years, but it was the shortest lunch they ever had. They would both enter the 1986 primary.

Both men were popular favorites within the small world of civil rights veterans and professionals, Bond because of his immense charm, wit, and innate grace, Lewis because he was so true to the

Movement and to himself, so singularly hardworking and fair. At first
Bond seemed the prohibitive favorite. He was infinitely more charming, scion of a distinguished family of black educators. (When his
father, Horace Mann Bond, a professor at Atlanta University, heard
that his son was about to run for the Georgia House of Representatives, he said, "My God, I didn't raise my boy to be a Georgia legislator. I'd hoped he'd go into a more academic occupation."[2]) Bond was
far better known nationally, charismatic as Lewis was not, he had
greater access to money, and he was good on television as Lewis was
not. Journalists had always been drawn to him, and he was unusually
rich in friendships with the nation's rising media stars, those reporters
who themselves had been gradually propelled to greater prominence
by their own coverage of the events of the sixties. Although some of
the older reporters knew John Lewis from the earliest days of the
Movement, he was not in the trade considered as good an interview,
nor, in a phrase beginning to enter the vocabulary, as good a sound
bite. Although Andy Young, now mayor of Atlanta, was pledged to
neutrality, Lewis felt that behind the scenes Young was tilting toward
Bond, and certainly most of his top people were openly for Bond.
That meant the odds were heavily in Bond's favor. By all rights John
Lewis knew, he should have folded and not even bothered to run. But
he felt he had every right to run. He had given as much to the Movement and he had taken as many risks as anyone in the country. He
decided he would run hard, but he would refrain from any personal
attacks on his old friend, though at one point he did use a phrase he
later regretted: The people of the district, Lewis said, needed a work-
horse, not a show horse.

Money was a problem at first for him, but gradually a few old
friends rallied and helped out. Eventually he got the AFL-CIO
endorsement. Rarely had those in the old civil rights world been faced
with so difficult a choice. There had been divisions before, of course,
over strategy and tactics and personalities, but they had been relatively minor; this campaign was about personalities and it was public—you had to make a choice between two of the best-loved figures
of the Movement. It was very painful for many people who were
friends of both candidates. Of all the calls that Lewis got, the one he
resented the most was from Stokely Carmichael, who called to say that
the race was dividing the community and that one of them should get

out. Lewis was surprised to get the call, for in the past Carmichael had rarely deigned to talk to him, and had treated American elective politics with obvious disdain. "Stokley," he told him, "you are not a person who has the right to tell me to drop out."

During the primary one of the minor candidates, a state senator named Mildred Glover, suggested that all elected candidates ought to take drug tests. Bond was unalterably opposed. "Jar wars," the issue was called at the moment. Because she, like Bond, had been in the state legislature, there were those in the Atlanta community who thought her statement was aimed at Bond. For a time the drug question just sat there; not quite an issue, and not quite a nonissue. Lewis said nothing about it.

Most people thought Bond would win handily, and that he would get the requisite 50 percent of the vote in the primary so that there would be no need for a runoff. Andy Young was in Washington on the day of the primary and he gave a late-afternoon interview to an Atlanta television station which said in effect that he had voted for Bond. Lewis was furious. When the results of the primary were in, Bond had fallen just short of 50 percent; he had gotten 47 percent to Lewis's 35. That meant there would have to be a second primary. Still, it seemed like an insurmountable lead. But Lewis was encouraged, and he gave an old-fashioned, evangelical speech when he got the news of the runoff saying that he would fight and win: Go and tell Julian Bond, go and tell Andy Young, go and tell Maynard Jackson that here we come and we are going to win, he told his supporters. He decided that he would simply work harder than anyone else. No one would outwork him. He had learned that from Robert Kennedy. He would start the day outside different Atlanta workplaces and he would visit the black district during the day, house by house, knocking on doors himself, and he would end the night outside movie theaters and shopping centers, and any other place which was still open.

To his considerable surprise Julian Bond challenged him to a series of debates. That went against the cardinal rule of politics, which was that if you were ahead you did not do anything which brought publicity and visibility to your opponent. But there appeared to be a quantum difference in their ability to speak on television. Bond was obviously more attractive and more graceful in expressing his thoughts, and the opportunity to debate seemed, despite the wisdom of the past, an obvious asset for him. In that decision Bond was both right and wrong: He was more articulate, and he was more graceful, but what came through with Lewis was how constant and how steadfast he was. Lewis had a sixth sense as the campaign neared its end that he was gaining quickly on Bond; a few days before the election, he knocked on the door of a black home and a young boy opened the door and yelled to his parents, "It's John Lewis." That made him sure he was getting the badly needed name recognition.

On the Friday before the election he and Bond appeared on a local broadcast, facing two local reporters assigned to question them. What transpired then was something both of them regretted. One of the smallest issues in the race was the fact that Lewis had accepted a $100 contribution from a cable television employee, a transaction which allegedly represented a conflict of interest for him. It was a small, dumb issue, Lewis thought, and when Bond, who was still his old friend, was asked about it, he expected Julian to swat it away. Instead Bond answered, "If it looks like a duck and quacks like a duck and waddles like a duck, then it must be a duck." Lewis was furious. Anyone, particularly a longtime friend, knew whatever else how clean he had been all those years, for he might as well have taken a vow of poverty when he entered the Movement.

Because Julian Bond's marriage was coming apart, and because his wife had confided a good deal of their marital problems to Lillian Lewis, John Lewis was all too aware of the chaos going on in his opponent's personal life at the time, but he had said nothing about it. But now, stung by Bond's answer, he decided to up the ante. At that moment he thought to himself, I'm not going to let this Negro get away with this. (In recounting the story years later, Lewis would emphasize that in his private description of Bond at that time, he had used the word *Negro,* not the slur word.) So he raised the drug issue. He had never bothered to do this before, never mentioned it during the campaign, but now, he said, Why don't we both step outside and take a urine test? With that the drug issue was out in the open. From then on Bond's fortunes declined. Lewis campaigned almost around the clock, and won 52–48, going up seventeen points in three weeks. But his friendship with Julian Bond was badly ruptured.

It would take nearly a decade, until they both revisited Mississippi in 1994 on the thirtieth anniversary of the Mississippi summer challenge, before the friendship was partially patched up. It had been a bitter moment for everyone involved. In the Movement, when they had all been at their best, the drive and the purpose had always been communal. But politics was a new and very different game, the members of the Movement who were entering it were beginning to learn, and in order to work for the same larger goals, you had to think only of what was good for you at the moment, and to be brutal, if need be, in your treatment of old colleagues. It was a lesson whites had learned long ago.

But there was a stain from that race. Lewis's old friend Chuck McDew, the second head of SNCC, had watched the escalating bitterness of the race from a distance, and had seen two of the most estimable members of their old group tear at each other. He was equally fond of both of them. What Lewis had done, McDew reminded himself, was the requisite proof that Lewis was not a saint as some of them had sometimes feared. It had not necessarily been his finest moment, but because it had finally showed his lesser side, McDew decided, it had also humanized him.

John Lewis had not been in Congress long before he attended a prayer breakfast on Capitol Hill. By chance as he was leaving it, a veteran white Mississippi congressman named Sonny Montgomery came over to see him. They had met, it turned out, once before some twenty-five years earlier. "Weren't you one of those Freedom Riders?" Congressman Montgomery asked Lewis.

"Sure was," said John Lewis, adding that he heard that Montgomery had been an officer in the Mississippi National Guard on that day in 1961 when the Freedom Ride buses had left Alabama and crossed over into Mississippi: "Someone said you were a general?"

"Still am," Montgomery said, "Mississippi National Guard."

They talked, and it turned out they both had been on the same bus. "You were on that bus?" Montgomery asked in disbelief, beginning to measure the time from that moment to this very different time and place.

"I was right up front," Lewis said.

"Isn't that something," Montgomery said. They talked a little more. Montgomery congratulated Lewis on his election. "You've come a long way, Congressman," Montgomery said.

"So have you, Congressman," John Lewis answered, "so have you."[3]

A few years after that John Lewis went back to Montgomery, Alabama, for the dedication of a civil rights memorial. He was by then a person of considerable substance, an increasingly influential congressman. As he was standing to the side waiting for the ceremonies to begin an older man who seemed vaguely familiar walked over to him. "You're John Lewis, aren't you?" Lewis said he was. "I remember you from the Freedom Rides," the man said. He held out his hand. "I'm Floyd Mann. I've kept up with you. Congratulations on becoming a congressman." *Floyd Mann,* John Lewis thought, finally matching the face in front of him with the face that went with the man who had raised his gun on that terrible day in Montgomery, Alabama, almost thirty years earlier when the mob had attacked him and he was sure he was going to die. "You saved my life," Lewis said, remembering as well what he had heard, that some of the Alabama authorities were not particularly happy with what Mann had done that day, that he had not been a hero in his own state, and that many powerful people in the Alabama political establishment believed he had gone too far in helping the Freedom Riders. Lewis reached over and hugged Floyd Mann, not exactly sure even now, almost thirty years after the fact, whether that was the right thing to do, whether black men hugged white men in contemporary Alabama, and then Mann hugged him back and Lewis began to cry. "I'm right proud of your career," Mann had said.

He remained true to his old course, even if in the nineties it was less and less fashionable. "The Last Integrationist," an excellent article by a Princeton professor named Sean Wilentz called him in *The New Republic.* It was important, he thought, for people to understand how much change had taken place, and how much more opportunity there was in America. He still spoke of the beloved community, the phrase he had first heard from his mentor Jim Lawson. The beloved community, he would say in speeches, might take more than a day to build, more than a week, more than a month, more than a year, more than one lifetime. But it would come. He was a remarkable living example of a passage from the Bhagavad Gita: "Man is a creature whose substance is faith. What his faith is, he is."

Lewis had become one of the most effective and influential black leaders in America, but of course, there was nothing charismatic about him. At the 1996 Democratic convention there was almost no coverage of his speech; to the degree that there was network interest in a black speaker, it was in Jesse Jackson, a far greater figure within the popular culture. It did not bother Lewis; he was used to it. By remaining, however involuntarily, out of the reach of the cameras, Lewis seemed as artless and uncorrupted as ever, and thereby marvelously authentic, while Jackson, a talented man who had gradually emerged as the number-one black leader, favored by television for any and all sound bites, began to seem like a man whose life was about being on television.

He and Lillian Miles Lewis had a strong marriage. She worked as the director of external affairs at Clark Atlanta University. Their one son dealt as best he could with the age-old problem of being the son of a famous father. He was told repeatedly by well-meaning strangers what a great man his father was and how much he had done for his people. That was a large shadow for a young boy to deal with, particularly in the black world, where increasingly among the young, good was bad and bad was good. Not surprisingly, John Miles Lewis decided in his late teens that he wanted to be a rap singer and a writer of rap songs. His father, the squarest of all men, was appalled. It was the most normal and most predictable kind of youthful rebellion imaginable, John Lewis decided later, but at the time he did not handle it particularly well. He hated the very idea of rap, the violence of the words and the black social dysfunctionalism they seemed to celebrate. Why, he said, when he was John Miles's age he had been in a nonviolent revolution against segregation. It was, he lamented later, precisely the wrong thing to say. "Oh, Dad, it's another day," his son answered. But he and Lillian finally waited it out, and John Miles gradually moved away from rap to more traditional studies at Clark Atlanta University.

71

In 1974 Bernard Lafayette, the proud possessor of two Harvard degrees in education, a master's and a doctorate, Dr. Bernard Lafayette now, set out for Gustavus Adolphus in St. Peter, Minnesota, a Lutheran College where the traditional belief in pacifism was unusually strong and where the college's administrators wanted someone steeped in the teaching of nonviolent political protest. In Minnesota his was the warmest of welcomes. Rarely in any community had so many people—other faculty members, businessmen in town—he decided, befriended a young academic. Soon after his arrival a local businessman decided that he should have a house, and when it turned out that Bernard did not have the money for a down payment, the businessman made it himself. The Lafayettes became, Kate Lafayette believed, the first black couple ever to own a house in that community. Lafayette was amused by the rather different concept of ethnicity of these good-hearted Lutherans compared with that which he knew best. When he talked about the need for integration in the South, some of the local people said that they too had integrated, and he asked in what way. Well, the answer came back, although they were primarily Swedish in their ancestry, they did hire some Norwegian faculty members a few years ago.

He and Kate spent several years there, and he was instrumental in bringing in many of the old Movement heroes to lecture there. Eventually he relocated to St. Louis to work with the National Institute for Campus Ministries, which ran a continuing education program for campus ministers. He liked St. Louis and taught part-time at Washington University.

But he and Kate began to miss the South. In 1980 they talked about moving to Atlanta, where he would take a job with the King Center.

By chance at the same time Kate's mother was dying and she wanted her family around her, and so in 1981 they moved back to Tuskegee, Alabama. There he found no shortage of job offers. Shortly after his return he was hired as dean of graduate studies and continuing education at Alabama State in Montgomery. There were four extension schools scattered throughout the region, and he loved the idea of bringing adult education programs to a region where so much had been denied to ordinary people for so long. That was truly doing God's work. He was impressed, but not surprised, by how many of them were willing to make significant sacrifices to improve themselves.

It was one of the happiest jobs in his life. In the few short years that he ran the program the number of people in it doubled, a figure of which he was inordinately proud. In time there was a power play against the man who had brought him in, a move driven primarily by complicated local politics. Eventually the people in the new regime offered him a job as head of the admissions office, but he did not like being offered a job which no one had even bothered to discuss with him. Too much of his life had been as a volunteer, he thought, for him to take a job which had been offered with a certain condescension.

He believed that he was luckier than most of his old colleagues; he could teach, he could preach, he had powerful connections with the SCLC in Atlanta, and, of course, he had those Harvard degrees, which could be used to open otherwise closed doors. He did not doubt that he would find a good job somewhere. While he was working at Alabama State, and commuting to Montgomery every day, he had by chance given a guest sermon at the black Presbyterian church in Tuskegee, Westminster Presbyterian, and the church elders had immediately asked him to be their regular pastor, even though he was a Baptist. He took the job and stayed there eight years.

Around 1985, he found himself pulled into a crisis at the local high school. One of his parishioners was the principal of Tuskegee High, a black school, and the stress of being the head of a school where the traditional system of authority was breaking down had made her desperate to get out. Bernard Lafayette, who had grown up in a black South, where the power of a school principal was ironclad, was amazed to find that in the small Southern town in which he now lived that era was over. Tuskegee High, to his astonishment, had turned into a modern urban war zone. If you walked down the hallway of the school, he discovered, you could get a high from the smell of marijuana. The principal could not call an assembly meeting without having the students virtually take over the school. There were gangs of boys and gangs of girls which seemed to dominate the hallways, threatening nonmembers. Some girls were afraid to go to the bathroom because they might be jumped by other girls who were members of a gang. The finances were a mess—Tuskegee was now an older community, there was an outmigration of talented, educated young people, and the older residents did not want to pay more taxes for education because they did not have children in school. Attempts to raise taxes for the school system were defeated. There was not enough money to buy textbooks. The windows in the school were broken, and the paint was peeling off the walls. He could hardly believe this was happening in the South. He had heard of situations like this in the North, but he had not realized that it had come home.

The principal told him that she had found another job and urgently needed to get out. But, she said, she could not leave until she found a successor. No one, she added, wanted to replace her. The idea of taking her place intrigued him, and pushed by Kate Bulls Lafayette, good daughter of this proud black community who also could not believe this was happening in her hometown, he decided to take the job.

The key to the breakdown, he soon discovered, was an odd reverse pattern of migration. The young people who were causing most of the trouble were students who had been raised in the ghettos of the North and the West, in New York or Chicago or Detroit or Los Angeles, more often than not in single-parent homes. Their parents, barely able to manage their own lives, and finding that they could no longer control their children, who were living increasingly dangerous lives, had eventually shipped them back home to be with their grandparents in the presumably gentler, less predatory, and less violent atmosphere of the small-town South. But, Lafayette discovered, they had brought the harsh new inner-city violence with them. "The new urban virus," as Kate Lafayette said later, "had moved back South."

Bernard Lafayette decided that Tuskegee High was going to be a great test. "Bernard's manner, that constant sweetness, fooled them," his wife noted years later, referring to both the students and the school board. "They thought that they were going to get this nice, soft little preacher, full of sweet talk about peace and nonviolence, and they were going to eat him up and spit out the pieces. They had no earthly idea how much he had been through in the past twenty-five years, how strong he was and how willing he was to be tough on an issue if toughness was required. They either forgot about Bull Connor and Jim Clark or they thought they were tougher than them." In a way she could understand that; Bernard postured so little about what he had done in the past, and seemed to have so little ego about those days, and seemed so mild in manner that it was easy to forget the pressures he had withstood.

But the students at the school learned quickly enough about him. He cleaned up the school in six months. He put teeth in the disciplinary codes. He was willing to expel students for the more serious disciplinary violations—no matter how powerfully connected their parents were in the community. He broke up the gangs. There would be no guns in his school, and he learned quickly that he was the man who was going to have to take the guns away from some of the students. In time he pulled the toughest, most difficult kids from class and put them on work details. He stopped the assaults, verbal and physical, on teachers. A student who had made denigrating remarks about a teacher's breasts found himself painting the entire cafeteria. He made the school's hallways safe. He stopped a new fad—he had no idea where it had started, but he thought it was from some movie that the students had seen—wherein the boys were allowed to slap their girlfriends. It was the worst kind of false, macho behavior and it was not going to take place in his school.

Because his students were behind the average on national test scores, he arranged on two Saturdays a month to have classes in math and English taught by his regular faculty and by faculty members from Tuskegee University, who came over to help out. The test scores started going up. Because the school was in terrible physical shape, he got local carpenters and plasterers and window men to come over and teach the students, so that the student body themselves could go to work fixing up the school. He believed that the students had to have a sense of living history as young American blacks and—against the wishes of a conservative school board—he took them on a reenactment of the Selma to Montgomery march, a march where everyone could now be treated with dignity but where he could readily recall the violence inflicted on himself and his friends.

Being principal of Tuskegee High was, he later decided, quite possibly the best job he ever had, the one which seemed to summon all his different experiences and talents and utilize them on behalf of needy young black kids. He had rarely felt so valuable; he loved going to work every day, in no small part because the results of what he was doing were so tangible. But in one way he had remained quite innocent: He had no idea that in a small town, so singular a success would create considerable jealousy. One morning just after the school year ended, Kate Lafayette got a call from her brother. "Is it true that Bernard's contract was not renewed at the board meeting?" he asked. Indeed it was true, though no one had bothered to tell him. The politics of a small-town school board, Bernard Lafayette later decided, were among the most vicious he had ever seen, rife with pettiness and jealousy. Every one of his successes, it seemed, had become a mark against him. Three members of the local board were former principals of the school who had failed in bringing any order and who had contributed to its decline, and they had had very mixed reactions to his rather considerable success in turning the school around. To them what he had done was something of a personal affront. "The problem with your husband," one member of the old guard told Kate Lafayette, "is that he was too successful too quickly and he scared a lot of people."

For a time Bernard Lafayette was, if not bitter, certainly wounded by the experience. But he had little time for self-pity since he needed work. Someone had once told him he could always be a salesman, that he had a magical ability to sell his ideas, and so for a time he tried selling cars, and turned out to be rather good at it. Then he got a call from old friends in the SCLC who asked him to come to work at the King Center. He worked there for a time, and then in 1987, he was asked to come back to American Baptist as vice president of academic affairs.

He was surprised how powerful the pull to his old school was. It was absolutely central to who he was and the person he had become. Returning there to visit and to consider whether or not to take the job, he was flooded by all the old memories—of the skinny young boy arriving there from Tampa, scared and poor, and of having to hold several jobs so he could afford to continue his studies. He could see himself and John Lewis and James Bevel, all of them young, all of them at once unsure of themselves and idealistic and ambitious, at first tentative with one another and tentative about their place in this school and city, and then gradually growing in confidence under the aegis of men like Kelly Miller Smith. It was clear, he realized as he thought about his future, that this was nothing less than a call.

It was the same school, small and poor as ever. Nothing had been changed and certainly nothing had been upgraded. There were 150 students, almost all of them poor. Funding from the Southern Baptists, around $300,000 a year, covered roughly 20 percent of the budget when he returned, and he was aware when he came back that there was a time limit on it, that by mutual agreement that funding was to end in 1996. Was there a poorer school in all America? he sometimes wondered.

He did well, and by 1992, to no one's surprise, he became the president of American Baptist. His problems were first and foremost financial, a daily fight just to keep the lights on and the water running. Each month he found that dealing with the school's finances was a cliffhanger. He had to decide which bills to pay first—electricity, food, and faculty—and then hope for the best on the others. There was no endowment. Getting money from the federal government was harder and harder in the more austere eighties. When he had first come back the school had needed roughly $1.5 million a year to run, and by the mid-nineties that had increased to $2 million. But he loved being back and he loved scratching for money; he still believed in the school's unique mission and he was proud of the school. It had, he believed, placed more people on Martin Luther King's executive staff than any other school: himself, John Lewis, and Bevel, as well as C. T. Vivian and Paul Brooks. Let other, wealthier schools ponder how and why that could happen, he thought—he knew the answer: It was about the absolute authenticity of the school and the people who went there.

The world had turned around many times since he had first arrived at American Baptist in the late fifties. He found himself on occasion teaching the grandchildren of some of the people who had been his classmates. In 1991, Bernard Lafayette returned to Selma, Alabama, on the occasion of the thirtieth anniversary of the Freedom Rides, this time to be given the keys to the city, and to receive a good-citizen's plaque. The mayor who made the presentation, Joseph Smitherman, was the same mayor who had headed the city back in those terrible days thirty years earlier, and he had spoken about a time when they had all been on different sides of the street, but now they were all on the same side of the street. Because of his daily responsibilities, Bernard Lafayette was, more than most Americans, aware of racial problems as yet unanswered, of the problems to be faced in the inner cities especially. But he was also aware of the differences in America, of the ability of ordinary black people everywhere in the South to be treated with elemental dignity, of the victories they had won, so much of which had been based on the ability to have the vote.

In addition to his job at American Baptist, he was the minister at a small church in Nashville, the Progressive Baptist Church; Kate Bulls Lafayette had stayed in her hometown of Tuskegee as the head of the Macon County Head Start program, and she and Bernard had to commute each weekend to see each other. He and Kate had no children of their own, but he had two children from his first marriage, Bernard and James. Bernard Lafayette III worked at American Baptist in maintenance, and took courses at Tennessee State, hoping soon to be an elementary-school teacher; James Lafayette, who had gone to Jackson State and SUNY, Albany, worked in the sheriff's office in Fulton County (Atlanta) as a communications man. In the fall of 1996 Bernard Lafayette's sixth grandchild was born, a boy named Katé (pronounced *Katay*) after his wife.

72

IN JANUARY 1977, RODNEY POWELL MOVED TO HONOLULU TO TAKE A job with the MEDEX Group, a nonprofit international health group at the University of Hawaii made up primarily of people who had once worked in the public sector and who were expert on designing public health programs for Third World countries. It was headed by Dr. Richard A. Smith, an old friend from the Peace Corps, and it seemed to offer Powell what he had always wanted: a chance to use his unusual bank of knowledge in an area which he cared about, and yet to exist outside of a traditional bureaucracy, of which he remained wary, and to remain relatively close to his family in California. In Honolulu he finally found the land he had sought, a place where the population was so varied that, as he once said, there was no majority culture to dictate its norms to the minority ones, a place well beyond the reach of the Puritan fathers where race and sexual orientation seemed to matter very little. Hawaii seemed, from the day he arrived, to be a haven for people like himself, whose sexuality had been defined by the larger, more conventional society as aberrant, but who did not want their sexuality to be the sole, defining aspect of their lives, and did not want to be forced into leading lives of sexual and emotional denial.

Some two months after arriving he was at a conference at the University of Hawaii when he met a man named Bob Eddinger, who had, despite a seemingly very different background, wrestled with many of the same problems. Bob Eddinger was white, he had grown up in a small town in western Pennsylvania, had done some missionary teaching in Burma, and had both his master's and Ph.D. in zoology. Aware from the time he was young that he was somehow different, he had gone out to Hawaii in the mid-sixties hoping to find greater personal freedom and acceptance. At the time that Rodney Powell met him he was a professor of zoology in the University of Hawaii system. He had always been aware, he told Rodney, that if he came out of the closet it would be extremely painful for his rather conservative, extremely religious family back east; it was true that when he first told his family of his homosexuality, their reaction had been searingly hostile. At the time he met Rodney Powell, Bob Eddinger felt terribly cut off from the people he loved, since they would not accept him for what he was, and judged him on something about which he had no control at all. Three months after they met in 1977, the two men started living together.

From the moment that Rodney Powell had told Gloria that he was gay they had both wrestled with what to tell their children. When they finally told them, April, the oldest, was fifteen, Allison was fourteen, and Daniel was eleven. It was not until 1973, Rodney Powell noted later, that the American Psychiatric Association removed homosexuality from its list of disorders. Gloria, uncertain of the waters they were entering, had been somewhat wary at first of telling their children the truth, but Rodney believed strongly that they could handle the truth. "The only thing I have to offer my kids," he reminded her, "is my love and who I am." They were particularly nervous about telling Daniel, who was the youngest and the only boy, but Daniel had handled it very well. "I don't care what my father is," he had said. "I love him very much and he'll always be my father." When the two girls received the news, they both, in different ways, said the same thing: *Oh, I always knew that, Dad—what took you so long to confide in us?* April had noted that Rodney had always told them that there was nothing that they as children could not tell him as a parent—why then, she asked, had he not felt the same way about them? Trust was a two-way street, she had said.

Daniel had wanted to move to Hawaii immediately to be with his father, but Gloria thought he was a bit young to live away from her and his sisters, and they decided he should wait until he was in the seventh grade, at which point he joined his father and Bob. For a time Gloria was ambivalent about the idea of her son living in a gay household, but gradually her reservations evaporated. (One of the things which contributed to making her so nervous, Rodney Powell later noted, was that almost everything that was written until then in textbooks referred to homosexuality as an illness.) She came in time to be grateful of how careful Bob Eddinger was as a member of this extended family, his ego always in control, trying in no way to replace either her or Rodney as a parent, but being kind and supportive, in sum, a generous, all-purpose extra uncle.

Bob Eddinger had always feared that if members of his own family knew about his homosexuality, they would cut him off, and he had told Rodney that in their eyes, being gay was worse than being a murderer or a rapist. When he had told his immediate family, his prediction proved all too accurate and what followed was virtually a complete separation. Rodney Powell, aware of what had happened, saw the terrible, almost impenetrable sadness that fell over his friend at certain times, when he would retreat deeply within himself. Finally, in 1995, Bob Eddinger decided that it was time to stop his family from treating him as if he were a social outlaw and time for them to stop judging him. So he wrote his mother saying in effect that unless she and the rest of the family accepted him completely and accepted his sexuality, that would be the end of their relationship. He would no longer tolerate a cold, essentially distant kinship in which they were permitted to define his morality. I pray that God will forgive you for rejecting me for who I am, a gay man, he had written her. If she could not accept him wholeheartedly as he really was, then she was no longer to contact him, he added.

Several months of silence ensued, and then his mother wrote saying that she would accept him. Visits on her part followed, and at one point she told him and Rodney that she only wished she had done this some twenty years earlier, that she would have saved herself and her son a great deal of heartbreak. The difference in his friend from then on, Rodney Powell believed, was dramatic. With the renewal of ties to his family, that dark cloud from the past seemed finally to have lifted.

73

GLORIA JOHNSON-POWELL HAD BEEN STUNNED BY HER NEAR SUICIDE. It was the opposite of everything she had been programmed to be and do in her life. That she, the most responsible of people, mother of three young children, accredited teaching psychiatrist, expert on the problems of children and their families, had very nearly succeeded in taking her own life *without even consciously thinking about it* was a staggering insight into how much real emotion she had been suppressing in her life and how deep was her own denial. Having had one therapist who had deliberately allowed her to bottom out in order to feel the totality of her depression, she now decided it was time to seek out another one, and this doctor treated her with far greater sophistication. Gradually, as she and her new therapist studied what had happened, she was stunned by how obvious the signs had been of her depression: She had been moody, she had been eating badly, she had slept poorly, and her thought processes, normally so clear, had become erratic.

The therapist was also helpful in discussing how she should handle the question of Rodney and the children. They studied the available literature about what happens to children in homes like this, and decided that they could not, despite her immediate anxiety, find anything negative. Bad things happened with bad people who were bad parents; good things happened with good people who were good parents. Helped by a sensitive therapist, and aided by antidepressants, she quickly began to pull herself together. At first there was some distance between her and Rodney, but in 1980 he and Bob Eddinger decided that she was working too hard and sent her a round-trip ticket to Hawaii to stay with them. On that trip she decided that Rodney was still very much her friend and that she liked Bob Eddinger—he was quiet, nice, studious, very much, she decided, like herself.

At almost the same time her career in child psychiatry was taking off at UCLA. She had gotten tenure in 1976, and she had created a psychiatric ambulatory care program for children which had dramatically cut the costs of the previous program. In 1973 she had published her first book, *Black Monday's Children,* about the first children to integrate the Nashville, Greensboro, and New Orleans school systems, and in 1983 her second book, *The Psycho-Social Development of Minority Group Children,* was published. By that time, she liked her life: Her children were all doing well, she liked the collegial atmosphere at UCLA Medical School, she had stabilized her relationship with Rodney, and she felt financially and emotionally secure again. Also, by the eighties, someone with her kind of achievements and credentials was a hot ticket and she was becoming accustomed to receiving offers from different universities and hospitals.

In 1988 Harvard Medical School came calling. The people there wanted a senior adviser for the Judge Baker Children's Center which, second only to Hull House in Chicago, was the oldest children's clinic of its kind in the country and which provided psychiatric care to inner-city children in Boston. In time she was brought back to Boston for an interview with Dr. Daniel Tosteson, the head of the school, who asked her a number of questions about herself and then asked her if she had any questions about Harvard. She did not, she said, because she had grown up in Boston, and therefore she knew a good deal about Harvard Medical School, both the up side and the down side: It was very good, it tended quite naturally to be smug about its excellence, but it was also very conservative, and it did remarkably little for the community around it, or at least the poor community around it. In 1990 her appointment as professor of child psychology was approved, and she was surprised to learn that Harvard was considerably behind UCLA Medical School in terms of its appointments of both blacks and women: A story in the Boston paper said she was the first black female tenured full professor at Harvard Medical School.

She was moved by the idea of coming back to Boston. This was the city where her mother, starting out as a teenage maid, had once dreamed seemingly unattainable dreams that her children would have a better life than her own, and now she was returning as a full professor at Harvard Medical School. That was a good deal more than a dream fulfilled. She bought a lovely home in Newton, a pleasant suburban area. She did not revisit Girls' Latin, where once she had both prospered and been punished for her political independence, because in the modern age it had been incorporated into Boys' Latin, a school in turn still wrestling with court orders over what percentage of minority children was appropriate and legal. But soon after arriving back in Boston, however, she drove back to the old neighborhood in Roxbury, now significantly the worse for wear, and terribly beaten down, like so many other once poor but stable communities, by the constant growth of the urban underclass. She had looked at the house on Elbert Street where she grew up, and was overpowered by the memories of those five children being raised by that fierce woman, part nurturing parent, part drill sergeant. But it had worked: All five of Mrs. Johnson's children had measured up. Barbara, Gloria believed, was the first black nurse trained at Children's Hospital in Boston; she had died at forty-eight of kidney failure. Alice was perhaps the first black court officer in the Massachusetts system, and had eventually moved to Los Angeles. Joyce had been a housewife and raised eight children; she too had died, of cancer. Gloria's brother Billy had worked for a technology company in Los Angeles before retiring. When Gloria's appointment was announced in the *Boston Globe,* she got a number of calls and letters, asking in effect if she was one of the Johnson sisters who had lived on Elbert Street. "Are you Alice's little sister Gloria?" several of them asked. Occasionally when she spoke at a dinner, someone who knew her from the old neighborhood would come up and tell her how proud they all were of her. She began working on a memoir which was mostly about her mother, which she tentatively called *The House on Elbert Street.*

She liked being back in Boston. Both the present and the past in her life seemed to be intertwined there. Harvard, not to any great surprise, seemed a rather cold place, offering less collegial kinship than UCLA, but she liked her work and in addition to her clinical supervisory role, she taught seminars on the most cost-effective way of providing child health services. By the nineties she and others like her who were struggling to provide desperately needed care to poor children in inner cities found themselves fighting against constant budget cuts, federal, state, and private. That made everyone's work infinitely harder. To her the problems facing the inner cities grew more formidable every year, while both the resources and the will to deal with them seemed to be steadily diminishing.

She and Rodney remained close friends. Their own children were doing well. The girls, April and Allison, both tall and attractive, received educations that would have made their grandmother proud, attending Westlake, an exclusive all-girls school in Los Angeles. April, now April Powell Willingham, went on to UCLA, where she got her undergraduate, master's, and law degrees. She was committed to public interest law, had married, had two children, and then was divorced. She lived in Sacramento. Allison, a year younger, who had almost died at birth because of the poor medical treatment in Tanganyika, also went to UCLA, where she received a master's in film production, but, falling in love with a young German film student named Paul Schueler, and knowing that she was going to live in Hamburg, went on to NYU Law School, getting a degree in international law, and lived with her husband and their one child in Hamburg, practicing international law there.

Of the three, Daniel struggled the most with the issue of race. Perhaps, his parents thought, it was because at the school he had attended there were so few other blacks, perhaps because he was the youngest member of a family with two achieving parents and two gifted sisters, and perhaps because, they often wondered, he was a boy and the direct price of race was heavier on men in this country than on women. When he was about seven and the miniseries *Roots* had been shown, he had refused to watch: Why, he had asked them at the time, do they always beat up on black men in this country? In the tenth grade he had decided to wear dreadlocks, and there had been something of a struggle among the school and the parents and the boy over the issue of his hair, a contest which Daniel Powell had won, though not without some price in terms of the school's definition of him. He had gone on to the University of Hawaii at Hilo, where he got a degree in political science, had become a Rastafarian, and did not entirely share his parents belief in nonviolence. If he was provoked by some incident, his parents worried, he might quickly lash back. The degree of racial tension in contemporary urban settings, the almost sure mathematical possibility that there would be constant, unnecessary racial incidents in daily life, made him edgy. In time Daniel Powell, a black Rastafarian with a white wife, moved to the most unlikely of settings, Kemmerer, a small town in Wyoming, where he was a builder, and where he found that despite the innate, old-fashioned conservatism of the region, he was accepted for what he was, a hardworking young entrepreneur. When his father, at heart a city boy, ill at ease in settings so demonstrably bucolic, visited him in Wyoming, and showed his uneasiness, Daniel Powell was amused. "Dad," he said, "out here we count the number of square miles per person rather than the people per square mile."

In 1994 Rodney Powell began the process of retirement, gradually cutting back on his full load at MEDEX. He remained partially active in the field of public health, and no one, Gloria Johnson-Powell thought, was as good at writing proposals to different foundations and to the government asking for grants than Rodney Powell. So a couple of times a year, he would fly to Boston and stay with his ex-wife while they worked jointly on proposals for inner-city health care. Some thirty years earlier, at a time when it was not yet fashionable, he had grown a beard. The first time he had shown up at UCLA Medical School wearing it in the late sixties, the dean, Roger Egeberg, had looked at him during a full faculty meeting and had said, "If I had known you were going to grow that beard I wouldn't have hired you." "If I had known you were going to take that position," Rodney Powell had answered, "I'd have grown it a few years earlier." Now that he had passed his sixtieth birthday, the beard had turned completely gray, and he looked like an Old Testament prophet. Though he had looked forward to this part of his life as a time to travel and enjoy some of the things he had worked so hard for, he found himself focusing more on issues of being gay in America. He remained grateful for his experiences in the civil rights movement. It had not merely saved him at Meharry at a time when he was desperate, but it had shaped his life, and given him, he believed, a life which had been fuller of purpose than he might otherwise have enjoyed.

Soon after he and Bob Eddinger had gotten together, they had bought a beautiful home on a high hill in the Tantalus section of Honolulu, and because Eddinger was a gifted amateur landscaper and gardener, they had created their own strikingly beautiful tropical garden. Rodney's parents, who had left Los Angeles and moved to Honolulu shortly after he did, took a small apartment at the bottom of the

hill and every day at the end of work, Rodney and Bob would drop by
and visit them. Raymond Powell, a hard and exacting man when Rodney had been a boy, had softened over the years. When Rodney was
ten his parents had had a fourth child, Antonia. By that time Raymond
had advanced to the best of his jobs, one in which he was both secure
and in a supervisory capacity. Antonia Powell had grown up in a time
of what was significantly greater affluence and therefore security in
the Powell household, the house finished and paid for. That greater
economic confidence seemed to permeate the younger sister's life;
when she and Rodney compared stories of growing up it was as if they
were talking about completely different households and different
fathers, hers being a more affluent home, with a more confident and
relaxed and loving father.

Rodney was pleased with the way his own family had handled the
news when he had come out of the closet, not surprised by his
mother's love and sensitivity, but delighted by the way his father, for
whom it was the most alien of news, took it in stride. In those last
years his father's health began to fade, but even as it did, he seemed to
be ever more at ease with this talented son whose life was so much different from his own. One day near the end of his life, when Raymond
Powell's health was slipping badly, Rodney and Bob dropped by to
visit, and Bob asked the older man how he was feeling, and Raymond
Powell answered, "I'm doing fine, thanks to the man upstairs . . ." He
paused for a moment, and then he added, pointing at Rodney,
". . . and that boy over there." It was the first time that he had ever
come close to saying something affectionate about his son, for words
like this were very difficult for a man that stern, and Rodney Powell
was deeply moved and was barely able to speak for the rest of the day.

If Rodney's success, and that of his younger sister Toni, who went
on to Washington University and Michigan Law, had given their hardworking parents a sense of the validity of their lives, then the great
sadness in Raymond and Norma Powell's lives had been watching
their next to the oldest child, Raymond Junior, self-destruct. He had
always been bright and gifted, but from the time he was young,
thought Rodney, he had always believed that he could beat the system.
He had lived a life based on the primacy of drugs, eventually heroin,
and his had become a life devoted to producing just enough money to

keep himself in drugs, inevitably one of small-time crime—car theft and moving cars over state lines. Early on, Rodney thought, perhaps as far back as when he was a teenager, his parents had probably sensed that he was incorrigible, or at least so singularly addictive that he was beyond their limited resources, and they had felt powerless to help.

The drain he put on their fragile means was enormous, and even when they were older and nearing retirement, Raymond would on occasion end up in jail, and they would be faced with the question of whether or not they could—or should—bail him out. This had led to intense arguments between them; ironically, his always stern father was the soft one, and his ever gentle mother the hardliner, his despairing father telling his mother, "Norma, go get that boy out of jail," and his mother arguing how vulnerable they were and that they could not risk everything on someone who was bound to let them down once again. Raymond Powell, Jr., was, by the time he was an adult, a shell of a man, his will and his abilities burned out by drugs. He died in his fifties; the family was notified some time after his death by people who knew him because in the terribly painful, losing process of dealing with him, they had finally lost contact. Raymond Powell, Sr., died in September 1981, and Norma Powell, ever radiant and caring, ever accepting of the complexity of human life, had reached out in her final years to bring Bob Eddinger into her family. When his own family had at first scorned him because of his sexuality, she had told him not to worry, she had enough love for two sons. She died in October 1994.

In the spring of 1997, Gloria Johnson-Powell received a phone call from the president of Mount Holyoke advising her that thirty-nine years from the month that she had graduated from there, her old college wanted to give her an honorary degree. Rarely had she been so overwhelmed by her own emotions, at once thrilled by the honor, but remembering as well the singular heroism of the person for whom Mount Holyoke had always remained such a special place, her mother. On that day, hanging up the phone after the president's call, she recalled one particular day years earlier which had always seemed to symbolize the difference between the life of her mother, who had gone to work as a domestic as a young teenager and spent her life working primarily as a maid, and her own vastly more privileged life as an esteemed professional woman. It centered around the moment in her senior year in high school when the day's mail had brought a letter announcing that Gloria had won a full scholarship to Mount Holyoke.

Her mother as a young girl had worked for a family in Cambridge, where the father was an academic. The family had a daughter named Emily, roughly the same age as the then young Elizabeth Hendren, and the two girls had become quite close. The two of them had remained friends over the years despite the immense gap of wealth and race and professional possibilities which separated them, and Emily had gone on to become a professor at Bryn Mawr. On the day that Mount Holyoke had written announcing her daughter's scholarship, Mrs. Johnson had remembered the moment long ago when Emily had been a senior in high school and her family had made a grand tour of all the girls' colleges with their daughter. They had taken along Elizabeth Hendren, their maid but their daughter's friend as well, as much for companionship as anything else. At the end of the tour, Emily had turned to this young black girl and had asked her which college she had liked best, which one she would go to if she could, and Elizabeth had said, "Oh, Emily, Mount Holyoke. It's so beautiful—I just love it."

When it had come time for her own daughter to apply to college, Mary Elizabeth Hendren Johnson had not dared tell Gloria how much she favored Mount Holyoke, for fear she might not get in or that they would not be able to afford it. Then when the first letter had come from Mount Holyoke suggesting that she apply, Mrs. Johnson had again held back her own enthusiasm for fear it would somehow not work out. But when the news had finally arrived—that Gloria Johnson had been accepted at Mount Holyoke with a full scholarship—she had picked up the phone to call Emily at Bryn Mawr to tell her the exciting news, and the two women had both been moved to tears. It had been, Gloria realized, a moment which seemed to justify all the hardship and sacrifice and rejection in her own mother's life.

Now here she was, journeying back to that same beautiful small college to receive yet another exceptional honor; as she drove back to South Hadley, Massachusetts, for the ceremony, her thoughts were both of her own career, and her days as a young and impressionable freshman arriving on campus forty-three years earlier. The 1997 Mount Holyoke commencement was truly a Johnson-Powell family

celebration: Among those accompanying her back were both daughters, several grandchildren, her former husband, Rodney Powell, and
his friend Bob Eddinger. Though her name at first meant little to the
graduating seniors, there was just enough information in the commencement program to give them some sense of the constant struggle
her life must have been—and that she had spent most of her life as a
pioneer in her profession. Until she was called forth to be hooded, the
graduation ceremonies had been somewhat restrained, but when
Joanne Creighton, the president of Mount Holyoke, mentioned that
Gloria was a graduate of the school herself, a loud, thundering
applause began, and when Ms. Creighton uttered the words "the first
African-American woman to achieve the rank of full professor at Harvard Medical School," the entire senior class was standing and cheering.

74

CURTIS MURPHY FOUND THAT HE DID NOT HUNGER GREATLY TO BE A school principal. When he first went to Carver in 1973, he had intended to stay only a few years. Instead, he has been there ever since. He liked his job and he liked his life. It struck him that his cup was surprisingly full: He was married to a woman he loved, they were raising a son he adored, and he liked being an assistant principal, which offered him a considerable amount of freedom to work with the kids he was interested in, and spared him a good deal of time struggling with an oppressive school bureaucracy. With the changes taking place in the Chicago school system, the politics of the schools were, he believed, becoming more intense every year, and he was glad to be out of the main line of political fire. The pension was not quite as good as that of a principal, but the job allowed greater personal freedom.

He had a few wondrous toys worthy of the new American middle class: an old Honda motorcycle, which symbolized personal freedom to him, and a handsome Lexus. More important, he had a strong family. He and Rayna loved being parents; in time Kevin Murphy graduated from Illinois State, where he studied criminal justice, and took a job working as an investigator in the public defender's office in Joliet, in neighboring Will County. Rayna was the assistant principal at the Burnside Scholastic Academy on the South Side, which seemed to her a surprisingly good and strong school, above average in parental support. Curtis decided he had most of the things a man could want.

In 1989 he went through a serious scare with his health when he suffered congestive heart failure. He returned from a Christmas vacation to find himself constantly out of breath. At first it appeared that he had pneumonia, and he visited a doctor and took some antibiotics.

But he did not get better, and one night he went to bed and he heard the sound of water in his chest. He was rushed to a hospital and they found the heart literally hanging out of the cavity. Part of the problem, he was told, was stress. On his doctor's orders he quickly changed his diet, giving up salt and most red meat, and he started to exercise. He soon lost eighteen pounds and his health improved dramatically.

He was proud of the fact that he had lived up to his father's exacting standards. After Curtis had bought the house in Glenwood and when Kevin was young, Buck Murphy had flown to Chicago to visit his son and daughter-in-law and his grandson in their handsome suburban home. He was obviously impressed. He had eyed the house carefully, walking back and forth around it several times, trying to figure out how something so modest could be worth so much money. "Son, you've got yourself a good home and a good piece of land here," he had finally said. It was the highest praise he could give his son. Curtis was aware that every success in his life was the same as a success for Buck.

In 1981 Buck Murphy had sensed he was dying of cancer. He came to visit his children in Chicago one last time. There he had made Curtis take him to one of the city's best department stores and he bought one last suit, telling his son this was the one he would be buried in. Though nominally he never touched his good suits after he bought them, this time he had the requisite alterations done so it would fit him that final time. In all ways Buck Murphy had prepared carefully for his own death. A few years earlier, sensing his own mortality, he had taken out an additional life insurance policy, one that would give his family extra protection and would guarantee that none of his precious land would have to be sold for taxes. As he was dying he gave his son, off the top of his head, a complete rundown on every bit of his finances—what he owed to others and what was owed to him. The land, of course, was owned in the clear, and it had turned out that his finances were in brilliant condition, better even than his own rough estimate of them had suggested. He had died in 1982. His wife, Duggar, continued to live in a simple but quite modern house near the country home outside of Whiteville in which Curtis had grown up.

After his close call with congestive heart failure the doctors told Curtis Murphy that part of the problem was the degree of stress in his life. Lessening it, however, was not so easily done. In the late seventies and eighties he watched the steady decline of the inner city with a profoundly melancholy sense. He, after all, had to deal with the results—the casualties of that decline—every day at work. He was the one who faced the reality of two historic forces coming together, first the great migration of blacks to the North, and second the terrible pain borne by those who had arrived as the entry-level jobs had begun to dry up. What were to most other people merely the grim statistics of that combination of forces was for him the terrible reality of daily life in the schools. Whatever else that was going wrong in the city, as the family system continued to break down, a world now, in his words, of babies having babies, became the everyday problem not for politicians and the social theorists, but for the school administrators and teachers. Every social ill in the city, he believed, would work itself around to becoming a problem in the schools. He came to hate conservative lawmakers in the state legislature who spoke casually about the need for law and order in the schools, but who in no way would empower the people who ran the schools to separate the truly violent young people from those who braved desperate conditions to try and improve their lives.

He was intrigued by the difference between his life and that of many of these inner-city youngsters. When on occasion—such as the celebration of the birthday of Martin Luther King—he spoke at a school assembly about what he and the pioneer sit-in kids had done to end segregation in the South, he could feel the lack of resonance in the auditorium. Occasionally a student would come up to him afterward and say that he and his friends had to have been crazy to do something like that. What Curtis and his friends had challenged, the harsh, segregated rule of another age in another place, was something these young people could not comprehend, as he in turn could barely comprehend their lives. In his mind some of these young people were, in ways that were often harder to calibrate, even more courageous. The world they dealt with every day was infinitely more violent than the one Curtis and his friends had known. All the odds were against these children of the inner cities: They grew up in broken homes, they rarely knew their fathers, they lived on gang-infested streets and attended schools where the undertow of drugs and crime and neglect was endlessly powerful; they had few traditional role models and few people explaining the need for discipline to them. They often arrived without a meal in the morning. It took a special kind of inner courage to stand up to the taunting they received when they dared to try and get good marks and to better themselves. And yet a surprising number of them somehow managed despite such cruel odds and such a marginal support system to try and better their lives. He never managed to immunize himself to the sheer injustice of that which he witnessed every day inflicted as it was on children.

His job at Carver got harder every year. That was a given of his life. The social problems were greater, and the tools which he and others like him had to work with were ever more limited. In September 1996, Carver and thirty-nine other Chicago high schools were placed on probation because of declining test scores and an increasing dropout rate. Curtis Murphy was not a man lightly given to bitterness, but it seemed to him one more occasion in which the politicians who ran the city and ran its school system, having rather skillfully shortchanged a generation of children, now seemed to be blaming the people working at the bottom of the system rather than working to fix the system itself. He was, he had come to realize over the years, the assistant principal of a school where a good 75 percent of the children came from poverty-level homes, and almost as many came from one-parent homes. In a school of 900 with about 450 girls, there were, by his rough estimate, as many as 35 or 40 teen pregnancies a year.

It was a gang-infested school and much of his day went into trying to limit the power of the gangs within the school. There were three or four fights a day, and it was a major job to control the violence. One of the great problems in the school was stealing, and any kid who wore anything nice to school had to be aware that he was advertising for it to be stolen. Not surprisingly, one of his main responsibilities was to try and limit student abuse of teachers.

He was aware that all of these young people already knew much more about violent death than he and his friends had when they were growing up. They were increasingly cynical about life itself. They became at quite young ages oddly immune to violence. When some boy was showing an ever greater tendency toward violence, slipping gradually into membership in a gang, Curtis Murphy would try and talk to the young man, and warn him that if he kept it up he was going to die young. "So what, Mr. Murphy," the young person would answer. "I was born to die."

On a Monday evening in October 1996, this reporter dropped by to see Curtis Murphy for one last interview. For once his normal ebulliance was gone. He had been through a terrible scene at Carver that day. There had been a crisis intervention, he reported, because a nineteen-year-old student named Cassandra Scales had been shot to death in a gang killing at 12:30 A.M. on the previous Sunday. She was the unmarried mother of a three-year-old daughter, and Murphy had thought of her as a good kid who, against all odds, was trying to make a success of herself. She had intended to finish school, go into the army, and then use her army training to perhaps become a nurse or a doctor. That Saturday she had had her hair done late in the evening and, accompanied by a half sister and her young daughter, had stopped off to get a piece of fried chicken from a fast-food place on the South Side of Chicago. A car filled with three gang members had pulled up, and the young men, according to bystanders, flashed the sign of their gang, and then pulled out .45 automatics and shot her.

The assailants did not seem to have known the victim. It appeared to be just an aimless killing. "Just random," Murphy said, "another child at the wrong place at the wrong time." There had been a story about what happened in the *Chicago Sun-Times,* but the *Chicago Tribune,* more accepting of this kind of killing as commonplace, had not even bothered to report it. Murphy's day that Monday had been given over to dealing with the effect of the killing on other students; he and a team of specialists from his and other schools were trying to help Cassandra Scales's best friends. The worst thing about it, he said, was the degree to which the young people—and he himself—had become in some way immunized to violence. He was somewhat shaken by it, he said, but the terrible thing was the degree to which he was *not* shaken, because violence was now an inevitable part of the way they all lived.

75

JAMES BEVEL'S FRIENDS THOUGHT THAT MARTIN LUTHER KING'S MURder hit him the hardest. There was, they thought, an odd dependency to Bevel, that he was most comfortable and most free when he was working for someone like Dr. King, whom he greatly admired. If many of the other senior people in the SCLC had remained wary of Bevel, then King was always intrigued by him, sensing that whatever else Bevel said and did, no matter how outrageous his personal behavior, no matter how many others he made angry, there was always a compelling quality to him, a sense that nothing he said could ever be disregarded, and that there was always a larger truth to his words. One dared not ignore him. His was the goading which King knew he needed, lest he become too moderate and centrist, too complacent, and finally, too political. Their relationship was a complicated and often contorted one: It gave Bevel the right to push as hard as he could for moral absolutes, leaving the delicate political balancing act between the different black and white political constituencies for others like Andy Young to worry about. Bevel was content to be a moral force, nothing less.

When Martin King was killed, Bevel's friends thought he was particularly vulnerable. Not only had he enjoyed a special relationship with King, culminating in his crucial role in helping to push King forward in his challenge of the Vietnam War, but he now had many powerful enemies within the SCLC. Bevel's idiosyncratic nature, his systematic disregard for the feelings of people he disagreed with, even when his opponents thought themselves more senior in the organization's hierarchy, had not bothered King very much. Perhaps the problem with Bevel, Andy Young later noted, was in the way he had been brought into the Movement by Jim Lawson: Lawson's decision making had always been the most communal kind imaginable, whereas most of the other top people in the SCLC had come there long after ascending to top places in the Baptist church, a most hierarchical institution, where they were not accustomed to being challenged, particularly by people younger than they were. Thus Bevel, the most outspoken of men, constantly offended many of his elders.

Within the SCLC leadership he was, quite predictably, not regarded as very much of a team player. Not many prophets are. He seemed to hear no one's voice and honor no one's vision save his own. He had always had his own unique clarity of vision; in the words of Andy Young, whose job it was to get on with everyone, he was "ideologically pure to the point of irrationality."[1] His conflicts with Hosea Williams and other top King aides were memorable, and unrelenting. "I don't know if the problem is that Brother Bevel is marching ahead of us, or whether it's that we are marching behind him," an exhausted Ralph Abernathy, King's closest friend in the SCLC, once said of him, "but I do know we are not marching together."[2] Even back in the Selma days when he was working for the SCLC, when the tensions between the SCLC and his old colleagues in SNCC had gotten out of control, Jim Forman had complained that he was angrier at Bevel than he was at the local cops.[3] Now with King dead, his emotional state was not only more fragile than ever, some of his friends thought, but worse, the one person with both enough loving tolerance and strength to reign him in was gone. Bevel was now a target.

He clashed openly with Ralph Abernathy not long after King's murder. Abernathy, who had been King's closest friend, had taken his place as the head of the SCLC after the assassination. Within the SCLC it was generally believed that King would have wanted Abernathy as his replacement; it was also widely assumed within the organization that Abernathy lacked the intellect, the selflessness, and the shrewdness to lead the organization. So there was something of a communal understanding that Abernathy would get the job but that it would be everyone else's responsibility to try and protect him not just from the terrible pressures which would face any successor to King but, equally important, from himself and his not insignificant limitations. At first Bevel was one of the leaders in trying to rally the others around Abernathy, but gradually he decided that Abernathy lacked

the ability not just to lead the Movement, but perhaps more important, to speak to the rest of the nation on behalf of what remained of
King's constituency. He went to Abernathy himself to explain his
change of mind, to tell him that he was a wonderful man but lacked
the ability to lead their group, and that it was time for him to move
aside for Jesse Jackson, younger, obviously more charismatic, and in
those days something of a Bevel protégé. Jackson was precisely the
kind of man the SCLC needed at that point, Bevel decided, a man
whose voice could reach millions. But many of the people close to
King had already been put off by the obvious nature of Jackson's soar-
ing ambition, a belief that he had barely kept his ambition in check
when King was alive, and a resentment over the way that Jackson,
wearing a shirt still stained with King's blood, had gone on television
right after the murder. The older Baptist ministers in the SCLC were
not about to turn the organization over to Jesse Jackson. What Bevel
had said about Abernathy was not that different from what a number
of other young people in the SCLC were thinking and saying privately,
but he had said it too openly and too soon, and he had made his position in the SCLC, where he was already vulnerable, more endangered.
For Bevel's personal behavior within the SCLC had always been
judged as erratic, outside the reach and control of everyone else. Not
everyone was enthusiastic about what seemed to his peers his odd
mixture of theology and sexuality, his voicing of ideas which they
thought of dubious legitimacy, particularly about subjects they felt
best never spoken of. The other SCLC executives were not thrilled
about the idea of one of the organization's most prominent people
constantly voicing his belief that traditional monogamy was restric-
tive, and therefore the more open a person's sex life, the healthier he
was. In 1970 there was an incident which seemed to show that he had
snapped. "An emotional breakdown," Andy Young wrote of the incident, "battle fatigue from a decade of stress and pressure."[4] "Combat
fatigue," John Lewis added, "it might as well have been a war for him,
all those years in the Movement. He was badly exhausted, more than
we realized, and when Dr. King was killed it was all too much."[5]

In the summer of 1970 Bevel was the chapel speaker at Spelman,
which was the prestigious black women's college in Atlanta. He
started at 11:00 A.M. on a Friday and his talk was supposed to end at

noon. But at noon Bevel wasn't finished talking. Indeed, he had barely begun. The lunch bell rang, but he kept on talking. "Niggers don't need to eat, you been eating all your lives, anybody who wants to be free needs to just stay here and listen. I'm not through yet," he told the young women listening to him. When the school chaplain said that they had to close the chapel building, Bevel said that they could continue the talk under a tree. In his version, his speech was largely about the need for James Earl Ray to have a fair trial; in the view of others, much of it was about the need for greater sexual freedom. His sermon continued all afternoon, the young women missing lunch and classes. When evening approached, Bevel was told he would have to leave the campus; he thereupon took the young women with him back to his digs at Paschals, a restaurant and motel which was a big SCLC hangout, where he had a two-room suite. There, with some fifteen or so young women in attendance, he spent the entire weekend continuing the sermon, writing on the walls of the rooms with a Magic Marker, and ordering in food. None of this, he later said, was very different from what he had often done before. The difference was that this time he had run out of paper on which to write, and so because he was using a Magic Marker he had written on the walls. ("All it needed," he said later, "was a $15 paint job to fix it up—no big deal."[6]) On Monday, Andy Young got a call from the somewhat distraught motel owner asking who would be responsible for Bevel's expenses; Young, having no idea what the damage was, said the SCLC would be. Then James Orange, another SCLC member, called Young to tell him that Bevel was really out of control this time.[7] The other SCLC executives, believing that Bevel was exhausted and had suffered a breakdown, arranged to put him in a hospital for two days so he could rest. He was furious that they chose to put him in the psychiatric ward of the hospital and turned on Andy Young, who had arranged the rest, thinking that Young had done this to discredit him within the Movement. There, in addition to resting, he also began to organize the hospital staff politically.

A meeting was called almost immediately to discuss whether or not to fire Bevel from the SCLC. Ralph Abernathy had already marked him as a troublemaker and was ready to get rid of him. At the meeting Andy Young, one of Bevel's few defenders, argued that Martin King had always favored a nonhierarchical type of leadership, and that it was precisely that kind of tolerance which had allowed so much talent to flower over the past dozen years. In fact, Young pointed out, King had believed that the greater someone's personal idiosyncracy, the more talented he was likely to be in the Movement, and that King had always complained that Young himself was far too normal. No one doubted, he said, that Bevel was in some kind of very serious personal trouble, but no one doubted that he was also one of the most talented and important staff members they had ever had. And no one should doubt as well, he added, that the Movement owed Bevel something, that it was his years as a battlefield leader which had helped bring him to this point. But at the meeting only Young and Lewis voted to keep him on. Lewis, watching the scene, felt a sadness: Not only was his old friend in trouble because of the death of his leader, but he was about to be cut off from his family—the SCLC—at a moment of his greatest vulnerability. It was, Lewis thought, a terribly sad scenario and it was not going to play out happily; he thought the SCLC had made a terrible mistake in not taking care of one of its own, someone who was in bad shape largely because of how high a price he had paid being in the Movement.

The fertility of Bevel's mind was amazing: It was Bevel whose idea for a march of schoolchildren from Alabama to Washington had, in the minds of some SCLC people, become mutated into the March on Washington; it was Bevel who had thought up the Selma march; it was Bevel, who when the campaign in Birmingham had faltered, had argued that they had to go into the schools for children to give them the mass army they needed and had helped turn Birmingham into a success; and it was Bevel, more than anyone else on the inner staff, who had pushed King in the mid-sixties to speak out on Vietnam.

In the years after King's death, cut off from his base, more eccentric but just as brilliant as ever, his old allies thought, he moved around a good deal, running projects in different cities, a school here and a cooperative farm there. He remained different from everyone else in the Movement. He was always Bevel, always true to his own ideas, and never unhappy when he seemed to be out of sync with the rest of the leadership. Earlier than most he differed from the other SCLC people over the question of James Earl Ray's guilt in the murder of Dr. King. Bevel, like Jim Lawson, believed Ray to be at best a small player in the murder and he was outspoken on the subject. That too angered many of his former colleagues. But he believed that nothing Hoover's FBI said—it had pursued Martin Luther King viciously during his life-time—could be believed now that he had been murdered.

In 1984 he ran for Congress in Chicago as a Republican candidate, and when friends questioned him, he pointed out that his father had always been a Republican. He got almost 22 percent of the vote. He refused offers from Republican headquarters to help fund his race. In time Lyndon LaRouche, the eccentric head of the Democrats for Economic Recovery Party, contacted him and asked him to run with him, Bevel to be the vice-presidential candidate. That LaRouche had already been in prison in no way bothered Bevel. The two men met, and Bevel decided that he thought LaRouche had been unfairly victimized by the government, something he could readily sympathize with, and agreed to be his vice-presidential candidate in 1992. The ticket was not elected. Many of Bevel's old friends were appalled by the LaRouche connection but Bevel reassured them that he was still Bevel and no one could tell him what to think or what to do. Certainly, thought his friends, none of whom had ever won an argument with him. In 1993 Bevel heard Minister Louis Farrakhan speak and thought he detected a change in Farrakhan's voice, particularly when he spoke about Martin Luther King. The two men met later that night and Bevel found that he liked Farrakhan. Farrakhan, in Bevel's eyes, showed that he now understood the importance of nonviolence as a scientific principle. Why don't you, Bevel suggested, sponsor a latter-day celebration in Washington, a kind of second coming of the March on Washington, albeit for black men? The idea would be about taking more responsibility for what they did as men and becoming more God-conscious, a kind of day of atonement. Farrakhan agreed that it was a good idea and that, he believed, was the origin of the Million Man March of 1995. A few years later, when the local Farrakhan representative came by the offices of *The Washington Post* to complain about the paper's coverage of the minister, Bevel accompanied him, although he said little at the meeting. But anyone who thought that he was a dutiful soldier in either Farrakhan's or LaRouche's army was wrong—he was, thought his old friends, simply Bevel, as brilliant, and idiosyncratic and mystical as ever. When a researcher for this writer named Kate Lardner called Bevel during the requisite fact-checking, she asked him how many children he had. Seventeen, he answered proudly, the same number as his father. There was a certain justice in that, he said. He was, after all, part Choctaw Indian, and white men had taken the lives of many of his people. He, in turn, was merely replenishing the race. The youngest was an infant named Jamerica, a combination of Bevel's and his wife Erica's names.[8]

76

In 1995, on the thirtieth anniversary of the battle of Selma, the Reverend James Luther Bevel returned to that city along with Jamese, his sixteen-year-old daughter, to be a part of the ceremonies commemorating both the past and the future. There he had received a surprisingly warm welcome from one of his old adversaries, Joseph Smitherman, who was still the mayor, and who told Jamese, "All of us were more afraid of your father than we were of any of the others. Your father's a small man physically, but when he would ride that bike by himself in the morning, with that hard look on his face, it scared us, not only because we had no idea what he was up to on those rides, but because we knew he didn't fear us. I mean, he was not supposed to be riding around by himself—Selma was dangerous for black people in those days, but he didn't seem to know it. We were more scared of him than of Dr. King.[1]

Amazingly enough Smitherman, by 1997, had been mayor for thirty-two years. He was exhausted by the job, he said, but he wanted to hold on to it at least until the year 2000. He had long ago made his accommodation to the region's new political forces, which he had once so strenuously fought. He numbered John Lewis, he said, as one of his close friends, and on occasion during political events, the two of them would ride together in open cars.

Smitherman presided over a city of some 27,000 people, which was 55 percent black and 45 percent white, with slightly more whites in the voting age population. His transition from old, hard-line segregationist to new-age racial pluralist had been steady over the past thirty years, starting with simple things—paving streets and bringing decent lighting as well as a sewage system to the black neighborhoods: "One thing Joe Smitherman can do that George Wallace could always do is count votes," said James Chestnut, the black attorney.[2] Over the years Smitherman, pushed by local black politicians, learned how to sell Selma's past. He would promote the town's unique history—it was, the promotional campaign emphasized, the place where the 1965 Voting Rights Act was born. That, after all, he added, "was the most important piece of legislation to be passed by the Congress in one hundred years."[3] There was a monument to Martin Luther King now, and tourists visiting the city were told of the importance of the Pettus Bridge.

Smitherman turned out to be extremely skillful in tapping into the federal bureaucracy and getting money for integrated public housing units. Accompanied in Washington by local black officials, he became gifted at telling some of the black HUD officials he met that they got their jobs because of what happened in Selma. Therefore, like it or not, Selma was a showplace city, and the feds owed the city. Over the years, with significant help from local black leaders, he was able to tap into the federal treasury for some $75 million in federal funds, a remarkable amount for so small a town, enough to build seven integrated housing units, which by HUD decree were scattered throughout the city, in rich white neighborhoods as well as poor black ones.

77

THERE WAS NOTHING PLEASANT OR EXHILARATING ABOUT THE CASE OF the *United States* v. *Barry*. From the very start there was something uniquely tawdry about the entire process. It began with a sting run against the mayor of Washington in January 1990, almost twenty-five years after he had first arrived in the city as the idealistic representative of SNCC. On the night of January 18, 1990, the mayor had all too willingly been picked up in an operation set up by the feds. They had, knowing their man and his special weaknesses, baited their trap not with money, for there were no suitcases filled with hundred-dollar bills to bring him in. Rather in his case the bait was the promise of sex and cocaine, courtesy of a beautiful young woman who had a long history both as a Barry girlfriend and as one of his principal suppliers of drugs. There had always been a certain dynamic to their past assignations. The money for the drugs had come from him, often handed to her in an envelope which was hidden in a magazine. Thereupon she did the buys (sometimes riding in his official limo and driven by the city police, who were assigned as his security team). Then the couple would reconnect later at some hideaway and enjoy the drugs together. The bait, Hazel Diane (Rasheeda) Moore, was a strikingly beautiful young woman. She had been born to a middle-class Washington family, had gone to Fisk, and, finishing there, had immediately set out to be a model. That had taken her to New York and for a short time she had done rather well. Among other successes, in December 1977, there had been an appearance on the cover of *Essence* magazine. She had looked so stunning in that photo that Marion Barry, then a rising young politician in Washington, had called her up and invited her to come to his city as his guest. She had not taken him up at the time. Soon her own fortunes had begun to decline, and she had started to slip into an increasingly unforgiving world of late-night action and drugs, of user and used. Around 1980 her then boyfriend, the father of one of her three children, had been arrested in England for trying to ship $18 million dollars' worth of heroin into the country. That and her testimony on his behalf had not helped her career. The world of modeling was brutal enough, a place where unless you were the rare superstar whom the designers absolutely loved, there were always destined to be younger, prettier girls coming up just behind you. But if you were tainted with drugs, then the powerful people in that world were going to keep their distance. When you fell in that world, you could fall quickly and you could fall a long way.

By the time Barry finally met Rasheeda Moore in 1986, nearly a decade after he had first seen her picture, he was on his way down personally and she was on her way down professionally and personally. She was by then in her mid-thirties, still quite striking, but her luck was turning bad. All three of her children had been born out of wedlock, and both of their fathers were reported drug dealers. Her days as a star model in New York on the wane, she had come back to Washington hoping to open a modeling agency. She and Barry met at a party and they quickly became involved, a relationship formed in mutual parts of drugs and sex. He was by then deep into his habit. He loved smoking crack cocaine, the newest, most fashionable, and most dangerous of drugs; he knew how to free base, to mix the cocaine with water and baking soda. In fact, he had a favorite way of doing it, she later testified, taking the tobacco out of a cigarette, mixing it with the crack, and then smoking it. An M.B. Special, it was called by his intimates. She soon became his favorite partner in this, all the while supported by the good citizens of Washington. For she and her sister and a third friend quickly received $180,000 from the city of Washington to teach a summer program to young Washingtonians on modeling. Project Me, it was called.

Her own drug usage was becoming ever more obsessive in this period. By 1989 she had come on even harder times, in no small part because she had started smoking crack herself, a drug which was virulently addictive. She was somewhat bothered, she later said, about having a prolonged affair with a married man—for they had met hundreds of times and in some twenty different locations. When she

refused to perform oral sex on him at one point, he cut off the funding
for her modeling course. The feds, following up on endless reports on
the rampant corruption in the city government, including his skilled
corrupting of the local police force as well as his well-known if not
quite so well-publicized drug abuse, had been moving against him for
a long time. But until then they had only succeeded in nailing his aides
and one paramour, a woman who was a major supplier for him and
who eventually spent eight months in jail rather than give him up.
(She said later that she was given $25,000 by city contractors for
remaining silent.) In time they stumbled across his connection to
Rasheeda Moore, and by checking phone numbers, and noting the
hundreds of calls between the two, they decided she was Barry's number one sex-and-drug connection. As such they began to squeeze her.
At her first meeting with government agents she testified that she
knew the mayor only casually, and had never seen him use cocaine.
They in turn, aware of how many phone calls there were from him to
her home number and of his recreational preferences, were sure she
was perjuring herself, and they so warned her. She was beginning to
fall into their net. They thought she might be the critical link in bringing down the mayor.

Her funding for Project Me cut off, she moved to Los Angeles in
1989. She was a full-fledged crack addict by then; a woman with three
young children, no husband, and no job possibilities. In Los Angeles
she and her children were living in a homeless shelter, and she was
taking welfare checks, cashing them, and using the money for drugs
and alcohol. She had come a long way from the cover of *Essence.* On
December 31, 1989, the Los Angeles police picked her up for drunk
driving; at the time the feds, sure she was the weapon they could use
against Barry, were already looking for her. That night the computer
linked the arrest in Los Angeles with the search then going on in
Washington. Their squeeze of her became merciless. If she did not
cooperate with them, they said, they would get her on perjury and she
would lose custody of her children. There was no longer any way out
for her, and she cooperated with them.

The job of going after Barry had fallen to the feds because the local
police, who normally should have been in charge and who would have
had ample evidence of his drug abuse and the corruption which it led

to, had long ago been tainted by his planting of loyalists within the force. If there was nothing attractive about the government of the United States mounting a vast, expensive videotaped sting against one of its citizens, what was unveiled about Marion Barry as the case played out in federal court was even less attractive. An endless series of witnesses got up and told of Barry's desperate need for cocaine and how they had helped supply it to him. Many of the witnesses were women, who told of his constant attempts to leverage his power and position for sexual favors. As the videotape of the sting itself was played out in court, Tom Shales, the talented television critic of *The Washington Post,* wrote, "The videotape was grimly compelling. The encounter between Barry and Moore seemed joyless and furtive and there was no evidence of any euphoria produced by the drug. As for the bust, it had little resemblance to the glamorous arrests in cop shows and action movies. This was not exciting. This was degrading and pathetic."[1]

The trial took place in the city which Barry had helped bring in all ways and with all services virtually to its knees. It was almost exclusively about race. To all too many in the city, particularly poor blacks, the people who had gone after Barry were not just feds, they were *white* feds. The jury was predominantly black, ten African-Americans and two whites. The judge, hardly amused by the attempts of Barry and his attorney to play the race card to obscure the overwhelming nature of the evidence, was white. The evidence against Barry, including the videotape, was devastating. A large number of men and women testified with great expertise about Barry's drug use, including Rasheeda Moore, who said that she had used cocaine with him more than one hundred times. But then she had seen the light. (Why had she participated in the sting? Barry's defense attorney asked her. "I agreed to participate in the sting because the Lord put it in my heart to participate in the sting," she answered.)

Inside the jury room, to no one's surprise, race was a dominating issue; in the end when the jury voted, the high-water mark on a vote for conviction on any of the felony charges was seven of its members. On all the felony charges against Barry, the jurors were badly deadlocked. In the end he was convicted on only one of the twelve counts, possession of cocaine, a misdemeanor. The judge, enraged by the entire process and the way in which the jury had behaved, called the evidence overwhelming, and angered by some of the jurors' behavior, gave Barry the maximum, six months. For a time he was gone from the city's politics. But then, inevitably, he began his comeback, first as a city councilman. In 1994 he ran again for mayor and was elected. He spoke of being reborn, but there seemed little remorse to him, nor did he exhibit much in the way of an improved capacity to govern. The city which he governed seemed more chaotic than ever, crime and drugs rampant, the schools a national embarrassment, the services ever more marginal. Its finances were so badly managed and so corrupt that an outside control board had been appointed to run them, and to minimize the damage done by Barry and his people to the city's residents; in time the same control board took over the city's school system as well.

No one with any knowledge of contemporary American social problems would underestimate how difficult it was to be the mayor of a big city in modern America, nor unaware that the problems often seemed greater than both the available resources and the capacity to deal with them even in the best circumstances. But most big-city mayors, whatever the limits of their resources, had made what were often gallant attempts to reverse devastating social trends. But the city of Washington, because of Marion Barry, stood apart on the contemporary landscape.

For even if there was a long history of American political rogues, particularly scoundrels, serving as mayor, Barry was different from the rascals of the past. Certainly there had been many rogues who had come to power belonging to once scorned minority or ethnic groups, eager to stick their finger in the eye of the representatives of the once dominating and seemingly superior ethnic group. But their behavior paled in comparison with his. Once elected they might have taken a certain revenge on those who had once repressed them, mocking in the process would-be reformers of higher station and better breeding and education. Perhaps on occasion they had used their new position and their rage to avenge old wrongs; they cloaked themselves, when things went wrong, in the ethnicity of previous victimhood. The Irish pols who had gotten even with the Brahmins of Boston had added several rich chapters all their own to American urban history. But these rogues had always taken care of their own, particularly the most vulnerable among their own. But Marion Barry was something new; it was not just that as things got worse he played the race card, but the fact that he ran a government so selfishly and incompetently that his primary victims in the end were the most vulnerable of his own people. That set him apart.

78

WHEN IT WAS TIME FOR HANK THOMAS TO BE DISCHARGED FROM WAL-
ter Reed hospital, he decided to go back to Atlanta because he
thought it was going to be the best city in America in which to be a
middle-class black. He knew he had to go to work because he had too
many responsibilities to return to school and get his degree. He was
lucky, he thought, for he had regained most of the use of his hand.
Very soon he had a number of jobs. A job in the civil service was marginal, so he switched to the Atlanta Fire Department, where his service record helped; he took a night job at a McDonald's in nearby
Decatur, Georgia, where he insisted on working the cash register, even
though that was supposed to be a white job in those days. When some
white people complained about his working the register, he was
always ready to spring his I-fought-for-you-and-got-a-Purple-Heart-
for-you story, but it never quite came to that. Determined as he was to
succeed, he faithfully read every book he could about rags-to-riches
business successes. He befriended another black fireman who was
also a veteran and who had comparable dreams, and the two of them
decided to pool their resources and go into business together. They
were going to have their own small slice of capitalism. Their first step
was to buy a Laundromat. Thomas had a loan of about $8,000 and a
tiny bit of savings from Vietnam and he put almost all of it into the
business.

That meant that he was holding down two jobs. He was doing well,
he and his partner kept expanding their operations, and in time they
owned six Laundromats, but he was far short of becoming rich.
About that time a local television station was doing a piece on ambitious young men who held down full-time jobs and were trying to
become entrepreneurial owners at the same time; they had the names

of several white would-be Horatio Algers, and one of its reporters asked Julian Bond for the names of any blacks who might fit that category. Bond, an old friend from the Movement, gave them Thomas's name. When the story appeared on the evening news a man named Gerald Reed, a local dentist, a white man who had once been active in the civil rights movement, saw it and contacted Hank Thomas.

Reed had, it turned out, been trying for some time to get blacks interested in getting into the world of small businesses, believing that this was the next stop on the road toward racial progress. The way out of poverty was to be a businessman, he believed, and he had been waiting patiently to find the right black partner. Reed owned a number of pieces of valuable property and he had been investigating the possibilities of using one as the locale for a franchised food operation. He was sure he had the right location. He proposed a fifty-fifty deal with Thomas: Reed would supply the location, which meant that he was putting up the lion's share of the capital, Thomas would actually run the business, and they would split the profits; Thomas would get credit for his work, and with the profits would gradually buy Reed out. At first Thomas was skeptical of the proposal, and he wondered why Reed would make so generous an offer. All of the money and thus all of the risk was Reed's. "I've become very wealthy and there's nothing I need personally," Reed answered; "it's my way of making a contribution, and of giving something back. Besides, I've watched you, and the way you've built up your Laundromat business, and I know you'll work hard."

So Hank Thomas sold his Laundromat shares to his partner and put the money into a business with Gerald Reed. They started with a Dairy Queen in a very tough section of Atlanta. Thomas decided to go at this as if it were an extension of the civil rights movement, and he was once again a pioneer. He would assume that he was always on alien ground, that the odds were quietly against him, but that if he listened and learned and committed every fiber of his being to its success, he might be able to pull it off. Reed tutored a very eager Thomas on the basics of being a small businessman: work harder than you've ever worked in your life, live with it and sleep with it, and whatever profits you make, pour back into the business. Always make your business better. If you do that, people will surely know, and you will succeed. Hank Thomas realized that this was probably the only chance he was ever going to get to enter a world of privilege and success, and he worked maniacally; in that sense he was like all successful franchise food operators, ma and pa owners willing to pay an enormous price in terms of their personal labor in order to have this one successful shot at proprietorial capitalism. He had nothing but time: His first marriage had broken up soon after he had returned from Vietnam; he and his wife had been, he decided, children who did not know each other when they were first married. All he had to do now was work, and he did. In three years they were successful enough for Thomas to buy Reed out, and he did, although they remained close friends. By 1978, Burger King was looking for black franchisees in Atlanta. That year he sold his Dairy Queen and bought a Burger King.

The location was once again in a very tough neighborhood, but he knew how to operate by then, and he turned it into a very successful operation. It was obvious that he was good at this, tough and resourceful and completely committed the way a franchise owner had to be. Since all the franchise food operators were learning in this period that blacks were very good customers, in time Hank Thomas was contacted by some McDonald's people who had checked out his operation and who offered to sell him a McDonald's. As far as he was concerned the equation was simple: McDonald's owners made more money than Burger King owners, and as he said, he followed the trail of the money. He sold his Burger King and in 1982 he bought his first McDonald's. Again he worked hard and again he was a stunning success: He bought his second franchise in 1985, his third in 1986, his fourth in 1991. At one point he owned six. A particularly sweet moment came in 1991 when he bought the McDonald's operation in Decatur where they had once debated whether or not he would be allowed to operate the cash register.

He was a millionaire by the nineties. He was a shrewd and careful manager, determined to give back to others as Gerald Reed had given back to him. He tried to wean his managers to capitalism and he worked out a program for them by which he would bring them into the stock market and teach them to save. He would put a sum equal to 10 percent of their annual salary into a mutual fund for them; if they stayed five years, the fund would be theirs. They would not have to contribute anything.

He was always aware of prejudice, both deliberate and unconscious, as it was manifest in American society, and he realized that no matter how successful you were, you could never entirely escape it. But he also thought it was possible to have a life which was rich and where you could have friends and associations of all kinds, and where the sum of the good things which happened each day was far greater than the indignities of the bad things that happened. In 1980 he had married again and in the late eighties he decided to build a home in the exclusive Stone Mountain suburb of Atlanta. He bought the property with the help of a black bank, but it was a bank which did not like to give long-term financing. When it was time to get a loan to build the house itself, he ran into the kind of prejudice which had bedeviled blacks for ages in the South, and particularly in Atlanta, where redlining by banks was a particular specialty of the house. He was rejected by four white banks on his application for a loan, even though his net worth at the time was around $2.5 million. Finally he decided to use his own cash to build the house. By chance, at almost the exact moment that he was being rejected, the *Atlanta Constitution,* momentarily invigorated by a tough new editor named Bill Kovach, ran a long series of stories on redlining, and within days two of the banks called to tell him he could have his loan—and he did not even have to come in; they would send the papers out to him.

Hank Thomas stayed active in veterans' affairs and was one of a group of veterans who not only went back to Vietnam to visit with former foes, but who sponsored North Vietnamese officers on their visits to America. On one of his trips back to Vietnam he and a group of other American veterans were staying in a hotel in Ho Chi Minh City, and one of the whites, a former officer, had pointed at the guest book and had said, "Hey, Hank, put your *X* right here." He had seethed with anger at the moment, and because he had brought some of his paperwork from his business along with him, he had later called the man over and showed him a check he was writing. "I'm writing a check," he had said, "and I need your help. You see the check is for three hundred thousand dollars, and I need to be sure that I get the number of zeroes right. Is it five or six?" It was not the most generous thing he had ever done, he realized, but once in a while you had to teach a man a lesson he should have learned a long time earlier.

At one McDonald's conference in the early nineties he met a man who was the son of the owner of a McDonald's in High Point, North Carolina. It happened to be a place where in 1961, Hank Thomas and a bunch of other activists had protested segregation, and they had momentarily at least closed it down. The son was now the owner, and he listened to his fellow McDonald's owner's story with great interest. "Hank," he had said, "that's just a great story." So it was, Hank Thomas thought, so it was.

In many ways it was not easy being a black millionaire. Early on as he became more successful, he brought a younger member of his family into the business and into his home, eager to share some of his good fortune, but the intensity of purpose Thomas himself had brought to this kind of life was not shared by his young relative, and the relationship did not pan out very well. His mother, who had had a particularly difficult life doing menial work, was proud of his success, and she liked to tell the white people she worked for as a domestic that her son had a job at McDonald's. That, Hank Thomas was sure, made them think he was probably some guy in the back flipping hamburgers, although when she told them that he had built a home in the swank Stone Mountain community, they began to get the picture. He tried to get her to give up her job, but she was a proud, dignified person and much of her self-esteem was invested in working, and she was reluctant to stop, even if it was work as a domestic. She was, he thought, somewhat ill at ease when she visited his quite grand house in Stone Mountain, because there was not enough for her to do, and she was most comfortable when she was able to put in a hard day of work. The source of her strength was her religious background, he believed; she liked her job not just because it gave her dignity, but because she knew that she was helping other people.

In the early nineties, through some intermediaries, he made contact with the man who was his blood father; in time his father showed up in Atlanta. At their meeting Hank Thomas, seeing this stranger for the first time, began to cry. His father thought they were tears of joy. They were not. They were tears, Thomas decided later, of conflict and confusion and rage, of wondering why this man had run off and deserted his family, and of wondering how much better and healthier his and his mother's lives might have been had this stranger stayed home.

One of the things which bothered Hank Thomas was the way so many of his old colleagues in the Movement treated entrepreneurial capitalism, putting it down, as if to be successful financially in this country was to betray the goals of the Movement. Financial success— living well with dignity and having many of the good things that so many white people had—was, as far as he was concerned, just as much a part of the Movement as ending voter discrimination. But, he believed, it was hard to make blacks see that, as if they felt that some-how their own personal success might seem to be a betrayal of other, less successful blacks. That was crazy, he thought: For too long in this country, blacks had supplied the labor but had not gotten the benefit of their labor. Now that the opportunities to benefit from their own labor were opening up, it was a mistake to hold up a kind of reverse prejudice against those who worked hard and were successful.

He thought one of the great vulnerabilities of the black middle class both in Atlanta and in other cities was that too many of their jobs were in government and civil services, which put a certain ceiling on the future of everyone involved. If they were in the private sector, there might be less of a ceiling. He thought the sooner that black people broke out of that cycle, the freer they would be within the middle class. He decided he would not be ashamed of his success. When peo-ple referred to him as being upper middle class, he corrected them: No, he said, he was actually in the elite; he was not just upper middle class, he was rich.

As a wealthy businessman he remained inordinately proud of his days as a demonstrator—it had been his graduate school, and he felt closer to the young people who had formed the Nashville group than to the men and women he had gone to college with at Howard. He returned faithfully to all the Nashville reunions, which were held every five years, and he was stunned by how pleased he was when, at the thirty-fifth anniversary reunion in 1995, Bernard Lafayette announced that they had made him an honorary Nashville sit-in kid.

79

ROBERT CHURCHWELL, THE *NASHVILLE BANNER*'s FIRST BLACK REPORTER, and his wife, Mary, stayed the course, he as a journalist, she as a teacher. In 1997 they still lived in the simple home in east Nashville which they had bought in 1959 for $9,500 with a $600 down payment and where they had raised their five children. Mary Churchwell thought that Robert was in his own way a heroic figure, a stoic man who over a long career had borne burdens that almost no one else could see or measure. Every week, she thought, the paper would write about someone who was a hero, a fireman or a policeman who had saved some child or some pet. But the real heroes in this life, she believed, went largely unnoticed. To her, Robert was a true hero. He went out every day and did something that was extremely difficult and he always retained his dignity in the face of constant slights. She had encouraged him in those difficult years, telling him on those Monday mornings when he could barely bring himself to go to work that it was going to get better, not just in the future but in his lifetime. "Robert," she would say, "you can conquer anything. *I know you!*" But it never really got better for him. When finally after Dick Battle had helped push the publisher to integrate the paper's Christmas party, Mary Churchwell had refused to go the first year. It was her own private protest against the way the *Banner* treated her husband.

Even in the seventies after Jimmy Stahlman sold the paper and new owners, less burdened by the issue of race, arrived, Robert Churchwell remained wary of his longtime surroundings. He had felt too much anxiety about his job for too long, and now that his position was far more secure, he was still unable to feel greater job security. He was convinced that he still might lose his job because of some editor's whim. When the paper finally got computers, he was scared because he was an older man now, well into his fifties, and he was sure he could not deal with something as modern as a computer. But Mary had again encouraged him and convinced him that a computer was just a somewhat smarter typewriter. Soon he had made the transition and was saying that these computers weren't so hard to handle after all.

He had one major nervous breakdown in those years with the *Banner*. He had been exhausted, worn down by his depression; his doctor had told him to take some time off, that he was badly overworked, but fearing that he would lose his job if he stayed out too long, he had not taken the prescribed rest. As such he had returned to work after too short a rest, and a more serious breakdown had taken place. This time he rested a bit longer, and his doctor was able to prescribe pills which helped alleviate the depression. On the occasion of the first breakdown, Mary Churchwell had opened the Bible for her husband and turned it to Psalm 121: "I will lift up mine eyes unto the hills, from whence cometh my help. My help cometh from the Lord, which made Heaven and Earth. He will not suffer thy foot to be moved; He that keepeth thee will not slumber . . . the Lord shall preserve thy going out and thy coming in from this time forth, and even for evermore." The doctors had told him his problem was simple, that he had worked too hard for too long in a state of too much loneliness, and that he had to cut back on his workload. When Mary Churchwell argued with him to cut back his responsibilities, he told her he was sure that the *Banner* editors would let him go if he did not work hard enough.

He had always worked hard. He even had a small sideline selling photos of black social occasions, particularly Sunday church functions. He and Jack Gunter, the *Banner* photographer, would cover any number of black social events each Sunday, and Gunter would take extra photos, and Churchwell would have them printed up, take them to the appropriate people and take orders, and he and Gunter would split the money. It was a pleasant additional income for a man raising five children, sometimes adding up to as much as $40 a week. Sometimes when they were on assignment for the *Banner* Churchwell would tease Gunter: "You know, Jack," he would say, "I'm an integrated man." Gunter would ask what he meant. "Well, I'm a black man working for a white newspaper and I'm a black man in a white man's car, which, by the way, a white man is driving. And we're going out to Fisk, which is a black university, and we're going to interview the head of General Motors, who is very white and who is going to give one million dollars to this very black school. That's pretty integrated."

In 1981 when he was 64, he retired from the *Banner*. The paper gave him a cake, a cash gift of $2,000, and a watch. He still worked several days a week for the National Baptist Publishing Board, which was the black Baptist publishing organization. As Nashville changed and became more integrated, he became something of a local icon, a man who had been the first to integrate the world of Tennessee journalism. One day in the eighties, the new publisher of the *Banner*, aware of the low esteem with which the paper was held in black Nashville, asked him to come and work for them, if not as a reporter, at least as a consultant. "Robert, you're too valuable a resource to waste," one of the *Banner* executives said, "and this is a different paper from the one you worked for." The offer they were making seemed quite handsome, but then Churchwell looked out at the city room where he had felt such pain, and the thought of coming in here once again to work regularly seemed more than he could bear. He decided that though he might occasionally write for them, he would not be a regular part of the paper's organization. He and Mary Churchwell, who taught school all those years, raised five children on their limited resources, and all five went to college, two to Tennessee State, one to Vanderbilt, one to MIT, and one to Harvard; three of their children became doctors, serving in different Nashville hospitals, and two of them became teachers.

80

JIM ZWERG, THE YOUNG TRANSFER STUDENT AT FISK FROM BELOIT who was badly beaten along with John Lewis in Montgomery in 1961, went through a difficult period in his personal life in the year following the Freedom Ride. He felt that he had acted as he had because of the teachings of his parents, who had always spoken of a society where race did not matter. But when he had put his life on the line for his beliefs, his father had turned away from him, and told him he had been manipulated by black people. From then on, still seeking their approval, when he tried to explain his actions his father simply blew up at him. His inability to convince his father and mother that he had acted on his conscience, formed as it was by their own teachings, weighed heavily for a time on Zwerg, and during the next year at Beloit he had taken his comfort and solace from alcohol; it was a year in which he was clearly out of control.

Still, Zwerg believed in some way that the events in Montgomery had changed his life dramatically for the better. A year after the beating he and the nine others who had been in the first bus were given the Freedom Award of the SCLC, and he had a chance to talk for half an hour with Martin Luther King. He had spoken of the choice he faced in his personal life—of taking a job which had been offered him as a white field worker for the SCLC or of going on and getting a graduate degree from the Methodist seminary at Northwestern and becoming a minister. King had urged him to continue his studies and become a minister, telling him he could help more people that way. He followed King's advice and got his degree from Northwestern, and served as a minister in Wisconsin before moving to the Southwest. Eventually he worked for the Tucson Chamber of Commerce in some of their governmental affairs programs, and in 1979 when IBM arrived in Tucson, he went to work for them as an expert on local affairs. He remained involved in a variety of community social issues in his years there. He suffered periodic pain from the beating he had received that day in 1961, when three vertebrae were broken and he also lost many of his teeth.

He remained proud that he had been a Freedom Rider. He knew that it had profoundly affected his outlook on life. How much the riders had changed history, he did not know—he was not, he would point out when the subject came up, a historian. But in 1986, on the twenty-fifth anniversary of the Freedom Rides, an incident took place which helped him to understand how much they had changed things. The Canadian Broadcasting Company had looked him up and had asked him to be a part of a documentary that it was doing on the Freedom Rides twenty-five years later. As part of the documentary he would ride the same bus from Birmingham to Montgomery. Some of what the television producers asked him to do that day as they retraced his steps struck Zwerg as hokey—they would, for example, tell him he had turned the wrong way when he stepped off the bus. But one thing struck him as true. When he had first boarded the bus they had asked him to sit next to a young black boy about fifteen years old, who was also riding the bus to Montgomery, on his way to visit his aunt. Zwerg began talking to the boy, asking him if he understood what the camera crew was trying to reenact. The boy said he did not. Well, Zwerg asked, have they ever taught you in school about the Freedom Rides? No, sir, the boy answered, they had not. "Did you know," Zwerg continued, "that twenty-five years ago we could not sit here together on this bus, a white person and a black person without being arrested or beaten or perhaps both?" The young boy said he did not know that, and Zwerg thought, yes, things have changed; some of what we fought for has been achieved, and even taken for granted. Just then the bus arrived in Montgomery and he descended. Almost as soon as he stepped down, the CBC interviewer asked, "Do you feel you made a difference?" The question, he thought, had just been answered for him on the bus. "Yes," he said, "I know we did."

81

PAUL LAPRAD, THE YOUNG FISK TRANSFER STUDENT FROM MANCHESter College who was beaten during the sit-ins, a beating captured for the nation by a Nashville photographer, thought years later that all in all he had lived the most ordinary of lives. He had returned to college in Indiana, graduated, and gone on to graduate school in the field of social services at Indiana University. Upon graduation he worked for a number of years in the Indiana and Ohio prison systems. From there he worked for a mental health organization. Eventually he decided he wanted to run a business of his own, which he did with a startling lack of success. But he took a job with Frontier Airlines, finding himself finally in Colorado, where he fell in love with the sheer beauty of the land, and where he decided that this was the place where he had always wanted to live. After a time, when Frontier folded he went back into the criminal justice system. The first question asked of him was whether he had a record, and he had answered yes, as a sit-in student in 1960. Eventually he became a parole officer, working in the Denver area, which amused some of his old friends from the Movement. He liked the work—most of it was with people who had somehow been unproductive all their lives and it was a challenge for him to see whether he could help them become more productive. What gave his life distinction, he believed, was that amazing moment in February 1960 when he had been the target of a white racist in Nashville; he remained inordinately proud of that moment.

82

ANGELINE BUTLER, THE STRIKINGLY BEAUTIFUL YOUNG WOMAN WHO had been one of the most important figures in the early sit-in days and who with her sweetness had given the meetings a certain joyousness, had always thought of a career in show business. She had originally intended to go to Oberlin because of its strong music department but her father had lost the papers which might have won her a scholarship there, and she had ended up at Fisk. By the time she arrived at Fisk she had already won a talent contest as the black Miss South Carolina, and her friends thought she had a wonderful voice to go with an ebullient, sparkling personality. After Fisk she went to New York to enter show business, where for a time it looked like she might make a breakthrough. She made a number of television appearances, including one on the old *Bob Newhart Show,* and one on the Johnny Carson show, as well as doing a commercial for a hair preparation. Johnny Carson seemed to like her very much; pleased by her considerable charm and talent during her first appearance, he invited her back again. On one of her appearances the song she chose was "They're Going to Hear From Me." Carson, obviously impressed, turned to her and said, "I don't say this very often, but you're going to be a big star." Thirty years later in her home in Los Angeles, she played a film clip of her old appearance to a friend and said, "I wish it had been true." Of her talent and beauty there seemed little doubt, but she had come to the entertainment world at a moment when despite the dramatic changes beginning to take place in the South, the people who ran Hollywood still thought of this as a white country, where white people sat in white movie theaters watching white actors play white people, a country where there was one slot for a black actor (Sidney Poitier, if possible) and one slot for a black actress (Dorothy Dandridge), and those slots were already filled. Had she arrived twenty years later, her friends thought, it might have been a very different story. As it was, her career was harder than Johnny Carson had prophesied on *The Tonight Show*. She continued to work in different theatrical productions over the next thirty years, but the big strike never took place.

83

In 1994, a bunch of old colleagues from the Movement held a party in Atlanta to celebrate C. T. Vivian's seventieth birthday. It was a joyous occasion made all the happier by the fact that except for a relatively small amount of gray in his hair, he seemed not to have aged at all, and still bore a striking resemblance to the younger man who almost thirty years ago on the steps of the Dallas County courthouse had engaged in a debate with Jim Clark about Clark's place in history, a debate which had ended with Clark breaking his hand on Vivian's head. He and Octavia lived in Atlanta, where they had raised their family of five children, and it appeared that she had finally forgiven him for going off on the Freedom Ride not just to Alabama but to Mississippi without talking to her. Over the years Vivian had never wavered in his beliefs, and had stayed committed to nonviolence throughout his life; his career remained rich and varied. He had served for a time as the dean of religion at Shaw University, and he had stayed on the board of the SCLC throughout the years. His interests were many—he advised some large companies on their executive hiring practices with blacks, he helped organize another group to expand the number of black-owned businesses in American cities, and in the mid-nineties when the Klan started burning black churches in the South, he helped organize a group of people to combat the Klan. C. T. Vivian not only looked youthful, he seemed as boyish as ever, ready as ever, his friends noted affectionately, to answer any question with a complete sermon.

84

CANDIE ANDERSON, THE YOUNG WHITE SUBURBAN EXCHANGE STU-
dent at Fisk who had been an enthusiastic early sit-in demonstrator
and had written one of the early sit-in songs, "They Go Wild Over
Me," fell in love with Guy Carawan, the white radical troubadour
from the Highlander Folk School, who helped bring "We Shall Overcome" to the Movement. They had met in 1960 and were married
within a year, and they stayed married; they spent their lifetimes working at Highlander for a variety of social and political causes that were
rarely popular. From the start being at Highlander meant that they
were in harm's way as far as the local and state authorities were concerned. The school, which was a teaching center for integration when
that was not only not fashionable but against the state law, was both
literally and figuratively a red flag to local politicians, who were constantly trying to close it down. Many of the leaders of the Movement,
both the older generation and the students, had attended Highlander
workshops over the years; it had been the site of historic early SNCC
meetings and it was where Rosa Parks of Montgomery had attended
early workshops before deciding she would no longer ride a segregated bus in December 1955.

Highlander was situated on some two hundred acres in Monteagle,
Tennessee. In 1959 the local authorities had raided the school and
arrested most members of its staff, including Guy Carawan; that
began a two-year legal battle on their part to close down the school by
taking away its land. A series of charges, some bogus, some reflecting
the prejudice of the time, were leveled at it: Highlander was holding
integrated classes and integration was illegal in Tennessee. Myles Horton, its director, was running it for profit. Horton was illegally selling
beer without a license. In time the charge about holding illegal inte-

gration classes was dropped. But the overall campaign against Horton and his school was successful, the land was sold at public auction, and the Highlander people were forced to set up shop in Knoxville. Eventually, in the changing climate of the seventies, they were able to move back and reopen in a more bucolic setting on some land in New Market, Tennessee. The original Highlander land moved back and forth between different owners in different sales. Recently, in one of those wonderful ironies wherein places which were once scenes of violence in the South have now been designated as historical landmarks, some of the land was offered for sale again. The advertisement for the land in the local paper noted that this was a historically valuable piece of land, one "where the New South was born."

85

HARVIE BRANSCOMB RETIRED AS CHANCELLOR OF VANDERBILT IN 1962, two years after the fiasco of the Lawson affair. His replacement was a political scientist at the University of North Carolina named Alec Heard, who was generally considered more liberal, so much so that Heard's supporters on the Vanderbilt board had to warn the editors of the liberal *Tennessean* to stop referring to Heard as a liberal because it would antagonize Jimmy Stahlman and only serve to make Heard's job harder. The one stain on Branscomb's tour as chancellor was the Lawson affair. Though he had done much to upgrade and modernize the university, it had taken years to bring the divinity school back to where it had been before that debacle, and it was widely believed in both educational and religious circles that Branscomb had blown the most important call of his administrative career.

As Branscomb grew older, he seemed to many friends increasingly obsessed by the Lawson affair, unable to let go, often managing to bring it up in conversation or in memos. In the memoir of his life, which was privately printed (lest, some friends thought, the book go out into the public domain, and the entire affair once again be rekindled and he be once again attacked), his recounting of the affair was curiously legalistic and sanitized; in no way did it mention the critical political pressures he was responding to, nor did he in any way accept that what Lawson and his students were doing was somewhat more serious and more spiritually driven than a panty raid. Branscomb's friends tried to tell him to let go, that he had done a good job at Vanderbilt, that what had happened had happened, and that he had to forget the Lawson incident, but he seemed to find that impossible.

Harvie Branscomb lived to a remarkable old age. In 1994, he celebrated his hundredth birthday. He had always taken his religion seriously, and as he became older he began to think of what he wanted
done with his ashes and those of his wife. He was proud of the new
divinity school chapel which had been completed and dedicated in
the midst of the Lawson turmoil. When as a young man he had visited
England as a Rhodes scholar, he had been impressed by the way the
British did certain things, particularly the little plaques they put up in
their chapels celebrating the lives of prominent people connected to
that institution. Branscomb decided that he and his wife were going to
be cremated and he wanted their ashes spread at the divinity school,
with a small modest plaque in the British style inside the chapel used
to mark both their lives, celebrating, in his case, the fact that he had
been the fifth chancellor of Vanderbilt University. So he set out to
arrange this but he did it very carefully, indeed secretively, clearing it
with the president of the university and the proper authorities in a
very low-key manner because he was afraid if the faculty at the divinity
school knew of it, there might be a protest because of the Lawson
affair and he could not bear to go through that again.

Late in his life he expressed a desire to close friends to meet with
Jim Lawson, as if to deal with the one issue which still cast a shadow
on him. But though Lawson was amenable to a meeting and returned
to Nashville periodically, the meeting could not be arranged, because
on the occasions when Lawson came back, Branscomb's health prevented the two of them getting together. In October 1996, however,
Jim Lawson was asked to come back to Vanderbilt and to receive the
divinity school's distinguished alumnus award, an honor which struck
him as not without its own special irony, since he was not an alumnus
of the school. But he came back and this time the efforts of intermediaries to arrange a meeting with the former chancellor who had
expelled him thirty-six years earlier proved successful. A luncheon
was arranged and it was a surprisingly pleasant meeting; Branscomb,
if he did not exactly apologize for what had happened in those tense
days, had come as close as a man could to an apology. He had made a
terrible mistake back then in allowing the decision to go to the board,
he told Lawson. In fact it was the worst decision he had made as chancellor. It was a decision he should have made in his office, and it

should have stayed there, particularly, as he told Lawson, because his board had two men on it who were "hard-core rednecks." One of them, he said, was Jimmy Stahlman. The harshness of Branscomb's phrase surprised Lawson somewhat. The former chancellor did not say, but he clearly implied, that he should have met with Lawson at the time and dealt with the issue personally; implied again was the idea that if they had met personally the questions would have been settled equitably and justly in the chancellor's office.

Jim Lawson was pleased to have all of this finally behind him. With that, as far as he was concerned, the issue was finished. He and his wife had forgiven Branscomb long ago, but he felt a great deal better after their meeting, aware that if what had happened back in 1960 no longer weighed on him, it had continued to burden this other, older man for more than a third of a century.

Jim Lawson remained remarkably unchanged in his beliefs after nearly four decades of social activism in contemporary America. He looked little different from the young man who had arrived in Nashville in the late fifties so eager to be a part of social change; he was to be sure a little heavier, and his hair had gone completely white and he wore it somewhat longer now. In his political persona he still defied fashion: He had been an integrationist back in the late fifties when it was unfashionable in the white community, and now he remained an integrationist when it was unfashionable in much of the black world. He remained, as he had been as a young man, at once a radical Christian and an integrationist, a man who both believed in and yet constantly questioned the American Dream—the difference was that his dream was significantly less materialistic than the one conjured up by most of his fellow citizens. The intense materialism of modern American society disturbed him more than ever, as, in a different way, did the increasing force for separatism within certain parts of the black community. When Minister Louis Farrakhan's Million Man March took place in November 1995, Jim Lawson was openly critical of it, both in what he said from the pulpit and what he wrote. But later as he spoke to people who had been there, he began to change his mind, certainly not about Farrakhan's role and speech, but about what the march had meant to those who had gone, many of whom, he believed, had actually paid little attention to Farrakhan. It had been, he decided, a day of affirmation for black men, of fathers affirming their relationships to their sons, and it had filled a tragic vacuum in black life at the time.

One subject which he remained absolutely passionate about was the murder of Martin Luther King. Though he was not in other areas given to conspiracy theories, Jim Lawson remained completely convinced that King had been murdered by a group of people and that James Earl Ray was a mere figurehead for a larger, almost surely well-financed group. As such he devoted a large amount of his time to pressing the government to reopen the case.

86

___

Sitting next to Lawson at that lunch with Branscomb was Will D. Campbell, the white civil rights minister who had been a close friend of both Kelly Miller Smith and Lawson in those early days. There seemed a certain inevitability to that; he, after all, had been the man who, when Lawson was dutifully ready to resign, had urged the young black student to hold the line and force Vanderbilt to expel him. Campbell, a truly ubiquitous figure of the early civil rights movement, had stayed on in a rural setting just east of Nashville in the ensuing years, turning down a series of jobs which would have led him to a seemingly more prestigious career. As the Movement had grown more powerful his own role as a white adviser inevitably became smaller and smaller, which was just as he wanted it. He was always quick to point out that in the Movement there had been no white heroes, but plenty of black ones, and that the black church had been far ahead of the white church in its nobility and in its essential concept of Christianity.

As for his own role in those dangerous days, he liked to say that the only thing he had ever done of note was to lend the students in the Freedom Rides his National Council of Churches telephone credit card, thereby keeping them from having to travel around the South with pockets full of change. He was, he liked to boast, a racist, but not a bigot, thereby letting whoever it was that he had spoken to unravel that particular conundrum. Campbell was by birth a Southern Baptist, but, irritated by the conservatism of the church into which he had been born, he liked to say that he was a Baptist preacher of the South, but not a Southern Baptist preacher. Late in life he started referring to himself as a Seventh Day Horizontalist. A quirky contrarian at heart, quick to let others know that his Yale divinity degree was not the defining part of him, uneasy when he was lauded for his role in the past, he nonetheless became something of a folk hero to a younger generation of people writing about the civil rights movement.

For a time, convinced that the problem in the South was not the blacks but the poor whites, Campbell tried pastoring to poor Klansmen and trying to deal with their religious and social problems, a role which offended some of his old allies who thought themselves purer of heart, but something which seemed to be perfectly in keeping with his unusual style. His long black Amish hat and his cane became something of a personal trademark, and a cartoonist named Doug Marlette created a comic strip called "Kudzu" in which a character named Preacher was said to be patterned on him. The comic strip was syndicated in a number of newspapers and brought Campbell additional fame, albeit a notoriety he did not seem particularly pleased with, and in order to disassociate himself from the figure in the strip, he gave up the hat. He also became a writer of distinction and a number of his books, including an autobiographical memoir, *Brother to a Dragonfly,* were published to exceptional reviews. He believed, however, that his true skill was not so much as a writer or a minister but as a six-string guitar player, a view not shared by all of his close friends, and in time he became very close to a number of Nashville's most prominent country singers. His capacity for forgiveness was not always as great as that of some of the black leaders who were his colleagues, and for what it had done to Jim Lawson and for its only partial support of Kelly Miller Smith, he did not lightly forgive Vanderbilt University. In the fall of 1996, when Vanderbilt played a close football game with highly favored Notre Dame, he found himself rooting for the Fighting Irish, something he was quick to admit was not easy for a Southern Protestant to do.

87

JOHN LAWSON, THE SON OF JIM AND DOROTHY LAWSON, INTEGRATOR of the Memphis Zoo at two years old, early black pioneer of the Memphis elementary school system, lived a life significantly different from that of his parents. He had clear memories of going on marches with his father in Memphis, of standing prayer vigils when his father had been arrested at different demonstrations for disturbing the peace, and, at the age of seven, marching with him in the sanitation men's strike and wearing an I AM A MAN pin. He was twelve years old when the family moved to Los Angeles in 1974. There the Lawsons took a house in a pleasantly middle-class black area around Crenshaw and LaBrea. He was bused to predominantly white schools from the moment he arrived in Los Angeles, first to a junior high school in the Westchester area near the Los Angeles airport, a white area on the very margin of the middle class, where some of the residents clearly did not fancy the idea of black children being sent into their neighborhood, and often lay in wait for them after school. Because of that, if John and some of his friends stayed late and missed their school bus, and had to use public buses, they sometimes had to dodge older white men chasing them with sticks and bats.

Pacific Palisades, where he was bused to high school, was different, a dramatically more affluent area, and here the local residents seemed more relaxed about the prospect of some black children being bused in. He liked Pacific Palisades High a good deal, and because he was not merely a good student but a good athlete and a linebacker on the football team, he was able to have a wide selection of friends. When he graduated in 1979, he won an academic scholarship to Oberlin, the Ohio school where more than twenty years earlier his father had been a divinity student and had first met Martin Luther King. At Oberlin, a school smaller than Pacific Palisades High, he again had a broad selection of friends, choosing not to be a part of the nascent black separatist movement and not to live in the all-black dorm. He would, he had decided, have friends of all kinds. When he finished college he decided to apply to law school, wanting, he sensed, in some way to carry on some of the things his father had been involved with in the Movement, although as a member of a very different generation facing different problems, and armed with a law degree. Because he realized he had lived an uncommonly privileged life for a young black man, John Lawson decided to go to Howard Law School, because it was time to experience life at a predominantly black school.

Howard had a powerful effect on him. Living in Washington, the nation's capital, seeing so many physical symbols of the power of the richest country in the world, which were surrounded by neighborhoods of terrible poverty, made him aware of the awful downward pull on so many blacks which he had been fortunate enough to escape. He would sometimes drive through the city at night, and see monuments to the nation's heroes, and buildings which housed the offices of its most important public officials, and across from them, the black homeless getting ready for the night, and then he would drive a few short blocks to black neighborhoods where people were beginning to prepare for an evening in which most of the street corner energy went into the search for drugs. In his last year there he was a part of a seminar which worked in the District of Columbia criminal justice system and in which he handled misdemeanor cases. He watched an endless series of black people entangled in a system which seemed to them, and increasingly to him, all about the flaws of a world where poverty and race were mixed together in a deadening combination and which created a terrible downward undertow.

He decided that given the way he had been raised, the only honorable career would be one in the criminal justice system, working in public service law. Corporate law was out of the question. When he graduated in 1986 he moved back to Los Angeles, and a year later, in 1987, he went to work in the Los Angeles County public defender's office. He had no illusions about what he was doing, how hard it would be, nor what his chances were of making a very deep impact on many people's lives. But someone, he thought, had to be a foot soldier here, even on the smallest scale, working within a system which did not offer the people ensnared in it very much hope of a better life. He thought he would measure his success not on any grand scale, but on his ability a few times a year to effect a handful of lives in some small way which might make them a little more bearable.

If, in 1995, much of the nation's attention was focused on the O. J. Simpson double murder case then taking place in Los Angeles, a celebrity case of rare high visibility, populated as it was with famous, well-paid, media-conscious lawyers, then John Lawson worked the other end of town and the other end of the spectrum, fighting an endless, silent, unnoticed series of battles for blacks and Latinos of marginal abilities and strengths who were overwhelmed by the forces working against them in late twentieth-century America. A great many of his cases had their roots in drug abuse. Drugs alone, he believed, made a mockery of the Constitution of the United States. They were all dealing with nothing less than an epidemic, a powerful, relentless disease with a contagiousness all its own, and it was spewing its casualties into the criminal justice system. Here was a system set up to deal with individual cases of legality, and of individual rights and wrongs, and it was absolutely overloaded by the product of what was, as far as he could tell, a modern plague. Many of his clients were relatively young mothers who had been arrested as welfare cheats. They were women between twenty-five and thirty-five, often with two or three children, and they had been deserted by their men; these women had bottom-end, minimum wage jobs which did not allow them to feed or care for or house their families properly. So they kept on cashing their welfare checks, even when they should have stopped. It was his responsibility to keep them from going to jail, and much of his day was given over to bargaining their way out of prison. Instead they went on probation, which meant that they were now part of the criminal justice system, that a critical part of their safety net, such as it was, was gone. They were people who were not normally criminals, but who had taken the first perilous step toward becoming criminals. The chances that they would not once again bob up in this system, pulled in by something more serious the next time, were slim. John Lawson still believed passionately in what he did, he was still, as he noted, his father and mother's son, but if anything he had, because of what he saw every day, become more radical every year. He had originally decided to give the public defender's office ten years and in 1996 he was coming up on that; he thought he could give it a few more years before he wore out completely.

88

THIRTY-FIVE YEARS TO THE DAY AFTER THE GREAT MOMENT IN APRIL
when Diane Nash had in the most personal way imaginable challenged Ben West in front of the courthouse to end racism at the lunch
counters, a new young white mayor of Nashville named Phil Bredesen
invited a group of the original activists back to Nashville to mark the
occasion. The group that returned included, among others, Jim Lawson, John Lewis, and Diane Nash, and they were all to participate in a
ceremony commemorating that historic day. At that spot Bredesen
had erected a plaque and on the plaque he had inscribed the words
from Joshua: "And the people shouted with a great shout; so that the
wall fell down." Of the many speeches that day, perhaps the most
moving was given by Diane Nash. She was a grandmother now, her
life had not been easy, but she spoke that day with a rare kind of modesty and elegance. She had been proud, she said, to be a part of something noble and generous, something which was larger than herself.
She had spoken not so much for herself on that day when she confronted Ben West, she said, but for all of her colleagues in the Movement, and perhaps even more, for all of those black people who had
gone before and who had never been given a chance to speak or who
had never been listened to.

AUTHOR'S NOTE

I suppose I started work on this book some forty-three years ago. In June 1955, I graduated from college, and set off to begin my journalistic career in Mississippi. It was one year after the Supreme Court had ruled in *Brown* v. *Board of Education,* and I believed that powerful social forces would now be set into play in the South, and I wanted, as a young reporter, to have a chance to cover them. There was a Nieman fellow at Harvard that year named Tom Karsell who was the operative editor of Hodding Carter's Greenville, Mississippi, *Delta Democrat-Times.* He and I became friends and at one point that spring during a quite liquid lunch he delivered startling news: He had been hired as the editor of a new, more enlightened start-up paper in Jackson, the *State Times.* More important, he thereupon hired me to come down and be his star reporter. A few weeks later, when I graduated, I packed all my belongings—one suitcase, a relatively primitive hi-fi record player, a handful of 33-rpm long-playing records, and a copy of Gunnar Myrdal's *An American Dilemma,* the most important and influential book I had read at the time and probably have read since. Then I got into my banged-up 1946 Chevy and drove off to Jackson, Mississippi, ready to be a heroic reporter.

On arrival in Jackson I discovered that Karsell was not the editor of the enlightened *State Times* as I thought, but in fact had taken a job as assistant to Fred Sullens, the famously racist editor of the famously racist *Jackson Daily News.* Karsell hoped, he said, to take the paper over in a coup in the near future. This was not the best of news for me; I was some thirteen hundred miles from home and had no job. But Karsell arranged a job for me as the one reporter on the smallest daily in the state, in West Point, a town of eight thousand. The choice was mine. I could put my tail between my legs, drive back to Boston, and try to find a more conventional job, or I could drive over to West Point. The job there paid $46 a week; actually $45 a week, with one dollar extra for expenses because I covered the weekly Kiwanis club meetings. The circulation of the West Point, Mississippi, *Daily Times Leader* was said to be four thousand people. To me, there was no choice—I drove to West Point.

It was a rich year (or to be exact, ten months) for me before I exhausted my welcome there. I made a lot of friends, and I was treated with uncommon courtesy by most people; I also wrote a number of freelance pieces for *The Reporter,* a biweekly liberal magazine of considerable status and influence. Of several of those early pieces I still remain quite proud—in particular, one which a young man named Medgar Evers helped me on, was an early report from Yazoo City where the local black people who had signed an NAACP petition demanding integration of the local school system had all lost their jobs. My arrival in Yazoo City, arranged by Medgar Evers, was made of cloak-and-dagger stuff; I was met outside of town and smuggled by different local black guides from car to car so that I could talk to those who had lost their jobs. I loved the process, of course, and was also properly terrified by it. My story detailed the economic pressures used by members of the local Citizens Council to force these people to withdraw their names from the petition.

Stories like that and a few local stories of the same sort greatly irritated my editor in West Point, Henry Harris. (He harbored, it turned out, dreams of running for statewide office as lieutenant governor, and perhaps one day governor, and feared, I suppose, that I would cost him not only advertising revenues but perhaps the governorship.) He asked me to stop writing for *The Reporter,* and said he would give me a considerable raise if I stopped. I would not. One day in March 1956, my successor already hired and on his way, he called me in and told me it was time to go. "David," he said in words I still remember, "you're free, white, and twenty-one." On occasion now I am asked to give commencement addresses at different colleges, and I usually point out that it is A) a good idea in any career to start small instead of big, West Point, Mississippi, instead of New York City, and B) it is permissible to fail early on—that I was fired from even that small a paper.

I went from there to become a reporter for *The Nashville Tennessean,* on the recommendation of my friend Hodding Carter, who told me it was the best stepping-stone paper in the country. The *Tennessean,* in the mid- and late fifties, was arguably the best and most aggressive paper in the South; it had a truly dazzling staff, full of audacious, courageous reporters. It was also a very generous staff: If a journalistic career is a process of continuing education, then the *Tennessean* in 1956 was the greatest graduate school in the country, and I was taught every day by some of the profession's most skilled practitioners. I was then, and I remain to this day, proud of its role in breaking the old Crump machine in Memphis and helping to bring the franchise to blacks and poor whites across the state. I spent four wildly happy years there. I covered everything: police, courts, and a good deal of racial confrontation.

The pace of racial change was in the late fifties extremely slow. The essential Southern strategy was to force the NAACP to make its assault child by child, school by school, and voter by voter in each Southern town. Therefore when the young students whom I have written about went into the streets, it represented a dramatic change from the past. Suddenly the best of a generation of young black students, frustrated in the six years since *Brown* by the lack of change in their lives, were taking things into their own hands.

There is a good deal of talk about journalistic political correctness these days, and political correctness is odious in any form. It should be noted, however, that there was an old political correctness in those days, and it was both very powerful and very pernicious. The key to the old political correctness was in the skillful use of silence at critical times. Under the old journalistic political correctness, as manifested throughout the South, when blacks gave any demonstration of grievance, there was a decision by consensus—the ruling white oligarchy of the town in concert with the editor of the paper—to take either no note of what had happened, or to write a tiny inoffensive story and bury it somewhere in the middle of the paper. If black heads had been cracked during a protest demonstration then it was still unlikely to make the paper. Thus blacks were faced with taking great risks in trying to change things, all too aware that even as they tried, the local authorities might take no note at all of their grievances, and the community would be spared any reports on what had happened.

The *Tennessean,* under Coleman Harwell, its flinty editor, was, by that standard, quite politically incorrect. We would be witnesses to this mounting crisis, he had decided at the very start, no matter what the cost in terms of social discomfort to himself and his family at whatever social gatherings they attended, and no matter which advertisers threatened to withhold advertising from us. We *would* cover it, and we *would* let our readers know the consequences of living in an age when segregation was under assault. Because of that, and because when the demonstrators had started out, the last thing the young people expected was fair and just coverage from a Southern paper, the *Tennessean*'s coverage turned out to be a significant bonus for them. That the paper's main reporter was young, virtually their own age, and very much at ease with them helped me greatly. Bernard Lafayette told me, some twenty years later, that when they had been beaten up downtown, they would sometimes wonder whether they could go on, and then there would be the morning story in the *Tennessean* giving the details of exactly what had happened. The fact that the rest of the community now had to witness the price of segregation helped them to keep going, he said.

I was twenty-five that winter when the sit-ins began, which meant that I was only a few years older than some of the demonstrators, two years older than Rodney Powell and Jim Bevel, for example. Though over the next few weeks a number of different reporters covered the story, I was the principal reporter, and it was to no small degree my story. I suppose, like most young and ambitious reporters, I was eager for fame, not journalistic fame as it is so unhealthily manifested today because of television, with multi-million-dollar salaries awarded star reporters (the very nature of which necessarily precludes the famed reporter from covering any real story), but a more old-fashioned fame, serious recognition within my profession that I was a budding star. I hungered, not to be famous or rich, but to be a great reporter and even more, to cover stories which mattered, and to be a witness to history. Starting in February 1960, the latter part of my ambition was more than fulfilled.

I think that I knew in some instinctive way from the first time I watched the young people walk from Kelly Miller Smith's church to the Woolworth's counter that I was watching the beginning of something historic, that these young people were not going to be turned around, nor were they likely to stop once they won their first localized victory at the lunch counters. It was a heady time for me, my first big story, one with, it seemed to me, a larger social significance. I worked hard, knew and liked the sit-in kids, as they were then known, and I readily gained their trust. A few years ago, Larry Brinton, who was my opposite number on the *Nashville Banner*—he and I really hated each other in those days in the way that competing reporters used to hate each other—told me that when the *Banner* reporters had been warned off the story by their publisher, Jimmy Stahlman, they simply followed me around, knowing that I knew where the action would be. My stories, looking back, seem quite clinical. We did little to try and humanize the demonstrators. There was very little editorializing in the news columns, particularly on a story like this; there was a belief, editor down to working reporter, that the story told itself. Indeed it did. Nonetheless I obviously felt a considerable amount of sympathy for their aims and their grievances; this was, I suppose, the story I had always hoped to cover when I first set out for Mississippi.

I was impressed by these young people from the start, by their courage and their dignity and their awesome inner strength, and in an odd way, by their relentless *innocence*—for they had set out to do what older, wiser, more experienced people told them they could never do. They knew nothing of the city and its politics; they had no comprehension of the seemingly overwhelming might of the forces arrayed against them in the beginning, and I, who knew those forces all too well, was moved by this simplicity. I was not surprised, a year later, having left the *Tennessean* to go to the *Times* (my ambitions beginning to come true) as I set out for the first of a series of foreign assignments as a newly minted *New York Times* reporter, that a number of these same young people whom I knew so well had taken over the Freedom Rides at the very moment when Klan violence threatened to shut them down.

My four years in Nashville were uncommonly rich and full, and I have dedicated this book to three men whose lives had a singular impact on mine. One of them, Coleman Harwell, I have already mentioned in this author's note; he ran an admirable paper, aggressive, fearless, and he understood, as few editors in the South did at the time, the transcending nature of this one story. He knew we would be judged on how we covered this story and nothing else. In personal terms he was not a particularly easy man to deal with; I do not believe we ever had a relaxed social conversation until some twenty-five years after I left the paper. But four years after leaving the *Tennessean,* when I won a Pulitizer Prize for covering Vietnam, the first telephone call I made, other than to members of my family, was to him. The second dedicatee, Jennings Perry, was in some ways his opposite number. Jennings was consummately graceful and charming, probably the most courtly man I ever met. He was a former chief editorial writer for the *Tennessean,* and he had led the fight in the thirties and forties to end the poll tax in Tennessee. That one campaign had a great deal to do with the significantly greater quality of political—and social—civility in Tennessee compared with its sister states in those years. To a young man just entering the profession, the victory in the poll tax struggle was a handsome lesson in what the uses of a newspaper could be. The third dedicatee is the Reverend Kelly Miller Smith, who is mentioned frequently in this book, and who was the principal leader of the black community in Nashville in those overheated days, and who was one of the most tolerant, generous, and enhancing men I have ever met. Kelly had a remarkable capacity to evoke the best of all people around him even in the worst of times; I still treasure his personal kindnesses to me in those years and I find it impossible to forget the singular richness of his smile.

In some ways because the story was so important to me, I have remarkably clear memories of that late winter and early spring in Nashville. I remain proud of the reporting I did that year; it is one of the things in my own mind which helps validate a lifetime in this profession, and over the years I have kept up my contacts (and, in a few cases, friendships) with the people I knew from those days. I have gone to several of their reunions in Nashville; some ten years ago it became clear in my mind that I would write this book. Though relationships between blacks and whites are edgier these days than ever before for a variety of reasons, I think some of the trust and the friendships which were established in 1960 served me well once I started doing the book's interviews. In deciding which young people I would write about I have chosen the ones I knew best in those days, and I have tried at the same time to give a representative sampling of them, balancing out from the leadership group a fair representation of the different levels of success they attained in the succeeding years.

Any experienced reporter who has covered social conflict over what is now five decades takes a kind of private sustenance, I think, from certain things. In my own case that sustenance comes from, for lack of a better phrase, the courage and nobility of ordinary people in times of stress. If you believe in that concept, I think, you are inclined to believe in democracy, despite endless examples of its weaknesses and flaws. I can think of no occasion in recent postwar American history when there has been so shining an example of democracy at work because of the courage and nobility of ordinary people—people hardly favored at the time of birth by their circumstances—than what happened in those days in the South. By that I mean the five years which began in February 1960 with the sit-ins and ended with the Voting Rights Act of 1965 after the Selma protests.

ACKNOWLEDGMENTS

I owe a debt of gratitude to a large number of people who helped me in different ways on this book. In particular I want to thank Kate Medina, my editor, and Meaghan Rady, her assistant, at Random House. Both Kate Lardner in New York and Jeremy Leaming in Nashville were extremely helpful in fact checking, as were the members of the staff of the *Tennessean* Library, particularly Nancy St Cyr and Annette Morrison. Vicky Phelps was invaluable in making arrangements for me in Nashville. I am indebted as well to Carolyn Parqueth, who typed my notes, and Philip Roome, who, as in the past, made my travels much easier. Marty Garbus and Bob Solomon, my lawyers and agents, were a constant source of support, as were my friends Ken Starr and Tom Weinberg. Bruce Davidson, a personal friend and one of America's most distinguished photographers, mentioned casually to me one night that he had taken some photos during the time of the Freedom Rides, and I am fortunate enough to be able to include some of them in this book.

I am grateful as well to old colleagues on the *Tennessean* for friendship given then and recollections of past events granted now: in particular Wallace Westfeldt (who I always thought should have won a Pulitzer Prize for his coverage of the civil rights story back then), John Seigenthaler, Bill Kovach, Jack Corn, and my old roommate from those days, Fred Graham. Will Campbell has been both friend and source since we first met in Holmes County, Mississippi, in November 1955 (both of us soon to be asked to leave that state by our respective employers). The Hodding Carters of Greenville, Mississippi, Big and Little (that is the late Hodding Jr., who connected me to the *Tennessean*'s editors in 1956, and his son, Hodding III, the former State Department spokesman) aided and abetted my career and offered me friendship and sustenance at critical times when I was most vulnerable.

In the years when I worked on the *Tennessean* I was lucky enough to partner up with two particularly gifted photographers, Joe Rudis and Jack Corn, who helped teach me how to talk to ordinary people while on assignment. Not many people know that among the best classes in journalism are those given by experienced photographers to beginning reporters. I am indebted to both of them for their kindnesses to a young man struggling to come to terms with his professional abilities; it was my particular good fortune during much of the coverage of the events recorded in this book to work with Jack Corn (who took a number of the photographs used in this book), and his courage and gentleness were a considerable source of strength for me in an edgy and dangerous time.

In those years I was from time to time a part of an uncommon group of reporters who covered the civil rights beat. It was one of those rare moments when American journalism was enhanced by an exceptional group of professionals who took uncommon daily risks to cover a difficult and demanding story. Because I went off to the Congo and Vietnam in the middle of the story I was not a lifer as some of them were, but I was enriched by their friendship—their generosity when I was just a kid, and their continued collegial generosity when I returned from overseas as a peer. I particularly want to mention and thank the six nonpareils of that time, John Popham, Bill Minor, Claude Sitton, Karl Fleming, John Herbers, and Jack Nelson.

AUTHOR INTERVIEWS
FOR *THE CHILDREN*

In writing the book, I was able, of course, to call on my memory of those events which took place thirty-eight years ago, and to use the old *Nashville Tennessean* clips. But to a large degree this book was based on interviews. In the case of the principals, I tended to see each of them seven or eight times for two or three hours at a time. In the case of some of the other names listed here the interviews usually lasted an hour or two although occasionally what took place was a simple interview to confirm some existing facts. Obviously, I am in addition indebted to all those other authors who have written on this subject, most notably Taylor Branch for *Parting the Waters,* and David Garrow, for both *Bearing the Cross* and *Protest at Selma.*

The list of interviews follows: Adele Alexander, Cliff Alexander, George Barrett, Marion Barry, Jr., Bob Battle, Dick Battle, Carl Bernstein, James Bevel, Creed Black, Julian Bond, Alex Bontemps, LaBarbara Bowman, Cecil Branstetter, Larry Brinton, Arthur Brisbane, Lucius Burch, Catherine Burks, Angeline Butler, Will Campbell, Candie Anderson Carawan, Guy Carawan, Hodding Carter III, Mary Churchwell, Robert Churchwell, Colia Liddell Lafayette Clark, David Clarke, Milton Coleman, Jack Corn, Mattie Barry Cummings, the Rev. William Sloane Coffin, Richard Cohen, Harry Cook, Morris Dees, John Doar, Bob Eddinger, Karl Fleming, Sam Fleming, Marian Fuson, Nelson Fuson, Jack Gunter, Carroll Harvey, Rob Harwell, Alex Heard, Frankie Henry, Bob Ingram, Ray Jenkins, Ben Jobe, Gloria Johnson-Powell, Kate Jones, Eddie Jones, Bob Kaiser, Herb Kaplow, Bill Kovach, Bernard Lafayette, Kate Bulls Lafayette, Paul LaPrad, Dorothy Lawson, the Rev. James Lawson, John Lawson, Morris Lawson, Julius Lester, John Lewis, Lillian Lewis, Ore Lewis Crawley, David Levering Lewis, Willie Mae Lewis, Chuck McDew, Bob McGaw, Bill Moyers, the Rev. Robert Curtis Murphy, Lucille (Duggar) Murphy, Rayna Ristow Murphy, Robert Murphy,

Diane Nash, the Rev. Robert Nelson, Jack Nelson, District Judge John T. Nixon, Peter Paris, John Patterson, Dr. Chester Pierce, Gary Pomerantz, Rodney Powell, Vincent Reed, the Rev. Metz Rollins, Reggie Robinson, Arvid (Bud) Sather, Arlie Schardt, John Seigenthaler, Tom Sherwood, Claude Sitton, Alice C. Smith-Key (widow of Kelly Miller Smith), Joy Smith, Mayor Joseph Smitherman, Jim Squires, Hank Thomas, Yvonne Thomas, Everett Tilson, Richard Valeriani, Zere Lynn Smith Verner, C. T. Vivian, Octavia Vivian, Dr. Matthew Walker, Ann Harwell Wells, Dorothy Webster, Sherman Webster, Wallace Westfeldt, Wayne Whitt, DeLois Wilkinson, Roger Wilkins, Joan Bontemps (Mrs. Avon) Williams, Jr., Avon Williams III, Bob Woodward, James T. Wooten, Mateen Wright, Andy Young, Bob Zellner, Jim Zwerg.

BIBLIOGRAPHY

Abernathy, Ralph David, *And the Walls Came Tumbling Down: An Auto-biography.* New York: HarperCollins, 1991.

Agronsky, Jonathan I., *Marion Barry: The Politics of Race.* Latham, New York: British American Publishing, 1991.

Anderson, Jervis, *Bayard Rustin: Troubles I've Seen: A Biography.* New York: HarperCollins, 1997.

Beifuss, Joan Turner, *At the River I Stand.* Memphis: St. Lukes Press, 1990.

Brisbane, Arthur, "Marion Barry Just Wants to Be Loved," *The Washington Post Magazine,* April 26, 1987.

Branch, Taylor, *Parting the Waters: America in the King Years, 1954–63.* New York: Simon & Schuster, 1988.

Branscomb, Harvie, *Purely Academic.* Nashville: Vanderbilt University, 1978 (private edition).

Burner, Eric, *And Gently He Shall Lead Them: Robert Parris Moses and Civil Rights in Mississippi.* New York: New York University Press, 1994.

Cagin, Seth, and Philip Dray, *We Are Not Afraid: The Story of Goodman, Schwerner and Chaney and the Civil Rights Campaign for Mississippi.* New York: Macmillan, 1988.

Campbell, Will, *Brother to a Dragonfly.* New York: Seabury, 1977.

Carawan, Guy, and Candie Carawan, *Sing for Freedom: The Story of the Civil Rights Movement Through Its Songs.* Bethlehem, PA: Sing Out Corporation, 1992.

Carmichael, Stokely, and Charles V. Hamilton, *Black Power: The Politics of Liberation in America.* New York: Random House, 1967.

Carson, Clayborne, *In Struggle: SNCC and the Black Awakening of the 1960s.* Cambridge: Harvard University Press, 1981.

Chestnut, J. L., Jr., and Julia Cass, *Black in Selma: The Uncommon Life of J. L. Chestnut, Jr.* New York: Farrar, Straus & Giroux, 1990.

Cobbs, Elizabeth, and Petric Smith, *Long Time Coming: An Insider's Story of the Birmingham Church Bombing That Rocked the World.* Birmingham: Crane Hill, 1994.

Conkin, Paul, Henry Lee Swint, and Patricia S. Miletich, *Gone With the Ivy: A Biography of Vanderbilt University.* Knoxville: University of Tennessee Press, 1985.

Curry, Constance, *Silver Rights.* Chapel Hill, NC: Algonquin Books, 1995.

Dittmer, John, *Local People: The Struggle for Civil Rights in Mississippi (Blacks in the New World).* Champaign, IL: University of Illinois Press, 1994.

Doyle, Don H., *Nashville Since the 1920s.* Knoxville: University of Tennessee Press, 1985.

Farmer, James, *Lay Bare the Heart: An Autobiography of the Civil Rights Movement.* New York: Arbor House, 1985.

Forman, James, *The Making of Black Revolutionaries.* Seattle: Open Hand Press, 1985.

Frady, Marshall, *Jesse: The Life and Pilgrimage of Jesse Jackson.* New York: Random House, 1996.

———, *Southerners: A Journalist's Odyssey.* New York: New American Library, 1981.

———, *Wallace.* Cleveland: New American Library, 1968.

Garrow, David J., *Bearing the Cross: Martin Luther King, Jr., and the Southern Christian Leadership Conference.* New York: William Morrow, 1986.

———, *Protest at Selma: Martin Luther King, Jr. and the Voting Rights Act of 1965.* New Haven, CT: Yale University Press, 1978.

Halberstam, David, *The Best and the Brightest.* New York: Random House, 1972.

———, *The Powers That Be.* New York: Knopf, 1979.

Haygood, Wil, *King of the Cats: The Life and Times of Adam Clayton Powell, Jr.* Boston: Houghton Mifflin, 1993.

Horton, Myles, with Herbert and Judith Kohl, *The Long Haul: An Autobiography.* New York: Doubleday, 1990.

Jaffe, Harry, and Tom Sherwood, *Dream City: Race, Power, and the Decline of Washington, D.C.* New York: Simon & Schuster, 1994.

Kasher, Steven, *The Civil Rights Movement, A Photographic History, 1954–68.* New York: Abbeville Press, 1996.

King, Martin Luther, Jr., *Stride Toward Freedom: The Montgomery Story.* New York: Harper and Row, 1958.

Lyon, Danny, *Memories of the Southern Civil Rights Movement.* Chapel Hill: University of North Carolina Press, 1992.

Mann, Robert, *The Walls of Jericho: Lyndon Johnson, Hubert Humphrey, Richard Russell, and the Struggle for Civil Rights.* San Diego: Harcourt Brace, 1996.

Mills, Kay, *This Little Light of Mine: The Life of Fannie Lou Hamer.* New York: Plume, 1994.

Morris, Aldon D., *Origins of the Civil Rights Movement: Black Communities Organizing for Change.* New York: Free Press, 1984.

Navasky, Victor, *Kennedy Justice.* New York: Atheneum, 1971.

Newfield, Jack, *A Prophetic Minority.* New York: New American Library, 1966.

Nossiter, Adam, *Of Long Memory: Mississippi and the Murder of Medgar Evers.* Reading, MA: Addison Wesley, 1994.

Oates, Stephen, *Let the Trumpet Sound: The Life of Martin Luther King.* New York: Harper and Row, 1982.

O'Reilly, Kenneth, *Black Americans: The FBI Files.* New York: Carroll and Graf, 1994.

————, *Nixon's Piano: Presidents and Racial Politics from Washington to Clinton.* New York: Free Press, 1995.

Oshinsky, David, *"Worse Than Slavery," Parchman Farm and the Ordeal of Jim Crow Justice.* New York: Free Press, 1996.

Payne, Charles, M., *I've Got the Light of Freedom: The Organizing Tradition and the Mississippi Freedom Struggle.* Berkeley: University of California Press, 1995.

Pepper, William, *Orders to Kill: The Truth Behind the Murder of Martin Luther King, Jr.* New York: Carroll and Graf, 1995.

Perry, Jennings, *Democracy Begins at Home: The Tennessee Fight on the Poll Tax.* Philadelphia: Lippincott, 1944.

Pomerantz, Gary, *Where Peachtree Meets Sweet Auburn: The Saga of Two Families and the Making of Atlanta.* New York: Scribner, 1996.

Powledge, Fred, *Free at Last?: The Civil Rights Movement and the People Who Made It.* Boston: Little, Brown, 1991.

Raines, Howell, *My Soul Is Rested: The Story of the Civil Rights Movement in the Deep South.* New York: Penguin, 1997.

Reeves, Richard, *President Kennedy: Profile of Power.* New York: Simon & Schuster, 1993.

Rowe, Gary Thomas, *My Undercover Years with the Ku Klux Klan.* New York: Bantam, 1976.

Schlesinger, Arthur M., Jr., *Robert Kennedy and His Times.* Boston: Houghton Mifflin, 1978.

Silver, James, *Mississippi: The Closed Society.* San Diego: Harcourt Brace, 1963.

Smith, Kelly Miller, *Social Crisis Preaching: The Lyman Beecher Lectures, 1983.* Macon, GA: Mercer University Press, 1984.

Smith, W. O., *Sideman: The Long Gig of W. O. Smith: A Memoir.* Nashville: Rutledge Hill Press, 1991.

Squires, James, *The Secrets of the Hopewell Box: Stolen Elections, Southern Politics, and a City's Coming of Age.* New York: Times Books, 1996.

Sumner, David, *Beloved Community,* unpublished manuscript.

Urquhart, Brian, *Ralph Bunche: An American Life.* New York: Norton, 1993.

Watters, Pat, *Down to Now: Reflections on the Southern Civil Rights Movement.* New York: Pantheon, 1971.

Wilkins, Roger, *A Man's Life.* New York: Simon & Schuster, 1982.

Wilkins, Roy, with Tom Mathews, *Standing Fast: The Autobiography of Roy Wilkins.* New York: Da Capo Press, 1994.

Williams, Juan, *Eyes on the Prize: America's Civil Rights Years, 1954–1965.* New York: Penguin, 1988.

Wofford, Harris, *Of Kennedys and Kings.* New York: Farrar, Straus & Giroux, 1980.

Wolff, Miles, *Lunch at the 5 & 10.* Chicago: Ivan R. Dee, Elephant Paperbacks, 1990.

Young, Andrew, *An Easy Burden: The Civil Rights Movement and the Transformation of America.* New York: HarperCollins, 1996.

Zinn, Howard, *Albany: A Study in National Responsibility.* Atlanta: Southern Regional Council, 1962.

Notes

Chapter One

1. Jervis Anderson, *Bayard Rustin: Troubles I've Seen: A Biography.* New York: HarperCollins, 1997, p. 192

Chapter Two

1. Interview with Wallace Westfeldt, who had interviewed Clement at the time for *Time* magazine

Chapter Four

1. Interview with Wallace Westfeldt, who worked closely with Cecil Sims over several years as *The Nashville Tennessean*'s reporter on that story

Chapter Five

1. Interview with Ben Jobe
2. Interview with Bernard Lafayette
3. Interview with Lillian Moses Lewis
4. Interview with David Levering Lewis
5. Interview with Julius Lester

Chapter Eight

1. Miles Wolff, *Lunch at the 5 & 10.* Chicago: Ivan R. Dee, Elephant Paperbacks, 1990, pp. 11–16
2. Pat Watters, *Down to Now: Reflections on the Southern Civil Rights Movement.* New York: Pantheon, 1971, p. 74
3. Wolff, p. 12, and from Fred Powledge, *Free at Last?: The Civil Rights Movement and the People Who Made It.* Boston: Little, Brown, 1991, pp. 199–201

4. Aldon D. Morris, *Origins of the Civil Rights Movement: Black Communities Organizing for Change.* New York: Free Press, 1984, p. 206 (quoted from David Sumner, unpublished manuscript on the Nashville sit-ins, *Beloved Community,* p. 28)

CHAPTER TEN

1. Interview with Dr. Matthew Walker
2. I talked with Neil Cunningham in the summer of 1960 when we both covered the last state campaign of Estes Kefauver together, and he took great delight in recounting the pressures to which Stahlman had subjected Ben West
3. Interview with Jack Gunter
4. Interview with Alec Heard
5. Interview with Bill Kovach, former *Tennessean* reporter
6. Interview with Jack Gunter
7. Interview with John T. Nixon
8. Interview with Bob Battle
9. Interview with Eddie Jones
10. Interview with Eddie Jones and Bob Battle
11. Interview with Jack Gunter

CHAPTER ELEVEN

1. Interview with John T. Nixon

CHAPTER TWENTY-ONE

1. Interviews with Dick Battle, Robert Churchwell, and Mary Churchwell
2. Interview with Larry Brinton

CHAPTER TWENTY-TWO

1. Interview with Will Campbell
2. Interview with Robert Nelson
3. Paul Conkin, Henry Lee Swint, and Patricia S. Miletich, *Gone With the Ivy: A Biography of Vanderbilt University.* Knoxville: University of Tennessee Press, 1985
4. From the Robert Nelson papers, a paper by Woodrow Eddins, Jr.
5. Conkin, p. 545
6. Conkin, p. 544

7. Conkin, p. 540

8. Sumner, p. 184

9. Interview with Alec Heard

10. Interviews with Alec Heard and Sam Fleming, former head of the Vanderbilt University Board of Trust

11. Interview with Bob Battle, who still had his rifle when I interviewed him and Larry Brinton

12. *The British Weekly,* March 23, 1961

13. Conkin, pp. 422–43

14. Nelson papers, Eddins's thesis

CHAPTER TWENTY-FOUR

1. Interviews with C. T. Vivian, Will Campbell, and Kelly Miller Smith, as well as various students

2. Interview with Wallace Westfeldt

3. Since I was the principal reporter on the story for the *Tennessean,* and since Whalen most assuredly did not want to be recommended by people at the *Banner,* he asked me to intervene and explain the importance of a *Time* cover. I was more amused by their lack of interest than he was. *Time* eventually did a report, but not a cover on the story.

CHAPTER TWENTY-FIVE

1. Interview with Julian Bond

2. Taylor Branch, *Parting the Waters: America in the King Years, 1954–63.* New York: Simon & Schuster, 1988, p. 291

3. Interview with Mattie Barry Cummings, mother of Marion Barry

4. Quoted in Jonathan I. Agronsky, *Marion Barry: The Politics of Race.* Latham, New York: British American Publishing, 1991, p. 80

5. Interview with Marion Barry

6. Agronsky, p. 90

7. Agronsky, p. 91

CHAPTER TWENTY-SIX

1. The narrative of the confrontation is largely taken from *The Nashville Tennessean* report of that remarkable day in its April 20, 1960, edition, which I wrote

CHAPTER TWENTY-SEVEN

1. Interviews with Willie Mae Carter Lewis, John Lewis's mother, and Ore Lewis Crawley, his oldest sister

2. Interview with Ore Lewis Crawley

3. Interview with Willie Mae Carter Lewis

4. Interview with Lillian Miles Lewis

5. Harris Wofford, *Of Kennedys and Kings.* New York: Farrar, Straus & Giroux, 1980, p. 166

6. Richard Reeves, *President Kennedy: Profile of Power.* New York: Simon & Schuster, 1993, p. 125

7. Branch, p. 417

CHAPTER TWENTY-EIGHT

1. Interview with Wayne Whitt

CHAPTER THIRTY

1. Branch, p. 430

2. Interviews with Diane Nash, John Seigenthaler, and George Barrett; Branch, pp. 429–30

3. Interviews with Diane Nash and John Seigenthaler; Reeves, p. 126

CHAPTER THIRTY-ONE

1. *Newsweek,* April 15, 1963, p. 29

2. Interview with Catherine Burks

3. Seth Cagin and Philip Dray, *We Are Not Afraid: The Story of Goodman, Schwerner and Chaney and the Civil Rights Campaign for Mississippi.* New York: Macmillan, 1988, p. 113

4. Interview with Catherine Burks

CHAPTER THIRTY-TWO

1. Marshall Frady, *Wallace.* Cleveland: NAL, 1968, p. 127

2. Interview with former Governor John Patterson

3. Interview with Ray Jenkins

4. Interview with Ray Jenkins

5. Powledge, p. 270

CHAPTER THIRTY-FOUR

1. Interview with Herb Kaplow
2. Interview with Jim Zwerg
3. Interview with Ray Jenkins
4. Powledge, p. 270; interview with Bob Ingram

CHAPTER THIRTY-FIVE

1. Wofford, p. 153
2. Wofford, p. 126
3. Interviews with Susan Wilbur Wamsley and John Seigenthaler
4. Interview with Ray Jenkins, former senior executive of the *Alabama Journal*
5. Powledge, pp. 273–74
6. Interview with John Seigenthaler
7. Interview with John Seigenthaler

CHAPTER THIRTY-SIX

1. Interview with Diane Nash
2. Arthur M. Schlesinger, Jr., *Robert Kennedy and His Times.* Boston: Houghton Mifflin, 1978, p. 297; Branch, p. 460

CHAPTER THIRTY-SEVEN

1. Branch, p. 467

CHAPTER THIRTY-EIGHT

1. David Oshinsky, *"Worse Than Slavery," Parchman Farm and the Ordeal of Jim Crow Justice.* New York: Free Press, 1996, pp. 141–48 (plus additional information in unnumbered photo section)

CHAPTER FORTY-THREE

1. Interviews with Sander Vanocur, Fred Dutton, and Pierre Salinger for *The Powers That Be,* pp. 383–88

CHAPTER FORTY-FOUR

1. Interview with Catherine Burks
2. Interview with Julian Bond

CHAPTER FORTY-FIVE

1. Interview with Chuck McDew

2. Interview with John Doar

3. Interview with Julian Bond

4. Interview with Chuck McDew

5. Cagin and Dray, p. 148

6. Interview with Reggie Robinson

7. Cagin and Dray, p. 146

8. Interview with Reggie Robinson

9. Interview with Chuck McDew

10. Charles M. Payne, *I've Got the Light of Freedom: The Organizing Tradition and the Mississippi Freedom Struggle.* Berkeley: University of California Press, 1995, pp. 120–22

11. Interview with John Doar

12. Interview with John Doar

CHAPTER FORTY-SIX

1. Wofford, pp. 111–12

2. Interview with Colia Liddell Lafayette Clark

3. Interview with Colia Liddell Lafayette Clark

4. J. L. Chestnut, Jr., and Julia Cass, *Black in Selma: The Uncommon Life of J. L. Chestnut, Jr.* New York: Farrar, Straus & Giroux, 1990, p. 166, and interview with Bernard Lafayette

CHAPTER FORTY-SEVEN

1. Interview with Karl Fleming

2. Andrew Young, *An Easy Burden: The Civil Rights Movement and the Transformation of America.* New York: HarperCollins, 1996, p. 207, and also author interview with him

3. Interview with James Bevel

4. Interview with Andrew Young

5. Interview with Andrew Young

6. Branch, p. 735

7. Branch; interviews with James Bevel and Andrew Young

8. Interviews with Bernard Lafayette and James Bevel

9. Interview with James Bevel

CHAPTER FORTY-EIGHT

1. Interview with Julian Bond

2. Interview with John Lewis; James Farmer, *Lay Bare the Heart: An Autobiography of the Civil Rights Movement.* New York: Arbor House, 1985, p. 239

3. Kenneth O'Reilly, *Black Americans: The FBI Files.* New York: Carroll and Graf, 1994, p. 41

4. Reeves, pp. 580–83; Roy Wilkins with Tom Mathews, *Standing Fast: The Autobiography of Roy Wilkins.* New York: Da Capo Press, 1994, pp. 292–93; Branch, pp. 869–74

5. Interview with Andy Young

CHAPTER FIFTY-THREE

1. David Halberstam, *The Best and the Brightest.* New York: Random House, 1972, p. 436

2. Interview with Karl Fleming

3. David J. Garrow, *Bearing the Cross: Martin Luther King, Jr., and the Southern Christian Leadership Conference.* New York: William Morrow, 1986, p. 368; interviews with C. T. Vivian and John Lewis

4. Interview with Bill Moyers

5. Interviews with John Lewis and C. T. Vivian

6. Interviews with John Doar and Bud Sather

7. Reeves, p. 531; interview with John Lewis

8. Interview with Karl Fleming, who as a senior reporter on the civil rights story was aware that King never went anywhere that television correspondents could not readily reach and report from

9. Interview with Joseph Smitherman

10. Interview with Joseph Smitherman

11. Interviews with Karl Fleming and John Chancellor of NBC, who also covered the civil rights movement. The quote itself is from Chancellor.

12. Interview with Karl Fleming

13. Interview with Karl Fleming

14. Interview with John Nixon

15. Interview with Diane Nash

16. David J. Garrow, *Protest at Selma: Martin Luther King, Jr., and the Voting Rights Act of 1965.* New Haven, CT: Yale University Press, 1978, p. 34

17. Interview with Joseph Smitherman

18. Garrow, *Protest at Selma,* p. 35

19. Chestnut, p. 185

20. Interview with John Nixon

21. Chestnut, p. 179

22. Chestnut, p. 196

23. Chestnut, p. 215; interview with John Lewis

CHAPTER FIFTY-FOUR

1. Interviews with C. T. and Octavia Vivian

CHAPTER FIFTY-FIVE

1. In an interview with the author in March 1967 for *Harper's* magazine

2. Interview with Arlie Schardt

3. Garrow, *Protest at Selma,* pp. 163–64

4. Juan Williams, *Eyes on the Prize: America's Civil Rights Years, 1954–1965.* New York: Penguin, 1988, p. 272

5. Williams, p. 272

6. Williams, p. 272

7. Interview with Russell Baker

8. Interview with Bill Moyers

CHAPTER FIFTY-SIX

1. Danny Lyon, *Memories of the Southern Civil Rights Movement.* Chapel Hill: University of North Carolina Press, 1992, p. 149

2. Interview with Arlie Schardt

CHAPTER FIFTY-SEVEN

1. Interviews with Lawson, Lewis, and Lafayette; Garrow, *Bearing the Cross,* pp. 610–11

2. Interview with Arlie Schardt

3. Interview with Jim Lawson

CHAPTER FIFTY-EIGHT

1. From *Katallegete* magazine, published by Will Campbell, fall-winter 1972, Nashville, p. 42

2. Interview with Diane Nash

3. Interview with Bernard Lafayette

4. Interview with James Bevel

5. Interview with Claude Sitton

6. Andrew Young, p. 425, quotes the spirit as saying: "James Bevel, my children are dying in Vietnam, my children are suffering. They are your brothers and sisters too. You must help them."

7. Young, p. 434

CHAPTER FIFTY-NINE

1. Interview with Marion Barry

2. Interview with Julian Bond

3. Interview with Roger Wilkins

4. Interview with Bob Kaiser

5. Interview with Carroll Harvey

6. For the portrait of Marion Barry, a subject of great sensitivity with many black people in the Movement and in Washington, I am indebted to Harry Jaffe and Tom Sherwood for their excellent book *Dream City,* and in particular their account of Barry's early days in Washington, as well as interviews with Clifford Alexander, Adele Alexander, Julian Bond, Carl Bernstein, LaBarbara Bowman, Arthur Brisbane, David Clarke, Richard Cohen, Milton Coleman, Carroll Harvey, Bob Kaiser, Chuck McDew, John Seigenthaler, Tom Sherwood, Vincent Reed, Reggie Robinson, Roger Wilkins, Bob Zellner, Mattie Barry Cummings (the mother of Marion Barry), and Marion Barry himself, as well as interviews with his old colleagues from the sit-in days about those years, most notably John Lewis and Bernard Lafayette. In addition a number of black officials in Washington who once were close to Barry and who later broke with him, but still have to transact business with the city, spoke to me with the agreement that I not use their names. I am indebted as well to Jonathan Agronsky for his book *Marion Barry: The Politics of Race.* Latham, NY: British American Publishing, 1991.

7. Interview with Bob Kaiser

8. Harry Jaffe and Tom Sherwood, *Dream City: Race, Power, and the Decline of Washington, D.C.* New York: Simon & Schuster, 1994, pp. 31–33 and 50–51

CHAPTER SIXTY

1. Joan Turner Beifuss, *At the River I Stand.* Memphis: St. Lukes Press, 1990, p. 35

2. Beifuss, p. 24

3. Beifuss, p. 50

4. Beifuss, p. 180

5. Beifuss, pp. 257–58

6. Beifuss, p. 295

CHAPTER SIXTY-ONE

1. Interview with Dr. Chester Pierce

CHAPTER SIXTY-SEVEN

1. Interview with Carroll Harvey

2. Jaffe and Sherwood, p. 57

3. Carson, p. 148

4. Jaffe and Sherwood, pp. 48–49

5. Jaffe and Sherwood, p. 97

6. Interview with David Clarke

7. Interview with Tom Sherwood

8. Interview with LaBarbara Bowman

9. Interview with LaBarbara Bowman

10. Jaffe and Sherwood, p. 125

11. Interview with Milton Coleman

12. Interviews with Vincent Reed and David Clarke; also Jaffe and Sherwood, pp. 152–53

13. Interview with Vincent Reed; Jaffe and Sherwood, p. 153

14. Interview with Julian Bond

15. Interview with LaBarbara Bowman

16. Arthur Brisbane and Milton Coleman, "Success Story's Tragic Twist; Private Life Tempted Fate," *The Washington Post,* January 21, 1990

17. Interviews with Richard Cohen, Bob Kaiser, Milton Coleman, Arthur Brisbane, and Tom Sherwood

18. Interview with Milton Coleman

19. Interview with Arthur Brisbane

20. Interview with Tom Sherwood

21. Arthur Brisbane, "Marion Barry Just Wants to Be Loved," *The Washington Post Magazine,* April 26, 1987

CHAPTER SIXTY-NINE
1. Interview with Will Campbell
2. Peter Paris, *The Journal of Religious Thought,* Howard University School of Divinity, Vol. 48, summer-fall 1991, pp. 10–11
3. Interview with Mateen Wright

CHAPTER SEVENTY
1. Interview with John Lewis
2. Marshall Frady, *Southerners: A Journalist's Odyssey.* New York: New American Library, 1981, p. 171
3. Interview with John Lewis; Jim Wooten

CHAPTER SEVENTY-FIVE
1. Young, p. 299
2. Interview with Will Campbell
3. Garrow, *Bearing the Cross,* p. 409
4. Young, pp. 503–4
5. Interview with John Lewis
6. Interview with James Bevel
7. Interviews with John Lewis, Bernard Lafayette, and C. T. Vivian; Young, pp. 503–4
8. Kate Lardner interview with James Bevel

CHAPTER SEVENTY-SIX
1. Interview with Joseph Smitherman
2. Jack Nelson, "Once-Violent Selma Now Proud of Racial Harmony," *Los Angeles Times,* August 27, 1989
3. Jack Nelson, *Los Angeles Times*

CHAPTER SEVENTY-SEVEN
1. Agronsky, p. 269

INDEX

ABOUT THE AUTHOR

DAVID HALBERSTAM graduated from Harvard, where he had served as a managing editor of the daily *Harvard Crimson*. It was 1955, a year after the Supreme Court outlawed segregation in public schools. Halberstam went south and began his career as the one reporter on the West Point, Mississippi, *Daily Times Leader*. He was fired after ten months there and went to work for *The Nashville Tennessean*. When the sit-ins broke out in Nashville in February 1960, he was assigned to the story as principal reporter. He joined *The New York Times* later that year, winning the Pulitzer Prize in 1964 for his early reports from Vietnam. He has received every other major journalistic award, and is a member of the Society of American Historians. His previous nine books have all been bestsellers.

ABOUT THE TYPE

This book was set in Simoncini Garamond, a typeface designed by Francesco Simoncini based on the style of Garamond that was created by the French printer Jean Jannon after the original models of Claude Garamond.